The Bribery Act 2010
A Practical Guide

The Bribery Act 2010
A Practical Guide

Eoin O'Shea
of the Inner Temple and of King's Inns, Barrister
Solicitor of the Senior Courts of England and Wales

Published by Jordan Publishing Limited
21 St Thomas Street
Bristol BS1 6JS

Whilst the publishers and the author have taken every care in preparing the material included in this work, any statements made as to the legal or other implications of particular transactions are made in good faith purely for general guidance and cannot be regarded as a substitute for professional advice. Consequently, no liability can be accepted for loss or expense incurred as a result of relying in particular circumstances on statements made in this work.

© Jordan Publishing Limited 2011

All rights reserved. No part of this publication may be reproduced, stored in a retrieval system, or transmitted in any way or by any means, including photocopying or recording, without the written permission of the copyright holder, application for which should be addressed to the publisher.

The moral rights of the author have been asserted.

Crown Copyright material is reproduced with kind permission of the Controller of Her Majesty's Stationery Office.

United Nations Convention against corruption, copyright United Nations, 2004. Reprinted with the permission of the United Nations.

OECD (2010), Convention on Combating Bribery of Foreign Public Officials in International Business Transactions and Related Documents, www.oecd.org/daf/nocorruption/convention, reproduced with the permission of OECD.

British Library Cataloguing-in-Publication Data

A catalogue record for this book is available from the British Library.

ISBN 978 1 84661 194 0

Typeset by Letterpart Ltd, Reigate, Surrey

Printed in Great Britain by CPI Antony Rowe, Chippenham and Eastbourne

To Margaret

FOREWORD

Bribery and corruption have been an affliction of many societies from time immemorial. In 1693, William Penn pithily expressed a view many may share:

> 'The taking of a bribe or gratuity should be punished with as severe penalties as the defrauding of the state.'

In more recent times in 2004, Kofi Annan, the then UN Secretary General described its effects:

> 'Corruption is an insidious plague that has a wide range of corrosive effects on societies. It undermines democracy and the rule of law, leads to violations of human rights, distorts markets, erodes the quality of life and allows organised crime, terrorism and other threats to human security to flourish. This evil phenomenon is found in all countries – big and small, rich and poor – but it is in the developing world that its effects are most destructive. Corruption hurts the poor disproportionately by diverting funds intended for development, undermining a government's ability to provide basic services, feeding inequality and injustice and discouraging foreign aid and investment. Corruption is a key element in economic underperformance and a major obstacle to poverty alleviation and development.'

No-one could but agree with these remarks, for reasons the author clearly explains in Chapter 1.

Much more difficult is finding the right means of preventing and punishing bribery and corruption, particularly where these crimes cross national boundaries. The Bribery Act of 2010 is the response of the United Kingdom by setting its law in a modern context and in line with its international obligations.

The preparatory work by the Law Commission was thorough. The Act is based on its draft proposals and draft bill. After some political controversy and the publication of the guidance under s 9 issued by the Secretary of State, it comes into force as this comprehensive book is published.

The book has been the product of immense industry, reflection and thought. It carefully traces the history of the legislation and then sets out in successive chapters a detailed and clear analysis of the legislation. It helpfully contains a number of appendices, containing not only the text of the Act and the explanatory notes but the guidance given under s 9, the DPP's guidance and the OECD Convention and its commentary. One helpful feature is that it contains references to broader principles which provide a useful introduction to areas of the law with which some readers might not be familiar, but which are necessary to understand the operation of Act.

This book identifies the difficult issues of interpretation and attempts to answer them, as the author modestly claims. I have no doubt it will be of considerable assistance to the courts when such issues arise for decision, even if the answers given may sometimes differ from those elegantly suggested by the author.

It helpfully examines the practical implications of the legislation for companies and individuals in a way many will find useful. It tackles the issues relating to the likely policy of enforcement and prosecution. This last is an area to which much thought is now being given, for without effective, speedy and appropriate methods of enforcement and punishment, the Act will be seen as having failed its purpose.

Lord Justice Thomas
June 2011

PREFACE

After a very long gestation period, the Bribery Act 2010 comes into force on 1 July 2011. The main purpose of this book is to provide a guide to the Act for those in the commerce and public service, as well as their advisers. This involves some analysis of the most important parts of the Act and discussion of the guidance material on adequate procedures and prosecution priorities which have been published recently.

Of course, the previous criminal law of bribery and corruption no longer applies to events occurring after 1 July 2011. Nevertheless, the old law may have some relevance, especially in providing context for the principles underlying the Act. As the law develops it will be interesting to see whether concepts central to the previous law, such as corrupt intent, re-emerge through interpretation of the new statutory language.

Although it is a criminal statute, the main effects of the Bribery Act will be on the conduct of business. Those applying the Act are likely to require an understanding of how businesses are run and the legal principles which apply to them. In many cases, questions of jurisdiction or liability will be difficult to determine without considering, for example, the law of agency, or the law of companies. So civil law will keep breaking in to most discussions of the criminal law of bribery. This phenomenon is especially evident in Chapters 4, 8 and 9. Chapter 13 summarises the separate civil law of bribery (ie civil claims available to victims), which is not changed by the Act but may be important to many.

The text does not dwell on elements of the Act which are irrelevant to the majority of readers. The supplementary provisions in ss 16–20 of the Act are not discussed. The detailed processes for consent to prosecution, the specific defences available to those working in defence or intelligence and questions of procedure are all passed over quickly.

Throughout the text I have sought to illustrate some of the more important points by using hypothetical examples. As well as assisting in the analysis, I hope this makes the law appear a little less abstract to the general reader.

The final chapter focuses on specific problem areas such as hospitality and facilitation payments and employs more detailed illustrative scenarios. I have not included solutions to all the questions raised in the scenarios. This is partly to encourage readers to re-examine the Act and other sources for themselves and partly to help stimulate discussion in a seminar or training environment.

Propositions of law are stated as at 30 April 2011.

Eoin O'Shea

London, 16 May 2011

ACKNOWLEDGMENTS

I am very grateful to Lord Justice Thomas for finding time to write the Foreword.

During the writing process I have benefited from discussion of ideas and various parts of the manuscript with many practitioners and public servants who have been very generous with their time. These include Jeremy Andrews, John Bray, Steven Elliott, Richard Everett, Professor Jeremy Horder, Amanda Pinto QC, Gareth Rees QC, Vivian Robinson QC and Nick Van Benschoten.

Many others have assisted me with research and proofreading. I owe thanks to Michelle Davis, Katherine Farthing, Alicia Kim, Charlotte Knight, Nicola McLeod, Natalie Roberts, Alex Shattock, James Sidwell, Naomi Snider and Attika Valli. Harpreet Paul has also provided assistance, in particular with elements of Chapter 11. Bridgette de Bourbon has been stalwart in her typing and editing of parts of the manuscript. Andrew Witts and several of my other partners have been very supportive. Kate Hather and the commissioning and editorial staff at Jordan Publishing have been helpful and professional. Naturally, any errors are my responsibility alone.

I am grateful for the assistance and patience of the librarians of the Lawrence Graham Library and the Inner Temple Library. Others have given timely logistical support, among them John Fitzgerald and Dr Paul McHugh. Aidan O'Shea kindly provided me with a retreat where I could write central elements of the text. I am glad to acknowledge my debt to Nick Benwell, who stimulated and supported my early interest in this subject.

My children have had to put up with the absences, sacrificed weekends and holidays which are the result of combining full-time practice with a project of this kind. I appreciate their constant cheerfulness as well as their suggestions on how to speed up the writing process.

I could not have written this book without the generosity and solidarity of my wife Margaret, to whom it is gratefully dedicated.

CONTENTS

Foreword	vii
Preface	ix
Acknowledgments	xi
Table of Cases	xxiii
Table of Statutes	xxxiii
Table of Statutory Instruments	xxxix
Table of European Material	xli
Table of International Material	xliii
List of Abbreviations	xlv

Chapter 1
Introduction and Historical Background — 1
Introduction — 1
  The radicalism of the Bribery Act — 1
  Why now? — 2
  The case for fighting transnational bribery — 3
  Are there counter-arguments? — 5
The existing criminal law of bribery and corruption — 8
  Common law bribery — 8
  The statutory offences — 9
    The Public Bodies Corrupt Practices Act 1889 — 9
      Public body — 10
      'Corruptly' — 10
    The Prevention of Corruption Act 1906 — 11
    The Prevention of Corruption Act 1916 — 14
  Anti-terrorism, Crime and Security Act 2001 — 15
Recent developments — 17
Previous attempts at reform — 17
Conclusion — 19
  'Bribery' or 'corruption'? — 19
  Interpreting a new Act of Parliament — 20

Chapter 2
General Offences: Active Bribery — 23
Bribery Act 2010: section 1 — 23
Introduction — 23
  Threshold conditions — 24
  Actus reus and mens rea — 24

Case 1: inducing or rewarding improper performance	25
Offer, promise or give	25
Financial or other advantage	27
To another person	29
Intending to induce improper performance	29
Intention	29
Intention and improper performance	30
'Induce'	32
Relevant function or activity	33
Intending to reward improper performance	33
Example	34
Case 2: compromise of position	34
Knows or believes	35
Acceptance itself improper	35
Examples	36
Indirectness and third parties	38
Offences by bodies corporate and their senior officers (section 14)	38
The innocent abroad?	40

Chapter 3
General Offences: Passive Bribery — **43**

Bribery Act 2010: section 2	43
Introduction	44
Case 3	45
'Requests, agrees to receive or accepts'	45
Example	47
Financial or other advantage	47
Intending that relevant function or activity is performed improperly in consequence	47
In consequence	48
Example	48
Offence complete without actual improper performance	49
Lack of intention as to improper performance	49
Case 4	50
Case 5	52
As a reward	52
For improper performance	53
Example	53
Case 6	54
In anticipation of or in consequence of	56
Position of person performing function or activity at R's request	56
Example	57

Chapter 4
Relevant Functions and Activities — **59**

Bribery Act 2010: section 3	59
Introduction	59

Summary of section 3 threshold condition	60
Two-stage definition	61
Public sector and private sector	61
Functions of a public nature	62
Existing English law	62
Core and hybrid public authorities	63
Relevance of section 6 'public function'	63
Members of Parliament	64
Activities connected with a business	66
Activities performed in the course of a person's employment	66
Activities performed by or on behalf of a body of persons	67
Example	68
Expectations applicable to the function or activity	69
Condition A: expectation of good faith	69
Example	70
Condition B: expectation of impartiality	70
Example	71
Condition C: position of trust	72
Examples	73
Fuzziness at the margins?	74
Another example	74
Can civil law be ignored?	75
Connections to the UK	76

Chapter 5
Improper Performance   **77**

Bribery Act 2010: section 4	77
Introduction	77
Relevant function or activity	77
Breach of relevant expectations	78
Breach of expectation of good faith	79
Example	79
Breach of expectation of impartiality	80
Example	80
Breach of expectation arising from position of trust	81
Examples	83
Connections to past protected functions	84
Examples	84
What is a reasonable person?	84

Chapter 6
The Expectation Test   **85**

Bribery Act 2010: section 5	85
Introduction	85
An objective test	85
Two questions for the reasonable person	86
What is a 'reasonable person'?	86
Breach of expectations	87

Examples	88
Performance of functions outside the UK	88
Local law informs expectations of reasonable person	89
Local customs	90

Chapter 7
Bribery of Foreign Public Officials — 91

Bribery Act 2010: section 6	91
Introduction	92
Compliance with the OECD Convention	93
Scheme of section 6	94
Actus reus and mens rea	94
Role of the OECD Convention in interpreting section 6	95
Article 1 of the OECD Convention	95
Definition of 'foreign public official'	97
Institutional definition	97
A legislative, administrative or judicial position	97
Support staff	98
Political candidates and officials of political parties	99
Territory outside the UK	100
Functional definition	100
Exercising public function for a foreign country	101
Public agency	102
Public enterprise	102
Example	104
Sovereign wealth funds	105
Officials of public international organisations	106
Intention to influence F in official capacity	106
Advantage need not be for 'improper performance'	107
The same mens rea as section 1?	107
Hospitality and promotional expenses	108
Private relationships with FPOs	110
Omissions and actions exceeding authority	110
Intending to obtain or retain business/an advantage in the conduct of business	111
Providing the advantage	112
Directly or through a third party	112
Offers promises or gives	112
Any financial or other advantage	113
To F or another at F's request, etc	113
Role of local law	114
Example	115
Applicable law	115
'Facilitation' payments to foreign public officials	116
Section 14 and offences under section 6 by bodies corporate and their senior officers	118
Comparison of Article 1 of the OECD Convention with section 6 of the Bribery Act 2010	119

Chapter 8
Failure of Commercial Organisations to Prevent Bribery — 129
Bribery Act 2010: section 7 — 129
Bribery Act 2010: section 8 — 130
Introduction — 130
Liability of corporate bodies — 131
   Corporate criminal liability and mens rea — 131
   Corporate liability under section 7 — 132
   Status of section 7 offence — 133
   Expanded jurisdiction — 134
   Corporate liability for other Bribery Act offences — 134
   Key issues — 134
   'C': a relevant commercial organisation — 135
   UK corporations and partnerships — 136
   Non-UK corporations and partnerships — 137
      Carrying on a business — 137
      Part of a business — 138
      Stock exchange listing — 140
      UK subsidiary of foreign company — 141
      The corporate veil — 142
      Must the UK subsidiary have a hand in the bribery? — 143
'A': a person associated with C (section 8) — 144
   What is an associated person? — 144
      Performing services for or on behalf of C — 144
      What does section 8(4) add? — 145
   Categories of associated person — 146
      A 'bribery only' relationship? — 146
      Shareholders — 147
      Employees, directors, partners — 147
      Agents — 147
      Suppliers — 148
      Contractors and subcontractors — 149
      Subsidiaries — 150
      Joint ventures — 152
      Example — 153
      Joint venture not incorporated — 155
      Other considerations — 156
Bribery by A to obtain/retain business or business advantage for C — 156
   Section 1 offence by A — 157
   Section 6 offence by A — 157
   Additional mens rea required by section 7(1) — 158
   No need for A to be prosecuted — 158
   No need for A to have UK connection — 159
The defence of adequate procedures — 159
   Burden of proof of adequate procedures is on C — 159
   Object is prevention of bribery by associated persons — 160
   Procedures must be 'adequate' — 160

Chapter 9
Defence of Adequate Procedures, Defence Under Section 13, Defences of Duress and Necessity — 163

Introduction	163
Adequate procedures	163
Bribery Act 2010: section 9	163
Meaning of 'adequate'	164
The status of the Ministry of Justice Guidance	166
The guidance document	166
Quick Start Guide	167
'Government policy' on interpretation of the Act	167
Six principles for prevention of bribery by associated persons	168
Principle 1: proportionate procedures	169
Sub-principles and specific topics	169
Proportionality	170
Clear, practical and accessible	173
List of topics	174
Gifts/hospitality	175
Facilitation payments	175
Recruitment/employment	176
Financial controls	176
Speak up procedures	176
Investigations and conflicts of interest	177
Principle 2: top level commitment	178
Principle 3: risk assessment	180
Methodology	181
Incentives	182
Regulatory environment	183
How much information is enough?	183
Principle 4: due diligence	184
Varying due diligence according to incorporation?	185
Red flags	186
Principle 5: communication (including training)	188
Principle 6: monitoring and review	189
Recording the procedures at work	189
Outline ABC policy	190
Defence for military and security service personnel –section 13	190
Bribery Act 2010: section 13	190
Relevant bribery offence	192
Armed forces and intelligence services	192
Proper exercise of any function	193
Police and informants	193
Defences of duress and necessity	194
Duress	194
Necessity	195
Outline ABC policy	197

Chapter 10
Consent to Prosecution, Enforcement Priorities and Penalties — 211
Bribery Act 2010: sections 10 and 11 — 211
Introduction — 213
Role of the Attorney-General and directors of prosecuting agencies (section 10) — 213
Prosecutors' priorities — 215
    Prosecution of individuals — 216
        2011 Joint Prosecution Guidance — 218
Giving assistance to prosecutors — 220
    Corporate prosecutions — 221
        Attorney-General's Guidance — 221
        Serious Fraud Office policy — 224
        Effect of Innospec on SFO policy — 224
        2011 Joint Prosecution Guidance — 226
Section 11: penalties — 227
    Mode of trial — 227
    Sentencing — 228
Maximum sentences provided in the Act — 228
Ranges of sentence: individuals — 229
Suspended sentences? — 230
Range of sentences: companies — 231
Innospec and sentencing — 232
    Ancillary orders — 233
        Compensation order — 233
    Confiscation order — 234
    Financial reporting order — 234
    Serious crime prevention order — 235
    Civil recovery orders under the Proceeds of Crime Act 2002 — 235
Agreements with SFO to accept civil penalties — 236
Disqualification as a director — 238
Other sentences — 239
Debarment from public procurement — 248
Proposed amendment of UK regulations — 249
Role of the Financial Services Authority — 250

Chapter 11
Territorial Application — 253
Bribery Act 2010: section 12 — 253
Introduction — 254
Sections 1, 2 and 6: territorial jurisdiction — 254
    Section 1 – provision of bribes — 256
    Section 2 – receipt of bribes — 257
    Section 6 – providing bribes to a foreign public official — 258
Sections 1, 2 and 6: nationality jurisdiction — 258
    British citizen — 259
    British overseas territories citizen — 260
    British national (overseas) — 260

British overseas citizen	260
British subject under the British Nationality Act 1981	261
British protected person	261
Individual ordinarily resident in the UK	261
UK incorporated body	262
British overseas territories/Crown dependency incorporated bodies	262
Section 7: failure of commercial organisations to prevent bribery	263
Specific provisions in relation to Scots criminal procedure	264

Chapter 12
Accessory Liability, Inchoate Offences, Related Offences and Extradition — 265

Introduction	265
Accessory liability for bribery offences	265
Aiding and abetting, counselling and procuring	266
Encouraging or assisting crime – Serious Crime Act 2007	268
Conspiracy	270
Fact of agreement	270
Impossibility	271
Intention to agree and fulfil agreement	271
The uses of conspiracy	272
Attempt	273
More than merely preparatory	273
Specific intent	274
Fraud	274
Fraud by abuse of position	276
Conspiracy to defraud	276
Money laundering	277
Criminal property	277
Main offences	278
Regulated sector	279
False accounting	280
Failure of companies to keep accurate records	281
Misconduct in public office	281
Extradition	283

Chapter 13
Civil Liability — 285

Introduction	285
Civil procedure	286
Jurisdiction	287
Arbitration	287
Key principles	287
Bribery as a civil wrong	287
The agent/principal relationship	288
Fiduciary duties	289
Definition of civil bribery	290
Proof of bribery	290

Knowledge of principal	292
Overview of claims	292
Claims against an agent	293
Breach of contract	293
Civil fraud	294
Unjust enrichment and restitution	295
Breach of fiduciary duty: account of profits and constructive trust	296
Conspiracy	297
Claims against the briber	298
Transaction void	299
Rescission	299
Bars to rescission	300
Damages for fraud and inducing breach of contract	301
Unjust enrichment claim against the briber	302
Dishonest assistance in a breach of fiduciary duty	302
Recovery of briber's profits	303
Conspiracy	303
Election and tracing	304
Election	304
Tracing	304
Claims against third parties other than the agent or briber	305
Claims by parties other than the principal of the agent	305
Unlawful means conspiracy	306
Breach of implied term of contract	306
Collusion in anti-competitive behaviour	307
Interim relief	307
Freezing order	308
Search order	309
Form and content of the search order	310
Supplemental orders	310
Civil recovery by states against former officials	311

Chapter 14
Particular Problems: Hospitality, Promotion, Facilitation Payments,
Extortion and Mergers — 313

Introduction	313
Corporate hospitality and promotional expenses	314
Private sector hospitality	315
Hospitality and the UK public sector	317
Hospitality and foreign public officials	318
Scenario A	319
Travel and events	321
Conference	322
Hedge fund fees	322
Next steps	323
Facilitation payments, extortion and mergers and acquisitions	325
Mergers and acquisitions	327

Scenario B 328
　　　　Port services fees 330
　　　　Cash for speedy visas 332
　　　　Inspection costs rebate 332
　　　　Austeristan airport – visa problems 333
　　　　Austeristan airport – threat of imprisonment 334
　　　　Subsequent allegations 334
　　　　Next steps 335

Appendix A
The Bribery Act 2010 337

Appendix B
The Bribery Act 2010: Explanatory Notes 355

Appendix C
Ministry of Justice Guidance, Section 9 of the Bribery Act 2010 ... 371

Appendix D
Ministry of Justice Guidance, The Bribery Act 2010, Quick Start Guide ... 405

Appendix E
Joint Prosecution Guidance on the Bribery Act 2010 411

Appendix F
OECD Convention on Combating Bribery of Foreign Public Officials in International Business Transactions ... 423

Appendix G
Commentaries on the OECD Convention 435

Appendix H
United Nations Convention Against Corruption 467

Appendix I
List of Useful Websites 523

Index **527**

TABLE OF CASES

References are to paragraph numbers.

A-G of Zambia (for and on behalf of the Republic of Zambia) v Meer Care & Desai (a firm) [2008] EWCA Civ 1007, [2008] All ER (D) 406 (Jul) [2008] EWCA Civ 754, [2008] All ER (D) 106 (Jul), CA, *Reversing*, [2007] EWHC 952 (Ch), [2007] All ER (D) 97 (May), Ch D ... 13.103

A-G v Blake (Jonathan Cape Ltd third party) [2001] 1 AC 268, [2000] 4 All ER 385, [2000] 2 All ER (Comm) 487, [2000] 3 WLR 625, [2000] IP & T 1261, [2000] NLJR 1230, [2000] 32 LS Gaz R 37, 144 Sol Jo LB 242, [2000] EMLR 949, [2001] 1 LRC 260, [2000] All ER (D) 1074, HL, *Affirming on other grounds* [1998] Ch 439, [1998] 1 All ER 833, [1998] 2 WLR 805, [1998] 04 LS Gaz R 33, [1998] NLJR 15, 142 Sol Jo LB 35, [1998] EMLR 309, CA, *reversing* [1997] Ch 84, [1996] 3 All ER 903, [1996] 3 WLR 741, [1996] FSR 727, [1996] EMLR 382, Ch D ... 13.42

A-G's Reference (No. 1 of 1975) [1975] QB 773, [1975] 2 All ER 684, [1975] 3 WLR 11, [1975] RTR 473, 61 Cr App Rep 118, 139 JP 569, 119 Sol Jo 373, CA ... 12.12

Adams v Cape Industries Plc [1990] Ch 433, [1991] 1 All ER 929, [1990] 2 WLR 657, [1990] BCLC 479, [1990] BCC 786, [1990] 11 LS Gaz R 36, CA, Ch D ... 8.55

Alexander v Webber [1922] 1 KB 642, 91 LJKB 320, 126 LT 512, 38 TLR 42, KBD ... 13.16

Arab Monetary Fund v Hashim [1993] 1 Lloyd's Rep 543, Comml Ct ... 13.9

Armagas Ltd v Mundogas SA, *The Ocean Frost* [1986] AC 717, [1986] 2 All ER 385, [1986] 2 WLR 1063, [1986] 2 Lloyd's Rep 109, 2 BCC 99, 197, 130 Sol Jo 430, [1986] LS Gaz R 2002, [1986] NLJ Rep 511, HL, *affirming* [1986] AC 717, [1985] 3 All ER 795, [1985] 3 WLR 640, [1985] 1 Lloyd's Rep 1, 129 Sol Jo 362, [1984] LS Gaz R 2169, CA, *reversing* [1985] 1 Lloyd's Rep 1, QBD ... 13.40, 13.49, 13.85

Aston Cantlow and Wilmcote with Billesley Parochial Church Council v Wallbank [2003] UKHL 37, [2004] 1 AC 546, [2003] 3 All ER 1213, [2003] 3 WLR 283, [2003] 33 LS Gaz R 28, [2003] NLJR 1030, (2003) *The Times*, 27 June, 147 Sol Jo LB 812, [2003] All ER (D) 360 (Jun), HL ... 4.16

Att-Gen for Hong Kong v Reid [1994] 1 AC 324, [1994] 1 All ER 1, [1993] 3 WLR 1143, [1993] NLJR 1569, 137 Sol Jo LB 251, PC, *On Appeal from* [1992] 2 NZLR 385 (NZ CA) ... 13.10, 13.41, 13.69, 13.78

Attorney General's Reference (No. 3 of 2003) [2005] 1 QB 73 ... 12.80, 12.82, 12.83

Bank Mellat v Nikpour [1985] FSR 87, [1982] Com LR 158, CA ... 13.90

Bank of Credit and Commerce International (Overseas) Ltd (in liq) v Akindele [2001] Ch 437, [2000] 4 All ER 221, [2000] 3 WLR 1423, [2000] Lloyd's Rep Bank 292, 2 ITELR 788, [2000] BCC 968, [2000] NLJR 950, [2000] 26 LS Gaz R 36, CA, affirming [1999] BCC 669, Ch D ... 13.80

Bankers Trust v Shapira [1980] 3 All ER 353, [1980] 1 WLR 1274, 10 LDAB 235, 124 Sol Jo 480, CA	13.101
Barlow Clowes International Ltd (in liquidation) & Ors v Eurotrust International Ltd [2006] 1 All ER 333 [2005] UKPC 37, [2006] 1 All ER 333, [2006] 1 All ER (Comm) 479, [2006] 1 WLR 1476, [2006] 1 P & CR D46, [2006] 1 Lloyd's Rep 225, 8 ITELR 347, [2005] 44 LS Gaz R 32, [2006] 1 LRC 667, [2005] All ER (D) 99 (Oct), PC	13.67
Baxter v Governor of HM Prison Brixton [2002] EWHC 300 (Admin), [2002] All ER (D) 218 (Jan), DC	12.74
Blackpool & Fylde Aero Club v Blackpool Borough Council [1990] 3 All ER 25, [1990] 1 WLR 1195, 88 LGR 864, [1990] 26 LS Gaz R 37, CA	13.86
Bodmin Case (1869) 1 O'M & H 117, 20 LT 989, pre-SCJA 1873	2.20
Bolton Partners v Lambert (1889) 41 Ch D 302, *affirming*(1889) 41 Ch D 295, 58 LJ Ch 425, 37 WR 434, 60 LT 687, 5 TLR 357, CA	13.53
Boston Deep Sea Fishing and Ice Co v Ansell (1888) 39 Ch D 339, [1886–90] All ER Rep 65, 59 LT 345, CA	13.30
Bowman v Fels [2005] EWCA Civ 226, [2005] 4 All ER 609, [2005] 1 WLR 3083, [2005] 2 Cr App Rep 243, [2005] 2 FLR 247, [2005] Fam Law 546, [2005] NLJR 413, (2005) *The Times*, 14 March, 149 Sol Jo LB 357, [2005] All ER (D) 115 (Mar), CA	12.67
Bradlaugh v Gossett (1884) 12 QBD 271, 53 LJQB 209, 32 WR 552, 50 LT 620, DC	4.25
Brauch (a debtor), *Re*, *ex parte* Britannic Securities and Investments Ltd [1978] Ch 316, [1978] 1 All ER 1004, [1977] 3 WLR 354, 121 Sol Jo 117, CA	8.34
Brinks MAT v Elcombe [1988] 3 All ER 188, [1988] 1 WLR 1350, CA	13.93
Bristol and West Building Society v Mothew (t/a Stapley & Co), *sub nom* Mothew v Bristol & West Building Society [1998] Ch 1, [1996] 4 All ER 698, [1997] 2 WLR 436, 75 P & CR 241, [1996] NLJR 1273, 140 Sol Jo LB 206, [1997] PNLR 11, CA	13.15
Brown v London and North Western Rly Co (1863) 27 JP 711, 4 B & S 326, 32 LJQB 318, 10 Jur NS 234, 2 New Rep 447, 11 WR 884, 122 ER 481, [1861-73] All ER Rep 487, 8 LT 695, Ct of QB	8.34
Cain v Butler [1916] 1 KB 759, 85 LJKB 804, 66 Sol Jo 539, 114 LT 698, 32 TLR 310, KBD	8.34
Car and Universal Finance Co Ltd v Caldwell [1965] 1 QB 525, [1964] 1 All ER 290, [1964] 2 WLR 600, 108 Sol Jo 15, CA, *affirming* [1965] 1 QB 525, [1963] 2 All ER 547, [1964] 2 WLR 600, 107 Sol Jo 738, QBD	13.58
CBS Songs Ltd v Amstrad Consumer Electronics plc [1988] AC 1013, [1988] 2 All ER 484, [1988] 2 WLR 1191, [1988] RPC 567, 132 Sol Jo 789, HL, *affirming* [1988] Ch 61, [1987] 3 All ER 151, [1987] 3 WLR 144, [1987] RPC 429, 131 Sol Jo 534, [1987] LS Gaz R 1243, CA	13.44
Churchman v Churchman [1945] P 44, [1945] 2 All ER 190, 114 LJP 17, 89 Sol Jo 508, 173 LT 108, 61 TLR 464, CA	2.72
Clough v London and North Western Rly Co (1871) LR 7 Exch 26, 41 LJ Ex 17, 20 WR 189, [1861-73] All ER Rep 646, 25 LT 708, Ex Ch	13.58
Conroy v Kenny [1999] 1 WLR 1340, [1999] All ER (D) 46, CA	8.31
Consul Development Pty Ltd v DPC Estates Pty Ltd [1975] 132 CLR 373, 5 ALR 231, 49 ALJ 74, Aus HC	13.68
Cooper v Slade (1858) 22 JP 511, 6 HL Cas 746, 27 LJQB 449, 4 Jur NS 791, 6 WR 461, 31 LTOS 334, Ex Ch	1.38
Corporacion National del Cobre de Chile v Sogemin Metals Ltd [1997] 2 All ER 917, [1997] 1 WLR 1396, [1996] 46 LS Gaz R 29, [1997] NLJR 161, [1997] CLC 435, Ch D	13.33, 13.38
Credit Lyonnais Bank Nederland NV (now known as Generale Bank Nederland NV) v Export Credits Guarantee Department, *sub nom* Generale Bank Nederland NV (formerly Credit Lyonnais Bank Nederland NV) v Export Credits Guarantee Department[2000] 1 AC	

Credit Lyonnais Bank Nederland NV (now known as Generale Bank Nederland NV) v Export Credits Guarantee Department, *sub nom* Generale Bank Nederland NV (formerly Credit Lyonnais Bank Nederland NV) v Export Credits Guarantee Department[2000] 1 AC —*continued* 486, [1999] 1 All ER 929, [1999] 2 WLR 540, [1999] 1 Lloyd's Rep 563, 143 Sol Jo LB 89, HL, *affirming* [1998] 1 Lloyd's Rep 19, [1997] 34 LS Gaz R 29, 141 Sol Jo LB 194, CA, *affirming* [1996] 1 Lloyd's Rep 200, 13 LDAB 194, [1996] CLC 11, QBD	13.44
Daraydan Holdings Ltd v Solland International Ltd [2004] EWHC 622 (Ch), [2005] Ch 119, [2005] 4 All ER 73, [2004] 3 WLR 1106, [2004] All ER (D) 507 (Mar), Ch D	13.20, 13.41
Devenish Nutrition Ltd v Sanofi-Aventis SA (France) and others [2008] EWCA Civ 1086, [2009] 3 All ER 27, [2009] 3 WLR 198, [2009] Bus LR 858, (2008) *The Times*, 4 November, 152 Sol Jo (no 41) 32, [2008] All ER (D) 117 (Oct), CA, *Affirming* [2007] EWHC 2394 (Ch), [2008] 2 All ER 249, [2008] 2 WLR 637, [2008] Bus LR 600, [2007] All ER (D) 293 (Oct), Ch D	13.87
Director General of Fair Trading v Pioneer Concrete (UK) Ltd, *sub nom* Supply of Ready Mixed Concrete (No 2), *Re*, Director General of Fair Trading v Pioneer Concrete (UK) Ltd [1995] 1 AC 456, [1995] 1 All ER 135, [1994] 3 WLR 1249, [1995] ICR 25, [1995] IRLR 94, [1995] 1 BCLC 613, [1995] 01 LS Gaz R 37, [1995] NLJR 17, HL, *reversing* [1994] ICR 57, [1994] IRLR 21, CA	8.6
DPP v Armstrong [2000] Crim LR 379	12.17
DPP v Holly, DPP v Manners, *sub nom* R v Manners, R v Holly [1978] AC 43, [1976] 2 All ER 96, [1976] 2 WLR 709, 64 Cr App Rep 143, 140 JP 364, [1976] Crim LR 255, 120 Sol Jo 96, CA	1.36, 4.14, 7.47
DPP v K & B [1997] 1 Cr App Rep 36,, [1997] Crim LR 121, KB	12.5
DPP v Shannon, *sub nom* R v Shannon [1975] AC 717, [1974] 2 All ER 1009, [1974] 3 WLR 155, 59 Cr App Rep 250, 138 JP 587, 118 Sol Jo 515, HL, *reversing* [1975] AC 717, [1974] 2 All ER 1009, [1974] 3 WLR 155, CA	12.27
El Ajou v Dollar Land Holdings plc [1994] 1 All ER 685, [1994] 1 BCLC 464, [1994] BCC 143, CA, *reversing* [1993] 3 All ER 717, [1993] BCLC 735, [1993] BCC 698, Ch D	13.79
European Roma Rights Centre v Immigration Officer at Prague Airport (United Nations High Commissioner for Refugees intervening) [2004] UKHL 55, [2005] 2 AC 1, [2005] 1 All ER 527, [2005] 2 WLR 1, [2005] IRLR 115, [2004] NLJR 1893, (2004) *The Times*, 10 December, 149 Sol Jo LB 27, 18 BHRC 1, [2005] 3 LRC 657, [2004] All ER (D) 127 (Dec), HL	7.17
Ex parte Winters 140 P 164 (1914) (Criminal Court of Appeals of Oklahoma)	4.33
Experience Hendrix LLC v PPX Enterprises Inc [2003] EWCA Civ 323, [2003] 1 All ER (Comm) 830, [2003] FSR 853, [2003] 22 LS Gaz R 29, (2003) *Times*, 19 April, 147 Sol Jo LB 509, [2003] EMLR 515, [2003] All ER (D) 328 (Mar), CA, *reversing* [2002] EWHC 1353 (QB), [2002] All ER (D) 100 (Jul), QBD	13.42
F v West Berkshire Health Authority [1990] 2 AC 1, [1989] 2 WLR 1025; *sub nom* F (Sterilisation: Mental Patient), Re [1989] 2 FLR 376, [1989] 2 All ER 545, CA and HL 9.143	9.145
Federal Republic of Nigeria v Santolina Investment Corp, Solomon & Peters, and others [2007] EWHC 3053 (QB), [2007] All ER (D) 11 (Dec), Comp Ct	13.104
Fyffes v Templeman [2000] 2 Lloyd's Rep 643, [2000] 25 LS Gaz R 40, (2000) *The Times*, 14 June, Comml Ct	13.40, 13.66, 13.69

Gammon (Hong Kong) Ltd v A-G of Hong Kong [1985] AC 1, [1984] 2 All
ER 503, [1984] 3 WLR 437, 80 Cr App Rep 194, [1984] Crim LR
479, 128 Sol Jo 549, [1984] LS Gaz R 1993, 26 BLR 159, PC ... 8.3
Gillick v West Norfolk and Wisbech Area Health Authority [1986] AC 112,
[1985] 3 All ER 402, [1985] 3 WLR 830, [1986] 1 FLR 224, [1986]
Crim LR 113, 129 Sol Jo 738, 2 BMLR 11, [1985] LS Gaz R 3551,
[1985] NLJ Rep 1055, HL, *reversing* [1986] AC 112, [1985] 1 All ER
533, [1985] 2 WLR 413, [1985] FLR 736, [1985] Fam Law 165, 129
Sol Jo 47, [1985] LS Gaz R 762, [1985] NLJ Rep 81, CA, on Appeal
from [1984] QB 581, [1984] 1 All ER 365, [1983] 3 WLR 859, [1984]
FLR 249, [1984] Fam Law 207, 147 JP 888, 127 Sol Jo 696, [1983] LS
Gaz R 2678, 133 NLJ 888, QBD ... 9.145
Grant v Gold Exploration and Development Syndicate Limited [1900] 1 QB
233, 69 LJQB 150, 48 WR 280, 44 Sol Jo 100, 82 LT 5, 16 TLR 86,
[1895-9] All ER Rep Ext 1304, CA ... 13.65
Great Western Insurance Co of New York v Cunliffe (1874) 9 Ch App 525,
43 LJ Ch 741, 30 LT 661, CA ... 13.23

H (Minors), *Re* [1996] AC 563 ... 13.5
Heinl v Jyske Bank, (Gibraltar) Ltd [1999] Lloyd's Rep Bank 511, (1999)
The Times, 28 September, (CA) ... 13.53
Hovenden & Sons v Millhoff [1900-3] All ER Rep 848, 83 LT 41, 16 TLR
506, CA ... 13.9, 13.19, 13.32
Hurstanger Ltd v Wilson [2007] EWCA Civ 299, [2007] 4 All ER 1118,
[2007] 2 All ER (Comm) 1037, [2007] 1 WLR 2351, [2008] Bus LR
216, [2007] NLJR 555, (2007) *The Times*, 11 May, [2007] All ER (D)
66 (Apr), CA ... 13.18, 13.23, 13.61

Immucor Inc and Gioacchino De Chirico, *Re*, SEC Administrative
Proceeding File No 3-12846 (27 September 2007), File No 3-11933
(2005) ... 7.42
Indicii Salus Ltd (in receivership) v Chandrasekaran [2006] EWHC 521
(Ch), [2006] All ER (D) 187 (Feb), Ch D ... 13.98
Industries and General Mortgage Co Ltd v Lewis [1949] 2 All ER 573,
[1949] WN 333, 93 Sol Jo 577, 99 L Jo 468, KBD ... 13.18
IRC v Marine Steam Turbine Co. Ltd [1920] 1 KB 193, 12 TC 174, 89
LJKB 49, 121 LT 368, 35 TLR 599, KBD ... 8.34
Island Records Ltd v Tring International plc [1995] 3 All ER 444, [1996] 1
WLR 1256, [1995] FSR 560, Ch D ... 13.71

Johnson v Phillips [1975] 3 All ER 682, [1976] 1 WLR 65, [1976] RTR 170,
140 JP 37, [1975] Crim LR 580, 119 Sol Jo 645, DC ... 9.143
Johnson v Youden [1950] 1 KB 544, [1950] 1 All ER 800, DC ... 12.6

Kensington International Ltd v Republic of Congo [2005] EWHC 2684
(Comm), [2006] 2 BCLC 296, [2005] All ER (D) 370 (Nov), Comml
Ct ... 8.55
Kirkwood v Gadd [1910] AC 422, 79 LJKB 815, [1908–10] All ER Rep 768,
54 Sol Jo 599, 102 LT 753, 26 TLR 530, HL ... 8.31
Kuwait Oil Tanker Co SAK v AL Bader [2000] 2 All ER (Comm) 271, CA ... 13.83

Levene v IRC [1928] AC 217, 97 LJKB 377, [1928] All ER Rep 746, HL
11.34 ... 11.34
Lister & Co v Stubbs (1890) 45 Ch D 1, 59 LJ Ch 570, 38 WR 548,
[1886–90] All ER Rep 797, 63 LT 75, 6 TLR 317, CA ... 13.41, 13.69
Lister v Hesley Hall [2001] UKHL 22, [2001] 1 AC 215, [2001] 1 WLR 1311,
[2001] 2 All ER 769, HL ... 4.30
Logicrose Ltd v Southend United Football Club Ltd [1988] 1 WLR 1256,
132 Sol Jo 1591, (1988) *The Times*, 5 March, Ch D ... 13.30, 13.55

Table of Cases xxvii

Lonrho Ltd and others v Shell Petroleum Co Ltd and others (No 2) [1981] 2
    All ER 456, HL, (No 1) (unreported) 6 March 1981, CA   13.46
Lonrho plc v Fayed [1992] 1 AC 448, [1991] 3 WLR 188, [1991] BCC 641,
    HL 13.83   13.46, 13.83, 13.85

Mahesan S/O Thambiah v Malaysia Government Officers' Co-operative
    Housing Society Ltd [1979] AC 374, [1978] 2 All ER 405, [1978] 2
    WLR 444, 122 Sol Jo 31, PC   13.32, 13.33, 13.62, 13.71
Mareva Compania Naveria SA v International Bulk Carriers SA (*The
    Mareva*) [1980] 1 All ER 213, [1975] 2 Lloyd's Rep 509, 9 LDAB 393,
    119 Sol Jo 660, CA   13.91
Massey v Boulden [2002] EWCA Civ 1634, [2003] 2 All ER 87, 93, 103,,
    [2003] 1 WLR 1792, [2003] 1 P & CR 354, [2003] 1 P & CR D23,
    [2003] 1 EGLR 24, [2003] 03 LS Gaz R 34, [2003] 11 EG 154, [2002]
    48 EGCS 139, (2002) *The Times*, 27 November, 146 Sol Jo LB 264,
    [2002] All ER (D) 188 (Nov), CA   1.73
Meretz Investments NV v ACP Ltd [2007] EWCA Civ 1303, [2008] Ch 244,
    [2008] 2 WLR 904, [2007] All ER (D) 156 (Dec), CA, *Reversing in
    part* [2006] EWHC 74 (Ch), [2007] Ch 197, [2006] 3 All ER 1029,
    [2007] 2 WLR 403, [2006] 2 P & CR 391, [2006] 06 EG 170 (CS),
    (2006) *The Times*, 27 April, [2006] All ER (D) 234 (Jan), Ch D   13.83
Meridian Global Funds Management Asia Ltd v Securities Commission
    [1995] 2 AC 500, [1995] 3 All ER 918, [1995] 3 WLR 413, [1995] 2
    BCLC 116, [1995] BCC 942, [1995] 28 LS Gaz R 39, PC   8.6
Moorcock (The) (1889) 14 PD 64, 58 LJP 73, 6 Asp MLC 373, 37 WR 439,
    [1886–90] All ER Rep 530, 60 LT 654, 5 TLR 316, CA, *affirming*
    (1888) 13 PD 157, P, D and Admlty   13.29
Morgan Grenfell & Co Ltd v Welwyn Hatfield District Council, Islington
    London Borough Council (Third Party) [1995] 1 All ER 1, Comml
    Ct   4.27, 8.32

Newman v Oughton [1911] 1 KB 792, 80 LJKB 673, 55 Sol Jo 272, 104 LT
    211, 27 TLR 254, KBD   8.34
News International plc v Clingerand others [1998] All ER (D) 592,
    (unreported) 17 November 1998, QB   13.83
Ninemia Maritime Corpn v Trave Schiffahrtsgesellschaft mbH & Co KG,
    The Niedersachen [1984] 1 All ER 398, [1983] 1 WLR 1412, [1983] 2
    Lloyd's Rep 600, [1984] LS Gaz R 198, CA, *affirming* [1984] 1 All
    ER 398, [1983] 1 WLR 1412, [1983] 2 Lloyd's Rep 600, [1983] Com
    LR 234, 127 Sol Jo 824, QBD   13.92
Norris v Government of the United States [2010] UKSC 9, [2010] 2 AC 487,
    [2010] 2 All ER 267, [2010] 2 WLR 572, (2010) *The Times*, 25
    February, [2010] All ER (D) 256 (Feb), SC, *affirming* [2009] EWHC
    995 (Admin), [2009] All ER (D) 144 (May), DC   12.89
Norwich Pharmacal Co v Customs and Excise Commissioners [1974] AC
    133, [1973] 3 WLR 164, [1973] 2 All ER 943, HL 13.101   13.101

O'Sullivan v Management Agency & Music Ltd [1985] 1 QB 428, [1985] 3
    All ER 351, [1984] 3 WLR 448, 128 Sol Jo 548, CA   13.59
OBG Ltd v Allan; Douglas v Hello! Ltd (No 3); Mainstream Properties Ltd
    v Young [2007] UKHL 21, [2008] 1 AC 1, [2007] 4 All ER 545, [2008]
    1 All ER (Comm) 1, [2007] 2 WLR 920, [2007] Bus LR 1600, [2007]
    19 EG 165 (CS), (2007) *The Times*, 4 May, 151 Sol Jo LB 674, [2007]
    EMLR 325, [2008] 1 LRC 279, [2007] All ER (D) 44 (May), HL   13.64, 13.65, 13.84
Ocular Sciences Limited v Aspect Vision Care Limited [1997] RPC 289   13.41

Panama and South Pacific Telegraph Co v India Rubber, Gutta Percha and
    Telegraph Works Co (1875) 10 Ch App 515, 45 LJ Ch 121, 23 WR
    583, 32 LT 517, CA in Ch   13.18, 13.30, 13.54

Parkdale (The) [1897] P 53, 66 LJP 10, 8 Asp MLC 211, 45 WR 368, 75 LT
597, 13 TLR 82, DC ... 13.22
Pepper (Inspector of Taxes) v Hart [1993] AC 593, [1992] 3 WLR 1032,
[1992] STC 898, [1993] 1 All ER 42, [1993] ICR 291, HL ... 1.73
Petrotrade and others Inc v Smith and others [2000] All ER (D) 264, QBD ... 13.19
Piller (Anton) KG v Manufacturing Processes Ltd [1976] Ch 55, [1976] 1 All
ER 779, [1976] 2 WLR 162, [1976] FSR 129, [1976] RPC 719, 120
Sol Jo 63, CA ... 13.97
Polly Peck International plc v Nadir (No 2) [1992] 4 All ER 769, [1992] 2
Lloyd's Rep 238, [1992] NLJR 671, CA, reversing [1993] BCLC 187,
Ch D ... 13.101
Practice Direction (Criminal Proceedings: Consolidation) [2002] 1 WLR
2070 ... 10.48
Premium Nafta Products Ltd (20th Defendant) & Ors v Fili Shipping
Company Ltd & Ors [2007] UKHL 40, [2008] 1 Lloyd's Rep 254, HL ... 13.7

R (on the application of Al-Skeini) v Secretary of State for Defence [2007]
UKHL 26, [2008] 1 AC 153, [2007] 3 All ER 685, [2007] 3 WLR 33,
[2007] NLJR 894, (2007) *The Times*, 14 June, 22 BHRC 518, [2008] 1
LRC 618, [2007] All ER (D) 106 (Jun), HL, *affirming* [2005] EWCA
Civ 1609, [2007] QB 140, [2006] 3 WLR 508, [2006] NLJR 112,
(2006) *The Times*, 6 January, [2005] All ER (D) 337 (Dec), CA,
affirming [2004] EWHC 2911 (Admin), [2005] 2 WLR 1401, [2005] 03
LS Gaz R 30, [2005] NLJR 58, (2004) *The Times*, 20 December,
[2004] All ER (D) 197 (Dec), DC ... 11.3
R (on the application of Corner House Research) v Director of the Serious
Fraud Office (BAE Systems plc, interested party) [2008] UKHL 60,
[2009] AC 756, [2008] 4 All ER 927, [2009] Crim LR 47, [2008]
NLJR 1149, (2008) *The Times*, 31 July, 152 Sol Jo (no 32) 29, [2009]
1 LRC 343, [2008] All ER (D) 399 (Jul), HL ... 7.13, 10.4
R (on the application of Daly) v Secretary of State for the Home
Department [2001] UKHL 26, [2001] 2 AC 532, [2001] 3 All ER 433,
[2001] 2 WLR 1622, [2001] 26 LS Gaz R 43, 145 Sol Jo LB 156,
[2001] 4 LRC 345, [2001] All ER (D) 280 (May), HL ... 9.32
R (on the application of N) v Mental Health Review Tribunal (Northern
Region) [2005] EWCA Civ 1605, [2006] QB 468, [2006] 4 All ER 194,
[2006] 2 WLR 850, 88 BMLR 59, [2005] All ER (D) 360 (Dec), CA,
affirming on other grounds [2005] EWHC 587 (Admin), (2005) *The
Times*, 18 April, [2005] All ER (D) 71 (Apr), Admin Ct ... 13.5
R v A (prosecution application for permission to appeal under s 58 of the
Criminal Justice Act 2003) [2007] EWCA Crim 2868, [2007] All ER
(D) 36 (Dec), CA ... 1.50
R v Anderson (Malcolm John) [2003] 2 Cr App Rep (S) 28 ... 10.109
R v Andrews-Weatherfoil Ltd [1972] 1 All ER 65, [1972] 1 WLR 118, 70
LGR 105, 56 Cr App Rep 31, 136 JP 128, 115 Sol Jo 888, CA ... 1.39, 2.4, 2.43, 3.38, 8.5
R v BAE Systems Plc (unreported) 21 December 2010 ... 10.85, 10.109, 12.78
R v Bembridge (1783) 3 Doug KB 327, 22 State Tr 1, (1783) 99 ER 679 ... 12.79
R v Boal [1992] QB 591, [1992] 3 All ER 177, [1992] 2 WLR 890, 95 Cr
App Rep 272, [1992] ICR 495, [1992] IRLR 420, 156 JP 617, [1992]
BCLC 872, [1992] 21 LS Gaz R 26, 136 Sol Jo LB 100, CA ... 2.73, 7.123
R v Bowden [1995] 4 All ER 505, [1996] 1 WLR 98, 94 LGR 137, 159 LG
Rev 649, 159 JP 502, [1996] Crim LR 57, CA ... 1.28, 12.81
R v British Steel plc [1995] 1 WLR 1356, [1995] ICR 586, [1995] IRLR 310,
[1995] Crim LR 654, CA ... 8.8
R v Bryce [2004] EWCA Crim 1231, [2004] 2 Cr App Rep 592, [2004] Crim
LR 936, [2004] All ER (D) 255 (May), CA ... 12.8
R v Bush [2003] 2 Cr App R (S) 117 ... 10.109
R v Carr [1956] 3 All ER 979n, [1957] 1 WLR 165, 40 Cr App Rep 188, 121
JP 58, 101 Sol Jo 112, Ct MAC ... 3.22, 3.23

R v Carr-Briant [1943] KB 607, [1943] 2 All ER 156, 41 LGR 183, 29 Cr
App Rep 76, 107 JP 167, 112 LJKB 581, 169 LT 175, 59 TLR 300,
CCA 8.139
R v Chaytor [2010] UKSC 52, [2011] 1 All ER 805, [2010] 3 WLR 1707,
[2011] 1 Cr App Rep 274, [2010] NLJR 1718, 174 CL&J 782, (2010)
The Times, 6 December, [2010] All ER (D) 19 (Dec), SC 1.5, 4.26
R v De Puy International (2011) (not yet reported) 10.47
R v Dearnley [2001] 2 Cr App R (S) 201 .... 10.109
R v Dias [2001] EWCA Crim 2986;, [2002] 2 Cr App Rep 96, [2001] All ER
(D) 198 (Dec), CA 12.5
R v Donald [1997] 2 Cr App R (S) 272 .... 10.109
R v Dougall [2010] EWCA Crim 1048, [2011] 1 Cr App Rep (S) 227, [2010]
Crim LR 661, 174 CL&J 365, (2010) *The Times*, 1 June, [2010] All
ER (D) 113 (May), CA 1.56, 10.47, 10.74, 10.104, 10.109, 12.34
R v Forsyth; R v Mabey [2011] 2 All ER 165, (2011) *The Times*, 24
February, [2010] EWCA Crim 2437; [2010] All ER (D) 25 (Nov)
Southwark Crown Court 23 February 2011 .... 10.109
R v Garner (1988) 10 Cr App R (S) 445 .... 10.109
R v Gaunt [2003] EWCA Crim. 3925, [2004] 2 Cr App Rep (S) 194, [2003]
All ER (D) 287 (Dec), CA 12.13
R v Ghosh [1982] QB 1053, [1982] 2 All ER 689, [1982] 3 WLR 110, 75 Cr
App Rep 154, 146 JP 376, [1982] Crim LR 608, 126 Sol Jo 429, CA ... 12.51
R v Godden-Wood [2001] Crim LR 810, [2001] EWCA Crim 1586, CA ... 4.10
R v Goodyear [2005] EWCA Crim 888, [2005] 3 All ER 117, [2005] 1 WLR
2532, [2005] 2 Cr App Rep 281, [2006] 1 Cr App Rep (S) 23, [2005]
Crim LR 659, (2005) *Times*, 21 April, 149 Sol Jo LB 512, [2005] All
ER (D) 266 (Apr), CA 10.48
R v Greenway (1992) *The Times*, December 8, 15, 22 .... 4.25
R v Gurney (1867) 31 JP 584, (1867) 10 Cox CC 550, pre-SCJA 1873 ...... 1.30, 2.36
R v Hall (1985) 81 Cr App Rep 260, [1985] Crim LR 377, 129 Sol Jo 283,
[1985] LS Gaz R 1485, [1985] NLJ Rep 604, CA 2.52
R v Harvey [1999] Crim LR 70, CA 1.39, 1.42, 4.10
R v Hasan, *sub nom* R v Z [2005] UKHL 22, [2005] 2 AC 467, [2005] 4 All
ER 685, [2005] 2 WLR 709, [2005] 2 Cr App Rep 314, [2006] Crim
LR 142, (2005) *The Times*, 21 March, 149 Sol Jo LB 360, [2005] All
ER (D) 299 (Mar), HL, reversing [2003] EWCA Crim 191, [2003] 1
WLR 1489, [2003] 2 Cr App Rep 173, [2003] Crim LR 627, (2003)
The Times, 26 March, [2003] All ER (D) 386 (Feb), CA 9.139
R v Heath (unreported) 23 September 2008 .... 1.56
R v Hurrell (Francis) [2003] EWCA Crim 3470, [2004] 2 Cr App Rep (S)
119, CA 10.109
R v Innospec Ltd [2010] EW Misc 7 (EWCC), [2010] Crim LR 665, Crown
Ct 1.56, 8.16, 10.39, 10.75, 10.78, 10.82, 10.103, 10.108, 10.109, 12.34
R v JF Alford Transport Ltd [1999] RTR 51, [1997] 2 Cr App Rep 326,
[1997] Crim LR 745, [1997] 15 LS Gaz R 27, 141 Sol Jo LB 73, CA 12.10, 12.13
R v Kellogg (MW) (2011) (not yet reported) 10.47, 10.100, 12.64
R v Mabey & Johnson Ltd (unreported) 29 September 2009 .... 1.56, 8.16, 10.77, 10.84, 10.87,
10.94, 10.108, 10.109, 12.34
R v Martin (Colin) [1989] 1 All ER 652, [1989] RTR 63, 88 Cr App Rep
343, 153 JP 231, [1989] Crim LR 284, CA 9.145
R v Messent (unreported) 26 October 2010 .... 1.56, 10.109
R v Millray Window Cleaning Co Ltd [1962] Crim LR 99 .... 1.40
R v Mills (1978) 68 Cr App R 154, 159, CA 1.39, 3.22, 3.23, 3.32
R v Moloney [1985] AC 905, [1985] 2 WLR 648, [1985] 1 All ER 1025, HL ... 2.24
R v Montila, *sub nom* R v M [2004] UKHL 50, [2005] 1 All ER 113, [2004]
1 WLR 3141, [2005] 2 Cr App Rep 425, [2005] Crim LR 479, [2005]
03 LS Gaz R 30, (2004) *The Times*, 26 November, [2004] All ER (D)
386 (Nov), HL 2.51
R v Natji [2002] EWCA Crim 271, [2002] 1 WLR 2337, [2002] 2 Cr
App Rep 302, (2002) *The Times*, 12 March, 146 Sol Jo LB 63, [2002]
All ER (D) 177 (Feb), CA 1.36

R v Ozakpinar ([2008] EWCA Crim 875, [2009] 1 Cr App R (S) 8, CA ... 10.109
R v P & O European Ferries (Dover) Ltd (1990) 93 Cr App Rep 72, [1991] Crim LR 695, CCC ... 8.6
R v P; R v Blackburn [2007] EWCA Crim 2290, [2008] 2 All ER 684, [2008] 2 Cr App Rep (S) 16, [2008] Crim LR 147, 151 Sol Jo LB 1438, [2007] All ER (D) 325 (Oct), CA ... 10.32
R v Quayle; A-G's Reference (No 2 of 2004) [2005] EWCA Crim 1415, [2006] 1 All ER 988, [2005] 1 WLR 3642, [2005] 2 Cr App Rep 527, [2006] Crim LR 148, 89 BMLR 169, (2005) The Times, 22 June, 149 Sol Jo LB 712, [2005] All ER (D) 447 (May), CA ... 9.145
R v Raud [1989] Crim LR 809 (CA) ... 7.5
R v Richards & Leeming (on appeal from 81 Cr App R 125) (unreported) 10 July 1986, HL ... 9.145
R v Saik [2006] UKHL 18, [2007] 1 AC 18, [2006] 4 All ER 866, [2006] 2 WLR 993, [2006] 2 Cr App Rep 368, (2006) The Times, 5 May, [2006] All ER (D) 24 (May), HL, reversing [2004] EWCA Crim 2936, (2004) The Times, 29 November, [2004] All ER (D) 383 (Nov), CA ... 12.31
R v Siracusa (1989) 90 Cr App Rep 340, [1989] Crim LR 712, CA ... 12.32
R v Smith [1960] 2 QB 423, [1960] 1 All ER 256, [1960] 2 WLR 164, 44 Cr App Rep 55, 124 JP 137, 104 Sol Jo 69, CCA ... 1.39
R v Smith (Wallace Duncan) (No 1) [1996] 2 Cr App Rep 1, [1996] Crim LR 329, [1996] 2 BCLC 109, [1995] 44 LS Gaz R 31, 140 Sol Jo LB 11, CA ... 11.5
R v Smith (Wallace Duncan) (No 4) [2004] QB 1418 (CA), [2004] All ER (D) 514 (Mar), (2004) The Times, 29 March, CA ... 11.5
R v Tobiasen, Tumukunde (unreported), HHJ Wasworth QC, Southwark Crown Court 2009 ... 10.30, 10.109
R v Walker [1962] Crim LR 458, CCA ... 12.26
R v Webster [2010] EWCA Crim 2819, [2011] 1 Cr App Rep 207, [2010] All ER (D) 05 (Dec), CA ... 1.50, 3.23
R v Welcher [2007] EWCA Crim 480, [2007] 2 Cr App Rep (S) 519, [2007] Crim LR 804, [2007] All ER (D) 33 (Mar), CA ... 10.109
R v Wellburn (1979) 69 Cr App Rep 254, 1 Cr App Rep (S) 64, CA ... 1.38
R v Whitaker [1914] 3 KB 1283, 10 Cr App Rep 245, 79 JP 28, 84 LJKB 225, 24 Cox CC 472, 58 Sol Jo 707, 112 LT 41, 30 TLR 627, CCA ... 1.28, 1.47, 12.81
R v Wilson (1982) 4 Cr App R (S) 337 ... 10.109
R v Woollin [1998] UKHL 28; [1999] AC 82; [1998] 4 All ER 103; [1998] 3 WLR 382; [1998] Crim LR 890; [1999] 1 Cr App Rep 8 (21st July, 1998), HL ... 2.24, 3.16, 7.69
Reading v A-G [1951] AC 507, [1951] 1 All ER 617, 95 Sol Jo 155, [1951] 1 TLR 480, HL ... 13.16
Redgrave v Hurd (1881) 20 Ch D 1, 57 LJ Ch 113, 30 WR 251, [1881-5] All ER Rep 77, 45 LT 185, CA ... 13.58
Royal Brunei Airlines Sdn Bhd v Philip Tan Kok Ming [1995] 2 AC 378, [1995] 3 All ER 97, [1995] 3 WLR 64, [1995] BCC 899, 13 LDAB 98, [1995] 27 LS Gaz R 33, [1995] NLJR 888, PC ... 13.67

S v Deal Enterprises (Pty) Ltd (1978) 3 SA 302, SA SC ... 1.29
Salomon v A Salomon & Co Ltd [1897] AC 22, 66 LJ Ch 35, 4 Mans 89, 45 WR 193, 1 LDAB 240, [1895-9] All ER Rep 33, 41 Sol Jo 63, 75 LT 426, 13 TLR 46, HL, reversing [1895] 2 Ch 323, 64 LJ Ch 689, 2 Mans 449, 12 R 395, 43 WR 612, 39 Sol Jo 522, 72 LT 755, 11 TLR 439, CA ... 8.54
Sarflax Ltd, Re [1979] Ch 592, [1979] 1 All ER 529 31, [1979] 2 WLR 202, 143 JP 225, 123 Sol Jo 97, Ch D ... 8.34
Serious Crime Agency v Agidi [2011] EWHC 175 (QB), [2011] All ER (D) 68 (Feb), QBD ... 12.62, 12.63

Table of Cases xxxi

Sinclair Investments (UK) Ltd v Versailles Trade Finance Ltd (in admin)
  [2011] EWCA Civ 347, [2011] All ER (D) 321 (Mar), CA, *affirming*
  [2010] EWHC 1614 (Ch), [2011] 1 BCLC 202, [2010] All ER (D) 10
  (Jul), Ch D ... 13.41, 13.69
Singh (Jagdeo) v R, *sub nom* Singh v State of Trinidad and Tobago [2005]
  UKPC 35, [2005] 4 All ER 781, [2006] 1 WLR 146, 68 WIR 424,
  [2006] 2 LRC 409, [2005] All ER (D) 18 (Aug), PC ... 1.39, 3.23
Smith New Court Securities Ltd v Scrimgeour Vickers (Asset Management)
  Ltd (Roberts, third party) [1994] 4 All ER 225, [1994] 1 WLR 1271,
  [1994] 2 BCLC 212, [1994] 15 LS Gaz R 35, 138 Sol Jo LB 77, CA,
  reversing [1992] BCLC 1104, Ch D ... 13.59
Stone & Rolls Ltd (in liq) v Moore Stephens (a firm) [2009] UKHL 39,
  [2009] 4 All ER 431, [2010] 1 All ER (Comm) 125, [2009] 3 WLR
  455, [2009] Bus LR 1356, [2009] 2 Lloyd's Rep 537, [2009] 2 BCLC
  563, [2009] NLJR 1218, (2009) *The Times*, 11 August, 153 Sol Jo (no
  31) 28, [2010] 2 LRC 773, [2009] All ER (D) 330 (Jul), HL, *affirming*
  [2008] EWCA Civ 644, [2008] 3 WLR 1146, [2008] Bus LR 1579,
  [2008] 2 Lloyd's Rep 319, [2008] 2 BCLC 461, [2008] All ER (D) 225
  (Jun), CA, *reversing* [2007] EWHC 1826 (Comm), [2008] Bus LR 304,
  [2008] 1 BCLC 697, [2007] NLJR 1154, [2007] All ER (D) 448 (Jul),
  Comml Ct ... 13.56

Tang Man Sit (Personal Representatives) v Capacious Investments Ltd
  [1996] AC 514, [1996] 1 All ER 193, [1996] 2 WLR 192, [1996] 05 LS
  Gaz R 32, 140 Sol Jo LB 29, PC ... 13.71
Temperley v Blackrod Mrg Co Ltd (1907) 71 JP Jo 341, Ct tbc ... 13.19
Tesco Stores Ltd v Pook [2003] EWHC 823, [2004] IRLR 618, Ch D ... 13.19, 13.29, 13.30
Tesco Supermarkets Ltd v Nattrass [1972] AC 153, [1971] 2 All ER 127,
  [1971] 2 WLR 1166, 69 LGR 403, 115 SJ 285, HL; *reversing* [1971] 1
  QB 133, [1970] 3 All ER 357, [1970] 3 WLR 572, 68 LGR 722, 114
  SJ 664, DC ... 2.69, 7.120, 8.4
Tesler v Government of the United States of America [2011] EWHC 52
  (Admin), [2011] All ER (D) 145 (Jan), DC ... 12.90
Total Network SL v Revenue and Customs Comrs [2008] UKHL 19, [2008]
  1 AC 1174, [2008] 2 All ER 413, [2008] 2 WLR 711, [2008] STC 644,
  (2008) *The Times*, 13 March, [2008] BPIR 699, [2008] SWTI 938,
  [2008] All ER (D) 160 (Mar), HL, *reversing* [2007] EWCA Civ 39,
  [2008] 1 AC 1174, [2007] 2 WLR 1156, [2007] STC 1005, (2007) *The
  Times*, 6 February, [2007] SWTI 291, [2007] All ER (D) 309 (Jan),
  CA, *reversing* [2005] EWHC 1 (QB), [2005] STC 637, [2005] SWTI
  105, [2005] All ER (D) 77 (Jan), QBD ... 13.46
Transport and General Credit Corpn Ltd v Morgan [1939] Ch 531, [1939] 2
  All ER 17, 108 LJ Ch 179, 83 Sol Jo 338, 160 LT 380, 55 TLR 483,
  Ch D ... 8.34
Twinsectra Ltd v Yardley and Others [2002] UKHL 12, [2002] 2 AC 164,
  [2002] 2 WLR 802, [2002] 2 All ER 377, HL ... 13.67

Ultraframe (UK) Ltd v Fielding, Northstar Systems Ltd v Fielding [2005]
  EWHC 1638 (Ch), [2005] All ER (D) 397 (Jul), Ch D ... 13.69
United Australia Ltd v Barclays Bank Ltd [1941] AC 1, [1940] 4 All ER 20,
  109 LJKB 919, 46 Com Cas 1, 5 LDAB 274, 164 LT 139, 57 TLR 13,
  HL, On Appeal from [1939] 2 KB 53, [1939] 1 All ER 676, [1939]
  WN 81, CA ... 13.71
US v Kahn, 472 F 2d 272 (2d Cir 1973) ... 9.147
US v Kay, United States Court of Appeals (5th Circuit), 359 F 3d 738, 4
  February 2004 ... 7.90, 7.91
US v Lee, 846 F 2d 531 (9th Cir 1988) ... 9.147
US v Noriega et al US District Court, Central District of California
  (Western Division – Los Angeles), Case # 2:10-cr-01031-AHM-4 ... 7.40, 7.57

Wheen v Smithman European Homes Ltd [2000] All ER (D) 836,
    (unreported), 20 June 2000, CA; ... 13.30
Woodward v Maltby [1959] VR 794, Vic SC ... 1.31
WWF-World Wide Fund for Nature (formerly World Wildlife Fund) v
    World Wrestling Federation Entertainment Inc [2007] EWCA Civ
    286, [2008] 1 All ER 74, [2008] 1 All ER (Comm) 129, [2008] 1 WLR
    445, [2007] Bus LR 1252, [2008] IP & T 136, [2007] All ER (D) 13
    (Apr), CA, *reversing* [2006] EWHC 184 (Ch), [2006] FSR 663, [2006]
    All ER (D) 212 (Feb), Ch D ... 13.42

YL v Birmingham City Council [2007] UKHL 27, [2008] 1 AC 95, [2007] 3
    All ER 957, [2007] 3 WLR 112, [2008] LGR 273, [2007] HLR 651, 96
    BMLR 1, [2007] NLJR 938, 151 Sol Jo LB 860, [2007] All ER (D)
    207 (Jun), HL ... 4.17

TABLE OF STATUTES

References are to paragraph numbers.

Accessories and Abettors Act 1861	12.4
s 8	8.122, 12.4
Anti-terrorism, Crime and Security Act 2001	1.52–1.54, 7.5
Pt 12	1.7, 1.26, 1.53
s 108	1.54, 7.5
s 108(2)	1.41
s 109	1.54
s 110	1.51, 1.54
Arbitration Act 1996	
s 7	13.7
Armed Forces Act 2006	9.125
Bill of Rights 1689	
Art 9	4.24
Bribery Act 2010	1.1–1.4, 1.6, 1.7, 1.25, 1.26, 1.47, 1.52, 1.62–1.65, 1.67, 1.69, 1.71, 1.72, 2.2, 2.3, 2.7, 2.10, 2.14, 2.17, 2.18, 2.20, 2.23, 2.28, 2.31, 2.33, 2.34, 2.36, 2.55, 2.59, 2.63, 2.77, 2.81, 3.7, 3.10, 3.32, 3.33, 4.4, 4.9, 4.14, 4.23, 4.26, 4.28–4.30, 4.39, 4.44–4.46, 4.49, 4.60, 4.63, 4.64, 4.73, 5.5, 5.7, 5.10, 5.24, 5.25, 6.6, 6.7, 6.25, 7.1, 7.2, 7.5, 7.13, 7.20, 7.34, 7.35, 7.43, 7.45, 7.50, 7.54, 7.56, 7.60, 7.64, 7.65, 7.76, 7.89, 7.90, 7.95, 7.103, 7.113, 7.120, 7.121, 8.1, 8.7, 8.14–8.17, 8.30, 8.31, 8.38, 8.48, 8.57, 8.58, 8.60, 8.72, 8.76, 8.83, 8.91, 8.93, 8.95–8.97, 8.99, 8.132, 9.1, 9.13, 9.21, 9.24, 9.34, 9.43, 9.54, 9.131, 9.133, 9.153, 10.1, 10.2, 10.19, 10.20, 10.25, 10.28, 10.34, 10.63, 10.82, 10.83, 10.105, 10.108, 10.109, 10.117, 11.6, 11.19, 11.20, 11.24, 11.34, 11.40, 11.45, 12.20, 12.33, 12.37, 12.44, 12.71, 12.78, 13.1, 13.5, 13.67, 14.1, 14.2, 14.12, 14.37, 14.49, 14.61, 14.71, 14.72, 14.95
s 1	1.47, 2.2–2.5, 2.7, 2.8, 2.13, 2.29, 2.31, 2.33, 2.69, 2.70, 2.74–2.76, 3.1, 3.3–3.5, 3.7, 3.8, 3.11, 3.15, 4.1, 4.9, 4.21, 4.33, 4.55, 4.76, 5.1, 5.11, 5.12, 5.34, 6.4, 6.18, 6.19, 6.26, 7.2, 7.9, 7.31, 7.71–7.76, 7.78, 7.95–7.97, 7.103, 7.115, 7.120–7.122, 7.124, 8.7, 8.11, 8.13,

Bribery Act 2010—*continued*	
s 1—*continued*	8.14, 8.16–8.18, 8.22, 8.52, 8.66, 8.76, 8.108, 8.120–8.127, 8.130, 8.136, 9.17, 9.67, 9.76, 9.81, 9.125, 9.126, 9.128, 9.129, 9.138, 9.148, 10.16, 10.23, 10.24, 10.58, 10.63, 10.64, 10.90, 10.114, 10.116, 11.1, 11.6–11.8, 11.11, 11.13, 11.19, 11.20, 11.40, 11.42, 11.43, 11.45, 12.10, 12.13, 12.21, 12.30, 12.76, 14.16, 14.24, 14.25, 14.38, 14.46, 14.52, 14.81
s 1(1)	2.2
s 1(2)	2.44
s 1(3)	2.49, 3.24
s 1(4)	2.21, 2.45, 2.65
s 1(5)	2.65, 11.12
s 1(a)	9.125
s 1(b)	9.125
s 2	1.47, 2.2–2.5, 2.29, 2.70, 3.1, 3.3–3.5, 3.7, 3.56, 4.1, 4.7, 4.9, 4.21, 4.33, 4.55, 4.76, 5.1, 5.13, 5.32, 5.34, 6.4, 6.18, 6.19, 6.26, 7.9, 7.103, 7.120–7.122, 7.124, 8.7, 8.13, 8.14, 8.16, 8.17, 8.22, 8.122, 8.136, 9.67, 9.76, 9.125, 9.128, 9.138, 10.24, 10.58, 10.63, 10.64, 10.90, 11.1, 11.6, 11.7, 11.10, 11.13, 11.15, 11.20, 11.40, 11.43, 12.13, 12.76, 12.87, 13.22, 14.24, 14.25, 14.38, 14.43, 14.46
s 2(2)	4.65, 4.66
s 2(6)	3.5
s 2(6)(a)	4.65
s 2(6)(b)	3.9, 4.65
s 2(7)	2.30, 3.25, 3.37, 3.45, 3.50, 3.55
s 2(8)	3.55
s 3	1.47, 2.5, 2.34, 2.39, 2.59, 3.2, 3.3, 4.1, 4.3, 4.6–4.8, 4.13, 4.21, 4.33, 5.1–5.4, 5.22, 6.1–6.3, 7.9, 7.41, 8.22, 8.123, 9.125, 9.137, 14.19
s 3(1)(b)	4.65
s 3(1)(c)	4.65
s 3(2)	2.31, 2.35, 4.6, 4.13, 4.38, 5.22, 9.137
s 3(2)(a)	3.28
s 3(2)(b)	4.31
s 3(2)(c)	3.28
s 3(3)	2.31, 2.35, 4.29, 4.41, 9.137
s 3(4)	2.31, 2.35, 3.28, 4.29, 4.41, 9.137

Bribery Act 2010—*continued*
s 3(5)   2.31, 2.35, 3.28, 4.29, 4.41, 9.137
s 3(6)   4.75, 9.137
s 3(7)   4.27, 7.90, 8.30
s 4   1.47, 2.5, 2.27, 2.54, 2.59, 3.3, 3.18, 3.23, 4.6–4.8, 4.20, 4.21, 5.1, 5.3, 5.4, 6.1, 7.9, 8.22, 8.123, 14.16
s 4(1)   5.5, 7.115
s 4(1)(a)   3.18, 5.21, 5.23
s 4(1)(b)   3.18, 5.30
s 4(2)   5.5
s 4(2)(a)   3.28
s 4(2)(b)   3.28, 5.23
s 4(2)(c)   6.3
s 4(3)   5.33, 5.34
s 5   1.47, 2.5, 2.54, 2.59, 3.3, 4.6, 4.8, 4.21, 4.42, 4.48, 5.4, 5.36, 6.1, 6.17, 6.19, 6.26, 7.9, 7.115, 8.22
s 5(1)   2.40, 3.18, 3.28, 4.8, 5.4, 5.6, 6.2
s 5(2)   7.103, 12.69
s 5(a)   7.39
s 5(b)   7.39
s 5(b)(i)   7.43
s 6   1.2, 2.2, 2.3, 2.10, 2.70, 3.3, 4.12, 4.17, 4.20, 4.21, 4.23, 4.25, 4.28, 4.75, 4.76, 6.19, 6.20, 6.26, 7.1, 7.2, 7.7–7.11, 7.13, 7.15, 7.16, 7.18, 7.34, 7.35, 7.39, 7.41, 7.47, 7.57, 7.68, 7.71, 7.72, 7.74–7.76, 7.78–7.81, 7.90, 7.91, 7.104, 7.105, 7.107, 7.110, 7.115, 7.116, 7.120–7.122, 7.124, 8.7, 8.11, 8.13, 8.14, 8.16–8.18, 8.22, 8.30, 8.52, 8.66, 8.76, 8.108, 8.120–8.122, 8.124, 8.127, 8.130, 8.136, 9.17, 9.67, 9.76, 9.81, 9.125, 9.126, 9.128, 9.129, 9.137, 9.138, 9.148, 10.16, 10.23, 10.25, 10.58, 10.63, 10.64, 10.90, 10.114, 10.116, 11.1, 11.6, 11.7, 11.18–11.20, 11.40, 11.42, 11.43, 11.45, 12.10, 12.13, 12.21, 12.29, 12.35, 12.69, 12.76, 14.16, 14.24–14.27, 14.52, 14.81
s 6(1)   7.10, 7.12
s 6(2)   7.11, 7.12
s 6(3)   7.10, 7.12, 7.105
s 6(3)(a)(ii)   7.62
s 6(3)(b)   7.10, 7.105, 7.124, 9.148, 12.69
s 6(4)   7.12, 7.84, 7.87
s 6(5)   4.18, 7.12, 7.20, 7.22, 7.31, 7.56, 7.124, 8.124
s 6(5)(a)   7.20, 7.22
s 6(5)(b)   7.20, 7.22
s 6(5)(b)(ii)   7.44
s 6(6)   7.12, 7.65
s 6(7)   7.12, 7.108
s 6(7)(a)   7.124
s 6(7)(b)   7.124
s 6(7)(c)   6.21
s 6(8)   7.12, 7.90, 8.30
s 7   1.2, 1.47, 1.63, 2.2, 2.3, 2.5, 2.7, 2.69, 2.71, 4.1, 4.55, 4.75, 5.11, 7.1, 7.2, 7.74, 7.90, 7.94, 7.120, 7.122, 8.1, 8.2, 8.9–8.18, 8.20, 8.26, 8.30, 8.46,

Bribery Act 2010—*continued*
s 7—*continued*
    8.48, 8.52, 8.61, 8.120, 8.122, 8.130, 8.131, 8.133, 8.134, 8.136, 8.144, 9.1, 9.2, 9.6, 9.9, 9.17, 9.68, 9.130, 9.138, 10.23, 10.35, 10.51, 10.58, 10.65, 10.90, 10.115–10.119, 10.125, 11.1, 11.3, 11.6, 11.7, 11.39, 11.40, 11.43, 11.44, 12.10, 12.14, 12.15, 12.21, 14.57
s 7(1)   8.18, 8.19, 8.60, 8.63, 8.71, 8.99, 8.100, 8.127, 8.135, 9.1, 9.15, 11.42, 11.45, 14.53
s 7(2)   8.1, 8.11, 8.17–8.19, 8.52, 8.134, 8.138, 9.1–9.3, 9.15, 9.81, 9.152, 10.51, 10.127, 11.42, 14.53
s 7(3)   8.18, 8.19, 8.108, 12.21
s 7(3)(a)   8.130
s 7(3)(b)   8.15, 8.133
s 7(4)   8.19
s 7(5)   7.90, 8.15, 8.18, 8.20, 8.22, 8.30, 8.47, 11.44, 11.45
s 7(5)(a)   8.20, 8.25
s 7(5)(b)   8.20, 8.37, 8.47
s 7(5)(c)   8.20
s 7(5)(d)   8.20, 8.37, 8.47
s 8   1.2, 1.47, 8.1, 8.2, 8.10, 8.18, 8.52, 8.63, 8.64, 8.80, 8.87, 8.113, 9.17
s 8(1)   7.44, 8.64, 8.66, 8.75
s 8(2)   8.68, 8.69, 8.71, 8.93
s 8(3)   8.67, 8.69, 8.71, 8.72, 8.80, 8.93, 8.97
s 8(4)   8.69, 8.71, 8.93, 8.95, 8.105
s 8(5)   8.78–8.80
s 9   1.63, 1.64, 1.73, 8.46, 8.143, 9.1, 9.3–9.5, 9.15, 9.17, 9.23, 9.25, 10.117
s 10   1.4, 10.1, 10.2, 10.7
s 10(1)   10.8, 10.36
s 10(2)   10.8
s 10(3)   10.9
s 10(4)   10.9
s 10(5)   10.9
s 10(6)   10.9
s 10(7)   10.9
s 10(8)   10.9
s 10(9)   10.9
s 10(10)   10.9
s 11   1.4, 10.54, 10.55, 10.63
s 11(1)   10.58
s 11(3)   8.13, 10.58
s 12   1.3, 4.75, 4.76, 7.2, 9.17, 11.1, 11.40, 12.22, 12.33
s 12(1)   11.1, 11.6
s 12(2)   11.1, 11.20, 11.43
s 12(2)(b)   11.21
s 12(2)(c)   12.21
s 12(3)   2.73, 11.1, 11.20, 11.43
s 12(4)   2.73, 6.18, 7.35, 7.123, 8.132, 11.1, 11.16, 11.20, 11.43, 12.21
s 12(5)   8.15, 8.108, 8.111, 8.133, 11.1, 11.2, 11.6, 11.43
s 12(6)   11.1, 11.21
s 12(7)   11.46

Bribery Act 2010—*continued*	
s 12(8)	11.46
s 12(9)	11.46
s 13	1.4, 2.5, 9.1, 9.125, 9.127, 9.129, 9.130, 9.133, 9.135
s 13(1)	9.133
s 13(1)(a)	9.132
s 13(2)	9.132
s 13(3)	9.132
s 13(4)	9.132
s 13(6)	9.128
s 14	2.69, 2.70, 7.120–7.122, 7.124, 8.47, 8.52, 8.120, 8.136, 9.67, 9.76, 9.138, 10.16, 11.7, 12.10, 12.13, 12.76
s 14(3)	7.123
s 14(4)	7.123
s 15	8.26
s 15(1)	8.26
s 15(3)	8.26
s 16	4.22
s 17	1.69
s 17(1)	1.69
s 17(1)(a)	1.69
s 17(1)(b)	1.69
s 19(1)	1.63
s 19(2)	1.63
Sch 1, para 14	8.14
Sch 2	1.69
British Nationality Act 1981	1.54, 11.25, 11.28, 11.30, 11.31
Civil Evidence Act 1968	
s 11	13.5
Civil Procedure Act 1997	
s 7	13.89
Companies Act 1985	11.37, 12.78
s 221	10.102, 10.109, 12.78
Companies Act 2006	4.53, 8.8, 12.77
s 386	10.102, 12.77
s 387	10.102, 12.77
s 1159	8.96
s 1159(1)	8.96
s 1159(1)(a)	8.96
s 1159(1)(b)	8.96
s 1159(1)(c)	8.96
Company Directors Disqualification Act 1986	
s 2	10.107
Competition Act 1998	
s 47A	13.87
Corporate Manslaughter and Corporate Homicide Act 2007	8.8
Criminal Attempts Act 1981	12.29, 12.38
s 1	7.124, 12.38
s 1(1)	12.38
s 1(2)	12.43
s 1)	12.40
s 1A	12.44
Criminal Justice Act 1967	
s 8	2.25
Criminal Justice Act 1987	
s 1(2)	10.11

Criminal Justice Act 1987—*continued*	
s 2	10.13
Criminal Justice Act 1988	10.109
s 47	10.109
Criminal Justice Act 1993	11.7, 12.33, 12.44
Criminal Justice Act 2003	10.62
s 142(1)	10.61
s 143(1)	10.67
Criminal Justice (Scotland) Act 2003	
s 68	1.53
Criminal Justice and Immigration Act 2008	
s 59	10.13
Criminal Law Act 1967	
s 4	12.13
s 5	12.13
Criminal Law Act 1977	12.25, 12.33
s 1	7.124, 12.24, 12.25
s 1A	12.33
s 3	12.37
Customs and Excise Management Act 1979	1.32
s 15	2.57, 3.28, 3.29
Employment Rights Act 1996	
Pt IVA	9.59
Enterprise Act 2002	
s 188	13.87
Extradition Act 2003	12.88
Financial Services Act 1986	4.27, 8.32
Financial Services and Markets Act 2000	4.27, 8.32
s 6	10.120
s 22	10.120
s 206	10.122
Fire Precautions Act 1971	
s 23	2.73, 7.123
Fraud Act 1968	
s 12	2.71
Fraud Act 2006	12.46, 12.53, 12.57
s 1	12.47, 12.48
s 1(2)	12.47, 12.51
s 2	12.47, 12.48, 12.52
s 3	12.47, 12.48, 12.52
s 4	4.57, 4.59, 4.64, 12.47, 12.48, 12.52, 12.54, 12.56
s 5(2)	12.52
s 12	7.122
Health and Safety at Work etc Act 1974	8.8
s 2(1)	9.153
Honours (Prevention of Abuses) Act 1925	1.32
Human Rights Act 1998	4.13
s 6(3)(b)	4.14
Income and Corporation Taxes Act 1988	
s 577A	1.7

Intelligence Services Act 1994
  s 3(3) 9.125
Interpretation Act 1978
  s 5 7.109, 7.120
  Sch 1 2.69, 7.109, 7.120, 10.107
  Sch 2 7.35, 11.4

Licensing Act 1964 1.32
Limited Partnerships Act 1907
  s 4 8.27
Local Government Act 1972 1.32
Local Government (Scotland) Act 1973
  s 68 1.26

Magistrates' Courts Act 1980
  s 44 12.4
Magna Carta 1215
  Art 40 1.65
Moneylenders Act 1900 8.31

Partnership Act 1890 11.38
  s 1 8.25
  s 1(1) 8.25, 11.38
  s 4(2) 11.39
Powers of Criminal Courts (Sentencing) Act 2000
  s 130 10.84
Prevention of Corruption Act 1906 1.26, 1.32, 1.37, 1.41–1.43, 1.48–1.50, 1.54, 1.59, 1.69, 3.22, 3.23, 3.32, 10.2, 10.9, 10.64, 10.66, 10.109, 10.112, 13.11
  s 1 1.41, 1.54
  s 1(3) 1.54
  s 1(4) 1.41
  s 2 10.2
  s 3 10.2
Prevention of Corruption Act 1916 1.26, 1.32, 1.36, 1.43, 1.45, 1.48, 1.49, 1.54, 1.69, 3.23, 4.10, 10.2
  s 2 1.49, 1.54
  s 4(2) 1.35, 1.43, 1.54
  s 4(3) 1.43
Proceeds of Crime Act 2002 10.36, 10.49, 10.95, 10.103, 10.104, 12.59, 12.68, 12.70, 13.27
  Pt 2 10.96
  Pt 5 10.41, 10.97, 13.8
  Pt 6 14.94
  Pt 7 12.59, 12.64, 14.57
  s 2A 10.36
  s 6 10.86
  s 7 10.86
  s 241 12.64
  s 327 12.66, 12.68, 14.57
  s 327(3) 12.66, 12.68
  s 328 12.67, 12.68, 14.57
  s 328(3) 12.68
  s 329 12.68
  s 329(2)(c) 12.66
  s 329(3) 12.68

Proceeds of Crime Act 2002—*continued*
  s 333A 12.70
  s 338 12.67
  s 340(2) 12.61
  s 340(3) 12.60
Prosecution of Offences Act 1985
  s 3(1) 10.11
Public Bodies Corrupt Practices Act 1889 1.26, 1.32–1.37, 1.41–1.43, 1.45, 1.48–1.50, 1.54, 1.69, 2.18, 2.43, 3.38, 4.2, 4.10, 4.14, 7.47, 10.83, 10.109, 10.112, 12.81
  s 1 1.33, 1.54, 3.23
  s 2 1.33
  s 2(b) 10.83
  s 4 10.2
  s 7 1.35, 1.54
Public Interest Disclosure Act 1998 9.59

Representation of the People Act 1983 1.32

Sale of Offices Act 1551 1.32
Sale of Offices Act 1809 1.32
Senior Courts Act 1981
  s 37(1) 13.89
  s 37(3) 13.89
Serious Crime Act 2007 12.10, 12.16, 12.17, 12.21, 12.22
  Pt I 8.14
  Pt II 9.149, 12.13, 12.15, 12.16, 12.21
  Pt 1 10.92
  Pt 2 9.125
  s 1 10.92
  s 2 10.92
  s 6 10.93
  s 7 10.93, 10.101
  s 8 10.93
  s 9 10.93
  s 10 10.93
  s 11 10.93
  s 12 10.93
  s 13 10.93
  s 14 10.93
  s 15 10.93
  s 44 7.124, 12.16
  s 45 7.124, 12.16
  s 46 7.124, 12.16
  s 50 9.149, 12.19
  s 52 12.22
  Sch 4, para 5 12.22
Serious Organised Crime and Police Act 2005 10.31, 10.75, 12.68
  Pt 2, Ch 2 10.31
  s 71 10.31
  s 72 10.31
  s 73 10.32
  s 74 10.32
  s 76 10.90
  s 76(3) 10.90, 10.91

Theft Act 1968 12.46
  s 17 4.26, 9.57, 12.72, 12.76
  s 17(1)(b) 12.75

Theft Act 1968—*continued*		Theft Act 1978	12.46
s 18	2.71, 7.122, 12.76		
s 19	4.36		

TABLE OF STATUTORY INSTRUMENTS

References are to paragraph numbers.

Civil Procedure Rules 1998,
   SI 1998/3132
     Pt 25.1(f)   13.89
     Pt 25.1(h)   13.89

Financial Services and Markets Act
   2000 (Regulated Activities)
   Order 2001, SI 2001/544   10.120

Public Contracts Regulations 2006,
   SI 2006/5
     reg 23   10.112–10.114, 10.116

TABLE OF EUROPEAN MATERIAL

References are to paragraph numbers.

Convention on the Protection of the European Community's Financial Interests	
Second Protocol, Art 3(2)	7.18
Council Act 26 May 1997, corruption in the public sector	10.110
Council Joint Action 98/742/JHA, corruption in the private sector	10.110
Council of Europe's Civil Law Convention on Corruption of 1999	
Art 1	13.2
Council of Europe's Criminal Law Convention on Corruption	
Art 18(2)	7.18
Directive 2004/18/EC of the European Parliament and of the Council on the coordination of procedures for the award of public works contracts, public supply contracts and public service contracts	
Art 45	10.36
EC Treaty	
Art 39	11.26
EU Commission Recommendation 2003/361/EC on Small and Medium Enterprises	9.38
EU Defence Procurement Directive, Directive 2009/81/EC	
Art 39	10.113
European Convention for the Protection of Human Rights and Fundamental Freedoms	
1956	4.15
Art 5	9.153
Art 6(2)	1.50
Art 6)	8.131
European Council's Framework Decision 2003/568/JHA	
Art 5(2)	7.18
Public Procurement Directive EC 2004/18	10.110, 10.114, 10.116, 10.117
Art 45	10.110–10.113, 10.115

TABLE OF INTERNATIONAL MATERIAL

References are to paragraph numbers.

False Claims Act
  31 USC ss 3729–3733   13.82

OECD Convention on Combating Bribery of Foreign Public Officials In International Business Transactions   1.6, 1.7, 1.25, 1.68, 1.71, 1.73, 2.1, 2.10, 2.12, 4.20, 4.21, 7.2–7.6, 7.14, 7.16, 7.18, 7.21, 7.29, 7.34, 7.38, 7.41, 7.46, 7.50, 7.54, 7.55, 7.71, 7.88–7.90, 7.116, 7.124, 10.3, 10.5, 10.22, 10.23
  Art 1   1.53, 2.10, 2.18, 6.21, 7.6, 7.9, 7.13–7.16, 7.39, 7.55, 7.75, 7.95, 7.96, 7.124
  Art 1.4   4.20, 7.21
  Art 1.4(a)   7.28, 7.31
  Art 2   7.16, 8.9
  Art 3   7.16, 10.79
  Art 5   10.3, 10.4, 10.23, 10.36

Racketeer Influenced and Corrupt Organisations Act
  18 USC ss 1961–1968   13.82

UN Convention against Corruption/ 08-50026   1.14, 1.68
  Art 2(a)   7.28
  Art 2(b)   7.28
  Art 16   7.13, 7.18
  Art 35   13.2

US Foreign Corrupt Practices Act   7.42, 7.57, 7.115, 7.116, 7.124, 8.12, 9.14, 9.60, 9.66, 9.123, 10.80, 10.81, 12.71, 13.42, 14.51, 14.71, 14.87
  s 78 dd-1(a)(2)   7.34
  s 78 dd-1(b)   7.115, 14.51
  s 78 dd-1(c)(1)   6.21, 7.101, 7.124
  s 78 dd-1(f)   7.115, 14.51
  s 78 dd-1(f)(1)   7.40
  s 78 m(b)   7.115, 14.51

US Securities Exchange Act of 1934
  s 21F   9.60

18 USC
  s 201(a)(2)   4.9
  s 201(b)(1)   4.9

LIST OF ABBREVIATIONS

CP 185	Law Commission Consultation Paper no 185, *Reforming Bribery: A Consultation Paper*, 2007
Explanatory Notes	The Stationery Office, *Bribery Act 2010, Explanatory Notes*, 2010
FCPA	Foreign Corrupt Practices Act 1977, 15 USC s 78
Joint Committee Report	House of Lords, House of Commons, Joint Committee on the Draft Bribery Bill, *Draft Bribery Bill, First Report of Session 2008–09*, 2009, HL Paper 115-II, HC 430-II, vols 1 and 2
Joint Prosecution Guidance	Serious Fraud Office, *Bribery Act 2010: Joint Prosecution Guidance Of the Director of the Serious Fraud Office and the Director of Public Prosecutions*, 2011
LC 313	Law Commission Report no 313, *Reforming Bribery*, 2008
MOJ Guidance	Ministry of Justice, *Guidance About Procedures Which Relevant Commercial Organisations Can Put Into Place To Prevent Persons Associated With Them From Bribing (Section 9 of the Bribery Act 2010)*, 2011
OECD Convention	OECD Convention on Combating Bribery of Foreign Public Officials in International Business Transactions, 1997
UN Convention	United Nations Convention Against Corruption, 2004

Chapter 1

INTRODUCTION AND HISTORICAL BACKGROUND

INTRODUCTION

The radicalism of the Bribery Act

1.1 The Bribery Act 2010 ('the Act') has attracted an extraordinary amount of comment since being enacted in April 2010. Some of this has been well-informed, some less so. But there is no doubt that the Act is a radical measure. When it comes into force on 1 July 2011 it will uproot the tangled crop of laws which have grown up piecemeal over the centuries and replace them with a single statute which has been described as one of the most draconian anti-corruption measures in the world.[1]

1.2 The Act has redefined existing offences of paying and receiving bribes. It has created two entirely new offences – bribery of a foreign public official[2] and failure by a commercial organisation to prevent the payment of bribes.[3] The former offence is a (partial) transplant of a law first developed in the US and domesticated in many other countries by international convention. The latter offence imposes both strict and vicarious liability on corporate bodies though allowing effective due diligence as a defence.

1.3 The Act widens the UK's jurisdiction well beyond its normal territorial limits. The law of bribery now applies to the actions, anywhere in the world, of a large class of individuals and businesses who can be said to have a 'connection to the United Kingdom' or who have a business presence there.[4]

1.4 The Act severely limits the role of the English Attorney-General in relation to bribery cases giving prosecutors effective autonomy.[5] The maximum sentence for bribery is increased to 10 years' imprisonment and/or an unlimited fine.[6] The Act is also unusual in expressly recognising that certain parts of the

---

[1] Vivian Robinson QC, General Counsel, Serious Fraud Office, interview published at www.sfo.gov.uk/bribery–corruption/bribery-act—what-does-it-all-mean.aspx.
[2] Section 6 of the Act.
[3] Sections 7, 8 of the Act.
[4] Sections 12, 7(5) of the Act.
[5] Section 10.
[6] Section 11.

state (intelligence agencies and the armed forces) may engage in bribery to achieve their objectives and in creating a specific defence to take account of this.[7]

Why now?

1.5 Why has such a strong measure been taken, and why now? After all, bribery and corruption have been with us for millennia. Public life in Britain is relatively clean compared to other places, despite recent scandals concerning the expenses claims of some members of Parliament.[8] Of course, domestic corruption still happens too often. Back-handers and secret commissions are known to occur. But, unlike in some countries, they are not seen as a normal part of public life. The 2009 Corruption Perceptions Index published by Transparency International, ranked the UK as the seventeenth least corrupt out of 180 countries.[9] Though hardly a paragon, this makes the UK comparable to other large Western countries which are not regarded as fundamentally corrupt.[10]

1.6 So it is hard to argue that this reform is driven by urgent domestic requirements. However, as economics and politics reflect the trend towards globalisation, so does the law. The problems of international corruption now loom very large on the international stage. Governments, international organisations and many NGOs see corruption, especially in developing countries, as de-stabilising and dangerous.[11] The consensus among these groups is that the 'supply side' must be tackled if endemic corruption is to be reduced. Businesses which pay bribes abroad should be criminalised by their home states. The Bribery Act can be seen as part of a wider trend towards developing a system of international norms in this area.

1.7 This consensus raises questions. Twenty years ago many countries, including the UK, were much more tolerant of bribes to foreign public officials. Some treated them not as criminal conduct but as tax-deductible business expenses.[12] Corruption overseas was seen by some business people and

---

[7] Section 13, coyly entitled 'Defences for Certain Bribery Offences, etc'.
[8] Dishonestly making a false expenses claim is not bribery but probably is fraud and/or false accounting. Although some parliamentarians accused of false accounting attempted to invoke the principle of parliamentary privilege in search of immunity from prosecution, in *R v Chaytor* [2010] UKSC 52 the Supreme Court ruled that no privilege applied.
[9] See www.transparency.org/policy_research/surveys_indices/cpi/2009/cpi_2009_table.
[10] The UK's score of 7.7 out of 10 was the same as that of Japan, slightly above the US, slightly below Germany. By 2010 the UK had slipped back to 20th. Of course such measures as the CPI are snapshots of perceptions, rather than empirical evidence of corruption, however they are nevertheless seen as important indicators. One should not be complacent about bribery within the UK, which is a serious problem in certain areas and more dangerous because it is too often ignored.
[11] A key element in the movement against international corruption is the OECD Convention on Combating Bribery of Foreign Public Officials in International Business Transactions (hereafter 'the OECD Convention'), discussed in more depth in Chapter 7. The Convention can be found at: www.oecd.org/dataoecd/4/18/38028044.pdf.
[12] Because of the territorial limits of the previous law, the official position of the UK seems to

politicians as just another cost of overseas commerce, only slightly more unwelcome than import duties or currency controls. Overseas corruption was not really seen as being 'our problem'. Now, plainly, it is our problem, and it is not surprising that some people question why this must be so. Some resent the change and the effects it might have on their business practices or relationships. Some think the new approach is naive or ultimately damaging to British national interests.[13] It is worth attempting a brief explanation of why this shift has happened, which will also draw out the underlying policy goals of the Act.

The case for fighting transnational bribery

1.8 The benefits of any bribe are private – they go to the recipient and the payer of the bribe, each of whom receives a quid pro quo. However, the harms done by a bribe are socialised, not least because, once bribery takes place, others dealing with the recipient who do not pay bribes are disadvantaged.

1.9 But the harm goes wider than this. A bribed official cannot be trusted by their employer, colleagues, customers or clients. As an administrator they become dysfunctional. They are less likely to do their job properly, or at all, and are more likely to be primarily self-interested and unfair in their actions or opinions. If they are senior or influential then others are likely to emulate them with the result that the phenomenon spreads. Soon the institution affected by corruption is no longer fulfilling its purpose of service to the public, but merely fulfilling the private purposes of its officials.

1.10 It is not surprising that corruption is often described as insidious, or compared to a cancer. Left unchecked, it undermines social trust in a way that is extremely difficult to repair. It is noticeable that most people, of whatever political or cultural stripe, recognise the distinctively harmful nature of bribery. It seems to offend against a sense of duty and fairness which is common across different groups and societies. Corruption, though often acquiesced to in a fatalistic way in those countries where it is endemic, is generally despised, especially by those too powerless or too honest to obtain any personal benefits from it.

---

have been that bribes outside of UK jurisdiction were not caught by the prohibition on deductibility of payments constituting criminal offences under s 577A of the Income and Corporation Taxes Act 1988, at least until implementation of Part 12 of the Anti-Terrorism, Crime and Security Act 2001. Other states said to have permitted the deduction of overseas bribes against tax include Australia, Austria, Belgium, Denmark, France, Germany, Luxembourg, Netherlands, New Zealand, Norway, Sweden and Switzerland – see Pieth, Low, Cullen (eds) *The OECD Convention on Bribery, A Commentary* (Cambridge, 2009) at p 539.

[13] For example, Charles Moore 'Moralising Crusades That Will Succeed Only in Doing Harm' available at www.telegraph.co.uk/comment/columnists/charlesmoore/8247054/Moralising-crusades-that-will-succeed-only-in-doing-harm.html.

1.11 So, for a concerned citizen, the need to prevent bribery in one's own country will be common sense. Few thinking people wish to live in a society undermined by corruption since they recognise the waste, social breakdown and poverty which results.[14]

1.12 However, this line of argument does not fully address the case for dedicating British resources to fighting a crime which has most of its damaging effects abroad. Why is the bribery of a procurement official in, say, Tanzania, any concern of people in Britain? The Tanzanian police can charge any Briton involved and he can be tried in the local courts. If the police or courts lack the will or resources to do so this is a matter for the sovereign people of Tanzania to address. Is it not better for the UK to leave the problems of foreign countries to resolve themselves?

1.13 If there were no international trade, immigration, sport or crime then such a view might be more understandable. In the real world, where economic and social contacts are not confined by national borders, action against overseas bribery is justified both on humanitarian grounds and on grounds of national interest.

1.14 It is widely acknowledged that corruption is a major contributor to poverty and conflict in developing countries.[15] Someone wishing to reduce these effects will naturally wish to prevent their own nationals from contributing to them. They will wish to provide justice for disempowered people everywhere, even if little or no benefit accrues to their own country.

1.15 Even those unmoved by such altruistic concerns might recognise that corruption distorts markets, increases the cost of trade, raises the credit and political risks of overseas investment, facilitates crime, and contributes to economic instability and the phenomenon of entirely or partially failed states. Failed states tend to provide a breeding ground for transnational crime and political extremism which is often exported to Britain or damages British interests. It can fairly be argued that corruption, even in far-away places, has damaging effects on the economy and the security of the UK.

---

[14] For an in-depth analysis of the justification for the criminalisation of bribery, based on the principle of deterrence of remote harm, see Horder *Bribery As Form of Criminal Wrongdoing* [2011] LQR 37.

[15] The former Secretary General of the United Nations, Kofi Annan, wrote this in the foreword to the UN Convention against Corruption (www.unodc.org/documents/treaties/UNCAC/Publications/Convention/08-50026_E.pdf): 'Corruption is an insidious plague that has a wide range of corrosive effects on societies. It undermines democracy and the rule of law, leads to violations of human rights, distorts markets, erodes the quality of life and allows organized crime, terrorism and other threats to human security to flourish. This evil phenomenon is found in all countries – big and small, rich and poor – but it is in the developing world that its effects are most destructive. Corruption hurts the poor disproportionately by diverting funds intended for development, undermining a Government's ability to provide basic services, feeding inequality and injustice and discouraging foreign aid and investment. Corruption is a key element in economic underperformance and a major obstacle to poverty alleviation and development.'

Are there counter-arguments?

1.16 It is occasionally said that corruption is part of human nature and/or a 'victimless crime'. It could be said that the employer of the recipient of a bribe either knows about and tolerates bribery, in which case he effectively approves, or he does not care enough to find out or prevent it, in which case he is partly to blame and does not deserve the benefit received by the recipient, whose need is greater. Of course these arguments can be made about many crimes against property, such as fraud, theft and so on. They are either entirely cynical or, perhaps, naive about the social and economic effects which tolerance of corruption would create.

1.17 A slightly more sophisticated argument is that one should not criminalise at least 'petty' bribery of lower-grade officials because it arises out of unfair social conditions. Someone paying a bribe can do so only because the recipient is incentivised to seek one, and those incentives arise out of low pay or social inequality. There is no doubt that, in many countries, state officials are badly paid compared to those in developed countries and that this and other facts may well contribute to petty corruption. However, the relationships between criminality and particular social and economic conditions are very complex. It could just as easily be argued that tolerance of corruption among low-paid officials perpetuates the status quo and inhibits the kind of change which would improve governance and civil society. It is very difficult to believe that permitting the bribery of particular categories of official would alleviate these problems. Of course, many wealthy and powerful people are at least as corrupt as any 'petty' official.

1.18 A third argument runs as follows: There are some places where practices which people in the UK might see as corrupt are, in fact, sanctioned by local culture. In such places, it is said, governments or institutions are little more than ciphers for particular interest groups, and the individuals in power have the implicit consent of the population to earn what rents they can from their positions. If they do not do this they are disparaged by their peers and quickly lose influence. Such people are themselves subject to obligations to a clan or a client-base which they feel duty-bound to fulfil.[16] Many of them are broadly well-intentioned on matters of policy and it is better to support them because, no matter who is in power, the influence of the 'big man' will be unavoidable.[17] To do business in these places one has to adapt to the local culture and that means, in effect, paying personal tribute to those in power. Regrettable though this state of affairs is, outsiders cannot effect reform and should not try. When in Rome, say the apologists, one must do as the Romans.

---

[16] For fascinating accounts of the roots and effects of corruption in different countries see Wrong, *It's Our Turn To Eat* (London, 2009) which focuses on the career of John Githongo, a former anti-corruption official in Kenya and Peel, *A Swampful of Dollars* (London, 2009), which deals with the effects of oil-wealth in West Africa.

[17] This phenomenon is not restricted to developing countries of course. Many politicians and businessmen in Europe and the US have been caught up in corruption scandals.

1.19 A supplementary point, often kept till last, is that if one is not prepared to fit in with this assumed culture of corruption then rivals will, giving Britain fewer opportunities to trade, and allowing less scrupulous countries to scoop the benefits.

1.20 Let us deal with the last point first. The view that bribery is tolerable if it means that a UK company wins a major contract ahead of the champion of some other country is (at least for now) out of favour in an era when trade, corporate governance, labour and environmental standards are increasingly the subject of internationally applicable rules and agreements.[18] More fundamentally, the beggar-thy-neighbour argument that 'if we don't do it the other lot will' is familiar but it is hardly principled. It is a rationalisation of self-interest, which does not answer the economic and social arguments about the long-term effects of bribery, or the moral argument that cheating is not justified by the fact that others also cheat.

1.21 The more general 'cultural' defence of overseas bribery is the most seductive, in part because it attempts to clothe realpolitik in the colours of cultural sensitivity. However it falls foul of certain important facts. Among these are the following:

(1) There are no countries in which bribery of state officials is legal. It is expressly illegal in the vast majority of countries. Although the law is often not enforced because of the weakness of institutions such as the police or judiciary, this is a fact which the citizens do not approve and that legal institutions are supposed to prevent. It hardly needs to be pointed out that non-enforcement does not change the law. Burglary is wrong whether or not the burglar manages to escape detection, and bribery is no different.

(2) Those who seek and provide bribes, whatever their culture or nationality, almost always do so surreptitiously. It is a strange cultural practice which hides itself from other members of the culture. If the Minister for Oil really was expected to gain huge personal wealth because of his job then he would gladly disclose his fortune and all his dealings to his compatriots. He would make it clear that he was using his office mainly to benefit himself or his family, not the country. Those paying him, or the persons connected to him, would disclose their payments and the reasons for them in their public filings. But this never happens. Elaborate steps are taken to disguise the true nature of corrupt payments. That is because both sides of such transactions are well aware that what they are doing is both illegal and immoral in whatever cultural context might apply.

1.22 The 'corruption as culture' position relies on the belief that the 'culture' in a particular country is both homogeneous and static. It tends to conflate the

---

[18] 'At least for now' because there is no guarantee that this movement towards internationalising business standards will continue.

attitudes of ruling elites with the views of the majority of people in the country in question. It is probably a mistake to assume that most citizens of these countries support practices which corrode public institutions and are of no benefit to them.[19]

1.23 From the ethical perspective, it is not easy to accept the assumption which is at the heart of the cultural defence of overseas corruption. That assumption is that people of certain nations or cultures do not share key moral values or rights with those of other nations or cultures, and that one should draw moral distinctions between national or cultural groups. Translated into policy, this comes down to the ethically unattractive proposition that there should be one rule for 'us' but another rule for 'them'. Such a principle is contrary to most of today's political and legal thinking.

1.24 We can conclude that a law criminalising bribery, at home or away, is necessary in an increasingly interconnected world and that it is wrong to see bribery of non-nationals as acceptable just because others do so or because there is not much chance of getting caught. This is now an assumption of international policymaking which is unlikely to change in the foreseeable future.

1.25 To accept this is also to accept that an anti-bribery law needs to be effective. By the end of the twentieth century, many actors in this field, including influential bodies such as the OECD Working Group on Bribery, felt that existing law in the UK, substantially unchanged for almost a hundred years, was no longer fit for purpose.[20] The law was seen as fragmented, unclear and not suited to present-day international business. The Bribery Act is the culmination of several recent initiatives towards reform. One can gain a deeper understanding of the purpose and policy of the Act by examining the existing law and outlining the attempts to change it.

---

[19] Recent events in some North African and Middle Eastern countries seem to have been motivated at least in part by popular anger at corruption among government officials and business elites. These make the case against the 'corruption as culture' argument more eloquently than any textbook could.

[20] For example see: *Follow-up Report on the Implementation of the Phase 2 Recommendations on the Application of the Convention and the 1997 Recommendation on Combating Bribery of Foreign Public Officials in International Business Transactions (July 2007)* at www.oecd.org/dataoecd/43/13/38962457.pdf; and *Phase 2 bis (October 2008)* at www.oecd.org/dataoecd/23/20/41515077.pdf.

THE EXISTING CRIMINAL LAW OF BRIBERY AND CORRUPTION

1.26 Prior to the coming into force of the Act, the law of bribery and corruption arose out of English (and Scots)[21] common law, and specific statutes.[22]

Common law bribery

1.27 The classic formulation of common law bribery is contained in a textbook of criminal law, the last edition of which was in 1964:[23]

> 'Bribery is the receiving or offering [of] any undue reward by or to any person whatsoever, in a public office, in order to influence his behaviour in office, and incline him to act contrary to the known rules of honesty and integrity.'

There are various instances of common law bribery which go under different names such as 'embracery' (bribery of a juror), bribery of a coroner and others, but these appear to have fallen into disuse.

1.28 Someone in a 'public office' is someone who discharges any duty in which the public is interested. So the colonel of a regiment is a public officer and he may not accept money in connection with the placement of a contract for the benefit of his regiment.[24] An officer of a local authority is also in a public office.[25] Of course a person in a public office who receives a bribe and who abuses his powers as a result may also be guilty of the separate offence of misconduct in public office.

1.29 'Undue reward' is a concept which has not been definitively explained but it is very likely to mean a reward to which the recipient is not otherwise entitled.[26]

1.30 So, under the common law, the provider of the bribe must intend to do two things: (1) to influence the behaviour of the public officer in relation to doing his duty and (2), in doing (1), to incline the public officer to act contrary to the known rules of honesty and integrity. It is enough to intend to produce

---

[21] Scottish common law also prohibited bribery, in particular of judicial officers. There are also specific statutory offences relating to bribery in Scotland, such as the Local Government (Scotland) Act 1973, s 68.
[22] Specifically the Public Bodies Corrupt Practices Act 1889, the Prevention of Corruption Act 1906, the Prevention of Corruption Act 1916 and Part 12 of the Anti-terrorism, Crime and Security Act 2001, as to which see below.
[23] Russell, *Crime* (12th edn, 1964) p 364.
[24] *R v Whitaker* [1914] 3 KB 1283.
[25] *R v Bowden* [1996] 1 WLR 98, CA.
[26] In a South African case it was held that whether something is 'undue' in this context depends on all the facts of the case such as the relationship between the provider and recipient: *S v Deal Enterprises (Pty) Ltd* (1978) 3 SA 302.

any effect at all, however minor, on the mind of the public officer.[27] For the recipient, it seems, no specific mental element is required once the reward sought is undue.[28]

1.31 There is no de minimis limit for an 'undue reward'. However, mere entertainment and 'treats' of a minor value may well not be seen as having been provided in order to influence the recipient, or 'incline him to act contrary to the known rules of honesty and integrity'.[29]

The statutory offences

1.32 Most recent prosecutions have been brought under the main statutory offences – the Public Bodies Corrupt Practices Act 1889 ('the 1889 Act') and the Prevention of Corruption Act 1906 ('the 1906 Act'). The Prevention of Corruption Act 1916 ('the 1916 Act') is relevant to both. It is best to deal with each Act separately.[30]

The Public Bodies Corrupt Practices Act 1889

1.33 The relevant provisions are in s 1, which provides:

> **'1 Corruption in office a misdemeanor**
>
> (1) Every person who shall by himself or by or in conjunction with any other person, corruptly solicit or receive, or agree to receive, for himself, or for any other person, any gift, loan, fee, reward, or advantage whatever as an inducement to, or reward for, or otherwise on account of any member, officer, or servant of a public body as in this Act defined, doing or forbearing to do anything in respect of any matter or transaction whatsoever, actual or proposed, in which the said public body is concerned, shall be guilty of a misdemeanour.
>
> (2) Every person who shall by himself or by or in conjunction with any other person corruptly give, promise, or offer any gift, loan, fee, reward, or advantage whatsoever to any person, whether for the benefit of that person or of another person, as an inducement to or reward for or otherwise on account of any member, officer, or servant of any public body as in this Act defined, doing or forbearing to do anything in respect of any matter or transaction whatsoever, actual or proposed, in which such public body as aforesaid is concerned, shall be guilty of a misdemeanor.'

---

[27] *R v Gurney* (1867) 10 Cox CC 550.
[28] See Nicholls et al, *Corruption and Misuse of Public Office* (Oxford, 2006) at para 2.08.
[29] See the Australian case of *Woodward v Maltby* [1959] VR 794.
[30] Other statutes touching on potential liability for bribery or corruption include the Sale of Offices Act 1551, the Sale of Offices Act 1809, the Honours (Prevention of Abuses) Act 1925, the Licensing Act 1964, the Local Government Act 1972, the Customs and Excise Management Act 1979 and the Representation of the People Act 1983. For reasons of economy, none of these are considered here.

Public body

1.34 The 1889 Act, though attempting comprehensiveness in its wording, has not always been easy to interpret. One problem has been in applying the definition of 'member, officer, or servant of a public body'. This is not the same as a 'public officer' stipulated by the common law offence.

1.35 The definition of 'public body' in s 7 of the 1889 Act is:

> '... any council of a county of a city or town, any council of a municipal borough, also any board, commissioners, select vestry, or other body which has power to act under and for the purposes of any Act relating to local government, money raised by rates in pursuance of any public general Act, and includes any body which exists in a country or territory outside the United Kingdom and is equivalent to any body described above.'

It was supplemented by the definition in the Prevention of Corruption Act 1916, s 4(2) which additionally provided that:

> '... in this Act and in the Public Bodies Corrupt Practices Act 1889, the expression "public body" includes in addition to the bodies mentioned in the last-mentioned Act, local and public authorities of all descriptions ...'

1.36 A 'public body' in general is a body which has public or statutory duties to perform and which performs those duties for the benefit of the public and not for private profit.[31] However, some confusion as to the nature a public body for the purposes of the 1889 Act prevailed even after the 1916 Act adopted more general language. It seems that members of the civil service proper and others technically serving 'under the Crown' were excluded, despite working for what most people would consider to be a 'public authority'. In *R v Natji*,[32] an immigration official was charged under the 1889 Act as a public officer. It was held that such an officer was a servant of the Crown and therefore not subject to the 1889 Act.[33]

'Corruptly'

1.37 Another problem in applying the 1889 Act relates to the definition of the term 'corruptly'. The concept has proved stubbornly resistant to satisfactory definition, under either the 1889 or the 1906 Act, to which it is common.

1.38 The leading authority on what is or is not done corruptly is *R v Wellburn*[34] in which the Court of Criminal Appeal adopted the statement that 'corruptly' means 'purposefully doing an act which the law forbids as tending to corrupt'. Unfortunately the explanation of 'corruptly' comes close to being

---

[31] *DPP v Holly* [1978] AC 43.
[32] [2002] EWCA Crim 271.
[33] As regards the new Bribery Act, any confusion in this regard is cleared up by s 16 which applies the Act to 'individuals in the public service of the Crown'.
[34] (1979) 69 Cr App R 254. The Court of Appeal examined the previous authorities and approved the direction of the trial judge that: 'Corruptly is a simple English adverb and I am

circular – doing something corruptly means doing something which tends to corrupt. It seems clear that the accused required an extra element of intention involving 'corruption', but one can understand the nervousness of a prosecutor whose task it is to explain this to judge and jury. Uncertainty about the meaning of 'corruptly' may have led to a lack of success in investigating or charging corruption under the old law.

1.39 It seems clear that for something to have been done corruptly there is no need for the accused to have been dishonest,[35] no deal needs to have been done before an offence is committed[36] and it is irrelevant that the intended recipient of the bribe was not aware of it.[37] A supposedly noble motive (such as the exposure of corruption by means of a 'sting' operation) may or may not suffice to negative the necessary mental element (mens rea) – of course a great deal will depend on the facts.[38] An undercover police officer may not be committing an offence if his purpose in offering a bribe was to investigate crime, however a private person with a grudge against a local official might not be so easily excused.

1.40 It is possible that a recipient of a benefit intended to corrupt him could be innocent because lacking a corrupt intent, but the provider might still be guilty, or indeed vice versa.[39]

The Prevention of Corruption Act 1906

1.41 The 1906 Act is the statutory provision with the widest scope. It applies to corruption both in the private sector (ie between two private parties) and in the public sector and applies to a wider category of officials than the 1889 Act. The most relevant provision is s 1 which provides:

'**1 Punishment of corrupt transactions with agents**

(1) If any agent corruptly accepts or obtains, or agrees to accept or attempts to obtain, from any person, for himself or for any other person, any gift or consideration as an inducement or reward for doing or forbearing to do, or for having after the passing of this Act done or forborne to do, any act in relation to his principal's affairs or business, or for showing or forbearing to show favour or disfavour to any person in relation to his principal's affairs or business; or

If any person corruptly gives or agrees to give or offers any gift or consideration to any agent as an inducement or reward for doing or forbearing to do, or for having after the passing of this Act done or forborne to do, any act in relation to his

---

not going to explain it to you except to say that it does not mean dishonestly. It is a different word. It means purposefully doing an act which the law forbids as tending to corrupt.' See also *Cooper v Slade* [1858] 6 HL 746.

[35] *R v Harvey* [1999] Crim LR 70.
[36] *R v Andrews-Weatherfoil Ltd* [1972] 1 WLR 118.
[37] *Jagdeo Singh v The State of Trinidad and Tobago* [2006] 1 WLR 146.
[38] *R v Smith* [1960] 2 QB 423, *R v Mills* (1978) 68 Cr App R 154, 159.
[39] *R v Millray Window Cleaning Co Ltd* [1962] Crim LR 99.

principal's affairs or business, or for showing or forbearing to show favour or disfavour to any person in relation to his principal's affairs or business; or

If any person knowingly gives to any agent, or if any agent knowingly uses with intent to deceive his principal, any receipt, account, or other document in respect of which the principal is interested, and which contains any statement which is false or erroneous or defective in any material particular, and which to his knowledge is intended to mislead the principal:

he shall be guilty of a misdemeanour, and shall be liable—

(a)   on summary conviction, to imprisonment for a term not exceeding 6 months or to a fine not exceeding the statutory maximum, or to both; and
(b)   on conviction on indictment, to imprisonment for a term not exceeding 7 years or to a fine, or to both.

(2)   For the purposes of this Act the expression "consideration" includes valuable consideration of any kind; the expression "agent" includes any person employed by or acting for another; and the expression "principal" includes an employer.

(3)   A person serving under the Crown or under any corporation or any … borough, county, or district council, or any board of guardians, is an agent within the meaning of this Act.

(4)   For the purposes of this Act it is immaterial if—

(a)   the principal's affairs or business have no connection with the United Kingdom and are conducted in a country or territory outside the United Kingdom;
(b)   the agent's functions have no connection with the United Kingdom and are carried out in a country or territory outside the United Kingdom.'[40]

1.42 The 1906 Act overlaps with the 1889 Act to some degree. The definition of 'corruptly' is the same[41] and of course the same problems arise. The 1889 Act refers to provision of a 'gift, loan, fee, reward or advantage' compared to a 'gift or consideration' in the 1906 Act but there is nothing to suggest that these differences are significant.

1.43 The most important difference between the 1906 Act and the 1889 Act, and between the 1906 Act and common law bribery, is that an offence under the 1906 Act depends on the recipient of the bribe being in a specific type of legal relationship, that of 'agent' to a 'principal', and that the purpose of the

---

[40] Subsection (4) was inserted by virtue of s 108(2) of the Anti-terrorism Crime and Security Act 2001, of which see below.
[41] *R v Harvey* [1999] Crim LR 70.

bribe is to influence the agent's actions in relation to the affairs of his principal. It does not matter whether the agent is the agent of a public body or a private person or enterprise.[42]

1.44 The agent/principal model of bribery is consistent with the approach of the law to civil liability in this area.[43] In civil law a claim for bribery is based on the idea that an agent (such as an employee, director, trustee or fiduciary) owes their principal (such as an employer or company or beneficiary or client) duties of loyalty. Accepting a bribe damages or destroys that loyalty and therefore the provider of the bribe will be liable to the principal for the damage done, as, of course, will the agent.

1.45 However, the agent/principal model has been subject to significant criticism as the basis for criminal liability. One criticism is that the victim of bribery may not easily be defined as the principal of the recipient. A beneficiary under a trust may not be the principal of a corrupt adviser, whose client could be the legal trustee, not the beneficiary himself. More significantly perhaps, it is straining language to define someone who is in a very elevated constitutional position, like a senior politician, as being as the agent of an identified principal or even 'serving under a public body' as provided by the 1889 and 1916 Acts.

1.46 Government ministers, military officers or judges may have *de facto* superiors but these can hardly be described as their principals, at least as English law traditionally understands these relationships. Such people have great responsibilities but it is not obvious that they owe them to a single identified principal in the same way that most employees or company directors do. The issue is particularly acute when approaching allegations of bribery of foreign public officials. Attempting to say that the head of the armed forces of state A is the agent of some other body or individual (the President? the King? the People?) runs into serious problems because it involves interpreting foreign constitutional settlements and then translating these into concepts rooted in English or Scots private law.

1.47 The agent/principal model also carries with it the following consequence: if bribery consists of an agent being paid, corruptly, to act in a particular way in relation to the affairs of his principal (assuming such a person or body can be identified), what is the effect of the approval, or at least knowledge, of the principal or a representative of the principal? This question has not been answered in case-law to date. However, there must at least be a risk that an agreement between principal and agent that the agent may receive personal benefits arising out of his work would mean that the agent receiving such a

---

[42] Section 4(3) of the Prevention of Corruption Act 1916 provides that a person serving under any public body as defined in s 4(2) 'is an agent within the meaning of the Prevention of Corruption Act 1906 ...'.
[43] See Chapter 13.

benefit would not have done so 'corruptly'. It might well not be corrupt, or tend to corrupt (to use the formula in *Whitaker*) to do something expressly licensed by one's principal.[44]

The Prevention of Corruption Act 1916

1.48 We have already seen that the 1916 Act amended the definition of 'public body' for the purposes of the 1889 Act and made it clear that a person serving under a public body was an agent for the purposes of the 1906 Act.

1.49 Another measure introduced by the 1916 Act was a presumption of corruption where any valuable consideration was given to a public official by anyone seeking to obtain a contract from the public body. Section 2 of the 1916 Act reads as follows:

> 'Where in any proceedings against a person for an offence under the Prevention of Corruption Act 1906, or the Public Bodies Corrupt Practices Act 1889, it is proved that any money, gift, or other consideration has been paid or given to or received by a person in the employment of His Majesty or any Government Department or a public body by or from a person, or agent of a person, holding or seeking to obtain a contract from His Majesty or any Government Department or public body, the money, gift, or consideration shall be deemed to have been paid or given and received corruptly as such inducement or reward as is mentioned in such Act unless the contrary is proved.'

1.50 The presumption of corruption is limited to payments made by a contract seeker directly to a government employee, not to an intermediary person which may pass the bribes on and which is not acting as an agent or as part of a joint enterprise.[45] It seems that placing a defendant at such a disadvantage merely because of his position as a state employee is contrary to the principle of presumption of innocence, and, among other things, unlawful under Art 6(2) of the European Convention on Human Rights.[46] The issue might be avoided by means of charges of conspiracy to commit offences under the 1889 or 1906 Acts since the presumption of corruption does not apply to charges of conspiracy.

1.51 The presumption of corruption was expressly excluded in cases where the offence is said to have been committed abroad, no doubt because it was felt

---

[44] The Bribery Act does away with any formal test for an agent/principal relationship. However, it may be difficult for any law purporting to regulate commercial conduct to escape the concept of agency completely. For example, the 'failure to prevent bribery' offence applicable to commercial organisations in ss 7 and 8 of the Bribery Act depends on a relationship between the commercial organisation and persons 'performing services for or on behalf of' the organisation (s 8(1)), which most lawyers would recognise as a relationship of agency, and which bears comparison to the definition of 'agent' in s 1(2) of the 1906 Act. See Chapter 8 herein. These provisions do not affect the main definition of the nature of bribery itself in ss 1–5, although a close examination of key elements of the definition reveals concepts which can be seen as overlapping the law of agency.
[45] *R v A* [2007] EWCA Crim 2868.
[46] This has recently been confirmed in *R v Webster* [2010] EWCA Crim. 2819.

that the burden of proving that a foreign official was entitled to receive the advantage in question would be too harsh for a UK-based defendant.[47]

1.52 This raises the more general problem of the traditional geographical limits on criminal jurisdiction. The usual rule is that only offences committed within the UK can be tried here. Although the rule is subject to certain exceptions,[48] it caused further problems for the application of the law to the bribery of foreign public officials, which were only partially addressed by the Anti-terrorism, Crime and Security Act 2001, discussed below. The Bribery Act is founded on a far wider jurisdictional base, as discussed in Chapter 11.

Anti-terrorism, Crime and Security Act 2001

1.53 Part 12 of the Anti-terrorism, Crime and Security Act 2001 (ATCSA 2001) was enacted in response to concerns that the UK was not compliant with Art 1 of the OECD Convention. It was intended to widen the jurisdiction of existing law so as to catch the corruption of persons abroad. It made explicit that corruption under the existing law which occurs outside the UK is an offence in UK law, and that officials of overseas bodies which are equivalent to public bodies as defined by the UK legislation are included in that legislation.[49]

1.54 The relevant provisions are:

'108 Bribery and corruption: foreign officers etc.

(1) For the purposes of any common law offence of bribery it is immaterial if the functions of the person who receives or is offered a reward have no connection with the United Kingdom and are carried out in a country or territory outside the United Kingdom.

(2) In section 1 of the Prevention of Corruption Act 1906 (c. 34) (corrupt transactions with agents) insert this subsection after subsection (3)—

"(4) For the purposes of this Act it is immaterial if—

(a) the principal's affairs or business have no connection with the United Kingdom and are conducted in a country or territory outside the United Kingdom;

(b) the agent's functions have no connection with the United Kingdom and are carried out in a country or territory outside the United Kingdom."

(3) In section 7 of the Public Bodies Corrupt Practices Act 1889 (c. 69) (interpretation relating to corruption in office) in the definition of "public body" for "but does not include any public body as above defined existing elsewhere than

---

[47] Anti-terrorism, Crime and Security Act 2001, s 110.
[48] Such as sexual offences against children, terrorism and other offences – see, in general, Archbold, *Criminal Pleading, Evidence and Practice,* Chapter 2.
[49] As to the situation in Scotland see s 68 of the Criminal Justice (Scotland) Act 2003.

in the United Kingdom" substitute "and includes any body which exists in a country or territory outside the United Kingdom and is equivalent to any body described above".

(4) In section 4(2) of the Prevention of Corruption Act 1916 (c. 64) (in the 1889 and 1916 Acts public body includes local and public authorities of all descriptions) after "descriptions" insert "(including authorities existing in a country or territory outside the United Kingdom)".

109 Bribery and corruption committed outside the UK

(1) This section applies if—

(a) a national of the United Kingdom or a body incorporated under the law of any part of the United Kingdom does anything in a country or territory outside the United Kingdom, and
(b) the act would, if done in the United Kingdom, constitute a corruption offence (as defined below).

(2) In such a case—

(a) the act constitutes the offence concerned, and
(b) proceedings for the offence may be taken in the United Kingdom.

(3) These are corruption offences—

(a) any common law offence of bribery;
(b) the offences under section 1 of the Public Bodies Corrupt Practices Act 1889 (c. 69) (corruption in office);
(c) the first two offences under section 1 of the Prevention of Corruption Act 1906 (c. 34) (bribes obtained by or given to agents).

(4) A national of the United Kingdom is an individual who is—

(a) a British citizen, a British Dependent Territories citizen, a British National (Overseas) or a British Overseas citizen,
(b) a person who under the British Nationality Act 1981 (c. 61) is a British subject, or
(c) a British protected person within the meaning of that Act.

110 Presumption of corruption not to apply

Section 2 of the Prevention of Corruption Act 1916 (c. 64) (presumption of corruption in certain cases) is not to apply in relation to anything which would not be an offence apart from section 108 or section 109.'

1.55 As pointed out by the Law Commission,[50] these amendments, though going some way to closing jurisdictional loopholes as regards overseas bribery, did not bring non-UK nationals or non-UK incorporated companies into the net of the existing law.

RECENT DEVELOPMENTS

1.56 The sketch of the existing law attempted above has focused on some of the difficulties encountered in applying it. However, it would be misleading to suggest that the law until now has been entirely impotent. There have been many successful prosecutions of domestic corruption offences. Even offences involving overseas countries have been successfully investigated and prosecuted in recent years.[51]

1.57 However, as we have seen, the doubts about the suitability of the old law to combat bribery, especially bribery overseas, were of real concern to policy-makers and there has been a strong movement towards reform, which is discussed below.

PREVIOUS ATTEMPTS AT REFORM

1.58 The modern movement towards reforming the law of bribery and corruption has roots in the reports on the need to improve standards in public life dating from the mid-1970s.[52] The Law Commission Report entitled *Legislating the Criminal Code: Corruption* marked the start of a more concerted and comprehensive effort at law reform driven in part by the requirements of the OECD Convention.[53]

1.59 On the strength of that Report in 1998 a draft bill was put forward by the government. A Parliamentary Joint Commission was highly critical of key aspects of the bill, in particular the definition of corruption on the agent/principal model which had survived from the 1906 legislation.[54] The government did not agree with the criticisms of the Joint Committee but it appeared that the current draft bill would not receive the support of Parliament.[55]

---

[50] Law Commission Consultation Paper No 185 (hereafter 'CP 185'), para. 1.24.
[51] Such as, for example, *R v Heath* (unreported) 23 September 2008, Birmingham Crown Court; *R v Mabey & Johnson Ltd* (unreported) 29 September 2009, Southwark Crown Court; *R v Innospec Ltd* [2010] EW Misc 7 (EWCC); *R v Dougall* [2010] EWCA Crim 1048; *R v Messent* (unreported) 26 October 2010, Southwark Crown Court.
[52] Royal Commission on Standards in Public Life (1976) Cmnd 6524, Committee on Standards in Public Life (1995) Cm 2850.
[53] *Legislating the Criminal Code: Corruption*, Law Com No 248 (1998).
[54] *Joint Committee on the Draft Corruption Bill, Session 2002–2003*, HL Paper 157, HC 705 (2003).
[55] At one point Transparency International drafted a Private Members Bill intended to effect reform (the Corruption Bill), which was introduced in the House of Lords in 2006 but did not become law.

1.60 It was then decided to commence another consultation exercise on the subject of reform. The eventual result was for the government to ask the Law Commission to produce a second report which took account of the consultation and the criticisms of the Joint Committee. This led to the 2007 Law Commission Consultation Paper, a further public consultation process pursuant to that paper, and then the 2008 Law Commission Final Report.[56]

1.61 A draft bill was published by the government in March 2009.[57] The bill did not implement certain elements of the reforms suggested by the Law Commission (such as a defence of reasonable belief in the legality of a payment made to a foreign public official) but was broadly in line with the draft bill which formed part of the Law Commission Report of 2008. Another Parliamentary Joint Committee considered the draft bill and engaged in another process of consultation. The final Report of the Joint Committee was broadly supportive of the terms of the draft.[58]

1.62 As the bill went through Parliament various minor amendments were made to it. Much of the attention was given to the corporate offence and what guidance could be given on the subject of adequate procedures, the position of the Attorney-General and the position of the security services and armed forces. The bill was passed by both the House of Lords and the House of Commons and received Royal Assent, thus becoming an Act of Parliament, on the last day before Parliament was prorogued for the general election, 8 April 2010.

1.63 The passage of the Act was not the end of the law-making process, although it was perhaps the beginning of the end. The main parts of the Act were not self-executing and required a further Order from the Secretary of State before they entered into force.[59] Section 9 of the Act also required the Secretary of State to publish guidance on the subject of adequate procedures for commercial organisations to prevent bribery and provide a defence to a charge under s 7, and the government had committed to doing this before the Act came into force.

1.64 After the general election of May 2010 the new coalition government was required by s 9 to issue the said guidance. It had been expected that this would occur by July 2010 but a decision was taken to undergo another consultation process, this time on the subject of what the guidance might be. A draft of the guidance was issued on 14 September 2010. There followed an intense campaign of lobbying of the Secretary of State and commentary in the media, which frequently took the line that the Act was too uncertain in its effects, especially in relation to the provision of corporate hospitality or gifts and promotional expenses. The final guidance, which contained considerable

---

[56] *Reforming Bribery*, Law Com No 313, 19 November 2008 (hereafter 'LC 313').
[57] Cm 7570, 25 March 2009.
[58] *Joint Committee on the Draft Bribery Bill, First Report, Session 2008–2009*, HL 115, HC 430 – I & II, 28 July 2009 (hereafter 'Joint Committee Report').
[59] Section 19(1) and (2).

differences in both tone and content from the original draft, was issued by the Secretary of State on 30 March 2011.[60] The Act itself will come into force on 1 July 2011.

CONCLUSION

1.65 What conclusions can we draw from the history of the previous law and the rather tortuous process of reform? It is clear that bribery has been seen as wrongful for centuries.[61] It is also clear that it has not always been easy to formulate the elements of the offence. Bribery or corruption are usually easy to recognise but hard to define, at least in terms which provide complete legal certainty. The Bribery Act contains comprehensive formulations of bribery offences but it remains to be seen whether it has managed to abolish these problems completely.

1.66 The slow pace of reform is not only due to difficulties attending formal legal definitions or worries about uncertainty of application. Some will have been hostile to meaningful reform because of the impact it might have on business practices and political relationships. The present reforms are partly the result of pressure from international organisations, advocacy groups and those businesses which recognise the virtues of a level playing field. Not all agree with these ideas, or agree with them only to the extent that they do not impede their own interests. Considering the tolerance towards overseas corruption of the recent past, and the previous political decisions about investigations seen as politically inconvenient, the slow pace of reform is less surprising. It is perhaps more surprising that such a far-reaching measure has finally been planted in what many will have seen as unpromising soil.

'Bribery' or 'corruption'?

1.67 Anyone reading about this topic may be curious about the uses of the terms 'bribery' and 'corruption'. For example, this chapter has tended to use the terms interchangeably, but the Act refers only to 'bribery'. Is there a difference?

1.68 As we have seen, the previous UK statutes related to the prevention of 'corruption'. However, the UK common law offence and the civil law refers to 'bribery'.[62] Internationally, the relevant UN and Council of Europe Conventions are on corruption, but the OECD Convention is on 'Combating the Bribery of Foreign Public Officials'.

1.69 As far as British criminal law is concerned it is clear that the term 'bribery' has won the day. The 2010 Act repeals the Public Bodies Corrupt

---

[60] See the detailed discussion in Chapter 9.
[61] For example Article 40 of Magna Carta, 1215, provides: 'To no one will we sell, to no one deny or delay right or justice.'
[62] See Chapter 13.

Practices Act 1889 and the Prevention of Corruption Acts of 1906 and 1916.[63] Therefore, the offences on the statute book from July 2011 will only be offences of bribery. It will not be technically correct to describe them as corruption offences, although, at least as far as the general offences are concerned, the new Act plainly covers the same ground.

1.70 As a matter of general language, both 'bribery' and 'corruption' can refer to the same phenomenon, that is the specific event whereby an advantage is given in exchange for an improper performance of duties. The term 'bribe' is rarely used to mean anything apart from this.[64] But 'corruption' and 'corrupt' seem to go wider. They can be used, quite loosely, to describe an unwholesome and improper state of affairs within institutions or groups. They can refer to unethical behaviour such as partisanship, self-interest, nepotism or unfairness without suggesting that specific bribes or corrupt transactions have taken place. Corruption can also be used to mean the degeneration of standards generally, especially the act of 'corrupting' others in terms of morals.[65] So it seems that bribery tends to mean something more specific and corruption tends to mean something more general.

1.71 Coming back to the Act, the decision to define this group of offences as bribery rather than corruption may reflect a wish to use terminology with a narrow connotation,[66] and to emphasise the specific elements making up the offence as well as a wish to escape the difficulties associated with defining the term 'corrupt' or 'corruptly' which affected the previous legislation. It may not be coincidental that 'bribery' is the preferred term in the OECD Convention.

Interpreting a new Act of Parliament

1.72 There has already been an enormous amount of discussion about what specific provisions of the Bribery Act mean or might mean. However, the only authoritative sources of interpretation of UK statutes are the decisions of the courts of the UK. Only the courts apply the law and only the courts' interpretations are binding.

1.73 In discussing new legislation it is now common to refer to parliamentary statements and debates, explanatory notes, the conclusions of bodies such as

---

[63] Section 17 and Sch 2 of the Act. Section 17 also provides: '(1) The following common law offences are abolished – (a) the offences under the common law of England and Wales of bribery and embracery, (b) the offence under the law of Scotland of bribery and accepting a bribe.'
[64] Although sometimes sales incentives offered to customers or fiscal measures attractive to groups of voters are referred to (inaccurately) as 'bribes', the usage still seems to be transaction-specific.
[65] There are also more technical uses of 'corrupt' and 'corruption' in the fields of textual analysis and information technology. The adaptability of the term perhaps results from the Latin derivation of '*cor*' (altogether) and '*rumpere*' (to break).
[66] See, for example, the oral evidence of Professor Jeremy Horder to the Joint Committee, Joint Committee Report, 28 July 2009, Ev 1.

parliamentary joint committees and the Law Commission.[67] This book makes reference to such sources, as well as to the government's guidance on adequate procedures pursuant to s 9, other statutes, the OECD Convention and its Commentaries, case-law under the previous law, case-law from other jurisdictions, textbooks, articles and even blogs. Although these may provide context and insight into contemporaneous thinking and assist in the purposive approach to interpretation which is now the norm, none are fully authoritative sources of interpretation.

1.74 Commenting on new legislation in the absence of any judicial authority provides many opportunities for being proved wrong. But the reader of any legal text is entitled to something which both identifies difficult interpretive questions and attempts to answer them. A lack of decided authorities is no excuse. Therefore this book often enters uncharted waters. Whether the course plotted proves true or false, it should, hopefully, aid the navigation of others.

---

[67] The statements of ministers and other promoters of a bill, including explanatory notes, can be used in the courts to assist in identifying the intention of Parliament in relation to legislation which is ambiguous – *Pepper (Inspector of Taxes) v Hart* [1993] AC 593, though some doubt has been expressed as to the application of the rule to criminal statutes where it runs up against the principle that these are to be narrowly construed – *Massey v Boulden* [2002] EWCA Civ 1634, [2003] 2 All ER 87, 93, 103.

Chapter 2

GENERAL OFFENCES: ACTIVE BRIBERY

BRIBERY ACT 2010: SECTION 1

'**1 Offences of bribing another person**

(1) A person ("P") is guilty of an offence if either of the following cases applies.

(2) Case 1 is where—

(a) P offers, promises or gives a financial or other advantage to another person, and
(b) P intends the advantage—
   (i) to induce a person to perform improperly a relevant function or activity, or
   (ii) to reward a person for the improper performance of such a function or activity.

(3) Case 2 is where—

(a) P offers, promises or gives a financial or other advantage to another person, and
(b) P knows or believes that the acceptance of the advantage would itself constitute the improper performance of a function or activity to which section 3 applies.

(4) In case 1 it does not matter whether the person to whom the advantage is offered, promised or given is the same person as the person who is to perform, or has performed, the function or activity concerned.

(5) In cases 1 and 2 it does not matter whether the advantage is offered, promised or given by P directly or through a third party.'

INTRODUCTION

2.1 The provision of bribes is sometimes known as 'active bribery', and their receipt as 'passive bribery'.[1] In this book, when discussing bribery, the term 'provider' (or sometimes 'P') is used as shorthand for the party who offers,

---

[1] The active/passive categorisation is a convenient shorthand and is used in certain international instruments such as the OECD Convention. However, it can be misleading because it gives the impression that the paying party is dominant or more culpable, which is not always the case.

promises, gives or pays, and 'recipient' (or sometimes 'R') for the party who requests, agrees to receive or accepts. Such people can also sometimes be described as 'bribe payers' and 'bribe seekers'.

2.2 Section 1 of the Act deals with the behaviour of the provider rather than the recipient.[2] It sets out two 'cases' which are deemed to be offences by s 1(1) (although case 1 in fact provides two different scenarios). The essence of case 1 is providing an advantage intending to induce or to reward improper performance of functions by the recipient, or another person. The essence of case 2 is providing an advantage to someone who occupies a position in which mere acceptance of the advantage would in itself be improper performance. The receipt offences are dealt with by s 2 of the Act, which outlines four further cases.

2.3 Unlike the two other main 'provision of bribes' offences in the Act (ss 6 and 7), s 1 offences and s 2 offences do not have to be connected to business. Although most bribery occurs in a commercial context, these general offences of bribery can be committed for purely personal reasons, or even with no intention of obtaining a personal gain, although the latter case can be expected to be rare.

2.4 Of course, the provision and receipt offences will often go hand in hand as a matter of fact. However, in law they are not interdependent and a provision offence does not logically require there also to be a receipt offence. So an offer of a bribe contrary to s 1 is an offence whether or not the intended recipient actually accepts it (and thus commits an offence under s 2). Similarly, requesting a bribe is an offence under s 2 whether or not it is ever agreed to or given.[3]

Threshold conditions

2.5 For both s 1 cases to apply there are two threshold conditions. The first condition is that the alleged bribe is related to the performance of certain 'relevant' functions or activities, defined by s 3. The second condition is that the performance to be carried out or rewarded by the advantage is 'improper performance' according to ss 4 and 5. It will not be possible to gain a complete understanding of the general offences under ss 1 and 2 without understanding the operation of ss 3 and 4 of the Act. These threshold conditions are examined in Chapters 4 and 5 and it may help to read these together.

Actus reus and mens rea

2.6 Discussion of criminal offences is often in terms of a conduct element, known in Latin as the 'actus reus' (or guilty act), and a mental element, known

---

[2] Bribery of foreign public officials and failure of a commercial organisation to prevent bribery under ss 6 and 7 of the Bribery Act can also be characterised as 'active' or provision offences.
[3] This was also the case under the previous law – *R v Andrews Weatherfoil Ltd* [1972] 1 WLR 118, CA.

as 'mens rea' (guilty mind).[4] A crime is committed by a person when a certain act is carried out by him while possessing a particular mental state. If one of either the actus reus or the mens rea cannot be proved then the commission of a crime cannot be established. This is the general rule. The exception is crimes of strict liability, where there is no requirement to establish mens rea.[5]

2.7 One approach to bribery might have been to set up a particular mens rea (such as intention to corrupt or intention to act corruptly) which would apply across various offences and fact-situations. However, the Bribery Act provides that different offences require different mental states. So the Act contains offences of specific intention such as s 1, case 1 (provision of advantage with intention to induce or reward improper performance of functions) as well as offences of knowledge or belief (s 1, case 2) and offences of essentially strict liability (s 7).

CASE 1: INDUCING OR REWARDING IMPROPER PERFORMANCE

2.8 Case 1 provides for two distinct factual scenarios. The first is the making of an offer, promise or gift of an advantage with the intention to induce the recipient or another person to perform relevant functions or activities improperly. We can call this the 'inducement' offence. The second is the offer, promise or gift of an advantage with the intention to reward improper performance of a relevant function or activity – the 'reward' offence. Several elements are common to both and these will be examined first.

Offer, promise or give

2.9 The offer, promise or gift of an advantage will be the active element of the offence, the actus reus.

2.10 The terms 'offer', 'promise' and 'give' are not defined in the Act and should be given their ordinary meaning.[6] They all seem to involve P taking some voluntary action to communicate or provide the advantage. However, they are obviously not synonymous, and each requires some analysis.

2.11 An offer can be defined as a statement to the effect that an advantage is available to the recipient contingent upon the recipient taking some other step. Sometimes the words used are clear, but sometimes an offer is not spelled out

---

[4] Some see Latin tags as unhelpful jargon, but these terms remain convenient short hand and they are used throughout this text.
[5] For example many traffic offences.
[6] The words 'offer, promise or give' also appear in s 6 of the Act. The formulation has roots in Art 1 of the OECD Convention, which employs the phrase 'intentionally offer, promise or give' in describing the offence of bribery of foreign public officials which the Convention requires states to criminalise. The courts can be expected to attempt to take a consistent approach to the interpretation of these terms.

but merely hinted at.[7] Words and actions will need to be understood in their context. A remark such as, 'If you can help us, we can help you' may be innocent in some contexts, but damning in circumstances where an envelope full of cash is being placed on the table. Even conduct alone, without any words being spoken, may amount to an offer. At a meeting between a purchasing official and a bidder, the placing of an envelope of cash on the table may well be enough to amount to an offer of a bribe, even if the envelope is never handed over, or even discussed.[8]

2.12 A promise is conceptually different to an offer, in that it is usually understood as involving a commitment or undertaking by the promisor which is not contingent on action by the promisee.[9] 'If you can help us, we can help you' is an offer but not a promise. A promise might be: 'I guarantee I will make this worth your while.'[10]

2.13 Although the Act is silent on this point, it is likely that any offer or promise would have to be communicated to the person in question to form the basis of an offence, or at least transmitted so that it is capable of being received by the recipient.[11] So an offer made in a letter or e-mail which was never sent to the offeree might indicate a plan to commit bribery but would not constitute the act of making an offer or an offence under s 1 (although it might be evidence of a conspiracy or attempt to commit such an offence – see Chapter 12). Of course, whether one has offered or promised something does not depend on whether the offer or promise has been accepted.

2.14 To 'give' is to do more than to offer or promise. It involves the transfer of at least an element of control of something specific (such as money or goods) from the giver to the recipient. Placing an envelope on a table may not be 'giving' it – it may depend on how far across the table it goes. If the intended recipient can take possession of it without the giver doing anything else then it will have been given. Of course, placing an item in someone's hand or pocket, delivering it by post or e-mail, or transferring money to their bank account will amount to 'giving' for the purposes of the Act.

---

[7] The Law Commission recognise that offers and promises can be implied as well as express – LC 313, para 3.46.

[8] During parliamentary debate of s 1 of the Bill an example was given of a hand gesture which on its own and in the correct context might amount to either the offer or request of a 'backhander' (*Hansard*, HL, col GC22 (7 January 2010).

[9] 'A declaration or assurance by which a person undertakes a commitment to do or refrain from doing a specified act or gives a guarantee that a specified thing will or will not happen, be done, etc.' (*Shorter Oxford English Dictionary* (*SOED*), 6th edn).

[10] In the context of the OECD Convention, Pieth et al discuss the difference between an offer and a promise. An offer is 'a declaration by the bribe-giver, on his own initiative, indicating his *readiness to pay* for the official act in question. By promising to do so he makes a *definitive commitment*'. Pieth, Low and Cullen (eds) *The OECD Convention on Bribery: A Commentary* (Cambridge, 2007) at p 109.

[11] That is certainly the position in the civil law – an offer is not made until it is capable of acceptance.

2.15 In this context, the term 'give' is probably not limited to a transfer of possession or control of something. It might be understood as any act involving the provision of the advantage in question. Someone wishing to improperly influence a businessman might use their influence within a private club or association to ensure his election to an important post. A teacher might award a higher grade to a student in exchange for some other favour from her parents. These are not 'gifts' in the traditional sense, but amount to the provision of advantages.

2.16 By the same reasoning, it may not be necessary for the recipient to be aware that they have received the advantage in question for a 'giving' offence to be complete, although, of course, the donor's plans to influence the recipient will almost always depend on the recipient coming to learn of the gift.[12]

Financial or other advantage

2.17 It is clear that the Law Commission wished the concept of 'advantage' in the Act to remain undefined, the view being that a jury would have little difficulty in understanding what is or is not an advantage in a particular case.[13] Parliament has not defined 'advantage' and it, like other terms, will be analysed by juries in its ordinary sense.

2.18 There may be scope for disagreement about whether a particular set of circumstances amount to an advantage.[14] The analysis is not especially helped by the phrase 'financial or other advantage'. It may be that 'financial' is included so as to give the jury a flavour of the sorts of advantages which the authorities are expecting to be identified.[15] As a matter of logic, the whole set of advantages includes financial advantages, so that providing for these in the alternative seems to introduce a distinction without a difference.[16]

2.19 As a practical matter, advantages should not be difficult to identify in most cases. A sum of money is clearly an advantage, as are securities such as

---

[12] Charging bribery in the case of the private club would not be straightforward of course. Alongside the evidential difficulties, one may question whether it would be drawing the limit of bribery too widely to criminalise someone for using social or personal influence who has not yet asked for anything specific in return.
[13] LC 313, paras 3.38–3.39.
[14] The Law Commission intended 'advantage' to be understood in the widest possible sense, claiming that virtually anything offered to a recipient in exchange for a favour would qualify as an advantage. LC 313, para 3.39.
[15] We are a long way from the prolix approach of the 1889 Act, which provided that: 'The expression "advantage" includes any office or dignity, and any forbearance to demand any money or money's worth or valuable thing, and includes any aid, vote, consent, or influence, or pretended aid, vote, consent, or influence, and also includes any promise or procurement of or agreement or endeavour to procure, or the holding out of any expectation of any gift, loan, fee, reward, or advantage, as before defined.' It seems reasonable to assume that the same term in the present Act was intended to cover at least these circumstances.
[16] It is probably not coincidental that the OECD Convention, Art 1, contains a similar construction, referring to 'any undue pecuniary or other advantage'.

shares or bonds, job offers, free gifts or entertainment. A non-exhaustive list of advantages typically found in bribery cases might include:

- cash;
- securities or valuable contractual rights such as options;
- free or discounted goods or services;
- real property such as a lease or a freehold of land;
- occupation of an apartment or house free or at a below-market rent;
- payment of bills, credit cards or prepaid cards;
- employment for the recipient or a friend or relative;
- payment of education costs;
- payment of medical expenses;
- payment of legal expenses;
- office or other valuable services;
- transportation or accommodation;
- sport or concert tickets, or tickets to other attractions;
- commercially valuable information such as pricing data, trade secrets or price-sensitive information;
- benefits to insurance, savings or pension schemes;
- loans;[17]
- an agreement to fix or coordinate prices, bids or other market behaviour.

2.20 The Act does not provide a de minimis limit for advantages. In strict theory a free cup of coffee might amount to an advantage, although no prosecutor with common sense would base a charge on such an exchange.[18] To any properly directed jury, an advantage should have the characteristic of being something with the potential to influence the mind of the recipient or

---

[17] Although a loan will involve repayment obligations and interest, credit is usually valuable of itself. Cheap loans are obviously advantageous.

[18] Provision of an advantage of such negligible value would be extremely weak evidence of the necessary intention to induce or reward improper performance.

decision-maker, whether or not it actually did so.[19] Such influencing potential may vary widely, according to circumstances and cultures. There may be room for debate as to whether something very commonplace and of low value in one culture might have significant influencing potential in another.

To another person

2.21 Another person in this context includes a legal person such as a company. Note the important provision of s 1(4) to the effect that 'in case 1 it does not matter whether the person to whom the advantage is offered, promised or given is the same person as the person who is to perform, or has performed, the function or activity concerned'. So a gift to a relative of a civil servant is a bribe if it is intended to induce the civil servant improperly to favour the giver when carrying out her functions.

Intending to induce improper performance

2.22 P's intention to induce improper performance is the mens rea necessary for the inducement offence under case 1. We can break this element down a little further by examining intention and inducement of improper performance separately.

Intention

2.23 Intention is a particular concept in criminal law about which there has been considerable judicial and academic debate. Many serious offences require that the accused intends to cause the undesirable outcome in question and is not merely reckless or negligent. So, for example, someone is not guilty of murder unless he intends to cause death or grievous bodily harm to the victim. The same is true of certain offences relating to property, sexual offences and so on. Not every offence under the Bribery Act requires intention as the mental element. However, the s 1, case 1 offences both require intention, and the burden of proving the accused's intention will be on the prosecution.

2.24 The present state of the law as to proving intention can be summarised as follows: usually, an accused intends to cause a result when it is his purpose to cause that result. In the unusual case where it is not the accused's purpose to cause that result, but the result is a virtually certain consequence of his action, and the accused knows this, the accused may also be found to have intended the result.[20]

---

[19] Compare the previous position at common law. It was stated by Willes J in the *Bodmin Case* (1869) 1 O'M & H 117 that he had been required to swear that he would not take any gift from a man who had a plea pending unless it was 'meat or drink, and that of small value'.

[20] See *R v Woolin* [1999] AC 82. This case, like so many leading cases on intention, was concerned with the law of murder, for which intention is a condition precedent to guilt. However, it is reasonable to assume that these principles apply to all crimes requiring intent – see, for example, the speech of Lord Bridge of Harwich in *R v Moloney* [1985] AC 905 at 925D–926B and 928F.

2.25 In assessing whether someone intended to cause a particular result it is proper for a jury to draw inferences from the surrounding circumstances as established by the evidence, including (but not limited to) whether they are satisfied that the outcome in question was a natural and probable consequence of the actions in question.[21]

2.26 <u>So the test for intention is subjective</u> – the question is what was the accused's purpose at the time of the offer, promise or gift. It does not matter what another person, or a theoretical reasonable person, might have intended. However, a jury can and should draw inferences from the evidence and in practical terms will usually see through a bare denial of intention when the evidence does not support it.

Intention and improper performance

2.27 Improper performance in this context is defined by s 4 of the Act – a performance of a relevant function or activity contrary to the expectations of good faith or impartiality arising out of the function or activity in question, or the expectations arising out of a position of trust. See Chapter 5 for a more detailed discussion.

2.28 Must P's mens rea extend to the impropriety of the performance? It might be arguable that it is enough for P to intend only that a certain performance is carried out, not knowing or caring whether that performance is improper, which should be a matter of law only.[22]

2.29 The previous law included the requirement that P's giving of gifts, etc was done 'corruptly', as well as to induce favours, etc from the recipient. In other words, there was a further purpose on the part of P – that the transaction be 'corrupt'.[23] There is no evidence in the parliamentary record, or in other relevant pre-legislative material, that s 1, case 1 (or s 2, case 3) were intended to involve a significant dilution of the necessary mens rea for active bribery.

2.30 Indeed, the evidence seems to go the other way. Intention extending to the impropriety of the performance is the only construction which sits comfortably with case 2, which expressly refers to P's knowledge or belief that acceptance of the advantage by R is itself improper performance. It would be odd for Parliament to construct a case 1 offence of an entirely different character to that in case 2. This would also sit oddly with the provision for passive bribery, in particular s 2(7) which provides that: 'In cases 4 to 6 it does not matter whether R knows or believes that the performance of the function or activity is improper.' This suggests that in other cases lacking such a qualification what R (or, by extension, P) knows or believes about the propriety of the conduct does matter.

---

[21] Criminal Justice Act 1967, s 8.
[22] See Sullivan, 'The Bribery Act 2010: An Overview' [2011] Crim LR 87.
[23] Although exactly what 'corrupt' meant remained problematic. See *R v Wellburn* (1979) 69 Cr App R 254.

2.31 The view of the Law Commission was that the fault element of P in the general offence of bribery was the intention that R behave improperly.[24] This is arguably the distinguishing feature of bribery – an intention to purchase the judgement or discretion of a decision-maker. The issue was only addressed obliquely in parliamentary debate, probably because it was seen as uncontroversial.[25] Nevertheless, the Explanatory Notes to the Act provide as follows:

> '16. Case 1 concerns cases in which the advantage is intended to bring about an improper performance by another person of a relevant function or activity, or to reward such improper performance …
>
> 17. It is sufficient for the purposes of the offence that P intended to induce or reward impropriety in relation to a function or activity falling within section 3(2) to(5).'

2.32 If P genuinely believed that the performance induced by a payment would not be improper, then his moral culpability would be doubtful because he would not know that he was doing anything wrong. The same will be true of the offence of rewarding improper performance or indeed a case 2 'compromise of position' case.

2.33 So we can conclude that the general provision offences in s 1 appear to be aimed at situations where P intends to provide the advantage so as to induce or reward the improper performance of relevant functions, or knows or believes his actions will do so.[26]

2.34 It would go too far to suggest that the Act allows P to make his own mind up about whether the performance in question is proper or not. Improper performance is defined in the Act as conduct which breaches the relevant expectations of good faith, impartiality or arising under a trust.[27] The question of what is expected is a test of what a reasonable person in the UK would expect.[28] So P will not be able to set up a defence based on his own personal system of morality. If P knew or believed that a reasonable person in the UK would consider the performance which he intended to induce or reward to be

---

[24] LC 313, paras 3.67–3.70, and LC CP 185, paras 6.85–6.88.
[25] Although the House of Lords committee stage of the bill involved some debate as to whether the word 'corruptly' should be added to the definition of P's offence under s 1, it seems to have been assumed that whether or not 'corruptly' or similar additional mens rea was added, P's intention must extend to the impropriety of R's performance. See, for example, the contributions of two distinguished lawyers to the debate at *Hansard* HL, col GC27 (Lord Goodhart), col GC28 (Lord Mackay of Clashfern) (7 January 2010).
[26] This is also the conclusion reached by Professor Sullivan, [2011] Crim LR 87 at 93. In his view, the difference in mens rea between P in cases 1 and 2 and R in case 3, and R in cases 4–6 is unjustified. However, the level of knowledge to be expected as to the nature of the performance is likely to differ significantly between P and R, with R being quite reasonably subject to the presumption that he understands the rules and standards applicable to his functions. The same should not be presumed of P.
[27] Bribery Act, ss 3 and 4.
[28] Bribery Act, s 5.

improper then he will be guilty. If P made a genuine mistake about this, and did not think that what he was asking R to do was improper according to UK standards, then he is not guilty.

2.35 The test of propriety, although objective because based on the standard of the reasonable person, is formulated at a high level. It is most unlikely that the prosecution will be required to prove that P actually considered whether the function or activity is among the list of specific functions or activities in s 3(2), or the detail of which of the expectations set out in s 3(3)–(5) apply or would be breached. Such an approach would be artificial. A person accused of causing serious bodily harm is not required to have considered in advance the detailed medical effects which his assault will cause the victim. On the same principle, it should be sufficient to prove that P intended to induce or reward behaviour relating to R's functions or activities which he knew or believed to be improper in some way, according to the standards of a reasonable person.

'Induce'

2.36 The term 'induce' is not defined in the Act. In ordinary language, an inducement is something said or done which could persuade the recipient to act improperly. It need not necessarily be the only or even the primary cause of any improper behaviour.[29] It is not necessary for the advantage to be the 'primary' reason for the improper performance, rather than just one of several reasons.[30]

2.37 For example, assume a supplier knows that a customer's manager is already well-disposed to him and is likely to put business his way for legitimate reasons. The supplier decides to offer a sweetener payment to the manager in any case, just to make sure of the business. It seems clear that the payment is intended to influence how the manager approaches the performance of his functions, and it can be seen as an intended inducement to the manager.

2.38 It is not part of the offence that the offer or provision must in fact induce the recipient to perform improperly. The offence is committed even if the manager is not in fact induced or if he refuses to accept the advantage. It is enough that the provider *intended* to induce him, however hopeless that task.

---

[29] There is a pleasing symmetry with the old law here – in *R v Gurney* (1867) 10 Cox CC 550 the relevant intention was an intention to produce any effect at all on the mind of the recipient, in that case a magistrate.

[30] As had originally been proposed by the Law Commission. During the consultation process this proposal was opposed by several consultees, who felt that the need to prove the dominance of the advantage as a reason for the action in question would provide recipients in particular with the excuse that although they had received an advantage from the provider, the decision in the provider's favour was primarily for other reasons.

Relevant function or activity

2.39 For the purposes of the general offences, a relevant function or activity is defined by s 3 of the Act.[31] These can be summarised as functions of a public nature, or activities which are either connected to business, performed in the course of employment or performed on behalf of a body of persons.

2.40 The function or activity in question should carry with it expectations of either good faith or impartiality or expectations arising from a position of trust imposed by the function or activity. These expectations are assessed by reference to what a reasonable person in the UK would expect in relation to the performance of the type of function or activity concerned.[32] The vast majority of activities carried out by public servants and those in responsible positions in the private sector are likely to be covered by this definition.

Intending to reward improper performance

2.41 Just as it is wrong to induce improper performance in advance, so also it is wrong to reward it retrospectively, and thus create incentives for improper performance. There is an obvious public interest in preventing office holders being tempted into performing their functions improperly in the hope that they will receive some sort of personal benefit.

2.42 The actus reus of the offence is the same as the inducement offence – an offer, promise or gift of a financial or other advantage. The mens rea is, again, intention, but a different intention – to reward a person (not necessarily the recipient) for the improper performance of a relevant function.

2.43 What is meant by a 'reward'?[33] In normal usage it presumes that there has in the past been some action advantageous to the provider and that a gift or benefit is paid in connection with that action.[34] A reward is not necessarily something agreed in advance of performance by the recipient.[35]

2.44 It is not quite clear whether it is necessary for improper performance to have actually taken place before P falls within the reward offence in case 1. One view, reading s 1(2) by itself, is that all that is necessary is for P to make the offer, promise or gift and for P to intend the advantage to reward a person for improper performance. P may be mistaken about the fact of the improper performance, or deceived by the recipient of the advantage – if so he will still have committed the offence. This approach fits with an earlier purpose of the

---

[31] See the discussion at Chapter 4.
[32] Bribery Act, s 5(1).
[33] The *SOED* has: 'A return or recompense, esp. for service or merit.'
[34] LC 313, para 3.48: 'In such cases, the corrupt conduct comes first, and the advantage is conferred afterwards.'
[35] This was clearly the case under the old law, at least the use of the term 'reward' in the Public Bodies Corrupt Practices Act 1889 could be 'given the natural meaning of an *ex post facto* gift without any antecedent agreement' *R v Andrews Weatherfoil Ltd* [1972] 1 WLR 118, CA.

Law Commission in its consultation paper which considered it undesirable for P to have a defence based on a mistake as to the facts of R's conduct.[36]

2.45 However, s 1(4) seems to contemplate only two types of counterparty for P – someone who 'is to perform' the function or activity (presumably in the context of the inducement offence) or someone who 'has performed' it (presumably in the context of the reward offence). This leaves out someone who P pays as an intended reward for impropriety but who has in fact not done what P wanted. Because this is new law, a definitive interpretation eludes us for now. It may be that s 1(4) will be read down for the purpose of defining the reward offence, since that is not its primary purpose.

Example

2.46 Inducement and reward offences could easily occur as part of a connected series of events. Imagine that Bob is a building control officer employed by a local authority. He inspects a building site on which a large office development is under construction. He finds a number of faults with the work. These faults are potentially dangerous and should result in construction being stopped and remedial work being done, resulting in major delays and extra costs.

2.47 Edmund, the project manager, approaches Bob the day before the report is due to be produced and says: 'What about forgetting all about this? We can sort it out quietly and there will be something in it for you.' Bob's report omits to mention the faults. A week later, Edmund meets Bob for a drink. When Bob looks in his coat at the end of the meeting he finds an envelope which contains £5,000 in cash. Edmund had been given the cash by a director of the development company for the purpose of giving it to Bob. Bob says nothing and keeps the money.

2.48 On these facts, Edmund has committed an 'inducement' offence under s 1(2)(b)(i) (by offering Bob a benefit intending that, in exchange, Bob will ignore the faults). Both he and the director of the development company and/or the company itself have committed a 'reward' offence under s 1(2)(b)(ii) (by providing cash in exchange for Bob ignoring the faults in his report). Of course Bob himself has committed recipient offences under s 2,[37] as will be discussed in Chapter 3.

CASE 2: COMPROMISE OF POSITION

2.49 The actus reus of case 2 (s 1(3)) is the same as that of case 1 offences – an offer, promise or gift of an advantage. Case 2 applies to what are sometimes called 'compromise of position' cases. There are certain circumstances where money or other advantages are offered or provided to people in positions of

---

[36] CP 185, para 5.118.
[37] Under cases 4, 5 and 6 and, arguably, the separate offence of misconduct in public office.

influence without asking for (or even necessarily expecting) something specific in return – there is no mention of a quid pro quo. However, the positions held by such people are such that it is improper for them to accept advantages of this kind, because to do so would or could, compromise them in the performance of their duties.

Knows or believes

2.50 Case 2 requires proof of a different (and less strict) mental state than that required for case 1. Case 2 applies if P 'knows or believes' that the acceptance of the advantage would constitute improper performance of relevant functions or activities by the recipient. Unlike case 1, there is no requirement that P 'intends' R to perform his duties improperly.

2.51 To know something is to believe something to be true which is in fact true, a state of mind often referred to as 'true belief'.[38] To establish knowledge one must first establish that the fact believed by the accused is true, and then establish that the accused believed it to be true.

2.52 To believe something is not the same as to know it. Belief does not require the truth of the fact in question – it has been described as a state of mind which is 'something short of knowledge'[39] but which exists when a person has no doubt that something is the case. However, belief is more than having a suspicion or wilfully closing one's eyes to the obvious. It requires a real commitment to the truth of the proposition in question.

2.53 In case 2 the test of the provider's mental element is knowledge *or* belief. Therefore the minimum burden for the prosecution is the actual belief of P that it is improper for the recipient to accept the advantage. It is clearly a subjective test – even if a reasonable person would have known or believed that it was improper for the recipient to receive the advantage, the burden remains on the prosecution to show that P actually knew or believed it. A very ignorant accused may not have sufficient mens rea and will not be guilty. Of course, it will not necessarily avail a defendant simply to say 'I never realised' – there will be many circumstances in which such a statement is incredible.

Acceptance itself improper

2.54 Whether the acceptance of the advantage is itself improper must, again, be addressed in light of the provisions of ss 4 and 5. The key question is whether a reasonable person would regard expectations of good faith, impartiality or arising from a position of trust ('the relevant expectations') as applying to the recipient's function or activity and whether the jury take the view that such expectations are breached by the recipient accepting the advantage.

---

[38] *R v Montila* [2004] 1 WLR 3141.
[39] *R v Hall* (1985) 81 Cr App R 260 at 264.

2.55 Sometimes of course there will be clear rules governing the employment of the recipient which regulate acceptance of gifts, such as corporate codes of conduct. However, the Act does not expressly refer to such rules and they may not always be determinative of P's state of mind. It will be a question for the jury whether the accused knew or believed that it was improper for the recipient to accept the advantage.

Examples

2.56 Imagine a case where Ben works as a customs officer at a ferry port. Jenny is passing through the port. She approaches Ben and takes him to her car. She hands him a valuable watch, saying 'sorry I forgot your birthday – hope this makes it up to you'.

2.57 A reasonable person will see Ben as being subject to expectations of impartiality between persons passing through the port and being in a position of trust by virtue of his role. The acceptance of expensive gifts from members of the public in these circumstances is a breach of the relevant expectations. Jenny might claim to be ignorant of the rule or expectation that customs officers should not accept gifts while on duty, but a jury may not accept this. Most people are likely to realise that law-enforcement officers should not accept gifts in the course of their work, even if the giver is known to them already. For case 2 to be made out it is irrelevant whether Jenny intended to influence Ben in the performance of his duties. It is enough if she knew or believed that Ben should not accept gifts from her in the course of his duty.[40]

2.58 Take another hypothetical situation. George, a government minister, is asked to address a conference in an exclusive ski resort. He will not be paid for speaking though his travel and accommodation costs will be covered. Boris, the event organiser, is Albanian by background but lives in London. He is sincerely grateful to George and his PA rings up George's office to ask which wines he enjoys. On hearing that, as a government minister, George cannot accept any gifts Boris says to his PA: 'what rubbish – that can't be right. It's just a token of thanks. Send a case of Haut Brion to his wife, at their home address'.

2.59 Let us assume that George's functions constitute relevant functions for the purposes of s 3 of the Act and that, as his office has stated, he cannot accept the wine without being in breach of the ministerial code. Let us also assume that an acceptance of the wine in breach of the code will be treated by a court as constituting the improper performance of functions.[41]

---

[40] A scenario of this nature may qualify as an offence under s 15 of the Customs and Excise Management Act 1979 which criminalises the receipt by a customs officer of payments or rewards not lawfully due to him. However, the offence is triable summarily and sentence is limited to a fine.

[41] Though that assumption might be debatable in some cases. The author has seen civil servants refuse a gift of a small branded paperweight commemorating a particular event, on the ground that acceptance was against the rules (although another motivation may have been aesthetic). If such a gift, which probably had a value of less than £5, were to be accepted, would the giver

2.60 This scenario is not within case 1 – there is little evidence of intention to induce or reward improper performance of George's duties.

2.61 If the wine is sent, is Boris (or indeed his assistant) guilty of a case 2 offence? Boris might say he genuinely did not believe, or know, that George's acceptance of the gift was improper, despite being told about the rule. He might say this is not how things work in Albania – it would be rude not to offer a gift of this sort. The burden will be on the prosecution to convince a jury that Boris's reaction of disbelief disguised his real knowledge or belief that George's acceptance would be improper.

2.62 Boris might be said to have been guilty of 'wilful blindness' – deliberately ignoring the evidence in front of him, or even perhaps of recklessness as to the existence of the rule. An unsubtle clue is the fact that Boris decided to direct the wine to George's home. If his state of mind was that he did not believe there was anything wrong with George accepting the gift then why not send it to the office? One reply might be that Boris was not really sure of the nature of George's duties. He thought the information he had about the rules was probably wrong, but he wanted to avoid the risk of George getting into some minor bureaucratic trouble. Ultimately, a jury would have to come to a view as to Boris's truthfulness.

2.63 In these 'compromise of position' cases there is no requirement for the provider to have any intention to seek something in return, or for the recipient to intend to provide something in return. To offer the advantage in circumstances where one believes the recipient should not accept it is enough to establish liability. The policy goal of this part of the Act is to draw a bright line between acceptable and unacceptable behaviour both towards and by those in positions of responsibility.

2.64 Such an approach has the effect of insisting that the acts of officials must be completely beyond suspicion. As with all new laws, there is a risk of over-zealous application. Resource constraints and the consideration of the public interest in prosecution are likely to mean that a one-off case such as Boris's might well need to be linked to other more serious wrongdoing, for example a pattern of using gifts to influence officials, before becoming a priority for police or prosecutors.[42] That said, the desire of government is to change the culture around gifts to officials and it would be unwise to ignore rules applying to them, especially if dealing with ministers of the Crown. Moreover, whatever the reaction of the SFO, the general public might take a less forgiving view if it became known that George had kept the gift for himself.

---

and the recipient be guilty of offences under the Act? It is questionable whether the paperweight could properly be seen as an 'advantage'. Moreover, acceptance of such a minor item may not be seen by a jury as performance of functions contrary to the relevant expectations provided by s 4. A reasonable person as provided in s 5 might not necessarily expect the official automatically to refuse such a very minor gift despite what the letter of the rule might say.

[42] See the discussion of prosecution priorities in Chapter 10.

INDIRECTNESS AND THIRD PARTIES

2.65 It is worth briefly considering the effect of s 1(4) and (5) on the common scenario of advantages being provided to friends or family of a person performing relevant functions or activities.

2.66 In cases of intention to induce or reward improper performance of functions (case 1) it does not matter if the advantage is given to someone other than the person who performs the protected function. An advantage to a family member, business partner or employer is a bribe if it is offered promised or given with the relevant intention.

2.67 However, this does not apply in cases of compromise of position. In those cases only the obligations which apply to the functionary in question are relevant.

2.68 Both in cases of intention to induce or reward (case 1) and in cases of compromise of position (case 2), it does not matter that the provider uses a third party such as a company, a friend or an assistant to make the offer, promise or gift of the advantage. This is an entirely sensible provision without which the law could be circumvented simply by using third parties to commit the conduct element.

OFFENCES BY BODIES CORPORATE AND THEIR SENIOR OFFICERS (SECTION 14)

2.69 It is clear that an offence under s 1, either case 1 or case 2, can be committed by legal persons, such as corporate bodies, as well as natural persons (ie individuals).[43] As the law currently stands, a corporate body can only commit an offence if a person who is identifiable with the company, sometimes called the 'directing mind', is effectively in the position of P – ie possesses the requisite mental element while committing the actions in question.[44]

2.70 Section 14 of the Act provides, in part:

'(1) This section applies if an offence under section 1, 2 or 6 is committed by a body corporate or a Scottish Partnership;

(2) If the offence is proved to have been committed with the consent or connivance of—

(a) a senior officer of the body corporate or Scottish partnership, or

---

[43] The Interpretation Act 1978, Sch 1 provides:'"Person" includes a body of persons corporate or unincorporate.'

[44] *Tesco Supermarkets Ltd v Nattrass* [1972] AC 153. Of course, as we shall see, the situation is very different for offences under s 7, which can be committed by corporate bodies without the need for involvement of any directing mind. See the discussion in Chapter 8.

(b) a person purporting to act in such a capacity,

the senior officer or person (as well as the body corporate or partnership) is guilty of the offence and liable to be proceeded against and punished accordingly.'

2.71 The purpose of the section is not to create a second offence of consent or connivance. The body corporate and senior officer are guilty of the main bribery offence.[45] This does not apply to s 7 offences, which can only be committed by commercial organisations. These provisions mirror those of s 12 of the Fraud Act 2006.[46]

2.72 The key terms are 'consent' and 'connivance'. At first sight there is no striking difference between them. However, connivance is likely to involve a degree of active participation either in the action itself or its facilitation. Consent may encompass a situation where a director may not have any active involvement in the provision but sufficient knowledge to have prevented it or at least attempted to do so. It is difficult to imagine an example of connivance without consent, but a little easier to imagine consent without connivance.[47]

2.73 Section 12(3) makes it clear that the senior officer or person purporting to act in that capacity will need to have a close connection to the UK within the meaning of s 12(4).[48] Section 12(4) defines a 'senior officer' as a director, manager, secretary[49] or other similar officer of the body corporate, or a partner in the Scottish partnership.

2.74 How might a senior officer consent to or connive in the commission of a s 1 offence by a corporate body? Examples will not be difficult to imagine. Returning to our example of Bob the building inspector who is paid to suppress parts of his report, the bribe money seems to have come from the development company. Assume that company's CEO authorised the use of company funds in the knowledge that it was for the purpose of bribing Bob. If the CEO can be identified as the directing mind of the company then the company is guilty of a s 1 offence and the CEO may be liable pursuant to s 14. If the finance director becomes aware of the scheme and agrees with it he will have at least consented to the company's actions,[50] and be similarly liable.

---

[45] See *Hansard*, HC, col 149 (18 March 2010).
[46] And, previously, s 18 of the Theft Act 1968.
[47] For the meaning of connivance in the context of the previous law of divorce see *Churchman v Churchman* [1945] P 44, 51. The gist seems to be that connivance denotes an active role as accessory or at least corrupt acquiescence in the offence.
[48] As to which see Chapter 11.
[49] In the sense of company secretary or other officer of an organisation, rather than in the sense of a personal assistant. In *R v Boal* [1992] 1 QB 591, 597–598, a case under s 23 of the Fire Precautions Act 1971 which contains the same formulation of 'director, manager, secretary or other similar officer of the body corporate', it was said by the Court of Appeal that the intention of the wording was only to make those 'in a real position of authority, the decision-makers within the company who have both the power and responsibility to decide corporate policy and strategy' liable.
[50] The CEO may also be liable as an accessory and/or for various inchoate offences – see Chapter 12.

THE INNOCENT ABROAD?

2.75 As already mentioned, s 1 offences can be committed outside the commercial sphere by those seeking personal advantages, or indeed by those seeking to avoid personal disadvantages or inconveniences. Section 1 offences may be committed even though the provider did not originally plan to pay a bribe and has found himself facing uncomfortable and undesired circumstances. It is no part of the offence that the provider must be dishonest, greedy or 'corrupt' himself.[51]

2.76 During parliamentary debate, examples were given of a person who wishes to obtain a service for which he has already paid (such as boarding a flight) but who is obstructed by an official demanding an illegal personal payment.[52] Many people would understand the frustration of the passenger and the temptation to pay a small amount of money in exchange for boarding, however distasteful they might find it. Many would resist the idea that the person paying is personally corrupt or blameworthy, especially if there are extenuating circumstances making it urgent for him to board the flight.

2.77 However, as was made clear by the government and other parliamentarians during debate, the purpose of the Act is to 'change culture' and to discourage the making of such demands by making both the demands and compliance with them criminal offences. Parliament seems to have accepted that there may be hard cases at the margins of the law but that this is a price worth paying for the benefits of a clear line in the moral sand. See the further discussion of facilitation payments in the context of the bribery of foreign public officials seeking to retain or obtain business advantages in Chapters 7, 9 and 14.

2.78 The 'bribes for boarding' case may not qualify as an inducement or reward offence because the intention is not to induce or reward improper performance – after all, the passenger already has a right to board. However, depending on the passenger's knowledge, it might well qualify as a 'compromise of position' case under case 2 because it will be improper performance for the official to demand and accept a payment. It would be surprising if the SFO or other authorities prosecuted the passenger in a one-off case such as this, but, strictly speaking, that option will remain open. The position of the government seems to be that the public can rely on prosecutorial discretion to prevent an over-harsh application of the law.

---

[51] See the debate on amendments 1–4 unsuccessfully proposed by Lord Lyell of Markyate, *Hansard*, HL, cols GC21–GC39 (7 January 2010).

[52] A good deal of debate at the House of Lords committee stage concerned the effect of s 1 on the difficult question of 'facilitation payments'. Some colourful examples involving barges transiting canals, airport baggage handlers, chauffeurs, stevedores and others were debated. As recognised by at least some of their Lordships who spoke in the debate, many of these cases amounted to queue-jumping by those able to afford it and/or denial of proper public services to those of lesser means, and as such should be within the ambit of the law, however frustrating to those accustomed to purchasing such preference when travelling overseas. See in general *Hansard*, HL, cols GC21–GC45 (7 January 2010).

2.79 Of course certain situations may amount to blackmail or extortion. For example, corrupt police officers sometimes target foreign motorists by alleging a real or imaginary breach of traffic regulations or immigration laws. They ask for a cash 'fine' and threaten arrest and prison as an alternative. The tourist will know or suspect that the officer is not entitled to the money and for the officer to accept it amounts to improper performance of his public functions.

2.80 Therefore for the tourist to pay the money, given his knowledge, may again amount to a 'compromise of position' offence. Yet few tourists would risk upsetting the officer so as to suffer a spell in a foreign prison of uncertain duration. How many British travellers would, in such circumstances, say: 'I won't pay a fine until convicted in a court of law, however long that takes'? Only the bravest.

2.81 The reality is that in such a situation, and many others where corrupt officials abuse their powers for personal enrichment, the tourist is the victim of a crime. Anyone making a payment in these circumstances, though perhaps technically guilty of a case 2 offence, is highly unlikely to be prosecuted by the UK authorities. Such a prosecution would not be in the public interest and would rapidly bring the law into disrepute.[53]

---

[53] See Serious Fraud Office, *Bribery Act: Joint Prosecution Guidance For the Director of the Serious Fraud Office and Director of Public Prosecutions* March 2011 (hereafter 'Joint Prosecution Guidance'). Page 9 of the Joint Prosecution Guidance mentions the vulnerable position of the payer as a factor indicating that prosecution of a 'facilitation payment' is not in the public interest. There may also be an argument that the defendant can raise a defence of duress or necessity, see the discussion in Chapter 9.

Chapter 3

GENERAL OFFENCES: PASSIVE BRIBERY

BRIBERY ACT 2010: SECTION 2

'2 Offences relating to being bribed

(1) A person ("R") is guilty of an offence if either of the following cases applies.

(2) Case 3 is where R requests, agrees to receive or accepts a financial or other advantage intending that, in consequence, a relevant function or activity should be performed improperly (whether by R or another person).

(3) Case 4 is where—

(a) R requests, agrees to receive or accepts a financial or other advantage, and
(b) the request, agreement or acceptance itself constitutes the improper performance by R of a relevant function or activity.

(4) Case 5 is where R requests, agrees to receive or accepts a financial or other advantage as a reward for the improper performance (whether by R or another person) of a relevant function or activity.

(5) Case 6 is where, in anticipation of or in consequence of R requesting, agreeing to receive or accepting a financial or other advantage, a relevant function or activity is performed improperly—

(a) by R, or
(b) by another person at R's request or with R's assent or acquiescence.

(6) In cases 3 to 6 it does not matter—

(a) whether R requests, agrees to receive or accepts (or is to request, agree to receive or accept) the advantage directly or through a third party,
(b) whether the advantage is (or is to be) for the benefit of R or another person.

(7) In cases 4 to 6 it does not matter whether R knows or believes that the performance of the function or activity is improper.

(8) In case 6, where a person other than R is performing the function or activity, it also does not matter whether that person knows or believes that the performance of the function or activity is improper.'

INTRODUCTION

3.1 Section 2 of the Act provides for further general offences, those where the defendant is the one who is bribed rather than offering or providing bribes. In this book these are described as passive bribery or the receipt offences. Section 2 follows a similar scheme to s 1 – it outlines the nature of the offences by describing four cases, each of which amounts to a separate offence.

3.2 To summarise the receipt offences: the accused, 'R', commits offences if any of cases 3–6 apply:

- case 3 involves the request, agreement to receive or acceptance of an advantage by R, intending the improper performance of a relevant function or activity as a consequence;

- case 4 relates to compromise of position cases – R's request or receipt of an advantage in circumstances where such a request or receipt is itself an improper performance of a relevant function or activity. Note that there is no requirement of knowledge or belief by R that this is the case, unlike case 2, and no requirement of intention, unlike cases 1 and 3;[1]

- case 5 relates to reward cases, involving R requesting, agreeing to receive or accepting a reward for improper performance of a relevant function or activity. Again there is no apparent requirement of intent, knowledge or belief that this is a reward for improper performance, although see the discussion below; and

- case 6 is a case where R performs a relevant function or activity improperly, in anticipation of requesting or receiving an advantage. Again there is no specified mental element although whether, as a matter of fact, the prosecution will be required to prove a form of knowledge by R is discussed below.

3.3 As with the providing offences, all the receipt offences provided for in s 2 are controlled by the application of the threshold conditions in ss 3–5. Only relevant functions or activities as defined by ss 3–5 can attract a charge of bribery under ss 1 or 2. A person requesting or accepting an advantage in relation to a function or activity not within s 3 may be acting unethically or even illegally in other ways, but he is not guilty of a bribery offence under these sections.[2]

---

[1] In pre-legislative deliberations, the Law Commission and the Joint Committee took the view that, in essence, anyone in R's position ought to know what improper performance is by virtue of their being in the role and that to require proof of such knowledge was 'superfluous', a view shared by the Secretary of State for Justice and the Attorney-General, see Joint Committee Report, pp 22–23.

[2] The s 6 (bribery of foreign public official) offence, which applies to providing bribes only, does not apply the threshold conditions under ss 3–5 but exists as a distinct regime.

3.4 We have also seen already that the general provision and receipt offences are not interdependent, so each provision offence does not logically require a receipt offence. An offer of a bribe contrary to s 1 is an offence whether or not anyone actually accepts it (and thus commits an offence under s 2). Similarly, requesting a bribe is an offence under s 2 whether or not it is ever agreed to, or given.

3.5 The cases in s 2 do not refer the actions of the accused to 'another person' in the same way as the s 1 cases. This is probably unnecessary – it is difficult to conceive of a case in which a request or agreement could take place without there being another person involved. For both the providing and receiving offences, the particular transaction or conversation does not have to be with the person who is going to benefit from the improper performance. For the receiving offences, a request of, agreement with or acceptance from someone (for example, an agent or relative of the person expected to benefit from the improper performance), accompanied by the other elements of each case, is all that is required.[3]

CASE 3
'Requests, agrees to receive or accepts'

3.6 The request, agreement to receive or acceptance of an advantage will be the conduct element of the offence, the actus reus. As explained in Chapter 2, this is the action by the accused which, when combined with the mental element (mens rea), constitutes the offence.

3.7 The terms 'request', 'agree to receive' and 'accept' are not defined in the Act and should be given their ordinary meaning. However, like 'offer, promise or give' they have different meanings, and each requires some analysis.[4]

3.8 What is a request for an advantage in this context?[5] A request requires some voluntary action by R. As a minimum such action will need to amount to an articulated suggestion that some action is taken by someone other than the person making the request. One would not expect any words used to always be explicit, since those seeking bribes may well try to maintain 'plausible deniability'. However, even ambiguous language, in context, can be understood by a jury as a request for an advantage. 'What can you do for me?' may be innocent in some contexts, but damning in circumstances where the speaker is pointing to his wallet. There are many euphemisms for bribes in different places

---

[3] Section 2(6) makes the somewhat different but equally important provision that it does not matter whether R's request, agreement or acceptance occurs 'directly or through a third party'.
[4] Of course, 'request, agree to receive or accept' in s 2 are clearly not the corollaries of 'offer, promise or give' in s 1.
[5] The *Shorter Oxford English Dictionary* (SOED), defines request in this context as 'the action or an instance of asking or calling for something'.

and languages.[6] Circumlocutions and hints will amount to requests if their import is clear from the context. Even conduct alone, without any words being spoken, may amount to a request.[7]

3.9 In more sophisticated cases the request may well involve various methods to disguise the provision of the advantage. For example, if a company is seeking the approval of a government official, R, for a bid to supply services, R might suggest that a third party be appointed by the company to act as an intermediary, a consultant or a subcontractor, in the knowledge that the third party will pass on to R some or all of its earnings. Is this a request for an advantage? The appointment by the company of someone who will provide a kickback is clearly an advantage to R. Indeed, as is clear from s 2(6)(b), the benefit of the advantage need not flow to R – R may be guilty of the case 3 offence by requesting that an advantage is provided to a relative, colleague or company, as long as R is the person making the request and R possesses the relevant intention, as to which, see below.

3.10 The Act does not require that the request is communicated to the person who is being asked to provide the advantage. Many cases of bribery involve a series of intermediaries and if it can be established that a communication with an intermediary was expected to be passed on to the person providing the advantage then that is likely to suffice. However, as with the providing offence in case 1, it is suggested that for the offence to be committed there must be some sort of communication. Private schemes to get rich through corruption, if not acted upon, are no crime, unless they amount to attempts, conspiracies or other inchoate offences.[8]

3.11 An agreement to receive an advantage is different to a request for one. It will involve a meeting of minds between the recipient and someone else (who may not necessarily qualify as a provider under s 1) to the effect that an advantage will be received. Again, it requires some voluntary action from R, although there is no need for R to expressly request an advantage – he may merely assent to a proposal from others. It would be wrong to read the term 'agreement' as requiring the traditional elements of a binding contract (such as an intention to be legally bound), not least because as a matter of civil law an agreement to pay or receive a bribe is not legally binding. So, for these purposes, how might we define an agreement? It is suggested that if R and the other party believe that they have agreed or if a reasonable person aware of all the evidence would believe that they had agreed, then this should suffice.

---

[6] For example, English slang contains several euphemisms for a bribe including 'bung' (often heard in the context of football transfers) and 'backhander'. In East Africa a common request of petty officials is for 'tea' or 'tea-money'. For an entertaining tour around such euphemisms see 'The Etiquette of Bribery', *The Economist*, 19 December 2006.
[7] Of course requests, like offers and promises in s 1, can be implied as well as express – LC 313, para 3.80.
[8] As to which see Chapter 12.

3.12 To 'accept' an advantage is more than to merely receive it.[9] Again, it will involve an element of voluntariness – knowledge that one is in possession of the advantage and at least some factor (perhaps merely the passage of time while knowing of the receipt) which indicates an intention to retain it.

Example

3.13 Take the case of Ben the customs officer discussed in Chapter 2. If Ben had asked Jenny to give him something valuable such as a watch then obviously this would be a request for it. If he had asked and she had consented to give it to him next week then that would be an agreement to receive it.

3.14 Imagine instead that the watch is never discussed but Jenny slips it into the pocket of Ben's coat. Ben may not have noticed this. By the time he puts his hand in his coat pocket Jenny is long gone. If Ben keeps the watch, sells it or gives it to his brother as a Christmas present then he may well have accepted it. But until he is conscious of being in possession of it there is no acceptance. One can imagine cases in which criminals attempt to compromise police officers or other officials by providing benefits to them or others without their knowledge or where they are deceived as to the true source or nature of the advantage. Until the truth is known to R such cases are most unlikely to involve the acceptance of an advantage by R under case 3.

Financial or other advantage

3.15 We have already explored the concept of 'financial or other advantage' in Chapter 2. Suffice to say here that, although the concept is intended to be a wide one, advantages should not be difficult to identify in most cases. A sum of money is clearly an advantage, as are securities such as shares, bonds or options, hospitality, entertainment or other free goods or services.[10] Although there is no lower or de minimis limit to the value of an advantage it is suggested that for R, as for P under s 1, the advantage should be something which has at least the potential to influence his mind – this will depend on the particular facts of each case.

Intending that relevant function or activity is performed improperly in consequence

3.16 Intention is a particular concept in criminal law and has been discussed in more detail in Chapter 2. As explained in that chapter, usually D intends to cause a result X when it is his purpose to cause result X. In the unusual case where it is not D's purpose to cause result X, but X is a virtually certain consequence of D's action, and D knows that X is a virtually certain consequence of his action, D may also be found to have intended X.[11]

---

[9] See discussion at LC 313, paras 3.82–3.84.
[10] For a non-exhaustive list of typical advantages see Chapter 2.
[11] *R v Woollin* [1999] AC 82.

3.17 'Relevant functions and activities' have also been briefly discussed in Chapter 2 and are dealt with in detail in Chapter 4. They are functions or activities of a public nature or connected to a business, trade or profession, or performed in the course of employment or performed on behalf of a body of persons. These functions or activities must also carry with them expectations of good faith, impartiality or expectations arising from a position of trust arising from the performance of the function or activity.

3.18 Improper performance of relevant functions and activities is defined in s 4 of the Act and is discussed in Chapter 5. Improper performance can be summarised as performance in breach of the expectations mentioned above – ie not in good faith or impartially or not in accordance with the expectations arising from the position of trust.[12] A failure to perform the function or activity can also be improper performance.[13] The test of what is expected is answered by looking to what a reasonable person in the UK would expect in relation to the activity in question.[14]

In consequence

3.19 The particular intention which R must possess in case 3 is that there will be improper performance (not necessarily by R himself) in consequence of R's request, agreement to receive or acceptance of an advantage.

3.20 Therefore R must intend there to be a causal link between his action and the improper performance. What is the degree of causation to be intended by R? The term 'in consequence' leaves this question open.[15] The words seem to allow the possibility that the advantage is an intended cause of the improper performance but not the only such intended cause. Therefore it might well be possible for R to commit an offence by seeking a payment as a quid pro quo for something he was likely to do anyway, but where the bribe helped him to make up his mind.

Example

3.21 Returning to the example of Ben the customs officer, assume he accepts the gift of the watch from Jenny who has, after all, said it is a birthday present. The critical question now is what was his state of mind when doing so? Was he intending that, as a consequence, a relevant function or activity would be performed improperly? Of course if and when confronted he may well deny any wrongful purposes and claim that this was just a gift from a friend and that he treated her no differently than if she had not given him anything. If he

---

[12] Section 4(1)(a).
[13] Section 4(1)(b).
[14] Section 5(1).
[15] See Chapter 2. It had previously been proposed by the Law Commission that the relevant intention should be that the advantage be the 'primary' reason for the improper performance, rather than just one of several reasons, but this was dropped and the bill contained no such stipulation.

subjected Jenny and her vehicle to the usual processes or, perhaps more powerfully, allowed a colleague who was not aware of the gift to do so then it may be difficult to infer the relevant intention unless there is some other evidence of it.[16] If he took unusual steps to make sure Jenny was not searched, or had been or started to do other favours for Jenny or her friends over time then negative inferences as to his intentions are likely to be drawn. Ben's later behaviour in this context is relevant because it may evidence his state of mind, his intention, not because it is necessary for the commission of the offence under case 3.

Offence complete without actual improper performance

3.22 Case 3 does not require that the request, agreement to receive or acceptance should in fact lead to a specific incident of improper performance.[17] It may be that R has not yet carried out his intention before he is discovered, or has never been in a position to do so. It may be that the payer, or R, changes their plans. This will not affect whether the offence has been committed in the first place. The offence is complete once R makes the request or agreement or accepts the advantage while intending consequential improper performance. If R is struck by a fit of conscience and changes his mind a minute later, he has nevertheless committed the offence.

Lack of intention as to improper performance

3.23 Because case 3 requires R to intend that improper performance is a consequence of the request, agreement or acceptance, it follows that case 3 is not made out when R makes a request or agreement but does not intend to engage in or cause improper performance of a relevant function or activity. R may wish merely to enrich himself and deceive his counterparty by giving the false impression that relevant functions will be performed improperly as a result.[18] Unlike under the previous law, there is no 'presumption of corruption' if R is a public officer.[19] It is not enough that R has solicited the advantage on the pretext of improper performance when in fact no such improper performance was intended. One would expect that in most cases the quid pro quo offered in exchange for an advantage would be reasonably explicit and R may have a difficult task convincing a court that he was engaged in a double

---

[16] Although, of course, it may be that a case 4 offence has been committed – see below.
[17] As was the case under the old law (the 1906 Act) – see *R v Carr* [1957] 1 WLR 165, *R v Mills* (1979) 68 Cr App R 154.
[18] A 'double-cross' situation, as alleged by the defendants to charges under the 1906 Act in *Carr* and *Mills* above. In *Jagdeo Singh v State of Trinidad and Tobago* [2006] 1 WLR 146 (PC) it was held that the effect of legislation in Trinidad and Tobago similar to s 1 of the 1889 Act was that even though the accused lawyer did not intend to offer a bribe to a magistrate he solicited money from a client alleging this was his purpose, and so was guilty of an offence by doing so. Under the new Act these facts would not be sufficient to establish an offence under case 3 but would be likely to amount to an offence under case 4.
[19] As discussed in Chapter 1, the original Prevention of Corruption Act 1916 provided for a presumption of corruption if the recipient was in a public office, although this is no longer the case since *R v Webster* [2010] EWCA Crim 2819.

cross or a fraud, but not in bribery. Whatever about that, many such cases are likely to amount to offences under case 4.

CASE 4

3.24 Like the providing offence under case 2 (s 1(3)), case 4 applies to what are sometimes called 'compromise of position' cases. There are certain circumstances where money or other advantages are sought by people in positions of influence without intending to take any specific action in return. The positions held by such people are such that it is wrong for them to seek advantages of this kind, because to do so would, or could, compromise them in the performance of their duties and bring their employers, or principals, or functions or activities into disrepute. Obvious examples are politicians, civil servants, police officers or judges but one could name many more.

3.25 Unlike the compromise of position case applicable to a provider in 'active' bribery cases (ie s 1, case 2), the position of the recipient is different from the point of view of mens rea or mental element. In the case of a recipient there is no requirement on the prosecution to prove that R knew or believed that seeking or receiving the advantage would constitute improper performance of a relevant function or activity. In fact, as provided by s 2(7): 'In cases 4 to 6 it does not matter whether R knows or believes that the performance of the function or activity is improper.'

3.26 It seems that the rationale for this distinction is that, unlike a provider who should not be assumed to understand the expectations applicable to R's duties, R herself should be expected to know them and any ignorance of them should not excuse her.

3.27 In the example of George and Boris outlined in Chapter 2, Boris, the organiser of an event at which George spoke, sends expensive wine to George, purportedly by way of thanks. The question of Boris's liability under s 1, case 2 will depend on his state of mind as to whether George's acceptance of the gift would amount to a breach of the relevant expectations applying to George. Boris might be able to plead ignorance. However, George will have no such defence to a charge under s 2, case 4 if he accepts the gift and if (as the example assumes) to do so is a breach of relevant expectations. George, a government minister, will be subject to rules preventing the acceptance of gifts in connection with his public duties. Even if George was somehow ignorant of these rules this ignorance will not avail him. As soon as he becomes aware of the wine he should return it or otherwise deal with it as advised by the relevant code.

3.28 In our customs officer case, we can assume that Ben is prohibited from accepting gifts from members of the public while on duty.[20] Other things being

---

[20] Customs and Excise Management Act 1979, s 15.

equal, his acceptance is likely to constitute improper performance of a relevant function, because: (i) the function is of a public nature,[21] (ii) is subject to an expectation of impartiality,[22] and/or (iii) subject to expectations as to the manner in which the function as defined by ss 3–5 of the Act will be performed arising from the officer's position of trust.[23] The (hypothetical) reasonable person in the UK can be expected to believe both that his job is subject to the expectations above and that accepting a valuable gift in these circumstances is a breach of them, in particular the expectations of impartiality or the expectations arising from his position of trust.

3.29 This would, at least, be the analysis if the person providing the advantage was a stranger to the officer. In this case the provider claims to be a friend, Jenny, who says the gift is for his birthday. Let us assume the birthday is in fact within a few days of the gift. We have not explored the nature of the relationship between Ben and Jenny or the exact details of the gift. Jenny may be a mere acquaintance who happens to remember Ben's birthday is around this time and uses this as a pretext for a bribe. But what if the two people in question are madly in love? In the case of the watch, it may be hastily slipped into a pocket as contraband or it may be tastefully wrapped and accompanied by a gift receipt and a birthday card. Would a jury consider that Ben accepting such a gift from someone so intimate while happening to be on duty was, by itself, a breach of a relevant expectation?[24]

3.30 Of course one would expect most cases charged to involve other supporting evidence of wrongdoing, such as attempts to disguise payments, secretiveness, or other factors pointing to guilt. The point of this example is to illustrate that even the outcome of cases which are apparently cut-and-dried when seen in outline will frequently depend on the detailed facts. A customs officer who happens to meet his girlfriend returning from a business trip and who is persuaded to accept her birthday gift on the spot will not seem like someone who is doing his job improperly. The issue may be one of perception and the inferences which can be drawn from the facts. A gift from a stranger looks like a breach of duty. A gift from a spouse or girlfriend does not.[25]

3.31 What of the 'double-cross' situation discussed above? Under case 4 the state of mind of R is irrelevant – if it is improper for R to request, agree to receive or accept the advantage then the fact that R did so without intending to take any action on the strength of the bribe is irrelevant. It is improper for a council officer to say 'I'll need £5,000 if you want planning permission' even if he has no intention of misusing his powers.

---

[21] Section 3(2)(a), and/or it is an activity performed in the course of the officer's employment – s 3(2)(c).
[22] Section 3(4).
[23] Section 3(5).
[24] Section 15 of the Customs and Excise Management Act 1979 does not criminalise acceptance of a payment or reward which the officer is lawfully entitled to claim or receive.
[25] Although, of course, it is possible for spouses and other intimates to bribe or corrupt each other.

3.32 One could imagine a scenario in which R is seeking to obtain evidence of propensity to offer bribes by specific individuals or businesses and intends to provide evidence to the police as soon as P offers or agrees to pay a bribe – a situation discussed but not decided in relation to the 1906 Act in *R v Mills*.[26] Under the Bribery Act this scenario will still amount to an offence under case 4 unless R's actions would not be regarded as being in breach of a relevant expectation of a reasonable person in the UK – for example if R is a detective charged with investigating corruption.

3.33 The strictness of case 4 illustrates again the policy priority – to draw a clear line establishing that office holders (in both the public and private sector) should not seek illicit personal gains from their office.[27]

CASE 5

3.34 Case 5 involves the request, agreement to receive or acceptance of a financial or other advantage as a reward for improper performance of relevant functions or activities. There is an obvious public interest not only in criminalising the seeking of bribes in advance of improper conduct but also the misperformance of duties in the expectation of subsequent rewards. A situation whereby rewards are sought for favourable decisions would be almost as damaging as one where advantages are sought in advance.

As a reward

3.35 Unlike the reward offence applying to a provider under case 1, no specific mental element is specified for the recipient in case 5. However, as discussed above, there is of course an element of voluntariness by R in requesting, agreeing to receive or accepting an advantage. Moreover, the advantage must be requested, agreed or accepted 'as a reward' for improper performance. This seems to mean that the terms of R's request or agreement must be to the effect that: (a) there has already been improper performance of a relevant function or activity, and (b) the advantage requested would reward that performance.

---

[26] (1978) 68 Cr App R 154.
[27] See the Joint Committee Report, para 46, p 23: 'On balance we support the provisions in the draft Bill that enable a person to be convicted of being bribed (clause 2) without proof of knowledge or intention, notwithstanding that subjective fault should ordinarily be required by the criminal law. This policy forms an important part of changing the culture in which taking a bribe is viewed as acceptable. In particular, we think that it should encourage anyone who is expected to act in good faith, impartially or under a position of trust, to think twice before accepting an advantage for their personal gain.' This perhaps begs the question of whether a 'culture' of acceptability of bribes actually exists in the UK (which is the place that this part of the Act is most likely to be relevant to) and, if so, whether disapplying the usual rules of mens rea will be so effective in changing such a culture that it merits extending criminal liability to negligent rather than deliberate wrongdoing.

For improper performance

3.36 The natural reading of case 5, in particular the phrase 'as a reward for the improper performance (whether by R or another person) of a relevant function or activity', implies that the request etc is for more than just a reward on its own, but is for a reward for improper performance. In other words, a representation as to the impropriety of performance seems to be a necessary element of the request, agreement or acceptance.

3.37 However, this sits rather uncomfortably with s 2(7). That provides: 'In cases 4 to 6 it does not matter whether R knows or believes that the performance of the function or activity is improper.' It leads to something of a paradox. How could R request a reward for improper performance if he did not know or at least believe that the performance was improper? The answer is not entirely clear from the wording of the Act and debate in Parliament and other sources do not offer much enlightenment. It might be that s 2(7) is intended merely to remove the requirement that the prosecution prove a specific mental element of R (knowledge or belief as to impropriety) although the request is still on the terms that the reward is for impropriety. It may be intended to cover a 'double-cross' situation as discussed above where R requests a reward said by him or believed by the payer to be for improper performance although R was of the view that the performance was in fact proper.

3.38 As discussed in Chapter 2, in normal usage the word 'reward' presumes that there has, in the past, been some action advantageous to the provider and that the advantage is provided in connection with that action.[28] A reward is not necessarily something agreed in advance of performance by the recipient.[29]

3.39 For the purposes of case 5 it does not seem to be necessary to prove that the improper performance by R has in fact taken place. All that is required is that R requests, agrees to receive or accepts the advantage 'as a reward for the improper performance' – ie that the ostensible basis of the advantage is that it is a reward for past improper performance.

Example

3.40 An example given in Chapter 2 was of Bob, a building control officer who was induced towards and/or rewarded for improper performance of his duties. Changing the facts, let us assume Bob was not approached by Edmund the project manager after mentioning faults in the building. Instead, after submitting his report, he approaches Edmund and says he had found some faults but left them out of his report. He also says that he is hoping to take

---

[28] LC 313, para 3.48: 'In such cases, the corrupt conduct comes first, and the advantage is conferred afterwards.'
[29] This was clearly the case under the old law, at least the use of the term 'reward' in the Public Bodies Corrupt Practices Act 1889 could be 'given the natural meaning of an *ex post facto* gift without any antecedent agreement' – *R v Andrews Weatherfoil Ltd* [1972] 1 WLR 118, CA.

early retirement soon but would like to do some consultancy work. Edmund says 'I think we could use someone like you'. Six months later, after he has retired, a company owned by Bob is appointed to provide 'consultancy services' to the project on a 3-year contract. It is made clear that the company is not actually required to achieve any specific outcomes or targets, although it files generic time sheets and invoices every month.

3.41 Let us assume that both Bob and Edmund knew that what Bob did in amending his report was contrary to the relevant expectations. If we accept that Bob's words were a request for an advantage (ie employment with the project company) there seems to be a clear connection between his request and his statement that he had suppressed evidence detrimental to the project company. His request constitutes the offence since it seeks an advantage 'as a reward' for the improper performance.[30] The case seems to fulfil the elements of the offence under case 5.[31]

3.42 What if Bob had in fact submitted a full report which outlined all the faults, but had disguised this fact from the project company? It seems that the offence would still have occurred because the request (or acceptance) was in terms that the advantage in question would be 'as a reward for improper performance'. It does not matter that, in fact, the impropriety which was the basis of the request or acceptance never happened.

CASE 6

3.43 Case 6 addresses a somewhat different situation, that of the person responsible for performance of a relevant function or activity who positions himself to obtain bribes before anyone has actually approached him or responded to a request from him. It is a more complex provision which requires some analysis.

3.44 The conduct element of the offence is wider than in cases 3 to 5. To have committed the conduct element (actus reus) R must either:

- perform a relevant function or activity improperly; or

- request another person to perform a relevant function or activity improperly, so that the function or activity is performed improperly by that other person; or

- assent to another person performing a relevant function or activity improperly; or

---

[30] Even if he does not request the advantage it seems that as and when he accepts the employment he accepts an advantage as a reward.
[31] Indeed, an offence under case 6 has also been committed – see below.

- acquiesce in another person performing a relevant function or activity improperly.

3.45 The improper conduct by R, or R's request, assent or acquiescence in the improper conduct by another, must be either in anticipation of or in consequence of a request for, agreement to or acceptance of an advantage by R. So it seems that although there is not a specified mental element such as intention,[32] the question of R's state of mind must come into consideration at least in relation to whether R's action is in anticipation of or in consequence of the request, agreement or acceptance.

3.46 By this stage it will, hopefully, be clear what is meant by a request, agreement to receive or acceptance of a financial or other advantage, and the improper performance of a relevant function or activity.

3.47 In this case, more specific provision is made for the possibility that it may not be R who performs the relevant functions or activities. There will be no difficulty in understanding how R himself performs in an improper way. R requesting another person to carry out improper performance also seems straightforward – it assumes some sort of communication between R and the other person in which R's wish for improper performance is expressed.

3.48 What of R's 'assent or acquiescence' when another person's improper performance is in question? The terms are not synonymous. 'Assent' is more active and denotes both a consciousness of the improper performance in question and some action indicating approval of or agreement to it.[33] 'Acquiescence' is more passive, although again it seems that knowledge of the improper performance is a prerequisite.[34] It seems likely that knowledge of improper performance by another person in anticipation or consequence of R's request, agreement to receive or acceptance of an advantage, combined with either an endorsement of the improper performance or a failure by R to act to protest against that improper performance would suffice.

3.49 Again, although no specific mental element (such as intention or knowledge or belief) is specified for a case 6 offence, there can be little doubt that the prosecution will have to prove that R's state of mind was such that it is consistent with assent or acquiescence in the other person's improper performance.

3.50 That said, as with cases 4 and 5, it is clear from s 2(7) that it is not necessary for R to know or believe that the performance in question is improper – it is the making by R of a link between the advantage and the performance of relevant functions or activities which is the target of the offence.

---

[32] And, as with case 5, s 2(7) expressly provides that it does not matter whether R knows or believes that the performance of the function or activity is improper.
[33] The *SOED* has 'express approval or agreement'.
[34] The *SOED* has 'the reluctant acceptance of something without protest'.

In anticipation of or in consequence of

3.51 This case envisages R's actions occurring before his request or agreement or acceptance of the advantage. It assumes that R's actions are either actuated by anticipation of such a request, etc or happen as a consequence.

3.52 As one might expect, no definitions of these terms are offered by the Act, no doubt for the usual reason that it is for the jury to decide whether the behaviour in question is within the meaning imparted by the terms of the section.

3.53 In this context, to act in anticipation of a particular event (such as a request, agreement or acceptance of an advantage) is to act in the awareness or belief that the event may take place in the future.[35] So for R to be guilty of bribery under case 6 (rather than any other offence such as misconduct in public office) he need not have had any contact whatsoever with a provider, or potential provider, of a bribe. All that is necessary is for R to misperform relevant functions or activities expecting that this will lead to his being rewarded in future.

3.54 An action 'in consequence of' the request, agreement or acceptance will be treated in the same way as under case 3. As we have already seen in relation to case 3 and indeed the case 1 'inducement' offence,[36] the policy of the Act is that the prospect of an advantage need not be the primary cause of the improper performance. It is reasonable to assume, therefore, that the request, agreement or acceptance need not be the only matter which causes the improper performance as a consequence. There may be other causes, but the offence is committed if the request, etc is one of them.

Position of person performing function or activity at R's request

3.55 As is made clear by s 2(8), if a person other than R is requested to misperform relevant functions or activities by R (or R assents or acquiesces in this) it does not matter whether that other person knows or believes that the performance is improper, just as R's state of mind as to impropriety is also irrelevant.[37]

3.56 It is quite possible that the person performing the function or activity is a subordinate of R or a colleague, friend or relation. That person may trust or rely on R or follow his guidance for other reasons. The policy of the Act is not to criminalise such people but to target the person who is the nexus between the request, agreement or acceptance and the improper performance. Of course if R's colleague is aware of the full facts and in particular that his performance

---

[35] The *SOED* has 'action taken beforehand in awareness of a possible or likely event'.
[36] Chapter 2.
[37] Section 2(7).

will be improper and is linked to R's request, agreement or acceptance then he may be guilty of the offence itself or of conspiracy, with R, to commit one of the s 2 offences.

Example

3.57 To return to our example of Bob the building inspector, when we left him he had amended his report to cover up faults in the project and then asked for a reward from the project company. A case 5 reward offence will have been committed when he asked for the reward. But a case 6 offence of 'anticipation' will have occurred as soon as it occurs to him to seek a reward and so, anticipating the reward, he amends the report.[38] There may be a gap of days or weeks before he has the opportunity to request a reward, or accept it, but the case 6 offence is complete if a link can be shown between Bob's wrongful amendment of the report and his anticipation of a reward for it.

3.58 It may be a rare case in which such anticipation could be proven unless there is evidence of a later request, agreement or acceptance of a reward. It may be possible to establish Bob's anticipation of the request agreement or acceptance from the evidence of third parties or from documents.

3.59 If Bob has asked for the job with the project company before he amends his report, but Edmund (the project manager) says 'I will think about it, let's see what you can do for us first' then his amendment of the report will not have been made in anticipation of his request. If he amends the report subsequently to the request, so as to provide evidence of his usefulness to the project company then his action will have been as a consequence of his request, and equally within case 6.

---

[38] Or at least as soon as he submits it to his superior or finalises it in some other way.

Chapter 4

RELEVANT FUNCTIONS AND ACTIVITIES

BRIBERY ACT 2010: SECTION 3

'3 Function or activity to which bribe relates

(1) For the purposes of this Act a function or activity is a relevant function or activity if—

(a) it falls within subsection (2), and
(b) meets one or more of conditions A to C.

(2) The following functions and activities fall within this subsection—

(a) any function of a public nature,
(b) any activity connected with a business,
(c) any activity performed in the course of a person's employment,
(d) any activity performed by or on behalf of a body of persons (whether corporate or unincorporate).

(3) Condition A is that a person performing the function or activity is expected to perform it in good faith.

(4) Condition B is that a person performing the function or activity is expected to perform it impartially.

(5) Condition C is that a person performing the function or activity is in a position of trust by virtue of performing it.

(6) A function or activity is a relevant function or activity even if it—

(a) has no connection with the United Kingdom, and
(b) is carried out in a country or territory outside the United Kingdom.

(7) In this section "business" includes trade or profession.'

INTRODUCTION

4.1 As we have seen in Chapters 2 and 3, fulfilment of the 'threshold condition' set out in s 3 is required before any of the bribery offences under s 1 or 2 are committed.

4.2 By placing this threshold condition at the centre of the definition of bribery Parliament has broken away from concepts central to the previous law. Unlike under the previous law, the formal title or legal category into which a recipient may personally fit[1] is far less relevant than the recipient's actual duties[2] and effect which the actions in question have, or are intended to have, on the exercise of those duties.

SUMMARY OF SECTION 3 THRESHOLD CONDITION

4.3 The 'threshold condition' can be summarised as follows:

(a) only functions of a public nature, or activities connected with a business, or employment, or performed on behalf of a body of persons are relevant to offences of bribery;

(b) any such function or activity must also satisfy one of three further conditions relating to the expectations upon the person performing the function or activity. The conditions are, either:

  (i) an expectation of good faith in performance; or
  (ii) an expectation of impartiality in performance; or
  (iii) that performance of the function or activity puts the person performing in a position of trust;[3]

(c) the question of what specific expectations apply is answered by reference to what a reasonable person in the UK would expect in relation to the performance of the type of function or activity concerned.

4.4 There has been disagreement on the subject of whether it was necessary to include this level of detail in the Act. Some felt that the requirement of proof of various expectations applying to the role of the recipient made the offence more complicated than it need be.[4] Proposed alternatives included the idea that the inducement be linked only to a 'breach of duty', or, mere 'improper' performance of functions, without further elaboration.

4.5 However, the Parliamentary Joint Committee considering the Bill rejected these ideas.[5] It was felt that to make the offence depend on concepts of duty which themselves depend on private law (such as director's duties, or employee's duties) would create difficulties typical of the 'agent/principal' model, now intended to be abandoned.[6]

---

[1] Whether 'agent', or 'member, officer, or servant of a public body' (per the 1889 Act) or otherwise.
[2] Or the duties of others who may be affected by the recipient's seeking or receiving bribes.
[3] Not limited to a trust in the formal legal sense.
[4] Notably the Council of HM Circuit Judges.
[5] Joint Committee Report, p 20.
[6] How successful the attempt to avoid private law concepts might be is considered towards the end of this chapter.

Two-stage definition

4.6 It is clear that a function or activity can only be relevant if it satisfies *both* s 3(2) *and* any of the three 'conditions' set out in subsections (3) to (5). There is a two-stage test for determining relevance.

4.7 The first stage is applying subsection (2), which sets out four legal tests as to the status of the functions or activities – whether of a public nature, connected with a business and so on. They are not subject to the 'reasonable person' test which applies to the conditions of good faith and impartiality in subsections (3) and (4). One can expect there to be a degree of consistency among future cases which relate to the applicability of the s 3(2) tests.[7]

4.8 The second stage is to determine whether any of the 'conditions' set out in subsections (3) to (5) apply to the function or activity. Whether the conditions apply is more likely to depend on the facts of each case. The first two conditions (expectations of good faith or impartiality) are to be established by means of the s 5(1) reasonable person test. By contrast the last condition (person in a position of trust) is not subject to any test of what a reasonable person expects. Instead, the question is whether performance of the function actually does give rise to a position of trust. This will ultimately be a question of fact for a jury, although if the issue were in doubt it may well provide fertile ground for debate.

Public sector and private sector

4.9 No distinction is made between the public and private sectors when defining the relevant functions and activities. This is a deliberate policy of the Act, so that, at least as far as the s 1 and s 2 offences are concerned, 'public' and 'private' bribery is treated in the same way. This is in contrast to the laws of certain other countries which sometimes limit the scope of bribery to public officials.[8]

4.10 There is a view that bribery of public officials is more heinous than bribery in the private sector. This may have to do with a once popular idea that one should have lower expectations of people in the commercial world, and/or that public service involved the highest possible trust because of its potential to affect society more widely than private commercial activity. The previous law made special provision for public sector bribery by means of the Public Bodies Corrupt Practices Act 1889 and the Prevention of Corruption Act 1916, although separate considerations did not apply to private sector bribery.[9]

4.11 In today's society it seems plain that many private sector functions are important enough to justify the fullest protection from bribery. Finance, insurance, medicine and legal services are vital to the common good but some

---

[7] Since whether they are satisfied can be expected to be raised as a preliminary point of law.
[8] Such as US federal law – see, for example, 18 USC s 201(a)(2), 201(b)(1).
[9] *R v Harvey* [1999] Crim LR 70, *R v Godden-Wood* [2001] Crim LR 810.

or all of the providers of these services are private concerns. Large scale bribery of bankers, accountants or credit-rating agencies could have disastrous results for the wider economy, and some would argue that the financial crisis of 2007–09 evidences systemic conflicts of interest among actors in financial markets.

4.12 Whatever the truth of such claims, when contemplating potential harm, it is difficult to accept that bribery of financial market makers in the private sector should be treated more leniently than bribing a traffic warden. The special importance of some public sector functions remains protected by the separate domestic offence of misconduct in public office[10] and the specific problem of bribing foreign public officials is of course dealt with separately in s 6.

4.13 The distinction drawn in subsection (2) between *functions* of a public nature and *activities* relating mainly to the private sector seems to derive from a desire for consistency with the terminology of the Human Rights Act 1998, which uses the term 'functions of a public nature' in the definition of 'public authority'.[11] The terminology does not appear to have any other special significance. For the sake of brevity, the functions and activities provided for in s 3 are frequently described in this work as 'relevant functions and activities'.

FUNCTIONS OF A PUBLIC NATURE

Existing English law

4.14 This term is not defined in the Act, although the Explanatory Notes to the Act refer to the definition of a public authority under the Human Rights Act 1998, s 6(3)(b), which uses the term 'functions of a public nature'. The formulation appears to replace the old concept of corruptly influencing a member or officer of a 'public body' under the Public Bodies Corrupt Practices Act 1889, the definition of which gave rise to some difficulty.[12]

4.15 There has been a considerable amount of litigation and scholarship on the subject of public authorities in the context of human rights law in particular. Jurisprudence as to the nature of public authorities and, hence, functions of a public nature is evolving quickly.[13] Key principles which have emerged from the English authorities are that both obviously governmental bodies, such as the civil service, and those more independent of government are

---

[10] For a brief discussion of which see Chapter 12.
[11] Explanatory Notes, para 28.
[12] The definition of public *body* (not public function) under the previous law was a body which had public or statutory duties to perform and which performs those duties for the benefit of the public and not for private profit – *DPP v Holly* [1978] AC 43. Although of course there will be some considerable overlap, it would be wrong to equate a public authority under the Bribery Act with a public body in the old law. The definitions are not the same.
[13] Both in England and the European Court of Human Rights. See in general: Clayton & Tomlinson *The Law of Human Rights* (2nd edn, Oxford, 2009) ch 5.

public bodies if they exercise public functions. Of course, English law in this area is heavily influenced by the law of the European Convention on Human Rights, emanating from the Court of Human Rights in Strasbourg.

Core and hybrid public authorities

4.16 'Core' public authorities exercise functions which are 'governmental' in nature, and which are distinguished by, for example, the possession of special powers, democratic accountability, public funding in whole or in part, an obligation to act only in the public interest and a statutory constitution.[14] So those working in government departments, HMRC, police forces, local authorities or the armed forces are very likely to be exercising functions of a public nature whenever they do their work.

4.17 'Hybrid' public authorities also exist. These are bodies which carry out certain public functions although they are not wholly governmental in nature. In the UK context they might include, for example, the BBC, Network Rail, or privatised water companies. The law on hybrid public authorities is still developing, but relevant factors in establishing whether a body might be a hybrid authority include:

- whether the body is performing a task which a core public authority must perform but has delegated to the body in question;

- whether the function in question is 'of a governmental nature';

- whether the body's exercise of the function in question can be subject to judicial review;

- whether the body has any special statutory powers, in particular powers of compulsion, in relation to the function in question;

- whether public funds have been used to fund the body.[15]

Relevance of section 6 'public function'

4.18 Section 6(5) of the Act defines a 'foreign public official' for the purposes of that section as, among other things, someone who 'exercises a public function —

(i) for or on behalf of a country or territory outside the United Kingdom (or any subdivision of such a country or territory), or
(ii) for any public agency or public enterprise of that country or territory (or subdivision).'

---

[14] *Aston Cantlow v Wallbank* [2004] 1 AC 546.
[15] *YL v Birmingham City Council* [2008] 1 AC 95.

4.19 It might be argued, somewhat counterintuitively, that the terms 'public function' and 'function of a public nature' should be seen as conceptually separate, despite both being used to describe the functions of officials in the same Act of Parliament.

4.20 It is true that there are differences between the terms. We have already seen the scope of 'function of a public nature' at least insofar as it appears in existing English jurisprudence. However, 'public function' is a term based directly upon Art 1.4 of the OECD Convention.[16] The Official Commentaries to the Convention define a 'public function' as including 'any activity in the public interest, delegated by a foreign country'.[17] Thus it may well be that 'public function' in s 6 seems to be of a somewhat narrower scope than 'function of a public nature' in s 4.

4.21 This apparent anomaly might be dealt with by distinguishing the general offences under ss 1–5 from the specific offence of bribery of foreign public officials under s 6 and referring to the distinct origins of each of the terms.[18] However, in cases where an accused is open to being charged with both offences – ie both a s 1 offence and a s 6 offence – there is the potential for confusion if the nature and status of the recipient of the advantage were in issue.

4.22 In practice, there are unlikely to be many cases which will turn on debates about the precise interpretation of this term. In most cases the answer will be obvious. Civil servants, local government staff, military and police personnel, judges and court staff and those employed by bodies exercising public functions such as the NHS, regulatory authorities and others will all be exercising functions of a public nature. So will government ministers, ministerial advisers and, arguably, leading members of the royal household, governors-general and volunteer-members of official advisory bodies.[19]

Members of Parliament

4.23 Members of the Scottish Parliament and Welsh and Northern Irish Assemblies are likely to be subject to the Act when carrying out their functions – there is little doubt that they are of a public nature. The same is true of members of foreign legislatures.[20]

---

[16] See Chapter 7 for a discussion.

[17] *Commentaries on the Convention on Combating Bribery of Foreign Public Officials in International Business Transactions* (OECD, 1997) ('Commentaries'), 12.

[18] Though query whether this is entirely legitimate given the expectation that very similar terms in the same Act of Parliament should have the same meaning and given that it is at least arguable that the OECD Convention forms part of the relevant interpretive context for the general offences as well as the s 6 offence.

[19] The Act also applies to crown servants – see s 16. The phrase used is 'individuals in the *public* service of the Crown' (emphasis added). This formulation may be intended to include someone such as a military officer, but exclude, say, a housekeeper at one of the royal palaces.

[20] For a discussion in the context of the s 6 offence see Chapter 7.

4.24 Members of the UK Parliament at Westminster are in a somewhat different constitutional position because of the effect of parliamentary privilege and the historic liberties of the UK Parliament, which have their origin in the political settlement between Parliament and the Crown in the seventeenth century. Article 9 of the Bill of Rights of 1689 provides: 'That the freedom of speech and debates or proceedings in Parliament ought not to be impeached or questioned in any court or place out of Parliament.' This provision is known as parliamentary privilege. Some have argued that parliamentary privilege has the effect of preventing at least some of the conduct of parliamentarians while in parliament from being used as evidence in proceedings for bribery or corruption. In 2009 an allegation of corruption against members of the House of Lords was not investigated by police citing this among other 'difficulties'.[21]

4.25 The draft Bill produced by the Law Commission contained a specific provision[22] which made it clear that MPs could not rely on parliamentary privilege to exclude evidence relating to charges of bribery. The Parliamentary Joint Committee rejected this clause as inconsistent with other attempts to reform parliamentary privilege more widely and on the further ground that legislation on the subject should not be made 'piecemeal'.[23] This is perhaps an example of the perfect being made the enemy of the good, but nevertheless the Act now makes no specific derogation from the general principle of parliamentary privilege. Of course, even under the old law, it was clear that parliamentary privilege did not act to prevent a charge relating to a crime occurring within the precincts of Parliament.[24] There is at least some authority that parliamentary privilege did not apply to suppress a charge, in any event in the case of common law bribery.[25]

4.26 In 2010, certain MPs and a member of the House of Lords were charged with false accounting contrary to s 17 of the Theft Act 1968, based on public revelations to do with their claims for expenses and allowances. They claimed to be immune from prosecution in the Crown Court on the ground of parliamentary privilege because their claims amounted to 'proceedings in Parliament'. The matter came before a nine-judge Supreme Court in *R v Chaytor & Others*[26] in which the Supreme Court ruled that no privilege applied. That finding will apply to most charges of bribery under the Bribery Act and so we can take it that Members of Parliament are subject to the Act in the same way as other citizens, although there may be a residual question of whether evidence of speeches made in the parliamentary chambers or committees could be adduced.

---

[21] 'Police Decide Against Peers Probe', BBC News Website, 11 February 2009, http://news.bbc.co.uk/1/hi/uk_politics/7884091.stm.
[22] Clause 15.
[23] Joint Committee Report, paras 204–228.
[24] *Bradlaugh v Gossett* (1884) 12 QBD 271.
[25] *R v Greenway* (1992) *The Times*, December 8, 15, 22.
[26] [2010] UKSC 52.

Activities connected with a business

4.27 No definition of these terms is offered by the Act, save that 'business' includes trade or profession (s 3(7)). A definition may not be necessary in most cases. The words can be given their everyday meaning. In the context of the Financial Services Act 1986 (now replaced by the Financial Services and Markets Act 2000) it has been held that the term 'business' should not be given a technical construction but rather one which conforms to what would in ordinary language be described as a business transaction as opposed to something personal or casual.[27]

4.28 'Activity connected with a business' does not necessarily mean activity carried out for profit. So, for example, someone volunteering at a charity shop is engaged in an activity connected with a business,[28] as is someone employed by a school or university or state agency such as an NHS Trust. A self-employed consultant may be carrying out a business, a trade and a profession at the same time, depending on the nature of the consultancy.

4.29 It is an interesting question whether people carrying out commercial but unlawful activities (perhaps drug dealing or the sale of illegal arms) are subject to the Act. Maintaining the integrity of such transactions is an unlikely goal of the Act or of public policy generally. Perhaps more importantly, in this context, those engaged in these activities are unlikely to be subject to the relevant expectations in s 3(3)–(5).

Activities performed in the course of a person's employment

4.30 Again, no definition of 'in the course of a person's employment' is offered. In the vast majority of cases a person's employment status will be obvious and easily established.[29] There is no stipulation that the employment requires payment of a salary or proof of the existence of a written contract of employment.[30]

4.31 There may be cases where a person is in a position similar to that of an employee but not directly employed by the entity to which his activity relates. So, for example, locum staff in a hospital are often employed directly by a staffing agency, not the hospital. This is irrelevant – the locum is employed and his activities at the hospital during work hours will, usually, be things done in

---

[27] *Morgan Grenfell & Co v Welwyn Hatfield DC* [1995] 1 All ER 1.
[28] In consultations on the Bill it was assumed that non-governmental organisations would be subject to the Act, although the discussion focused on the vexed issue of facilitation payments and the s 6 offence of bribery of foreign public officials, which has a requirement that the bribe is provided with the intention of obtaining or retaining business or a business advantage.
[29] In civil cases where the vicarious liability of an employer for the acts, even illegal acts, of an employee is in issue the test is also whether the employee is acting 'in the course of his employment'. The question is whether the employee's conduct is so closely connected with the employment that it would be fair and just to hold the employer liable as relating to any action, see *Lister & Others v Helsey Hall* [2001] UKHL 22.
[30] Though of course this may be required under employment legislation.

the course of the employment. Such activities can be the subject of bribery. The same applies in the case of independent contractors who provide services via a limited company. In most of these cases there will be a service agreement between the limited company and the individual, and this should suffice. Of course activities governed by such arrangements are very likely to be connected to a business (or trade or profession) in any event.[31]

4.32 Activities which have nothing to do with an employment will not qualify under this head. For example, someone conducting his personal affairs during work hours, using facilities provided by his employer (such as internet facilities) may not be performing activities in the course of his employment. Depending on the activity, it may fit into one of the other categories.

4.33 It is not obvious that someone falsely holding themselves out as having a particular employment (such as bogus doctors or lawyers) will be acting in the course of employment. On one view the purported employment (or business, trade or profession) does not exist and it is impossible for the accused to be acting in the course of a non-existent employment. Under the common law it may have been possible to be guilty of common law bribery while falsely holding oneself out as a public officer,[32] but it is difficult to read the terms of ss 1–3 of the Act as encompassing such circumstances. Whatever about bribery, a person in such a position may well be guilty of one of the inchoate offences of attempt or conspiracy, to which impossibility is not a defence.[33]

Activities performed by or on behalf of a body of persons

4.34 Again, no definition is offered of a 'body of persons'. The sense in which the term is used is obviously intended to refer to aggregations of individual persons which can be identified collectively.[34]

4.35 A body of persons may, of course, be incorporated, for example, a town council or a professional institute. Officers of such bodies, even if not employed, and even in the unlikely event that they are not performing activities connected with a business, trade or profession, will usually be performing activities on behalf of the body.

4.36 Groups of people may also be members of unincorporated associations. The classic examples are sports clubs. The example cited by the Law

---

[31] Section 3(2)(b).
[32] See the Oklahoma case of *Ex p Winters* 140 P 164 (1914) (Criminal Court of Appeals of Oklahoma), cited in Lanham 'Bribery and Corruption' in Smith (ed) *Criminal Law Essays In Honour of JC Smith* (London, 1987).
[33] See Chapter 12.
[34] The *Shorter Oxford English Dictionary (SOED)*, has: 'An artificial person created by legal authority; a corporation; an officially constituted organization, an assembly, an institution, a society.'

Commission in its report is a golf club,[35] and it is clear that the membership secretary of such a club would be guilty of bribery if he offered to take money to allow people to jump the queue for membership.[36] Other clubs or societies with some sort of structure or rule are also likely to fall within the term 'body of persons'. Religious orders, residents' associations, youth clubs or campaign groups will all qualify.

4.37 However, a body of persons is probably something more than a random group of individuals. Friends who meet to play music most Saturdays are probably not a 'body of persons'. However, if they decide to play regular gigs or go on tour they may become something more than the sum of their parts – perhaps an unincorporated association or at least a body of persons.[37]

4.38 Section 3(2) makes it clear that people acting in capacities outside the categories listed, ie in a purely private capacity, are not subject to a charge of bribery. There is no wish to enforce morality in such contexts.[38]

Example

4.39 To take an example of a situation likely to fall outside the Act, let us imagine that Fran has invited friends to form a book group which meets informally to discuss contemporary fiction. None of the existing participants pays anything towards joining or membership. Each pays for her own book.

4.40 An acquaintance asks Fran to propose to the others that she joins the group. Corrupted by a particularly degenerate novel, Fran offers to do so for £100. This is shabby, but it is probably not bribery. It is not activity connected with a business. It is not a function of a public nature or an activity performed in the course of Fran's employment. It is not even an activity performed by or on behalf of a body of persons. Even assuming the book group could be seen as a body of persons, proposing a new member is not something performed *by or on behalf* of the group. It is performed by Fran, on behalf of herself or, perhaps, on behalf of the proposee. The law of bribery should not concern itself with this type of situation.[39]

---

[35] There seems to be more suspicion of golf as a hotbed of corruption compared to other sports. This may have to do with the social cachet supposedly associated with the game, in England at least, or it may just be an unfair prejudice.
[36] According to the Law Commission the provision was included 'to avoid obvious gaps and for the sake of consistency with other closely related legislation' (the example cited is s 19 of the Theft Act 1968): LC 313, para 3.25.
[37] So bribery could be committed if, for example, one member of the band took and kept for himself payments in exchange for backstage passes or bootleg recordings.
[38] LC 313, paras 3.12 3.17, Joint Committee Report, para 29.
[39] Contrast a situation where Fran tries to negotiate a discount for the group with a bookshop. There, arguably, she is acting as their representative and on their behalf. Subject to the 'body of persons' point, if she accepts a secret commission to recommend one shop over another then she may be guilty of bribery, as well as being liable to compensate the others in the group.

EXPECTATIONS APPLICABLE TO THE FUNCTION OR ACTIVITY

4.41 As we have seen, the more formal questions of the status of the person performing the function or activity in question are only the first step. The second step is considering the function or activity itself and whether any of conditions A to C in subsections (3)–(5) apply to a person performing it.

4.42 The question of whether conditions A or B apply to a particular function or activity is to be answered by reference to what a (hypothetical) reasonable person in the UK would expect in relation to the performance of the type of function or activity concerned.[40] This is intended to be a question of fact for the jury in each case.[41]

4.43 Before entering a detailed examination of these concepts one should keep in mind how they might be seen by and presented to a jury. It is likely that the arguments will be framed at quite a high degree of generality, at least by prosecutors, but there may be cases towards the margins in which defendants can argue for special factors which modify or circumscribe reasonable expectations of the particular role of the recipient.

4.44 The Act makes explicit that the question of what expectations apply is to be judged according to the standards of a reasonable person in the UK. This is a jury question, as it should be, since it ultimately has to do with social mores, ie what should be expected of a person in a particular position.[42] However, the expectations contained in the three conditions are distinct. Even though they may overlap in many cases, each requires a separate examination.

Condition A: expectation of good faith

4.45 Good faith is undefined by the Act, probably deliberately.[43] In common usage it seems to approximate to honesty and lack of malice. The *SOED* defines good faith as 'honesty of intention, sincerity'.

4.46 In the context of the Act, acting in good faith can be seen as acting in a way in which one does not knowingly mislead the person affected by one's actions. It is not the same as acting impartially, since it is frequently possible to be partial but nevertheless act in good faith.

---

[40] Section 5 – see Chapter 6.
[41] Although the trial judge may be capable of determining, on a preliminary basis, whether the facts are capable of giving rise to a relevant expectation, and, if so, leaving to the jury the question of whether the relevant expectation existed, and whether it was breached. See LC 313, paras 3.134, 3.170–3.173.
[42] In Parliament the government took the view that concepts such as 'good faith', 'impartiality' and 'position of trust' would be sufficiently clear to a jury from the context so as not to require further definition – *Hansard*, HL, col GC35 (7 January 2010), per Lord Bach.
[43] In certain other legal systems the concept of good faith has an important role to play in the law of private obligations, but the Act does not import these concepts.

Example

4.47 For example, imagine a company which wishes to develop new proprietary software. Ted, the company's IT Director, reports to Len, his CEO, on which software developers the company should engage. The candidates are Netco and Webco. Ted says: 'Netco did a great job for my last company. Webco are pretty new to this sector of the market and don't have much of a track record.'

4.48 Such a statement is hardly impartial. However, it is probably not expected to be by Len the CEO or, one would argue, by a hypothetical reasonable person. The expectation of Ted in exercising his functions as an adviser to the company in this situation is less that he is strictly impartial, and more that he does not mislead his superiors in a material way. If Ted's statement is made in the belief that it is accurate then he will not be in breach of the expectation of good faith.

Condition B: expectation of impartiality

4.49 Impartiality is more conveniently defined negatively, as a lack of bias. Being impartial involves not, without justification, showing favour between those over whom one has some power or influence or those for whom one acts or represents.[44] It could be described as treating like cases alike, uninfluenced by personal preferences. Again, it is a term which is not defined in the Act. The concept is close to but not the same as that of being disinterested – ie not being influenced by the fact of a personal interest in the outcome of a process or transaction.[45]

4.50 One expects impartiality from those exercising functions which involve an element of adjudication. Obviously, the functions of judges, arbitrators and others are within this category. The same is true of many roles within regulatory bodies (such as the Financial Services Authority, OFCOM, OFGEM, etc) and many functions within professional bodies such as the Law Society or British Medical Association. Trade union officials would be expected to be impartial as between members, as would officials of friendly societies, building societies, political parties and representative associations.

4.51 National, regional or local government officials may have roles which require them to be impartial as between those interested in their functions.

---

[44] The *SOED* defines impartiality as: 'treating all disputants equally'.
[45] For example in an arbitration between two football clubs it would be reasonable to expect an arbitrator to at least inform the parties if she was a regular supporter of one of them because she might be thought less than impartial as a result of her allegiance. This will be the case even if strictly speaking she is disinterested (ie like most supporters, has no financial interest in the club). To turn the example around, the arbitrator may know nothing about football but may happen to have inherited a small number of shares in one of the clubs. One might still expect a professional arbitrator to be impartial between the clubs, although not formally disinterested in the outcome of the arbitration. Of course, in both cases it would be wise for the arbitrator to declare her interest.

People such as planning officers, buildings inspectors, health and safety inspectors, housing officers, trading standards officers, police and prison officers, probation officers, trustees of charities and others whose independence is an essential part of their role will be subject to an expectation of impartiality, although the degree or content of the impartiality required may well vary according to the job description. Doctors, nurses, teachers, academics, social workers, school governors, clerics and others may well also be expected by a reasonable person to exercise at least some of their functions and activities impartially, at least insofar as they involve the allocation of resources.

4.52 People in commercial organisations may well have obligations of impartiality, especially if they have a role in disciplinary or grievance procedures, performance evaluation or perhaps recruitment.[46] Company directors will be expected to be impartial as between shareholders. No doubt there will be some expectations of impartiality on professionals who are charged with representing or advising groups of individuals or clients, though these may well be modified by contracts or other legal requirements such as fiduciary duties and regulatory codes of conduct. Sometimes the rules as to impartiality will be set out in written policies but sometimes they will fall to be inferred from the circumstances.

4.53 It would be going too far to say that company executives have duties of impartiality to all those they deal with. Classical economics has it that trade competitors, suppliers and even customers should expect nothing less than enlightened self-interest on the part of economic actors.[47] Of course these general precepts are subject to the plethora of laws governing the proper conduct of business and finance.

Example

4.54 Let us imagine Chris, a junior official charged with enforcing competition law at the Office of Fair Trading (OFT). He is tipped off that there is a price-fixing cartel between companies hosting children's parties – Playland and Funland, and is instructed to work on the investigation. Chris's brother is an executive at Funland and asks what Chris knows of rumours that the OFT is aware of the cartel. Chris truthfully tells his brother that 'you didn't hear it from me, but you should really think about coming clean with us, and quickly'.

4.55 Chris may have acted in good faith – he has not lied or misled anyone. But he has not been impartial in discharging his duties because he has favoured

---

[46] Of course general duties of impartiality will very often be contained within specific legal requirements, such as those imposed by employment law and the law applying to race and/or sex and/or age discrimination.

[47] At least in certain circumstances. The situation may be different for regulated professionals, who have to conform to their professional standards of ethics as well as any fiduciary duties upon them. For example, those acting as trustees may well have duties of impartiality towards the beneficiaries. The Companies Act 2006 provides for detailed duties on company directors which include, for example, a duty to avoid conflicts of interest not consented to by the company.

one firm and one individual in circumstances where he is expected to be impartial. If Chris were later rewarded by Funland or by his brother he would be guilty of an offence under s 2, case 5.[48]

Condition C: position of trust

4.56 Condition C applies if the performance of a particular function or activity puts the person performing it into a position of trust. 'Position of trust' is, again, not a defined term. Lawyers, at least from common law jurisdictions, might expect the term to mean that the person in question had certain legally defined duties, such as fiduciary duties, arising under the law of trusts. However, the Law Commission Report states that:[49]

> '... a "position" of trust should not be construed narrowly as if it was a recognised "relationship" of trust, such as exists between banker and client, doctor and patient and so forth. People can be in a position of trust in some respect (say, with regard to access to documents or premises) whatever the nature and level of their duties.'

4.57 The concept bears some comparison with that underlying the offence of 'fraud by abuse of position' introduced by s 4 of the Fraud Act 2006.[50] That section provides in essence that it is a fraud for a person who is in a position involving an expectation that he will safeguard the financial interests of another person dishonestly to abuse that position, intending to make a gain or cause a loss.

4.58 Although the offence of fraud by abuse of position offence contains crucial differences to the offence of bribery of someone in a position of trust (such as the former's requirements of personal dishonesty and intention to make a gain or cause a loss) there may be an overlap between the offences in many factual situations.

4.59 Those engaged in corrupt business practices in particular will often be in relationships which satisfy both categories. Examples could include relationships between a trustee and beneficiary, a director and company, a

---

[48] Funland or an individual executive may also be guilty of offences under ss 1 and/or 7.
[49] LC 313, para 3.157. In Parliament the government took the view that concepts such as 'good faith', 'impartiality' and 'position of trust' would be sufficiently clear to a jury from the context so as not to require further definition. See *Hansard*, HL, col GC35 (7 January 2010), per Lord Bach.
[50] Fraud Act 2006, s 4:
'(1) A person is in breach of this section if he—
(a) occupies a position in which he is expected to safeguard, or not to act against, the financial interests of another person,
(b) dishonestly abuses that position, and
(c) intends, by means of the abuse of that position—
(i) to make a gain for himself or another, or
(ii) to cause loss to another or to expose another to a risk of loss.
(2) A person may be regarded as having abused his position even though his conduct consisted of an omission rather than an act.'

professional person and client, an agent and principal and an employee and employer and between business partners.[51]

Examples

4.60 An example given by the Law Commission of a 'trust' relationship which is outside the traditional trustee/beneficiary category is that of a security guard who, in exchange for money, looks the other way while someone looks through confidential files held in the office where he works.[52] Such a person may not be within the traditional category of fiduciary or trustee, but will still be in a position of trust as provided by the Act.

4.61 An important point is that the position of trust arises by virtue of the performance of the function or activity. It is not merely a question of people who are trusted by friends, family or colleagues. For example, spouses (usually) trust each other to remain faithful, but a husband who had an affair as a result of some inducement would not be guilty of bribery, no matter how much his wife felt he acted contrary to her trust.

4.62 By contrast, the security guard is in a position of trust because his job (one might also say his duty) is to control access to the premises according to his employer's instructions. It is no good for the security guard to argue, for example, that he works for an agency, that the owner of the premises or the property in it have no idea who he is and that there is no specific person at the employer who trusts him personally. It is also irrelevant to say that he has no idea of what was in the files, or to say that the files, as opposed to the premises, were not entrusted to him. The activity of being a security guard involves preventing access to the premises to authorised people. This activity places the guard in a 'position of trust' which is capable of being compromised if he allows access to someone unauthorised in exchange for an advantage.

4.63 Someone might be in a position of trust arising from a particular function or activity even if they are not employees or under any contract. Imagine Daphne says to her neighbour Velma that she is going on holiday and asks Velma to 'look after the front door key, in case anything strange should happen'. Velma agrees. That circumstance seems to amount to the creation of a position of trust in the sense intended by the Act. Velma has taken on a responsibility to take care of the key, and in doing so is in a position where she is trusted not to use it to enter, or allow anyone else to enter.

---

[51] However one should not push the similarities too far. There are likely to be many more relationships which theoretically satisfy condition C of the Bribery Act than s 4 of the Fraud Act.
[52] LC 313, paras 3.158–3.161.

FUZZINESS AT THE MARGINS?

4.64 Many cases will clearly fall within condition C. However, the condition seems considerably more elastic, and more vague, than the others. It has the flavour of a 'sweep up' provision. The relatively loose way that the word 'trust' is used in general conversation means that its use in defining the threshold condition of bribery could cause problems in marginal cases.[53]

Another example

4.65 Consider Miranda, the general manager of a chain of children's nurseries. She agrees to allow a confectionery company to install vending machines in the nurseries. The nursery chain will be paid 20% of sales. The revenue generated will ensure the manager's personal budget target is met and that she earns a bonus as a result. Could the manager or the company be guilty of a bribery offence?[54]

4.66 Miranda has agreed to arrangements which will lead to her receiving an advantage (the chance of earning a bonus) intending that, in consequence, she will perform her functions/activities in a particular way (allowing the machines to be installed).[55] The key question is whether the intended performance by Miranda is improper – ie contrary to the relevant expectations. It is unlikely that expectations of good faith or impartiality will have been breached. The relevant expectation is more likely to be one connected to the fact that Miranda is in a position of trust.

4.67 Some parents might say that the management of a nursery puts a person in a position of trust in relation to the well-being of the children and the wishes of their parents. As a result of her position, the manager is expected to maximise the children's health and well-being by not encouraging unhealthy eating. She is trusted to do so.

4.68 But Miranda may argue that this is too wide a definition of 'trust'. The person with whom she has a trust relationship is her employer, and no one else.[56] She has no such relationship with the parents – their contract is only with the nursery itself, and still less the children who have no expectations of her. She may also point out that she is not doing anything which endangers the children and that many are given sweets and sugary drinks every day by their

---

[53] Although it may be tempting to regard the case as being close to the person in a position who is expected to safeguard, or not to act against, the financial interests of another person (as in s 4 of the Fraud Act 2006) the 'position of trust' test in the Bribery Act is not as specific as this.
[54] Miranda has agreed to arrangements which will at least indirectly lead to her receiving an advantage intending that, in consequence, she will perform her functions/activities in a particular way (s 2(2), case 3). Her functions/activities are within s 3(1)(b) (connected with business) and/or (c) (in the course of employment). Because of s 2(6)(a) and (b) the facts that funds do not go directly to her or that there is also a benefit to the nursery itself do not matter.
[55] Section 2(2), case 3.
[56] Condition C does not specify whether there can be more than one 'position of trust' or whether it can take different forms depending on the counterparty.

parents. She is accounting to her employer for the revenues from the machines, and is not breaking any other element of the law.[57]

4.69 If Miranda is not in breach of any civil law duties and is not in any formal legal relationship with the parents can it be right that she might nevertheless be found guilty of bribery? Such an outcome would be the result of an approach to the term 'trust' which was completely open-ended.

Can civil law be ignored?

4.70 One goal of the Law Commission Report which seems to have been accepted by Parliament was to try to avoid the importation of civil law concepts into the definition of bribery.[58] But the potential difficulties of defining the nature of expectations arising from a position of trust illustrate that this may be easier said than done.

4.71 It is not easy to imagine circumstances where persons are in positions of trust *by virtue of* performing either public functions or activities connected to a business but are not under existing legal duties which relate to their functions. The security guard is very likely to be required by his employment contract not to allow access to unauthorised persons. Chris of the OFT is in a position which will carry with it obligations of confidentiality concerning his casework. Velma is almost certainly a bailee of Daphne's key.[59]

4.72 Indeed, although condition C illustrates the proximity of civil law concepts most clearly, it is also difficult to imagine a person in public service or in business who is not in breach of a legal duty under the civil law (such as an employment contract, professional rules or duties under the law of tort) if he breaches expectations of impartiality or good faith in exchange for some personal benefit.

4.73 The point is that, in each case, the court may be invited to consider the specific rules governing the performance of a particular role in deciding whether the function or activity in question is subject to relevant expectations and/or whether those expectations have been breached. Civil law rules and concepts form the background to professional life. In real cases no thorough discussion of relevant expectations can occur without considering them. The courts can be expected to continue to have to deal with legal issues connected to the accused's status, responsibilities, authorisation and so on, even under the Bribery Act.[60]

---

[57] It may be that a statutory inspectorate such as OFSTED discourages provision of sweets at nurseries, but such a policy may not mean that the manager's actions are illegal per se.
[58] LC 313, paras 3.88–3.125.
[59] A bailee is someone who takes voluntary possession of goods belonging to another. As such the bailee is required to take some care of the goods and may be liable to the owner for the consequences of loss or damage to the goods even if there is no contract between them. See *Palmer on Bailment* (3rd edn, London, 2009), ch 10.
[60] It will be interesting to see whether, in practice, debates as to the nature of a position of trust

4.74 The case of the nursery vending machines is an attempt to illustrate the complications following from an entirely open approach to the definition of a position of trust. Of course, the case is relatively trivial. Miranda, though perhaps crass, does not seem to have been particularly venal and has not sought to conceal the truth. The criminal law probably should not concern itself with such a situation and aggrieved parents are unlikely to receive a sympathetic hearing from their local fraud squad.[61] As we have already seen, the social or business context in which actions occur can magnify or diminish the seriousness of facts which may technically satisfy the terms of the legislation.

CONNECTIONS TO THE UK

4.75 Section 3(6) makes it clear that relevant functions or activities need not have any connection with the UK. The Act provides for nationality and residence jurisdiction at s 12[62] and these are the only jurisdictional limitations which apply to offences under ss 1, 2 and 6. Once the accused is subject to the court's jurisdiction by virtue of s 12 (for example by being a UK-registered company or by carrying out any act or omission forming part of the offence in the UK) then it is irrelevant that the protected functions or activities have no connection with the UK. Therefore, a company registered in England may commit an offence if its non-resident chief executive offers money to a politician in, say, Australia, so that the company can obtain a licence to operate there.[63] Similarly, a US citizen ordinarily resident in England commits an offence if he makes a money transfer through his London bank for the purpose of inducing a US official to breach his duties.

4.76 These provisions make clear that it is not only offences under s 6 of the Act (bribery of foreign public officials) which can be committed by acts occurring outside the UK. Bribery of foreign public officials, or private entities, may also amount to an offence under s 1. Receipt offences occurring abroad may also be chargeable under s 2 once R is subject to UK jurisdiction under s 12.

---

or expectation of impartiality are clarified as part of the evaluation of whether a case can go before a jury based on the strength of the evidence – ie are the subject of judicial rulings on the law, or are the subject of appeals.

[61] This is not to suggest that the parents lack good reasons to be aggrieved. Their remedy may ultimately be to remove their children or at least not to provide them with pocket money.

[62] See Chapter 11.

[63] Subject to the 'directing mind' test for corporate criminal liability – see the discussion at Chapter 8. These facts may also engender liability under ss 6 and 7.

Chapter 5

IMPROPER PERFORMANCE

BRIBERY ACT 2010: SECTION 4

'**4 Improper performance to which bribe relates**

(1) For the purposes of this Act a relevant function or activity—

(a) is performed improperly if it is performed in breach of a relevant expectation, and
(b) is to be treated as being performed improperly if there is a failure to perform the function or activity and that failure is itself a breach of a relevant expectation.

(2) In subsection (1) "relevant expectation"—

(a) in relation to a function or activity which meets condition A or B, means the expectation mentioned in the condition concerned, and
(b) in relation to a function or activity which meets condition C, means any expectation as to the manner in which, or the reasons for which, the function or activity will be performed that arises from the position of trust mentioned in that condition.

(3) Anything that a person does (or omits to do) arising from or in connection with that person's past performance of a relevant function or activity is to be treated for the purposes of this Act as being done (or omitted) by that person in the performance of that function or activity.'

INTRODUCTION

5.1 Section 4 of the Act sets out the means by which a relevant function or activity, as defined by s 3, is performed 'improperly' for the purposes of the general offences under ss 1 and 2. The key concept in defining what is improper is a breach of the three expectations which apply to a 'relevant function' as defined by s 3.

RELEVANT FUNCTION OR ACTIVITY

5.2 As we have seen in Chapter 4, a relevant function or activity is one defined by s 3 of the Act. This is broadly either:

(a) a function of a public nature, or an activity which is either connected with a business, performed in the course of employment or performed by or on behalf of a body of persons; which also

(b) involves 'relevant expectations' of good faith or impartiality in performance; or

(c) involves the person performing the function or activity being in a position of trust by reason of the performance.

5.3 So the concept of relevant expectations is at the centre of both the definition of a relevant function or activity in s 3 and the definition of improper performance of such an activity in s 4.

5.4 In analysing relevant expectations it is important to remember the 'reasonable person' test required by s 5(1). That section applies the test of 'what a reasonable person in the UK would expect in relation to the performance of the type of function or activity concerned' to both ss 3 and 4.[1] So both the question of what expectations apply and whether those expectations have been breached are answered by an objective test: what would a reasonable person in the UK expect? These will be questions for the jury in a particular case.

Breach of relevant expectations

5.5 It seems clear that the purpose of Parliament was to make a 'breach' of an expectation cognate with a failure to fulfil such an expectation. Although the Act does not expressly define 'breach' it is safe to assume that an action or omission which does not satisfy an expectation of good faith or impartiality or expectations arising under a position of trust will amount to a breach of those expectations.[2]

5.6 The issue of breach is to be tested by reference to the 'reasonable person' test applied by s 5(1). It is a classic jury issue.

5.7 The 'reasonable person' test for whether a task is performed in breach of expectations is an objective one. It applies even if the person performing the task believes he is not doing anything wrong. The Act makes no provision for

---

[1] Although the language of the sections admits some ambiguity. Section 5(1) says 'for the purposes of sections 3 and 4 *the test of what is expected* is a test of what a reasonable person ... etc.' (emphasis added). However, s 4 does not speak of 'what is expected' but of a relevant function or activity 'performed in breach of a relevant expectation'. Strictly, whether something is performed in breach of an expectation is not the same question as the question of 'what is expected' in the first place. However, it would be perverse to apply the s 5 test to s 4 if it were not intended to apply to the question of impropriety – ie breach of expectation. If the reasonable person test were intended only to apply to the question of what relevant functions and activities are, rather than how they are improperly performed, its application could and should have been limited to s 3.

[2] This is the only logical interpretation of s 4(1) and (2).

the actual state of mind of the person performing the functions or activities. To do so would make the offence much more difficult to prove.[3]

5.8 Arguments as to whether a particular action or omission was or was not a breach of a particular expectation could, and no doubt will, be framed in different ways. For example does a breach of the expectation of good faith involve proof of a specific lie or merely a failure to tell the whole truth? Such questions will depend on the factual context in each case. It is doubtful whether it was the intention of Parliament to make the process of establishing a breach of a relevant expectation into an overly technical exercise. The jury should be invited to decide the question of breach of expectation in a common-sense way, according to what they think a reasonable person would expect and without the need for further formulae or tests.

5.9 Having said this, it may still be interesting to discuss how a court could approach the question of establishing breach of the three types of relevant expectation.

Breach of expectation of good faith

5.10 It is probably inappropriate to describe a breach of an expectation of good faith in some other form of words. Such a breach is not necessarily the same as 'bad faith' although the concepts must be closely related. The Act does not mention bad faith, merely a breach of an expectation of good faith, and it is possible that the latter may be different from the former.

Example

5.11 It might help the analysis of breach of an expectation of good faith if we return to one of our examples in Chapter 4. Ted, the IT director has recommended Netco over a rival bidder, Webco. Let us assume that Jack, an executive of Netco, had offered Ted a commission if he recommends Netco and Netco wins the business. If Jack and/or Netco were charged with bribery of Ted under s 1 it would be necessary to establish what performance of Ted's activities Jack wished to induce or reward and whether that performance was contrary to expectations.[4]

5.12 The performance in question is Ted's recommendation of a bidder to his employer. Jack and Netco would be guilty of intending to induce improper behaviour by Ted if their intention was to induce Ted to make a false or misleading statement about Netco, or about a rival bidder. A reasonable person in the UK would see a deliberate lie to the company as a breach of an

---

[3] See Chapter 6 for a discussion of the relevant person test.
[4] Netco as a company may be liable if the actions of the person in question are attributable to the company or, even if not, under s 7 if the bribe is to obtain a business advantage and the adequate procedures defence is not available to it. See Chapter 8 for a discussion.

expectation of good faith,[5] and an offer of money by Jack, or Netco, intended to induce or reward such a lie as bribery under s 1.

5.13 The analysis in relation to the receiving offences in s 2 will be different. Here, the state of mind of Ted (ie 'R' under s 2) is relevant to establishing whether the performance is in breach of the expectation of good faith.

5.14 In our example, Ted's statements were that Netco had performed well in the past and that Webco were new to the market. If these statements were believed by Ted to be true then, on the face of it, a reasonable person would not consider that he had acted in breach of the expectation of good faith.

5.15 If statements were believed by Ted to be untrue (for example if he knew or believed that Netco had actually performed poorly on the previous project or that Webco was just as good as Netco) then Ted will have acted in breach of the expectation of good faith.

5.16 What if Ted was mistaken about some of the details of his statement? For example he might somehow have forgotten that the previous Netco project had failed. If established, such facts suggest negligence or incompetence, though not a breach of an expectation of good faith. Even if Ted should have remembered these facts, and should have amended or even reversed his opinion, without knowledge that his statement is untrue he will not have acted in breach of an expectation of good faith.

5.17 It is irrelevant whether, in fact, Netco is superior to Webco. Ted's lie remains a breach of a duty of good faith even if he claims he did so for valid reasons or its effects were for the benefit of his employer.

Breach of expectation of impartiality

5.18 In Chapter 2 we saw that impartiality amounts to an absence of bias, or not showing favour between those over whom one has some power or influence or those for whom one acts or represents. Where one is expected to be impartial it is obvious that partiality or bias will amount to a breach of such an expectation.

Example

5.19 We can illustrate a case of breach of the expectation of impartiality by returning to the example in Chapter 4 of Chris the OFT official. He is

---

[5] As we have seen in our analysis of s 1, it is not necessary for Jack to know in advance of the offer or payment exactly what Ted intends to do or say. As discussed in Chapter 2 it may not even be necessary for Jack to have identified with any precision the expectations upon Ted or which of them Ted will break if he improperly uses his influence to ensure Netco wins the contract. Further, even if Ted himself never intended to breach his duty of good faith towards his employer, Jack will still be guilty if he intended to induce him to or reward him for doing so.

investigating an alleged cartel between Playland and Funland. We can quickly assume that a reasonable person would regard Chris's functions as carrying with them expectations of impartiality between companies who he is investigating.[6] In Chapter 4 we posited a tip-off by Chris to his brother who was an executive of Funland.

5.20 Again, in approaching the question of breach of expectation we must identify the particular conduct which could amount to breach. In Chris's case this is the provision of information about an investigation to one party being investigated but not another. A reasonable person would consider this to be a breach of the expectation of impartiality. If Chris is offered money by Funland as a reward for his assistance then the offer will be seen by a reasonable person as a reward for a breach of the expectation of impartiality, ie for improper performance.

Breach of expectation arising from position of trust

5.21 In Chapter 4 we saw that a 'position of trust' was to be construed widely as referring to more or less any relationship in which one person is trusted with valuable property or assets or to safeguard the interests of another person. It is worth remembering that unlike the other two conditions, the expectations of reasonable people are irrelevant to the initial question of whether the defendant is in a position of trust. They are only relevant to deciding whether the defendant has breached a relevant expectation.[7]

5.22 However, breach of a 'position of trust' expectation is considerably more involved than the other two. To recap: s 3 defines relevant activities as those satisfying subsection (2) (function of a public nature, activity connected with business, employment, on behalf of body of persons) and satisfying conditions A to C. Condition C is that: 'a person performing the function or activity is in a position of trust by virtue of performing it.'

5.23 In s 4(1)(a), improper performance involves performance 'in breach of a relevant expectation'. The relevant expectations which apply to a 'position of trust' case are described as:[8]

> '... any expectation as to the manner in which, or the reasons for which, the function or activity will be performed that arises from the position of trust mentioned in that condition.'

---

[6] This does not mean that the OFT cannot treat one company more leniently than the other if there are objective reasons for doing so such as a policy of treating those self-reporting cartel offences more leniently.
[7] Section 4(1)(a).
[8] Section 4(2)(b).

5.24 One way to unpack this rather dense formulation is as follows:

- Identify whether the defendant's function or activity involves being in a 'position of trust' *by virtue of performing it*. It is the performance of the job or role which gives rise to the position of trust, not the fact that one may have a particular title or official position. The Act does not specify any test to determine whether someone is in a position of trust by virtue of performing a particular function or activity.[9] It seems to be a matter for common sense.

- Identify whether that position of trust itself gives rise to expectations as to the manner in which, or the reasons for which, the function or activity will be performed, and identify what those expectations are.

- Identify whether any of the expectations have been breached by the defendant, in the eyes of a reasonable person in the UK.

5.25 One might summarise the central principle by saying that functions or activities which give rise to a relationship of trust must be performed in accordance with expectations of a reasonable person about how such functions or activities should be performed by a person in that position.[10]

5.26 Note that the actual expectations of a person who had trusted the defendant to carry out the role are not relevant.[11] It is general expectations attaching to the role which matter in establishing whether the relevant expectation has been breached.

---

[9] Parliamentary debate and material such as the reports of the Law Commission are also unenlightening in this regard.

[10] This may suffice as a working summary, but it is not completely satisfactory when one considers the way in which the position of trust is said by the Act to relate to the expectations as to performance, and vice versa. There is a risk of circularity in the approach to these issues. The most likely, perhaps only, reason that the performance of a particular function might give rise to a position of trust is that there is something about the way in which or the reasons for which it is performed which requires trust in the person performing it. Justification of a position of trust arising *by virtue of performance of a function* must depend on expectations as to how the function should be performed. So the relevant expectations are likely to be prior to the trust, and to be what calls the position of trust into being in the first place. However, for the purpose of establishing improper performance, it seems to be the position of trust which then defines any relevant expectations as to how the function is to be performed ('any expectation ... that *arises from the position of trust* mentioned in [condition C]'). It may be that the real target of the legislation is a party who, objectively, is in a position where he is trusted by others to act in a certain way and fails to do so. That failure might amount to improper performance of his functions or activities which, combined with a connection to the provision or seeking of advantages, adds up to bribery. However, the terms of the Act are some way from this and one can see potential for real confusion in attempts to sum these considerations up for a jury.

[11] It is not hard to imagine a person with great faith in the person entrusted to look after his interests but who does not understand the functions sufficiently to be able to criticise their performance.

5.27 The explanation above deals with expectations relating to 'the manner in which' the function or activity is carried out. But what of the alternative expectation in the text – an expectation as to 'the reasons for which' the function or activity is carried out?

5.28 At first sight this test is confusing. One can have expectations about behaviour and methodology (fairness, due process, making disclosures, etc). However, it is less easy to conceive of expectations about the justification for a particular state of affairs. The reasons behind the carrying out of a particular activity may be obscure or various. They are likely to be difficult to prove save in certain well-defined legal situations such as wills or express trusts. It may be that this form of words was added as 'belt and braces' to cover situations where it is difficult to establish expectations as to methodology but it is clear that the defendant has betrayed an agreed purpose which was the reason for his being in a position of trust.[12]

5.29 Despite the conceptual difficulties discussed above, there are many categories of function or activity where it will be clear that those performing them are in positions of trust as a result. Many if not all of those whose role it is to protect or further the interests of others are likely to be in a position of trust, and a breach of their well-established duties will amount to breach of expectations and improper performance. The finance director who fiddles the books, the solicitor who steals client funds, the doctor who issues false diagnoses, all will be engaging in improper performance of relevant functions.

Examples

5.30 One example discussed in Chapter 4 was of a security guard who is offered an advantage if he allows access to a property he is responsible for. It is suggested to him that on an agreed evening he neglects to lock or alarm a specific door thus allowing access to unauthorised people. On the night in question he acts as suggested.[13] Such an act seems clearly to be a breach of an expectation, arising from his position of trust, as to the manner in which the 'trusted' activity was to be performed.

5.31 There was also the example in Chapter 4 of Velma temporarily holding Daphne's key. Let us imagine that while Daphne away, Velma is approached by a mysterious stranger who says he will make it worth her while if she 'loans' him the key. This she does, and, of course, the house is burgled.

5.32 Velma knew, or ought to have known, that she was trusted to keep the key because Daphne did not want it to fall into the wrong hands. When Velma

---

[12] The difficulties attending this topic are a further illustration of the point argued in Chapter 4, that defining 'position of trust' entirely independently of established civil-law concepts is a challenging task.
[13] Though this is technically an omission to carry out a particular activity it is of course still improper performance under s 4(1)(b) – a failure to perform the activity which is itself a breach of an expectation as to the manner in which the activity is to be performed.

agreed to hold the key a reasonable person would agree that she was being trusted to act towards it in specific ways, such as to keep it out of the hands of strangers. Although she was a volunteer and not under any legal duty to accept Daphne's key in the first place, once she accepted it there was an expectation as to the manner in which she would hold the key. By handing over the key she breached those expectations and by doing so in anticipation of a reward she has committed an offence under s 2.[14]

Connections to past protected functions

5.33 Section 4(3) is intended to provide for circumstances where people leave particular positions but either continue to exercise influence over how they are performed or accept rewards after leaving for improper performance while in post.

Examples

5.34 For example, imagine a government minister involved in a political or financial scandal. The minister resigns, but is called to give evidence to a public enquiry. He is approached by the company being investigated and asked to give untrue testimony about meetings which occurred while he was a minister. It is clear from s 4(3) that if the ex-minister were to agree to the scheme it would amount to improper performance. As a well as a charge under s 1 against the company there could be a charge under s 2 against the ex-minister, even though he no longer exercises relevant functions.

5.35 There could be many other examples, such as the security guard who leaves his job and later offers to divulge what he knows about the vulnerabilities of the site to thieves.

What is a reasonable person?

5.36 The analysis of breach of expectations above, and some of that in Chapter 3 about whether or not a particular function or activity is 'relevant', all depend on the test of what a 'reasonable person in the United Kingdom' would expect under s 5, which will be examined in the next chapter.

---

[14] At least under case 5 – agreeing to receive an advantage as a reward for improper performance of a relevant function or activity, if not also cases 4 and 6.

Chapter 6

THE EXPECTATION TEST

BRIBERY ACT 2010: SECTION 5

'**5 Expectation test**

(1) For the purposes of sections 3 and 4, the test of what is expected is a test of what a reasonable person in the United Kingdom would expect in relation to the performance of the type of function or activity concerned.

(2) In deciding what such a person would expect in relation to the performance of a function or activity where the performance is not subject to the law of any part of the United Kingdom, any local custom or practice is to be disregarded unless it is permitted or required by the written law applicable to the country or territory concerned.

(3) In subsection (2) "written law" means law contained in—

(a) any written constitution, or provision made by or under legislation, applicable to the country or territory concerned, or
(b) any judicial decision which is so applicable and is evidenced in published written sources.'

INTRODUCTION

6.1 The effect of s 5 of the Act has already been discussed when discussing the s 3 relevant expectations and the s 4 definition of improper performance in Chapters 4 and 5, so our separate discussion of the expectation test can be relatively brief.

AN OBJECTIVE TEST

6.2 Tests of whether certain behaviour or states of mind are within particular standards can be subjective or objective. To apply a subjective test is to put oneself into the mind of the individual in question – it is his understanding and beliefs which are relevant. To apply an objective test is to consider how the conduct would be regarded according to a general standard. The standard most usually applied is that of the reasonable person. The reasonable person test in s 5(1) is just such an objective test.

Two questions for the reasonable person

6.3 The reasonable person test is applied to two distinct questions. The first is what is expected of persons performing a particular function or activity. Do the conditions A (expectation of good faith) or B (expectation of impartiality) in s 3 apply so as to make the function or activity a relevant one for the purposes of the general offences?[1] This first question does not apply to the existence of condition C (position of trust).[2] The second question is whether, if those expectations do apply, or if there is a position of trust, would the performance sought or carried out amount to a breach of expectations?[3]

6.4 If a reasonable person would not see the function or activity as being subject to an expectation of good faith or impartiality or if there is no position of trust then the second question as to breach of those expectations is irrelevant – the general offences (ss 1, 2) cannot be committed. If an expectation of good faith or impartiality or arising under a trust exists but a reasonable person would not see the performance as involving a breach of any relevant expectation then none of the general offences have been committed.

WHAT IS A 'REASONABLE PERSON'?

6.5 The question of what a reasonable person might expect is one for the jury. It is not one which a jury is likely to struggle with. However, because it is so critical for the working of the offence, some further discussion may be of assistance.

6.6 In criminal law, and in civil law, the reasonable person test is used in different ways in different contexts. It is dangerous to transpose definitions across categories. For example, factors relevant to, say, how a reasonable person would react to a particular provocation (so as to establish a defence of provocation), or how a reasonable person would drive a car (to establish road traffic offences), are quite distinct both from each other and from the issue of expectations under the Act. Perhaps the only common theme across various categories of offence is that they all seek to apply an objective standard of behaviour. Ultimately, the reasonable person test indicates that the jury is being asked to impose the norms and standards of contemporary society as they understand them.

6.7 As one would expect, the reasonable person is not defined further in the Act. In a particular case it will be a matter for the prosecution and/or the defence to explain how the reasonable person test will apply to the facts. However we can venture some working assumptions:

---

[1] Fulfilment of condition C (position of trust) is not subject to a test of expectations.
[2] Establishing a position of trust is not subject to the reasonable person test.
[3] Improper performance in position of trust is defined as breach of an expectation, as provided by s 4(2)(c).

- The reasonable person is a hypothetical construct. The reasonable person is not R, or another actual person performing or expected to perform the activity.

- The reasonable person should be assumed to be someone of moral integrity.[4]

- Such a person is not necessarily the same as an individual member of the jury. The question for a juror is not 'what do I expect of a person performing the function or activity?' but 'what do I believe a reasonable person in the UK would expect of a person performing the function or activity?'

- Because the purpose of the reasonable person test in the context of Act is to apply a wholly objective standard to the existence of expectations, and whether certain conduct would be a breach of those expectations, any particular personal characteristics, abilities or disabilities of R or P or the person who is to perform the activity are irrelevant.

BREACH OF EXPECTATIONS

6.8 We have already discussed potential breaches of expectations in Chapter 5. That discussion was based on assumptions as to what a reasonable person would make of particular types of conduct.

6.9 To say that a reasonable person would expect an executive to be honest in his dealings with his company is, for present purposes, the same as saying that a reasonable person would expect him to carry out his functions in good faith. By extension, a reasonable person would see a lie by the executive about company business as a breach of the same expectation of good faith.

6.10 Similarly a failure to be impartial in circumstances where impartiality is expected will, to a reasonable person, amount to a breach of the expectation of impartiality.

6.11 The situation for 'position of trust' cases may be particularly fact-sensitive, since the central concept of a position of trust is harder to pin down. However, as explained in Chapter 5, once the expectations of a reasonable person as to how a function or activity is to be performed can be established then a failure to meet such expectations is likely to be seen by a reasonable person as a breach of the same expectations.

---

[4] See LC 313, para 3.176 – at one point the Law Commission sought to specify a test of the expectations of a 'person of moral integrity' but that suggestion did not make it into the government bill.

6.12 Each function or activity will be subject to its own expectations and the prosecution will have to establish what the relevant expectations are in each case.

Examples

6.13 To use one of our previous examples, we can predict that a reasonable person would expect Ted the IT director not to mislead his employer about which is the better contractor to use. In other words there will be an expectation that he performs his duties in good faith. If he lies to the company about the suitability of potential contractors, or if such a lie is the purpose of a transaction between Ted and one of the contractors, then a jury can be expected to accept that this is a breach of the expectation of good faith.

6.14 The same analysis can be applied to our example of expectations of impartiality (such as the competition official who tips off one of the subjects of his investigations) and breach of expectations arising out of a position of trust (such as the security guard who allows access).

6.15 Any discussion of offences based on objective 'reasonable person' tests will tend to fall back on one's general impressions of prevailing attitudes and common sense. Though it makes it more difficult to establish hard and fast rules, this allows the application of the law to align with and evolve alongside society.

6.16 A court may find it difficult to distinguish between the question of the defendant's state of mind (what he intends or knows or believes), the question of what a reasonable person might expect of someone performing a particular activity and the question of what was actually permitted by specific rules of conduct applicable to the activity. There may be activities where the relevant expectations are not clear and whether a particular action or omission amounts to breach of a relevant expectation is even less so.[5] The fact that events occur overseas or have a significant overseas connection may make these questions even more difficult.

6.17 This leads us on to consider whether local standards can ever apply to the objective test under s 5 – ie the case where performance of the function or activity occurs outside the UK.

PERFORMANCE OF FUNCTIONS OUTSIDE THE UK

6.18 Section 12 of the Act extends the territorial application of the general offences under ss 1 and 2 to acts committed anywhere in the world as long as the accused has a close connection to the UK, as defined in s 12(4). The Act aims to criminalise the act of providing or seeking incentives towards

---

[5] Certain types of financial intermediation such as market-making or broking come to mind.

impropriety, not so much the impropriety itself. Its main target is those with a connection to the UK rather than local officials who are not subject to UK jurisdiction. No matter where the bribery takes place, the definition of the offence (the provision or receipt of advantages in exchange for improper performance of relevant functions or activities) remains constant.

6.19 It follows that improper performance of functions should be considered according the same standards wherever they occur or are expected to occur. If this were not the case then it might be considered a crime to offer a bribe to an official in Brasilia but not in Berlin.[6] If such an incoherent outcome is to be avoided then local customs or practices about how functions be carried out should be ignored when applying the 'reasonable person' test.[7]

Local law informs expectations of reasonable person

6.20 If the conduct in question is legal in the country in which it is performed then this can be taken into account in establishing the expectations of the reasonable person in the UK. A reasonable person in the UK is likely to expect people to obey the laws of countries in which they happen to be visiting, and to consider it reasonable, in most cases, to do things which the local law requires or permits.[8]

6.21 For the general offences the local law exception is limited to the 'written law' of a country or territory.[9] Examples of written law include a constitution, legislation or judicial decisions, as long as they are in written form and/or published.[10] To allow unwritten laws to be taken into consideration would create a very difficult evidential situation. A law which is not recorded somewhere in written form is very unlikely to be sufficiently established or certain to qualify as a law recognisable to the UK legal system.[11]

---

[6] The Joint Committee considered the issue of cultural variations and reliance on local custom, and said: 'While we accept that while it may occasionally be acceptable to consider cultural variations on issues such as hospitality, a careful line needs to be drawn. The draft Bill must in general prevent individuals from relying on local customs to justify corrupt practices, otherwise its effectiveness will be seriously undermined.' Joint Committee Report, p 21.

[7] Of course, s 6 of the Act makes separate provision for the offence of bribing a foreign public official. In cases with a foreign element there may be an overlap between a s 6 offence and the general offences under ss 1 and 2. The test for improper performance outlined in s 5 is only relevant to the general s 1 and s 2 offences.

[8] There are likely to be certain obvious exceptions to this such as varying laws on sexual equality, freedom of speech, etc.

[9] The reference to territory will include both subdivisions of a nation-state which may have distinct laws as well as geographical areas which may not have full statehood under international law.

[10] The same formulation as to the sources of written law appears in s 6(7)(c) of the Act. The requirement that the law be 'written' echoes the US FCPA, 15 USC §78 dd-1(c)(1), and is also echoed in the Official Commentary on Art 1 of the OECD Convention.

[11] This is perhaps a grapho-centric approach. Historically, many societies lacked writing but were nevertheless governed by laws which were learned and transmitted orally. However, few if any such societies survive as separate political entities today.

6.22 The effective burden of proof of the existence of written law is likely to fall upon the defendant. A person seeking to excuse conduct on the basis of legality in local law will wish to introduce evidence in support of that position and will not succeed in making the position good unless capable of doing so.

Local customs

6.23 It is clear that purely customary activities which are not given express written legal sanction by institutions of the state or territory are not to be taken into account in considering what a reasonable person in the UK would believe. As discussed in Chapter 1, it is sometimes said that certain practices which would amount to corrupt favours by officials if committed in the UK are officially tolerated in particular countries. It could be argued by a defendant that the conduct in question is not illegal in the state in question, or at least that it should not be seen as improper or unlawful by a reasonable person in the UK, because it is culturally insensitive or unrealistic to challenge it.

6.24 In many such cases, the practice being debated is likely to be illegal under local law and is usually carried out in secret for the very reason that it is not, in fact, 'tolerated'. A plea that 'the official was expected to favour companies who paid him some commission – it was normal in that country' will not assist a defendant unless that expectation was expressed in a binding written law. The fact that corruption is well known and it can be shown that the superiors of the official expected him to do favours in exchange for commissions will not matter. The question will remain – would a reasonable person in the UK see it as a breach of a relevant expectation for the official to act in this way?

6.25 It may be that some difficulty is encountered in circumstances where the reasonable person in the UK would have no experience of the particular function or activity in question, because it does not occur in the UK. It may be difficult to apply the expectations of good faith, impartiality or impose the concept of trust in such circumstances. However, one can expect cases of this sort to be extremely rare. The working assumption should be that the saying 'when in Rome do as the Romans' is, in this context, quite inapt. Whether in Rome, or in whatever corner of a foreign field, the conscience of anyone subject to the Act is deemed never to have left the UK.

6.26 Section 6 of the Act makes separate provision for the offence of bribing a foreign public official. In cases with a foreign element there may be an overlap between a s 6 offence and the general offences under ss 1 and 2. The test for improper performance outlined in s 5 is only relevant to the general s 1 and s 2 offences. One inconsistency between the general offences and the offence of bribing a foreign public official under s 6 is that the local legality exception is much wider for the general offences than for the s 6 offence, which only makes an exception for circumstances where the local law permits or requires the recipient to be *influenced by* the offer, promise or gift of the advantage.[12]

---

[12] See Chapter 7.

Chapter 7

BRIBERY OF FOREIGN PUBLIC OFFICIALS

BRIBERY ACT 2010: SECTION 6

'6 Bribery of foreign public officials

(1) A person ("P") who bribes a foreign public official ("F") is guilty of an offence if P's intention is to influence F in F's capacity as a foreign public official.

(2) P must also intend to obtain or retain—

(a) business, or
(b) an advantage in the conduct of business.

(3) P bribes F if, and only if—

(a) directly or through a third party, P offers, promises or gives any financial or other advantage—
  (i) to F, or
  (ii) to another person at F's request or with F's assent or acquiescence, and
(b) F is neither permitted nor required by the written law applicable to F to be influenced in F's capacity as a foreign public official by the offer, promise or gift.

(4) References in this section to influencing F in F's capacity as a foreign public official mean influencing F in the performance of F's functions as such an official, which includes—

(a) any omission to exercise those functions, and
(b) any use of F's position as such an official, even if not within F's authority.

(5) "Foreign public official" means an individual who—

(a) holds a legislative, administrative or judicial position of any kind, whether appointed or elected, of a country or territory outside the United Kingdom (or any subdivision of such a country or territory),
(b) exercises a public function—
  (i) for or on behalf of a country or territory outside the United Kingdom (or any subdivision of such a country or territory), or
  (ii) for any public agency or public enterprise of that country or territory (or subdivision), or
(c) is an official or agent of a public international organisation.

(6) "Public international organisation" means an organisation whose members are any of the following—

(a) countries or territories,
(b) governments of countries or territories,
(c) other public international organisations,
(d) a mixture of any of the above.

(7) For the purposes of subsection (3)(b), the written law applicable to F is—

(a) where the performance of the functions of F which P intends to influence would be subject to the law of any part of the United Kingdom, the law of that part of the United Kingdom,
(b) where paragraph (a) does not apply and F is an official or agent of a public international organisation, the applicable written rules of that organisation,
(c) where paragraphs (a) and (b) do not apply, the law of the country or territory in relation to which F is a foreign public official so far as that law is contained in—
  (i) any written constitution, or provision made by or under legislation, applicable to the country or territory concerned, or
  (ii) any judicial decision which is so applicable and is evidenced in published written sources.

(8) For the purposes of this section, a trade or profession is a business.'

INTRODUCTION

7.1 Section 6 stands rather apart from the other main provisions of the Bribery Act. It deals specifically, and exclusively, with the provision of bribes to foreign public officials. It does not apply to the receipt of bribes, or to the behaviour of foreign public officials themselves, or to the provision of bribes to anyone other than a foreign public official. Unlike s 7, it does not adopt definitions arising in other parts of the Act.

7.2 It could be argued that the provisions of s 6 are not strictly necessary. Given the width of the jurisdictional provisions in s 12 of the Act, most forms of bribery of public officials outside the UK are likely to be offences within the terms of ss 1 or 7, or both. Nevertheless, legislation specifically and separately prohibiting the bribery of foreign public officials was an important objective of the UK Government in the last Parliament. Even more than other parts of the Act, s 6 should be seen in the context of the emerging international law on transnational bribery and in particular the 1997 OECD Convention on Bribery[1] ('the OECD Convention' or 'the Convention').

---

[1] The full title of which is 'Convention on Combating Bribery of Foreign Public Officials in International Business Transactions', OECD 1997b.

Compliance with the OECD Convention

7.3 In 1998 the UK ratified the OECD Convention. The Convention requires criminalisation of the bribery of foreign public officials by persons subject to the jurisdiction of the member states. It does not specify how this is to be done by each state, since each will have a separate legal system, but defines the desired outcome as 'functional equivalence' among the measures taken by each state.[2]

7.4 The Convention has, in a short time, had a considerable influence on both the content, the enforcement and the profile of the law of bribery, both in the UK and in other countries which have ratified it.

7.5 For example, in 1998 it was doubtful whether the existing UK laws of bribery and corruption extended directly to the bribery of foreign public officials. This state of affairs was considered to amount to a breach of the UK's obligations under the Convention.[3] In 2002, s 108 of the Anti-Terrorism, Crime and Security Act 2001 came into force. Section 108 extended the existing law to acts taking place outside the UK. However, legitimate doubts about the overall effectiveness of UK law remained.[4]

7.6 These doubts were exacerbated by the UK's poor record of investigating and prosecuting overseas bribery. This record, and the harm done to the UK's reputation by the very public abandonment of the Al Yamamah investigation,[5] led to a strong feeling among policy-makers that the UK had fallen badly behind in its approach to the Convention. Reforming the law on bribery of foreign public officials came to be seen as an important element of the UK's efforts to improve its record on corporate governance generally. It is difficult to

---

[2] The official 'Commentaries to the OECD Convention adopted by the Negotiating Conference on 21 November 1997' (hereafter 'Commentaries' or 'Commentary') can be treated as *travaux preparatoires* of the Convention text – in other words a highly authoritative interpretation and explanation of key elements of the Convention. Commentary 2 states: 'This Convention seeks to assure a functional equivalence among the measures taken by the Parties to sanction bribery of foreign public officials, without requiring uniformity or changes in fundamental principles of a Party's legal system.' So local differences are tolerated as long as they achieve the same ends.

[3] Although conspiracy to engage in corrupt conduct together with a foreign public official was an offence – see *R v Raud* [1989] Crim LR 809 (CA).

[4] The OECD Working Group on Bribery, UK Phase II Report (www.oecd.org/dataoecd/43/13/38962457.pdf) took the view that, even after the extension of the previous law to bribery of foreign officials by means of the 2001 Act, the legal situation in the UK remained 'characterised by complexity and uncertainty'. However, there is scope for argument about whether the existing law presented as many difficulties as was suggested. A number of important cases of overseas bribery have been prosecuted recently, all under the previous law. There are likely to be more prosecutions under the previous law which of course still applies to events occurring before the Act comes into force, once appropriate resources are made available to the authorities – see in general Chapter 1.

[5] See the discussion in Chapter 10.

escape the impression that, whatever the case for law reform on its own merits, a new offence, closely aligned with the terms of Art 1 of the Convention, was felt to be a political necessity.[6]

7.7 The Law Commission and the Parliamentary Joint Committee[7] certainly took the view that a separate offence was useful, if not necessarily essential, in demonstrating compliance with the UK's obligations under the Convention and this was not seriously challenged in parliamentary debate.

Scheme of section 6

7.8 As already mentioned, s 6 only applies to the providers of bribes. It does not apply to recipients. It also only applies to cases in which the recipient is a foreign public official or the nominee of such an official.[8]

7.9 The s 6 offence does not grow directly out of the legal concepts or language established by ss 1–5 and it should therefore be approached independently of those sections. The structure of the section is also different to the general offences. Section 6 appears to follow the scheme of Art 1 of the OECD Convention, so far as is possible. Unlike ss 1 and 2, s 6 does not proceed by setting out 'cases' which, if satisfied, constitute the offence. Instead, s 6 declares P to be guilty if he 'bribes' a 'foreign public official' while possessing a specific mental element.

Actus reus and mens rea

7.10 Subsections (1) and (3) of s 6 provide for the conduct element (or actus reus) of the offence. Subsection (1) provides that it is an offence if any person (which will include a legal person such as a corporation) 'bribes' a foreign public official (F). Subsection (3) defines what is meant by 'bribes' in subsection (1) as the offer, promise or gift of a financial or other advantage to F, or another person at the request of F or with F's assent or acquiescence. Subsection (3)(b) contains the qualification that F must be neither permitted nor required to be influenced by the advantage, according to the written law applicable to F.

7.11 The mental element of the s 6 offence (mens rea) is set out in subsection (2). It involves intention alone. To commit the offence, P's intention in bribing F must be both to influence F in F's capacity as a foreign public official and, by so doing, to obtain or retain business or an advantage in the conduct of business.

---

[6] LC 313, para 5.62, although the government expressly denied that the existing law was not compliant with Convention obligations – *Hansard*, HL, col 1087 (9 December 2009). See also the MOJ Guidance, p 11.
[7] LC 313, para 5.61–5.70, Joint Committee Report, paras 51–64.
[8] The critical term 'foreign public official' will be analysed below.

7.12 Subsections (4) to (8) define and explain the terms used in subsections (1) to (3) and subsection (5). They provide definitions of the terms 'foreign public official', 'influencing F in his capacity as a foreign public official' and 'written law applicable to F'.

ROLE OF THE OECD CONVENTION IN INTERPRETING SECTION 6

7.13 Although the existence and purpose of the OECD Convention are important to understanding the context of the Bribery Act as a whole, s 6 appears to be a provision designed specifically to fulfil the UK's obligations under the Convention. Prior to the Act, it was not entirely clear whether the Convention as a whole or even Art 1 had been incorporated into UK domestic law.[9] However, given the terms of s 6 and the legislative history of the section, there is little doubt that at least Art 1 of the Convention has now been so incorporated.[10] Therefore an understanding of Art 1 is useful in considering s 6, especially if there is or could be any uncertainty in interpreting it.

Article 1 of the OECD Convention

7.14 The critical article of the OECD Convention in this context is Art 1, which provides:

> '1. Each Party shall take such measures as may be necessary to establish that it is a criminal offence under its law for any person intentionally to offer, promise or give any undue pecuniary or other advantage, whether directly or through intermediaries, to a foreign public official, for that official or for a third party, in order that the official act or refrain from acting in relation to the performance of official duties, in order to obtain or retain business or other improper advantage in the conduct of international business.
>
> 2. Each Party shall take any measures necessary to establish that complicity in, including incitement, aiding and abetting, or authorisation of an act of bribery of a foreign public official shall be a criminal offence. Attempt and conspiracy to bribe a foreign public official shall be criminal offences to the same extent as attempt and conspiracy to bribe a public official of that Party.
>
> 3. The offences set out in paragraphs 1 and 2 above are hereinafter referred to as "bribery of a foreign public official".
>
> 4. For the purpose of this Convention:

---

[9] The better view seems to be that it had not – see *Corner House Research & Ors, R (on the Application of) v The Serious Fraud Office* [2008] UKHL 60, para 43, per Lord Bingham of Cornhill.
[10] See, for example, *Hansard*, HL, col 1087 (9 December 2009); *Explanatory Notes*, para 34. Although it receives far less attention in the pre-legislative process, a similar obligation of criminalisation of bribery of foreign public officials applies by virtue of the UN Convention Against Corruption, Art 16.

a. "foreign public official" means any person holding a legislative, administrative or judicial office of a foreign country, whether appointed or elected; any person exercising a public function for a foreign country, including for a public agency or public enterprise; and any official or agent of a public international organisation;
b. "foreign country" includes all levels and subdivisions of government, from national to local;
c. "act or refrain from acting in relation to the performance of official duties" includes any use of the public official's position, whether or not within the official's authorised competence.'

7.15 Section 6 is not identical to Art 1. For obvious reasons it does not reproduce the clause requiring the parties to 'take measures'. There are also differences between some elements of offence provided for in Art 1 and the offence stipulated by s 6. These differences can be most economically illustrated by means of a table, which is set out at the conclusion to this chapter.

7.16 Since, as we have seen, the purpose of the OECD Convention is only to achieve 'functional equivalence' between the criminal laws of the ratifying parties, the differences between Art 1 and s 6 are not such as to put the UK in breach of its obligations under Art 1 of the Convention. It is clear that s 6, and indeed the Act as a whole, satisfy the requirement of functional equivalence with the terms of Art 1.[11]

7.17 It is well established that once Parliament has given effect to international treaty obligations by incorporating them into domestic legislation the courts must interpret the provisions of that legislation in the light of those obligations.[12] In interpreting such legislation the courts apply the presumption that Parliament intended to legislate in a manner which is consistent with the international instrument concerned.

7.18 Therefore, the relevant provisions of the Convention provide a particularly strong guide to the meaning that Parliament intended s 6 to bear. If the courts consider the wording of the section to be ambiguous for any reason, the presumption is that the courts must construe it to avoid conflict with the Convention and any other related international laws.[13] However, where the wording of the Act is not ambiguous, the courts have no choice but to interpret

---

[11] Of course there are other important and binding articles of the Convention, such as provision for the responsibility of legal persons which bribe FPOs (Art 2), provision for 'effective, proportionate and dissuasive criminal penalties' for such bribery (Art 3) and others. Some of these provisions are discussed in other chapters. However, to do justice to the interesting topic of whether the UK is in conformity with *all* the provisions of the Convention would require another book. A leading work on the Convention generally is Pieth, Low and Cullen (eds) *The OECD Convention on Bribery, A Commentary* (Cambridge, 2009) (hereafter Pieth et al).

[12] *Regina (European Roma Rights Centre and Ors) v Immigration Officer at Prague Airport and Anor (United Nations High Commissioner for Refugees intervening)* [2005] 2 AC 1.

[13] For example, the UN Convention Against Corruption. Other relevant provisions of international instruments to which the UK is a party include Art 3(2) of the Second Protocol of the Convention on the Protection of the European Community's Financial Interests; Art 18(2) of the Council of Europe's Criminal Law Convention on Corruption; and Art 5(2) of

it in the manner in which Parliament intended, regardless of any conflict with the Convention or other related international laws.

DEFINITION OF 'FOREIGN PUBLIC OFFICIAL'

7.19 Before the offence of bribery of a foreign public official (FPO or F) can be understood it is, of course, essential to establish who qualifies as such an official.

7.20 The Act provides definitions of a foreign public official at subsection (5). There are two elements – *an institutional definition* in subsection (5)(a) and a *functional definition* in subsection (5)(b). A person qualifies as an FPO if they satisfy one or other of these definitions.

7.21 The definitions are intended to be broad in scope. They cover a wide range of people who have influence over the conduct of state institutions or the management of state assets, as well as the management of international institutions. These definitions are very similar to those of the OECD Convention (Art 1.4) and many of the key concepts used to define a foreign public official are expressed in the same terms. It was plainly the purpose of Parliament to ensure consistency with the Convention in this regard.

Institutional definition

7.22 The institutional definition in subsection (5)(a) applies to state officials outside the UK. For F to qualify as such an official F must 'hold a legislative, administrative or judicial position of any kind, whether appointed or elected, of a country or territory outside the United Kingdom (or any subdivision of such a country or territory)'. It seems clear that the domestic law of the state in question is relevant only to the question of whether F holds the position in question.[14] That domestic law is not relevant to whether a person in such a position qualifies as a foreign public official for the purposes of the Act. It will usually not be difficult to prove that, as a matter of the law of, say, France, a particular person is a member of the legislature, judiciary or administration, and in most cases this is unlikely to be controversial.

A legislative, administrative or judicial position

7.23 These words should be given their ordinary meaning. They seem to be intended to reflect a widely accepted classification of the main branches of government – the legislature, the executive (or administrative branch) and the judiciary.

---

the European Council's Framework Decision 2003/568/JHA. None of these appear to be incorporated directly into UK law, although their provisions may inform interpretation of the law in relevant circumstances.

[14] See Pieth et al, pp 57–58.

7.24 Someone in a legislative position will hold a position which entitles her to a role in the creation or amendment of legislation, of whatever sort. So a member of a legislature, whether national, state, regional or local, will be in a legislative position. She may be 'appointed or elected'.[15] In territories where the power to legislate lies with a monarch, governor or other person outside a specific legislative assembly such persons will nevertheless qualify as being in a legislative position. The fact that a particular person does not exercise her powers as a legislator is irrelevant.

7.25 A person authorised by the state to adjudicate on disputes or to rule on the application of existing law to specific cases, or to rule on constitutional matters will be in a judicial position. Of course this will include judges, of whatever level in the state court system, including someone whose appointment to a judicial role is temporary, part time or subject to supervision. Support staff whose role is to assist judges to carry out their duties, such as a court clerk or research assistant, should also qualify, as will a juror. Indeed anyone with influence on the functioning of the judicial system, however minor, is likely to qualify.

7.26 An arbitrator not employed by the state, although in an adjudicative position, probably is not in a 'judicial' position given that his powers are essentially controlled by the private contract between the parties.

7.27 An 'administrative position' could cover a multitude of roles, but it seems to refer to the executive branch of government which runs the day-to-day business of the state. Government ministers, civil servants, police and military officers will all qualify, as will any state or local employee with responsibility for influencing the actions of the governing institution with which he is connected. All forms of administration are included, not merely national or federal governments.

Support staff

7.28 Might all state employees fulfil the institutional definition? Probably not. The subsection refers not to those in a particular employment relationship but to those in a particular position, whether legislative, administrative or judicial. In other words, the position itself must have a legislative, administrative or judicial function attached to it. There are many state employees who have no influence whatsoever over the role or functions of the state or their part of it. For example, maintenance, catering and IT staff provide essential services, without which most institutions could not function at all. However, they will rarely have any say on how the institution carries out its key tasks. They provide services to those in legislative, administrative or judicial positions, but their own positions cannot be so categorised.[16]

---

[15] For example, where membership of a second legislative chamber is by appointment or where there are other bodies with a formal role in creating legislation.

[16] See OECD Convention, Art 1.4(a), though note this applies to 'persons' not 'individuals' and to 'holding a legislative, administrative or judicial *office*' rather than a 'legislative,

7.29 In relation to the OECD Convention, Pieth et al take the view that 'only persons who have some substantive association with the policy or mandate of the institution are covered in this institutional sense', and that people such as a secretary who 'simply types what is put in front of her, or a clerk who is responsible only for photocopying and shredding documents' are 'borderline cases'.[17]

7.30 This borderline may sometimes be difficult to draw. One can imagine situations in which those whose roles are not normally influential might in fact have considerable personal influence. Even those without such influence may be capable of providing third parties with information or access to premises, goods or services. A person paying money to a secretary for a copy of documents which she has typed for her boss is as morally culpable as if he had paid the boss himself. If the payment was made with the requisite mens rea then there seems to be no good reason to exclude this situation from the offence.

7.31 It may just be arguable that the wider terminology employed in s 6(5) (a 'legislative, administrative or judicial *position of any kind*') compared to Art 1.4(a) ('holding a legislative, administrative or judicial *office*') has the effect of including support staff who are corrupted from their duties by bribery of this nature. The pre-legislative process did not disclose any clues in this regard and the issue must be regarded as doubtful. Bribery of such individuals with the requisite mens rea may well amount to a general offence under s 1.

Political candidates and officials of political parties

7.32 A candidate for public office who does not hold any existing office and does not exercise a public function seems to be outside the definition of foreign public official. To a layperson this might be surprising. Obviously, such candidates have the potential to exercise enormous influence once they are elected or appointed and therefore are quite influential even before this happens. Providing candidates with payments or other advantages in circumstances where one expects illegal or improper favours in future is likely to be just as damaging to public life as paying off people presently in office.

7.33 The same exclusion seems to apply to officials of political parties, despite the fact that such officials can be extraordinarily influential even in democracies, and even more so in single-party states.

---

administrative or judicial *position of any kind*. The position under the UN Convention Against Corruption is that Art 2(b) provides: '"Foreign public official" shall mean any person holding a legislative, executive, administrative or judicial *office* of a foreign country, whether appointed or elected; and any person exercising a public function for a foreign country, including for a public agency or public enterprise' (emphasis added). Contrast the definition of 'public official' (which applies to domestic officials) at Art 2(a) of the UN Convention.

[17] Pieth et al, p 70.

7.34 It has been said that such cases are difficult because it is not easy to identify the sense in which the payment to 'Candidate F' is improper. Candidate F may not have any specific duties as a foreign public official at the date on which the offer, promise or gift is made by P.[18] The OECD Convention contains a similar lacuna.[19] Neither of these are quite satisfactory explanations for reproducing the lacuna in the Act. The US Foreign Corrupt Practices Act (FCPA) specifically includes 'any foreign political party or official thereof or any candidate for foreign political office' within the class of those who may not be bribed.[20] There seems to be no convincing reason for the Bribery Act not to have done likewise in relation to the s 6 offence.

Territory outside the UK

7.35 The 'United Kingdom', for the purposes of the Act, amounts to Great Britain and Northern Ireland,[21] therefore encompassing England, Scotland, Wales and Northern Ireland. Other entities governed by or constitutionally affiliated to the UK, but which are not part of the UK are not included. It follows that officials of British Overseas Territories, Crown Dependencies, and so on are 'foreign public officials' for the purposes of s 6.[22]

7.36 As is clear from the words 'territory or country', officials of territories which are not countries per se or whose status under international law is disputed (such as was historically the case with the territories seceding from existing states such as Bosnia–Herzegovina, East Timor, Western Sahara and others) are foreign public officials for the purposes of the Act.

7.37 Similarly, subdivisions of countries such as states or provinces of a federal country, regions or municipalities, often have officials in legislative, administrative and judicial positions. These are also included in the definition.

Functional definition

7.38 For the purposes of the OECD Convention, a foreign public official includes anyone who carries out a public function for another country or for an international organisation.[23] Being an official of a specific state body (such as the legislature, executive branch or judiciary) is likely to bring one within this definition. However, there may be many people performing such functions who are outside these three categories.

7.39 Similarly, for s 6 of the Bribery Act, the fact that a person may not fit within the institutional definition at subsection 5(a) does not mean that they are not carrying out functions which are for the benefit of the public and

---

[18] See LC 313, paras 5.53–5.57.
[19] See Pieth et al, p 67.
[20] See s 78 dd-1(a)(2)
[21] Interpretation Act 1978, Sch 2.
[22] Although nationals of British Overseas Territories are subject to the Act – see s 12(4).
[23] Pieth et al, p 59.

therefore require protection from bribery. Subsection 5(b) mirrors Art 1 of the Convention by providing that those exercising public functions, on behalf of a foreign country or territory or on behalf of a 'public agency' or 'public enterprise' of such a country or territory also qualify as foreign public officials.

7.40 In the FCPA a similar provision is made for those not in post as government servants but either officers or employees of an 'agency or instrumentality' of the foreign government, or acting in an official capacity for or on behalf of the government, agency or instrumentality.[24]

Exercising public function for a foreign country

7.41 The term 'public function' appears to catch functions which are delegated by governments to private individuals or businesses, or have traditionally been carried out by private sector entities acting on behalf of the state. It is not defined in s 6 of the Act.[25] The Official Commentaries to the OECD Convention may be of use. They state that public function 'includes any activity in the public interest, delegated by a foreign country, such as the performance of a task delegated by it in connection with public procurement'.[26]

7.42 Those doing work delegated by governments may not be in legislative, administrative or judicial positions. For example, in many countries, medicine is practised by self-employed doctors or privately owned clinics or hospitals which are paid by the state according to the services they perform.[27] States often contract with private firms or consultants to provide specific services in relation to state assets or provide advisory services in commercial matters, or instruct such entities to conduct inquiries, tenders or auctions.

7.43 So people acting in roles of this type are within the definition of foreign public official pursuant to subsection 5(b)(i). For the purposes of the Act, a specific individual must be identified with a specific public function. Like support staff of the legislative, administrative or judicial bodies, individuals who are not themselves charged with public functions should not fall within the definition. The prosecution will be required to adduce at least some evidence

---

[24] See s 78 dd-1(f)(1), although the scope of this provision is the subject of litigation, see, for example, the judgment of the Hon Judge Matz, 20 April 2011, in *US v Noriega et al* US District Court, Central District of California (Western Division – Los Angeles), Case 2:10-cr-01031-AHM-4.

[25] In Chapter 4 we discussed the relationship between the term 'function of a public nature' in s 3 of the Act which provides for the general offences and 'public function' in this section. Although the issue is far from clear, the better view may be that the two concepts are distinct, despite their semantic similarity, because of their differing provenances and purposes.

[26] Commentary 12.

[27] In the FCPA context see, for example, *In re Immucor Inc and Gioacchino De Chirico*, SEC Administrative Proceeding File No 3-12846 (27 September 2007) which concerned the director of a state-owned hospital in Italy; *In the Matter of Diagnostics Products Corporation*, SEC Administrative Proceeding File No 3-11933 (2005) which concerned doctors and laboratory employees at state-owned hospitals in China.

Public agency

7.44 According to s 6(5)(b)(ii) a foreign public official includes those exercising public functions for[28] a 'public agency' and a 'public enterprise'.

7.45 Like 'public function', 'public agency' is not defined in the Act. However, the term is likely to mean any organisation which is created or controlled by a foreign state even though it may not formally be part of the state itself.

7.46 The term also appears in the Convention, and Commentary 13 explains as follows: 'A "public agency" is an entity constituted under public law to carry out specific tasks in the public interest.' Pieth et al give as examples 'representative bodies of employees and employers, for universities or for certain religious communities, where they are organised not as private entities but as bodies subject to public law which are (co-) controlled by the government'.[29]

7.47 The concept of bodies such as these being organised under public law and controlled by the government is not entirely a familiar one in the UK. More familiar UK examples might include NHS Trusts or regulatory agencies such as OFSTED, OFCOM, the FSA and the like.[30] Of course, it is only such bodies that qualify as public agencies in foreign countries which are relevant to s 6.

7.48 It is only those individuals working for such a public agency who are also carrying out a public function as described above that amount to foreign public officials.

Public enterprise

7.49 Some enterprises take the form of a private entity, such as a company, but are in fact majority-owned or effectively controlled by a state. Many such enterprises have been set up or taken over by governments in different countries, for a variety of reasons.[31]

---

[28] Note not 'for or on behalf of' – contrast s 8(1).
[29] Pieth et al, pp 61–62.
[30] Compare the definition of a 'public body' under the Public Bodies (Corrupt Practices) Act 1889 which is a body which has public or statutory duties to perform and which performs those duties for the benefit of the public and not for private profit – *DPP v Holly* [1978] AC 43.
[31] Examples might include the national oil companies of many oil-rich states. In countries such as France, Germany or Italy it is common for states or subdivisions of states to own dominant shareholdings in private commercial or financial concerns such as utilities, banks or airlines.

7.50 Again, the Act does not define 'public enterprise' but, again, since the terms of the OECD Convention are identical one can turn to the official Commentaries on the Convention in case of any ambiguity.

7.51 Paragraph 14 of the Commentaries states:

> 'A "public enterprise" is any enterprise, regardless of its legal form, over which a government, or governments, may, directly or indirectly, exercise a dominant influence. This is deemed to be the case, inter alia, when the government or governments hold the majority of the enterprise's subscribed capital, control the majority of votes attaching to shares issued by the enterprise or can appoint a majority of the members of the enterprise's administrative or managerial body or supervisory board.'

7.52 Note that this text contains a definition, followed by examples deemed to be within the definition. The definition is extremely wide and extends well beyond the examples which follow it. Any enterprise may be a public enterprise, the key question in each case will be whether or not the government exercises a dominant influence over it.

7.53 One would expect an enterprise in which the government has 51% of the voting shares to qualify as a public enterprise. It is also possible that an enterprise in which the government itself owns no shares but in which the president, or the president's spouse, owns a large shareholding, might also qualify. An enterprise which receives very large loans from the state might amount to a public enterprise if it can be shown that the government exercises a dominant influence.[32] Even an enterprise in which there was no shareholding or debt owned by the government or its members or their families might be controlled by the state if its affairs are so heavily circumscribed by state regulation and intervention that the government's influence is dominant.[33]

7.54 A public enterprise as described above may well operate in a relatively free market and compete with other enterprises. Individuals working for a public enterprise may or may not be exercising public functions. As to this, again, the Act provides no guidance but the official Commentaries to the Convention do. Commentary 15 states:

> 'An official of a public enterprise shall be deemed to perform a public function unless the enterprise operates on a normal commercial basis in the relevant market, i.e. on a basis which is substantially equivalent to that of a private enterprise, without preferential subsidies or other privileges.'

7.55 This is one topic on which the official interpretation of Art 1 may differ from the usual approach of English law. The Commentaries take a very broad approach by deeming all the functions of a public enterprise to be public

---

[32] In this regard it seems arguable that the many banks and other financial institutions bailed out by national governments during the financial crisis of 2008/09 qualify as public enterprises as long as a government can exercise a dominant influence.

[33] See the discussion in Pieth et al, pp 62–66.

functions unless certain rather vague market-related criteria are met. To consider such questions, a criminal court may have to grapple with questions of substantial equivalence between the foreign public enterprise in question and 'a private enterprise'. This is not a very attractive prospect. The possible identity of such a private enterprise, or what its characteristics might be, are not specified – it may be a hypothetical construct.[34] In the UK, issues of this kind are generally reserved for specialist tribunals concerned with competition law, and one would not relish dealing with them before a jury.

7.56 It may be relevant that the key provision defining a foreign public official in s 6(5) is that such a person is 'an individual who ... (b) exercises a public function ... (ii) for any public agency or public enterprise of that country or territory (or subdivision)'. In the scheme of the Act, therefore, the question of whether an individual is exercising a public function comes before the question of whether this is done for a public agency or public enterprise. Putting the public function test first may act as a worthwhile filter because the public agency or public enterprise test will only be relevant once it is established that the individual in question exercises public functions for the agency or enterprise.

7.57 The issue of whether employees of private companies in which states own shareholdings amount to 'foreign public officials' under the US FCPA is currently the subject of litigation in the US courts.[35] The argument, though interesting, seems to hinge on the interpretation of provisions of the FCPA which are not mirrored in the Bribery Act.[36] Nevertheless, the identification of foreign public officials under s 6 of the Bribery Act could provoke considerable debate as cases come to be prosecuted.

Example

7.58 To take an example, let us imagine an airline, AirHelpus, which was once 100% owned by the state of Ivernia. Ten years ago AirHelpus was privatised, although 20% of its shares were retained by the government. AirHelpus controls 55% of the landing and take-off slots at the state's main airport, a legacy from its days as the national flag-carrier. It has also inherited a highly unionised workforce and a very large liability to pay the defined-benefit pensions of retired staff. It recently received a loan from the government on favourable terms.

---

[34] There is further useful analysis of this issue in Pieth et al's work on pp 63–66. The gist of the points made is that (for the purposes of the Convention) an enterprise which has a legal monopoly or is protected or regularly subsidised by the state or favoured by public authorities such that it has 'a special position within the domestic economy' is a public enterprise.

[35] *US v Noriega et al* US District Court, Central District of California (Western Division – Los Angeles), Case 2:10-cr-01031-AHM-4.

[36] In particular the terms 'foreign government or any department, agency or instrumentality thereof'.

7.59 The government wishes to develop a new airport and has set up a committee to study the feasibility of the project, recommend sites and design criteria. Raymond is a former government minister, now retired from public office and is a director of AirHelpus. He has been appointed as chairman of the committee, which will take up one day per week for a year. He is being paid a fee of €5,000, which is about 1% of his overall annual earnings.

7.60 Is Raymond an FPO for the purposes of the Act? He does not fit the institutional definition as he does not hold a legislative, administrative or judicial position of any kind. However, AirHelpus may amount to a public enterprise. Although it is not majority owned by the state it seems clear that as the provider of a subsidy and as a large shareholder the state will be influential over the business. How influential may depend on the relative size of the subsidy.

7.61 Let us assume for the moment that AirHelpus is a public enterprise (though in a real case that might be questionable). Is Raymond performing any public functions? If his role was confined to supervising commercial operations then this might be doubtful. However, his role as chairman of the new airport committee appears to be a public function. The committee has been delegated the task of studying and no doubt advising on the new airport project by the government. Such work is clearly in the public interest.

7.62 The practical upshot is that dealings with Raymond, in any of his capacities, should be handled carefully by someone interested in working on the new airport project. It is at least arguable that Raymond qualifies as a foreign public official. Even the provision of unusual advantages to other executives of AirHelpus in the hope of this influencing Raymond into advantageous decisions in relation to the airport project might amount to bribery of Raymond if he assents or acquiesces to the transaction.[37]

Sovereign wealth funds

7.63 Several countries, such as Norway, Kuwait and the United Arab Emirates, have established sovereign wealth funds. These funds receive cash or assets from the state or state enterprises and buy assets around the world, as well as investing in various projects.

7.64 Although the funds may take different legal forms it may well be that their officials are either directly employed by or at least responsible to the state for the management of state property. As such they appear to perform a public function on behalf of the state in question. Even if the funds are not part of the state itself (for example if they are, in law, autonomous companies or agencies) the funds are likely to qualify as public agencies or public enterprises

---

[37] Section 6(3)(a)(ii).

if the states in question have a dominant influence on how they are run. Therefore their officials may well be foreign public officials for the purpose of the Act.

Officials of public international organisations

7.65 For the purposes of the Act, a public international organisation is defined as an organisation whose members are countries, territories, governments of countries or territories, other public international organisations or a mixture of the above.[38] The United Nations and its various agencies are classic examples of public international organisations, as are bodies such as NATO, the European Union, WTO, ASEAN and the many hundreds of others spanning almost every sphere of activity.

7.66 Private organisations with international memberships, such as trade associations, professional bodies, academic associations, charities, groups of churches, etc are not public international organisations as defined because they do not have countries or governments as members.

7.67 Whether or not a particular person is an 'official' or 'agent' of a public international organisation may not always be an easy question to answer. It may depend on the rules of the international organisation in question and whether the organisation itself has a legal status in UK law by virtue of the UK having ratified the treaty or other instrument recognising it.

INTENTION TO INFLUENCE F IN OFFICIAL CAPACITY

7.68 In relation to s 6, the mental element required is in two parts – an intention to influence F in F's capacity as an FPO and also an intention to obtain or retain business or an advantage in the conduct of business.

7.69 We have already seen that intention is a specific concept in criminal law. Usually, an accused intends to cause a result when it is his purpose to cause that result. In the unusual case where it is not the accused's purpose to cause that result, but the result is a virtually certain consequence of his action, and the accused knows this, the accused may also be found to have intended the result.[39]

7.70 To be guilty, P must intend to influence F's function as an FPO. The degree of influence intended is not specified. It is clearly irrelevant whether, in fact, F was or was not influenced by what P did – the offence is located in P's seeking to influence F, successful or not.

---

[38] See s 6(6).
[39] See *R v Woolin* [1999] AC 82, and the discussion in Chapter 2.

Advantage need not be for 'improper performance'

7.71 A key difference between the general bribery offence under s 1 and the specific offence of bribery of a foreign public official under s 6 is that P's intention in providing the advantage to F need only be to *influence* F in his capacity as an official. There is no requirement that P wishes F to act improperly (as in s 1) or that the advantage provided is 'undue' (as in the OECD Convention).

7.72 This makes it easier for people in business to commit an offence under s 6 than under s 1. When it comes to foreign public officials, there is a particular risk that often minor benefits, such as hospitality or the payment of expenses to do with promotional events might fall foul of the offence.

7.73 It is submitted that 'influence' should not be interpreted in a way which leads to absurdity. An intention to influence someone in their official capacity would be extremely difficult to infer from the provision of benefits of negligible value. Nevertheless, the open nature of the concept of 'influencing' an official may cause difficulty in marginal cases.

The same mens rea as section 1?

7.74 In the MOJ Guidance of March 2011, the section headed 'Government Policy and Section 7 of the Bribery Act' discusses s 6 of the Bribery Act and contains the following passage:

> 'Sections 1 and 6 may capture the same conduct but will do so in different ways. The policy that founds the offence at section 6 is the need to prohibit the influencing of decision making in the context of publicly funded business opportunities by the inducement of personal enrichment of foreign public officials or to others at the official's request, assent or acquiescence. Such activity is very likely to involve conduct which amounts to "improper performance" of a relevant function or activity to which section 1 applies, but, unlike section 1, section 6 does not require proof of it or an intention to induce it. This is because the exact nature of the functions of persons regarded as foreign public officials is often very difficult to ascertain with any accuracy, and the securing of evidence will often be reliant on the co-operation of the state any such officials serve. To require the prosecution to rely entirely on section 1 would amount to a very significant deficiency in the ability of the legislation to address this particular mischief. That said, it is not the Government's intention to criminalise behaviour where no such mischief occurs, but merely to formulate the offence to take account of the evidential difficulties referred to above.'[40]

7.75 Although, as we have already noted, it is true that many cases under s 6 might also be chargeable under s 1 this passage risks giving the impression that the offences are essentially the same. Although evidential difficulty attaching to foreign official cases was said in Parliament to be one reason for the width of

---

[40] MOJ Guidance, p 11, para 23.

s 6, it was not the only reason. Another reason was the need to give effect of Art 1 of the OECD Convention in an unambiguous way.

7.76 This passage risks creating the impression that the s 1 test for mens rea is relevant to s 6, despite the obvious differences in wording between each section. Whatever the government's intention as of March 2011, it is clear that Parliament's intention when enacting the statute in April 2010 was to create two distinct offences. It would be unwise to proceed on any other assumption.

Hospitality and promotional expenses

7.77 Often, business people hosting foreign officials are doing so for the ultimate purpose of influencing the official to look favourably on the host's product or service. Of course the host may well not wish the official to do anything which he is not entitled to do, or anything which is improper. The host will no doubt believe it is important to build personal affinity and trust with officials who may be in charge of purchasing decisions by providing modest hospitality or, say, a traditional gift.

7.78 If the recipient were not a public official then these activities would not fall foul of s 1 because the host would lack the necessary mens rea. If the recipient of the hospitality were a domestic (ie UK) public official it would also not fall foul of s 1 or s 6, because s 6 relates only to foreign public officials.[41] However, in dealing with FPOs the Act lays down a far more ambiguous standard, which may well catch corporate hospitality or promotional expenses which would not be an offence if the recipient had a different status.

7.79 During parliamentary debate government ministers acknowledged that some corporate hospitality and promotional expenditure now seen as 'normal' might be within s 6 if it occurred in relation to a foreign public official. It was said that the wise use of prosecutorial discretion could be relied upon to prevent over-zealous application. During debate, the Parliamentary Under-Secretary of State Lord Tunnicliffe said:

> 'Those involved in international business activities should have ready access to legal advice on the legitimacy of payments to foreign officials and should think twice before offering, promising or giving advantage to foreign officials. The Joint Committee fully considered the impact of the Clause 6 offence on bona fide commercial activities such as corporate hospitality. In its report at paragraph 147 the Joint Committee noted that the prosecutorial discretion would be able to differentiate the good from the bad in respect of corporate hospitality and was content with this approach. The evidence of Professor Horder of the Law Commission was highlighted in the report, which stated:
>
>> "Might it not be said, then, that 'improperly' should be tacked on as an adverb after 'influence' so as to distinguish legitimate from illegitimate

---

[41] Unless P knew or believed that if the recipient received the advantage he would be acting improperly – s 1, case 2.

hospitality? ... The answer is 'no' because that would inevitably re-introduce questions about whether cultural norms and expectations can make a payment 'proper', and that is exactly the result that this offence is designed to prevent."

Should there be a defence for reasonable corporate hospitality? We do not believe one is needed. The offence applies only to advantages given to foreign public officials which are intended to influence officials and to obtain or retain business. This will not necessarily be the case in respect of hospitality. To the extent that any corporate hospitality might be caught by this division – which will certainly not generally be the case – it is appropriate for prosecutors to take a view on where the public interest lies. It is unlikely that reasonable hospitality to foreign officials will attract the interest or action of enforcement authorities.'[42]

7.80 A connected issue is promotional expenses, where a business will wish to demonstrate its products or facilities to a foreign official who is a potential customer, and pays for the official to travel for a site visit or other promotional event. Section 6 could criminalise such activity, at least if one classifies the site visit as a benefit to the official. However, there is considerable room for doubt about this. Whereas hospitality generally might be seen as a benefit, even if minor, the same may not be true of promotional activities such as site visits or product demonstrations. Travel to a conference, industrial facility, trade show or data centre should not automatically be regarded as personal benefits. They are not holidays and involve time away from one's home, family and the conduct of one's principal affairs.

7.81 Of course many promotional activities also involve the provision of some hospitality – for example a business meeting followed by dinner, a tour or a sports event. There is no doubt that those providing corporate hospitality must be more careful when dealing with foreign public officials than with their counterparts in the UK. However, s 6 should not be read as outlawing all hospitality to FPOs. There will be few cases in which a business will record a specific intention to influence an FPO in a form which can be used in evidence and most cases will be built on the inferences to be drawn from specific transactions. Transactions which are inconsequential are most unlikely to be able to support the necessary inference of intention to influence the FPO, especially if it is not possible to identify a specific decision of the FPO which the supposed bribery is intended to influence.

7.82 As to prosecutorial discretion, it is difficult to imagine that a prosecution would be in the public interest where a UK company paid for travel, food and accommodation connected only to a business meeting with a foreign public official or officials who are potential customers. Of course if the expenditure was for the provision of additional benefits, such as extravagant leisure

---

[42] *Hansard*, HL, col GC 41 (7 January 2010).

activities, and there were other factors suggesting these were not provided in a bona fide way the SFO may wish to prosecute.[43]

7.83 The Guidance issued by the UK Ministry of Justice on 30 March 2011 also suggests that present government policy is to allow a fairly wide margin of appreciation for such activities.[44]

Private relationships with FPOs

7.84 Subsection (4) states that 'references in this section to influencing F in F's capacity as a foreign public official mean influencing F in the performance of F's functions as such an official'. So offering a gift to F merely so as to gain membership of his private club or use of his personal holiday home does not qualify.

7.85 Of course it is possible for advantages such as gifts to be provided to FPOs without intending to influence them in their capacity as such. For example, friends or relatives of a foreign official will give personal gifts or other advantages. Usually these will be provided whatever job the recipient happened to do and are not connected to an intention to influence the FPO in any relevant way. However, pre-existing friendship or even kinship with an FPO does not vaccinate someone who attempts to provide an advantage with the intention of influencing the FPO in his official capacity.

7.86 Sometimes P may not know that F is a foreign public official. For example, it is possible that an official of a private company could also be an adviser to the national government, and for this to be unknown to the general public. If P, seeking commercial opportunities with the private company, provides F with a gift it is possible that its intention was to influence him in his commercial capacity and not his official one. The burden of proof would remain on the prosecution to show that P's intention was to influence F in F's official capacity.

Omissions and actions exceeding authority

7.87 Subsection (4) also makes clear that an intention to influence an official not to exercise functions (such, for example, as not pursuing investigations or not submitting reports), or an intention to get the official to exceed his powers or improperly use his position to influence other matters which are not his direct responsibility is sufficient mens rea for commission of the offence.

---

[43] This position seems to be broadly confirmed by the Joint Prosecution Guidance of 30 March 2011, p 10.
[44] MOJ Guidance, p 14.

Intending to obtain or retain business/an advantage in the conduct of business

7.88 This stipulation is known generally as the 'business purpose test'. Intending to 'obtain business' seems to mean intending to obtain something of economic or commercial value in business, usually, though not always, a contractual obligation to purchase goods or services from P. 'Retaining' business is included so that bribes paid to officials in the hope of avoiding detriment (such as the cancellation or modification of a contract) rather than simply achieving a gain, do not escape the net.

7.89 The concept of 'an advantage in the conduct of business' is wider than the OECD Convention which provides for an intention to obtain or retain business or 'other *improper* advantage in the conduct of international business' (emphasis added). The Bribery Act does not have a test of whether the advantage in the conduct of business is 'improper'. Such a test might import difficult considerations of local law on the subject of the propriety of the business or business advantage provided.[45]

7.90 Both 'business' and 'advantage in the conduct of business' are likely to be interpreted widely.[46] Although there is no UK case-law as yet, the important FCPA case of *US v Kay*[47] may well be influential, as it has been in the interpretation of the business purpose test in the context of the OECD Convention.

7.91 In *Kay* the facts were that the defendant's company ARI exported rice from the US into Haiti. The defendant was an officer of ARI. In an attempt to reduce the company's taxes and duties the defendant and another officer of the company paid bribes to staff of the Haitian tax and customs authorities. The FCPA has a narrower test than s 6 and only forbids the payment of bribes 'in order to assist [an issuer/domestic concern] in obtaining or retaining for or with, or directing business to, any person'. So the question was whether the bribes were to obtain or retain 'business' for the company. The defendants took

---

[45] And may also import similar problems of definition which the 'corruptly' test carried with it under the old law – see Chapter 1 for a discussion.
[46] The Act attempts to include the businesses carried out by trades and professions by means of s 6(8) but the wording used risks introducing some ambiguity. The first difficulty is that the subsection says that a trade or profession 'is a business'. The indefinite article makes the clause appear to refer to an enterprise of some sort. However, the section does not refer elsewhere to 'a business' in that sense, only to 'business' in the sense of contracts or economic advantages. The purpose of the subsection seems to be to include trades and professions in the class of those which may not bribe foreign public officials, although it is surprising that it was felt that this might be in doubt. The second difficulty is similar to that found in s 7(5) – by stating that a trade or profession 'is' a business, does the Act suggest that commercial activities which might not be deemed trades or professions are not 'a business' for the purposes of s 6? Contrast the clearer words of s 3(7): 'In this section "business" includes trade or profession'. It seems unlikely that Parliament intended to have the rather nebulous concepts of what may or may not constitute a trade or profession govern the application of such important parts of the Act as ss 6 and 7 but ideally the language in question would be clearer.
[47] *US v Kay*, United States Court of Appeals (5th Circuit), 359 F 3d 738, 4 February 2004.

a preliminary objection that tax reductions were not 'business' as normally understood and as provided in the legislation. The federal court of first instance agreed. However, on appeal, the Court of Appeals for the Fifth Circuit disagreed, holding that 'bribes paid to foreign officials in consideration for the unlawful evasion of customs duties and sales taxes could fall within the purview of the FCPA's proscription'.

7.92 After trial and conviction, the defendants then appealed on the ground that the alleged vagueness of the 'obtaining or retaining business' stipulation meant their conviction was unfair. The Court of Appeals disagreed again, holding that:

> 'Although ARI did not make corrupt payments to guarantee one particular contract's success ... ARI ensured, through bribery, that it could continue to sell its rice without having to pay the full tax and customs duties demanded of it. Trial testimony indicates that ARI believed these payments were necessary to compete with other companies that paid lower or no taxes on similar imports – in other words, in order to retain business in Haiti, the company took measures to keep up with competitors. The fact that other companies were guilty of similar bribery during the 1990s does not excuse ARI's actions; multiple violations of a law do not make those violations legal or create vagueness in the law.'

7.93 This reasoning takes a generous approach to the definition of 'obtaining or retaining business'. Its effect seems to be that the presence or absence of almost any factor which affects the operation of a business is capable of being either business or either an advantage or disadvantage in the conduct of business. The courts of the UK may well take a similar approach.

PROVIDING THE ADVANTAGE

Directly or through a third party

7.94 'Directly' in this context seems to mean not through a third party or intermediary. 'Through a third party' will include a case where anyone other than P offers promises or gives the advantage, whether that person is an intermediary, a company, an individual or even a government department. The offer promise or gift will have to be made with the knowledge of P if P is to be liable[48] – a gratuitous unauthorised offer is most unlikely to implicate P because P will lack mens rea.

Offers promises or gives

7.95 The formulation 'offers promises or gives' appears in Art 1 of the Convention, as well as in s 1 of the Act. As discussed at more length in Chapter 2, the essential characteristics of each are as follows:

---

[48] Contrast the lack of a knowledge requirement in s 7, if P is a relevant commercial organisation.

- an offer can be defined as a statement to the effect that an advantage is available to a recipient contingent upon the recipient taking some other step;

- a promise is usually understood as involving a commitment or undertaking by the promisor which is not contingent on action by the promise;

- to give something involves an element of transfer of control of something specific from the giver to the recipient. In the context of the Act it may be interpreted more widely as involving the actual provision of any advantage, material or non-material.

Any financial or other advantage

7.96 Again, this formulation mirrors that of s 1 and is discussed in more detail in Chapter 2. Article 1 of the Convention mentions 'any undue pecuniary or other advantage'. The difference between a 'pecuniary' and 'financial' advantage is unlikely to be significant.

7.97 Advantages are not limited to money or independently valuable assets. They can include a wide range of goods or services, including hospitality, gifts and so on. As with s 1 there is no minimum limit on value, but it will be relevant in each case whether the advantage in question was or could have been capable of influencing F in F's capacity as a foreign public official, so that minor offers of hospitality or items with little or no market value are extremely unlikely to be of interest to the authorities or the courts.[49]

To F or another at F's request, etc

7.98 This element is effectively self-explanatory. The advantage must be offered or provided to F or to another person at the request, assent or acquiescence of F. So a company passing on favours to the business of a relative of F is within the definition, at least if F requests, assents or acquiesces in this.

7.99 A request implies a positive communication by F which indicates that he wishes P to make the offer, promise or gift to the recipient. What of 'assent' or 'acquiescence'? The terms are not synonymous. 'Assent' is more active and denotes both a consciousness of the transaction in question and some action indicating approval of or agreement to it.[50] 'Acquiescence' is more passive, although again it seems that knowledge of the improper performance is a prerequisite.[51]

---

[49] As discussed above, as a matter of evidence, an 'advantage' of little or no value would tend to undermine any case of intention to influence F, and it is submitted that a prosecution would not be in the public interest unless connected with a wider pattern of criminality.
[50] The *Shorter Oxford English Dictionary* (SOED) has 'express approval or agreement'.
[51] SOED: 'the reluctant acceptance of something without protest'.

7.100 'Another person', includes natural persons and legal persons such as companies.

Role of local law

7.101 In some legal systems it is a defence to a charge of bribery of a foreign public official that the alleged bribe was legal under the law of the territory which governed the FPO. For example, it is an express affirmative defence to a charge under the anti-bribery provisions of the FCPA.[52]

7.102 The Law Commission had originally proposed that it should be a defence to a charge of bribery of a foreign public official if P could show that he reasonably believed that the provision of the advantage was required or permitted under the law local to the FPO.[53] This would have amended the necessary mens rea on the part of P. However, this proposal was rejected by the Joint Committee and was excluded from the Bill.

7.103 When it comes to the general offences, the Act specifically makes allowance for local customs or practices involving payment for the performance of protected functions and activities.[54] If a s 1 or s 2 offence is charged in which the actions in question took place outside the UK then local written law may be taken into account in deciding the expectations which apply, and thus in determining whether an offence has been committed.

7.104 However, commission of an offence relating to a foreign public official under s 6 does not depend on the expectation tests relevant to the general offences. The expectations of a 'reasonable person in the United Kingdom' do not come into consideration.

7.105 Instead of focusing on the state of mind of P, the Act contains a narrow defence to the s 6 offence based on the law applicable to the foreign public official.[55] If the written law applicable to F either permits or requires F to be *influenced by* the offer, promise or gift of the advantage in his capacity as an FPO then the offer promise or gift is not a bribe under s 6(3).

7.106 This provision may exist to make provision for particular circumstances known as 'offset' or 'counter-trade', in which a government purchaser requires sellers to provide collateral benefits to the state, as well as the items purchased. These benefits may include agreements to provide local facilities such as schools, to co-produce equipment with local companies, technology transfers, the purchase of components or services from local suppliers or simply the

---

[52] FCPA, s 78 dd-1(c)(1), although it seems that this defence has not yet been successfully relied upon in any reported case.
[53] LC 313, paras 7.2–7.49.
[54] Section 5(2) – see Chapter 6.
[55] Section 6(3)(b).

purchase of other goods, which may have no connection with the material being sold, from the state in question.[56]

Example

7.107 Let us imagine Wernham, a UK company seeking to sell fighter planes to the People's Republic of Slough. As part of its bid, it is told by Gareth, an official in charge of the tender process, that it should undertake to subcontract assembly or maintenance to an industrial concern in Slough. The company offers a contract to Brent plc, a local engineering firm. The offer to Brent is an offer of a financial or other advantage to another person at Gareth's request or with Gareth's asset or acquiescence, with the intention of influencing Gareth in his capacity as an FPO and seeking to obtain/retain business. The case would be a bribe, and contrary to s 6, unless it can be shown that Gareth is permitted by the written law applicable to him (in this example the law of Slough) to be influenced by the offer to Brent.

Applicable law

7.108 Which law is applicable to F is defined by s 6(7). If the functions of F which P seeks to influence are subject to UK law then the law of the relevant part of the UK applies. If F is an official of an international organisation then the rules of that organisation apply. If neither of these apply then the law is that of the country or territory of which F is a public official.

7.109 In each case, the laws or rules must be 'written'. This can be taken to mean recorded in any visible form.[57] In cases where the law of the UK or an international organisation do not apply the writing is limited to a written constitution, or provisions made by or under legislation[58] which is applicable to the place in question, or judicial decisions which are both applicable and 'evidenced in published written sources'.[59]

7.110 In the example above, the written law in question will be that of Slough. It should not prove difficult to find the sources of law applicable to the

---

[56] Some feel that offset as a practice distorts competition and leads to irrational decision-making by purchasers. Offset arrangements offer greater potential for corruption than normal sales because the local firms which gain contracts through offset may be connected to the governmental decision-makers and the local elements of decision-making tend not to be transparent. However, exporters believe they have little option but to offer offset as part of their sales proposition since it is a requirement of the purchasing state.
[57] Interpretation Act 1978, s 5, Sch 1: '"Writing" includes typing, printing, lithography, photography and other modes of representing or reproducing words in a visible form, and expressions referring to writing are construed accordingly.'
[58] Which appears to includes delegated or subordinate legislation.
[59] This seems to leave unpublished judgments as significantly poorer relations. It would be difficult to justify a situation where a relevant and binding legal judgment had to be ignored because of a lack of a comprehensive system for the reporting of judgments or because subject to reporting restrictions. It may be that the term 'published' can be given the maximum flexibility so as to include, for example, an entry in a court or other official record.

transaction. If Gareth is subject to rules permitting offset arrangements to influence his decision then Wernham's arrangement with Brent, intended to influence Gareth, will not be contrary to s 6.[60]

7.111 However, even in a transaction involving offset it is unlikely that the written law of the state will allow an official to be influenced by the offer or receipt of any direct personal benefits from bidders. To do so would undermine the integrity of the tendering process and state procurement as a whole.

7.112 There is a short discussion of offset cases in the 'Government Policy' section of the MOJ Guidance. Most of this is uncontroversial. However, the following passage rather leaps out:

> 'In circumstances where the additional investment would amount to an advantage to a foreign public official and the local law is silent as to whether the official is permitted or required to be influenced by it, prosecutors will consider the public interest in prosecuting. This will provide an appropriate backstop in circumstances where the evidence suggests that the offer of additional investment is a legitimate part of a tender exercise.'[61]

7.113 Unfortunately, this statement has to be treated with considerable caution. If the local law is silent on the subject then there is no written law which permits or requires F to be influenced by the promise offer or gift. The Act has nothing extra to say about whether an offer is 'legitimate' according to some other criteria, or 'part of a tender exercise'. Even if it did, it seems rather unlikely that a personal advantage to the FPO would be part of any official tender criteria.

7.114 Although there may well be other facts which suggest that a prosecution may not be in the public interest, the (admittedly skeletal) case outlined does not seem to fit within the list of 'factors tending against prosecution' set out by the DPP and Director of the SFO in their own guidance document.[62]

'FACILITATION' PAYMENTS TO FOREIGN PUBLIC OFFICIALS

7.115 Facilitation payments can be defined as payments made with the purpose of expediting or facilitating the provision of services or routine government action which an official is normally obliged to perform.[63] Such

---

[60] Exporting companies already have access to sources of detailed information on various national offset laws and regulations, often maintained by the trade agencies of their own states of origin
[61] MOJ Guidance, p 12.
[62] Joint Prosecution Guidance, p 9.
[63] The FCPA has the following definition: 'any facilitating or expediting payment to a foreign official, political party, or party official the purpose of which is to expedite or to secure the performance of a routine governmental action by a foreign official, political party, or party official' (s 78 dd-1(b)). A more detailed definition of routine government action, which

payments amount to bribery under s 1 or s 6 because they are made either with the intention of inducing or rewarding improper performance of a relevant function or activity,[64] or in the knowledge that the acceptance of the advantage by the official itself involves improper performance of his functions. If such payments are made in the course of business they will often be made with the intention of influencing F in his capacity as such.[65]

7.116 Unlike the FCPA, the Bribery Act makes no exception for facilitation payments, in s 6 or elsewhere. Such payments were not subject to exceptions under previous law and the approach of the Law Commission, the Joint Committee and the government has been to hold this line, essentially on the ground that tolerance of such payments would send the wrong signal as to the seriousness of even 'petty' bribery in poor or developing countries.[66]

7.117 The UK government has previously attempted to mitigate the effect that UK law might have on those wishing to invest or do business overseas. For example it has previously stated that it is not the government's policy to seek prosecution of UK businesses paying facilitation payments. In parliamentary debate the government acknowledged that it might not be in the public interest to prosecute in many circumstances in which facilitation payments arise.[67] Such circumstances might include circumstances of extortion or blackmail.

7.118 The Joint Prosecution Guidance of March 2011 mentions the public interest considerations attaching to prosecution of facilitation payments, the gist being that single small payments may not be prosecuted and companies which make good faith efforts to prevent facilitation payments may also be treated leniently. The issue of prosecutorial priorities is discussed in more detail in Chapter 10 and a hypothetical scenario involving facilitation payments is considered in Chapter 14.

7.119 Nevertheless, facilitation payments to FPOs intended to procure faster processing of paperwork or similar administrative tasks will be offences under

---

excludes such actions as the awarding of business, is at s 78 dd-1(f). Note that businesses might still fall foul of the FCPA if they do not record facilitation payments accurately in their books and records – s 78 m(b).

[64] Section 1, case 1. The impropriety in question may depend on the facts of each case, but might typically involve the official acting in a manner contrary to an expectation of good faith (not accounting to his employer for the payment), or impartiality (allowing P to 'jump the queue'), or in breach of an expectation arising from a position of trust (if the official would be trusted to exercise his power even-handedly) (s 4(1)). The test is that of the reasonable person in the UK, not local custom, although local written law permitting the activity can be considered (s 5).

[65] The view of the commentaries to the OECD Convention (para 9) that facilitation payments do not pass the business purpose test is, with respect, unconvincing.

[66] The OECD has also hardened its line against facilitation payments, seeking to discourage toleration of them by Convention States generally – see OECD *Recommendation of the Council for Further Combating Bribery of Foreign Public Officials in International Business Transactions,* 2009.

[67] *Hansard*, HL, col 135 (2 February 2010).

s 6, absent highly unusual circumstances, and those doing business overseas should conduct themselves accordingly.

SECTION 14 AND OFFENCES UNDER SECTION 6 BY BODIES CORPORATE AND THEIR SENIOR OFFICERS

7.120 It is clear that a s 6 offence can be committed by legal persons, such as corporate bodies, as well as natural persons (ie individuals).[68] As the law stands, a corporate body can only commit an offence if a person who was identifiable with the company, sometimes called the 'directing mind', possesses the relevant mental state when the company commits the act or omission in question. Of course this position has been amended in relation to the s 7 offence by the Act. However, in relation to other offences under the Act, as provided by ss 1, 2 and 6, the standard rule applies.[69]

7.121 The Act makes further provision for the senior officers of bodies corporate. Section 14 of the Act provides, in part:

> '(1) This Section applies if an offence under section 1, 2 or 6 is committed by a body corporate or a Scottish Partnership;
>
> (2) If the offence is proved to have been committed with the consent or connivance of —
>
> (a) a senior officer of the body corporate or Scottish partnership, or
> (b) a person purporting to act in such a capacity,
>
> the senior officer or person (as well as the body corporate or partnership) is guilty of the offence and liable to be proceeded against and punished accordingly.'

7.122 The purpose of this provision is to make senior people who are key players in an offence committed by the business as liable as the business itself. The provision mirrors s 12 of the Fraud Act 2006 in this regard.[70] Section 14 does not create a second offence of consent or connivance. Rather it makes clear that both the body corporate and the relevant senior officer who consents and connives are guilty of the s 6 offence as well as the general offences under ss 1 and 2.[71] This does not apply to s 7 offences, which can only be committed by commercial organisations.

7.123 The key terms are consent and connivance, which have been discussed in Chapter 2. Section 14(3) makes it clear that the senior officer or person purporting to act in that capacity will need to have a close connection to the

---

[68] Interpretation Act 1978, s 5, Sch 1: '"Person" includes a body of persons corporate or unincorporate'.
[69] *Tesco Supermarkets Ltd v Nattrass* [1972] AC 153. See the discussion in Chapter 8.
[70] And, previously, s 18 of the Theft Act 1968.
[71] *Hansard*, HL, col 149 (18 March 2010).

UK within the meaning of s 12(4).[72] Section 14(4) defines a 'senior officer' as a director, manager, secretary[73] or other similar officer of the body corporate, or a partner in the Scottish partnership.

7.124 How might a senior officer consent to or connive in the commission of a s 6 offence by a corporate body? Examples will not be difficult to imagine. As discussed in Chapter 2, if a company's finance director authorises a scheme by his company to pay inflated 'consultancy fees' to third parties so that they may in turn be used to bribe an FPO, then, although the company will be guilty of a s 6 offence, the finance director will also be guilty, having consented to or connived in the company's actions.

COMPARISON OF ARTICLE 1 OF THE OECD CONVENTION WITH SECTION 6 OF THE BRIBERY ACT 2010

7.125 The table below sets out some of the more relevant points of comparison between the Bribery Act and the OECD Convention.

	Item	Article 1	Section 6	Remarks
1	Mens rea part 1	1.1 Intentionally [to offer, promise or give any undue pecuniary or other advantage to F/third party].	No express requirement of intention to offer, promise or give, although voluntariness as to actions is implicit.	In Art 1 it is clear that P must intend to make the offer, etc as well as intend to make it with the corrupt purpose of affecting F's conduct in office.
				In s 6 the stipulated 'intention' of P only expressly relates to the purpose of the offer, etc. However, the section should be taken to require voluntariness on the part of P in making the offer, etc.

---

[72] As to which see Chapter 11.
[73] In the sense of company secretary or other officer of an organisation. In *R v Boal* [1992] 1 QB 591, 597–8 a case under s 23 of the Fire Precautions Act 1971 which contains the same formulation of 'director, manager, secretary or other similar officer of the body corporate' it was said by the Court of Appeal that the intention of the wording was only to make those 'in a real position of authority, the decision-makers within the company who have both the power and responsibility to decide corporate policy and strategy' liable.

	Item	Article 1	Section 6	Remarks
2	Mens rea part 2	1.1 in order that the official act or refrain from acting in relation to the performance of official duties ...	6(1) Intention [to influence F in F's capacity as a foreign public official] ...	Note that in both texts this test relates only to the state of mind of P – P's intention must be to influence F in the manner stated.
		1.4.c. 'act or refrain from acting in relation to the performance of official duties' includes any use of the public official's position, whether or not within the official's authorised competence'.	6(4) References in this section to influencing F in F's capacity as a foreign public official mean influencing F in the performance of F's functions as such an official, which includes—	It does not matter whether F is actually open to influence or was actually influenced. 'Influencing' F in his capacity as an FPO may be somewhat wider than the Art 1 wording:
			(a) any omission to exercise those functions, and	'[providing advantages, etc] in order that the official act or refrain from acting'. However, the difference seems to be cosmetic.
			(b) any use of F's position as such an official, even if not within F's authority.	
3	Mens rea part 3	1.1 in order to obtain or retain business or other improper advantage in the conduct of international business.	6(2) P must also intend to obtain or retain—	Article 1's 'intention' appears to stretch as far as the business purpose test set out here. Section 6 makes this express, so the provisions as to intention at least appear identical.
			(a) business, or	
			(b) an advantage in the conduct of business.	
				There are differences on the question of what needs to be intended by P. Both Art 1 and s 6 have the intention to 'obtain or retain business' in common.
				Section 6 goes further than Art 1 by including 'advantage in the conduct of business' but avoiding the qualifications 'improper' or 'international' contained in Art 1

Item	Article 1	Section 6	Remarks
			Under s 6 there is no need to establish whether receipt or provision of the advantage was proper or improper (ie legal or illegal) under the law of the foreign country in question.[74]
			A connected issue is that of facilitation payments. The Commentaries to Art 1 provide that facilitation payments do not constitute payments made 'to obtain or retain business or other improper advantage'.[75]
			There is no exception for facilitation payments in UK law.
4	Actus reus part 1	1.1 Offer promise or give.	6(3) P bribes F if and only if:	Identical.
		(a) directly or through a third party P offers promises or gives ...	
5	Actus reus part 2	1.1 undue pecuniary or other advantage.	6(3)(a) ... any financial or other advantage	'pecuniary' should be read as meaning the same as 'financial' in this context.
			The requirement that the payment be 'undue' in Art 1 means that it would be possible for a defendant to show that the payment was required or allowed by local law, as is the case under the US FCPA and other national laws.[76]

---

[74] Save for the 'influencing' question under s 6(3)(b).
[75] See Commentaries, para 9: 'Small "facilitation" payments do not constitute payments made "to obtain or retain business or other improper advantage" within the meaning of paragraph 1.' This must be doubtful in circumstances where speedy processing of paperwork is an important requirement of a business, and jumping the queue to obtain this is hardly proper.
[76] Including those of Canada, France, Germany and others.

Item		Article 1	Section 6	Remarks
				However, a stipulation that the payment be 'not legitimately due', though recommended by the Law Commission and Parliamentary Joint Committee,[77] was abandoned in the draft Bill and does not appear in the Act.
				See also the 'written law' requirement below.
6	Use of third parties	1.1 [... offer, promise or give any undue pecuniary or other advantage], whether directly or through intermediaries.	6(3)(a) [P bribes F if and only if (i) directly or through a third party, [P offers, promises or gives any financial or other advantage ...	Effectively identical. Although 'intermediary' in Art 1 seems to have a narrower meaning than 'third party' in s 6 any third party which is involved in offering, promising or giving a bribe on behalf of someone else seems to be an intermediary.
7	Benefits to parties other than F	1.1 ... to a foreign public official, for that official or for a third party.	6(3)(a) [P offers, promises or gives any financial or other advantage ...]	The Convention stipulates that the advantage goes to F, is for F or a third party. Although these scenarios may have been intended to be put as alternatives, the English language text omits the critical word 'or' which would have made this clearer.
			(i) ... to F, or	
			(ii) to another person at F's request or with F's assent or acquiescence.	
				Section 6 makes clear that an advantage going 'to' a third party is part of the actus reus, but only if this is done, in essence, with the knowledge of F.

---

[77] Joint Committee Report, Part I, para 64.

Item		Article 1	Section 6	Remarks
				This may make cases, where benefits go to friends, relatives or clients of F in order to influence F, more difficult to prove, given that it will be necessary to prove the state of mind of F as well as of P.
8	Complicity/ Conspiracy/ Attempt	1.2 Each Party shall take any measures necessary to establish that complicity in, including incitement, aiding and abetting, or authorisation of an act of bribery of a foreign public official shall be a criminal offence.	None, save for s 14.	It was not necessary for the Bribery Act to make specific provision for offences of conspiracy, attempt or incitement given the existing common law and statute.[78]
		Attempt and conspiracy to bribe a foreign public official shall be criminal offences to the same extent as attempt and conspiracy to bribe a public official of that Party.		Section 14 provides for the liability of senior officers of corporate bodies which consent or connive in offences under s 6 and ss 1 and 2 committed by the body corporate.
9	Definition of FPO	1.4.a 'foreign public official' means any person holding a legislative, administrative or judicial office of a foreign country, whether appointed or elected;	6(5) 'Foreign public official' means an individual who— (a) holds a legislative, administrative or judicial position of any kind,	The apparent intention of the drafter of s 6 was to model the definition of an FPO on Art 1 as closely as possible to maintain the 'autonomous' nature of the definition.

---

[78] For example, the Criminal Law Act 1977, s 1, Criminal Attempts Act 1981, s 1, Serious Crime Act 2007, ss 44–46.

Item	Article 1	Section 6	Remarks
	any person exercising a public function for a foreign country, including for a public agency or public enterprise; and any official or agent of a public international organisation; ...	whether appointed or elected, of a country or territory outside the United Kingdom (or any subdivision of such a country or territory),	However, there are some minor differences of language.[79]
			Section 6 is limited to any 'individual' (s 6(5)).
		(b) exercises a public function—	and plainly does not apply to bodies corporate.
	1.4.b. 'foreign country' includes all levels and all subdivisions of government, from national to local.	(i) for or on behalf of a country or territory outside the United Kingdom (or any subdivision of such a country or territory), or	Article 1 refers to any 'person', which could in theory include a legal person such as a company.
		(ii) for any public agency or public enterprise of that country or territory (or subdivision), or	Section 6 refers to a legislative, administrative or judicial position of any kind which is potentially somewhat wider than an 'office'.
		(c) is an official or agent of a public international organisation.	There may be some in such positions who are not holders of particular 'offices' per se.[80]
			The functional definitions relating to carrying out public functions for foreign countries, public agencies or public enterprises are effectively identical in both texts.

---

[79] These may well arise from the fact that the Convention is an international instrument, not drafted in the common law tradition and requiring terms which can be readily translated between various languages.

[80] That there will be differences between national legal systems in this regard is noted in the Commentaries, para 16, which recognises that certain legal systems may treat such persons as foreign public officials.

	Item	Article 1	Section 6	Remarks
10	Local written law exception.	1.1 Advantage provided must be 'undue'.[81]	6(3)(b) [P bribes F if and only if] F is neither permitted nor required by the written law applicable to F to be influenced in F's capacity as a foreign public official by the offer, promise or gift.[82]	Section 6's only deference to the 'local law exception' which appears in the FCPA expressly.[83]
				and in the Convention by implication (from 'undue') is this provision which
				emphasises not a permission/requirement in relation to receipt[84] of the advantage, but in relation to being influenced by it.
				This appears to be intended to make provision for sales involving offset – ie connected spending within a purchasing state.
				It is conceivable that a particularly corrupt state could pass a law which allowed its officials to be influenced by personal bribes.
				The recognition such a law would receive in the UK courts can only be a matter of speculation.

---

[81] As to 'undue', see item 5 above.
[82] This wording was not foreshadowed in the draft Bill put forward by the Law Commission or considered by the Joint Committee.
[83] See s 78 dd-1(c)(1).
[84] Or, of course, the offer or promise of the advantage.

Item		Article 1	Section 6	Remarks
11	Definition of local written law.	None.[85]	6(7) For the purposes of subsection (3)(b), the written law applicable to F is—	These provisions of s 6 have a flavour of 'belt and braces', making clear and limiting the local law, for the apparent purpose of excluding what may be said to be unwritten toleration of corrupt practices, customs relating to courtesy and so on.
			(a) where the performance of the functions of F which P intends to influence would be subject to the law of any part of the United Kingdom, the law of that part of the United Kingdom,	
			(b) where paragraph (a) does not apply and F is an official or agent of a public international organisation, the applicable written rules of that organisation,	
			(c) where paragraphs (a) and (b) do not apply, the law of the country or territory in relation to which F is a foreign public official so far as that law is contained in—	
			(i) any written constitution, or provision made by or under legislation, applicable to the country or territory concerned, or	
			(ii) any judicial decision which is so applicable and is evidenced in published written sources.	

---

[85] Although note Commentaries, para 7: 'It is also an offence irrespective of, inter alia, the value of the advantage, its results, perceptions of local custom, the tolerance of such payments by local authorities, or the alleged necessity of the payment in order to obtain or retain business or other improper advantage.'

	Item	Article 1	Section 6	Remarks
12	Definition of public international organisation.	None[86]	6(6) 'Public international organisation' means an organisation whose members are any of the following—	
			(a) countries or territories,	
			(b) governments of countries or territories,	
			(c) other public international organisations,	
			(d) a mixture of any of the above.	

---

[86] Though see Commentaries, para 17: '"Public international organisation" includes any international organisation formed by states, governments, or other public international organisations whatever the form of organisation and scope of competence, including, for example, a regional economic integration organisation such as the European Communities.'

Chapter 8

FAILURE OF COMMERCIAL ORGANISATIONS TO PREVENT BRIBERY

BRIBERY ACT 2010: SECTION 7

'7 **Failure of commercial organisations to prevent bribery**

(1) A relevant commercial organisation ("C") is guilty of an offence under this section if a person ("A") associated with C bribes another person intending—

(a) to obtain or retain business for C, or
(b) to obtain or retain an advantage in the conduct of business for C.

(2) But it is a defence for C to prove that C had in place adequate procedures designed to prevent persons associated with C from undertaking such conduct.

(3) For the purposes of this section, A bribes another person if, and only if, A—

(a) is, or would be, guilty of an offence under section 1 or 6 (whether or not A has been prosecuted for such an offence), or
(b) would be guilty of such an offence if section 12(2)(c) and (4) were omitted.

(4) See section 8 for the meaning of a person associated with C and see section 9 for a duty on the Secretary of State to publish guidance.

(5) In this section—

"partnership" means—

(a) a partnership within the Partnership Act 1890, or
(b) a limited partnership registered under the Limited Partnerships Act 1907,

or a firm or entity of a similar character formed under the law of a country or territory outside the United Kingdom,

"relevant commercial organisation" means—

(a) a body which is incorporated under the law of any part of the United Kingdom and which carries on a business (whether there or elsewhere),
(b) any other body corporate (wherever incorporated) which carries on a business, or part of a business, in any part of the United Kingdom,
(c) a partnership which is formed under the law of any part of the United Kingdom and which carries on a business (whether there or elsewhere), or

(d) any other partnership (wherever formed) which carries on a business, or part of a business, in any part of the United Kingdom,

and, for the purposes of this section, a trade or profession is a business.'

BRIBERY ACT 2010: SECTION 8

'8 Meaning of associated person

(1) For the purposes of section 7, a person ("A") is associated with C if (disregarding any bribe under consideration) A is a person who performs services for or on behalf of C.

(2) The capacity in which A performs services for or on behalf of C does not matter.

(3) Accordingly A may (for example) be C's employee, agent or subsidiary.

(4) Whether or not A is a person who performs services for or on behalf of C is to be determined by reference to all the relevant circumstances and not merely by reference to the nature of the relationship between A and C.

(5) But if A is an employee of C, it is to be presumed unless the contrary is shown that A is a person who performs services for or on behalf of C.'

INTRODUCTION

8.1 The offence of failure of a commercial organisation to prevent bribery is the most controversial element of the Bribery Act. Its effect is that businesses have a much higher risk of prosecution than under the previous law. Section 7 provides for the liability of a relevant commercial organisation (abbreviated to 'C') for active bribery by those essentially acting on its behalf ('A'), as defined in s 8. C's knowledge or participation in the bribery committed by A is irrelevant. However, C has an important potential defence under s 7(2) – the defence of 'adequate procedures'.

8.2 This chapter considers both the s 7 offence and the important definition of 'associated person' contained in s 8. The finer detail of what might amount to adequate procedures and recent government guidance on that subject are dealt with in Chapter 9.

LIABILITY OF CORPORATE BODIES

Corporate criminal liability and mens rea

8.3 In general, the common law assumes that all offences involve a mental element unless, in the case of offences created by statute, there is a clearly expressed intention to the contrary by the legislature.[1] Strict liability offences are, therefore, quite rare.

8.4 However, a body corporate such as a company does not have a mind of its own.[2] It only has the (borrowed, or rented) minds of its officers or employees. So it might be possible to argue that a corporate body cannot be guilty of a crime involving a mental element (mens rea). English law has attempted to solve this problem by what is known as 'the identification principle'. The identification principle is that if a corporate body, such as a company, commits the conduct element of a crime requiring mens rea, and there is an individual who can be identified as the 'directing mind' of the company who has the relevant mental element, then the company is criminally liable.[3]

8.5 Corporate liability for corruption offences under the previous law was the subject of *R v Andrews Weatherfoil Ltd*.[4] In that case the managing director and two other executives of a company were alleged to have made payments to an official of a local authority so as to influence him in favour of their firm. The conviction of the company at first instance was overturned by the Court of Appeal because the judge had not adequately directed the jury on whether the executives acted 'as the company' (ie satisfied the identification doctrine), and not merely as the company's servants or agents.

8.6 The directing mind need not necessarily be a person at the top of the company, such as a CEO or even a director. There have been several cases in which the doctrine has been distinguished on the basis that a particular statute allows a wider identification of employees or managers with the company.[5] However it is not possible to aggregate the mental states of several people in the organisation.[6]

8.7 Although the state of the law is not fully settled, we can say that the identification doctrine survives and generally makes it difficult to establish the liability of companies and other corporate bodies for crimes requiring mens rea, such as the s 1, s 2 or s 6 offences under the Bribery Act.

---

[1] *Gammon (Hong Kong) Ltd v Attorney General of Hong Kong* [1985] AC 1 (PC).
[2] Famously, a corporation has 'no soul to be damned and no body to be kicked' Baron Thurlow, LC *Oxford Dictionary of Quotations* (7th edn, 2009), ch 18.
[3] *Tesco Supermarkets Ltd v Nattrass* [1972] AC 153.
[4] (1972) 56 Cr App Rep 31.
[5] *Director General of Fair Trading v Pioneer Concrete (UK) Ltd* [1995] 1 AC 456; *Meridian Global Funds Management Asia Ltd v Securities Commission* [1995] 2 AC 500, PC.
[6] *R v P&O European Ferries Ltd* [1990] 93 Cr App Rep 72.

8.8 There are plans for a statutory reform of the law of corporate criminal liability although, so far, these have been unfruitful.[7] The identification doctrine is sometimes criticised on the ground that breaches of the criminal law by a company can often happen without the direct knowledge of people in senior positions, with the result that criminal conduct goes unpenalised. In the absence of more general reform, legislation has created exceptions to the identification doctrine in specific areas of activity.[8] There are also hybrid offences where strict liability is qualified by a particular defence, usually that the company has exercised reasonable care or due diligence.[9]

8.9 Article 2 of the OECD Convention provides that '[e]ach Party shall take such measures as may be necessary, in accordance with its legal principles, to establish the liability of legal persons for the bribery of a foreign public official'. There seems to be little doubt that, whatever criticisms could be made of the identification principle, s 7 satisfies this requirement.

Corporate liability under section 7

8.10 The Law Commission felt that the limitations on corporate criminal liability were hindering the objective of getting businesses to take positive steps against bribery. The introduction of ss 7 and 8 are an explicit circumvention of the existing law and create a specific regime in relation to bribery offences. Under ss 7 and 8 the offence can be committed without a company or one of its officers or a putative 'directing mind' having any knowledge, belief, intention or any mental state at all about the events in question. It is not even necessary for C or some senior officer of C to be negligent in relation to such events.[10]

8.11 For C to commit the s 7 offence merely requires the commission of offences under s 1 or s 6 of the Bribery Act by a 'person associated with' C, who intends to retain or obtain business or a business advantage for C.[11] Of course, for the associated person to commit a s 1 or s 6 offence the specific mens rea for each of these offences must also be proven.[12] But none of these stipulations extend to C under s 7. C need not request or know about or approve of the bribery. This is a good example of a strict liability offence.[13]

---

[7] See in general Pinto & Evans, *Corporate Criminal Liability* (London, 2008), ch 4.
[8] For example see Companies Act 2006, Corporate Manslaughter and Corporate Homicide Act 2007.
[9] *R v British Steel Plc* [1995] ICR 586, CA, which concerned the Health and Safety at Work Act 1974. In that case it was not a defence that senior management had taken reasonable care to avoid a breach, the staff in charge of a specific operation should also have done so.
[10] As had previously been suggested by the Law Commission in LC 313, Part 6.
[11] Although C retains the possibility of a defence of adequate procedures under s 7(2), as to which see below.
[12] Although one must assume that where A is a body corporate it is necessary to prove that A is liable for the actions of its servants or agents under the law applicable to A. If that law is English law then the identification doctrine seems to return via a side door.
[13] This was acknowledged by ministers in parliamentary debate – *Hansard*, HL, col GC 23 (7 October 2010) and HL, col 142 (2 February 2010). Subsequently, the government and prosecuting agencies have seemed uncomfortable with the idea that s 7 involves strict liability.

8.12 The s 7 offence can also be seen as instituting a form of vicarious liability, because C is liable as a result of the actions of the associated person, although C does not commit the same offence as the associated person (hereafter 'A').[14] Again, C's state of mind as to the actions of A is irrelevant. Other legal systems have utilised concepts of vicarious liability instead of the identification doctrine to attribute criminal responsibility to corporate bodies. The concept is one of the foundation stones of the application of the US Foreign Corrupt Practices Act (FCPA) to corporations.[15] Where companies can be liable for the actions of their agents (acting in the course of the agency), with no requirement of a mental element, it is very much in their interests to attempt to control the actions of those agents and this is an important policy objective underlying s 7.[16]

Status of section 7 offence

8.13 Note that, unlike the other offences under ss 1, 2 and 6, which are triable either summarily or on indictment, an offence under s 7 is triable only on indictment, that is only in a Crown Court before a jury.[17] In consequence, the penalty of a fine is unlimited in amount.

8.14 However, Parliament has not designated a s 7 offence as a 'serious crime' for the purposes of Part 1 of the Serious Crime Act 2007. This has the consequence that serious crime prevention orders, which are available to the courts for those committing offences under ss 1, 2 or 6 of the Bribery Act, are not available for commercial organisations guilty under s 7.[18] Moreover, the view of the present government seems to be that a s 7 conviction is not the same as a conviction for active corruption, at least for the purposes of UK procurement law.[19]

They point to the existence of a possible defence – adequate procedures (s 7(2)). But whether that defence is available is a matter of fact in each case and has nothing to do with mens rea in the commission of the offence itself.

[14] There has also been some resistance to the view that s 7 also involves vicarious liability – the Joint Prosecution Guidance asserts (without argument) that it does not (p 11). Such points of legal semantics are irrelevant to most business people – the essential point is that C can be liable for the crimes of third parties without any mental element in relation to the crime committed.

[15] In the US, the concept is known by the Latin tag 'respondeat superior'.

[16] See, for example, the speech of the then Secretary of State for Justice, Jack Straw to the 5th European Forum on Anti-Corruption (June 2009): 'A strong legal architecture is necessary in tackling corruption but in and of itself it is not sufficient. Ultimately our aim must be to bring about behavioural change within businesses themselves, creating corporate cultures in which no form of corruption is tolerated.'

[17] Section 11(3).

[18] Bribery Act, Sch 1, para 14.

[19] Hansard Written Ministerial Statements, 30 March 2011. See Chapter 10 for a discussion of the Bribery Act in the context of procurement law.

Expanded jurisdiction

8.15 In distinction to the usual rules of criminal jurisdiction, there is no need for the events forming part of the s 7 offence to occur within the UK.[20] Neither does A need to have a 'close connection to the United Kingdom', as is required for those accused of other offences under the Act.[21] However, as discussed in more detail below, C (the commercial organisation) must be involved in business and constituted in or carry on business or part of a business in the UK.[22] The inclusion of non-UK-domiciled enterprises which carry on business or part of a business in the UK expands the category of those subject to the Act far beyond the traditional geographical boundaries of UK law. It is likely to capture foreign-headquartered organisations with a relatively small presence in the UK, such as a sales or representative office.

Corporate liability for other Bribery Act offences

8.16 It is worth bearing in mind that the identification doctrine for corporate criminal liability has not been abolished for bribery offences. Section 7 creates a specific exception to it, but companies can still be guilty of offences under ss 1 and 2 (providing or receiving bribes) or s 6 (bribery of foreign public officials), or of secondary or inchoate offences (conspiracy, attempt, etc) through someone who is the company's directing mind. Companies have recently been charged and convicted of corruption offences under the old law, without the need for a strict liability offence.[23]

8.17 It may well be that cases under the Bribery Act involving commercial organisations involve several charges under different sections of the Act, as well as against individuals involved. The 'adequate procedures' defence in s 7(2), which is discussed below, will not apply to any charges outside s 7. So it will be possible for a UK company to be convicted of offences under s 1, s 2 or s 6, once the identification doctrine is satisfied, even though it has a defence of adequate procedures to any charge under s 7.

Key issues

8.18 The principal questions which arise when considering whether an offence under s 7 has been committed are:

(1) whether the organisation in question is a 'relevant commercial organisation', ie 'C'. This involves examination of the definition of a relevant commercial organisation in s 7(5);

---

[20] Section 12(5).
[21] Section 7(3)(b).
[22] Section 7(5).
[23] *R v Mabey & Johnson Ltd* (unreported) 29 September 2009, Southwark Crown Court; *R v Innospec Ltd* [2010] EW Misc 7 (EWCC).

(2) whether there exists a person associated with C, namely 'A'. This is determined by examining the definition of 'associated person' set out in s 8;

(3) whether A has bribed another person, intending to obtain or retain business or an advantage in the conduct of business for C within the meaning of s 7(1) and (3). This involves considering either or both ss 1 and 6 of the Bribery Act, and the mental state of A at the time he committed those offences;

(4) whether, even if elements (1) to (3) above are established, C can establish a defence that it had in place 'adequate procedures' to prevent bribery by persons associated with C, on C's behalf, under s 7(2).

8.19 To establish liability the prosecution must establish each of elements (1) to (3) above. The burden of proof of (4) (adequate procedures) is on C, not on the prosecution, although it is clearly a matter which prosecutors will take into account prior to a charging decision. Each of these elements will be examined in more detail below. The detail of what might constitute 'adequate procedures' is discussed separately in Chapter 9.

'C': a relevant commercial organisation

8.20 A s 7 offence can only be committed by a relevant commercial organisation ('C'). The offence is not applicable to individuals. For the purposes of s 7, a relevant commercial organisation is defined by s 7(5). Such an organisation is either:

(a) incorporated anywhere in the UK and carries on a business there or elsewhere; or

(b) incorporated anywhere else in the world and carries on a business, or part of a business, in the UK; or

(c) a partnership which:

  (i) is formed under the law of any part of the UK; and
  (ii) carries on a business anywhere in the UK or elsewhere; or

(d) a partnership formed anywhere else in the world which carries on a business or a part of a business in the UK.

The tests set out in items (a) to (d) must be satisfied at the time the conduct element of the offence takes place.

8.21 The question of whether any particular defendant is a relevant commercial organisation seems to be a mixed question of fact and law. Certain elements are likely to be dealt with as purely legal questions, for example whether C is incorporated and where. Others are more likely to be left to a jury as factual questions, for example whether C carries on a business or a part of a business in the UK.

8.22 It seems clear from s 7(5) that a relevant commercial organisation has to have a recognised corporate or partnership form. A sole trader, although he may have a large and profitable business in his own name, or in a trading name, is not a relevant commercial organisation because the business is not incorporated and the trader is not in partnership. The same seems to apply to any trusts which are neither incorporated or carried on in partnership, and to unincorporated associations. Whether these will prove significant gaps in the law remains to be seen. Individual traders, and trustees, remain subject to ss 1–6 of the Act.

UK corporations and partnerships

8.23 Category (a) (body incorporated in the UK and carrying on business) should not cause many difficulties. Records such as those of Companies House and the relevant legislation should normally suffice to establish whether a company or other body is incorporated in the UK. It does not matter whether the company is public or private, limited by shares or guarantee. It also does not matter whether the company carries on business in the UK – the only requirement is that it carries out some business, whether in the UK or elsewhere.

8.24 What 'carrying on a business' might mean is discussed below in the context of non-UK enterprises. In the case of UK companies or partnerships this should not be difficult to prove by reference to statutory filings and is most unlikely to be controversial in individual cases.

8.25 Category (c) (partnership formed under UK law and carrying on a business) also seems straightforward. The established definition of partnership is contained in s 1 of the Partnership Act 1890 and this is expressly applied by s 7(5)(a) of the Act. So a partnership is 'the relation which subsists between persons carrying on a business in common with a view of profit'.[24] Many partnerships advertise themselves as such, or, even if they do not, it should not be difficult to establish their nature as partnerships (for example by investigating their records and accounts).

8.26 Section 15 of the Act provides that proceedings for an offence under s 7 alleged to have been committed by a partnership must be brought in the name of the partnership (and not in that of any of the partners). Any fines must be paid from partnership assets,[25] rather than by individual partners.

---

[24] Partnership Act 1890, s 1(1).
[25] Section 15(1) and (3).

8.27 A 'limited partnership' is a particular species of partnership in which there are general partners who possess the standard rights and liabilities of normal partners and 'limited partners' who contribute capital but whose rights and liabilities are curtailed. It is a structure often used by private equity firms. The relevant definition is at s 4 of the Limited Partnerships Act 1907. Limited partnerships are registered at Companies House.

Non-UK corporations and partnerships

8.28 More difficulties may attend to category (b): 'any other body corporate (wherever incorporated) which carries on a business, or part of a business, in any part of the United Kingdom', and category (d) which applies the same test to partnerships formed outside the UK.

8.29 It should be relatively straightforward to establish whether and if so where a particular organisation is incorporated since virtually all territories allowing for the incorporation of companies have company registers and the like. However, whether or not an organisation 'carries on a business' or 'part of a business' in the UK may not be as clear.

Carrying on a business

8.30 As well as taking the necessary legal form, to qualify as a relevant commercial organisation the entity in question must carry on a business. The term 'carries on a business' is not defined in the Act or the explanatory notes. The Act makes clear that 'business' includes a trade or profession,[26] which will not come as a surprise.[27]

8.31 The words 'carry on a business' or variants thereon appear elsewhere in English law. Interpretations of this term in other contexts may provide at least some guidance relevant to the Bribery Act, although ultimately it is a matter of applying the words of the statute to the particular facts, and previous authorities relating to other statutes will not be determinative.[28]

8.32 In the context of the Financial Services Act 1986 (now replaced by the Financial Services and Markets Act 2000) it has been held that the term 'business' should not be given a technical construction, but rather one which

---

[26] Section 7(5).
[27] Although this formulation, 'a trade or profession is a business', may admit some ambiguity. It might be read as suggesting that commercial activities which might not be deemed trades or professions are not 'a business' for the purposes of s 7. Contrast the clearer words of s 3(7): 'In this section "business" includes trade or profession'. The same issue arises in relation to s 6(8). It seems unlikely that Parliament intended to have the rather nebulous concepts such as the nature of trades or professions govern the application of such important parts of the Act as ss 6 and 7, and it is notable that the Act does not say 'business means (ie is defined as) trade or profession'. Nevertheless, ideally, the language in question would be clearer.
[28] For example, see the discussions of how 'carrying on business' might be defined in the context of the Moneylenders Act 1900 in *Kirkwood v Gadd* [1910] AC 422; *Conroy v Kenny* [1999] 1 WLR 1340.

conforms to what would in ordinary language be described as a business transaction as opposed to something personal or casual.[29]

8.33 The term 'carries on' implies a degree of repetition or continuity. A company which only has highly infrequent dealings with anyone in the UK might not qualify as carrying on business there. A company executive who met a colleague in a London hotel 5 years before an alleged bribe would not thereby cause his company to have been carrying on a business or part of a business in the UK if no other activity of the company touched the jurisdiction. However, the issue will be different in each case. Relatively infrequent transactions or dealings in the UK may suffice as proof that a business was being carried on, especially if the dealings in question were of importance to the entity in question.

8.34 In most cases, a jury is likely to be capable of determining what activities amount to carrying on a business rather than doing something personal or casual. It is not merely a question of whether there is business involved in what people are doing. Case-law (admittedly derived from interpretation in different legal contexts) argues for treating the word 'business' as meaning an active occupation or profession continually carried on and where there is some degree of management and control.[30] The relative frequency of a specific activity may be a clue to whether it is carried on as a business.[31]

8.35 The seeking of profit is also an important indicator, but may not be the sole criterion, since people may seek profits in transactions which are not part of their business. Frequency of trading is also important, but this may not be the sole criterion either, since certain businesses may trade quite infrequently.

8.36 It seems more likely than not that charitable or academic organisations which engage in commercial activities (such as running shops or selling services) will be carrying on a business.

Part of a business

8.37 The formulation which applies to overseas-based commercial organisations in s 7(5)(b) and (d) of the Bribery Act is 'carries on a business, or part of a business' in the UK. The 'part of a business' element only applies to companies or partnerships incorporated or formed outside the UK.

8.38 There are no qualifying words so we must assume that 'part' means any part, not necessarily a substantial part or a specific part, such as sales or

---

[29] *Morgan Grenfell & Co v Welwyn Hatfield DC* [1995] 1 All ER 1.
[30] *Brown v London and North Western Rly Co* (1863) 32 LJQB 318, Ct of QB; *Cain v Butler* [1916] 1 KB 739 at 762; *Newman v Oughton* [1911] 1 KB 792; *Transport and General Credit Corpn Ltd v Morgan* [1939] Ch 531, [1939] 2 All ER 17; *Re Brauch (a debtor), ex p Britannic Securities and Investments Ltd* [1978] Ch 316, [1978] 1 All ER 1004, CA; *Re Sarflax Ltd* [1979] Ch 592, [1979] 1 All ER 529.
[31] *IRC v Marine Steam Turbine Co Ltd* [1920] 1 KB 193.

management. It may well include activities regarded as ancillary to the central business activities of a particular enterprise. The intention of Parliament seems to have been that a foreign commercial organisation with business operations of any kind in the UK would be subject to the Act.[32]

8.39 So, for example, a company communicating with clients, maintaining a bank account or accommodation address with reasonable regularity is likely to be carrying on business or part of a business in the UK.[33]

8.40 A straightforward case of a company or partnership which is incorporated in and managed from, say, Belgium and sells products in Scotland, is clearly within the definition. The making of sales, even if they only represent a small element of turnover, is the carrying on of part of a business in the UK.

8.41 Similarly, a foreign company or partnership operating in Dubai, but conducting regular board meetings in London, is carrying on part of its business in the UK. It could hardly be argued that the management of the business by the board is not part of the business.

8.42 A foreign company or partnership which has a representative office of its own in the UK but no sales or management operations may well be carrying out some part of a business in the UK, although it may be necessary to establish the function of the representative office and whether it was active at the material time (ie the time at which the actus reus of the offence occurred).[34] Often the representative office will be for the purpose of marketing, and, again, it will be hard to argue that this activity is not part of the business of a commercial organisation.

8.43 What about a foreign company which has no management, sales, marketing or representative activity in the UK, but which purchases goods or services there? Because of the width of the term 'part of a business', the answer is not obvious. Purchasing is as much 'part of' a business as sales. If the organisation regularly interacts with others in the UK to negotiate purchases or for other reasons connected to its business then it may well fall within a wide interpretation of the definition. Occasional purchases from UK suppliers may not qualify because they lack the required element of continuity.

---

[32] This seems to be the interpretation of the Director of the Serious Fraud Office – see 'Bribery Act: SFO chief Richard Alderman sees UK courts as a stumbling block', *Daily Telegraph*, 20 January 2011.
[33] *FSA v Fradley & Woodward* [2005] EWCA Civ 1183 (re Financial Services and Markets Act 2000, s 418). In the limited context of the FSMA 2000 and whether regulated activities are being carried out in the UK generally see FSA Handbook, PERG 2.4 'Link between activities and the United Kingdom'.
[34] The mere fact that a company had a postal address or a premises in the UK might not by itself suffice to establish that it was carrying out a business or part of a business there. But it is rare that corporations rent offices or utilise services for non-business reasons and any activity at or involving such a UK premises is likely to be evidence of the carrying on of part of a business there.

Stock exchange listing

8.44 Most foreign companies which are listed on a UK stock exchange are likely to be within the definition even if they do not conduct any sales activity within the UK. Such a company is not the same as a business which occasionally purchases stock or services from UK-based suppliers. It is likely to have ongoing relationships with UK entities to which it is responsible and the maintenance of a UK listing will usually be an important goal of the business, a part of its identity and attractiveness to investors, lenders, employees and counterparties. A UK listing is often sought after by companies from jurisdictions with less developed capital markets both as a means of increasing liquidity of its securities and gaining commercial respectability.[35]

8.45 Raising capital, dealing with shareholders and advisers (such as auditors, sponsors, nominated advisers or lawyers) or complying with the various ongoing obligations upon listed companies are all likely to be part of the business of such a company and to occur on a regular basis.[36] The same analysis should apply to a foreign company which issues other forms of security on UK markets, for example corporate bonds or other instruments.

8.46 It is therefore rather surprising to see the following passage in the MOJ Guidance issued under s 9 of the Act (adequate procedures):

> 'However the Government anticipates that applying a common sense approach would mean that organisations that do not have a demonstrable business presence in the United Kingdom would not be caught. The Government would not expect, for example, the mere fact that a company's securities have been admitted to the UK Listing Authority's Official List and therefore admitted to trading on the London Stock Exchange, in itself, to qualify that company as carrying on a business or part of a business in the UK and therefore falling within the definition of a "relevant commercial organisation" for the purposes of section 7.'[37]

8.47 These comments are not supported by any further analysis. Of course it may be that a mere listing does not engage s 7(5) if the courts were to adopt a restrictive reading of that section and were to hold, for example, that the words 'which carries on a business or part of a business in the United Kingdom' actually mean 'which has a demonstrable business presence in the United Kingdom'. It is just possible that the words 'carrying on a business or part of a business' were intended to mean, in essence, engaging in the main focus of the business, ie in many cases, making sales or trading. However, it would not be prudent for a listed company to assume that this is the best interpretation of s 7(5)(b) or (d), at least until the matter is the subject of binding authority through decided case-law.

---

[35] The same may not be true of a company whose securities are merely traded on an organised market in the UK, since it is possible to trade unlisted securities without the involvement of the company in question.

[36] See, for example, the continuing obligations on listed companies provided by the UK Listing Rules – http://fsahandbook.info/FSA/html/handbook/LR.

[37] MOJ Guidance, p 15, para 36.

8.48 More surprising is the impression given by this passage that the government (which of course is not the same as that which sponsored the Bribery Bill through Parliament) wishes to encourage the view that some foreign companies with a UK listing (but not UK-based companies) should not be subject to s 7 of the Act. Of course, constitutionally, the government's opinion on how the Act should be interpreted is irrelevant. However, it is unusual for members of the government to point out potential loopholes in legislation in this way. It is not quite clear whether it is government policy to encourage foreign-based but UK listed companies to seek to escape the provisions of the Act. If so, this should be made express.

UK subsidiary of foreign company

8.49 It is not immediately obvious whether the intention of Parliament was to hold parent companies of large international groups liable for bribery when the connection with the UK is only the existence of a UK subsidiary which has no connection with the alleged bribery. The better answer seems to be that it was not, but this is a relatively complex issue which may be better explained via a hypothetical example.

8.50 Let us imagine Robin Industries, a conglomerate based in India. It acquires a controlling interest in Peckham Vans, based in England. Peckham is de-listed from the London Stock Exchange after the acquisition, but remains a separate company with a separate board. Peckham's board of seven directors contains three executives of Robin, and the chief executive of Peckham reports directly to the CEO of Robin in Delhi. Peckham's financial statements are consolidated with those of Robin.

8.51 Two years after the acquisition, Derek, an executive of Peckham, offers a cash bribe to an official of an Indian state to persuade him to cause the state to buy Peckham's commercial vehicles. Derek claims Robin executives were aware of the deal and encouraged it. However no payment is made as the Indian authorities arrest the official shortly after his discussion with Derek. Peckham adopted detailed anti-bribery procedures before it was taken over. Robin has only very limited procedures at group level.

8.52 Let us assume that on these facts Derek is guilty of offences under s 6 and s 1 of the Act.[38] Peckham may be guilty under s 7 since Derek is clearly within the definition of someone associated with Peckham, as an employee.[39] However, depending on the nature of its procedures, Peckham may have an 'adequate procedures' defence under s 7(2).[40]

---

[38] Or potentially under s 14, if one of the companies in question is guilty under ss 1 or 6.
[39] See s 8, and below.
[40] Various other charging possibilities exist – for example, if Derek passes the 'directing mind' test then Peckham may be guilty of offences under ss 1 and 6. Anyone assisting Derek or agreeing with him to facilitate the offence may be liable as accessories or for inchoate offences such as conspiracy – see Chapter 12.

8.53 What of Robin – does it carry on a business in the UK via its subsidiary, Peckham? Peckham is a wholly-owned subsidiary of Robin, whose revenues and losses are directly relevant to Robin's own finances. Peckham's financial results are consolidated with those of Robin. The shares of Peckham are not merely an arm's length investment. It is plain that Peckham is controlled by Robin. One could fairly argue that in reality Peckham is merely a division of Robin and/or a part of the Robin group of businesses, so that the activities of Peckham are, ultimately, the activities of Robin.

The corporate veil

8.54 The UK law in relation to companies is that even a wholly-owned company is not the same person as its owner, and the liabilities of a subsidiary are not those of the parent. This principle, established since the late-nineteenth century, is known as the 'corporate veil'.[41]

8.55 In most cases it is very difficult to attribute the actions or assets of one company to another, or to those owning the company (ie pierce the corporate veil). There is one well-established exception, which is that if the corporate structure is a facade or a sham concealing the true facts then the veil may be pierced.[42] This is a rather vaguely defined test. It seems clear that companies created for the purpose of furthering criminality may not benefit from the corporate veil. But a corporate structure designed to avoid the risk of a liability accruing to the parent company continues to possess the corporate veil if the companies in question are legitimately constituted.[43] The fact that all companies in a group constitute a single economic unit does not change the way the principle is applied.[44]

8.56 Subsidiary or parent companies may act as agents for each other, thus fixing one or the other with liability. We will discuss the role of agency and 'performing services for or on behalf of' a commercial organisation below. However, on the bare facts outlined in our example, the fact that Robin owns Peckham would not, as a matter of existing law, be proof that Robin itself carries out business in the UK, unless there are other connecting factors.

8.57 Of course the Act must be interpreted on its own terms. If there were express words providing that a foreign company with a UK subsidiary is deemed to carry on a business or part of a business in the UK then the existing corporate law could not change that position. However, there are no such words in the Act. Indeed, as we shall see below, it seems clear that the Act does not change the existing law on the subject of the criminal liability of UK companies for the actions of their subsidiaries. It would be very surprising if

---

[41] *Salomon v Salomon* [1897] AC 22.
[42] *Adams v Cape Industries Plc* [1990] Ch 433. There is no comprehensive definition of what constitutes a 'mere facade', but a dishonest motive for setting up the company in question will be a relevant factor – *Kensington International Ltd v Republic of the Congo* [2006] 2 BCLC 296.
[43] *Adams v Cape Industries Plc* [1990] Ch 433 at 538.
[44] Ibid, at 536.

the Act maintained the corporate veil principle for UK companies which have foreign subsidiaries, but abolished it for foreign companies with UK subsidiaries.

8.58 The conclusion is that Robin, as a company, does not carry on business or part of a business in the UK just because it owns Peckham or, indeed, just because some of its directors are on the board of Peckham.[45] It may still be open to a prosecutor to argue that Robin is subject to the Act if it carries out any business activity in the UK independently of Peckham or that, while in the UK, the dual directors are in fact spending some of their time conducting the business of Robin. We will consider the application of the Act to overseas subsidiaries of UK companies in more detail below.

Must the UK subsidiary have a hand in the bribery?

8.59 There may be some confusion as to whether the involvement of the UK-subsidiary in the bribery is relevant to the test of whether a foreign parent carries on a business or part of a business in the UK. In parliamentary debate the government minister, Lord Tunnicliffe, said:

> 'With regard to foreign companies operating in the UK, I recognise that the Joint Committee voiced some concerns that the phrase "part of a business" might be difficult for the courts to interpret, but we believe the courts will interpret the term in a common-sense manner. Clearly, if a foreign corporation has part of its business in the UK, and that part is guilty of paying bribes, we would want the jurisdiction to prosecute the organisation concerned.'[46]

8.60 The emphasis here seems to be on whether the UK part of the business is itself involved in the bribery. However, the words of the Act go wider than this. The organisation is liable not only if the UK part of it pays bribes, but also if an associated person pays bribes within the terms of s 7(1) and if any part of its business as a whole is carried on in the UK. The Act does not provide that the UK part has to be involved before the organisation as a whole can be a relevant commercial organisation.

8.61 So, to change our example, if Derek's part of the Peckham business had been sold directly to Robin, so that he was a Robin employee when he offered the bribe, and his office remained in the UK, then Robin would be subject to s 7 because part of its business would be carried on in the UK.

8.62 Moreover, if the bribery were committed by Robin intending to provide a business advantage to Peckham (ie the parent acting so as to benefit the

---

[45] In legal theory, when acting as directors of Peckham they must act only in the interests of Peckham the company and in doing so must be independent of Robin, although it might be open to the prosecution to seek to prove a lack of independence by the directors in fact.
[46] *Hansard*, HL, col GC 61 (7 January 2010).

subsidiary) it is quite possible for Peckham to be liable, once it can be shown that Robin was performing services for Peckham or on its behalf – ie was an 'associated person'.

'A': A PERSON ASSOCIATED WITH C (SECTION 8)

What is an associated person?

8.63 Section 7(1) defines A as being 'a person ('A') associated with C'. The definition of associated person is in s 8, set out above, and comes down to whether, as a matter of fact, A performs services for or on behalf of C.

Performing services for or on behalf of C

8.64 The language of s 8 needs to be read carefully. Section 8(1) does not speak of 'providing' services 'to' C, but of *performing* services *for or on behalf of* C. The terms 'for' and 'on behalf of' usually import the concept of agency, especially when found together.[47]

8.65 The Law Commission's discussion of the point proceeds on the assumption that it will only be those representing a commercial organisation which can fix it with liability[48] and parliamentary debate seems to have proceeded on that same assumption.[49]

8.66 As discussed below, there is an additional mental element required for C to be liable for bribery conducted by A. As well as intending the predicate offences of bribery under ss 1 or 6 of the Act, A must intend by the bribery to obtain or retain business or an advantage in the conduct of business *for* C. Someone who performs services for or on behalf of C, and has either a general or specific purpose of benefiting C in transactions with third parties[50] seems as close to a traditional legal definition of an agent as makes no difference.[51]

---

[47] The *Shorter Oxford English Dictionary* (SOED) has: 'For ... Representing, as a representative of'; and 'on behalf of: ... as the agent or representative of (another)'. See also Greenberg, *Stroud's Judicial Dictionary of Words and Phrases* (7th edn, London, 2006), pp 1019, 1856 and the authorities cited therein.

[48] LC 313, Part 6 *passim*.

[49] See in particular *Hansard*, HL, col GC 59 (7 January 2010) per Lord Tunnicliffe: 'A person may be performing services for an organisation for the purposes of Clause 7 even though there is no formal relationship between them. This may be the case, for example, where the person is representing a number of organisations in a joint venture and has a formal relationship with the lead organisation but not with the commercial organisation charged with the Clause 7 offence. We believe that the words that the amendment seeks to remove are necessary and desirable as they signal to the courts, and indeed to organisations which the offence is intended to cover, that an organisation may be liable in circumstances where there is no formal relationship between A and C.'

[50] Leaving aside the interesting theoretical question of whether the payment of a bribe in connection with C's business should be analysed as actually constituting a benefit to C. For these purposes, it should be treated as such.

[51] See the definition at *Bowstead and Reynolds on Agency* (19th edn) 1-001. That definition

8.67 However, in s 8(3) an 'agent' is included as an example of a person who could satisfy the definition of associated person, rather than as the definition of such a person. It may be that the term 'agent' is used in s 8(3) in a non-technical sense to denote an independent third party acting for a commercial organisation but outside of any subsidiary or employment relationship with it. It seems quite clear that the intention of Parliament was not to focus on the formality of legal categories.[52]

8.68 This is made clear by the language of s 8(2) which states that the capacity in which A provides services on behalf of C does not matter. It does not matter whether A is a director, employee, subsidiary, agent or in another type of relationship with C, which might not involve a formal contract or official position. For example, if a civil servant who regularly promotes UK companies abroad develops an understanding with C that, if C wins certain key contracts as a result of the civil servant's lobbying, the civil servant will be offered a directorship, then he may well be associated with C for the purposes of the Act, despite the fact that there is no binding agreement between them.

What does section 8(4) add?

8.69 Section 8(4) provides that the test is to be determined by 'all the relevant circumstances' and 'not merely by reference to the nature of the relationship between A and C'. It does not seem to add very much to s 8(2) and (3) to stipulate that 'all the relevant circumstances' must be considered.

8.70 More confusing is the suggestion that there is a meaningful distinction between the question of whether A performs services for or on behalf of C and 'the nature of the relationship' between A and C. The question whether A performs services for C is surely a question about whether they have a relationship (if there were no relationship the issue would not arise) and whether that relationship involves specific elements (ie A performing services for or on behalf of C). It is a question precisely about the nature of the C/A relationship.

8.71 However, it may be unfair to parse this subsection too closely. The overall context suggests that the subsection was intended to emphasise that the test is substantive and not formal and, perhaps, as a further gloss on s 8(2) and (3). Section 8(4) seems to indicate, for example, that C's liability under s 7(1) cannot be excluded merely by a contract which appears to exclude A from being an associated person, although in reality that is A's position. The Explanatory Notes state that the section 'also ensures that section 7 relates to the actual activities being undertaken by A at the time rather than A's general position'.[53]

---

encompasses both a person with actual or apparent authority to bind the principal and a broker or introduction-only agent, and both these categories are clearly within the definition of A under s 8(1) of the Bribery Act.
[52] See, for example, the passage quoted above.
[53] Explanatory Notes, p 8.

8.72 The position of the government during parliamentary debate was that the degree of control which C might have over A can be a circumstance relevant to whether A is an associated person.[54] This must be right, although it may not be the only such circumstance.[55] Of course, control can come in different forms. It is clear from s 8(3) that A could be both within C's corporate structure (such as an employee or subsidiary) or an outsider (such as an external agent). A third party which is bound to C by a contract which involves acting as C's agent is likely to be sufficiently under C's control for the purposes of the Act, even though it is legally independent of C.

8.73 The best construction of the section as a whole seems to be that the question of whether A is associated with C is a question of fact in each case. It is essentially to do with whether, in fact, the person or entity in question was already in a relationship with C which involved it representing C's interests, at the time of the bribery in question. This is clearly a substantive test rather than a formal one, but should be easily explicable to a jury.

Categories of associated person

8.74 The following paragraphs discuss various types of relationships that commercial organisations may have, and whether they are likely to amount to 'associated persons'.

A 'bribery only' relationship?

8.75 It is clear from s 8(1) that the associated person test cannot be fulfilled merely by the act of bribery itself. If someone with no previous association with C decides to pay a bribe in the hope of assisting C's business then C cannot be liable for this. The C and A relationship must pre-exist the actual bribery if the test is to be fulfilled.

8.76 But what if C hired A for the sole purpose of using A to pay the bribe, with no pre-existing relationship? Potentially, this is a lacuna in the Act. However, if A is engaged by C for the purpose of providing bribes then an employee, director or other representative of C is likely to have been responsible for the engagement. Such an employee is himself likely to be within the definition of a person performing services for or on behalf of C. So by

---

[54] See, for example, *Hansard*, HL, col 142 (2 February 2010) per Lord Tunnicliffe: 'It goes without saying that "all the relevant circumstances" is likely to cover the extent of the organisation's influence over the person paying the bribes.' See also *Hansard*, HC, col 76 (16 March 2010) per Claire Ward MP.

[55] For example, a case in which C, as a legal entity, does not control A, but is owned by the same shareholders or is under the influence of the same director or shadow-director, such that A can be shown to act in C's interests and perform services for or on behalf of C.

trying to get around the law by hiring a third party specifically for bribery the employee may himself become 'A', hence potentially triggering liability for C, and for himself.[56]

Shareholders

8.77 The status of shareholder itself does not involve the performance of services for or on behalf of C. Owner-managers may be at more risk of acting in the role of A, since many of their actions in relation to the businesses they own are likely to be seen as being done for or on behalf of the business. Of course shareholders may also be officers or employees or in some other relationship with C through which they perform services for it or on its behalf, but the mere position of shareholder is not enough.

Employees, directors, partners

8.78 It is clear that an employee of a commercial organisation is capable of being in the position of A, and indeed s 8(5) makes it clear that it is to be presumed that any employee is in such a position, unless the contrary can be proven. The burden of proof that the employee was not so acting therefore shifts to the accused (C), although this will only be to the civil standard.

8.79 A director of a company or a partner in a partnership will often not be an employee of the organisation. Strictly speaking, therefore, the presumption arising from s 8(5) does not apply to people in these positions. However, it should be obvious in particular cases when people in those positions act as representatives of the company or partnership in question.

Agents

8.80 In some contexts the term 'agent' is a legal term of art, the definition of which can be relatively technical.[57] However, the context in which the term is used in s 8 suggests that a non-technical meaning is intended.[58] The usually accepted understanding of an agent is of a person who acts for another person in business or politics[59] and it is this general concept of 'an agent' which seems to be intended in s 8.

8.81 Many commercial organisations instruct individuals or companies to represent them in various contexts, both at home and abroad. Lawyers, bankers, tax advisers, PR consultants, lobbyists and others are all capable of

---

[56] Section 1 and s 6 offences may be committed directly or through a third party. The employee may be personally guilty of the offences of conspiracy or attempt to commit offences under s 1 or s 6, or both.
[57] For a discussion in the context of civil bribery, see Chapter 13.
[58] Because, for example, a senior employee of a commercial organisation may often be its 'agent' as a matter of law, yet s 8(3) and (5) draw a distinction between them.
[59] SOED.

qualifying as agents in a particular case. Similarly, local distributors acting on behalf of a manufacturer or an owner of designs or copyrights are likely to be agents.

8.82 In exporting businesses, it is common to instruct intermediaries to represent an exporter in overseas territories. Historically, these intermediaries have been seen as the most likely conduits for bribery. They can be used to disguise the true sources of payments, operate without the direct scrutiny of the auditors and regulators of the main business and allow their principals to claim 'plausible deniability' if misconduct is uncovered. Many of the bribery scandals of the recent past have involved allegations of the use of intermediaries.

8.83 Despite the risks associated with intermediaries in general, many are seen as essential for success in certain countries, and it is unlikely that use of these intermediaries will disappear. Sometimes they can be called 'consultants', or 'advisers', or 'local partners', but a specific title or label does not matter for the purpose of the Act. Any intermediary hired by a commercial organisation to represent or advise it in a particular territory or in relation to a particular transaction or class of business is likely to fall within the category of 'agent' and will be capable of being an associated person.

Suppliers

8.84 Those who merely supply C with goods or a service (such as selling components or providing IT support) will not usually be performing services for C or on C's behalf. Therefore C's suppliers generally are unlikely to qualify as A, at least so long as their contact with C does not extend to a representational role.

8.85 However, certain functions which might be seen as supplying a non-core service may be within a wide reading of 'performing services for or on behalf of'. For example travel agents, insurance brokers or estate agents can be the legal representatives of their clients even though they are not necessarily representing C in core elements of its business.

8.86 Providers of outsourced services might also be performing services for their customer. An example might be a call centre based in India but which provides services to customers of a UK utility. The company running the call centre is performing services for or on behalf of the utility by dealing with the utility's customers. If a bribe is paid for the purpose of obtaining advantages for the utility then the utility will be liable.

8.87 Moreover, if a person which normally acts as a mere supplier takes on responsibility for performing services for or on behalf of C then their previous or concurrent role as a mere supplier will not prevent them from becoming A for the purposes of s 8.

8.88 To take an example, imagine a bank which purchases stationery from a wholesaler. Though the account may be a large one, and though the wholesaler will be negotiating prices with manufacturers so that these may be passed on (at least in part) to its customers, the wholesaler does not perform services for or on behalf of the bank when dealing with third parties. It relationships with the manufacturers are on a principal to principal basis, and it sells to the bank also as a principal.

8.89 If the wholesaler agrees with the bank that it will go into the market to negotiate the best prices for the bank, which will then buy direct from a manufacturer, then the situation has changed. The wholesaler is now acting as an intermediary or broker, in other words for or on behalf of the bank. In relation to the manufacturers it is not dealing as a principal, at least on the transactions in question. It is in these circumstances that the bank might fairly be liable for the wholesaler's actions because it has a greater degree of control of, is aware of and is likely to benefit directly from, the actions of a person which it has engaged to act on its behalf.

Contractors and subcontractors

8.90 In many industries, such as construction or manufacturing, it is very common for projects to be carried on through long chains of contractual relationships. Often a public authority or property owner (an 'employer') will appoint a contractor to carry out a project, and the contractor (sometimes called a head-contractor or prime-contractor) will engage specialist subcontractors to carry out particular parts of the work.

8.91 Whether or not a contractor is associated with the employer under the Act will depend on the nature of its role at the time the events constituting the bribery took place. If its role is merely to provide a specific service, and not to engage or deal with others on behalf of its employer then it may not qualify as an associated person. However, if its role includes dealing with suppliers or subcontractors on behalf of the employer then the contractor may well be an associated person. The same is true of those charged with making representations or submissions on behalf of the employer to state authorities (for example, architects or planning consultants), or customers (such as sales agents).

8.92 Like head-contractors, subcontractors whose role does not involve acting for or on behalf of the employer are not associated persons. In most cases, the fact of being a subcontractor may make it less likely that a person is performing services for or on behalf of the employer. However, the mere fact that a particular person or company is a subcontractor rather than a head-contractor does not mean that it cannot be an associated person of the employer. Some subcontractors may develop a sufficiently close relationship with the employer so that, whether or not it is within the scope of their contractual duties, they do in fact begin to perform services for or on behalf of the employer.

8.93 If contractors, and their subcontractors are capable of being associated persons, what about those further down the chain, sub-subcontractors, or below? The answer, which may be disappointing to those businesses who wish to understand the limit of their risks and the reach of their anti-bribery procedures, is that, in principle, even those at two, three or more links further down the contractual chain are capable of being associated persons. Whether they actually are associated persons depends on the facts of each case. It is clear from the Act that contractual formalities do not matter if, in substance, a person is performing services for or on behalf of C. An associated person may be a sub-sub-subcontractor to C (although of course in practice this is very unlikely) or may not be acting pursuant to any contract whatsoever. This is the principle which appears to underlie s 8(2), (3) and (4).

8.94 The recent MOJ Guidance contains the following passage:[60]

> 'Where a supply chain involves several entities or a project is to be performed by a prime contractor with a series of sub-contractors, an organisation is likely only to exercise control over its relationship with its contractual counterparty. Indeed, the organisation may only know the identity of its contractual counterparty. It is likely that persons who contract with that counterparty will be performing services for the counterparty and not for other persons in the contractual chain.'

8.95 This is likely to be true in many cases. However, although control is undoubtedly one of the 'relevant circumstances' that must be considered pursuant to s 8(4), the Act itself does not expressly refer to the concept of control in defining an associated person. Nor does it refer to the need for C to know the identity of A.[61] Although the Secretary of State no doubt wishes to reassure businesses as to the likely scope of their liability, there may be cases in which it is unwise simply to assume that a party who fits the category 'subcontractor' cannot trigger liability for C.

Subsidiaries

8.96 Generally speaking, a subsidiary can be defined as an undertaking which is controlled by a parent company.[62] The Bribery Act gives no clues as to whether the test to be applied should be the percentage shareholding held by the parent. However, this issue is unlikely to be as important as that of control as a matter of fact. Although a shareholding of more than 50% is likely to

---

[60] MOJ Guidance, p 16, para 39.
[61] There may well be cases of bribery where C believes or suspects that someone is paying bribes on its behalf but does not know, or wish to know, who it is, with the transactions taking place through various undisclosed middlemen.
[62] The Companies Act 2006, s 1159 provides: '(1) A company is a *"subsidiary"* of another company, its *"holding company"*, if that other company—(a) holds a majority of the voting rights in it, or (b) is a member of it and has the right to appoint or remove a majority of its board of directors, or (c) is a member of it and controls alone, pursuant to an agreement with other members, a majority of the voting rights in it, or if it is a subsidiary of a company that is itself a subsidiary of that other company.'

carry with it the assumption of control, a shareholding of less than this does not necessarily prove the opposite if there are other indicators of actual control.

8.97 We have already considered the possibility that the conduct of a subsidiary company might cause its parent company to carry on a business in the UK. Of course subsidiaries may also perform services for or on behalf of the parent. Indeed s 8(3) makes it clear that a subsidiary is expressly within the contemplation of the Act as a person which might perform such services for a relevant commercial organisation.

8.98 Such services might include functions specifically delegated to the subsidiary within a group of companies. For example, in some groups a local subsidiary acts as a sales representative for the group in its territory. Some subsidiaries exist to provide specific services such as staffing or procurement, or to hold assets. In very complex groups there can be hundreds of subsidiaries, many taking different legal forms in different jurisdictions.

8.99 In relation to the Bribery Act, it matters less what a specific subsidiary is intended to do than what it actually does. If the subsidiary performs any services for or on behalf of its parent, for example if it buys or sells products for the parent, or lobbies governments, or markets the parent to customers, or arranges meetings or travel for the parent, then it may be associated with the parent for the purposes of the Act. If such a subsidiary satisfies the other elements of s 7(1) then C will have committed the offence, subject to the s 7(2) defence.

8.100 The fact that a company has a subsidiary, and that subsidiary bribes another person within the terms of s 7(1) does not automatically mean that the parent company is liable. It remains a question of fact whether the subsidiary, at the time in question, was performing services for or on behalf of C.

8.101 Parliament and the Law Commission seem to have quite deliberately avoided changing the rule of parent company liability for the actions of subsidiaries. The intention seems to have been to maintain the corporate veil principle, discussed above, pending further reform. It is worth quoting the Law Commission Report[63] on this subject:

> 'It would be anomalous if subsidiary companies were specifically to be excluded from the range of persons who may be considered to be acting on behalf of the company, for the purpose of establishing the company's liability in this respect.
>
> In that regard, the test of whether a subsidiary company is providing services "on behalf of" a main company should be a substantive rather than a formal test. In other words, the question of whether the test has been satisfied will depend on all the circumstances. It should not depend simply on whether, for example, the subsidiary company does business with foreign officials using papers that all say,

---

[63] LC 313, para 6.119.

"none of the (subsidiary) company's actions are done on behalf of the main company". It could be that, in such a case, there is clear evidence that the official sought, and received, an assurance that an advantage was to be conferred on behalf of the main company. If that were the case, then the advantage would be one to be conferred "on behalf of" the main company, notwithstanding the contrary indication on the paperwork.

This kind of situation is different from the situation in which a question arises whether liability should be imposed on a company for a failure adequately to supervise a subsidiary, when that subsidiary has committed bribery on its own account, and not specifically on behalf of the main company. It is this difficult question that we believe is best left to the general review of corporate liability.'

The view which Mr des Tombe, the legal adviser to the Secretary of State for Justice gave to the Parliamentary Joint Committee is also instructive. In his evidence he said:[64]

'So you have to look at whether, first, A was performing services for or on behalf of C. You then also have to look at whether the bribe was in connection with C's business. So, obviously, the jury and the court will be looking at those elements and, if it can be established that there was this connection, then it is fair that C shall be prima facie liable, but if the foreign subsidiary has no connection with the UK other than its parent company being located there, then we do not think it should be caught by the offence. We do not think that the question of ownership is sufficient justification for taking jurisdiction over foreign subsidiaries.'

Joint ventures

8.102 Many businesses operate joint ventures, especially in relation to large projects. Sometimes governments require foreign companies to operate by way of joint venture with a local partner or a state-owned company. Sometimes the joint venture is justified on business grounds as a way for businesses to pool resources and risks or to benefit from the contacts and experience of a local partner.

8.103 A joint venture often takes a separate legal form from the owners. It may be a separate company or a limited liability partnership. If so, it will have its own articles of association and there will be a written agreement between the owners and perhaps between the joint venture company and the owners, which set out the rights and responsibilities of each of the parties.

8.104 Of course if a company, C, participates in such a joint venture then the joint venture, or one of the joint venture parties, might be performing services on behalf of C and will therefore qualify as an associated person. This should not be presumed merely from the fact of the joint venture. The issue depends on the question of whether services are being performed for or on behalf of the owning company.[65]

---

[64] Joint Committee Report, Vol 2, p 109.
[65] See, for example, *Hansard*, HC, col 982–3 (3 March 2010): 'It will depend on the particular

8.105 There have been complaints that UK enterprises which participate in joint ventures may be liable for actions by the joint venture, or their partners in it, about which they knew nothing and over which they had no control. However, of course, this issue is to be determined by reference to 'all the relevant circumstances'.[66] In the case of joint ventures, this may mean that the degree of control which C has over A is likely to be relevant, at least as evidence of the relationship between C and A.[67]

Example

8.106 Imagine a Scots oil company, Happer Oil. It wishes to explore for oil in the waters off Texas, but lacks the capital to do this alone. It enters into a joint venture with a Texan company, Ferness Inc, and with Imperial Petroleum (a global oil major). They form a joint venture company called HFI. Ferness has 40% of the voting rights. Happer and Imperial have 30% of the voting rights each. Ferness will provide most of the staff to man the rigs and local administrative support. Costs and profits are split between the parties on the basis of their percentage shareholdings.[68]

8.107 During the course of the joint venture Gordon, a director of HFI who is also an employee of Ferness, provides 10 tickets to the Superbowl to a local official responsible for deciding whether the drilling rigs pass safety inspections. No one from Ferness or HFI attends: the tickets are at the official's exclusive disposal. If the rigs fail the inspections then exploration could be halted for several months, costing HFI and ultimately its members a considerable sum of money. Gordon intends the Superbowl tickets to influence the official when inspecting the rigs.

8.108 Let us assume that if the provision of tickets (worth many thousands of dollars) had occurred in the UK the joint venture (HFI) would be guilty of an

---

circumstances of the case, but it may be that a bribe by a person performing services for one company in a joint venture is rightly regarded as being paid in connection with the business if any of the company is involved in that venture. Equally, it may be the case that, on the facts, the necessary connections are not present to establish liability under clause 7 if a bribe is paid in the context of a joint venture. Ultimately, it will be a matter for the courts to determine where liability stands.' (Clare Ward MP, Minister of State). For a slightly more gung-ho approach by a government minister (at an earlier stage of parliamentary proceedings) see Lord Bach, *Hansard*, HL, col 1124 (9 December 2009): 'Our purpose is clear: we want to encourage organisations which are involved in joint ventures to ensure that they are satisfied that adequate procedures are built into the arrangements for their joint venture.'

[66] Section 8(4).
[67] *Hansard*, HL, col 142 (2 February 2010).
[68] For the purpose of exposition this example ignores the fact that the US federal and/or state authorities are most likely to take the lead in any investigation and US domestic law may well also apply to these facts.

offence under s 1 or s 6.[69] The first question is whether HFI was performing services for or on behalf of Happer or Imperial when it paid the bribes.[70]

8.109 On one view, it is arguable that HFI should be taken to be performing services on behalf of Happer by reason of its very existence. Happer and others created HFI so as to have it carry out certain activities. Happer will be a beneficiary of those activities. As such, it should not be able to disown the actions of HFI when they are inconvenient.[71]

8.110 However, the principle of the corporate veil means that HFI is a separate legal entity and its actions are not automatically attributable to Happer. Many companies own a minority share in other companies without assuming liability for their defaults. A pension fund would not be liable for bribery carried out by one of the thousands of companies in which it happened to hold some shares. There seems to be no reason of principle why an investor in a joint venture company should be in a worse position simply because it chose, with others, to found such a company rather than purchase existing shares in it.

8.111 As noted above, the Bribery Act did not change the substantive law in relation to the corporate veil principle, even for companies which own 100% of the shares in a subsidiary. Therefore a joint venture company is unlikely to be deemed to be 'A' to the 'C' of an investor such as Happer without further evidence. At least such an outcome is not obvious from the face of the Bribery Act, and existing law seems to militate against it. In our example, the fact that Happer appears not to have full control of HFI also suggests that HFI should not be assumed to be its agent or representative.

8.112 Since the test of 'performing services for or on behalf of 'is a substantive one, much will depend on identifying how the relationship of agency or representation between A and C (in our example HFI and Happer) took effect. Any agreements between Happer and HFI, or established or customary practices, or communications indicating that HFI will represent Happer will be relevant evidence.

8.113 However, the fact that HFI will, if profitable, contribute revenue to Happer, Ferness and Imperial may not be relevant. A subsidiary or joint venture company may well be providing services *to* each of the owners (such as

---

[69] As noted above, the fact that the events occurred outside the UK do not prevent C from being liable – s 12(5). Neither does A need to have a 'close connection with the United Kingdom' – s 7(3).

[70] It is also relevant to ask whether HFI paid the bribe with the requisite mens rea – that is the intention to obtain or retain business or an advantage in the conduct of business for Happer – this will be discussed below.

[71] See the view expressed by Mr David Howarth MP in parliamentary debate, *Hansard*, HC, col 72 (7 January 2010).

the administration of profit-yielding assets). But, as we have seen, the s 8 definition involves performance of services *for or on behalf of* C, a quite different idea.

8.114 Varying the example, what if the local partner, Ferness, gave the tickets to the official on its own initiative? It did not use the joint venture HFI's assets or staff to do so and did not discuss this with the HFI board or with its other partners. In that case one would have to look at the rules of attribution applicable to HFI as to whether an action by one of its owners could be attributable to it. In English law, the corporate veil principle would mean that this would very difficult. If Happer knew nothing of Ferness's plans or actions then it seems unlikely that the actions of Ferness would pass the 'performing services for or on behalf of' test.

8.115 Another variation: imagine that an independent agent is engaged by HFI to make the payments to the officials. Happer knows nothing about this at the time it occurs. Could that agent be performing services for or on behalf of Happer, as well as HFI? If Happer genuinely knew nothing of the services which the agent was engaged to provide then it seems unlikely that the agent was performing those services for Happer or on its behalf. If its client (in substance as well as in form) was HFI, not Happer, the corporate veil principle will apply to insulate Happer, absent complicity on its part.

Joint venture not incorporated

8.116 A final hypothesis: if the HFI joint venture was not a separate company but simply took effect by way of an agreement between the participants or as an unincorporated partnership then the corporate veil principle would not apply. There would, arguably, be a much closer connection between the acts of bribery and the joint venture partners. Again, the key question would be whether the person which paid the bribes was performing services for or on behalf of Happer (among others).

8.117 It might be argued that Gordon, the provider of the bribe, was the employee of Ferness, and that he did not act on behalf of Happer. This seems rather artificial since, in fact, his action was in the course of his employment and seems to have been directed to the joint venture operations which are the joint property of all participants. The conduct of the safety inspector would be seen as an advantage in the conduct of the business of all the partners, including Happer.[72] In a real case it seems quite likely that Gordon's action would be attributed to Ferness.[73] If Ferness has had any prior dealings with the

---

[72] Of course it is doubtful whether a report which wrongly passes an installation as safe, is a genuine advantage to the owners. The potential for harm which might result is immense. Nevertheless, on these assumed facts, the intention of the payer of the bribe (however foolish) was that the corruption of the official would be an advantage in the conduct of the joint venture's business.

[73] In US law generally, corporations are liable for the actions of their employees who act in the course of their employment, on the principle of respondeat superior.

authorities which related to the joint venture project then it would seem that, prior to the act of bribery itself, Ferness was performing services for or on behalf of the other partners.[74] It does not matter that this specific action was not authorised by the other partners.

Other considerations

8.118 A word of warning is necessary about these hypothetical examples. In the real world, the knowledge or likely knowledge of Happer, its directors, agents or employees, will be critical to the outcome of any case. One should expect these matters to be investigated extremely thoroughly. An investigator is likely to start from the assumption that Happer will have taken an interest in the business of HFI and will not have simply allowed others to control it. It may not be easy to convince such an investigator, or a jury, that Happer can have been kept completely in the dark about matters of importance to the business.

8.119 Once a matter is before a jury in a Crown Court some of the nicer distinctions of company law or carefully worded contracts may be less persuasive than cogent evidence of awareness of wrongdoing by specific people. The greater the degree of control or ownership which a commercial organisation has in a subsidiary or a joint venture, the less convincing any plea of ignorance or that the subsidiary or joint venture was not acting for the organisation is likely to be.

8.120 Leaving s 7 aside, a commercial organisation can still be guilty of s 1 and s 6 offences (subject to the identification doctrine) and can be guilty as a secondary participant, or of conspiracy with other individuals or companies.[75] This is to say nothing of the individual liability of managers or directors.[76] Therefore where companies can influence subsidiaries and joint ventures or even important suppliers to adopt or participate in appropriate anti-bribery policies and procedures, it may be prudent for them to do so. The subject of the procedures by which this may be achieved will be discussed in detail in Chapter 9.

BRIBERY BY A TO OBTAIN/RETAIN BUSINESS OR BUSINESS ADVANTAGE FOR C

8.121 The question of whether A's actions constituted an offence under ss 1 or 6 must naturally be analysed according to the terms of those sections. These offences are analysed in detail in Chapter 2 and Chapter 7 respectively.

---

[74] Although contacts prior to the formation of the joint venture would probably be excluded.
[75] See Chapter 12.
[76] Either as individuals under ss 1 or 6 or for consenting or conniving in an offence by the commercial organisation under s 14.

8.122 Note a few preliminary points: only 'active' bribery, ie the provision of bribes, under s 1 or s 6 are relevant. Section 7 does not criminalise failure to prevent receipt of bribes under s 2. If A is guilty of secondary offences, such as aiding, abetting, counselling or procuring an offence under ss 1 or 6 this also makes C liable.[77]

Section 1 offence by A

8.123 A s 1 offence by A involves A either:

(1) offering, promising or giving a financial or other advantage to another person, intending the advantage either to induce improper performance of a relevant function or activity[78] or to reward such improper performance; or

(2) offering, promising or giving a financial or other advantage to a person knowing or believing that the acceptance of the advantage would itself constitute improper performance of a relevant function or activity.

See Chapter 2 for a detailed discussion.

Section 6 offence by A

8.124 The s 6 offence of bribery of a foreign public official is different to the general offence of provision of a bribe under s 1. It will be necessary to establish that the official in question, F, fulfils the characteristics of a foreign public official, as defined in s 6(5) and that A intended to influence F in his capacity as such an official, for a business purpose.

8.125 The conduct element is similar to that of s 1, the offer, promise or gift of a financial or other advantage. However the recipient must be F (the foreign public official) or another person at F's request or with F's assent or acquiescence.

8.126 The mental element (mens rea) is different to that under s 1. The payer of the bribe (in this case A) must intend to influence F in his capacity as a foreign public official and must intend to obtain or retain business, or an advantage in the conduct of business. Unlike under s 1, it is not necessary to prove that A intends F to act 'improperly' in his official capacity. See Chapter 7 for a detailed discussion.

---

[77] Accessories and Abettors Act 1861, s 8. Explanatory Notes, para 51. See the discussion of secondary liability generally in Chapter 12.

[78] Relevant functions and activities and improper performance are defined by ss 3 and 4 of the Act respectively. See Chapters 4 and 5.

Additional mens rea required by section 7(1)

8.127 To make C liable under s 7(1), A must also commit the s 1 or s 6 offence with an additional mental element. A must intend the bribery either to obtain business, or an advantage in the conduct of business, not for himself (or not exclusively for himself) but for C.

8.128 The meaning of 'obtain or retain business or business advantage' has been discussed in more detail in Chapter 7. The conclusion was that almost any factor which affects the operation of a business is capable of being either 'business' or 'an advantage in the conduct of business'. So, for example, the award of a contract or concession is 'business', and the avoidance of business disadvantages, taxes, penalties under law or regulation are likely to amount to an advantage in the conduct of business.

8.129 A paradigm case will be that of the representative agent hired by a commercial organisation to further its interests in a particular territory. If the agent commits bribery of a foreign public official and by doing so the agent intends to assist C's business in some way (for example to win a contract for C) then C will be guilty, subject to the adequate procedures defence.

No need for A to be prosecuted

8.130 There may be some cases in which proof of these elements against a will be quite clear-cut and it might be possible to prosecute A (for example if A is within the court's jurisdiction). However, many cases involve associated persons who have no presence in the UK and who would be difficult to extradite. It would make the enforcement of s 7 against C very cumbersome if it were necessary to convict A of a s 1 or s 6 offence before C could be convicted. Therefore s 7(3)(a) makes clear that the test is not that A 'is' guilty of offences but that he 'would be' guilty, and that it is not necessary for A to have been prosecuted for the court to find that A has bribed another person.

8.131 So in making a finding that C is guilty the jury will be invited to find that A is also guilty, even though A may not have been prosecuted and may not be present to defend himself. It is doubtful that a conviction of C on this basis creates any legal effects for A. Under UK law A has a right to a fair trial which may not be abrogated in circumstances such as this.[79] The assumption must be that a conviction of C for a s 7 offence does not affect the status of A as a matter of law, and that A remains innocent until it is itself proven guilty.[80]

---

[79] European Convention on Human Rights, Art 6.
[80] Though, if A were subsequently charged, he might attempt to argue that the conviction of C and/or any publicity connected to it, make it difficult for A to receive a fair trial.

No need for A to have UK connection

8.132 The Act applies to a wide range of persons. The main test for those who commit relevant acts outside the UK is whether they have a 'close connection with the United Kingdom' as defined by s 12(4).

8.133 In the case of offences under s 7, it does not matter where the events take place.[81] There is no requirement that A has a close connection with the UK.[82] A need have nothing to do with the UK and his actions can have taken place anywhere in the world.

THE DEFENCE OF ADEQUATE PROCEDURES

8.134 Section 7(2) provides the commercial organisation, C, with a defence to a charge under s 7. The defence is that C had adequate procedures designed to prevent persons associated with C from undertaking such conduct (ie bribery). Section 7(2) does not expressly say that the procedures must have existed at the time of the bribery, though that is the obvious implication.

8.135 The 'adequate procedures' defence does not apply to any offences other than the failure to prevent bribery offence under s 7(1). Therefore the defence is not available to anyone other than C, and not even available to C in response to any other charges.

8.136 The defence is of no help to individual directors or employees of C who may be charged under ss 1, 2 or 6.[83] The defence does not apply to a person associated with C, or its directors or employees which may have been involved in the bribery. This means that where individuals or contractors working with or for C are charged with offences under ss 1, 2 or 6 they face a higher risk of conviction than C itself does if C is only charged with an offence under s 7.

8.137 What adequate procedures themselves might amount to and the government's guidance on this subject will be discussed in the next chapter. Here we consider the nature of the defence itself.

Burden of proof of adequate procedures is on C

8.138 Section 7(2) makes it clear that it is for C to prove that it had adequate procedures in place.

8.139 It is well established that, in criminal matters, where the burden of proof of a particular matter is on a defendant the standard which the defendant must

---

[81] Section 12(5).
[82] Section 7(3)(b).
[83] A charge under s 14 can only be made if the senior manager in question consents or connives in the commission of a s 1, 2 or 6 offence by a body corporate or Scottish partnership. It could not be brought if all C was charged with was a s 7 offence.

attain is not the usual standard applicable to the prosecution case (the traditional formulation of 'beyond reasonable doubt'), but a lower standard, usually required for civil proceedings.[84] That standard is usually called the 'balance of probability'. In other words the jury will only need to be convinced that it is 'more likely than not' that C had procedures designed to prevent bribery by persons associated with C which were adequate.

8.140 One can expect that any commercial organisation which has anti-bribery procedures in place will be able to provide evidence of their existence and their nature and how they were operated. Whether or not C has such procedures in place is a question of fact. This must mean that all the ingredients of the defence (whether C has procedures in place, what they are designed to do, whether they are adequate) are questions for a jury and about which a good deal of factual evidence, and probably expert evidence, will be relevant.

Object is prevention of bribery by associated persons

8.141 C's procedures must be primarily aimed at those who are in or could be in the category of associated persons – performing services for or on behalf of C. These will obviously include employees, subsidiaries or agents, and also, arguably, joint venture partners and others, depending on the nature of the services performed. It is more doubtful whether suppliers of goods or services which do not involve the representation of C need to be included in the scope of the procedures, unless there are special factors at play.

8.142 The procedures must be designed to prevent bribery, not merely to warn of it or disparage it. This seems to mean that the procedures must have as their object a system which can be expected to be effective in preventing bribery. The procedures must be developed or organised in such a way as to address the risk of bribery being committed by associated persons. It is likely to be important to be able to show a genuine belief by the commercial organisation that the procedures were, or were likely to be, adequate in preventing such bribery. A procedure which C believes is not fit for this purpose, or where C has not considered the question of fitness for this purpose, seems to fail the requirement that it is designed (ie intended) to prevent bribery by associated persons.

Procedures must be 'adequate'

8.143 Many businesses and organisations have considered the issue of what anti-bribery procedures could be adopted by those usually on the 'supply-side' of bribery. There is, probably, an identifiable standard of good practice, at least as it applies to the largest transnational companies. Pursuant to s 9 of the Bribery Act, the Secretary of State for Justice has issued the MOJ Guidance on this subject.

---

[84] *R v Carr-Briant* [1943] KB 607.

8.144 No guidance can hope to encompass all the different risks and business practices prevalent in the UK economy or, indeed, the other economies whose organisations may be subject to s 7 by virtue of carrying on part of their business in the UK. The MOJ Guidance is principles-based and is not definitive. It is not binding on the court as to the standard of what is adequate in a particular case.

8.145 It seems clear that the mere fact that a person associated with C committed bribery cannot amount to proof that any procedures in place were inadequate.[85] If the procedures could be described as inadequate merely because they had failed in relation to the facts charged then the defence would be deprived of all efficacy. In normal English 'adequate' does not mean 'perfect' or 'infallible'.[86]

8.146 Sensible commercial organisations which face a risk of bribes being paid on their behalf will wish to avoid even the possibility of being prosecuted for an offence under the Bribery Act. They will wish to know what they should do in the light of prevailing good practice and will wish to have some regard to the likely attitudes of the UK prosecuting authorities and how to apply the principles contained in the MOJ Guidance. It is to this difficult subject which we turn in the next chapter.

---

[85] See, for example, *Hansard*, HL, col 142 (2 February 2010): 'Our ultimate aim is of course to prevent bribery, but the defence recognises that a well run organisation will avoid liability, despite an isolated incident of bribery, if its procedures are otherwise adequate.' (Lord Tunnicliffe).

[86] The SOED has 'Commensurate in fitness; sufficient, satisfactory'.

Chapter 9

DEFENCE OF ADEQUATE PROCEDURES, DEFENCE UNDER SECTION 13, DEFENCES OF DURESS AND NECESSITY

INTRODUCTION

9.1 This chapter focuses on particular defences to charges under the Bribery Act. It is largely devoted to the adequate procedures which might be put in place by commercial organisations in response to s 7(2) of the Act and the guidance issued by the Secretary of State under s 9. The defence available to members of the military or security services under s 13 is also discussed although much more briefly. The defences of duress and necessity might also be relevant in some extreme circumstances and are outlined at the end of the chapter. The final part of the chapter gives an outline of policy material which might exist to support an anti-bribery and corruption ('ABC') programme.

ADEQUATE PROCEDURES

BRIBERY ACT 2010: SECTION 9

'**9 Guidance about commercial organisations preventing bribery**

(1) The Secretary of State must publish guidance about procedures that relevant commercial organisations can put in place to prevent persons associated with them from bribing as mentioned in section 7(1).

(2) The Secretary of State may, from time to time, publish revisions to guidance under this section or revised guidance.

(3) The Secretary of State must consult the Scottish Ministers before publishing anything under this section.

(4) Publication under this section is to be in such manner as the Secretary of State considers appropriate.

(5) Expressions used in this section have the same meaning as in section 7.'

9.2 As we have seen in Chapter 8, s 7(2) of the Bribery Act provides a commercial organisation ('C') with a defence to a charge of failure to prevent bribery under s 7. The defence is that C had (at the time the s 7 offence occurred) adequate procedures designed to prevent persons associated with C from undertaking such conduct (ie bribery). The burden of proving the existence and adequacy of the procedures is upon the organisation in question, on the 'balance of probabilities' standard.

9.3 Section 9 was inserted into the Bribery Bill during its passage through Parliament after various expressions of concern that the term 'adequate procedures' was too vague and that there was a need for businesses to have guidance about what to do in order to design anti-bribery procedures sufficient for s 7(2).[1]

9.4 The legal effect of s 9 is quite limited. It provides a statutory obligation on the Secretary of State (in this case the Secretary of State for Justice) to publish guidance about procedures which commercial organisations can put in place to prevent associated persons from carrying out bribery when acting for them. There are various requirements and permissions as to methodology and consultation which need not detain us here. Section 9 does not make following the guidance mandatory for UK businesses or anyone else.

9.5 The guidance was published by the Secretary of State for Justice on 30 March 2011[2] and, as a result, it can be said that the obligation imposed by s 9 has now been fulfilled.

9.6 Some may have hoped that the guidance would create a legal 'safe harbour' whereby, once certain formal steps were taken, a business would become immune from liability. This could never have been the case, given the terms of s 7. The issues of whether (i) a commercial organisation is guilty of an offence of failing to prevent bribery and (ii) the organisation has a defence based on 'adequate procedures' are clearly issues of fact and are substantive, not formal. They will depend on what organisations have actually done and what they should have done in their particular circumstances.[3]

Meaning of 'adequate'

9.7 'Adequate' is not defined in the Bribery Act. However, it has its own meaning. As already observed in Chapter 8, it cannot mean 'perfect', since if it did it would rob the defence of all effect as soon as bribery by A on behalf of C was proved. So the fact that an associated person has committed bribery does not mean that the procedures of the commercial organisation with which it is associated were not adequate.[4]

---

[1] *Hansard*, HL, col 143 (2 February 2010).
[2] Ministry of Justice, *Guidance about Procedures Which Relevant Commercial Organisations Can Put into Place to Prevent Persons Associated With Them From Bribing*, 30 March 2011 (hereafter 'MOJ Guidance'), a copy of which is at Appendix C.
[3] The guidance itself recognises this – MOJ Guidance, p 6, para 4.
[4] Although a number of earlier, unconnected incidents of bribery contrary to existing procedures might be evidence that the procedures were inadequate.

9.8 Although adequate does not mean perfect, it seems to indicate a quite high standard. The *Shorter Oxford English Dictionary* defines adequate as 'commensurate in fitness; sufficient, satisfactory'. It is difficult to imagine an adequate procedure which was not objectively suitable for its purpose, at least in terms of identifying and responding to risks and being operated effectively. Procedures which are not matched to obvious areas of risk, or which seem adequate on paper but are in fact ignored, are unlikely to be judged to be adequate.[5]

9.9 Prior to the introduction of the Bill, the government and Joint Committee rejected the recommendation of the Law Commission that the applicable standard for liability under s 7 should be the negligence of senior persons within the organisation.[6] So individual negligence is not relevant to liability under s 7.

9.10 In general, it seems plain that adequacy does not bear a direct relation to fault. Procedures which a business may implement in all good faith, believing (wrongly) that they are adequate may still not be adequate if they do not respond to clear and obvious risks. Similarly, a 'bad apple' at a senior level who subverts procedures which otherwise operate effectively will not necessarily destroy the adequate procedures defence.

9.11 It is interesting to consider the effect of an event of employee negligence in operating a procedure. An example might be a careless, but not deliberate, failure to notice highly relevant information emerging from a due diligence exercise. Human error occurs in every type of activity. Given that a deliberate action to avoid ABC procedures in committing bribery would not of itself render those procedures inadequate, a single event of negligence also should not, without more, mean that procedures were inadequate. However, if procedures were operated or monitored by staff who were not capable of doing so, perhaps because they are lacking appropriate expertise or experience or were not updated in face of an important new area of risk, they may well not be adequate.

9.12 The enormous variety of businesses and risks faced by organisations makes it impossible to lay down hard and fast rules on what is or is not adequate in the abstract. Establishing adequacy in individual cases is likely to be much more of an art than a science, which will require an understanding of business, an understanding of good practice and the application of informed judgment in equal measure.

---

[5] It seems to have been the view of the ministers proposing the Bill that 'adequate' should not be read as 'reasonable', at least in the sense of 'reasonable' which might be construed as meaning 'affordable' – see *Hansard*, HC, col 68 (16 March 2010).

[6] Joint Committee Report, Part I, p 5.

THE STATUS OF THE MINISTRY OF JUSTICE GUIDANCE

9.13 Because the publication of the guidance is required by the Act, its content is obviously relevant to the question of whether any particular procedures are adequate. In fact, any government guidance on this subject would be relevant evidence on the issue of adequacy, even if it were not required by statute.

9.14 The Secretary of State, although required to publish the guidance, will have no role in deciding its legal status or how it is relevant to any specific organisation.[7] In essence the guidance is an advisory document which sets out what the Secretary of State, no doubt on advice, believes to be current good practice. There may well be procedures which are in fact adequate but which are not described in the guidance.[8]

9.15 It might be thought that the fact that Parliament required the publication of guidance means that it must have intended that those who can demonstrate that their procedures follow such guidance will have satisfied the test of adequacy. This is probably going too far, on a proper reading of both ss 7(2) and 9.[9] It is noticeable that s 9 does not refer to s 7(2) (which provides for the defence) and does not even use the term 'adequate'.

9.16 The guidance itself makes it clear that it is not prescriptive[10] and expressly does not propose any detailed procedures. The guidance is principles-based, and whether any particular organisation has fulfilled the principles through its policies and procedures can, and will, be the subject of detailed argument in individual cases.

The guidance document

9.17 The document containing the MOJ Guidance can be divided into three main parts. The first part is entitled 'Government Policy and Section 7 of the Bribery Act'[11] and amounts to a summary of not only s 7 but also ss 1, 6, 8 and 12, and the views of the government as to how those sections are best interpreted. The status of this part of the guidance will be discussed further below. The second part is entitled 'The Six Principles' and sets out the view of the government as to the principles which should be reflected in procedures

---

[7] As already mentioned, the US authorities can provide individual companies with guidance or 'advisory opinions' as to the prospects of prosecution in specific situations, as occurs under the FCPA. No such facility exists in the UK.
[8] MOJ Guidance, p 6, para 5.
[9] Section 9 merely provides for a duty on the Secretary of State to publish guidance about procedures that relevant commercial organisations can put in place to prevent persons associated with them from bribing as mentioned in s 7(1). Note the use of 'can' rather than 'must'.
[10] MOJ Guidance, p 6, para 4.
[11] MOJ Guidance, pp 8–19.

designed to prevent bribery by associated persons.[12] This section is the s 9 guidance proper. The third part is an appendix which contains various case studies, designed to show how the six principles apply to real cases.[13]

Quick Start Guide

9.18 At the same time as the guidance itself was issued, the Ministry of Justice also issued something called a 'Quick Start Guide'. As far as one can tell, this document does not form part of the statutory guidance. It is a summary of the guidance, expressed in rather more breezy 'high level' language. The Quick Start Guide does not provide more than a surface outline of the guidance and it should not be necessary for it to be considered separately when designing ABC procedures.

9.19 There is no doubt that the six principles will have a role in determining the nature of adequacy in any case, primarily as strong evidence on the question of the standard of adequacy which a defendant's procedures should achieve. They will also be important in influencing prosecutors such as the SFO and others investigating allegations of bribery against a commercial organisation.

9.20 So, for most commercial organisations the six principles in the guidance should serve either as a starting point for the design of their anti-bribery procedures or a benchmark against which to measure existing procedures. The six principles helpfully distil a great deal of existing learning and good practice into principles which can be understood and applied across different industry sectors.[14]

'Government policy' on interpretation of the Act

9.21 A reader of the MOJ Guidance who was not familiar with UK constitutional law and in particular the doctrine of the separation of powers, might get the impression that a statement of government policy about an existing Act of Parliament was an authoritative interpretation of the Act. That is not the case. Only the courts can interpret legislation in an authoritative way. Governments do not generally have a stated 'policy' about how the courts will interpret existing legislation and the publication of a statement of government policy about how to interpret this particular piece of legislation came as something of a surprise.

---

[12] MOJ Guidance, pp 20–31.
[13] MOJ Guidance, pp 32–43.
[14] The guidance reflects various elements of existing material, such as the OECD Good Practice Guidance on Internal Controls, Ethics and Compliance (available at www.oecd.org/document/ 42/0,3746,en_2649_34855_41799402_1_1_1_1,00.html) and Part 8 of the US Federal Sentencing Guidelines (available at www.ussc.gov/Guidelines/2010_guidelines/Manual_ HTML/Chapter_8.htm).

9.22 The courts will not take into account what the government of the day happens to believe about the meaning of an Act of Parliament, unless, of course, the government is making submissions as a party to the proceedings. In criminal prosecutions, the government is not a party. The proceedings are brought on behalf of the Crown by the statutorily independent prosecution services such as the Crown Prosecution Service or the Serious Fraud Office, whose views on the law may well differ from those of the government

9.23 It is fair to say that the 'government policy' section of the guidance does not expressly claim to be authoritative, and that many, though not all, of its conclusions are clearly correct. Its main aim may be to provide information to members of the public and the media who have come to believe some of the more exaggerated claims about the effects of the Act on corporate hospitality and other practices. Reading this section, and comparing it to the previous draft,[15] it is hard to resist the impression that public relations considerations, in particular a wish to play down what some saw as the 'burdensome' effects of the Act on businesses, played a part in how the guidance was presented.

9.24 Since the courts and prosecuting agencies may not share the preoccupations of any particular administration, the government policy section has to be approached with caution. Some of its more debatable assertions (for example the view that foreign companies listed on a UK stock exchange may not be subject to the Act) are dealt with elsewhere in this book during discussion of the relevant parts of the Act.[16] The purpose of this chapter is to focus on the guidance proper, ie the six principles, and how they might apply to commercial organisations in practice.

SIX PRINCIPLES FOR PREVENTION OF BRIBERY BY ASSOCIATED PERSONS

9.25 The six principles which make up the s 9 guidance proper are:

(1) proportionate procedures;

(2) top level commitment;

(3) risk assessment;

(4) due diligence;

(5) communication (including training);

(6) monitoring and review.

---

[15] Ministry of Justice, Consultation on guidance about commercial organisations preventing bribery (section 9 of the Bribery Act 2010), Consultation Paper CP 11/10, September 2010.
[16] See in particular Chapters 7 and 8.

9.26 The structure of the six principles section of the guidance is to offer a short statement of each principle, followed by commentary. The commentary seems to be intended to explain the possible effects of the principle rather than to form part of the principle itself.[17] So, in a real case, one of the relevant questions in determining adequacy is whether the procedures which C had in place at the time of the alleged bribery reflected the six principles. In answering that question one might look at various materials, including, but not limited to, the commentary accompanying each principle.

9.27 The six principles section of the guidance is supplemented by Appendix A, which contains fictional scenarios in which the principles are demonstrated. Each scenario illustrates the operation of one or more of the principles. Again, the scenarios do not form part of the six principles themselves. They amount to further illustrative material which can be used by commercial organisations wishing to understand the effect of the six principles.[18]

9.28 The guidance is not legislation and it is probably a mistake to pick over each word in a forensic way. Many elements of the principles do not need extensive further exposition. Nevertheless, it may be useful to discuss certain elements in more depth.

PRINCIPLE 1: PROPORTIONATE PROCEDURES

9.29 The text of principle 1 is as follows:

'A commercial organisation's procedures to prevent bribery by persons associated with it are proportionate to the bribery risks it faces and to the nature, scale and complexity of the commercial organisation's activities. They are also clear, practical, accessible, effectively implemented and enforced.'

Sub-principles and specific topics

9.30 Principle 1 seems to contain a number of principles, or perhaps sub-principles. Among these are that:

- the procedures are 'proportionate to the bribery risks [a commercial organisation] faces';

- the procedures are proportionate to 'the nature, scale and complexity of the commercial organisation's activities';

- the procedures are clear;

- the procedures are practical;

---

[17] MOJ Guidance, p 20.
[18] MOJ Guidance, p 32.

- the procedures are accessible;
- the procedures are effectively implemented;
- the procedures are effectively enforced.

Proportionality

9.31 The guidance frequently refers to the need for proportionality and to the taking of a risk-based approach.[19] This can only be sensible. Not all commercial organisations face identical risks of bribery and few could argue against the proposition that any measure should be proportionate to the mischief it is intended to counter.

9.32 In certain areas 'proportionality' has acquired a specific legal meaning.[20] It seems plain that these specialist uses are not what the guidance is referring to. It seems to be referring, in a generalised way, to the idea that it is permissible to focus procedures on those circumstances which are genuinely likely to involve risks of payment of bribes by associated persons – what is known as 'risk-based approach'.

9.33 Principle 1 distinguishes between two types of proportionality applicable to the procedures. The first is in the relationship between the procedures and the actual risks faced by the organisation. As a principle, this must be right. Adequacy ought to be considered in relation to the risks which exist. An oil company with operations in countries notorious for corruption will face different risks to a chain of newsagents operating in the EU, and the anti-bribery measures each should be expected to take will be different.

9.34 The second type of proportionality mentioned relates to 'the nature, scale and complexity of the commercial organisation's activities'. At first sight this also seems reasonable. It seems counterintuitive to require a business which turns over £500,000 to implement the same procedures as one which turns over £5 billion.[21]

9.35 However, the size-based approach to proportionality gives rise to difficulties. For example, unlike the assessment of risk, which gets its own principle and commentary, the guidance does not suggest what measures are appropriate to judge the 'scale' of an organisation's activities. If X Co decides

---

[19] The word 'proportionate' was used three times in the original draft of the guidance, twice in the limited context of 'appropriate hospitality'. It is used 18 times in the final draft, excluding appendices.

[20] Such as in human rights law – see *R v Secretary of State For The Home Department, Ex Parte Daly* [2001] UKHL 26.

[21] A question which is sometimes asked is whether or not the profitability of a business ought to be relevant to the adequacy of its procedures. The short answer seems to be 'no'. It is not mentioned in the Act or in the guidance and does not feature in assessing the reasonableness or otherwise of corporate behaviour under other statutory regimes. It would be incoherent to have the standard of adequacy of a programme vary according to annual profit figures.

its activities are on a small scale, thus requiring less stringent procedures, by what standard should this be judged by a court or a prosecutor? The same question can be asked about the 'nature' and 'complexity' of X Co's activities.

9.36 It is also unclear what relationship the 'risk-based' concept of proportionality and the 'size-based' concept have with each other. Are they, or should they be, commensurable? If one is engaging in high-risk activities but is small in size does this justify very limited procedures? This issue is not dealt with head-on by principle 1 or the commentary. The commentary does contain the following passage:

> 'Adequate bribery prevention procedures ought to be proportionate to the bribery risks that the organisation faces. An initial assessment of risk across the organisation is therefore a necessary first step. To a certain extent the level of risk will be linked to the size of the organisation and the nature and complexity of its business, but size will not be the only determining factor. Some small organisations can face quite significant risks, and will need more extensive procedures than their counterparts facing limited risks. However, small organisations are unlikely to need procedures that are as extensive as those of a large multi-national organisation. For example, a very small business may be able to rely heavily on periodic oral briefings to communicate its policies while a large one may need to rely on extensive written communication.'[22]

9.37 The first two sentences make the proper point that proportionality should be judged in relation to risk and that risk assessment is the first step.[23] However, the remainder of the paragraph muddies these waters, suggesting that if one is a 'small' organisation (undefined) one is unlikely to need procedures as extensive as those of a 'large multi-national organisation' (again, undefined, and with an unstated level of risk). On the other hand, if one faces a high level of risk then procedures should be more extensive than a 'counterpart' (which perhaps means a business of the same size) which faces a limited risk. How the small, high-risk organisation's procedures should compare to those of a 'large multi-national' is not stated. However, it seems that if one is 'very' small one can rely heavily on oral briefings.

9.38 With respect, this does not really help. One could be forgiven for thinking that the Ministry has mixed up the desire to reassure small and medium-sized businesses about the burden of compliance with the proper analysis of the principle of proportionality.[24] One cannot estimate what is proportionate without making an assessment of risk. Although the number of an organisation's employees, or agents, or transactions may well have an effect on the level of risk, these are not the primary determinant of it. Some businesses with a handful of employees are engaged in very risky fields of activity which

---

[22] MOJ Guidance, p 21, para 1.3.
[23] To anyone considering what might or might not be a proportionate procedure it is quite obvious that this cannot be decided without a risk assessment. It is surprising that the guidance did not put the principle of risk assessment first, as was the case in the previous draft.
[24] It is possible to define what is a small or medium-sized or large business if necessary. See, for example, EU Commission Recommendation 2003/361/EC on Small and Medium Enterprises.

would, for example, require them to do very extensive due diligence on third party intermediaries. A business which is 20 times larger may face lower levels of risk which does not require the same degree of due diligence.

9.39 In practical terms, organisations seeking to develop adequate procedures should carry out their risk assessment before considering what is a proportionate response. It is notable that the types of risk identified in the commentary on principle 3 (risk assessment), do not include the size of the organisation, perhaps recognising the difficulties of taking size into account in any systematic way.

9.40 Businesses facing a high degree of risk would be unwise to reduce the strength of their responses merely because they are, or consider themselves to be, 'small' or even 'very small'. Procedures which are proportionate to a reasonable estimate of risk should be implemented. In an organisation with a small number of employees or other associated persons this need not be a costly exercise.

9.41 The statement in the commentary that 'a very small business may be able to rely heavily on periodic oral briefings to communicate its policies' seems both incongruous and not a little dangerous. Again, a 'very small business' is not defined by the guidance. Since the burden of proof of the existence of adequate procedures falls on a defendant it would be far safer, even for a business which only employs a handful of people, to record anti-bribery policies and the communication of them to staff/agents in writing, for example by e-mail. A failure to do this will make it more difficult to satisfy the evidential burden of proof and seems to cut against the other requirements of principle 1 that the procedures be accessible.[25]

9.42 These criticisms of the guidance have not addressed the issue identified earlier, that some businesses, even those with high degree of risk, may not be able to afford the 'Rolls-Royce' approach to compliance which is possible for very large companies.

9.43 In many cases, organisations with few employees or small turnover will not in fact face the level of risk of larger organisations, so that an approach which is proportionate to risk will lead to the same outcome as an approach which is proportionate to size. Where this is not the case, a purist might argue that an enterprise which cannot afford the compliance cannot afford to take part in risky transactions, and they should be avoided. But this is hardly satisfactory, either to those entrepreneurs who consider risk to be the lifeblood of profitable business or to the enterprise whose risks happen to increase through no fault of its own.

---

[25] Also note the expectation in principle 3 that the organisation's risk assessment is 'documented', with no exception for small or very small organisations.

9.44 It might have been possible to accommodate the likely mismatches between available resources and possible risks by providing that adequacy should be judged according to a 'reasonable person' standard. An organisation's procedures could have been considered in the light of what a reasonable person in the position of the organisation would have done, having carried out a risk assessment and in light of the other principles. The burden would remain with the defendant to satisfy a jury that the reasonable person standard had been met. However, unfortunately, this is not what the Act provides.

9.45 The difficulties resulting from the principle of proportionality, as formulated, may not be clarified until and unless they are dealt with in the courts. Whatever the legal arguments, at a trial, a jury may well be sympathetic to an enterprise with limited resources which made good faith efforts to put adequate procedures in place, even if they were not as extensive as those of larger organisations. It will be interesting to see whether a principle based on the reasonable conduct of a person in the position of the defendant, or one similar to it, emerges from decided cases or becomes established otherwise.

Clear, practical and accessible

9.46 The requirement that the procedures are clear seems to mean that they are capable of being understood by those to whom they are addressed. Obviously, documents which are too long or too complicated may not be effective because many staff will not wish to read them or find them confusing. On the other hand, some anti-bribery procedures may be quite detailed and require a good deal of explanation. Striking a balance between clarity and accuracy is never easy. A method which is often used is to create a user-friendly and quite short policy document which sets out the key rules and principles in straightforward language. This is then supplemented by material which set out the details of procedures which are relevant to specific departments or people within the organisation.

9.47 The requirement that the procedures are 'practical' may overlap the requirement of clarity. It is difficult to say in the abstract how a particular procedure might be judged to be either practical or impractical. Procedures which are too cumbersome or bureaucratic to be implemented effectively (for example because they are too time consuming or depend on over-legalistic or confusing documentation) will not do much good. The importation of generic procedures which bear no relation to the existing structures or procedures of the business is also likely to be impractical in effect. It is probably more effective for many businesses to create procedures which fit in with their existing structures and ways of doing things. Training and examples need to be adapted to the experiences, culture and roles of the audience rather than assuming that all staff share the experiences of senior managers, or lawyers.

9.48 As to accessibility, all procedures should be capable of being accessed by those to whom they apply, preferably in permanent written form (perhaps in hard copy or via company intranets). If necessary, documentation should be translated into the working languages of those being addressed.

List of topics

9.49 The commentary then suggests 'an indicative and not exhaustive list' of topics which might be dealt with in the procedures. Some of these are already dealt with in other six principles, such as:

- the involvement of the organisation's top-level management (principle 2);

- risk assessment procedures (principle 3);

- due diligence of existing or prospective associated persons (principle 4);

- the communication of the organisation's policies and procedures, and training in their application (principle 5);

- the monitoring, review and evaluation of bribery prevention procedures (principle 6).

9.50 Other topics on the list are about the actual content of an organisation's policies or procedures. These include:

- the provision of gifts, hospitality and promotional expenditure, charitable and political donations and demands for facilitation payments;

- direct and indirect employment, including recruitment, terms and conditions, disciplinary action and remuneration;

- governance of business relationships with all other associated persons including pre- and post-contractual agreements;

- financial and commercial controls such as adequate bookkeeping, auditing and approval of expenditure;

- transparency of transactions and disclosure of information;

- decision making, such as delegation of authority procedures, separation of functions and the avoidance of conflicts of interest;

- enforcement, detailing discipline processes and sanctions for breaches of the organisation's anti-bribery rules;

- the reporting of bribery including 'speak up' or 'whistleblowing' procedures;

- the detail of the process by which the organisation plans to implement its bribery prevention procedures, for example, how its policy will be applied to individual projects and to different parts of the organisation.

9.51 There is a great deal of expertise available on the detailed content of ABC procedures[26] and this book is not a 'how to' manual on the detail of procedures. However, it may be helpful to offer some comments on selected items in this list.

Gifts/hospitality

9.52 It is generally accepted as good practice for businesses to record all gifts and hospitality provided or received above a certain de minimis limit. That limit may vary according to region or according to the type of person receiving it (for example, a lower limit for a government official). It will rarely be necessary for senior managers to be involved in day-to-day decisions about gifts or hospitality which are 'normal' – ie where there is little to no risk of the recipient being influenced in the performance of his duties by the hospitality.

9.53 Many businesses have policies about charitable donations. These should be adapted to reflect bribery risk, so that a donation is verified as being bona fide and not used as cover for bribery.

Facilitation payments

9.54 Much more challenging is the policy which a business should adopt towards facilitation payments. A policy which expressly permitted such payments would probably not be considered adequate given the clear 'zero tolerance' policy of the Act. Many companies already prohibit these payments, but tend not to penalise staff who believe they have no option but to pay, preferring instead to insist that the incident be reported and that relevant records are not misleading.

9.55 Case study 1 of Appendix A to the guidance has some suggestions as to how a commercial organisation might respond to regular demands for facilitation payments. However, useful as these suggestions are, none are likely to provide a fully satisfactory solution to the problem, either individually or collectively. In practice this can be an extremely difficult area to police. It seems that the best policy is to outlaw facilitation payments on behalf of the business and try to work towards empowering staff or representatives to resist them wherever possible. There is further discussion of this topic in the remarks on the outline ABC policy, below.

---

[26] See Appendix I, 'List of useful websites'.

Recruitment/employment

9.56 As to recruitment and employment, it may be good practice in some circumstances to carry out specific due diligence on senior recruits or those whose actions might expose the business to bribery risk. Of course in many businesses this will happen anyway, certainly for those operating at a high level within the enterprise. Employment conditions will have to reflect relevant employment law but, subject to this, the 'staff handbook' or other material could make clear that a breach of the 'no bribery' policy may provide grounds for dismissal or other penalties. These sanctions should be enforced in appropriate circumstances. If they are not then the procedures will be seen to lack teeth and this may well affect an assessment of their adequacy.

Financial controls

9.57 The design and operation of the financial systems and controls of businesses is a specialised subject about which commercial organisations will no doubt have considerable knowledge and external advice. It is well outside the scope of this book. From the point of view of the criminal law, it is clear that the records of a commercial organisation should not permit accounting records to be 'doctored' in any way, including destruction, defacement, concealment or falsification and entries in accounts should not be 'misleading, false or deceptive in a material particular'.[27]

9.58 How best to enter transactions into accounts or monitor their accuracy is a question for each commercial organisation. An effective system of controls is likely to be capable of ensuring that transactions are authorised by appropriate people in the organisation, are accurately recorded and reported to those responsible for the relevant budgets or assets and that there are safeguards to prevent fraud, false accounting or misappropriation.

Speak up procedures

9.59 'Speak up' or 'whistleblowing' procedures whereby staff and others are encouraged to report wrongdoing are also very important. Without an effective procedure of this kind it will be far more difficult for commercial organisations to discover bribery by associated persons, to monitor the effectiveness of its procedures and to mitigate the possible consequences of bribery. The confidentiality of the reporter should be protected and it should be made clear that they will not be victimised in any way for a report or complaint made in good faith about the conduct of any co-worker or other party or the business itself.[28] It is likely that those investigating allegations of bribery will pay particular attention to what happened to anyone who made a credible report of wrongdoing to the organisation.

---

[27] Theft Act 1968, s 17.
[28] In UK law, see Part IVA of the Employment Rights Act 1996, as amended by the Public Interest Disclosure Act 1998.

9.60 In the US, the Securities and Exchange Commission is now permitted, via the recent Dodd-Frank Act, to offer financial incentives of up to 30% of sums recovered to those reporting violations of securities laws, including the FCPA. This is likely to lead to an increase in whistleblowing reports.[29]

9.61 The other items on the list (transparency, decision making, enforcement) may also be relevant in many circumstances, though perhaps not all. Avoidance of conflicts of interest is at the heart of corporate governance in general. The issue is dealt with below in the context of what to do if bribery is suspected. Of course businesses should strive to have efficient processes for dealing with breaches of internal rules, but these subjects are very complex and it may well be difficult to argue that technical deficiencies in disciplinary procedures, for example, impact directly on the efficiency or otherwise of ABC procedures.

Investigations and conflicts of interest

9.62 Conflicts of interest are dangerous for commercial organisations and lie at the heart of many economic crimes such as fraud and bribery. Ethics codes and ABC policies might benefit from highlighting the need to avoid such conflicts, in particular by requiring all those subject to the code to declare any interest in decisions or transactions.

9.63 A topic which is not specifically mentioned in the guidance but which might be very important to commercial organisations is what should be done if the organisation is provided with credible evidence of bribery by associated persons.

9.64 In such circumstances an organisation needs to understand the relevant facts and their legal consequences quickly. It will be necessary to investigate, and for the investigation to be managed in a way which is not compromised by the interests of people likely to be affected by it. For example, an allegation of bribery in a particular division of a business is likely to affect the position of the executive responsible for that division, and that executive should not be involved in any investigation. If the allegation has the potential to affect the position of senior management such as a chief executive or finance director then these individuals should also be excluded from the investigation.

9.65 Larger and listed companies tend to have non-executive directors (known in the US as 'independent directors') on the board. These may well be suitable parties to manage an investigation process and to receive reports from those investigating.

9.66 In serious matters where the commercial organisation is concerned about the possibility of criminal or other liability, it is good practice to instruct external lawyers to advise the organisation and conduct an investigation, responding to the non-executive directors or other suitably independent

---

[29] US Securities Exchange Act of 1934, s 21F.

persons.[30] The involvement of external professionals with experience of obtaining, testing and weighing evidence to a legal standard will assist in ensuring the investigation is both independent and seen as such by third parties such as prosecutors. Advice from lawyers in such circumstances will be confidential and will, in most circumstances, be subject to legal professional privilege, so that the organisation will not be required to disclose the report or interview notes or other communications to and from the lawyers.[31]

9.67 It may be good practice for the procedures to expressly provide for independent external parties to investigate any credible evidence of bribery (or other criminality) affecting the organisation, although this is not a prerequisite of adequacy. Any directors or others who face the risk of being personally liable alongside the organisation (for example under ss 1, 2, 6 or 14 or for inchoate or allied offences) may require separate legal representation. If directors' and officers' liability insurance is in place then the necessary notifications should be made.

9.68 Of course, external advisers such as lawyers, accountants or consultants can also suffer from conflicts of interest and will usually be subject to professional rules in relation to them. A firm which was involved in advising on a transaction which is now being impugned, or which is frequently retained by the company on other matters, or which performed an audit or due diligence checks which might be impugned if the bribery allegations are made out might lack, or at least be seen to lack, the requisite independence. If there is the possibility of a charge under s 7 an external firm which advised on the adequacy of procedures might also face a conflict.

PRINCIPLE 2: TOP LEVEL COMMITMENT

9.69 The text of principle 2 is as follows:

> 'The top-level management of a commercial organisation (be it a board of directors, the owners or any other equivalent body or person) are committed to preventing bribery by persons associated with it. They foster a culture within the organisation in which bribery is never acceptable.'

9.70 This element of the guidance is largely self-explanatory. Most commercial organisations are hierarchical and respond to the priorities set by senior management. An anti-corruption programme is unlikely to be effective unless the senior decision-makers both endorse it formally and are seen to support it in practical terms.

---

[30] This seems to be standard practice in the US when there are allegations relating to the FCPA.
[31] Of course privilege can be waived at a later point should the commercial organisation wish to do so. However, there is no requirement to give such a waiver and prosecutors are not entitled to insist on it or take the issue of waiver of privilege into account when considering the public interest in prosecution. This topic is quite separate from the issue of what public disclosures might be necessary for listed entities.

9.71 The commentary suggests that key responsibilities will be the authorisation of the risk-management process, communication of the policy[32] and the clear and effective communication of the resulting policies and procedures, as well as more general 'engagement' with elements of the procedures as necessary.

9.72 When major policies in this area are introduced the Chief Executive Officer, Chairman or other senior person will often make an announcement to staff and others affected by it, saying, in effect, that he personally endorses it and setting out the consequences of non-compliance. ABC programmes often take effect as part of larger codes of practice or ethical principles which cover various other subjects and which are designed to develop a specific corporate culture. There should be nothing objectionable about amalgamating an ABC programme into a wider code of ethics or behaviour, as long as the specific commitment to not tolerating bribery is clear.

9.73 More important than warm words from a CEO is actual support for the programme, in particular the provision of resources to those tasked with operating it. As suggested in the commentary, this may take the form of the personal involvement of top-level managers or directors in developing a code of conduct. It may also involve the appointment of a senior person to oversee the programme. Such a person is likely to be the day-to-day 'owner' of the programme, and will be a vital part of the overall effectiveness of the procedures. Some firms refer to this function as a compliance officer (CO) and for the sake of convenience this chapter does the same.

9.74 It will be important for senior management to provide the CO with appropriate assistance, budget, etc so that they can do their job. In a low-risk organisation responsibility for the programme may simply be added to the other responsibilities of management, with little need for separate specific resourcing. It is probably good practice for the CO to have a line of reporting to the board, although he may sit as part of the legal or compliance teams.

9.75 Perhaps most important of all is the role of senior management in establishing a culture in which bribery and other illegality is not tolerated. As usual, actions will speak louder than words. Companies which do not investigate or discipline a finance director, sales director, trader, broker, consultant or agent known to be engaged in questionable conduct may be facilitating the illicit activities in question, whether or not the specifics of those activities are known about or endorsed. A culture of 'making the numbers', whatever the cost, can lead to serious problems in the long term.[33]

---

[32] The commentary suggests that this might be done 'periodically'. One wonders whether this is likely to happen in practice, when most boards or chief executives consider that a directive, once given, is in force unless withdrawn.
[33] The case of Enron is an example. For a highly readable account of the culture of that company see McLean and Elkind *The Smartest Guys In The Room* (New York, 2003).

9.76 Of course, under s 14, senior officers who consent or connive in the commission of s 1, s 2 or s 6 offences by corporate bodies or Scottish partnerships will be personally liable.[34] Moreover, such conduct by those responsible for the ABC procedures may be evidence of the effectiveness or otherwise of the procedures.[35]

9.77 Certain elements of the commentary bear the hallmarks of a tendency to focus on very large organisations. For example, the suggestion that the top level of the business should demonstrate '[e]ngagement with relevant associated persons and external bodies, such as sectoral organisations and the media, to help articulate the organisation's policies' is less likely to be relevant to businesses with little or no involvement in sectoral organisations or the media. The adoption of anti-bribery procedures is hardly the stuff of headlines even in the trade press – the media tend only to be interested in such matters after a scandal has already occurred.

9.78 It has been suggested by some that the subject of ABC procedures should be a standing item on the agenda of every board meeting.[36] In most cases this probably goes too far. Time at board meetings is limited and it is for the directors to exercise their judgement about which subjects require discussion. The elimination of bribery is not the sole priority of all businesses, some of whom will reasonably consider that there is little risk of it affecting them in a material way or that, even if there is, the business faces even more important issues.

9.79 Of course boards should commit the organisation to an anti-bribery policy and procedure which is adequate for the business, and in some cases a regular item on the board's agenda may be very sensible. But each case will be different and it is submitted that the jury considering adequacy of procedures should be concerned with the substance of the procedures themselves, not how many meetings might have referred to them.

PRINCIPLE 3: RISK ASSESSMENT

9.80 The text of principle 3 is as follows:

> 'The commercial organisation assesses the nature and extent of its exposure to potential external and internal risks of bribery on its behalf by persons associated with it. The assessment is periodic, informed and documented.'

9.81 Risk assessment is at the heart of any anti-bribery and corruption policy or procedure. Without a risk assessment it will be very difficult to argue that

---

[34] Inchoate and secondary liability may also come into play – see Chapter 12.
[35] Though a single incident probably does not invalidate an adequate procedure defence, for reasons given in Chapter 8.
[36] Transparency International *Guidance on Good Practice Procedures for Corporate Anti-bribery Programmes* (2010) p 15.

any procedures are adequate for the purpose of s 7(2) because there will be little evidence that they have been 'designed to prevent persons associated with C [from committing bribery under ss 1 and 6]'.

9.82 It is also critical, as the principle points out, for the risk assessment not to be a one-off event which is never revisited. The nature and scale of bribery risk can change as an organisation changes.

9.83 That the risk assessment is documented is also common sense, not only because the process of writing it down can be expected to improve the assessment but also because of the need to have evidence of the process.

Methodology

9.84 The commentary makes the following suggestions for methodology to be employed in assessing risk:

- '• Oversight of the risk assessment by top level management.
- Appropriate resourcing – this should reflect the scale of the organisation's business and the need to identify and prioritise all relevant risks.
- Identification of the internal and external information sources that will enable risk to be assessed and reviewed.
- Due diligence enquiries (see Principle 4).
- Accurate and appropriate documentation of the risk assessment and its conclusions.'

9.85 The commentary also makes a distinction between 'external' risks, which are the focus of much discussion of bribery risk, and 'internal' risks which tend to receive less attention. The commentary identifies that both are relevant and provides a succinct summary of typical facts which a commercial organisation should consider.

9.86 In general, the commentary on this subject is both comprehensive and concise. On external risks it makes the point, again sometimes ignored, that 'country risk' – the (apparent) level of corruption prevalent in a particular country in which the business operates – should not be analysed alone, but in conjunction with risks arising in certain sectors, transactions, types of opportunity or types of business partner.

9.87 Some of these more 'macro' risks can be evaluated, at least to some extent, by reference to surveys and studies published by reputable organisations such as the World Bank or Transparency International.[37] There is no shortage of other material being published by consultancies, NGOs, think-tanks and governments. The actual experience of employees may also be very useful, since few will know the sector or types of business opportunity better than experienced staff.

---

[37] See Appendix I, 'List of useful websites'.

9.88 It follows from the commentary that categorisation of territories as 'high risk' or 'low risk' should not necessarily be a mechanistic process which merely follows the judgments in existing literature. A country which is high risk for an oil company may be less risky for a consumer goods company or a vendor of professional services. The same could be true of a country seen generally as low risk but where corruption is quite common in a particular industry.

9.89 In cases where a specific business opportunity is under consideration, the commercial organisation should consider whether the transaction gives rise to bribery risk and where that is most likely to occur. The nature of the services to be provided by the associated person and how the remuneration relates to the services is likely to be critical.

9.90 The question of commission-based remuneration can be important when assessing the risks associated with intermediaries in particular. To ensure that it will earn a 10% commission on a transaction involving C, a corrupt intermediary may be happy to pay 3% away in bribes to officials or others.

9.91 Therefore, excessive commissions which do not seem to be justified by any (legal) benefit to the payer are viewed with considerable suspicion. There is no golden rule that certain rates of commission are always acceptable while others always are not. That said an organisation might well be asked to explain a case where it agrees to commission which significantly exceeds industry norms (if these can be established). There might be good reasons for divergence from the norm, such as the particular expertise of the agent or the difficulty of the task in question or because C is less commercially attractive to the agent as a customer.

9.92 The specification of services often has an important role to play. Agents and others which are vague or secretive about the detail of their services, who do not produce regular reports or allow appropriate scrutiny of their activities or agree to appropriate project milestones will be more risky than those who are prepared to be more open.

Incentives

9.93 By highlighting internal risks the commentary also affirms the importance of considering incentives in assessing risk. As we have seen in the case of intermediaries, people who are strongly incentivised towards making sales or achieving margins at all costs, and who are not scrutinised or subject to a culture of transparency or accountability, are at greater risk of getting involved in unethical practices. Commission-based remuneration has traditionally been a source of concern for this reason, and this is a potential risk factor, especially where regulation or scrutiny is relatively lax. The same could be said for some financial and private-equity businesses where bonuses or a 'turn' is central to remuneration.

9.94 Of course, it is perfectly legitimate to reward those who provide valuable services by means of bonuses or commission. Performance-related pay is central to modern management practice and it is hard to imagine an effective business where those who create profits are not rewarded for doing so. Moreover, there is no shortage of corruption among those whose pay is fixed. All that said, the potential for temptation of an employee or other person who personally stands to earn large sums from a single deal should not be ignored as a potential risk factor. As personal stakes are raised, so is the risk that corners will be cut to get the deal done.

Regulatory environment

9.95 A factor not specifically referred to in the guidance but which is important to evaluating risk in general is the regulatory environment applicable to a particular business. Firms who work in fast-developing sectors where there is little or no regulation tend to face greater risks of bribery. Firms whose business is subject to established standards which are effectively enforced by regulatory bodies, or whose viability depends on a reputation for probity, may be at a lower risk of committing bribery, partly as a result of the more conservative organisational culture which tends to result and partly because short-termism is not as strongly incentivised as elsewhere.

How much information is enough?

9.96 Those carrying out the risk assessment should have the skill and resources to do so. In a large corporate environment these might be senior people with credibility and authority within the business but who are not seen as being too involved in any one element of it, such as the company secretary or general counsel, supported as appropriate and perhaps reporting to the board or a designated sub-committee of the board. Some firms appoint a 'compliance officer' or someone with a similar title to coordinate this work. In a smaller business this might be an executive with existing responsibilities, such as a finance director, company secretary or an owner-manager.

9.97 If a business faces a higher degree of risk then there will be a greater need for thoroughness. In some cases it will make sense to review relevant financial and employment information within the business, such as audit reports, information about existing contractors, as well as publicly available information about counterparties, agents, joint-venture partners, etc. Often, key staff are surveyed to gain 'on the ground' intelligence about market practices and perceptions of risk.

9.98 Some organisations combine this work with the commissioning of reports by outside consultancies, and consult industry bodies or international institutions. It is not uncommon to carry out specific due-diligence enquiries into prospective joint venture partners or intermediaries. Others rely on more informal methods, such as meetings to tap into the collective experience of their managers, advice from professional advisers such as accountants or consultants, or the views of members of the board.

9.99 A recent phenomenon has been a growth in private firms which offer specific 'due-diligence' services to businesses worried about compliance with anti-corruption laws. Some such firms offer privately sourced information about particular countries, industries, companies and individuals (usually accompanied by far-reaching disclaimers). Some offer standard or bespoke training or capacity-building programmes or accreditation or certification of compliance programmes. Such services are considered useful by many large businesses and no doubt the demand for them will continue to grow. However, in all dealings with private information, businesses should be careful to ensure that they and their agents abide by the law, including laws on data protection, confidentiality and personal privacy.

9.100 A failure to use all the sources of information that might be available in carrying out the risk assessment should not be seen as an indicator of inadequacy of the process. There is almost no end of information which is potentially relevant to any business decision. It is submitted that the reasonable judgement of a well-informed business as to the limits of its risk assessment should be respected in any analysis of the adequacy of the procedures employed.

PRINCIPLE 4: DUE DILIGENCE

9.101 The text of principle 4 is as follows:

> 'The commercial organisation applies due diligence procedures, taking a proportionate and risk based approach, in respect of persons who perform or will perform services for or on behalf of the organisation, in order to mitigate identified bribery risks.'

9.102 It naturally makes sense for businesses to carry out due diligence when considering a significant new transaction or business relationship, and well-run businesses do this as a matter of course. The commentary outlines the need for due diligence as an important part of ABC procedures and suggests practical methodologies and factors to be considered.[38]

9.103 It is clear that the level of due diligence which is necessary will vary according to each situation. As the commentary points out, many situations will not call for significant or any due diligence, especially transactions or relationships of a routine or minor nature. The examples highlighted in the commentary as calling for a higher degree of due diligence include the appointment of an intermediary for the purpose of developing business in a new territory and a merger or acquisition.

---

[38] A source of good practice is the Trace International Due Diligence Guidebook, available at www.traceinternational.org/news/TRACEDueDiligenceGuidebook.asp.

9.104 The reputation of agents, joint-venture partners and others acting on behalf of the commercial organisation should be investigated so far as reasonably possible. It is generally wise to consider media and other sources independent of the proposed business partner itself, if these are available.[39] It might be possible for embassy staff to assist in any due diligence investigation although in practice this seems to be rare. Trade associations and other bodies may be able to supply lists of approved subcontractors or other suppliers and of course, as with any important transaction, financial and personal references are potentially useful. As noted in our discussion of risk assessment, some suppliers will conduct more in-depth investigations using local sources or contacts within government or a wider range of public sources than might be accessible to an individual business.

9.105 It will frequently be the case that local businesses which are capable of acting as intermediaries or other associated persons do not have the sort of detailed policies and procedures which a major multinational might have, and it is simply unrealistic to expect this. It is submitted that the lack of a policy which is sure to be adequate in the UK should not be a disqualification so long as the commercial organisation has satisfied itself that the proposed partner is committed to the principles of its anti-bribery policy. A willingness to adopt the policy of the commercial organisation, or at least to abide by its principles, will be likely to evidence such a commitment.

9.106 There is a further discussion of due diligence in the outline ABC policy below.

Varying due diligence according to incorporation?

9.107 The commentary in the MOJ Guidance states:

> 'Generally, more information is likely to be required from prospective and existing associated persons that are incorporated (e.g. companies) than from individuals. This is because on a basic level more individuals are likely to be involved in the performance of services by a company and the exact nature of the roles of such individuals or other connected bodies may not be immediately obvious.'

9.108 The logic of this passage is a little difficult to follow. Whether a business partner is incorporated or not is unlikely to be an important indicator of the degree of due diligence needed. Some intermediaries or partners will be powerful individuals in host states. Other things being equal, one would expect these individuals to attract a higher degree of due diligence. Some genuine trading businesses which are incorporated might well have more public information available and risk-management systems and controls in place already and thus require a lower degree of due diligence. Each case should be approached individually.

---

[39] In many countries, of course, there are few independent media sources. Even in territories with a free media the coverage of business affairs often does not achieve the depth of that available in more developed markets.

Red flags

9.109 Various organisations have published material on matters which should be in the mind of those carrying out due diligence in relation to bribery risk, especially when using intermediaries in overseas countries.[40] Findings which indicate a heightened degree of risk have come to be known as 'red flags'. Among the more important of these are the following:

(a) Is the territory in question subject to a high level of bribery or corruption in business transactions?

(b) Is the intermediary from a country outside of that in which services are being rendered?

(c) Is it proposed that payment is made to a bank account of a country known for its strict bank secrecy laws or where ownership of companies or control of trusts is difficult to establish, or to a third party with no apparent connection to the intermediary?

(d) Does the intermediary have a reputation that raises suspicion and/or has the due diligence exercise uncovered information to this effect?

(e) Does the intermediary have any family or business connections with any member of the government or regulatory authorities in the territory in question?

(f) Is there any evidence of previous involvement by the intermediary in the payment of bribes?

(g) Are there any media reports of allegations of corruption, bribery, dishonesty, nepotism, connections with politicians known for such things or with other intermediaries with a poor reputation in this area?

(h) Was the intermediary recommended by a customer, or by a government official involved in the transaction?

(i) Is the intermediary appropriately qualified, for example in the case of technical products, does the intermediary have appropriate technical qualifications or a track record?

(j) Does the intermediary have appropriate resources to carry out the services in question?

(k) Has the intermediary requested payment of a commission before or immediately after the time of the award of the contract?

---

[40] For example, the Transparency International Guidance and Trace International Due Diligence Guidebook mentioned above.

(l) Has the intermediary made reference to the need for 'political contributions' or charitable contributions or other possible euphemisms for bribery?

(m) Is the intermediary aware of the law applicable to its activities in particular in relation to corruption and procurement?

(n) Has the intermediary been evasive or unreasonably slow to provide any information sought from it?

(o) Is the proposed remuneration of the intermediary out of line with normal commercial terms or industry norms?

(p) Is the proposed remuneration of the intermediary justifiable and proportionate to the services to be rendered?

(q) Does the intermediary fail to provide appropriate detail in reporting its activities, its claims for remuneration or expenses?

9.110 The list above is in no particular order. It may well be that the existence of one or more red flags does not necessarily make it unreasonable for the appointment to be made. It will be a question of balancing and attempting to mitigate risks in each individual case.[41] It may be necessary to carry out enhanced due diligence should red flags appear as a result of an initial enquiry. Businesses should not close their eyes to obvious dangers, and a failure to make reasonable and pertinent enquiries for fear of obtaining inconvenient answers may harm the case that a due diligence procedure was adequate.

9.111 There may well be cases where, although the associated person has certain risk factors attached to it, there are nevertheless good reasons for making or continuing the appointment, perhaps with enhanced vigilance over the activities in question or other measures to mitigate identified risks. The process by which any decision was reached should be carefully documented. It is submitted that the issue of whether to go ahead with a particular appointment, and on what terms, should be subject to the exercise of reasonable discretion.[42]

---

[41] For example, there may be intermediaries who have friends or relations who work in public service or government (as is the case with lobbying firms in the UK) but who have no record of bribery and to whom no other risk factors attach.

[42] After all, the UK, as a state, regularly licenses transactions with regimes whose officials have been accused of some very serious crimes, including bribery, no doubt on the basis that it is in the national interest to do so and that it has no direct knowledge of such transactions facilitating crime.

PRINCIPLE 5: COMMUNICATION (INCLUDING TRAINING)

9.112 The text of principle 5 is as follows:

> 'The commercial organisation seeks to ensure that its bribery prevention policies and procedures are embedded and understood throughout the organisation through internal and external communication, including training, that is proportionate to the risks it faces.'

9.113 This is essentially common sense. There is a good deal of overlap with principle 2 (top level commitment). An organisation which is committed to an ABC policy will demonstrate that commitment by communicating it throughout the organisation and to those others affected by it such as associated persons.

9.114 The commentary makes a straightforward case for the utility of training in communicating and reinforcing the ABC message. There are two elements of the commentary which may be a little more controversial, although these are couched in terms which are considerably less directive than in the previous draft.

9.115 The first is the suggestion that 'a commercial organisation may consider it proportionate and appropriate to communicate its anti-bribery policies and commitment to them to a wider audience, such as other organisations in its sector and to sectoral organisations that would fall outside the scope of the range of its associated persons, or to the general public'. It is clear from the language used that the Secretary of State does not consider such external communications as a prerequisite of adequacy, and this must be right. There will be all kinds of organisations with adequate procedures which are not advertising the fact, in the same way that other policies of the firm are not necessarily advertised. Of course this is not to say that public commitments of the type envisaged are not useful in many circumstances.

9.116 The second is the statement that:

> 'It may be appropriate to require associated persons to undergo training. This will be particularly relevant for high risk associated persons. In any event, organisations may wish to encourage associated persons to adopt bribery prevention training.'

Again, it is clear that such training of third parties is hardly considered essential. There will be many circumstances where it will not be commercially possible to dictate what training is necessary or desirable for associated persons, although perhaps an organisation in a very powerful commercial position may be able to do so.

PRINCIPLE 6: MONITORING AND REVIEW

9.117 The text of principle 6 is as follows:

'The commercial organisation monitors and reviews procedures designed to prevent bribery by persons associated with it and makes improvements where necessary.'

9.118 As the commentary states, bribery risks faced by an organisation will change over time and therefore, to be effective, the relevant procedures should do so as well.

9.119 The commentary recommends various methods by which this can be achieved such as staff surveys, questionnaires and feedback from training, as well as formal periodic reviews by the organisation's management.

9.120 The essential point is that procedures which are not managed and monitored are not going to be effective. This will be an important function of any compliance officer or person in a similar role. In high-risk organisations it is something which should be addressed proactively rather than in a reactive way. So, for example, a compliance officer could refresh their know-how by participating in industry or interest groups, manage and/or lead training sessions, sign up for e-mail or other alerts on subjects relevant to this type of risk, and convene regular feedback meetings with others involved in the procedures (such as people in audit or divisional or country managers).

9.121 The commentary mentions obtaining external verification or assurance of effectiveness of procedures from external agencies. For organisations facing a high degree of risk these measures may well be very helpful, although it is again clear from the commentary that the Secretary of State does not consider them to be an essential measure of adequacy.

Recording the procedures at work

9.122 An important test of the actual effectiveness of any set of procedures is likely to be evidence of how it operates in practice and, how it applies in specific situations. For example, if the corporate due-diligence process indicates a very high level of risk in a particular transaction, the outcome of the procedure may well be relevant to the question of how the procedures are really operating. A decision to go ahead with a very risky transaction with no additional safeguards, despite an apparently strong likelihood of bribery or, worse, a decision to try to disguise the true nature of a relationship with an associated person so as to distance the organisation from likely bribery will not speak well of the procedures.

9.123 Anyone reviewing a procedure which has been in effect for a period of time is likely to ask: 'What actual business decisions have been affected by the procedures, and how has that happened?' To this end, organisations would be well advised to maintain careful and complete records of not only the ABC procedures themselves but how they are being operated. They should record both evidence of compliance and key decisions in writing and in a readily accessible form.[43]

OUTLINE ABC POLICY

9.124 At the end of this chapter is a table outlining a hypothetical anti-bribery policy. This is offered with a good deal of diffidence, because the entire tenor of this chapter so far, and of virtually all writing on this topic, including the MOJ Guidance, is that one size does not fit all organisations.

9.125 Nevertheless, organisations which may be facing the task of creating ABC procedures for the first time sometimes benefit from a suggested list of topics, if only to stimulate thought about what is actually suitable for their own needs. The table can be found at **9.153** below.

DEFENCE FOR MILITARY AND SECURITY SERVICE PERSONNEL –SECTION 13

BRIBERY ACT 2010: SECTION 13

'**13 Defence for certain bribery offences etc.**

(1) It is a defence for a person charged with a relevant bribery offence to prove that the person's conduct was necessary for—

(a) the proper exercise of any function of an intelligence service, or
(b) the proper exercise of any function of the armed forces when engaged on active service.

(2) The head of each intelligence service must ensure that the service has in place arrangements designed to ensure that any conduct of a member of the service which would otherwise be a relevant bribery offence is necessary for a purpose falling within subsection (1)(a).

(3) The Defence Council must ensure that the armed forces have in place arrangements designed to ensure that any conduct of—

(a) a member of the armed forces who is engaged on active service, or
(b) a civilian subject to service discipline when working in support of any person falling within paragraph (a), which would otherwise be a relevant bribery offence is necessary for a purpose falling within subsection (1)(b).

---

[43] For a US perspective in the context of the FCPA, see Athanas, 'Demonstrating 'Systemic Success' in FCPA Compliance (American Bar Association, 2011) at www2.americanbar.org/sections/criminaljustice/CR121212/Pages/actf_athanas.aspx.

(4) The arrangements which are in place by virtue of subsection (2) or (3) must be arrangements which the Secretary of State considers to be satisfactory.

(5) For the purposes of this section, the circumstances in which a person's conduct is necessary for a purpose falling within subsection (1)(a) or (b) are to be treated as including any circumstances in which the person's conduct—

(a) would otherwise be an offence under section 2, and
(b) involves conduct by another person which, but for subsection (1)(a) or (b), would be an offence under section 1.

(6) In this section—

"active service" means service in—

(a) an action or operation against an enemy,
(b) an operation outside the British Islands for the protection of life or property, or
(c) the military occupation of a foreign country or territory,

"armed forces" means Her Majesty's forces (within the meaning of the Armed Forces Act 2006),

"civilian subject to service discipline" and "enemy" have the same meaning as in the Act of 2006,

"GCHQ" has the meaning given by section 3(3) of the Intelligence Services Act 1994,

"head" means—

(a) in relation to the Security Service, the Director General of the Security Service,
(b) in relation to the Secret Intelligence Service, the Chief of the Secret Intelligence Service, and
(c) in relation to GCHQ, the Director of GCHQ,

"intelligence service" means the Security Service, the Secret Intelligence Service or GCHQ

"relevant bribery offence" means—

(a) an offence under section 1 which would not also be an offence under section 6,
(b) an offence under section 2,
(c) an offence committed by aiding, abetting, counselling or procuring the commission of an offence falling within paragraph (a) or (b),
(d) an offence of attempting or conspiring to commit, or of inciting the commission of, an offence falling within paragraph (a) or (b), or
(e) an offence under Part 2 of the Serious Crime Act 2007 (encouraging or assisting crime) in relation to an offence falling within paragraph (a) or (b).'

9.126 Anyone interested in military history or the history of espionage will be aware that soldiers and spies sometimes pay for information, for favours or for military assistance. There are circumstances where this will amount to bribery as defined in s 1 or 6 of the Act.[44]

9.127 Section 13 of the Bribery Act provides any person charged with a 'relevant bribery offence' with a defence if he can establish that the conduct in question was necessary for the proper exercise of any function of an intelligence service or the armed forces on active service.[45] The main elements of the defence will be examined briefly below.

Relevant bribery offence

9.128 A relevant bribery offence is limited to the general bribery offences under ss 1 and 2 and the various inchoate offences listed in s 13(6). It does not extend to offences under s 6, or to offences charged under s 1 which would also be an offence under s 6.

9.129 As we have seen, s 6 offences involve the bribery of a foreign public official ('F') for a business purpose. As well as intending to influence F by means of the bribe, the defendant ('P') must also intend to obtain or retain business, or an advantage in the conduct of business. So a bribe offered, promised or given to a foreign public official for a non-business purpose (for example to obtain information relevant to matters of national security) would not be an offence under s 6, though it might well qualify as an offence under s 1. A charge under s 1 in such circumstances would be subject to the defence under s 13.

9.130 A s 7 offence, by a commercial organisation, cannot be the subject of a defence under s 13. Obviously, commercial organisations are not members of the intelligence services or armed forces and the element of the s 7 offence again includes a business purpose.

Armed forces and intelligence services

9.131 The intelligence services and armed forces are defined in the Act as the security service (otherwise known as MI5), the secret intelligence service (otherwise known as MI6) and GCHQ, which deals with electronic intelligence.

9.132 Sections 13(2) and (3) provide for duties on the heads of the various intelligence services, and on the Defence Council, to put in place arrangements designed to ensure that conduct by their staff which might amount to a relevant

---

[44] *Hansard*, HL, col GC88 (13 Jan 2010): 'We do not seek to hide the fact that certain arms of the state may need to offer financial or other inducements that may amount to a bribe in order that they can effectively carry out their difficult functions' (Lord Bach, Parliamentary Under-Secretary of State).
[45] As with most statutory defences, the burden of proof will be on the defendant, but only to the 'civil' standard of the balance of probabilities.

bribery offence is for a necessary purpose as defined by s 13(1)(a) and (b). This seems to require an administrative arrangement whereby conduct which might amount to bribery is considered and a decision is taken as to whether it is necessary for the relevant purpose. The implication of s 13(4) is that the Secretary of State (presumably, in this context, the Secretary of State for Justice) will consider and approve these arrangements, although he will not be involved in individual decisions as to the propriety of a particular transaction.

9.133 It is interesting that although various provisions are made for the governance of intelligence or military personnel, the Act does not actually specify that only serving members of the armed forces or intelligence services may avail of the s 13 defence. Section 13(1) seems to be available to any person who can establish that his conduct was necessary for the proper exercise of the functions of the respective services. This may have been an error, given the considerable detail given elsewhere in s 13 to provide for the controls on armed forces and intelligence personnel. Persons who are not members of the respective services can be expected to have a difficult task in establishing that their conduct was for the purposes of those services, absent exceptional circumstances.

Proper exercise of any function

9.134 The term 'proper exercise of any function' (of either the armed forces or security services) is not defined. It is very wide and no doubt will be referable to the published mission statements and duties of the services in question. It is likely to be treated as an objective requirement rather than merely the opinion of the accused or another person.

9.135 Interesting though these arguments might be in an academic seminar, they may not be tested in the courts in the near future. Although nothing is impossible, it seems most unlikely that cases in which the s 13 defence has a real chance of success would reach trial, both because of the sensitivity of the subject matter and the duty of prosecutors to protect the public interest.

Police and informants

9.136 The mere existence of the defence may appear to some to create a slippery slope. It has led to arguments that the proper performance of other functions (such as the police seeking to prevent crime) should also be protected by such a defence. Indeed, the original Bill included law enforcement agencies among those which could benefit from such a defence. This was withdrawn, after vehement debate.

9.137 The position of a police officer who, for example, pays for information from an informant who is not a foreign public official should be considered in the light of whether the payment was intended to induce improper performance of a relevant function or activity. The activities of an informant may not qualify as relevant activities under s 3(2) or may not be subject to relevant expectations under s 3(4)–(6). Even if an informant's activities are within tests spelled out by s 3, it is doubtful whether providing information to the police for the purpose of the investigation of crime would amount to improper performance. The situation in relation to foreign public officials may be somewhat different, and those investigating offences under s 6 of the Act (or other crimes requiring information from foreign public officials) should take care not to commit bribery in doing so.

DEFENCES OF DURESS AND NECESSITY

9.138 Other potential defences to charges of bribery, under any of ss 1, 2, 6, 7 or 14 of the Act, are duress and necessity.[46] They are particularly relevant to the concerns regularly expressed about the risk of extortion by foreign public officials.

Duress

9.139 The law has long recognised that where people are faced with a threat of death or serious injury unless they commit a crime this may be an excuse for their crime. The elements of the defence (which is not available for crimes of murder, attempted murder, or treason) are as follows:[47]

(1) there must be a threat of death or serious injury;

(2) the threat must have been made to the defendant or his immediate family or someone close to him or someone for whom D would reasonably regard himself as responsible;

(3) the defendant's perception of the threat and his conduct in response are to be assessed objectively. It must be reasonable for him to believe that he is under such a threat and his decision to commit the crime in response must be reasonable;

(4) the conduct in question must have been directly caused by the threats relied on;

(5) the defendant must not reasonably have been able to take evasive action;

(6) the defendant cannot rely on threats to which he has reasonably left himself open.

---

[46] Of course other defences exist within criminal law more generally, such as insanity, intoxication or mistake. These are not considered here as they are unlikely to be relevant to bribery offences.

[47] *R v Hasan* [2005] UKHL 22.

9.140 Only a threat of death of serious injury will suffice. Threats of minor injuries, pain or property damage such as arson or theft are irrelevant, as is the fact that the crime proposed is less serious than the threat.

9.141 A person under duress is expected to display 'the steadfastness reasonably to be expected of the ordinary citizen in his situation'. Age and sex may be relevant, depending on circumstances, as will psychiatric illness.

9.142 The defence of duress is well established in law and a person who was threatened with imminent serious violence to himself, or another person for whom he was responsible unless a bribe was paid would no doubt be able to rely on duress if later charged with the bribery.

Necessity

9.143 Closely connected to duress is the defence of necessity. The boundaries between necessity and what has been called 'duress of circumstances' are not fully clear but need not trouble us for present purposes.[48] The principle is that where a person is faced with two alternative evils, one of which involves harm to himself or others, the other involving a breach of the law, the defence of necessity should be available if he chooses the lesser evil, even if in doing so he breaks the law. For example, a fire engine is approaching a house which is fully ablaze. The traffic lights turn red. Must the driver wait for the green light in all circumstances? The answer the law gives is 'no', because it is permissible to break traffic regulations if that is reasonably necessary to preserve life and property.[49]

9.144 Many other examples could be given. An example in the context of bribery law is where a corrupt official threatens immediate and extremely serious consequences (perhaps imprisonment without trial for an indefinite period) unless a bribe is paid. In principle, could the defence of necessity apply even if there is little apparent risk of death or serious injury flowing from the threatened consequence?

9.145 The defence of necessity has applied in cases where the mental health of a person would suffer harm unless a certain medical procedure was done without consent or in circumstances of minority.[50] It seems that it is also a defence to trespass to land in some circumstances.[51]

9.146 It is notable that in these cases the alleged perpetrators of the offences were public authorities or police officers who were facing serious ethical dilemmas and stood to make no personal gains from the course of action which

---

[48] See *Smith and Hogan on Criminal Law* (12th edn, Oxford, 2008) pp 342–54.
[49] *Johnson v Phillips* [1976] 1 WLR 65.
[50] *F v West Berkshire Health Authority* [1989] 2 All ER 545, HL; *Gillick v West Norfolk & Wisbech AHA* [1986] AC 112.
[51] *R v Richards & Leeming* (on appeal from 81 Cr App R 125) (unreported) 10 July 1986, HL, summarised in *Smith and Hogan on Criminal Law* (12th edn, Oxford, 2008) p 346.

they took. Private citizens deciding for themselves which is the lesser of two evils and relying on necessity or duress of circumstances may have a more difficult case to make, perhaps because of the lack of any statutory or public law duty on them to act in the public interest or the interests of persons in their care.[52]

9.147 There is no case of such a defence being successfully employed against a charge of bribery which is known to the author. In most cases where bribes are sought the negative consequence of failure to comply is economic, such as loss of a contract or not receiving a service. This is not the emergency situation which has historically attracted the defence and to which it can be expected to be limited.[53] The editor of *Smith & Hogan* remarks:

> 'Despite the explicit recognition of the defence [of necessity] the courts adopt a persistently restrictive approach to its application. There is an underlying anxiety that the defence must be kept within strict limits to prevent defendants claiming generally that they thought their actions in breaking the law were reasonable and represented the lesser of two evils. This would be a Trojan horse for anarchy.'[54]

9.148 Recognising this, a case can nevertheless be made that the defence of necessity could apply to a charge of bribery in circumstances where, through no fault of his own, a person faces imprisonment without trial if he does not pay a bribe.[55] The loss of liberty, especially in circumstances where it is reasonable to believe there is little prospect of a fair trial or independent scrutiny of the lawfulness of the detention, would be an extremely daunting prospect for the average person, especially if he is a foreigner who cannot speak the local language. In some cases, such a threat could be seen as equivalent to the threat of serious injury in its effect on the mind of a person of reasonable steadfastness.

9.149 A defendant charged with assisting or encouraging a crime under Part II of the Serious Crime Act 2007 may defend himself on the ground that

---

[52] *R v Quayle* [2005] EWCA Crim 1415 (avoiding pain not sufficient defence to charge of cannabis possession), although see *R v Martin (Colin)* [1989] 1 All ER 652 where the direct threats of self-harm by the wife of the accused could have provided a necessity defence to a charge of driving while disqualified.
[53] In domestic cases, courts in the US have refused to allow a defence of 'extortion' to a charge of bribery – see *US v Kahn*, 472 F 2d 272 (2d Cir 1973), *US v Lee*, 846 F 2d 531 (9th Cir 1988).
[54] *Smith and Hogan on Criminal Law* (12th edn, Oxford, 2008) p 346.
[55] A payment would be a bribe under s 1, case 2, because P would know or believe that it is improper performance of a relevant function for the official to accept it. If R is a foreign public official the payment would be intended to influence the FPO in his capacity as such and if P was on a business trip then it is quite arguable that being allowed on his way is an advantage in the conduct of business, which might be part of P's intention in paying the bribe and thus the situation qualifies as a s 6 offence. In either case, it is most unlikely that the written law applicable to the official would either require or permit the payment (relevant to the view of the reasonable person when considering whether performance was improper for the purpose of s 1 offence) or require or permit the official to be influenced by the payment (relevant to whether the payment amounts to a bribe under s 6(3)(b)).

he was 'acting reasonably'[56] – for example because his actions were intended to prevent the commission or a more serious crime or to limit harm or to expose wrongdoing. The situation seems very close to that of an innocent person confronted with a criminal official who threatens to immediately deprive him of his liberty unless he makes a relatively small, though illegal, payment.

9.150 There seems to be no convincing reason of principle not to permit a defence of necessity to go before a jury in such circumstances. There would be little danger of a slippery slope. The number of such cases being prosecuted would be extremely small.[57] Permitting a defence would not incentivise wrongdoing since the defendant will not have made any gains by reason of his decision (to pay the bribe) but will have merely avoided a greater loss.[58]

OUTLINE ABC POLICY

9.151 This is an outline of an ABC policy which might be applicable to a UK-based company with, say 1,000 employees, with international operations, some in territories which are high risk and which uses intermediaries to make sales. The table below assumes that an adequate risk assessment has been carried out. It is essentially an annotated list of the materials which might be expected to emerge from such a process.

9.152 The limitations of a 'generic' document of this type will be immediately obvious – for example the subtleties of any particular market or industry sector, existing corporate culture or controls cannot be reflected in it. The outline is not put forward as a model or template. Any commercial organisation seeking to develop or improve ABC procedures should and develop policies which are suitable to their own circumstances.

9.153 In the outline, 'company' is shorthand for 'commercial organisation' and 'employee' is shorthand for 'associated person' (to include agents, intermediaries and other associated persons). 'CO' is shorthand for Compliance Officer.

---

[56] Serious Crime Act 2007, s 50.
[57] A prosecutor would have to give careful consideration to the public interest in bringing such a prosecution in any event. The terms of the Joint Prosecution Guidance, p 9, suggests that a prosecution would be unlikely.
[58] The Law Commission's original consultation paper proposed a specific 'emergency defence' along similar lines, however this was abandoned amid fears that a specific defence might dilute the nature of the general defences of duress and necessity. See LC 313, p 131.

TOPIC	CONTENT	REMARKS
Code of Ethics	Introduction/Endorsement of Board/CEO/Chairman	Many companies now have a general code or policy or statement of the business' approach to obeying applicable laws. It is sometimes called a code of conduct, integrity policy, anti-corruption policy or similar.
	Statement of principle – no bribery	
	The law	Such codes are often introduced by a senior figure such as the CEO, Chairman or similar and state the commitment of the board or other bodies to the principles contained in the code.
	Conflicts of interest	
	Definition of terms	Sometimes codes refer to a wide range of topics such as international sanctions, competition law, corporate governance, money laundering, employment, environmental standards, workplace conduct, labour standards and other subjects. They may be part of or attached to other materials such as employee handbooks.
	To whom code applies	
	Relationship to employment terms/employee handbook/other policies	
	'Wiring' – roles of CO or similar, reporting lines, contact details	There is nothing wrong with ABC being included in a more wide-ranging document or policy so long as relevant elements are identified. However, beware the risk of key messages getting lost if material is too scattered.
	Reference to ABC-specific procedures/policies	
	Reference to any trade association material/other relevant third party material	Statements of general principle can be put in a broad way such as 'we wish to uphold the very highest standards of legal and ethical conduct', or, more specifically 'we will not encourage or tolerate illegality in any form', or, more specifically again, 'bribery and corruption are not tolerated'.
	Risk assessment	
	Response to evidence of illegality	Whatever form of words are used the message should be that bribery is not permitted. It should be clear that the same standard applies across the organisations, notwithstanding local customs or expectations.
		The code could refer to specific laws such as the Bribery Act, although it is better to avoid being too legalistic or reductive. It might also make reference to the need to abide by local laws in each state the company operates in (without compromising the policy).

TOPIC	CONTENT	REMARKS
		It may be sensible to refer to a general principle of avoiding conflicts of interest – a concept which underlies a good deal of risk in the business world and can be an indicator of fraud, bribery and poor systems and controls more generally.
		The code should make specific reference to the specific policies and procedures which apply the ABC standards.
		The code should contain some definitions of terms relating to the nature of the business, who it applies to and key concepts. However, it should use language which the average employee can be expected to understand, and probably should not attempt any sort of detailed legal analysis.
		The code should explain the 'wiring' of the ABC procedure, how various procedures relate to each other and who is responsible for making key decisions. Often the code will introduce the role of the CO or other person whose job it is to manage the operation of the ABC process. The code should make clear that the most difficult or important decisions will be for the board or a sub-committee of the board, or for some similar senior decision-making body.
		If the company's procedures are part of a wider initiative or compliant with standards agreed by a trade association or sector body then this should be referred to.
		It is important that, if a risk-assessment on which the ABC policy has been carried out (as it ought to have been), the process should be recorded and underlying materials retained. It may or may not be necessary to make explicit reference to this in the code, as long as there are proper records of the risk-assessment process.
		It may be advisable to make a commitment to a speedy and independent investigation of credible allegations of illegality including bribery, for example by way of instructing an external body to investigate and report to an independent board sub-committee, the general counsel or similar.

TOPIC	CONTENT	REMARKS
		It probably is not necessary, and may be dangerous, to commit to 'self reporting' in every case. So far as possible, allegations should be investigated and legal advice obtained before taking such a significant step.
Policy on gifts	Definitions (gifts, hospitality)	Many ABC procedures contain a statement of policy in relation to giving and receiving gifts and/or hospitality (here, 'gift').
	Thresholds/authorisation	A model which is frequently used is to set a threshold for the value of any gift given or received by an employee. Before any gift above this value can be provided or received the employee must obtain authorisation from a superior and the gift, its value and the provider or recipient must be recorded. In some cases the thresholds vary according to geography.
	Records	
	Public officials	
		Many businesses limit the value of gifts which can be given to a recipient or received by an employee in a particular time period. The policy would not usually prevent gifts above the threshold figure, only require that they are justified and recorded. There is no ideal threshold figure – this must be a matter of judgement for each organisation.
		Some policies apply more stringent rules to gifts to public officials or foreign public officials and this is probably wise for most companies.
		Of course it is also in the interest of a company to make sure that their employees are not receiving gifts which make them subject to undue influence or perform their duties improperly by favouring the giver.
Policy on financial controls	Abide by law	The policy should make it clear that accounts and financial records must be kept to the applicable standards. No documents can be falsified and accounts should not be misleading. There must be no hidden or off-book accounts, since these obviously facilitate fraud generally and bribery in particular.
	No falsification or misleading material	
	Accounting according to applicable standards	
	No 'off-book' accounts	

TOPIC	CONTENT	REMARKS
Policy on charitable/political donations, sponsorship	Refer to any existing policy	Many ABC procedures limit charitable and political donations (including sponsorships) according to a pre-existing policy of the organisation in question and require all such donations, or donations above a threshold figure, to be authorised by senior persons such as the CO and recorded.
	Refer to risk of bribery	
	Threshold for authorisation/recording	Any thresholds should not be set too high if there is a risk that such donations or sponsorships might be a form of bribery, especially in poorer countries.
	Consider limiting political donations to board.	Some companies limit charitable donations to a pre-approved 'charity of the year' or similar.
	Make clear private charitable/political activities are not affected	Some companies prohibit political donations altogether or limit decisions in this area to the Board. Political donations are more common in other countries such as the US. It is good practice to draw attention to the risk that donations labelled as charitable or political may be cover for bribes.
		Personal donations to charities or political parties by employees are not the affair of employers save in very exceptional circumstances and in the UK it would not be lawful to prevent employees using their private resources in this way.
Policy on facilitation payments and extortion	Definitions	Some ABC procedures already attempt to assist employees faced with illegal demands for payments or other benefits by officials.
	Prohibit facilitation payments	These may urge employees to try to resist such demands by doing things like asking for receipts, referring to their company's policy of non-payment, providing their interlocutor with a laminated card which summarises that policy, threatening to inform the British Embassy and/or the official's superiors, and other such measures.[59]
	Suggest methods for resisting demands	

---

[59] See the case study attached to the MOJ Guidance at Appendix 1, which has been the subject to some trenchant commentary by a US-based anti-corruption practitioner, Howard Sklar, who blogs at www.openairblog.wordpress.com.

TOPIC	CONTENT	REMARKS
	Do not penalise staff who refuse to pay	Some offer training to employees which may be at particular risk or offer 'hotlines' to compliance officers or other colleagues such as senior management. Some might provide that employees which cause inconvenience to projects or business as a result of a refusal to pay a facilitation payment will not be penalised.
	Refer to training for staff at risk (if any)	
	Refer to hotlines, etc (if any)	Few will go as far as the suggestion made by Transparency International UK that 'employees may have to miss flights to make their point with airport officials or be prepared to incur the delay of a visit to a police station when a bribe is demanded for an alleged traffic offence'.[60]
	Permit payment if risk of harm	
	Require reporting of incidents	Such injunctions are easy to write down in a London corporate headquarters but difficult to follow at a roadblock or in an airport holding cell. The risk to people in such circumstances may be more than mere delay.
		Employers have a responsibility not to put their employees in harm's way and no employee should be obliged to put himself at personal risk protecting the interests of his employer unless, as with military or emergency service personnel, doing so is part of his official duty.[61]
		The policy might well accept that employees who are in situations where their well-being, or the well-being of others for whom they are responsible, is at risk then they must exercise their judgement and act to minimise the risk of harm to themselves or those others.
		If the alternative to paying up is disproportionate risk of harm to the employee or those others then they should pay. In those circumstances the employee is the victim of a crime and ought to be entitled to mitigate the harm which is likely to result.

---

[60] Transparency International *Adequate Procedures: Guidance to the UK Bribery Act 2010*, available at www.transparency.org.uk/working-with-companies/adequate-procedures.

[61] See, for example, Health & Safety At Work Act 1974, s 2(1). The situation is also likely to involve consideration of the right to liberty and security of person provided under Art 5 ECHR.

TOPIC	CONTENT	REMARKS
		They are most unlikely to be prosecuted.[62] It makes sense to require employees to report requests for facilitation payments and attempts at extortion so that the company can take such measures as it can to reduce this activity.
		The RESIST tool developed by the International Chamber of Commerce and various international organisations working in this area is a useful source of ideas for discouraging demand for facilitation or other bribe payments and methods of coping with them when made.[63]
Intermediaries[64]	Define intermediaries	The policy should make clear that intermediaries representing the company, including outsourced providers of services which involve such representation (hereafter simply 'intermediaries'), should be vetted and their activities monitored, depending on the level of risk associated with their activities.
	Include outsourced service providers if representing company	
	Require business justification for engaging intermediary	There should be a business justification for the engagement of any intermediary, which should be recorded. The policy could refer to specific procedures in this regard, including the items listed opposite.
	Spell out scope of engagement and detail of services	Depending on the services to be provided, fixed fees are less of a risk than commission-based remuneration, although these may not be appropriate for every engagement.
	Refer to need to vet intermediaries	The policy should require written contracts for intermediaries and require that such contracts contain terms prohibiting bribery. It should require that intermediaries are at least made aware of and preferably agree to abide by the ABC policies or principles of the company.
	Refer to detailed due-diligence procedures, to include:	

---

[62] See Joint Prosecution Guidance, p 9.
[63] See www.iccwbo.org/policy/anticorruption/index.html?id=37568.
[64] A source of good practice in relation to carrying out due diligence on intermediaries in particular is Trace International's Due Diligence Guidebook, available at www.traceinternational.org/news/TRACEDueDiligenceGuidebook.asp.

TOPIC	CONTENT	REMARKS
	• Geography risk	The contracts should make clear what the intermediary is engaged to do and specify the services to be provided in as much detail as possible.
	• Transaction risk	
	• Media/web searches	If possible, a right of termination in circumstances of bribery or breach of the anti-corruption term of the contract or the ABC policy should be reserved to the company, or apply to both parties. However, the details of these clauses can prove highly contentious, some intermediaries believing that certain terms might be used as a pretext for unjustified breaches of contract.
	• Capability information	
	• Commercial proposal and remuneration	
	• Corporate information (if any)	
	• Ownership information	
	• Affiliated businesses	Similar issues apply to terms which allow the company to examine/audit the records of the intermediary. Few western concerns would allow this level of access to a customer and it is not surprising that such clauses are often resisted. Moreover, to require such rights but then fail to pursue them might be counter-productive for the company.
	• Links to government/ regulators (inc family links)	
	• CVs of key people	
	• Specification of services	
	• References	The policy should draw attention to possible red flags arising from due diligence and provide a system for resolving issues arising from the process.
	• Third party verification	
	• Private intelligence	The company should consider whether the proposed remuneration of the intermediary (for example the rate of any commission) is in line with market norms or otherwise justifiable, and whether it presents a risk of bribery.
	• Embassy, trade association, other sources	
	Refer to red flags	The company should consider making all contracts with intermediaries limited in time and/or review due diligence at intervals.
	Require written contracts	
	Prohibit extra-contractual agreements (e g side letters)	An agreement which provides for governing law and particularly jurisdiction in countries where there is significant judicial corruption or an underdeveloped rule of law should be avoided if at all possible. If arbitration is selected it is preferable to choose an established arbitration jurisdiction and arbitration institution.
	Require anti-corruption provision in contract	
	Refer intermediary to ABC policy	

TOPIC	CONTENT	REMARKS
	If necessary hold face-to-face interview with intermediary	
	Keep full records of process	
	Consider periodic review/ re-tendering	
	Seek effective governing law and jurisdiction, dispute-resolution provisions	
	Consider extending training to intermediaries	
Joint ventures	As intermediaries, so far as possible	Joint ventures should, in principle, be approached with the same caution as overseas intermediaries.
	Maximum transparency of transactions, etc in JV agreement	However it is possible that certain potential JV partners (such as state companies without whose participation no project could happen) will either resent or ignore aspects of due diligence programmes which companies seek to follow, because they believe they have the economic or political power to do so.
	Seek significant board representation (though this will depend on commercial factors)	
	Anti-corruption commitment in JV agreement	In such cases companies have to make a good-faith evaluation of the risks associated with the JV.
	Seek effective governing law and jurisdiction, dispute-resolution provisions	A decision to ignore the procedures so as to participate in a lucrative project risks damaging or destroying the adequate procedures defence since a procedure which can be suspended when inconvenient can hardly be described as adequate.[65]
	Consider extending training to JVs	
		JV agreements should be as comprehensive as possible. There should be a commitment to anti-corruption in the JV agreement, and as much transparency in accounting and reporting as possible.

---

[65] Or 'effectively implemented and enforced' – MOJ Guidance, principle 1.

TOPIC	CONTENT	REMARKS
		An agreement which provides for governing law and particularly jurisdiction in countries where there is significant judicial corruption or an underdeveloped rule of law should be avoided if at all possible. If arbitration is selected it is preferable to choose an established arbitration jurisdiction and arbitration institution.
Mergers/ acquisitions	Refer to need for due diligence when acquiring company or business from third parties	The due diligence necessary when considering a merger or acquisition of another business is probably too complex a subject to be set out in the code or in any written procedure which is of general application. However, the code could mention that its principles on ABC are also applicable when considering mergers or acquisitions.
Speak up	Refer to speak up principle – reporting wrongdoing is required and encouraged	Some companies have extensive 'speak up' or 'whistleblowing' procedures, with considerable resources devoted to hotlines, external consultants or lawyers and other machinery.
	Provide support – who to speak to, protection of confidentiality, anonymous methods, no victimisation	Organisations with few employees may not need this. However, it should be clear to all employees that they are obliged to report breaches of the law or of procedures, including the ABC procedure. It should also be clear that they will not be victimised as a result. Methods for making reports which, if necessary, avoid the managers or others being complained about should be referred to.
Recruitment	Senior hires should be vetted. Bribery risk should be considered in sensitive positions	Naturally, the engagement of any person with a significant effect on an enterprise should be approached with care and due diligence should be done on that person. Employment, privacy and data protection law must be respected.
		However, in principle, companies should be aware of bribery risk and attempt to identify any factors which might indicate such a risk (for example media reports or government connections), especially in high-risk territories.

TOPIC	CONTENT	REMARKS
Human resources	Include ABC policy in employment terms	In principle, compliance with the ABC policy should be a term of employment. In English law terms, the payment or receipt of a bribe in the course of the employment could be defined as gross misconduct justifying immediate dismissal, perhaps with certain limited exceptions connected to facilitation payments where the employee complies with the ABC Policy.
	No loss for following ABC policy	
	Possibly consider incentive structures if significant contributor to risk	Where serious breaches are identified it is important that they are treated seriously, within the law. Criminal conduct such as bribery should not be tolerated.
		Employees should not be penalised in terms or remuneration, promotion or otherwise for abiding by the ABC policy even if this is seen to cause a loss of business or a business advantage.
		In some companies the ABC policy might be an opportunity to review the overall attitude to risk management including incentivising or discouraging certain behaviour through use of bonuses or commissions if that behaviour is seen as a significant contributor to risk.
Monitoring and review	Identify who is responsible for monitoring – CO?	The code should state the essential principle that the operation of the ABC procedures will be monitored and their effectiveness will be subject to review.
	Require staff/managers report to CO	
	What data is monitored?	The methodology of how to do this may be quite detailed and can be put into a separate procedure document.
	Consider monitoring particular high-risk projects or transactions (e g seek monthly reports on expenditure, etc)	That document should spell out who is responsible for monitoring and what actions they are expected to take, for example collating information which arises as a result of speak up procedures, surveys, legal advice or other sources.
	Annual report/certification by managers	Information and feedback coming out of training sessions can inform the monitoring and review.
	Periodic reviews as necessary	Staff and management in particular should be encouraged to work with the compliance officer function and to record and report breaches of the policy.
	Involve audit function	

TOPIC	CONTENT	REMARKS
	Record decisions, positive and negative, and evidence	Depending on risk, it can be good practice to require senior managers to report on compliance with the ABC policy by their division or business unit annually and/or to certify that the ABC policy has been complied with or that they are not aware of bribery involving the company.
		If there are identified high-risk projects or engagements then the compliance function could decide to monitor these closely, requiring regular reports on expenditure, activity of intermediaries, etc.
		Of course monitoring financial information is critical and will be necessary for the proper functioning of the business in any event.
		Audits, whether internal or external, should be planned with the risk of detecting bribery and fraud among the objectives, and those compiling and reviewing accounts should be vigilant for suspicious activity generally.
		Audit firms offer expertise in developing or optimising anti-bribery systems and controls.
		The company should retain records of how difficult issues and evidence of bribery, or bribery risk, were dealt with, how decisions of the CO, board or other decisions-makers were arrived at and the outcomes.
Training	Plan training programme	Training is seen as central to the effectiveness of ABC procedures at least in those companies where staff are likely to encounter requests for bribes. It is a specialist area and there are many organisations which offer training to companies, both in person and through the use of IT.
	Can be internal or external, web-based or face to face, depending on needs/risks	
	Tailor to business and risk associated with staff	
	Record and follow-up	Training should be targeted at those employees most in need of it. More senior staff who are likely to be taking big decisions about transactions may receive more in-depth training. Some companies make training mandatory.
	Use feedback as part of monitoring/review process	

TOPIC	CONTENT	REMARKS
		It is considered good practice to keep a record of the training and to pursue employees (often among the senior management) who do not participate.
		Feedback and information gained from training sessions can be used as part of the monitoring and review process.

Chapter 10

CONSENT TO PROSECUTION, ENFORCEMENT PRIORITIES AND PENALTIES

BRIBERY ACT 2010: SECTIONS 10 AND 11

'10 Consent to prosecution

(1) No proceedings for an offence under this Act may be instituted in England and Wales except by or with the consent of—

(a) the Director of Public Prosecutions,
(b) the Director of the Serious Fraud Office, or
(c) the Director of Revenue and Customs Prosecutions.

(2) No proceedings for an offence under this Act may be instituted in Northern Ireland except by or with the consent of—

(a) the Director of Public Prosecutions for Northern Ireland, or
(b) the Director of the Serious Fraud Office.

(3) No proceedings for an offence under this Act may be instituted in England and Wales or Northern Ireland by a person—

(a) who is acting—
  (i) under the direction or instruction of the Director of Public Prosecutions, the Director of the Serious Fraud Office or the Director of Revenue and Customs Prosecutions, or
  (ii) on behalf of such a Director, or
(b) to whom such a function has been assigned by such a Director,
except with the consent of the Director concerned to the institution of the proceedings.

(4) The Director of Public Prosecutions, the Director of the Serious Fraud Office and the Director of Revenue and Customs Prosecutions must exercise personally any function under subsection (1), (2) or (3) of giving consent.

(5) The only exception is if—

(a) the Director concerned is unavailable, and

(b) there is another person who is designated in writing by the Director acting personally as the person who is authorised to exercise any such function when the Director is unavailable.

(6) In that case, the other person may exercise the function but must do so personally.

(7) Subsections (4) to (6) apply instead of any other provisions which would otherwise have enabled any function of the Director of Public Prosecutions, the Director of the Serious Fraud Office or the Director of Revenue and Customs Prosecutions under subsection (1), (2) or (3) of giving consent to be exercised by a person other than the Director concerned.

(8) No proceedings for an offence under this Act may be instituted in Northern Ireland by virtue of section 36 of the Justice (Northern Ireland) Act 2002 (delegation of the functions of the Director of Public Prosecutions for Northern Ireland to persons other than the Deputy Director) except with the consent of the Director of Public Prosecutions for Northern Ireland to the institution of the proceedings.

(9) The Director of Public Prosecutions for Northern Ireland must exercise personally any function under subsection (2) or (8) of giving consent unless the function is exercised personally by the Deputy Director of Public Prosecutions for Northern Ireland by virtue of section 30(4) or (7) of the Act of 2002 (powers of Deputy Director to exercise functions of Director).

(10) Subsection (9) applies instead of section 36 of the Act of 2002 in relation to the functions of the Director of Public Prosecutions for Northern Ireland and the Deputy Director of Public Prosecutions for Northern Ireland under, or (as the case may be) by virtue of, subsections (2) and (8) above of giving consent.

11 Penalties

(1) An individual guilty of an offence under section 1, 2 or 6 is liable—

(a) on summary conviction, to imprisonment for a term not exceeding 12 months, or to a fine not exceeding the statutory maximum, or to both,
(b) on conviction on indictment, to imprisonment for a term not exceeding 10 years, or to a fine, or to both.

(2) Any other person guilty of an offence under section 1, 2 or 6 is liable—

(a) on summary conviction, to a fine not exceeding the statutory maximum,
(b) on conviction on indictment, to a fine.

(3) A person guilty of an offence under section 7 is liable on conviction on indictment to a fine.

(4) The reference in subsection (1)(a) to 12 months is to be read—

(a) in its application to England and Wales in relation to an offence committed before the commencement of section 154(1) of the Criminal Justice Act 2003, and
(b) in its application to Northern Ireland,
as a reference to 6 months.'

INTRODUCTION

10.1 This chapter discusses both the new law on the autonomy of prosecutors under s 10 of the Bribery Act, the likely approach of prosecutors to charges under the Act and the penalties available pursuant to s 11. The processes by which charges are laid, grounds for arrest and powers of investigators and prosecutors to obtain evidence are outside the scope of this book.

ROLE OF THE ATTORNEY-GENERAL AND DIRECTORS OF PROSECUTING AGENCIES (SECTION 10)

10.2 In the UK the Attorney-General (AG) acts as the chief government law officer, responsible for giving legal advice to the government and for the supervision of various prosecuting agencies, including the Serious Fraud Office. Prior to the Act, the permission of the Attorney-General for England and Wales was required before certain prosecutions could be brought under the Prevention of Corruption Acts.[1] The AG is not a civil servant as traditionally understood but a political appointment of the Prime Minister. Most AGs of recent times, although they have been lawyers, have also been parliamentarians and members of the cabinet.

10.3 Since the UK ratified the OECD Convention, matters relating to the economic or diplomatic interests of the UK should not be considered by the prosecuting authority or by the state in deciding whether to prosecute offences of bribery of foreign public officials.[2]

10.4 The issue came to the fore in the *Al Yamamah* affair, which involved allegations that bribes were paid to members of the Saudi Arabian government in connection with arms contracts. After having various representations made to him by the Prime Minister among others, the then Director of the SFO terminated the investigation in 2006, amid very considerable controversy. The decision was endorsed by the Attorney-General and the government.[3] The reason given was that to continue the investigation risked serious harm to the

---

[1] Prevention of Corruption Act 1906, ss 2, 3 (excepts Scotland), Public Bodies Corrupt Practices Act 1889, s 4 (includes Scotland, substituting the Lord Advocate for the AG of England and Wales).
[2] OECD Convention, Art 5 provides: 'Investigation and prosecution of the bribery of a foreign public official shall be subject to the applicable rules and principles of each Party. They shall not be influenced by considerations of national economic interest, the potential effect upon relations with another State or the identity of the natural or legal persons involved.'
[3] *Hansard*, HL, col 1711 (14 December 2006).

national security of the UK and thus to UK citizens (a matter outside the scope of Art 5 of the OECD Convention). The government denied that any commercial considerations played any part. An attempt at judicial review of that decision ultimately failed.[4]

10.5 Many felt that the case demonstrated that the UK did not take its obligations under the Convention seriously, or seriously enough, and that an official as closely connected to the government as the AG should have no role in deciding on prosecutions on matters which may in some cases be politically sensitive, such as bribery.

10.6 However, there is a case for locating decisions on the prosecution of bribery at a senior point in the prosecutorial hierarchy, even if not necessarily at cabinet level. Cases of official corruption are often to do with the functioning of governments and can attract both official interference and the risk of vexatious private prosecutions for political ends. It is idle to pretend that such cases should be treated in exactly the same way as burglaries or boiler-room frauds. The important discretionary power of the prosecutor ought to be exercised by those with the seniority to resist inappropriate pressure and to ensure that prosecutions not in the public interest are avoided.

10.7 Section 10 of the Act retains the need for the permission of a senior prosecutor before a prosecution is commenced and creates a specific scheme providing for (limited) delegation of powers of decision making on this subject. The prosecutors in question are the three directors of specific prosecuting bodies.

10.8 Under s 10(1) the three directors are named as:

- the Director of the Serious Fraud Office (SFO);

- the Director of Public Prosecutions (DPP);[5]

- the Director of Revenue and Customs Prosecutions.[6]

Their various equivalents in Northern Ireland are provided for by s 10(2).[7]

10.9 Pursuant to s 10(3)–(10) officials of each of the nominated prosecuting bodies can initiate prosecutions but must have the prior consent of the director and in case the director is not available a nominated and authorised alternate can exercise his power of consent.[8]

---

[4] *R (Corner House Research & Others) v Director of the Serious Fraud Office* [2008] UKHL 60.
[5] Who is in charge of the Crown Prosecution Service.
[6] Who is in charge of HM Revenue and Customs Prosecution Office.
[7] Section 10(1).
[8] No express provision seems to have been made for the Scots prosecuting agencies, perhaps because these authorities were already free of the requirement for the Attorney-General's

10.10 At the time of writing (April 2011) the government is said to be considering a reorganisation of the roles and responsibilities of various prosecuting authorities.[9] It may well be that the body currently charged with investigating and prosecuting significant corruption cases, the Serious Fraud Office (SFO), merges into another agency. However, it seems sensible to assume for present purposes that the general policies and priorities of the SFO will continue to be followed by whichever agency may succeed to its role.

10.11 By statute, the AG retains a supervisory role over the activities of the Director of the SFO and the other directors of the prosecuting bodies.[10] The precise nature of that responsibility is not entirely clear, although the AG seems to be responsible for appointment of the DPP and reports on his performance to Parliament. At least one former AG believed that she retained a 'power of direction' over the directors of prosecution services, albeit that this was a 'nuclear option' to be exercised rarely if ever.[11] In the present climate it would be quite extraordinary for an AG to interfere with a specific prosecution or investigation and such interference might well be the subject of judicial review.

PROSECUTORS' PRIORITIES

10.12 Prosecutors do not have an easy job. As public officials themselves their decisions are subject to considerable public scrutiny, potential judicial criticism, judicial review and frequently ill-informed media comment. The SFO in particular has the task of both investigating and prosecuting matters which are often extremely complex, usually with an international element, where the perpetrators tend to be much more motivated, sophisticated and well-funded than the average criminal suspect.

10.13 Although the SFO does have the benefit of certain specific powers of investigation not available to other agencies,[12] the difficulties attending the typical serious fraud case and limitations on budget mean that the SFO has to take considerable care in choosing which cases can be pursued.

10.14 UK prosecutors are also subject to an impressive range of codes, guidance, practice directions and other published material which must inform their decisions and practices. Not all of this material can be discussed here. However, there are specific publications applicable to the SFO and the prosecution of bribery in particular which are plainly relevant.

---

consent, at least in relation to the 1906 Act, or perhaps because the role of Scots prosecuting agencies is considered more of a devolved matter for the Scottish Parliament.
[9] 'Ministers defy their experts to kill Serious Fraud Office', *The Times*, 8 April 2011.
[10] Prosecution of Offences Act 1985, s 3(1), Criminal Justice Act 1987, s 1(2).
[11] See Joint Committee Report, Part 1, paras 165–76.
[12] For example, under the Criminal Justice Act 1987, s 2. Section 59 of the Criminal Justice and Immigration Act 2008 has extended the SFO powers to compel the production of documents at the earlier 'vetting' stage of foreign bribery cases.

10.15 Investigation or prosecution of bribery offences need not be conducted by the SFO. The City of London Police contains a specialised unit which is also tasked with investigating corruption which takes place overseas, and which supports the SFO in certain cases. Various other police forces and state agencies have units whose remit covers corruption in particular areas or sectors.[13] It is expected that the broad thrust of policy in this area will be determined by the SFO as the most specialised agency, in consultation with the others.

Prosecution of individuals

10.16 No crime of mens rea is committed without the involvement of one or more individuals. There is likely to be no greater deterrent to corporate crime than if the individuals responsible for it face a realistic risk of being convicted and sentenced. There is little doubt that the SFO will, in appropriate cases, seek the conviction of any individuals involved in bribery. These will of course include those receiving bribes as well as individuals paying bribes on their own behalf. Directors and managers of companies which are involved in bribery can also expect to have their personal culpability examined very closely since there are multiple routes by which they might be liable, whether directly (for example by way of ss 1, 6 or 14) as accessories or for inchoate offences.

10.17 All prosecutions in England and Wales are subject to the Code for Crown Prosecutors ('the Code')[14] which sets out the standards applicable to the work of the Crown Prosecution Service. The SFO also adheres to the Code. The Code sets out two central tests for a prosecution:

(1) that there is sufficient evidence to provide a realistic prospect of conviction of the suspect on the charge in question; and

(2) that a prosecution is in the public interest.

10.18 The evidence test speaks for itself and does not need further exposition here – detailed considerations as to how it will be applied can be found in the Code.

10.19 The 'public interest' test is particularly pertinent to discussion of the Bribery Act because of frequently expressed fears that very minor infractions fall within it and that well-intentioned people face heavy-handed prosecutions.[15]

---

[13] For example the Fraud Squad of the Ministry of Defence Police.
[14] Which can be found at www.cps.gov.uk/publications/code_for_crown_prosecutors.
[15] A recent case much celebrated in the media was that of Sprowston Bowls Club, Norfolk (*Daily Telegraph*, 20 February 2011), whose members were told by the Parish Council that the custom of giving a 'Christmas tip' to the club groundsman should be stopped because it might amount to bribery. This was quite wrong as a matter of law, assuming, as one does, that the gratuity was not intended to induce or reward improper performance of the groundsman's duties and

10.20 The Director of the SFO and the DPP have recently issued guidance as to the prosecution of offences under the Bribery Act,[16] which is dealt with in more detail below. We can say for now that it is clear, both from this material and from the main Code, that where there is sufficient evidence to establish a case of a breach of criminal law then it will usually be in the public interest to prosecute. Given the serious nature of bribery, the presumption in favour of prosecution is likely to be stronger.[17] All that said, the prosecutor must consider the public interest independently in each case.

10.21 Numerous factors are identified by the Code as favouring prosecution in the public interest. Among these, the following are especially relevant to bribery offences:

(a) a conviction is likely to result in a significant sentence;

(b) the offence was premeditated;

(c) there was an element of corruption of the victim in the way the offence was committed;

(d) the offence was committed in order to facilitate more serious offending;

(e) the suspect was in a position of authority or trust and he took advantage of this;

(f) a conviction is likely to result in an order of the court in excess of that which a prosecutor is able to secure through a conditional caution;

(g) the offence was carried out by a group;

(h) the suspect was a ringleader or an organiser of the offence;

(i) a prosecution would have a significant positive impact on maintaining community confidence;

(j) there are grounds for believing that the offence is likely to be continued or repeated.

10.22 Additional to these in cases of bribery of foreign public officials is the fact that prosecuting such bribery is a specific obligation of the UK under the

---

that it was not in itself improper performance for the groundsman to accept it. But even if the gratuity had been unlawful it would hardly have been in the public interest to prosecute it.

[16] Serious Fraud Office, *Bribery Act: Joint Prosecution Guidance For the Director of the Serious Fraud Office and Director of Public Prosecutions* March 2011 (hereafter 'Joint Prosecution Guidance'), attached at Appendix E.

[17] 'Bribery is a serious offence. There is an inherent public interest in bribery being prosecuted in order to give practical effect to Parliament's criminalisation of such behaviour' – Joint Prosecution Guidance, p 4.

OECD Convention. The expectation must be that a genuine and serious case of bribery of a foreign public official will be prosecuted.[18]

10.23 Among the factors which the Code identifies as militating against prosecution the following are especially relevant to bribery offences:

(k) the court is likely to impose a nominal penalty;

(l) the seriousness and the consequences of the offending can be appropriately dealt with by an out-of-court disposal which the suspect accepts and with which he complies;

(m) the suspect has been subject to any appropriate regulatory proceedings, or any punitive or relevant civil penalty which remains in place or which has been satisfactorily discharged, which adequately addresses the seriousness of the offending and any breach of trust involved;

(n) the offence was committed as a result of a genuine mistake or misunderstanding;

(o) the loss or harm can be described as minor and was the result of a single incident, particularly if it was caused by a misjudgement;

(p) the suspect played a minor role in the commission of the offence;

(q) the suspect has put right the loss or harm that was caused (but a suspect must not avoid prosecution or an out-of-court disposal solely because he pays compensation or repays the sum of money he unlawfully obtained);

(r) a prosecution may require details to be made public that could harm sources of information, international relations or national security.[19]

2011 Joint Prosecution Guidance

10.24 In relation to prosecution under ss 1 and 2, the Joint Prosecution Guidance published in March 2011 is supplementary to the main Code for Crown Prosecutors and makes it clear that the Code must be applied as a whole. The Guidance does not list all of the factors set out in **10.21** and **10.23** above. It lays particular emphasis on factors (a) to (e) as tending in favour of

---

[18] See OECD Report on United Kingdom: Phase 2bis Report, 16 October 2008, para 98, available at www.oecd.org/dataoecd/23/20/41515077.pdf.

[19] Although note Art 5 of the OECD Convention which provides that matters relating to the economic or diplomatic interests of a Convention state should not be considered by the prosecuting authority or by the state in deciding whether to prosecute offences of bribery of foreign public officials. This applies not only to offences under s 6 but also to offences under ss 1 or 7 which involve provision of bribes to foreign public officials.

prosecution.[20] Factors tending against prosecution specifically mentioned were (k) (nominal penalty likely) and (o) (minor harm, single incident).[21]

10.25 In relation to s 6 offences (bribery of a foreign public official), the Joint Prosecution Guidance states that 'prevention of bribery of foreign public officials is a significant policy aspect of the Act'. However, having said this, the prosecution guidance then concentrates its attention on the issue of facilitation payments. For non-facilitation-payment cases it seems more likely than not that the factors in favour of and against prosecution will be those outlined at **10.21** and **10.23** above.

10.26 In relation to facilitation payments the relevant factors are said to include the following factors in favour of prosecution:

(s) if payments are large or repeated and thus more likely to attract a significant sentence;

(t) facilitation payments that are planned for or accepted as part of a standard way of conducting business – indicating premeditation;

(u) an element of active corruption of the official;

(v) failure by an individual to follow a policy on facilitation payments which was applicable to the individual.

10.27 Factors against prosecution will include item (k) above (nominal penalty likely), as well as the following:

(w) the payments came to light as a result of a genuinely proactive approach involving self-reporting and remedial action;[22]

(x) that an appropriate policy concerning facilitation payments has been followed;

(y) that the defendant was in a vulnerable position arising from the circumstances in which the payment was demanded.

10.28 Of course, all cases are different and prosecuting authorities, properly, retain considerable discretion over which cases are in the public interest to prosecute.[23] Nevertheless it seems clear that breaches of the Act involving small amounts, committed through one-off errors made in good faith or where the penalties are likely to be nominal are very unlikely to require prosecution in the

---

[20] Joint Prosecution Guidance, p 7.
[21] The effect of self-reporting, etc mentioned in the Joint Prosecution Guidance is only relevant to corporate offending, as to which see below.
[22] This factor is only likely to be relevant to commercial organisations.
[23] Although any significant breach of relevant guidance and public law generally could be subject to judicial review.

public interest. Individuals lacking resources or experience who face urgent practical dilemmas and whose actions do not cause meaningful harm are unlikely to be considered important targets by the SFO.

10.29 However, people in positions of responsibility should not assume that they will be given the benefit of any doubt. Arguments can be and will be made that company directors, state officials, bankers, professionals and those with similar responsibilities should be held to high standards of probity and even cases which some would see as relatively 'minor' may be prosecuted to give effect to this principle. It should go without saying that deliberate and premeditated involvement in bribery is highly unlikely to escape prosecution once the evidential standard is achieved.

10.30 A good example of the policy, under the previous law, is the case *of R v Tobiasen and Tumukunde*.[24] In that case a UK-based director paid amounts in the tens of thousands (said to be 'tax') to an adviser to the President of Uganda in exchange for the awarding of government contracts to his company. Both the director and the Ugandan adviser (who was in Britain receiving medical treatment) were charged and sentenced to imprisonment, although the UK director's sentence was suspended.

GIVING ASSISTANCE TO PROSECUTORS

10.31 It is possible for prosecutors to offer various benefits to individuals once they cooperate with the investigation and give evidence as required. These powers (traditionally known as 'turning Queen's evidence') are now codified in the Serious Organised Crime and Police Act 2005.[25] The benefits include immunity from prosecution,[26] or that certain evidence will not be used against the accused in proceedings.[27]

10.32 In circumstances where an offender is convicted but has given cooperation to the prosecutor the sentencing court may take account of the extent of the offender's cooperation when sentencing.[28] The offender must abide by the conditions specified, failing which the sentence can be reviewed at a later date.[29] The process is not confined to offenders who provide assistance in relation to crimes in which they were participants, or accessories, or with which they were otherwise linked.[30] Discounts on sentence in the case of cooperation may be in the range between one-half and two-thirds. More than that will be unlikely.

---

[24] (Unreported) 2009, Southwark Crown Court.
[25] Serious Organised Crime and Police Act 2005, Part 2, Ch 2.
[26] Ibid, s 71.
[27] Ibid, s 72.
[28] Ibid, s 73.
[29] Ibid, s 74.
[30] *R v P & Blackburn* [2007] EWCA Crim 2290.

10.33 These provisions apply to 'any person', in other words to legal persons such as companies as well as to individuals, and there seems to be no reason of principle against companies benefiting from them if appropriate.

10.34 It is more likely than not that prosecutors will consider the exercise of these powers in cases under the Bribery Act, since, traditionally, a good deal of information about bribery cases has come from 'whistleblowers' and others with first-hand knowledge of the facts. It may well be possible even for individuals who are deeply implicated in the offences to escape conviction, depending on the level and standard of evidence which they are able to give.

Corporate prosecutions

10.35 Corporate prosecutions are much rarer than the prosecution of individuals, even in the field of economic crime. This is partly a function of the identification doctrine for corporate criminal liability discussed in Chapter 8, which has meant that corporate liability for the wrongdoing of officers or employees has been difficult to establish. Of course s 7 provides more opportunity to charge commercial organisations with bribery and there is no doubt that the authorities will do so in appropriate cases.

Attorney-General's Guidance

10.36 The Attorney-General's office has issued Guidance on Corporate Prosecutions.[31] It is applicable to each of the three directors of prosecutions listed in s 10(1) of the Act. It is a concise summary of certain issues facing prosecutors dealing with corporate prosecutions. Of particular interest is the section headed 'Charging Companies – Additional Public Interest Factors to be Considered', which is worth quoting at length:

> '30. Where the evidence provides a realistic prospect of conviction, the prosecutor must consider whether or not a prosecution is in the public interest, in accordance with the Code for Crown Prosecutors. The more serious the offence, the more likely it is that prosecution will be needed in the public interest. Indicators of seriousness include not just the value of any gain or loss, but also the risk of harm to the public, to unidentified victims, shareholders, employees and creditors and to the stability and integrity of financial markets and international trade. The impact of the offending in other countries, and not just the consequences in the UK, should be taken into account.
>
> 31 Prosecutors must balance factors for and against prosecution carefully and fairly. Public interest factors that can affect the decision to prosecute usually depend on the seriousness of the offence or the circumstances of the suspect. Some factors may increase the need to prosecute, but others may suggest that another course of action would be better. A prosecution will usually take place unless there are public interest factors against prosecution which clearly outweigh those tending in favour of prosecution.

---

[31] Which may be found at www.cps.gov.uk/legal/a_to_c/corporate_prosecutions.

[…]

Additional public interest factors in favour of prosecution:

a. A history of similar conduct (including prior criminal, civil and regulatory enforcement actions against it); failing to prosecute in circumstances where there have been repeated and flagrant breaches of the law may not be a proportionate response and may not provide adequate deterrent effects;

b. The conduct alleged is part of the established business practices of the company;

c. The offence was committed at a time when the company had an ineffective corporate compliance programme;

d. The company had been previously subject to warning, sanctions or criminal charges and had nonetheless failed to take adequate action to prevent future unlawful conduct, or had continued to engage in the conduct;

e. Failure to report wrongdoing within reasonable time of the offending coming to light; (the prosecutor will also need to consider whether it is appropriate to charge the company officers responsible for the failures/ breaches);

f. Failure to report properly and fully the true extent of the wrongdoing.

Additional public interest factors against prosecution

a. A genuinely proactive approach adopted by the corporate management team when the offending is brought to their notice, involving self-reporting and remedial actions, including the compensation of victims:

> In applying this factor the prosecutor needs to establish whether sufficient information about the operation of the company in its entirety has been supplied in order to assess whether the company has been proactively compliant. This will include making witnesses available and disclosure of the details of any internal investigation;[32]

b. A lack of a history of similar conduct involving prior criminal, civil and regulatory enforcement actions against the company; contact should be made with the relevant regulatory departments to ascertain whether investigations are being conducted in relation to the due diligence of the company;

c. The existence of a genuinely proactive and effective corporate compliance programme.

---

[32] It must be doubtful whether such a policy could lawfully require the waiver of legal professional privilege in any privileged material. See, for example, *R (Morgan Grenfell & Co Ltd) v Special Commissioner for Income Tax* [2002] UKHL 21, [2003] 1 AC 563, *Bowman v Fells* [2005] EWCA Civ 226.

d. The availability of civil or regulatory remedies that are likely to be effective and more proportionate:

> Appropriate alternatives to prosecution may include civil recovery orders combined with a range of agreed regulatory measures. However, the totality of the offending needs to have been identified. A fine after conviction may not be the most effective and just outcome if the company cannot pay. The prosecutor should refer to the Attorney's Guidance on Civil Recovery (see "Proceeds of Crime Act 2002: Section 2A [Contribution to the reduction of crime] Joint Guidance given by the Secretary of State and Her Majesty's Attorney General") and on the appropriate use of Serious Crime Prevention Orders.

e. The offending represents isolated actions by individuals, for example by a rogue director.

f. The offending is not recent in nature, and the company in its current form is effectively a different body to that which committed the offences – for example it has been taken over by another company, it no longer operates in the relevant industry or market, all of the culpable individuals have left or been dismissed, or corporate structures or processes have been changed in such a way as to make a repetition of the offending impossible.

g. A conviction is likely to have adverse consequences for the company under European Law, always bearing in mind the seriousness of the offence and any other relevant public interest factors.

> Any candidate or tenderer (including company directors and any person having powers of representation, decision or control) who has been convicted of fraud relating to the protection of the financial interests of the European Communities, corruption, or a money laundering offence is excluded from participation in public contracts within the EU. (Article 45 of Directive 2004/18/EC of the European Parliament and of the Council on the coordination of procedures for the award of public works contracts, public supply contracts and public service contracts). The Directive is intended to be draconian in its effect, and companies can be assumed to have been aware of the potential consequences at the time when they embarked on the offending. Prosecutors should bear in mind that a decision not to prosecute because the Directive is engaged will tend to undermine its deterrent effect.

h. The company is in the process of being wound up.

33. Prosecutors dealing with bribery cases are reminded of the UK's commitment to abide by Article 5 of the OECD Convention on Combating Bribery of Foreign Public Officials in International Business Transactions: investigation and prosecution of the bribery of a foreign public official shall not be influenced by considerations of national economic interest, the potential effect upon relations with another State or the identity of the natural or legal persons involved.

34. A prosecutor should take into account the commercial consequences of a relevant conviction under European law, particularly for self-referring companies, in ensuring that any outcome is proportionate.'

Serious Fraud Office policy

10.37 In July 2009 the SFO published a document aimed primarily at companies facing the risk of prosecution for overseas corruption. It was entitled 'Approach of the Serious Fraud Office to Dealing With Overseas Corruption',[33] and made it clear that companies which reported themselves to the SFO, and which demonstrated good faith efforts to improve their measures against bribery in the course of business were likely to be dealt with leniently. In those circumstances the SFO would consider seeking a civil penalty only.

10.38 This policy was seen by some as akin to the policy of plea-bargaining frequently used in the US. There is opposition to plea-bargaining among many UK lawyers and judges and although legislation to permit plea-bargaining has been suggested it has never been introduced. Be that as it may, it seems the Director of the SFO believed that the announced policy was the most efficient way to improved corporate behaviour whilst fulfilling the SFO's remit to crack down on overseas corruption. The nature of the specific jurisdiction to obtain civil recovery orders is discussed further below.

Effect of Innospec on SFO policy

10.39 Key elements of the SFO's policy were examined in the important 2010 case of *R v Innospec Ltd*.[34]

10.40 In that case the defendant company was a UK-based subsidiary of a US parent which manufactured an additive for leaded petrol. It was accused of a long-standing scheme to bribe officials in Indonesia so that Indonesia would not phase out leaded petrol, which would have damaged sales of the product. The company was also accused of paying bribes to officials of the Saddam Hussein regime in Iraq. The SFO and US Department of Justice and Securities and Exchange Commission cooperated in investigating the offences, and the independent directors of Innospec also provided cooperation.

10.41 As a result, the SFO, the US authorities and the company came to a complex agreement as to a plea of guilty and sentencing, the effect of which was that the UK company would pay £12.7m, split between a civil settlement order of £6m[35] and a confiscation penalty of £6.7m. This was much less than the company might have been liable to pay if found guilty after trial (on various bases of liability the figures in question ranged from US$101.5m to US$160m). However, the lower settlement was accepted because of the likely effect which higher penalties might have had on the solvency of the company. It was felt to

---

[33] Available at www.sfo.gov.uk/bribery–corruption/the-sfo's-response/self-reporting-corruption.aspx. The Joint Prosecution Guidance of March 2011 states that this document 'is currently being revised'.
[34] [2010] EW Misc 7 (EWCC).
[35] Pursuant to Proceeds of Crime Act 2002, Part 5.

make the company bankrupt would punish shareholders employees and creditors who had no moral culpability for the bribery.[36]

10.42 The settlement had to be approved by the Crown Court. It was not so approved. In his sentencing remarks Thomas LJ reminded the SFO of the primacy of the courts in deciding on sentence. The SFO belatedly accepted that a fine would be more appropriate than a confiscation penalty as a signal of the punitive nature of the sentence. Moreover it was noted that there was conflict of interest for the SFO when considering fines and confiscation orders in circumstances where the defendant cannot pay both.[37] In those circumstances, the judge said that a fine should always be preferred.

10.43 Thomas LJ stated that, as a matter of constitutional principle, the Director of the SFO was not permitted to enter into the plea agreement which was presented to the court.

10.44 Thomas LJ also made it clear that a civil penalty was inappropriate for a case of serious criminality, whatever the professed benefits of a policy to encourage self-reporting by companies by preferring civil penalties to criminal ones, stating that:

> 'It is of the greatest public interest that the serious criminality of any, including companies, who engage in the corruption of foreign governments, is made patent for all to see by the imposition of criminal and not civil sanctions.'

10.45 Ultimately, the court imposed a fine in the amount of £12.7m because in the circumstances it would have been unjust not to do so, although Thomas LJ made it clear that this was a unique case which would not be repeated.

10.46 At the time Thomas LJ held the position of Deputy Head of Criminal Justice. It was unusual for such a senior appellate judge to be allocated to deal with sentencing in a Crown Court and it may be that this was intended to signal the seriousness with which the senior judiciary now takes the subject of corporate corruption and the apparent approach of the SFO to settlement.

10.47 This authority, which the SFO has not sought to challenge, plainly compromises the SFO policy of rewarding self-reporting by companies with a process akin to plea-bargaining.[38] Despite this authority, the SFO clearly remains committed to a policy of encouraging self-reporting and reflecting this in its prosecution decisions, as the recent cases (albeit cases involving lower

---

[36] The US parent company was also penalised to the tune of US$14.1m.
[37] Because some of the fruits of a confiscation order are channelled back to the SFO, whereas a fine goes to central funds only.
[38] A similar approach, disapproving of the apparent attempt by the SFO to plead in favour of a defendant with whom a plea agreement has been reached, is evident in the judgment of the Court of Appeal in *R v Dougall* [2010] EWCA Crim 1048.

culpability by the defendant companies) show.[39] It remains to be seen whether the courts will continue to take a hard line if the SFO attempts to dispose of more serious cases by means of civil settlements.

10.48 It remains open to a defendant to seek the judge's view of sentence in circumstances where there is a guilty plea.[40] Such an indication will be non-binding.

10.49 Whether or not an effective plea-agreement might emerge, there are powerful arguments for considering such self-reporting, not least due to the effect of other laws such as the Proceeds of Crime Act and the risk of individuals committing other offences such as false accounting or fraud if the fact of the bribery is known to them but appropriate steps are not then taken.

2011 Joint Prosecution Guidance

10.50 The Joint Prosecution Guidance issued in March 2011 refers to the existing Attorney-General's Guidance on Corporate Prosecutions referred to above, and appears to adopts its principles.[41]

10.51 In relation to the s 7 offence and the possible defence of adequate procedures in particular the Joint Prosecution Guidance states the following:

> 'As stated in the Code (4.5) prosecutors must consider what the defence case may be, and how it is likely to affect the prospects of conviction, under the evidential stage. Clearly, the defence under s7(2) of adequate procedures is likely to be highly relevant when considering whether there is sufficient evidence to provide a realistic prospect of conviction. Prosecutors must look carefully at all the circumstances in which the alleged bribe occurred including the adequacy of any anti-bribery procedures. A single instance of bribery does not necessarily mean that an organisation's procedures are inadequate. For example, the actions of an agent or an employee may be wilfully contrary to very robust corporate contractual requirements, instructions or guidance.'[42]

10.52 On the role of the MOJ Guidance on procedures in prosecutorial decision-making the Joint Prosecution Guidance is clear. It states:

> 'Prosecutors must[43] take it [the MOJ Guidance] into account when considering whether the procedures put in place by commercial organisations are adequate to prevent persons performing services for or on their behalf from bribing.'

---

[39] Such as *R v MW Kellogg* available at www.sfo.gov.uk/press-room/latest-press-releases/press-releases-2011/; *R v De Puy International* available at www.sfo.gov.uk/press-room/latest-press-releases/press-releases-2011/, both of which are discussed further below.
[40] *R v Goodyear* [2005] 2 CAR 20, Practice Direction (Criminal Proceedings: Consolidation) [2002] 1 WLR 2070.
[41] Joint Prosecution Guidance, p12.
[42] Ibid.
[43] Emphasis added.

10.53 It is only the part of the MOJ Guidance which relates to the nature of procedures for commercial organisations (ie the six principles section, discussed in Chapter 9) which is directly relevant. The other parts of the document issued by the MOJ, which put forward certain interpretations of parts of the Act itself, do not bind prosecutors and will not bind the courts.

10.54 There is little doubt that considerable thought will be given to the nature and effect of the procedures which a commercial organisation may have had in place at the time the alleged bribery took place. In many cases the issue may well be determinative of whether a prosecution goes ahead.

SECTION 11: PENALTIES
Mode of trial

10.55 In England and Wales, criminal offences are tried either in a Magistrates' Court or in a Crown Court. A Crown Court is reserved for more serious offences. Some offences are triable 'either way', that is either in the Magistrates' Court or in Crown Court, depending on the decision of the prosecutor. Offences tried in a Magistrates' Court are known as summary offences, or offences tried summarily. Those in a Crown Court are known as indictable offences or as being tried on indictment.[44]

10.56 A Crown Court trial is almost always before a judge and jury.[45] A trial in the Magistrates' Court does not involve a jury and will be either before a professional district judge or a bench of three lay-magistrates.

10.57 Sentences in the Crown Court are unlimited up to the maximum provided for the offences in question. Sentences in the Magistrates' Court are generally limited to a maximum of 6 months' imprisonment and/or fines up to £5,000. Under the Bribery Act, the maximum sentence of imprisonment available in the Magistrates' Court is 12 months.

10.58 Offences under ss 1, 2 and 6 of the Bribery Act are triable either way. It can be expected that all but the most minor cases of bribery will be tried on indictment in a Crown Court.[46] Offences under s 7 are triable only on indictment,[47] and as a result commercial organisations which are subject to it can expect to receive significant fines if convicted.

---

[44] The indictment is the formal statement of the Crown's case.
[45] Save for highly unusual circumstances which are most unlikely to occur in bribery matters.
[46] Bribery Act 2010, s 11(1).
[47] Bribery Act 2010, s 11(3).

Sentencing

10.59 Criminal sentencing is a complex topic in itself and those seeking a detailed treatment of the governing principles should refer to specialist works on the subject.[48]

10.60 Of course there are no direct precedents or guidelines for sentencing for a new statute, so what follows is a discussion about the likely ranges of sentences applicable to offences under the Bribery Act which are tried on indictment, and the applicable principles.

10.61 Section 142(1) of the Criminal Justice Act 2003 provides:

> 'Any court dealing with an offender in respect of his offence must have regard to the following purposes of sentencing—
>
> (a) the punishment of offenders,
> (b) the reduction of crime (including its reduction by deterrence),
> (c) the reform and rehabilitation of offenders,
> (d) the protection of the public, and
> (e) the making of reparation by offenders to persons affected by their offences.'

10.62 The 2003 Act does not prioritise any one purpose over another. In an individual case, any or all of the purposes may be relevant to some degree and applying them will be for the judge. In bribery cases involving individuals, punishment, deterrence and reparation are likely to be of particular concern because it is more likely than not that an offender convicted of bribery is unlikely to be in a position to commit similar offences in the future.

MAXIMUM SENTENCES PROVIDED IN THE ACT

10.63 As provided in s 11 of the Act, the maximum sentence for an individual convicted on indictment of an offence under ss 1, 2 or 6 of the Bribery Act is 10 years' imprisonment, or the possibility of an unlimited fine.

10.64 The maximum sentence for an offence under ss 1, 2 or 6 tried summarily is 12 months' imprisonment (or 6 months' imprisonment in Northern Ireland) and/or a fine not exceeding the statutory maximum.[49]

10.65 For a s 7 offence the only available sentence for a commercial organisation is a fine, the amount of which is unlimited.

---

[48] For example Thomas, *Current Sentencing Practice* (London, 2010).
[49] Presently £5,000.

RANGES OF SENTENCE: INDIVIDUALS

10.66 Sentencing varies according to the facts of each case. At the time of writing there were no sentencing guidelines for Bribery Act offences and sentences for offences under the previous law cannot be relied on as direct precedents because the Act is intended to be a new code with a harsher sentencing tariff.[50]

10.67 Nevertheless, it is possible to identify factors going to the seriousness of an offence, ie aggravating or mitigating factors, which will move cases to one end of the scale or another. The key factors in deciding seriousness of offending are the culpability of the offender and the harm caused as a result.[51]

10.68 Aggravating factors relevant to bribery are likely to include the following, which are listed in no particular order:

(i) the offender's conduct caused significant harm to societies, communities or institutions – for example by corrupting senior politicians, officials, police officers or judges;

(ii) the offender played a central role in the bribery;

(iii) the offender used his position to intimidate or persuade others to participate;

(iv) the bribery involved large sums of money;

(v) the bribery occurred over a long period;

(vi) there were multiple offences;

(vii) the offender abused a position of trust or leadership;

(viii) the offender obtained personal advantages as a result of the bribery – for example by increasing his own earnings or used the proceeds for personal expenditure;

(ix) the offender hampered the investigation.

10.69 If all or several of these factors were present, without any or any significant mitigating factors, the case could well attract a sentence at or close to the statutory maximum.

---

[50] For example, under the Prevention of Corruption Act 1906 (as amended) the maximum sentences were 7 years' imprisonment for conviction on indictment and 6 months' imprisonment for summary conviction.

[51] Section 143(1) of the Criminal Justice Act 2003 provides: 'In considering the seriousness of any offence, the court must consider the offender's culpability in committing the offence and any harm which the offence caused, was intended to cause or might foreseeably have caused.'

10.70 Mitigating factors might include the following:

(x) the bribery was relatively minor in terms of amount;

(xi) the harm caused was limited in extent – for example because the recipient was not in a real position of power or because he did not in fact act improperly as a result of the bribery;

(xii) the offender relied on the (incorrect) advice of others as to the propriety of his actions;

(xiii) the bribery was ongoing at the time the offender came to it;

(xiv) the offender was relatively junior in the structure which was endorsed by his superiors;

(xv) the offender did not himself gain financial benefits from the bribery;

(xvi) the offender was of previous good character;

(xvii) the personal circumstances of the offender (such as health, age, family responsibilities, etc);

(xviii) cooperation with investigating authorities;

(xix) a plea of guilty in advance of trial.

10.71 If several of these factors were present, without any or any significant aggravating factors, the case could well attract a sentence at a much lower level.

10.72 If a custodial sentence is imposed an additional sentence of a fine will be relatively unusual. However, orders for confiscation and/or compensation of victims and orders for costs may well be imposed.

SUSPENDED SENTENCES?

10.73 Given the importance which bribery offences have now assumed it is probably going to be an unusual case where a custodial sentence is not at least considered in the case of an individual. However, a suspended sentence might be considered in appropriate cases.

10.74 In *R v Dougall*[52] (again, a case under the previous law) Mr Dougall was an employee of a multinational company which made payments to medical professionals in Greece to encourage them to purchase the company's goods. When he took up his responsibility for the company's Greek operation the

---

[52] [2010] EWCA Crim 1048.

corrupt scheme was ongoing, but he failed to prevent it from continuing over a 4-year period. He attempted to persuade others in the industry to end practices of this nature, but without success. He provided 'fulsome' cooperation to the SFO. He had no previous convictions.

10.75 The SFO made a 'plea agreement' with Mr Dougall, to the effect that only a suspended sentence would be sought. However, in the light of the sentencing remarks in *Innospec* the SFO recognised that the agreement could not be relied on before the court. The trial judge refused to suspend a sentence of 12 months' imprisonment. In the event, after an appeal, the sentence on Mr Dougall was suspended because it was found that the appropriate sentence in all the circumstances was 12 months' imprisonment or less, and that in circumstances of cooperation of this nature there was a 'very powerful' argument that such a sentence should be suspended. The Lord Chief Justice said:

> 'where the appropriate sentence for a defendant whose level of criminality, and features of mitigation, combined with a guilty plea, and full co-operation with the authorities investigating a major crime involving fraud or corruption, with all the consequent burdens of complying with his part of the SOCPA agreement, would be 12 months' imprisonment or less, the argument that the sentence should be suspended is very powerful.'

RANGE OF SENTENCES: COMPANIES

10.76 The sentencing of companies raises separate considerations to those relevant to individuals. Personal circumstances play no part. However, the key principles going to seriousness, those of culpability and harm, continue to apply.

10.77 In *R v Mabey & Johnson* the company had bribed government officials in Jamaica and Ghana in connection with bridge-building contracts, and had breached sanctions relating to trade with the government of Iraq. The company was ordered to pay a total of £6.6m in fines, confiscation orders, reparations to the countries harmed by the bribery and prosecution costs, and to undergo compliance monitoring.[53] The fines element was £750,000 per bribery offence in relation to Jamaica and Ghana and £2m in relation to the breach of Iraq sanctions. The court does not seem to have imposed a fine in respect of each incident of bribery, merely to cover programmes of bribery which occurred over time. The SFO seems to have agreed to these levels of fines and other penalties with the offender.

---

[53] (Unreported) 29 September 2009, Southwark Crown Court, SFO press release available at www.sfo.gov.uk/press-room/latest-press-releases/press-releases-2009/mabey–johnson-ltd-sentencing-.aspx

INNOSPEC AND SENTENCING

10.78 The seriousness of a bribery offence committed by companies should now be considered by reference to the sentencing remarks of Thomas LJ in *Innospec*.

10.79 Although relating to a case under the previous law, and although strictly *obiter* in that they did not relate directly to the reasons for the sentence actually imposed,[54] Thomas LJ's remarks are likely to indicate the future policy of the courts in relation to the sentencing of companies. Among other things,[55] Thomas LJ made the following points in respect of sentencing:

- corruption of foreign government officials is at the top end of serious corporate offending both in terms of culpability and harm;

- Art 3 of the OECD Convention requires states to apply penalties which are 'effective, proportionate and dissuasive';

- 'the level of fines now imposed in cartel cases is now measured in the tens of millions. It is self-evident that corruption is much more serious both in terms of culpability and harm caused';

- in this case, the penalty that the US court could have imposed was US$101.5m, with disgorgement of profits on top. There was no suggestion of a reason to differentiate between the UK and US in terms of the financial penalties to be imposed. There was every reason for states to adopt a uniform approach to fines;

- a fine comparable to that imposed in the US would have been the starting point in the *Innospec* case, with depriving Innospec of the fruits of its criminality potentially to come on top.

10.80 If the UK adopts a system similar in outcome to that applicable under US law, then the sentences available under the Foreign Corrupt Practices Act may well be relevant to UK sentencing practice. However, it would be surprising if quite such a financially specific scheme were adopted in full since UK courts are likely to wish to retain greater flexibility.

10.81 In brief, the FCPA provides for:

- fines of up to $2m per violation of the FCPA's anti-bribery provisions. This means $2m per bribe – if a company pays numerous bribes over a period of time the aggregate of such fines can become very large;

---

[54] It is not clear whether all the observations of the court had been the subject of detailed argument from counsel.
[55] Such as in relation to 'plea-bargaining' – discussed above.

- a fine of up to $25m for wilful violations of the Books and Records and Internal Control provisions of the FCPA for a company;

- it is common for the Securities and Exchange Commission also to seek civil penalties and disgorgement of any profits earned from the contracts or business obtained through the bribery. These can and often do run into tens of millions.

10.82 The upshot is that in cases where companies have earned tens or even hundreds of millions from contracts gained by bribery then, unless there are highly unusual circumstances, they can expect to have to pay at least such sums and considerably more by way of penalties.[56] The remarks of Thomas LJ in *Innospec* are a warning that, in cases under the new Act which do not face the fetters which seem to have attached themselves to the SFO in that case, the English courts can be expected to impose very large penalties, comparable to those applicable in the US.

Ancillary orders

10.83 The power of the court to require a person convicted under the Public Bodies Corrupt Practices Act 1889 to pay the amount of value of the bribe to the public body in question[57] is ended by the repeal of that Act pursuant to the Bribery Act. However, the courts generally have scope to make various ancillary orders to obtain compensation for victims, confiscation of ill-gotten gains and confiscation orders, financial reporting orders and similar measures. These are briefly summarised below.

Compensation order

10.84 A court must consider making a compensation order in any case where an offence has resulted in personal injury, loss or damage, and bribery is likely to qualify as such.[58] The purpose of the order is to compensate the victim of the crime. In *Mabey & Johnson Ltd*[59] various forms of order were made, including fines and confiscation orders (discussed below). Additionally, 'reparations' were agreed to be paid to the governments of Ghana and Jamaica, presumably pursuant to the jurisdiction to order compensation.

10.85 In another recent case BAE Systems agreed to pay the difference between £30m and any fine imposed on it to the people of Tanzania, as part of

---

[56] One such circumstance might be where the company is unable to pay the level of fine which the offence might merit and there were likely to be damaging effects on entirely innocent parties such as employees, shareholders and pensioners. This was the explanation offered by the SFO for its decision not to prosecute PWS Insurance in the case of *Messent*. Some might see this approach as introducing an inappropriate element of moral hazard, penalising profitable companies and favouring unprofitable ones.

[57] Public Bodies Corrupt Practices Act 1889, s 2(b).

[58] Powers of Criminal Courts (Sentencing) Act 2000, s 130.

[59] *R v Mabey & Johnson Ltd* (unreported) 29 September 2009, Southwark Crown Court, see www.sfo.gov.uk/press-room/latest-press-releases/press-releases-2009/.

its plea of guilty to an accounting offence relating to payments made in connection with the supply of an air-traffic control system to Tanzania.[60] This payment may not have been by way of a compensation order – it was described as an 'ex gratia payment', although it was contained in an agreement between SFO and BAE which was put before the court.

Confiscation order

10.86 Where there is evidence in a case before the Crown Court that the offender has benefited financially from his offending, the court can consider making a confiscation order, under s 6 of the Proceeds of Crime Act 2001. A confiscation order is intended to deprive the defendant of the benefit that he has obtained from crime. The recoverable amount for the purposes of s 6 is an amount equal to the defendant's benefit from the conduct concerned.[61] It is not necessary to identify a victim or his loss or damage for a confiscation order to be made.

10.87 So, for example, a confiscation order of £1.1m (among other penalties such as fines) was imposed on the corporate offender in *Mabey & Johnson*.

10.88 Where a confiscation order is in prospect the prosecutor may take steps in the High Court to preserve assets so that they are available to pay the order. Such steps include an order restraining assets (which may be obtained even before a charge is laid, providing that a charge is to be laid), an order requiring a defendant to give disclosure as to the location of assets, an order for repatriation of assets from outside the UK back to the UK and an order appointing a receiver.

10.89 If the order is not paid voluntarily then the courts may either enforce the order as if it were a fine or the prosecutor may apply to the High Court to appoint a receiver.

Financial reporting order

10.90 The Serious Organised Crime and Police Act 2005 (SOCPA), s 76, provides for the making of a financial reporting order. Such an order can be made when sentencing offenders convicted of one of the crimes listed in s 76(3) of SOCPA. Schedule 1 of the Bribery Act amends that section so as to include offences under ss 1, 2 and 6 of the Bribery Act. Note that s 7 offences applicable to commercial organisations are not so included.

10.91 A financial reporting order can be made if the court is satisfied that there is a risk of the offender committing another offence of the type listed in

---

[60] *R v BAE Systems Plc* (unreported) 21 December 2010, per Bean J, Southwark Crown Court, available at www.judiciary.gov.uk/media/judgments/2010/r-v-bae-systems-plc.
[61] Proceeds of Crime Act 2002, s 7.

s 76(3) of SOCPA. The effect of the order is to require the offender to report aspects of his financial affairs at specific intervals.

Serious crime prevention order

10.92 If the courts (in England and Wales and Northern Ireland) are satisfied that a person (including a legal person) 'has been involved in serious crime' (which includes committing, facilitating the commission of, or conducting himself in such a way as to facilitate the commission of a serious crime), they may make a serious crime prevention order (SCPO).[62] The court must have 'reasonable grounds to believe that the order would protect the public by preventing, restricting or disrupting involvement by the person in serious crime [in England and Wales or in Northern Ireland]'.[63]

10.93 The court may impose requirements to answer questions or provide information or documents to law enforcement agencies, as well as restrictions on financial, property or business dealings or holdings; restrictions on working arrangements, communications, access to premises, travel, trading and employment. Such orders can apply to corporate bodies as well as to individuals. There are various safeguards against abuse provided by the Serious Crime Act.[64]

10.94 One example of an order which might be made in the context of corporate bribery is the monitoring of the activities of a corporate offender. The use of a 'compliance monitor', usually for a fixed time period, is established practice in the US and there seems to be no reason of principle why this should not occur in the UK. In *Mabey & Johnson* the company agreed to submit its compliance programme to an independent monitor and to pay the costs of doing so (estimated at £250,000 for one year). This may well be a precedent for the future.

Civil recovery orders under the Proceeds of Crime Act 2002

10.95 The Proceeds of Crime Act 2002 (POCA) creates new state agencies responsible for fighting crime and new legal remedies for such agencies. The regime created is extensive and a proper treatment of it must be sought elsewhere.[65] Money laundering is a particular target of the legislation, and there is a brief discussion of the main money laundering offences in Chapter 12.

10.96 The wide powers of confiscation and restraint of assets provided to the courts under Part 2 of the Act apply to any person convicted of an offence in the Crown Court who has benefited from the criminal conduct for which he has

---

[62] Serious Crime Act 2007, s 1 and, in general, Part I.
[63] Serious Crime Act 2007, s 2.
[64] Sections 6–15.
[65] For a detailed treatment of this see *Millington and Sutherland Williams on The Proceeds of Crime* (3rd edn, Oxford, 2010).

been convicted.[66] So it is possible for the court to impose a confiscation order in relation to the proceeds of bribery as well as a sentence of imprisonment or fine.

10.97 Separately, Part 5 of POCA provides for civil proceedings by which the High Court can make a 'recovery order' in relation to property obtained through unlawful conduct. The proceedings may be brought by an Enforcement Authority, which includes the Serious Organised Crime Agency (SOCA), the DPP, the Director of Revenue and Customs Prosecutions and, most relevantly in the context of bribery, the Director of the SFO.

10.98 To enable the SFO to pursue proceedings for civil recovery it must establish that unlawful conduct has occurred which has led to the acquisition by the defendant of specific property. Unlawful conduct will certainly include either the payment or receipt of bribes. There is no need to prove that the defendant himself has committed any offence only that, on the civil balance of proof (ie the balance of probabilities), that the property in question represents the proceeds of crime.

10.99 If so satisfied the court will make a recovery order in relation to the property and that property will vest in a trustee for civil recovery nominated by the SFO – the defendant will no longer have title to it.

10.100 A recent example in the context of corruption is the case of MW Kellogg Ltd, which received dividends from a joint venture project in Nigeria that had obtained business through corruption.[67] Those dividends were alleged by the SFO to be property obtained through unlawful conduct. High Court recovery proceedings were settled by the company in the amount of approximately £7m, plus the SFO's investigation costs. The case did not seem to involve significant culpability on the part of MW Kellogg itself, which appears not to have been directly involved in the corruption, but merely involved as a conduit for its parent company.

AGREEMENTS WITH SFO TO ACCEPT CIVIL PENALTIES

10.101 Recently, the SFO has made agreements with companies under investigation for bribery that payments to the SFO would be accepted as settling civil recovery proceedings, pursuant to its policy to encourage

---

[66] Or from criminal conduct in general if he is deemed to have a 'criminal lifestyle'. This applies if the defendant is convicted of specific offences.
[67] See: /www.sfo.gov.uk/press-room/latest-press-releases/press-releases-2011/mw-kellogg-ltd-to-pay-%C2%A37-million-in-sfo-high-court-action.aspx.

self-reporting discussed above.⁶⁸ The alternative is a criminal charge against the company and the possibility of a criminal conviction for bribery. The latter is clearly undesirable, especially if the company is convicted for an offence other than under s 7, not least because of the risk that the company will be debarred from tendering for public procurement contracts if convicted of a corruption or bribery offence.⁶⁹

10.102 Balfour Beatty, the construction company, carried out an internal investigation and reported itself to the SFO in 2005. The SFO ultimately agreed to compromise any proceedings which might have been available to it by accepting a payment of £2.25m.⁷⁰ Another construction firm, Amec, has also settled civil recovery proceedings with the SFO by means of a consent order. Amec agreed to pay over £5m as part of the settlement.⁷¹ Both of these cases were said to relate to 'irregularities' in the maintenance of the company's books and records in breach of s 221 of the Companies Act 1985.⁷²

10.103 However, as we have seen, the use, or threatened use, by the SFO of its civil recovery powers under POCA has been challenged by the authority of *Innospec*, in which Thomas LJ stated:

> 'Those who commit such serious crimes as corruption of senior foreign government officials must not be viewed or treated in any different way to other criminals. It will therefore rarely be appropriate for criminal conduct by a company to be dealt with by means of a civil bribery order; the criminal courts can take account of cooperation and the provision of evidence against others by reducing the fine otherwise payable.'

10.104 This warning notwithstanding, it seems to be the clear policy of the SFO to use its civil recovery powers under POCA where appropriate, or where it believes charges are too risky or heavy-handed, especially in cases of self-reporting by companies. For example, in March 2011 another civil recovery order in the amount of £4.829m plus prosecution costs was imposed on De Puy International Ltd (the employer of the defendant in *Dougall*, above). De Puy's parent company, Johnson & Johnson, had reported itself to the US authorities, which had imposed a deferred prosecution agreement and a total of approximately US$51m in fines and compensation in that jurisdiction, with the Greek authorities restraining a further €5.7m.⁷³

---

⁶⁸ Serious Fraud Office, 'Approach of the Serious Fraud Office to Dealing With Overseas Corruption', available at www.sfo.gov.uk/bribery–corruption/the-sfo's-response/self-reporting-corruption.aspx.
⁶⁹ See the discussion below. Note that such an outcome does not preclude the possibility that individual directors or executives will face criminal prosecution for their role in bribery even if the company's penalty is merely civil.
⁷⁰ SFO Press Release, 6 October 2008.
⁷¹ SFO Press Release, 26 October 2009.
⁷² Now replaced by ss 386 and 387 of the Companies Act 2006.
⁷³ See www.sfo.gov.uk/press-room/latest-press-releases/press-releases-2011.

10.105 This is another example of a complex international case in which the prosecutorial traditions and priorities of more than one state were considered in attempting to achieve a global settlement. The SFO took the decision that the most efficacious use of its powers was the imposition of a civil recovery order, despite the fact that some criminal sanctions were imposed in the US. Despite the greater utility of the Bribery Act for prosecutors, it is possible that future cases of this nature will be disposed of in similar ways, especially if the culpability of the corporate entity is at the lower end of the scale.

DISQUALIFICATION AS A DIRECTOR

10.106 Company directors are fiduciaries from whom a high standard of probity is expected by the law. Those who are involved in bribery, whether as individuals or as part of their role as directors, are very likely to be disqualified from acting as a director for a lengthy period of time, whatever other sentence is imposed.

10.107 The Company Directors Disqualification Act 1986, s 2, provides as follows:

> **'Disqualification on conviction of indictable offence**
>
> (1) The court may make a disqualification order against a person where he is convicted of an indictable offence (whether on indictment or summarily) in connection with the promotion, formation, management liquidation or striking off of a company with the receivership of a company's property or with his being an administrative receiver of a company.
>
> (2) "The court" for this purpose means—
>
> (a) any court having jurisdiction to wind up the company in relation to which the offence was committed, or
> (b) the court by or before which the person is convicted of the offence, or
> (c) in the case of a summary conviction in England and Wales, any other magistrates' court acting for the same petty sessions area;
>
> and for the purposes of this section the definition of "indictable offence" in Schedule 1 to the Interpretation Act 1978 applies for Scotland as it does for England and Wales.
>
> (3) The maximum period of disqualification under this section is—
>
> (a) where the disqualification order is made by a court of summary jurisdiction, 5 years, and
> (b) in any other case, 15 years.'

10.108 Many of the recent cases of corporate corruption have led to the disqualification of company directors, including *Innospec* and *Mabey &*

Johnson. It will be a rare case in which a company director is convicted under the Bribery Act, but escapes disqualification.

OTHER SENTENCES

10.109 As the Act is a new code, sentences under the previous law should be treated with considerable caution. However, the table below summarises some relatively recent cases under the previous law which may at least provide a reference point. It should be borne in mind that the maximum sentence applicable to individuals on conviction under the 1889 or 1906 Acts was only 3 years' imprisonment prior to the application of the Criminal Justice Act 1988, and only 7 years thereafter.[74]

Other recent sentencing cases

YEAR	CASE	SENTENCE	FACTS	ADDITIONAL REMEDIES	REMARKS
2011	*R v Mabey & Forsyth* Southwark Crown Court 23 February 2011	21 months plus £75,000 prosecution costs for the managing director; 8 months plus prosecution costs of £125,000 for the sales director; 8 months, but sentence suspended for 2 years, for the sales manager.	Bribery of government officials in Iraq.	Disqualification from directorships for 5 years for the managing director; Disqualification from directorships for 2 years for the sales director.	The SFO seems to have agreed these levels of fines and other penalties with the offenders.
				Company ordered to pay £6.6m in fines, confiscation orders, reparations and costs, and to undergo compliance monitoring – see *R v Mabey & Johnson Ltd*, below.	

---

[74] Criminal Justice Act 1988, s 47.

YEAR	CASE	SENTENCE	FACTS	ADDI-TIONAL REMEDIES	REMARKS
2010	*R v Messent* Southwark Crown Court 26 October 2010	21 months plus payment of £100,000 compensation within 28 days, failing which another 12 months to be served.	Bribery of state insurance officials in Costa Rica to place insurance with the defendant's company. Substantial cooperation with SFO.	Disqualification as a director for 5 years.	Had it not been for cooperation with SFO, sentence would have been 4–5 years. Company involved not charged because in administration – burden of fine would fall on innocent creditors and pensioners.
2010	*R v BAE Systems Plc* Bean J, Case No S2010565 Southwark Crown Court 21 December 2010	Corporate prosecution. Total penalty £30m. Fine £500,000 plus prosecution costs. Balance paid to government of Tanzania as 'ex gratia payment'. SFO agreed to terminate all other investigations into BAE.	Charge was of failing to keep accurate accounting records, s 221 of the Companies Act 1985, in relation to payments made to middlemen dealing with contract for supply of air-traffic equipment to Tanzania. SFO did not charge corruption.	Payment to Tanzania apparently 'ex gratia', although part of agreement between SFO and BAE. Nature of offence means that compensation or confiscation orders not available.	Judge was clearly unhappy with settlement agreement, but decision not to charge corruption was within the discretion of SFO Director and thus upheld. BAE also fined US$400m for offences under US law and had implemented compliance programme.

YEAR	CASE	SENTENCE	FACTS	ADDI-TIONAL REMEDIES	REMARKS
2010	R v Dougall [2010] EWCA Crim 1048	12 months, suspended on appeal.	Employee of healthcare company continued existing scheme of bribery of doctors in Greece for 4 years.		The SFO had attempted to put forward a plea agreement and a suspended sentence. Trial judge refused to suspend. Court of Appeal upheld suspension in this case but made clear that this had nothing to do with the plea agreement which was irrelevant, as per *Innospec*.
			D not very senior in company. D attempted to 'clean up' industry as a whole seeking to prohibit corrupt practices in industry sector, though without success.		
			Significant cooperation with SFO.		

YEAR	CASE	SENTENCE	FACTS	ADDITIONAL REMEDIES	REMARKS
2009	*R v Mabey & Johnson Ltd* Southwark Crown Court, 25 September 2009	Corporate prosecution. Total penalties of £6.6m, broken down as follows: Fines: Ghana £750,000 Jamaica £750,000 Iraq £2 m Confiscation order £1.1m Reparations: Ghana £658,000 Jamaica £139,000 Iraq £618,000 Costs to the SFO £350,000 First year monitoring of compliance programme, cost £250,000	Bribery of officials to win contracts in Jamaica, Ghana. Bribes to Iraqi officials, breach of UN Sanctions. Self-reporting and cooperation with SFO, company implemented compliance programme as part of remediation.		The first corporate conviction for overseas corruption offences. Agreed basis of plea.

YEAR	CASE	SENTENCE	FACTS	ADDI-TIONAL REMEDIES	REMARKS
2009	R v Ozakpinar [2009] 1 Cr App R (S) 35	30 months, upheld on appeal.	Defendant was the chief procurement officer for the CPS. He was convicted of corruption in respect of employing persons who were personal friends and receiving payments in connection with three separate contracts.		The Court of Appeal did not accept an argument that the guidelines for theft in breach of trust were helpful in dealing with corruption cases.
2009	R v Tobiasen, Tumukunde (unreported), HHJ Wasworth QC, Southwark Crown Court 2009	D1 5 months (suspended for 1 year); D2 12 months.	D1 was director of UK company which made payments to D2 in connection with contracts from government of Uganda. Amounts of payments approx £80,000.		D1 was 65 years of age and of previous good character. It seems that D2 initiated the scheme.

YEAR	CASE	SENTENCE	FACTS	ADDITIONAL REMEDIES	REMARKS
2007	R v Welcher [2007] 2 Cr App R (S) 519	6-and-a-half years for each defendant, upheld on appeal.	Conspiracy to corrupt and conspiracy to defraud. The defendants had been involved in paying sums of money totalling £3mn to an employee of a major company in return for showing favour to their company by placing major orders and authorising overpayments to the company.		Example of serious 'private to private' bribery.
2004	R v Francis Hurrell [2004] 2 Cr App R (S) 23	3 months on appeal.	Attempted bribery of police officer prior to and following arrest for driving under the influence of alcohol. Man of 43, of previous good character.		Even attempted bribery of a police officer will attract a custodial sentence.

YEAR	CASE	SENTENCE	FACTS	ADDI-TIONAL REMEDIES	REMARKS
2003	*R v Anderson (Malcolm John)* [2003] 2 Cr App R (S) 28	6 months, having been reduced from 12 months on appeal.	Defendant, a strategic rail manager, had accepted a bribe in return for awarding business. He pleaded guilty to corruption.		
			Previous good character, the contracts involved were beneficial to his employer and his financial gain was relatively small.		
2003	*R v Bush* [2003] 2 Cr App R (S) 117	2-and-a-half years, reduced from 4 years on appeal.	Defendant was an officer in a local authority convicted of accepting payments and other services over a period of 6 years in return for putting company names on the authority's contracts list so that they could tender for large contracts with the authority.		

YEAR	CASE	SENTENCE	FACTS	ADDITIONAL REMEDIES	REMARKS
2001	R v Dearnley [2001] 2 Cr App R (S) 201	12 months, reduced from 18 months on appeal.	Defendant was a council employee and a supplier of security services to the council. He pleaded guilty to corruption in the form of supplying a car worth £5,445 and misrepresenting a loan in order to pay off a personal debt.		In the Court of Appeal, Rafferty J noted that a custodial sentence was required as a deterrent and was inevitable.
			Defendant, was previously of good character and now a 'broken man'. Further, there had been no lack of value for the security services paid for by the council.		

YEAR	CASE	SENTENCE	FACTS	ADDI-TIONAL REMEDIES	REMARKS
1997	*R v Donald* [1997] 2 Cr App R (S) 272	11 years.	Defendant was a detective constable who accepted various sums (totalling £18,500) from a man who was the subject of criminal proceedings in return for the disclosure of confidential information about the inquiry and to destroy surveillance logs. The officer had agreed to accept about £50,000.		The sentencing judge commented that the case was 'almost unique' in its seriousness. The Court of Appeal said the sentence was severe, but not manifestly excessive.
1988	*R v Garner* (1988) 10 Cr App R (S) 445	18 months; 12 months; and 12 months suspended for each defendant, upheld on appeal.	Defendants pleaded guilty to conspiracy to corrupt. They were involved in bribing a prison officer to take various items, including luxury foods, alcohol and cigars to one of the defendants who was serving a prison sentence at the time.		Maximum sentence 3 years.

YEAR	CASE	SENTENCE	FACTS	ADDITIONAL REMEDIES	REMARKS
1982	R v Wilson (1982) 4 Cr App R (S) 337	18 months, reduced from 3-and-a-half years on appeal.	Defendant was a purchasing agent and chief buyer with a manufacturing concern, accepted gifts of £2,500 in return for showing favour to a company supplying parts to his employer.		
			Mitigating factors included the break-up of D's family, the loss of his home and his business.		

DEBARMENT FROM PUBLIC PROCUREMENT

10.110 European law provides specific rules for the procurement of goods and services by public bodies by means of the Public Procurement Directive.[75] Article 45 of the Directive provides:

> 'Any candidate or tenderer who has been the subject of a conviction by final judgment of which the contracting authority is aware for one or more of the reasons listed below shall be excluded from participation in a public contract.'

10.111 The reasons listed include corruption,[76] which is defined elsewhere in European law[77] as follows:

> 'the deliberate action of whosoever promises or gives, directly or through an intermediary, an advantage of any kind whatsoever to an official for himself or for a third party for him to act or refrain from acting in accordance with his duty or in the exercise of his functions in breach of his official duties shall constitute active corruption'

---

[75] Directive EC 2004/18, [2004] OJ L134/114.
[76] As well as certain other offences including fraud and money laundering.
[77] Council Act of 26 May 1997, which relates to corruption in the public sector. See also Council Joint Action 98/742/JHA for a similar provision as to corruption in the private sector, which is also relevant to debarment under Art 45.

10.112 Article 45 of the Directive, which is incorporated into UK law by the Public Contracts Regulations 2006, provides for the mandatory exclusion of an economic operator convicted of corruption under the Acts of 1898 and 1906 and 'an offence of bribery', presumably common law bribery, as well as fraud and money laundering.[78]

10.113 The Directive and the Regulations which implement it do not provide for any discretion on the part of the public authority who are subject to it. There is no process for mitigation, consideration of matters which are de minimis or even a process by which past offences can be considered spent.[79]

10.114 The similarities between the definition of 'corruption' under the Directive, and under the existing law, and the definitions of active bribery applicable to ss 1 and 6 of the Bribery Act are clear.[80] It seems plain that the conviction of any person, individual or corporate, for a s 1 or s 6 offence would be treated as a corruption offence under the Procurement Directive, with the result that the person in question will be debarred from participating in public procurement work. For some businesses the effect of this could be devastating.

10.115 Section 7 offences do not appear to fit within the definition of corruption for the purposes of Art 45. Section 7 involves the liability of C for the actions of an associated person, A. It does not seem to involve any 'deliberate action' by C.

10.116 Of course if C is itself aware of and complicit in the actions of A it might be liable under ss 1 or 6, as well as under s 7. Liability under ss 1 or 6 would trigger debarment. However, as a matter of present UK law, a s 7 conviction, by itself, does not seem to trigger automatic debarment from public procurement under the Directive or the Regulations.

PROPOSED AMENDMENT OF UK REGULATIONS

10.117 Various government ministers have stated that the government is taking or will take action to address this with other member states or with the EU institutions so that the issue is satisfactorily clarified. On 30 March 2011 the Lord Chancellor issued a Written Ministerial Statement in relation to implementation of the Bribery Act and the s 9 guidance. The statement also addressed the issue of the procurement regulations and s 7 offences, in the following terms:

> 'The Government has also decided that a conviction of a commercial organisation under section 7 of the Act in respect of a failure to prevent bribery will attract discretionary rather than mandatory exclusion from public procurement under the

---

[78] Public Contracts Regulations 2006, SI 2006/5, reg 23.
[79] See also the EU Defence Procurement Directive, Directive 2009/81/EC, Art 39.
[80] The Public Contracts Regulations 2006 also provide for the mandatory exclusion of an economic operator convicted of 'an offence of bribery', ie common law bribery.

UK's implementation of the EU Procurement Directive (Directive 2004/18). The relevant regulations will be amended to reflect this'.

No timetable or specific amendment has been specified.

10.118 If such a measure is taken then a conviction of a commercial organisation under s 7 only would not lead to automatic debarment as far as UK authorities are concerned.

10.119 Of course such an amendment to the UK regulations will not affect the law in other EU states. There must be at least some risk that the authorities in other states may take a different view of whether the s 7 offences constitutes corruption. Ultimately the issue may be one for the European Court of Justice.

ROLE OF THE FINANCIAL SERVICES AUTHORITY

10.120 The Financial Services Authority (FSA) is the statutory regulator of the UK financial services industry. Of course only those financial services businesses or activities regulated by the FSA will be within its jurisdiction.[81] Among the objectives of the FSA are the reduction of financial crime, in particular fraud and money laundering.[82]

10.121 Bribery in the financial sector is relevant to the FSA because weak controls over third party relationships and payments leave firms vulnerable to becoming involved in bribery and corruption. This weakens the firms themselves and the markets regulated by the FSA. Bribery and corruption distort natural competition and make the UK a less attractive place for financial firms to conduct business.[83] The FSA is not the lead agency responsible for investigating or prosecuting bribery offences, but it retains the capacity to penalise financial institutions subject to its control.

10.122 In a recent case, the FSA imposed a significant financial penalty on Aon, an international insurance company, in connection with illicit payments to overseas intermediaries, the purposes of which were not clear, but which were suspected to involve bribery of some kind.[84] The penalty came to £5.25m, which figure included a considerable credit to Aon for having cooperated with the FSA, admission of liability and the implementation of an appropriate anti-bribery programme within the business.[85]

10.123 Neither Aon nor anyone else were proven to have been directly involved in or guilty of a corruption or bribery offence. Aon's 'offence' was a

---

[81] Financial Services and Markets Act 2000, s 22, Financial Services and Markets Act 2000 (Regulated Activities) Order 2001, SI 2001/544.
[82] Financial Services And Markets Act 2000, s 6.
[83] Financial Services Authority, *Anti-bribery and corruption in commercial insurance broking* (May 2010) para 9.
[84] Financial Services Authority, *Final Notice to Aon Limited* (6 January 2009).
[85] The penalty was imposed pursuant to s 206 of the Financial Services and Markets Act 2000.

failure to manage the risk of bribes being paid in suitable way, described as a failure to fulfil Principle 3 of the FSA's Statement of Business Principles.

10.124 Principle 3 provides: 'A firm must take reasonable care to organise and control its affairs responsibly and effectively, with adequate risk management systems.' The substance of the FSA's complaint was that Aon's internal controls had not prevented the payments. The FSA Notice, which repays careful analysis, goes into some detail as to why Aon's codes, policies, etc (which did contain some anti-corruption provisions) were not compliant with Principle 3. One can expect the very wide terms of Principle 3 to be used as the basis for similar investigations by the FSA in the future.[86]

10.125 The Aon case sets no precedent in relation to the Bribery Act. However, at least for regulated businesses, it is an important example of the type of collateral damage which a failure to combat commercial bribery effectively can have, even if there is no criminal prosecution.

10.126 Moreover, the critique of Aon's procedures in the Notice provides a strong indicator of the priorities of the UK authorities when considering such matters. It is telling that Aon, a very large US-headquartered business, with policies in place which were, no doubt, intended to be compliant with the US FCPA, still failed to satisfy a UK-based regulator on the adequacy of its policies and procedures.

10.127 There is an obvious overlap between the principles employed by the FSA as to what is sufficient for financial firms under Principle 3 and the issue of 'adequate procedures' under s 7(2) of the Bribery Act. Each authority will have to fulfil its statutory duties independently. It is interesting to consider whether a financial firm which was not compliant with the expectations of the FSA under Principle 3 could establish a defence of adequate procedures under s 7(2), or vice versa. In principle, the answer must be that it could. However, it is reasonable to hope the FSA, SFO and other authorities will adopt a joined-up approach to these subjects. One can imagine that the courts will wish to encourage consistency of standards where possible.

---

[86] In much the same way as the US SEC relies on the 'books and records' provisions of the FCPA in cases where there may be insufficient evidence of active bribery per se.

Chapter 11

TERRITORIAL APPLICATION

BRIBERY ACT 2010: SECTION 12

'12 Offences under this Act: territorial application

(1) An offence is committed under section 1, 2 or 6 in England and Wales, Scotland or Northern Ireland if any act or omission which forms part of the offence takes place in that part of the United Kingdom.

(2) Subsection (3) applies if—

(a) no act or omission which forms part of an offence under section 1, 2 or 6 takes place in the United Kingdom,
(b) a person's acts or omissions done or made outside the United Kingdom would form part of such an offence if done or made in the United Kingdom, and
(c) that person has a close connection with the United Kingdom.

(3) In such a case—

(a) the acts or omissions form part of the offence referred to in subsection (2)(a), and
(b) proceedings for the offence may be taken at any place in the United Kingdom.

(4) For the purposes of subsection (2)(c) a person has a close connection with the United Kingdom if, and only if, the person was one of the following at the time the acts or omissions concerned were done or made—

(a) a British citizen,
(b) a British overseas territories citizen,
(c) a British National (Overseas),
(d) a British Overseas citizen,
(e) a person who under the British Nationality Act 1981 was a British subject,
(f) a British protected person within the meaning of that Act,
(g) an individual ordinarily resident in the United Kingdom,
(h) a body incorporated under the law of any part of the United Kingdom,
(i) a Scottish partnership.

(5) An offence is committed under section 7 irrespective of whether the acts or omissions which form part of the offence take place in the United Kingdom or elsewhere.

(6) Where no act or omission which forms part of an offence under section 7 takes place in the United Kingdom, proceedings for the offence may be taken at any place in the United Kingdom.

(7) Subsection (8) applies if, by virtue of this section, proceedings for an offence are to be taken in Scotland against a person.

(8) Such proceedings may be taken—

(a) in any sheriff court district in which the person is apprehended or in custody, or
(b) in such sheriff court district as the Lord Advocate may determine.

(9) In subsection (8) "sheriff court district" is to be read in accordance with section 307(1) of the Criminal Procedure (Scotland) Act 1995.'

INTRODUCTION

11.1 Section 12 of the Bribery Act sets out the territorial application of the relevant offences under the Act, often referred to as the 'jurisdiction' of the Act. Section 12(1) to (4) deal with the general bribery offences and the foreign public official offence under ss 1, 2 and 6 of the Act. Section 12(5) and (6) relate to the s 7 (failure to prevent) offence.

11.2 The Act provides for both territorial jurisdiction (where the state applies its laws to all those present in its borders and all events occurring inside its borders) and nationality jurisdiction (where the state applies its laws to all its nationals,[1] wherever they may be).

11.3 In relation to the s 7 offence, the Act provides for an extended concept of territorial jurisdiction for commercial organisations, whereby commercial organisations with any business presence in the UK can be liable, even if the bribery does not occur in the UK and the persons committing the bribery have no connection to the UK. The use of both nationality and territorial principles is unusual for a criminal statute, since criminal law does not usually apply to acts committed outside the jurisdiction.[2]

SECTIONS 1, 2 AND 6: TERRITORIAL JURISDICTION

11.4 The United Kingdom includes England, Wales, Scotland and Northern Ireland.[3] It does not include the Crown dependencies of the Channel Islands of Jersey, Guernsey and their associated islands, or the Isle of Man. It also does

---

[1] 'Nationals' may be too narrow a term in the case of the Bribery Act, since the category includes anyone with a 'close connection to the United Kingdom' as defined, including residents and citizens of territories formally outside the UK.
[2] *Secretary of State for Defence v Al Skeini & Ors* [2007] UKHL 26.
[3] Interpretation Act 1978, Sch 2.

not include the various British overseas territories.[4] During parliamentary debate there was some discussion of the likelihood of the Crown dependencies and British overseas territories adopting similar legislation but whether this will happen is a matter of conjecture.

11.5 A broad principle of English law, in relation to economic crime generally, is that where 'a substantial measure of the activities constituting a crime' take place in England, and there are no reasons of international comity which prevent it, the English courts have jurisdiction.[5] Of course, in the case of offences created by statute, one must look to the wording of each individual statute and interpret these from first principles.

11.6 Under s 12(1) of the Bribery Act an offence is committed under ss 1, 2 or 6 when acts or omissions which 'form part of' the offences as defined by the Act take place in the UK. It is clear that the same rule applies to s 7 offences, although those offences are not limited to this jurisdictional basis.[6]

11.7 Acts or omissions forming part of the offences can be described as the conduct element or actus reus of each of the offences under ss 1,2, 6, and 7.[7] In each case it will be necessary to identify which acts or omissions formed part of the offence in question and whether any of these occurred in the UK.[8]

---

[4] These were formerly known as the British dependent territories. The territories are: Anguilla, Bermuda, British Antarctic Territory, British Indian Ocean Territory, Cayman Islands, Falkland Islands and dependencies, Gibraltar, Montserrat, Pitcairn, Henderson, Ducie and Oeno Islands, St Helena and dependencies, the Sovereign Base Areas of Akrotiri and Dhekelia, Turks and Caicos Islands, and the Virgin Islands. The sovereign bases of Akrotiri and Dhekelia do not count as qualifying territories for nationality purposes. South Georgia and the South Sandwich Islands were the dependencies of the Falkland Islands, but were not British overseas territories between 3 October 1985 and 3 December 2001. Hong Kong ceased to be a British overseas territory on 30 June 1997 when sovereignty returned to China. St Christopher and Nevis was a British overseas territory until 18 September 1983, when it became an independent Commonwealth country.

[5] *R v Smith (Wallace Duncan) (No 1)* [1996] 2 Cr App R1 (per Rose LJ), approved in *R v Smith (Wallace Duncan) (No 4)* [2004] QB 1418 (CA).

[6] Section 12(5).

[7] The Criminal Justice Act 1993 defines a similar test for a 'relevant event' which, if occurring in the UK, grounds jurisdiction, as 'any act or omission or other event (including any result of one or more acts or omissions) proof of which is required for conviction of the offence'. However, the 1993 Act is limited to certain specified offences which do not include bribery.

[8] Section 14 of the Act makes a senior officer of a body corporate (or partnership) also guilty of an offence under ss 1, 2 or 6 (not s 7) which is committed by the corporation with the officer's consent or connivance. It does not create a separate offence merely extends the range of persons who may be guilty in the event that a corporation is guilty. It seems to follow that there is no separate actus reus or conduct element involved in s 14, the conduct element being satisfied by the conduct of the corporation under ss 1, 2 or 6. Consent and connivance therefore seem to amount to mental states only, although of course evidence of such mental states (which will certainly involve evidence of knowledge by the officers) will be required.

Section 1 – provision of bribes

11.8 In the case of s 1 the prosecution will need to establish:

(a) any event through which the accused ('P') made the offer, promise or gift to the other person; and

(b) the place at which that event took place.

11.9 In Chapter 2 we considered a hypothetical example of a building inspector, Bob, who is asked by Edmund not to report on defects in a development (ie to perform a relevant function or activity improperly), in exchange for an unspecified advantage. At a later meeting, cash is surreptitiously provided to Bob.

11.10 At least two events relevant to the commission of offences have occurred. First Edmund makes an offer (or possibly a promise) of an advantage to Bob. Secondly, Edmund later gives Bob the advantage itself (the cash). A third event is Bob receiving the cash.

11.11 If the meeting where Edmund first makes the offer occurs in a part of the UK then this will be sufficient to make Edmund guilty of a s 1 offence – offering a financial advantage, etc (subject to proof of mens rea). The place where the meeting took place determines what part of the UK the offence occurred in (England and Wales, Scotland or Northern Ireland). So if the meeting happened in Belfast the offence occurs under the law of Northern Ireland.

11.12 Of course the offer does not need to be made in person to be an act forming part of the offence. A phone call or e-mail by Edmund to Bob, or the use of an intermediary to pass on the offer would also qualify. If Edmund's normal place of work was in Spain but he asked a friend or subordinate in Belfast to make an offer on his behalf by e-mail then the place of the offer is Belfast, because the offer to Bob does not exist until an e-mail containing the offer is sent.[9]

11.13 The scenario also describes a second meeting involving the actual provision of the financial advantage by Edmund, contrary to s 1 and the receipt of such an advantage by Bob contrary to s 2. If that meeting occurred in, say, Manchester, then those offences are subject to the law of England and Wales.

11.14 In circumstances where acts forming part of different offences occur in two different jurisdictions of the UK then it seems that each offence can be tried in whichever part of the UK it occurred in. As with all international offences, one can expect the prosecuting authorities to consult with each other

---

[9] As we have seen, it does not matter whether Edmund's offer is made directly or through a third party – Bribery Act, s 1(5).

as to the most efficient method of trial of all defendants in relation to the same facts so as to avoid unnecessary duplication.[10]

Section 2 – receipt of bribes

11.15 In the case of s 2 the prosecution will need to establish:

(a) for cases 3, 4 and 5 – an act through which the accused ('R') made the request for the advantage, or agreement to receive the advantage or accepted the advantage; or

(b) for case 6:

   (i) an act constituting the improper performance of the relevant function or activity by R, or

   (ii) in the case of an act constituting improper performance in (i) but carried out by another person at R's request assent or acquiescence, the act or omission carried out by that other person constituting R's request, assent or acquiescence; and

(c) the place at which the events in (a) or (b) took place.

11.16 To continue our hypothetical example, Bob, the building inspector, seems to have agreed to amend his report in exchange for an advantage. If he had originally offered to do so then the prosecution needs to establish the place where the offer is made. If what is alleged is an agreement by Bob, rather than an offer, then the facts may be more complicated. It might well be possible to make inferences from the evidence that an agreement was reached at a particular place and time, whether by express words or by conduct.[11]

11.17 In case 6, the actus reus is the improper performance of the function or activity or R's request for or assent or acquiescence to someone else's improper performance. If Bob drafted and submitted a misleading report (in the hope of currying favour with Edmund) while on a holiday in Florida then it is possible that no act forming part of the offence took place in the UK.[12] If Bob asks a colleague to amend the report in his absence then the same result is possible, always subject to the 'close connection' test.

---

[10] See, for example, the CPS practice at www.cps.gov.uk/legal/h_to_k/jurisdiction/#crossborder.
[11] Of course if Bob has a close connection to the UK under s 12(4) this may not matter.
[12] Although this seems unlikely in most cases since Bob is very likely to have engaged in other conduct necessary to disguise or legitimise his actions while at his usual place of work and/or to be liable as a secondary offender (ie for aiding, abetting, counselling or procuring).

Section 6 – providing bribes to a foreign public official

11.18 The actus reus is the act of bribery, which is when P, directly or through a third party, offers, promises or gives any financial or other advantage either to a foreign public official ('F'), or to another person at F's request or with F's assent or acquiescence.[13]

11.19 The principles relevant to the s 1 offences also apply to bribery under s 6. It will be necessary to establish the time and place at which a financial or other advantage is offered, promised or given. If any action within the UK amounts to such an offer, promise or gift then the offence will have occurred under the Act, with the particular place within the UK which is the location of the action determining jurisdiction.

SECTIONS 1, 2 AND 6: NATIONALITY JURISDICTION

11.20 Acts or omissions forming part of an offence occurring outside the UK may nevertheless amount to an offence under ss 1, 2 or 6 of the Act by virtue of s 12(2) to (4), which extends the application of the Bribery Act to any person (including legal person) with a 'close connection to the United Kingdom'.

11.21 As one would expect, it is a condition of the liability of someone with a close connection to the UK that the actions or omissions would form part of the offence in question if they occurred in the UK.[14] Proceedings in relation to offences where none of the acts or omissions took place within the UK may be taken at any place within the UK.[15]

11.22 If it has been established that none of the elements of the actus reus of an offence under these sections occurred within the UK the nationality jurisdiction can be considered.

11.23 The more urgent question in many cases of overseas bribery will be whether the alleged perpetrator qualifies as having a close connection with the UK. The category includes those with formal national status under UK law as well as residents and companies or partnerships.

11.24 The close connection test is to be applied at the date the acts or omissions occurred. Someone subsequently acquiring a close connection will not thereby acquire a liability under the Act for acts done prior to the connection existing.

---

[13] The mental element, irrelevant for the purposes of jurisdiction, involves an intention to influence F in F's capacity as a foreign public official and intention to obtain or retain business, or an advantage in the conduct of business.
[14] Section 12(2)(b).
[15] Section 12(6).

11.25 A person will be deemed to have a 'close connection' if at the material time they were:

- a British citizen;
- a British overseas territories citizen;
- a British national (overseas);
- a British overseas citizen;
- a person who under the British Nationality Act 1981 was a British subject;
- a British protected person within the meaning of that Act;
- an individual ordinarily resident in the UK;
- a body incorporated under the law of any part of the UK; or
- a Scottish partnership.

British citizen

11.26 A person is a British citizen if they were:

- born in the UK or qualifying territory (British overseas territory[16]) before 1 January 1983 (a person born to certain diplomatic staff of foreign missions who had diplomatic immunity are excepted);[17]
- born in the UK on or after 1 January 1983 and at the time of their birth, one of their parents was a British citizen or legally settled in the UK;[18]
- born in a qualifying territory[19] after 21 May 2002 and at the time of their birth, one of their parents was a British citizen or legally settled in the UK or that particular territory;[20]

---

[16] See n 4 above.
[17] UK Border Agency: 'What is British Citizenship?' at www.ukba.homeoffice.gov.uk/britishcitizenship/aboutcitizenship.
[18] UK Border Agency: 'What is British Citizenship?' at www.ukba.homeoffice.gov.uk/britishcitizenship/aboutcitizenship.
[19] These are the same as the British overseas territories listed in n 4 above.
[20] UK Border Agency: 'What is British Citizenship?' at www.ukba.homeoffice.gov.uk/britishcitizenship/aboutcitizenship.

- born in the UK on or after 1 January 1983 but before 2 October 2000, if, at the time of their birth, either of their parents were European Economic Area (EEA) citizens who were exercising Treaty rights[21] under European Community (EC) law;[22]

- born in the UK and their parents are family members of citizens of the EEA who were exercising Treaty rights and were settled in the UK by the time of the person's birth; or

- born in the UK on or after 1 June 2002 to parents one of whom is a Swiss citizen.

11.27 Where a person is born in the UK to parents neither of whom were British citizens or legally settled in the UK at the time of their birth they are not a British citizen.

British overseas territories citizen

11.28 A person is a British overseas territories citizen if they are connected with the British overseas territories. British overseas territories citizenship is a category of citizenship that was created by the British Nationality Act 1981, which came into force on 1 January 1983. A person became a British overseas territories citizen on 1 January 1983 if they were a citizen of the UK and colonies on 31 December 1982 and:

- did not become a British citizen on 1 January 1983; and

- had connections with a British overseas territory because they, their parents or grandparents were born, registered or naturalised in that British overseas territory. If they did not have these connections, they may have become a British overseas citizen.

British national (overseas)

11.29 Special rules were introduced in 1986 to allow British overseas territories citizens from Hong Kong to acquire the new status of British national (overseas). Those who did not register as British nationals (overseas) and had no other nationality or citizenship on 30 June 1997 became British overseas citizens on 1 July 1997.

British overseas citizen

11.30 British overseas citizenship is a category of citizenship that was created by the British Nationality Act 1981, which came into force on 1 January 1983.

---

[21] Article 39 of the European Communities Treaty.
[22] UK Border Agency: 'What is British Citizenship?' at www.ukba.homeoffice.gov.uk/britishcitizenship/aboutcitizenship.

A person became a British overseas citizen on 1 January 1983 if they were a citizen of the UK and colonies on 31 December 1982 and they did not become either a British citizen or a British overseas territories citizen on 1 January 1983. People from Hong Kong who did not register as British nationals (overseas) and had no other nationality or citizenship on 30 June 1997 became British overseas citizens on 1 July 1997.

British subject under the British Nationality Act 1981

11.31 Until 1949, nearly everyone with a close connection to the UK was called a British subject. All citizens of Commonwealth countries were British subjects until January 1983. Since that date, very few categories of people have qualified as British subjects.

British protected person

11.32 From 1 January 1983, the following categories of people became, or were able to become, British protected persons:

- certain citizens or nationals of Brunei;

- anyone who, immediately before 1 January 1983, was a British protected person; and

- anyone who would otherwise be born stateless, on or after 1 January 1983, in the UK or an overseas territory if, at the time of their birth, their mother or father was a British protected person.

11.33 In most cases, British protected persons lost that status when they gained any other nationality or citizenship, including British citizenship, British overseas territories citizenship or British overseas citizenship.

Individual ordinarily resident in the UK

11.34 The term 'ordinarily resident' is not defined for the purposes of the Act. It appears in different areas of law and may vary somewhat between them. However, it seems clear that ordinary residence involves a person being resident in a place 'with some degree of continuity and apart from accidental or temporary absences',[23] or an 'abode in a particular place or country which he has adopted voluntarily and for settled purposes as part of the regular order of his life for the time being, whether or short or long duration'.[24]

11.35 A person can be ordinarily resident in more than one country. The fact that a person might be said to have a home in another country does not mean

---

[23] *Levene v IRC* [1928] AC 217, 225.
[24] Collins (ed), *Dicey Morris and Collins on the Conflict of Laws* (14th edn, London, 2006), para 6-120 et seq.

that they cannot also be ordinarily resident in the UK. In considering whether a person is ordinarily resident, all the circumstances of the particular case will need to be addressed but factors such as the length of stay in the UK, presence of family, location of business interests, possession of property or accommodation, frequency of presence or absence will all be relevant.

11.36 To take an example, a businessman of Russian nationality who owns many properties around Europe but spends a significant amount of time at his house in London may qualify as ordinarily resident in the UK even though he spends the majority of his time outside the UK.

UK incorporated body

11.37 A body incorporated under the law of any part of the UK includes companies incorporated under the Companies Acts. It also includes incorporated public bodies such as local authorities and limited liability partnerships.

11.38 As to partnerships, the Partnership Act 1890 outlines the definition of a partnership which is 'the relation which subsists between persons carrying on a business in common with a view of profit'.[25]

11.39 A Scottish partnership is a partnership constituted under the law of Scotland. Section 4(2) of the Partnership Act 1890 states that in Scotland, 'a firm is a legal person distinct from the partners of whom it is composed', and it seems to have been for this reason that separate provision is made for Scottish partnerships. An unincorporated partnership under the law of England and Wales or Northern Ireland has no separate legal identity, so that partners in such firms are subject to the rules applicable to individuals.[26]

British overseas territories/Crown dependency incorporated bodies

11.40 Companies or other bodies incorporated in British overseas territories are not deemed to have a close connection to the UK under s 12. So a Cayman Islands-registered company is not subject to the Act unless it either commits an action or omission forming part of a s 1, 2 or 6 offence within the UK or unless it carries on a business or part of a business in the UK for the purposes of s 7.

11.41 The same applies to companies or other bodies incorporated in British Crown dependencies.

---

[25] Partnership Act 1890, s 1(1).
[26] Although of course the partnership will be a relevant commercial organisation for the purposes of s 7, and see s 15 of the Bribery Act for the liabilities of partnerships pursuant to s 7.

SECTION 7: FAILURE OF COMMERCIAL ORGANISATIONS TO PREVENT BRIBERY

11.42 As outlined in Chapter 8, the offence of failing to prevent bribery is committed by a commercial organisation ('C') when an associated person ('A'), commits offences under ss 1 and 6 intending either to obtain or retain business or an advantage in the conduct of business for C. C may benefit from a defence of adequate procedures to prevent bribery by persons associated with it.[27]

11.43 The territorial application of s 7 is extremely broad. Section 12(5) of the Act makes it clear that:

> 'An offence is committed under section 7 irrespective of whether the acts or omissions which form part of the offence take place in the United Kingdom or elsewhere.'

As a result, the traditional test of territorial jurisdiction does not apply. Further, the 'close connection to the United Kingdom' test set out in s 12(2)–(4) only applies to offences under ss 1, 2 and 6.

11.44 Hence the only limitation on the application of s 7 insofar as commercial organisations are concerned arises out of s 7 itself, in particular the question of whether the commercial organisation is a 'relevant commercial organisation' as defined by s 7(5).

11.45 The issues arising under s 7(5) have been explored in detail in Chapter 8. Here it suffices to say that:

- companies incorporated in the UK or partnerships formed under UK law which carry on business will be subject to the Act;

- bribery by foreign subsidiaries or joint ventures will not make a UK commercial organisation automatically subject to the Act. The issue will be whether at the time of the bribery the entity committing the bribery was performing services for or on behalf of the UK entity – ie representing the UK entity in some way;

- companies or partnerships incorporated or formed overseas may well also qualify if they carry on a business, or part of a business, in the UK. This is a wide definition, and may well catch businesses which conduct relatively little commercial activity in the UK. It is unlikely to catch a parent company with a UK subsidiary if the only business carried on in the UK is the business of that subsidiary, rather than the parent. However, each case will turn on its own facts and a UK business presence should alert non-UK enterprises to the risk of liability under the Bribery Act.

---

[27] Section 7(1), (2).

SPECIFIC PROVISIONS IN RELATION TO SCOTS CRIMINAL PROCEDURE

11.46 Section 12(7) to (9) provide specific measures for the allocation of jurisdiction to court districts within the Scottish criminal justice system, according to the determination of the Lord Advocate.

Chapter 12

ACCESSORY LIABILITY, INCHOATE OFFENCES, RELATED OFFENCES AND EXTRADITION

INTRODUCTION

12.1 Economic crimes such as bribery tend not to occur in isolation. They are frequently connected to or are the predicates of other offences. Where bribery occurs in a business context it is more likely than not that more than one person will be aware of it and as knowledge and participation spreads, so does the potential for liability.

12.2 This chapter seeks to provide a brief outline of certain other areas of liability which may be relevant to businesses people in particular. In no particular order these are: accessory liability (aiding, abetting, counselling and procuring), inchoate offences (assisting and encouraging offences, conspiracy and attempt), fraud, money laundering, false accounting and misconduct in public office.[1] There is also a very brief treatment of extradition.

ACCESSORY LIABILITY FOR BRIBERY OFFENCES

12.3 A person who aids, abets, counsels or procures the commission of any offence may be liable for the offence in the same way as the principal offender who actually commits the offence. This is known as 'secondary liability' or 'accessory liability'. Being an accessory is not a separate offence. It involves participation in the primary offence and so the range of penalties on conviction will be the same. It is not the same as the inchoate offences of attempt or conspiracy, which are committed independently of the principal crime.

12.4 Section 8 of the Accessories and Abettors Act 1861 is the main source for the law of secondary liability. As amended, it provides that anyone who 'shall aid, abet, counsel or procure the commission of any indictable offence … shall be liable to be tried, indicted and punished as a principal offender'.[2]

---

[1] For more detailed treatment of these subjects see Ormerod (ed) *Smith & Hogan on Criminal Law* (12th edn, Oxford, 2008). The leading practitioner works are *Archbold on Criminal Pleading, Evidence and Practice* (London, 2011) and *Blackstone's Criminal Practice 2011* (Oxford, 2011).

[2] The 1861 Act applies to offences tried on indictment only. For summary offences see the Magistrates' Courts Act 1980, s 44.

12.5 To be held liable as a secondary offender ('S') a principal offender ('P') must commit the principal offence.[3] However, it is not always necessary for P to be convicted for S to be guilty – it seems to be sufficient to prove that someone committed the primary offence and that S aided, abetted, procured or counselled it.[4]

12.6 The mental element for all the secondary offences is essentially the same. It involves:

(a) an intention to assist or encourage (for aiding, abetting and counselling) or bring about (for procuring) the conduct of the principal offender;

(b) knowledge of the essential elements of the offence including any necessary *mens rea* of the principal.[5]

Aiding and abetting, counselling and procuring

12.7 There is some doctrinal debate about whether each of these terms denotes a specific and separate offence. Over time the definitions offered in relation to each have become a little blurred and many now think that at least aiding, abetting and counselling can better be seen together as 'assisting and encouraging', although procuring still appears to be conceptually separate.[6]

12.8 In *R v Bryce*[7] the Court of Appeal held that the essential elements of liability which the prosecution had to prove for aiding, abetting, counselling or procuring were as follows:

(a) an act done by S which in fact assisted the later commission of the offence;

(b) that S did the act deliberately realising that it was capable of assisting the offence;

(c) that S at the time of doing the act contemplated the commission of the offence by P, ie he foresaw it as a 'real or substantial risk' or 'real possibility'; and

(d) that S when doing the act intended to assist P in what he was doing.

---

[3] *R v Dias* [2001] EWCA Crim 2986; [2002] 2 Cr App R 96.
[4] *DPP v K & B* [1997] 1 Cr App R 36.
[5] *Johnson v Youden* [1950] 1 KB 544.
[6] Smith, 'Criminal Liability of Accessories: Law and Law Reform' (1997) 113 *Law Quarterly Review* 453.
[7] [2004] EWCA Crim 1231.

12.9 To aid the commission of an offence is to give help, support or assistance before or at the time the offence is committed.[8] An example of such assistance in the context of bribery might be arranging a meeting where bribe money is to be handed over. In a corporate context, the creation of a secret 'slush fund' in order to finance the payment of bribes to foreign officials by P is likely to amount to aiding a bribery offence.

12.10 Abetting an offence is more in the nature of encouraging it than actually assisting in it.[9] It is not necessary for S to be present while P is committing the actus reus of the offence for S to encourage it.[10] In the context of bribery one can imagine a senior executive generally encouraging a subordinate to commit bribery, although the senior executive does not himself wish to participate in it. Such encouragement would be sufficient for secondary liability for the primary offence which is committed by the subordinate.[11]

12.11 Whatever the situation historically, there now seems to be little of substance that separates 'abetting' and 'counselling'. Counselling also means 'to advise, or solicit or encourage'[12] and it is difficult to envisage a modern case in which counselling could be charged but abetting could not.

12.12 To 'procure' an offence is to 'produce by endeavour' – in other words to work to cause a particular offence.[13] To be guilty of procuring one must intentionally act to cause the *actus reus* and know of the essential elements of the principal offence. In a corporate context, bribing an executive who misled a colleague into issuing a cheque payable to a corrupt official may have procured the commission of an offence by the company under ss 1 or 6.

12.13 What about a failure to act to prevent bribery by someone else? English law does not have a general 'good Samaritan' requirement, so that it is not an offence to stand by and fail to stop the commission of a crime by a third party.[14] However, where S is under a legal duty to act, failure to discharge the duty is capable of constituting assistance or encouragement, and where S is in a position to control the actions of P a failure to do so may also amount to such assistance or encouragement.[15] The latter aspect is particularly relevant in the business context. The turning of a blind eye will afford no defence where a

---

[8] *Smith & Hogan on Criminal Law* (12th edn, Oxford, 2008) p 186. Events occurring after the crime is committed do not amount to aiding, abetting, counselling or procuring it.
[9] *R v JF Alford Transport Ltd* [1997] 2 Cr App R 326.
[10] Although presence at the time the crime was committed may once have been what distinguished 'abetting' from 'counselling'.
[11] If the senior executive has sufficient responsibility this may involve the company itself committing a s 1 or s 6 offence, the executive being liable for complicity under s 14, and the company committing a s 7 offence, depending on whether its anti-bribery procedures were adequate. The scenario might also qualify as encouraging the commission of an offence under the Serious Crime Act 2007, as to which see below.
[12] *Smith & Hogan on Criminal Law*, p 187.
[13] *A-G's Reference (No 1 of 1975)* [1975] 2 All ER 684.
[14] Although it is an offence to impede the apprehension of offenders or to 'compound' an offence – Criminal Law Act 1967, ss 4, 5.
[15] *J F Alford Transport Ltd* (1997) 2 Cr App R 326; *R v Gaunt* [2003] EWCA Crim 3925.

defendant could have exercised control had he so desired. A senior manager or director who knows about but fails to stop bribery by someone reporting to him (or, in the case of a director, by anyone in the company) may well be guilty of aiding or abetting a s 1, s 2 or s 6 offence.[16]

12.14 Secondary liability for a s 7 offence may be more difficult to establish because s 7 is so limited in its scope. The offence (which only C can commit as a principal offender) does not involve C doing any positive act. It only involves C being 'associated' with A, as defined, and A committing bribery so as to benefit C. It is not easy to conceive of a secondary participant S doing something of assistance or encouragement to C in these circumstances. However, it may be sufficient for S to assist A to commit the bribery, thus causing the liability of C as well as A and thereby incurring secondary liability for both the offence committed by A and the offence committed by C.[17]

12.15 Perhaps a more likely scenario would be where S, an employee of C, deliberately sabotages or mis-applies C's systems and controls so as to facilitate the provision of bribes on C's behalf, and thus facilitates the commission of a s 7 offence. There seems no reason in principle why S should not be liable as an accessory in those circumstances, although more condign penalties may also be available if S is charged with assisting or encouraging a crime under Part II of the Serious Crime Act 2007, as to which see below.

ENCOURAGING OR ASSISTING CRIME – SERIOUS CRIME ACT 2007

12.16 The Serious Crime Act 2007, Part II, created a series of new offences which relate to the assistance or encouragement of crime.[18] The offences, under ss 44–46 of the Act can be summarised as follows:

(a) doing an act capable of encouraging or assisting the commission of an offence and intending to encourage or assist its commission (s 44);

(b) doing an act capable of encouraging or assisting the commission of an offence and believing that the offence will be committed and that his act will encourage or assist its commission (s 45);

---

[16] Again, if the company itself can be said to have committed the offence then the senior manager may be guilty under s 14 of the Act. There is also the risk of committing an offence of assisting or encouraging a crime, under Part II of the Serious Crime Act 2007 – see below.

[17] Although since the penalties for participation in the A offence (imprisonment and fine) are more severe than those available for C's offence (fine only) a s 7 charge may be redundant.

[18] These offences replace the previous common law offence of incitement. It was felt that there was a gap in the previous law, in particular in relation to persons who deliberately assisted in the commission of a crime who could not be convicted in circumstances where the main perpetrator, for whatever reason, did not go on to commit the offence. Part II of the 2007 Act is intended to close these loopholes. See Law Commission *Inchoate Liability for Assisting and Encouraging Crime*, LC 300, CM 6878, July 2008.

(c) doing an act capable of encouraging or assisting the commission of one or more of a number of offences and believing that one or more of those offences will be committed, though lacking a belief as to which and believing that his act will encourage or assist the commission of one or more of the offences (s 46).

12.17 The Act does not provide a definition of 'assisting' or 'encouraging' or indeed of 'doing an act capable of' either assisting or encouraging. These will be questions for the jury in every case. However, there is some reason to think that encouraging will have the same meaning as incitement under the previous law – ie seeking to persuade or encourage, or compel by threats, another person to commit an act which would constitute a crime. It does not matter if the person so encouraged is not in fact persuaded to take action.[19] 'Assisting' seems to include any conduct that, as a matter of fact, makes it easier for the principal offender to commit the principal offence. Such assistance might include giving advice as to how the offence could be committed or how to avoid detection.

12.18 Assisting and encouraging offences are inchoate offences in their own right. Like attempt and conspiracy, but unlike secondary participation offences, they do not require the actual commission of the principal offence for there to be liability. However, in many cases there is likely to be a considerable overlap between the necessary mens rea and actus reus for the assisting and encouraging offences and secondary liability for aiding and abetting, counselling or procuring.

12.19 There is a specific defence of 'acting reasonably',[20] to allow a person who assists or encourages crime to show that his act was reasonable in the circumstances – for example because it was intended to prevent the commission or a more serious crime or to limit harm or to expose wrongdoing.

12.20 Plainly, it will be possible for individuals (and corporate bodies) to be guilty of assisting or encouraging the commission of offences under the Bribery Act. The example given above in the context of abetting a crime, of the senior executive who encourages his subordinate to pay bribes, will also constitute an offence of encouraging a bribery offence even if the subordinate refuses to comply and/or informs the police.

12.21 Part II of the 2007 Act applies to all offences, including a s 7 offence. As discussed above in the context of aiding and abetting, someone deliberately sabotaging C's systems and controls, thus assisting or encouraging A to pay bribes for C's benefit, may well be guilty of the assisting/encouraging offences under the 2007 Act even if no actual bribery by A can be proved.[21]

---

[19] *DPP v Armstrong* [2000] Crim LR 379.
[20] Serious Crime Act 2007, s 50.
[21] Note in this regard s 7(3): 'For the purposes of this section, A bribes another person if, and only if, A—(a) is, or would be, guilty of an offence under section 1 or 6 (*whether or not A has been prosecuted for such an offence*), or (b) would be guilty of such an offence if section 12(2)(c) and (4) were omitted' (emphasis added).

12.22 As to jurisdiction, where there are specific jurisdictional rules applicable to the principal offence then these also apply to offences of assisting and encouraging under the 2007 Act. Therefore the jurisdictional regime established by s 12 of the Bribery Act also applies to these offences.[22]

CONSPIRACY

12.23 A criminal conspiracy is an agreement between two or more persons to carry out a course of conduct involving crime. Like encouraging and assisting the commission of a crime, a conspiracy is an inchoate offence – it does not require the commission of the offence which is the subject of the conspiracy in order for the defendant to be liable.

12.24 There are various forms of criminal conspiracy.[23] The most relevant for the purposes of bribery offences will be conspiracy to commit a criminal offence contrary to s 1 of the Criminal Law Act 1977 (CLA 1977).

12.25 Section 1 of CLA 1977[24] provides as follows:

> '(1) Subject to the following provisions of this part of the Act, if a person agrees with any other person or persons that a course of conduct will be pursued which, if the agreement is carried out in accordance with their intentions, either –
>
> (a) will necessarily amount to or involve the commission of any offence or offences by one or more of the parties to the agreement; or
> (b) would do so but for the existence of facts which render the commission of the offence or any of the offences impossible,
>
> he is guilty of conspiracy to commit the offence or offences in question.'

Fact of agreement

12.26 Agreement is the crucial element in conspiracy. Whether the understanding between the individuals concerned amounts to an agreement will often be a matter of degree. There is no criminal conspiracy if there are negotiations about the possibility of doing something but the outcome is that the parties do not in fact agree.[25] In most cases there is unlikely to be contemporaneous evidence of an agreement to do something illegal, however inferences as to agreement can be drawn from the later conduct of the accused.

12.27 The agreement must involve at least two persons, although it is possible to be guilty of a conspiracy with persons unknown. It is also possible to be guilty even if an accused co-conspirator is acquitted (for example due to lack of

---

[22] Serious Crime Act 2007, s 52, Sch 4(5).
[23] Which should be distinguished from conspiracy in civil law, as to which see Chapter 13.
[24] The CLA 1977 applies only to England and Wales.
[25] *R v Walker* [1962] Crim LR 458.

evidence of mens rea).[26] It is possible to have conspiracies in which some of the parties involved have not been in direct communication with one another.[27]

12.28 As an inchoate offence, it is not necessary for the agreement to be carried out – the conspiracy itself is the crime.

Impossibility

12.29 At common law it was possible for a defendant to rely on a defence that the object of the conspiracy was impossible to achieve. However, defences based on impossibility have largely been abolished.[28] So, for example, where two people agree to pay money to F who they wrongly believe to be a foreign public official for the purpose of influencing him in his capacity as such then, although they will not be liable under s 6, because F is not an FPO, they may nevertheless be liable for conspiracy to commit a s 6 offence.

Intention to agree and fulfil agreement

12.30 The mens rea requirements for conspiracy involve both an intention to make an agreement and an intention to carry the agreement out. If the principal offence involves knowledge of particular circumstances (such as, for example, that acceptance of a particular advantage would itself amount to improper performance of a relevant function or activity)[29] then such knowledge on the part of the alleged conspirator must also be proved.

12.31 However, it is not necessary for the conspirator to intend that a specific actual offence which is, in law, the subject of the conspiracy be committed. He may be indifferent as to whether that specific offence is committed. Nor is it necessary for him to know that what is planned is criminal – ignorance of the law is, famously, no defence. If the accused intends to make an agreement, and intends to go along with the course of action agreed, and he knows of circumstances which make the course of action unlawful, he will be liable for conspiracy.[30]

12.32 In *R v Siracusa*[31] it was held that participation in conspiracy can be active or passive. The defendant's liability is established when he enters the agreement, intending that the conspiracy be carried out and his failure to stop the criminal conduct is evidence of his agreement and intention.

---

[26] *DPP v Shannon* [1975] AC 717.
[27] For example, the so-called 'chain' and 'wheel' conspiracies. In either case, the conspirators must be shown to be party to a common design and they must further be aware that they are part of a wider scheme.
[28] See Criminal Attempts Act 1981.
[29] Bribery Act 2010, s 1, case 2.
[30] *R v Saik* [2007] 1 AC 18.
[31] (1990) 90 Cr App R 340.

12.33 Section 1A of CLA 1977 extends jurisdiction for conspiracy to agreements to commit offences outside the UK, as long as certain conditions are satisfied, including a condition of illegality under the law of the place in which the intended offence was to be committed and a condition that there was some conduct referable to the agreement which occurred in England and Wales. The wider principle of a close connection with the UK, as provided in s 12 of the Bribery Act, does not appear to apply to conspiracy charges.[32]

The uses of conspiracy

12.34 In the business world, a conspiracy to commit bribery is not difficult to imagine. To carry out any significant bribery in a business context will probably require the involvement of more than one individual and various meetings or at least communications, which result in an agreement or agreements to carry out conduct amounting to bribery. The large schemes to corrupt foreign officials on the part of businesses which have recently come before the courts have all involved charges of conspiracy to commit corruption offences under the previous law.[33]

12.35 In other chapters we have considered various examples of companies engaging in conduct which might amount to the principal offences of bribery, such as the hypothetical case of Peckham Cars discussed in Chapter 8. Peckham's executive, Derek, offered cash to an overseas official so as to win a contract for the company. If Derek discussed his plan to do this with Rodney, the CEO of Peckham, and they agreed that Derek should provide the advantage in question then, once that agreement is made, Rodney and Derek are guilty of conspiracy to commit bribery under s 6 of the Act and probably also under s 1. Since Rodney is the CEO it is quite possible that his participation was as the 'directing mind' of the company, making Peckham itself also a part of the conspiracy. The intervention of the Indian authorities might mean that the principal offences of bribery were not committed, but the conspiracy charge would still lie.

12.36 The more limited nature of what is required to be proved on a charge of conspiracy to commit a bribery offence makes it very attractive for prosecutors. Bribery cases can be difficult to prove, especially when the case involves an overseas element. In conspiracy cases the evidence needed only goes to the agreement to bribe and the state of mind of the parties at that time. Whether the person to be bribed actually qualified as a foreign public official or was subject to relevant expectations of impartiality, good faith, etc is not relevant as long as the accused knew or believed that the facts necessary to making the agreed transaction a bribe were true. The same applies to other inchoate offences.

---

[32] The Criminal Justice Act 1993 also extends jurisdiction for inchoate offences of attempt and conspiracy to commit certain offences, but this has not been amended to include offences under the Bribery Act.

[33] For example *R v Mabey & Johnson Ltd* (unreported) 29 September 2009, Southwark Crown Court; *R v Innospec Ltd* [2010] EW Misc 7 (EWCC); *R v Dougall* [2010] EWCA Crim 1048.

12.37 The sentences applying to conspiracy are the same as those of the main offence, so conspiracy to commit an offence under the Bribery Act attracts a maximum of 10 years' imprisonment and an unlimited fine on conviction.[34] On present form, it is reasonable to expect quite a few charges of conspiracy to commit bribery under specific sections of the Bribery Act to come before the courts after the Act is implemented.

ATTEMPT

12.38 The law relating to attempts in England and Wales is set out in the Criminal Attempts Act 1981 (CAA 1981). Section 1 of CAA 1981 provides as follows:

> '(1) If, with intent to commit an offence to which this section applies, a person does an act which is more than merely preparatory to the commission of the offence, he is guilty of attempting to commit that offence.
>
> (2) A person may be guilty of attempting to commit an offence to which this section applies even though the facts are such that the commission of the offence is impossible.
>
> (3) In any case where –
>
> (a) apart from this subsection a person's intention would not be regarded as having amounted to an intent to commit an offence; but
> (b) if the facts of the case had been as he believed them to be, his intention would be so regarded,
>
> then for the purpose of subsection (1) above, he shall be regarded as having an intent to commit that offence.'

More than merely preparatory

12.39 The offence requires that the accused has committed an act which is 'more than merely preparatory' to the offence attempted. The application of this test is left to the jury, once the judge has determined that there is sufficient evidence of an attempt. The question of whether the defendant has engaged in acts that are more than merely preparatory is a question of degree.

12.40 In the case of bribery, consider our previous example of Bob the building inspector.[35] Edmund, a building contractor, provides Bob with cash in order to prevent him from writing a critical report. He does so by placing an envelope full of cash in Bob's coat when both are at a restaurant. Imagine instead that on approaching Bob's coat Edmund notices someone he believes is a police officer and quickly turns away, without transferring the money. If there has been no prior conversation between Bob and Edmund about Bob being

---

[34] Criminal Law Act 1977, s 3.
[35] Chapter 2.

paid for amending his report then Edmund may not have committed the main offence under s 1, since he has neither offered, promised nor actually given the money to Bob. But by bringing such a large amount of cash with him to the meeting and by starting the process of giving it to Bob he may well have attempted to do it because his action was not merely preparatory to the gift. All that stopped him from giving the money was an extraneous circumstance – the unplanned presence of an observer.

12.41 There is no defence of voluntary withdrawal. Once the defendant has progressed beyond the stage of merely preparatory acts, he will be unable to avoid liability for attempt, though it may be relevant to mitigation of sentence.

Specific intent

12.42 Where a person is charged with an attempt, the prosecution must show that the accused, armed with the necessary knowledge of facts and circumstances, acted with specific intent to commit the crime attempted.

12.43 As with conspiracy, the impossibility of committing an offence (for example because of the existence of some unknown fact such as the position, or lack of position, held by the recipient of a putative bribe) is irrelevant to attempt.[36]

12.44 As to jurisdiction, actions within England and Wales which constitute attempts to commit offences outside England and Wales are likely to be subject to UK jurisdiction.[37]

FRAUD

12.45 Cases of bribery may also involve the offence of fraud, which may briefly be defined as dishonest conduct intended to make a gain, or cause a loss or a risk of loss to another person, by means of false representation, failure to disclose information or abuse of position.[38] It may well be possible for individuals in particular to face charges of fraud alongside charges of bribery, especially where there is evidence that the individual intended to enrich himself by means of the conduct in question.

12.46 The Fraud Act 2006 (FA 2006) came into force on 15 January 2007 and overhauled several of the criminal offences of fraud.[39]

---

[36] Criminal Attempts Act 1981, s 1(2).
[37] Criminal Attempts Act 1981, s 1A. The Criminal Justice Act 1993 also extends jurisdiction for inchoate offences of attempt and conspiracy to commit certain offences, but this has not been amended to include offences under the Bribery Act.
[38] This definition is not the same as for civil fraud, as to which see Chapter 13.
[39] Prior to the implementation of the Act, the statutory fraud offences were based on deception under the Theft Acts 1968 and 1978. The offences included obtaining property by deception, obtaining a money transfer by deception, obtaining a pecuniary advantage by deception and obtaining services by deception.

12.47 Section 1 of FA 2006 provides:

'(1) A person is guilty of fraud if he is in breach of the sections listed in subsection (2) (which provide for different ways of committing the offence).

(2) The Sections are –

(a) section 2 (fraud by false representation),
(b) section 3 (fraud by failing to disclose information), and
(c) section 4 (fraud by abuse of position).'

12.48 The new offence is intentionally wide so as to catch as much fraudulent behaviour as possible. Section 1 of FA 2006 creates a single offence, not three separate offences under ss 2–4. Since there is only one offence of fraud, a charge can possibly include breaches of more than one section. The offence is punishable on conviction on indictment with 10 years' imprisonment.

12.49 In all three instances of the offence, the accused must have:

(a) acted dishonestly; and

(b) have intended to make a gain or to cause a loss to another or expose another to a risk of loss.

12.50 Unlike the old deception offences, there is no requirement to prove that an actual gain or loss occurred, so long as the requisite intention is made out.

12.51 'Dishonesty' is an element common to all forms of the offence under s 1(2). It is one of those terms (like 'corruptly') which the common law has struggled to define satisfactorily. The present test of dishonesty is encapsulated in the well-known case of *Ghosh*.[40]

12.52 'Gain' and 'loss' for the purposes of ss 2–4 are defined by s 5(2). They:

'(a) extend only to gain or loss in money or other property;
(b) include any such gain or loss whether temporary or permanent;

and "property" means any property whether real or personal (including things in action and other intangible property).

(3) "Gain" includes a gain by keeping what one has, as well as a gain by getting what one does not have.

(4) "Loss" includes a loss by not getting what one might get, as well as a loss by parting with what one has.'

---

[40] *R v Ghosh* [1982] QB 1053.

12.53 Unlike theft, there is no requirement under FA 2006 that the accused acts with intent to deprive his victim permanently of any property. As mentioned above, it is sufficient that the accused intends that his victim will be exposed to the risk of loss. It will not be necessary for the prosecution to establish that the defendant had a more specific intention that his victim will lose.

Fraud by abuse of position

12.54 Section 4 of FA 2006 is of particular interest to those considering bribery. It provides:

> '(1) A person is in breach of this section if he –
>
> (a) occupies a position in which he is expected to safeguard, or not to act against, the financial interests of another person,
> (b) dishonestly abuses that position, and
> (c) intends, by means of the abuse of that position –
>   (i) to make a gain for himself or another, or
>   (ii) to cause loss to another or to expose another to a risk of loss.
>
> (2) A person may be regarded as having abused his position even though his conduct consisted of an omission rather than an act.'

12.55 The Explanatory Notes give examples of relevant 'positions' including those where the defendant is given access to his victim's assets, premises, equipment, and customers or where a care worker abuses their access to patient bank accounts.[41]

12.56 There are obvious parallels with the definition of bribery for the purpose of the general offences, especially with condition C in s 3(5).[42] Many professionals and public officials occupy positions in which they are expected to safeguard the financial interests of the people they serve. One can expect specific cases, especially charges of passive bribery, to involve allegations of fraud under s 4 as well as bribery and perhaps misfeasance in public office. However, these offences are all independent of each other and should be analysed separately.

CONSPIRACY TO DEFRAUD

12.57 The Fraud Act 2006 did not abolish the controversial common law offence of conspiracy to defraud. However, the Attorney-General has issued

---

[41] Explanatory Notes to the Fraud Bill, prepared by the Home Office, *Bill 7- EN*, note 18.
[42] See discussion in Chapter 4.

guidance on the use of the offence in the wake of the Fraud Act 2006 which indicates a very narrow range of circumstances in which its use in future is likely.[43]

MONEY LAUNDERING

12.58 The term 'money laundering' refers to the process by which funds derived from a crime or criminal conduct are given apparent legitimacy. It is a significant area of law in itself.

12.59 Money laundering offences apply to the proceeds of all crimes, even the most trivial. There are no de minimis limits in relation to the crimes in question or amounts involved. The most important UK legislation is the Proceeds of Crime Act 2002 (POCA). Part 7 of POCA provides for various offences which involve dealing with or failing to report dealings with 'criminal property'.

Criminal property

12.60 Criminal property is property constituting a person's benefit from criminal conduct or representing such a benefit (whether directly or indirectly). The alleged offender must also know or suspect that the property represents such a benefit.[44]

12.61 Criminal conduct is conduct which constitutes an offence in any part of the UK or would constitute an offence in any part of the UK if it occurred there, thus including conduct that occurred abroad but the proceeds of which come into the UK.[45]

12.62 Bribery, wherever it occurs, will constitute criminal conduct for the purposes of POCA. We can therefore take it that money (or other property such as gifts) provided by way of a bribe is almost certainly criminal property because it represents the benefit which the recipient of the bribe receives from his criminal conduct. The proceeds of such money (such as property or other assets) is also capable of being criminal property and may be made the subject of recovery proceedings. In *SOCA v Agidi*[46] the defendant was a government official in Nigeria who had accumulated huge sums of money as a result of corruption and had used some of the proceeds to purchase property in London. The court held that the contents of an English bank account and the London property could be claimed by the Serious Organised Crime Agency (SOCA) as representing criminal property. The increase in value of the London property since purchase was also claimable.

---

[43] Guidance on Conspiracy to Defraud: www.attorneygeneral.gov.uk/Publications/Documents/conspiracy%20to%20defraud%20final.pdf.
[44] POCA, s 340(3).
[45] POCA, s 340(2).
[46] [2011] EWHC 175.

12.63 *Agidi* was a case of a corrupt official who received cash bribes and invested them, or some of them. What about the more difficult case where a company or other person, pays a bribe and business is obtained as a result? If the business is profitable, are all the profits criminal property? This will depend on whether such profits can be said to represent a direct or indirect benefit from criminal conduct. The author's research has not uncovered a case where this has been definitively established, however, there seems to be no reason in principle why it should not be, so long as it can be proven that the profitable transaction would not have occurred but for the bribery.

12.64 Although the case was not one of money laundering under Part 7 of POCA, it is of interest that the Serious Fraud Office recently exercised its powers of civil recovery of the proceeds of unlawful conduct against MW Kellogg Ltd (MWK). MWK received (or is to receive) payments from a joint venture involved in the notorious Bonney Island project in Nigeria.[47] Several of the joint venture's contracts were said to have been obtained by bribery on a widespread scale. Thus it seems the dividends due to MWK from the joint venture amounted to 'property obtained through unlawful conduct' under s 241 of POCA and therefore subject to confiscation. It may be that MWK was not prosecuted for bribery and/or money laundering because, according to the SFO, MWK itself 'was used by the parent company and was not a willing participant in the corruption'.

12.65 It would be prudent for businesses in a similar position to consider their position very carefully. They should work on the assumption that funds received in such circumstances may well amount to criminal property and will at least amount to property obtained through unlawful conduct and therefore be subject to civil recovery by the authorities.

Main offences

12.66 The money laundering offences most relevant to bribery are likely to be:

(a) s 327 – concealing, disguising, converting or transferring criminal property or removing it from England, Wales, Scotland or Northern Ireland. Concealing or disguising criminal property is defined at s 327(3) as including 'concealing or disguising its nature, source, location, disposition, movement or ownership or any rights with respect to it'. Disguising the true nature of payments or receipts in the way of bribery, for example by false invoices or false accounting records, will be money laundering offences under s 327;[48]

(b) s 328 – entering into or becoming concerned in an arrangement which the defendant knows or suspects facilitates the acquisition, retention, use or

---

[47] See www.sfo.gov.uk/press-room/latest-press-releases/press-releases-2011/mw-kellogg-ltd-to-pay-%C2%A37-million-in-sfo-high-court-action.aspx.
[48] Amongst other potential offences, such as false accounting and/or secondary participation in bribery.

control of criminal property by or on behalf of another person. An estate agent or solicitor who assisted a government official to purchase property with the proceeds of corrupt activity who suspected the source of funds was illegitimate would be guilty of such an offence;

(c) s 329 – acquisition, use or possession of criminal property. The accused must have the requisite subjective knowledge or suspicion as to the origin of the property concerned. A person in possession of criminal property without the relevant knowledge or suspicion is not guilty of an offence under this section.[49]

12.67 Key features of all these provisions are that no offence is committed if the defendant makes a disclosure to the appropriate authorities pursuant to s 338 of POCA prior to the events charged or if the defendant intended to make such a disclosure but had a reasonable excuse for not doing so.[50] It is for the defendant to prove this on the balance of probabilities.

12.68 A person does not commit an offence under ss 327–329 if he knows or believes on reasonable grounds, that the relevant criminal conduct occurred outside the UK, and was not, at the time it occurred, unlawful under the criminal law then applying in that country or territory.[51]

12.69 Note that this defence of legality under local law is much less strict than the 'local law' defence potentially available to a s 6 Bribery Act offence,[52] which is a question of fact rather than a question of the defendant's knowledge or reasonable belief. It is also less strict than the consideration given to local written law in considering whether conduct is 'improper' in the case of the general offences.[53]

Regulated sector

12.70 Certain undertakings are deemed by the 2007 Money Laundering Regulations to be within the 'regulated sector' for the purposes of POCA, and are required to take detailed steps in relation to money laundering. These undertakings will commit an offence if they fail to make disclosures to appropriate persons if they suspect that any other person is engaged in money laundering. Those included in the regulated sector include credit institutions, financial institutions, auditors, insolvency practitioners, tax advisers, independent legal professionals, estate agents and casinos. Legal advisers learning of

---

[49] Section 329(2)(c).
[50] Also, a s 328 'arrangement' does not include the conduct of litigation by legal professionals and any information obtained by lawyers in these circumstances would be subject to legal privilege in any event – *Bowman v Fels* [2005] EWCA Civ 226.
[51] Sections 327(3), 328(3), 329(3) – added by Serious Organised Crime and Police Act 2005.
[52] Section 6(3)(b).
[53] Section 5(2).

information in legally privileged circumstances are exempt. 'Tipping off' the subject of an investigation that a disclosure has been made is also an offence.[54]

FALSE ACCOUNTING

12.71 In the United States, the 'books and records' provisions of the FCPA have been used to considerable effect. The Bribery Act does not contain any similar provisions, but the offence of false accounting is certainly wide enough to capture businesses and individuals who falsify records as part of a scheme to commit or avoid liability for bribery.

12.72 False accounting is criminalised by s 17 of the Theft Act 1968, which provides as follows:

> (1) Where a person dishonestly, with a view to gain for himself or another or with intent to cause loss to another—
>
> (a) destroys, defaces, conceals or falsifies any account or any record or document made or required for any accounting purpose; or
> (b) in furnishing information for any purpose produces or makes use of any account, or any such record or document as aforesaid, which to his knowledge is or may be misleading, false or deceptive in a material particular;
>
> he shall, on conviction on indictment, be liable to imprisonment for a term not exceeding seven years.
>
> (2) For purposes of this section a person who makes or concurs in making in an account or other document an entry which is or may be misleading, false or deceptive in a material particular, or who omits or concurs in omitting a material particular from an account or other document, is to be treated as falsifying the account or document.'

12.73 A 'person' will include a corporate body. It is most unlikely that the accounts of a business engaged in active bribery contain entries which are completely accurate and/or not misleading. As with other offences, for the corporate body to be guilty the 'directing mind' test has to be applied.[55]

12.74 The terms 'account', 'record' and 'document made or required for any accounting purpose' should be interpreted according to their ordinary meaning, not as technical terms. An account will obviously include computerised ledgers and financial accounts of all kinds. A document may be required for an accounting purpose even if that is not the primary purpose of the record. One useful test seems to be whether the document is one which the addressee would be likely to retain or throw away.[56]

---

[54] POCA, s 333A.
[55] See the discussion in Chapter 8.
[56] *Baxter v Governor of HM Prison Brixton* [2002] EWHC 300.

12.75 The relevant *mens rea* includes both dishonesty and intent to achieve a gain for the perpetrator or another, or intent to cause loss to another, and, in the case of s 17(1)(b), knowledge that the account, record or document is or may be misleading.

12.76 Section 18 of the Theft Act makes specific provision for circumstances where a company is guilty of false accounting under s 17. Where such an offence has been committed with the consent or connivance of any director, manager, secretary or other officer, or person purporting to act in any such capacity, he as well as the body corporate shall be guilty of the offence. This provision is very similar to, and seems to have been the model for s 14 of the Bribery Act which criminalises the consent or connivance of senior officers of a body corporate in the commission of offences under ss 1, 2 and 6 of the Bribery Act.

Failure of companies to keep accurate records

12.77 For companies constituted under UK law, the Companies Act 2006 has a more general requirement that companies keep accurate records,[57] and makes it an offence for a company to fail to do so.[58]

12.78 In a recent case, BAE plc had been accused of involvement in the bribery of the officials of several countries including Tanzania. BAE reached a settlement agreement with the SFO where investigations into other matters was dropped in exchange for a plea of guilty to a single charge of failure to keep accurate accounting records, under equivalent provisions of the former Companies Act[59] and an agreement to pay the difference between any fine and £25m to the people of Tanzania. There was also a prosecution in the USA in relation to the same or connected facts which led to a far larger fine. The case is quite unusual in many respects, not least the fact that the SFO seems to have been willing to give BAE a blanket indemnity in respect of all previous conduct, which is not a circumstance which other corporate defendants should expect to see repeated after the coming into effect of the Bribery Act.[60]

MISCONDUCT IN PUBLIC OFFICE

12.79 Misconduct in public office is a common law offence that owes its origins to the case of *R v Bembridge*[61] in 1783.[62]

---

[57] Companies Act 2006, s 386.
[58] Companies Act 2006, s 387.
[59] Companies Act 1985, s 221.
[60] See the sentencing remarks of Bean J, at www.judiciary.gov.uk/media/judgments/2010/r-v-bae-systems-plc.
[61] (1783) 3 Doug KB 327, 22 State Tr 1.
[62] See, generally, Nicholls et al, *Corruption and Misuse of Public Office* (2006), ch 3.

12.80 In *Attorney General's Reference (No 3 of 2003)*[63] the Court of Appeal defined the offence as follows:

> 'The elements of the offence of misconduct in a public office are:
> 1. a public officer acting as such;
> 2. wilfully neglects to perform his duty and/or wilfully misconducts himself;
> 3. to such a degree as to amount to an abuse of the public's trust in the office holder;
> 4. without reasonable excuse or justification.'

12.81 A 'public officer' is 'an officer who discharges any duty in the discharge of which the public are interested, more clearly so if he is paid out of a fund by the public'.[64]

12.82 In *Attorney General's Reference (No 3 of 2003)* the Court of Appeal held that there must be a breach of duty by the public officer which is wilful and which is such the conduct is an affront to the standing of the public office held.[65] It was noted that 'the threshold is a high one requiring conduct so far below acceptable standards as to amount to an abuse of the public's trust in the office holder'.[66] The breach may consist of an act of commission or of an omission to fulfil a duty.[67] The wilful misconduct must be deliberate and accompanied by an awareness of the duty to act or subjective recklessness as to the existence of the duty itself or to the conduct in question.

12.83 In order to assess whether the third element of the offence (as set out above) is satisfied, the court identified five relevant factors that ought to be considered in any case:

> 'I. the responsibilities of the office and the officer;
> II. the importance of the public objects they serve;
> III. the nature and extent of the officer's departure from those responsibilities;
> IV. the motive with which the officer acted; and
> V. the likely consequences of the misconduct.'[68]

12.84 In the guidance published on 19 November 2007, the Crown Prosecution Service advised that a charge of misconduct in public office should be reserved for cases of serious misconduct or deliberate failure to perform a duty which is likely to injure the public interest. It should always be borne in mind that it is a serious, indictable only offence which carries a maximum sentence of life imprisonment.[69]

---

[63] [2005] 1 QB 73.
[64] *R v Bowden* [1995] 4 All ER 505, adopting the definition of public officer for the purposes of the Public Bodies Corrupt Practices Act 1889 in *R v Whitaker* [1914] 3 KB 1283.
[65] [2005] 1 QB 73, at para 56.
[66] Ibid.
[67] *Attorney General's Reference (No 3 of 2003)* [2005] 1 QB 73.
[68] Ibid at paras 46 and 56–59.
[69] See www.cps.gov.uk/legal/l_to_o/misconduct_in_public_office/index.html.

12.85 If the acts complained of can properly be dealt with by another available statutory offence, that other charge should be preferred unless the facts are so serious that the court's sentencing powers would be inadequate, or if a charge of misconduct in public office would ensure the better presentation of the case as a whole.

12.86 Any person charged with the offence of misconduct in public office has a defence if they can demonstrate that they had a reasonable excuse or justification for acting as they did. For instance, it would be open for a defendant to claim that they were acting in the public interest.

12.87 Charges of misconduct in public office have become more prevalent in recent years. It may well be that domestic public servants will, in the appropriate cases, face charges both of misconduct in public office and charges under s 2 of the Bribery Act. A deliberate and determined seeker after bribes who abuses a public office in a serious way should expect no less.

EXTRADITION

12.88 Finally, a brief word about extradition. In the event that a person is charged with bribery, corruption or a similar offence by a foreign state then it is quite possible that that person will be extradited to that state if the UK authorities are unable or unwilling to prosecute them and the other tests in the Extradition Act 2003 are met.

12.89 It is very likely, for example, that an offence under the US Foreign Corrupt Practices Act satisfies the test of dual criminality so that an individual business person of British nationality or residence could be extradited to the US to face charges there. Similar cases of 'white collar criminals' have been subject to extradition, despite the theoretical possibility of a UK prosecution.[70]

12.90 It is not clear what the policy of the UK will be in cases where those subject to UK jurisdiction and who might be charged under the Bribery Act, but have not been, are made the subject of an extradition request. It seems that cases involving British citizens under the current law are not automatically to be allocated to the British courts. The sprawling Bonney Island affair (in which MW Kellogg paid a civil penalty to the SFO – see above) also involves allegations of criminality against an English citizen, Mr Tesler. Despite his residence in and citizenship of the UK, charges were laid against him in the United States rather than in the UK. His bid to escape extradition there was refused by the Court of Appeal in January 2011.[71] Mr Tesler was subsequently extradited.

---

[70] *Norris v Government of the United States* [2010] UKSC 9.
[71] *Tesler v Government of the United States of America* [2011] EWHC 52 (Admin).

Chapter 13

CIVIL LIABILITY

INTRODUCTION

13.1 Although not dealt with by the Bribery Act, which provides for criminal offences only, civil claims are likely to be relevant to many, especially those commercial organisations or governments which have encountered bribery.

13.2 Civil liability is often ignored in discussions of anti-corruption policy. Most of the current debate is focused on criminal offences and the general trend towards criminalisation of the business world. However, civil liability is important for at least two reasons. The first is the need for recompense in cases where bribery has caused loss to individuals, businesses or states. The second is that civil claims go towards filling the gap between the prevalence of bribery and the limited resources of the SFO and other investigating authorities. Not all cases of bribery can be investigated or prosecuted. Civil proceedings mean that corrupt individuals or groups which fall outside the criminal net, for whatever reason, could still face the significant personal and financial risks of being sued and this can be expected to have a deterrent effect.[1]

13.3 In the US, the Securities and Exchange Commission (SEC) regularly commences civil proceedings to recover the proceeds of bribery in conjunction with criminal charges laid by the Department of Justice. The recoveries made from the civil penalties are often larger than the fines imposed via the criminal process.

13.4 As a topic, the English civil law of bribery (to which this chapter is confined) is both very deep and very wide. This chapter can offer no more than a sketch of the key principles and an outline of certain remedies which may be available to claimants in the civil courts.[2] Because there is a lot to cover, the

---

[1] That civil remedies have an important role to play in reducing bribery is apparent from the terms of the UN Convention Against Corruption, Art 35 of which provides: 'Each State Party shall take such measures as may be necessary, in accordance with principles of its domestic law, to ensure that entities or persons who have suffered damage as a result of an act of corruption have the right to initiate legal proceedings against those responsible for that damage in order to obtain compensation.' Similar though not identical provisions are contained in the Council of Europe's Civil Law Convention on Corruption of 1999, Art 1.

[2] Bribery and other forms of financial impropriety are protean in their capacity to generate different perspectives on traditional legal categories, and even new or expanded remedies in civil law. In the last 20 years the topic has also been a testing ground for academic discussion of the nature and scope of some civil obligations and remedies. For example there has been a long battle, still, unfortunately, undecided, about whether there is a constructive trust of a

Civil procedure

13.5 Many readers of this chapter will either have some knowledge of the basic elements of English civil law or will have access to experienced legal advisers. However, there may be non-legal readers for whom it may be helpful to explain some preliminary points:

- civil claims have to be pursued as separate legal proceedings and cannot normally 'piggyback' on the criminal process;[3]

- the legal tests required to establish a civil claim for compensation are different to the tests under criminal law. The provisions of the Bribery Act are not directly relevant to a civil action;

- civil claims for bribery (as well as related claims such as fraud, dishonest assistance, etc) are likely to be within the jurisdiction of the High Court;[4]

- proceedings will be tried by a judge without a jury;

- evidence will be weighed on the civil standard of proof (ie that a fact is proved on the balance of probabilities rather than beyond reasonable doubt), although specific allegations of fraud or dishonesty will need to be established to a more onerous standard than usual[5] and judges are careful to ensure that there is strong evidence of fraud or bribery before making such findings;

- procedural and evidential rules in civil proceedings are on the whole less rigorous than in criminal proceedings, though this is perhaps counterbalanced by the fact that after a civil judgment is obtained it may not always be easy to enforce.

---

fiduciary's assets acquired by the proceeds of bribery. This chapter attempts to cross these troubled waters via as many established stepping-stones to relief as can be identified.

[3] Although, in civil proceedings, criminal convictions stand as evidence of the fact that the accused committed the offence for which he was convicted and the information, complaint, indictment or chargesheet on which the person in question was convicted is admissible in evidence for that purpose – Civil Evidence Act 1968, s 11.

[4] Unless the parties have agreed to arbitration or some other alternative form of dispute resolution or unless the figure claimed is less than the minimum limit of High Court jurisdiction, in which case it is a matter for the county courts.

[5] See *Re H (Minors)* [1996] AC 563, 586 per Lord Nicholls; *R(N) v Mental Health Review Tribunal* [2006] 4 All ER 194.

Jurisdiction

13.6 In cases with an international dimension the jurisdiction in which the claims may be determined is not necessarily clear-cut. The rules by which national jurisdiction may be established are outside the scope of a work of this nature. It suffices to say that in any civil claim for bribery with an international dimension a party should quickly establish which court or tribunal might have jurisdiction and, if there is any doubt, attempt to found jurisdiction in the most convenient forum.[6]

Arbitration

13.7 Many contracts now include arbitration clauses and allegations of bribery can be and are dealt with in arbitral proceedings. As with jurisdiction, the law of arbitration is too large a subject for this chapter.[7] If the law governing the relations between the parties is that of England and Wales then the principles outlined here will be relevant to the outcome of arbitration proceedings in the same way as in court proceedings. Note that in English law it is difficult to challenge the validity of a written arbitration agreement and such challenges should be heard in the first instance before the arbitration tribunal.[8] So even if it is alleged that the contract as a whole, including the arbitration clause, was brought about by means of the bribery of the principal's agent the court must stay jurisdiction so that the arbitrators can decide the matter.[9]

13.8 Finally, the SFO and other law enforcement authorities also have powers to bring proceedings for the civil recovery of the proceeds of crime.[10] This specialised subject is dealt with in Chapter 10.

KEY PRINCIPLES

Bribery as a civil wrong

13.9 English civil law has long regarded the taking or provision of bribes as wrongful and deserving of recompense. Someone suffering some direct loss as a result is entitled to sue. There has been some debate as to the correct classification of bribery under theories of the law of civil obligations. At least as far as the case-law is concerned, this debate about classification has often been driven by concern that certain remedies should, or should not, be available to the claimant in the case in question. Nevertheless there is a general

---

[6] See Dicey, Morris and Collins *The Conflict of Laws* (14th edn, London, 2008).
[7] See Blackaby and Partasides *Redfern & Hunter on International Arbitration* (Oxford, 2009). For an interesting treatment of corruption in the context of arbitration see Sayed *Corruption In International Trade and Commercial Arbitration* (The Hague, 2004).
[8] Arbitration Act 1996, s 7.
[9] *Premium Nafta Products Ltd (20th Defendant) & Ors v Fili Shipping Company Ltd & Ors* [2007] UKHL 40, [2008] 1 Lloyd's Rep 254.
[10] Proceeds of Crime Act 2002, Part 5.

consensus that bribery is a self-contained category of civil wrong[11] for which a wide range of remedies are theoretically available. Which remedies are in fact available will depend on the facts of each case. For bribery to be found there must first exist a relationship of agent and principal. If an agent/principal relationship exists, that relationship needs to be fiduciary in character if certain equitable remedies are to be relied on.

The agent/principal relationship

13.10 Most civil claims for bribery occur in a commercial context. The person accused of receiving a bribe is usually someone who represents the owners of assets – ie an agent. Since businesses and many others depend on the loyalty of those acting to further their interests it should not be surprising that a bribe has long been seen as an attack on these kinds of relationships.[12] The agent/principal paradigm has come to dominate the analysis of civil bribery.

13.11 As mentioned elsewhere in this book, the agent/principal relationship, which was the basis of the statutory offence under the 1906 Act, has been abandoned by the criminal law. It was seen as too narrow a platform on which to base criminal offences of bribery. There was a view that subtle questions of agency law or the law relating to other civil obligations inhibited the sort of robust risk assessment and analysis required by those seeking to prosecute such offences in the criminal courts.[13]

13.12 However, the agent/principal paradigm has proved quite effective in the civil realm. The reported cases demonstrate a satisfying record of obvious wrongdoing being properly identified and giving rise to a very wide range of remedies to victims.

13.13 In the context of civil bribery (or other claims such as civil fraud) the category of agent/principal relationship is very wide. One does not have to have formally defined oneself as an agent in order to qualify as one. For example, employees are seen as the agents of their employer, directors are seen as the agents of their company. Third party advisers such as brokers, lawyers or indeed anyone owing duties of loyalty to someone else are likely to qualify as agents in many contexts.

13.14 Whether a specific person or entity can be seen as an agent will, of course, depend on the facts of each case. Agency is an extremely flexible concept which has adapted to many circumstances over time.[14]

---

[11] *Hovenden & Sons v Millhoff* (1900) 83 LT 41; *Arab Monetary Fund v Hashim* [1993] 1 Lloyd's Rep 543, 564.
[12] Indeed, it has been described as 'an evil practice which threatens the foundations of any civilized society' – per Lord Templeman in *Att-Gen for Hong Kong v Reid* [1994] 1 AC 324, 330-1.
[13] As suggested in Chapter 4, civil law concepts may still be relevant to the proper analysis of bribery act offences although whether this is recognised in practice remains to be seen.
[14] *Bowstead and Reynolds On Agency* (19th edn, London, 2010) offers the following definition at

Fiduciary duties

13.15 What is a fiduciary relationship? Like many important legal categories, it is usually recognisable but not very easy to define. It can safely be said that a fiduciary owes certain duties of loyalty to his principal. These duties include the duty not to place himself in a position of conflict of interest or potential conflict of interest with his principal and a duty not to receive or retain secret profits. As Millett LJ put it in *Bristol & West Building Society v Mothew*:[15]

> 'A fiduciary is someone who has undertaken to act for or on behalf of another in a particular matter in circumstances which give rise to a relationship of trust and confidence. The distinguishing obligation of a fiduciary is the obligation of loyalty. The principal is entitled to the single-minded loyalty of his fiduciary. This core liability has several facets. A fiduciary must act in good faith; he must not make a profit out of his trust; he must not place himself in a position where his duty and interest may conflict; he may not act for his own benefit or the benefit of a third person without the informed consent of his principal. This is not intended to be an exhaustive list, but it is sufficient to indicate the nature of fiduciary obligations. They are the defining characteristics of the fiduciary.'

13.16 Where there is any relationship of trust there are usually also fiduciary duties.[16] Agent and principal relationships, if they involve an element of trust and/or discretion and/or the provision of advice by the agent to the principal, can be expected to be fiduciary in nature. Indeed, in the context of bribery at least, there is considerable conceptual overlap between a fiduciary relationship and an agency relationship. If an agent lacks the characteristics of a fiduciary there will be little reason to provide him with secret commissions and little harm to the principal if commissions are provided. A legal realist would say that the way that the courts deploy the categories of agency and fiduciary duty demonstrates that they are essentially quite flexible means to achieving a particular end.[17]

13.17 The receipt of a bribe places a fiduciary agent in a position whereby his interests conflict with his duty towards his principal. He obtains a benefit which is secret from his principal and places himself in a position whereby he risks not providing disinterested advice to his principal and not acting in good

---

Art 1: 'Agency is the fiduciary relationship which exists between two persons one of whom expressly or impliedly manifests assent that the other should act on his behalf so as to affect his relations with third parties, and the other of whom similarly manifests assent so to act or so acts pursuant to the manifestation.'

[15] [1998] Ch 1, 18.

[16] Like agency, the concept benefits from considerable flexibility. In *Reading v Att-Gen* [1951] AC 507 an ex-sergeant of the British Army who used his old uniform to prevent vehicles being used by smugglers from being searched qualified as a fiduciary. In *Alexander v Webber* [1922] 1 KB 642 a chauffeur on whom his employer relied for advice on buying a new car was a fiduciary.

[17] The end being to prevent those empowered to act in the interests of others from being improperly influenced or tempted to abuse their powers. For an influential treatment of the subject of fiduciary relationships in the context of bribery claims see Sir Peter Millett *Bribes & Secret Commissions* [1993] 1 RLR 1.

faith towards him. Therefore for an agent to receive or agree to receive a bribe entails a breach of his fiduciary duties to his principal.

Definition of civil bribery

13.18 Civil liability for bribery arises where:

(a) an agent/principal relationship can be said to exist; and

(b) a third party provides a benefit[18] to the agent in connection with the principal's business; and

(c) the principal is not told by the third party of the payment or benefit.[19]

The term 'secret commission' is sometimes used as shorthand for these circumstances.[20]

Proof of bribery

13.19 For liability for civil bribery to be established there is no need for proof of breach of the criminal law. There is no need for proof of corrupt or dishonest motives by either the agent or the third party. Nor is there any need to prove that the briber intended to influence or reward the agent. Nor is there any need to prove that the agent either took active steps to hide the payment from the principal[21] or actually was influenced by the secret commission to act in a way detrimental to the principal as a result of it.[22] These factors will be presumed once it is established that the agent received a secret commission.[23] Nor is it necessary to prove that any actual contract between the principals has been brought about by the bribed agent.[24]

---

[18] Which need not be money – any benefit capable of influencing an agent may suffice, see *Panama and South Pacific Telegraph Co v India Rubber, Gutta Percha and Telegraph Works Co* (1875) LR 10 Ch App 515.

[19] See, for example, *Industries and General Mortgage Co Ltd v Lewis* [1949] 2 All ER 573, 575 which offers the following definition which has been widely cited in other authorities: 'For the purposes of the civil law a bribe means the payment of a secret commission, which only means (i) that the person making the payment makes it to the agent of the other person with whom he is dealing; (ii) that he makes it to that person knowing that that person is acting as the agent of the other person with whom he is dealing; and (iii) that he fails to disclose to the other person with whom he is dealing that he has made that payment to the person whom he knows to be the other person's agent.'

[20] Although Bowstead and Reynolds, at 6-083 suggest that a secret commission may be distinguished from a bribe by virtue of its lack of corrupt intention. This distinction is relevant to the reasoning in *Hurstanger v Wilson* [2007] 2 All ER (Comm), CA which provides for a 'half-way house' mere equitable remedy to the principal in circumstances of partial disclosure of a commission.

[21] *Temperley v Blackrod Mrg Co Ltd* (1907) 71 JP 341.

[22] *Hovenden & Sons v Millhoff* (1900) 83 LT 41, 43.

[23] *Ibid* and *Tesco Stores Ltd v Pook* [2003] EWHC 823.

[24] *Petrotrade Inc v Smith* [2000] All ER (D) 264.

13.20 Lawrence Collins J provided a helpful summary of the principles applicable to proceedings against the payer of a bribe in *Daraydan Holdings Ltd v Solland International*:[25]

> 'In proceedings against the payer of the bribe there is no need for the principal to prove (a) that the payer of the bribe acted with a corrupt motive; (b) that the agent's mind was actually affected by the bribe; (c) that the payer knew or suspected that the agent would conceal the payment from the principal; (d) that the principal suffered any loss or that the transaction was in some way unfair: the law is intended to operate as a deterrent against the giving of bribes, and it will be assumed that the true price of any goods bought by the principal was increased by at least the amount of the bribe, but any loss beyond the amount of the bribe itself must be proved; (e) that the bribe was given specifically in connection with a particular contract, since a bribe may also be given to an agent to influence his mind in favour of the payer generally (e.g. in connection with the granting of future contracts).'

13.21 This is in contrast to the requirements of the criminal law. One difference, at least to the offences requiring specific *mens rea*, is that in civil proceedings the state of mind of the parties to the corrupt transaction is irrelevant. Another difference is the absence of any test of propriety by reference to the expectations of reasonable people. The working presumption of the civil law is that there are no circumstances in which an agent can legitimately receive a secret commission and that if such a receipt is proved then the law should provide the principal with remedies without his having to go to further proof.

13.22 Moreover, unlike most other areas of the law of private obligations, the principal does not have to prove any specific loss before being entitled to recover. As Lawrence Collins J pointed out in *Daraydan* there is a presumption that the value of the bribe should have been paid to the principal so that is an initial measure of loss. Beyond this, it is clear that as soon as an agent receives, or even expects to receive, a secret commission, he may no longer be in a position to act for or advise his principal in an objective or disinterested way.[26] This too is a loss to the principal, indeed it is a loss which may have more damaging effects than the presumed loss of the value of the bribe.[27] There can be little doubt that this loss arises as soon as an arrangement for a secret commission is entered into. A person interfering with the proper exercise of

---

[25] [2005] Ch 119 at para 53.
[26] This analysis assumes that the bribe (or at least the promise of a bribe) is received before the transaction in question, or its terms, are finalised. Unlike the 'reward' offence under s 2 of the Bribery Act, a gift to an agent after the transaction has gone through may not constitute a bribe as a matter of civil law if it was not promised or intimated in advance of the transaction and once there are no further transactions in prospect. This is because the gift does not create a conflict of interest in relation to any current duty of the agent – see *The Parkdale* [1897] P 53. Such circumstances can be expected to be rare. If another transaction comes about after the gift was given, in circumstances where the principal is unaware of the gift (and the gift is of a sort capable of influencing the agent), then the case may well amount to civil bribery.
[27] Although it may be considerably more difficult to prove separate damage in excess of the value of the bribe.

fiduciary duties so as to corrupt the loyalty of a fiduciary, is not allowed to insist that the victim prove more specific losses before being entitled to relief.

Knowledge of principal

13.23 What if the principal knew that the agent was seeking or receiving payments from third parties in connection with the principal's business? If the principal knew of the detail of the commission then it will not be secret and, ex hypothesi, will not amount to bribery. However, full disclosure by the agent is usually necessary. What amounts to full disclosure will depend on the facts of each case. If there is a well-known custom in a particular market that all agents receive commissions[28] and/or if the principal has authorised the agent to seek remuneration from third parties then it may be that the principal will have sufficient knowledge, although this will be a matter for the agent to prove.[29] After *Hurstanger v Wilson*[30] there may be a 'half-way house' where the agent makes limited disclosure so that his commission is not secret but not enough of a disclosure to fulfil his fiduciary duties, though it is not clear whether this principle will be accepted outside the particular facts of that case.

OVERVIEW OF CLAIMS

13.24 A feature of the civil law of bribery is the multiplicity of legal causes of action which may be available to a principal whose agent has been bribed. Many of these will overlap and not all are considered in this chapter.[31] These causes of action may lead to different results in terms of the nature of recovery made by the claimant. For example reliance on breach of fiduciary duty and/or constructive trusts may allow a claimant to gain recovery against third parties who have assisted in the bribery.

13.25 The claims outlined below are considered from the point of view of a company (or a public body) which has discovered bribery of its agent. The claims against the agent and the briber are treated separately, although their liability to the principal in many cases may be joint and several. Whether a third party which is not the principal of the bribed agent but has nevertheless been disadvantaged by bribery could make effective claims is considered separately.

13.26 A key point is that before the end of any trial the claimant may well need to elect which remedy he wishes the court to order, and against which

---

[28] For example, historically, in parts of the insurance industry – *Great Western Insurance Co of New York v Cunliffe* (1874) LR 9 Ch App 525.
[29] Bowstead and Reynolds at 6-057.
[30] *Hurstanger v Wilson* [2007] 2 All ER (Comm) 1037.
[31] Among the claims potentially open to a principal, but not discussed here, are claims in the tort of conversion, for misuse of confidential information and various claims available on winding up or insolvency of the principal or the briber. For a detailed treatment of some of the heads of claim accruing to the principal of a bribed agent see Berg, *Bribery – transaction validity and other civil law implications* [2001] 1 LMCLQ 27.

party, so as to prevent double recovery. Some defendants may not be capable of satisfying a judgment. Often, a briber, or a party dishonestly assisting in the bribery, may have considerably more resources with which to satisfy a judgment than a bribed agent. However, proving their knowledge and participation in the bribery may be more difficult than establishing the claim against the agent.

CLAIMS AGAINST AN AGENT

13.27 A principal bringing proceedings against an agent who receives a bribe can rely on several causes of action, many of which overlap each other.[32] Which of these are available in a particular case will, of course, depend on the facts. Among the key causes of action, which will be examined in more detail below, are:

- a claim for damages for breach of contract;

- a claim for damages for fraud;

- a claim for restitution of the agent's gain, based on unjust enrichment;

- a claim based on breach of fiduciary duty, seeking an account of profits and remedies under a constructive trust;

- a claim for damages for conspiracy.

Breach of contract

13.28 Most agents will be acting pursuant to some sort of contract with their principal. Acceptance of a bribe or secret commission is likely to amount to a breach of that contract.[33] The terms of the contract may or may not expressly prohibit the acceptance or payment of bribes, although of course many organisations have anti-corruption policies.

13.29 Each contractual relationship is different. That said, a defendant who argues that bribery is not a breach of contract because it is not expressly prohibited is unlikely to get very far. Even if not express, one would expect a term prohibiting bribery and/or conflicts of interest to be implied into the vast majority of contracts.[34] Any loss to the principal flowing directly from the breach of the agent's contract will be recoverable from the agent as damages. If

---

[32] The question of whether employers learning of the involvement of their employees or agents in bribery which might implicate the company should report this to the SFO or other authorities is considered elsewhere – see in particular Chapter 10. If the offence does not involve the company itself committing an offence the issue may be somewhat different. In English law there is no general positive duty to report a crime by others although this has been amended by specific legislation such as the Proceeds of Crime Act 2002 – see the discussion in Chapter 12.

[33] It follows that any activity by the briber to induce such a breach of contract is itself a tort and actionable at the suit of the principal.

[34] The relevant legal test is that set out in *The Moorcock* (1889) 14 PD 64.

the agent is an employee then accepting bribes will almost certainly amount to gross misconduct and provide grounds for dismissal.[35]

13.30 The principal may also be entitled to terminate a contract with a bribed agent who is not an employee.[36] In any relationship of trust, the agent, by accepting or even seeking a bribe, will most likely have destroyed the trust which is fundamental to the contract. This breach of the contract can be seen as being so serious and fundamental that it amounts to a repudiation of the contract itself, which the principal is capable of accepting, thus bringing the contract to an end.[37]

13.31 As discussed above, in some cases it may be open to the agent to argue that the principal was aware of and approved of the fact that the agent was receiving payments from other parties. If this were the case the arrangements would not qualify as civil bribery, since they lack the quality of secrecy from the principal. However, in a corporate context, the knowledge of a colleague or an immediate superior is not necessarily the knowledge of the principal, especially if any conflict of interest exists between the colleague or superior and the principal (for example, if there is something in the bribery for the colleagues too). Depending on the facts such individuals may be seen more as co-conspirators rather than as representing the company as a whole. These issues should be considered alongside the issues of corporate liability for crime which are examined in Chapter 8.

Civil fraud

13.32 Bribery amounts to the same thing as the tort of civil fraud, and the principal is entitled to damages as a result.[38] For such a claim to succeed a principal does not need to show any specific representation by the agent or any reliance on such a representation. There is a presumption that the loss is the same as the amount of the bribe unless the principal can prove some actual additional loss.[39] As is the case with other remedies, the claimant must elect between the remedy of damages and the profits said to have been gained by the agent. The briber is similarly liable as a joint tortfeasor even though he may not have had any direct contact with the principal.

13.33 Damages for fraud are intended to put the claimant into the position which he would have been in if the fraud had never happened, so that profits lost as a result of the fraud, or other losses, may be recoverable from the

---

[35] See, for example, *Tesco Stores Ltd v Pook* [2003] EWHC 823 (Ch).
[36] *Panama and South Pacific Telegraph Co v India Rubber, Gutta Percha and Telegraph Works Co* (1875) LR 10 Ch App 515, *Logicrose Ltd v Southend Utd FC* [1988] 1 WLR 1256.
[37] *Boston Deep Sea Fishing and Ice Co v Ansell* (1888) 39 ChD 339; *Wheen v Smithman European Homes Ltd* (unreported), 20 June 2000, CA; *Tesco Stores Ltd v Pook* [2003] EWHC 823 (Ch). For a general discussion of discharge of contracts for breach see *Chitty on Contracts* (30th edn, Sweet & Maxwell, London, 2008), Ch 24.
[38] *Mahesan v Malaysian Government Officers' Co-Operative Housing Society Ltd* [1979] AC 374, 383; *Hovenden & Sons v Millhoff* (1900) 83 LT 41.
[39] Ibid.

tortfeasors.⁴⁰ As in the tort of deceit, it is not a defence to claim that the principal's own negligence has contributed to the loss.⁴¹

Unjust enrichment and restitution

13.34 In circumstances of bribery the principal can make a claim for restitution of the amount of the bribe against the agent, relying on the unjust enrichment of the agent. The claim is personal rather than proprietary and is also known as a claim for 'money had and received'.

13.35 For a claim in unjust enrichment the claimant must establish, in respect of the particular events on which he bases his claim (in this case the bribery):

(a) that the defendant has been enriched;

(b) that this enrichment was at the claimant's expense;

(c) that the enrichment was 'unjust'.

13.36 Item (a) will of course depend on the available evidence but in a typical bribery scenario there will have been a benefit or payment of some kind to the agent.

13.37 On the face of it, item (b) is more problematic because, on one view, the whole purpose of the secret commission is that the principal does not know about it or get any of it. How can the claimant have lost out on a benefit which, had the agent done what he ought, would not have existed?

13.38 The law evades this problem, at least in the case of purchases, by assuming that the true price of the item (or service) includes the value of the bribe. In a transaction tainted by bribery a seller could have sold the item for the actual sale price plus the amount of the bribe had his agent not been bribed. Similarly, a purchaser could have bought at less than the actual sale price had his agent not been bribed. Therefore the agent has diverted an available mark-up, or discount, from his principal and to himself. That mark-up or discount can be valued at the amount of the bribe. The theory is that not only is the agent not entitled to that benefit but in fact it is rightfully the property of the principal and the agent must therefore account for it to the principal.⁴²

13.39 As to item (c), the injustice of the diversion of a bribe by the agent is not merely a matter of applying general standards of morality. Injustice in this context refers to specific recognised categories of circumstances which are accepted as 'unjust' and as providing grounds for restitution of the benefit. For

---

⁴⁰ *Mahesan v Malaysian Government Officers' Co-Operative Housing Society Ltd* [1979] AC 374, 383.
⁴¹ *Corporacion National del Cobre de Chile v Sogemin Metals Ltd* [1997] 1 WLR 1396.
⁴² Ibid.

example, that the claimant paid the defendant by mistake is a well-established category of injustice for these purposes. In a bribery case the principal will be mistaken and/or ignorant as to the true nature of the transaction and the true price which his counterparty was willing to come to and this is sufficient injustice to ground a claim for restitution of the bribe.

Breach of fiduciary duty: account of profits and constructive trust

13.40 There can be little doubt that an agent who is in a position of trust is in a fiduciary relationship to his principal. As mentioned above, the receipt of a bribe places an agent in a position whereby his interests conflict with his duty towards his principal. He obtains a benefit which is secret from his principal and risks being incapable of providing disinterested advice to his principal and not acting in good faith towards him.[43] In these circumstances the principal will be able to claim not only the amount of the bribes received by the agent but also an account of profits, which requires the agent to disclose and repay any profits made as a result of the breach of duty.[44]

13.41 Perhaps more useful from the principal's point of view is the fact that he may be able to enforce his claim against identifiable property which the bribed agent has acquired as a result of the bribery. This head of claim is known as the imposition of a constructive trust of the amount represented by the bribe. In *Att-Gen for Hong Kong v Reid*,[45] the Privy Council held that as soon as a bribe is received the agent holds it on a constructive trust for the principal. If the bribe money is invested at a profit, or is turned into other assets, then the profit earned and/or the assets acquired are also due to the principal. The facts of the case are enlightening: Reid was a crown prosecutor in Hong Kong who accepted bribes from local criminals during the course of his duties. The value of the bribes was estimated at NZ$2.5 million. He spent NZ$500,000 on properties in New Zealand. After his arrest and conviction the Hong Kong Government successfully sought orders preventing the sale of the properties from the New Zealand courts.

---

[43] It is also arguable that the unauthorised *payment* of a bribe by an agent is also a breach of the agent's fiduciary duty at least in circumstances where the agent believes he will gain a personal benefit (such as a bonus) as a result of the transaction effectuated by the bribe. This is not the same question as whether the principal can be found liable by reason of payment of a bribe by his agent even if that agent is not expressly authorised. As far as a claim by the principal of the bribed agent is concerned the question is whether the bribing agent is acting within the scope of his employment – if so then it is likely the bribing principal will be liable even if he was unaware of the agent's actions – see *Armagas v Mundogas* [1986] AC 717, 744-745, per Robert Goff LJ.

[44] *Fyffes v Templeman* [2000] 2 Lloyd's Rep 643, 668, col 2.

[45] [1994] 1 AC 324, contradicting the previous leading authority of *Lister & Co v Stubbs* (1890) 45 Ch D 1. Since *Reid* is a Privy Council decision it is not strictly binding on English courts ahead of *Lister*. Until recently there was a clear trend towards accepting the authority of *Reid*, by distinguishing *Lister* so far as possible (see, for example, *Daraydan*, above, *Ocular Sciences Limited v Aspect Vision Care Limited* [1997] RPC 289, 412-413). However, in *Sinclair Investments (UK) Ltd v Versailles Trade Finance Ltd* [2011] EWCA Civ 347 the Court of Appeal held that *Lister v Stubbs* remained binding as a Court of Appeal authority. The situation is hardly satisfactory and there is likely to be an appeal to the Supreme Court.

13.42 An account of profits may also be available based not on the claimant's losses but on the gains invalidly acquired by the defendant, at least in exceptional circumstances where justice requires the defendant not to profit from his wrongdoing and damages to the claimant are not a sufficient remedy.[46] There is little doubt that the receipt of a bribe gives rise to a liability to the principal even if no other harm is done. One might imagine this applying in a case where an agent has accepted small bribes in exchange for disclosure of confidential information to competitors or the media and has used the ensuing notoriety to gain far more valuable work for his own account.[47]

Conspiracy

13.43 The civil tort of conspiracy takes two forms: 'conspiracy to injure' and 'unlawful means conspiracy'. Both require an agreement (or 'combination') between two or more parties to injure the claimant. There are similarities with the criminal offence of conspiracy, the major difference being that for the civil claim to succeed the claimant has to show that it has suffered damage as a result of the conspiracy.

13.44 To qualify as an actionable civil conspiracy, the combination must result in the carrying out of actions which cause the damage complained of, as well as an intent on the part of the defendant to injure the claimant. There must be active involvement by the defendant in action pursuant to the combination, mere facilitation is not sufficient.[48] So, for example, manufacturing a machine which is capable of unlawful copying of copyright material is not active involvement in a conspiracy to breach copyright.[49]

13.45 To establish conspiracy to injure, a claimant must prove that the conspirators had the dominant purpose of injuring the claimant (or the person targeted by the conspiracy). This is difficult to prove and is unlikely to be the dominant purpose of most agreements between briber and agent, whose motives tend to be predominantly selfish rather than malicious.

13.46 However, to establish unlawful means conspiracy there is no need to establish that the intention to injure the claimant was the predominant one. An intention to injure is still required but this may well be subordinate to other intentions including of course the intention that the parties favour their own interests above those of the claimant. All that is necessary is that 'the conspiracy is aimed or directed at the claimant, and it can reasonably be

---

[46] *AG v Blake* [2001] 1 AC 268; *Experience Hendrix LLC v PPX Enterprises Inc* [2003] EWCA Civ 323; *World Wide Fund for Nature v World Wrestling Federation Entertainment Inc* [2007] EWCA Civ 286.
[47] In the US the SEC frequently takes or threatens civil proceedings requiring companies in breach of the FCPA to 'disgorge profits' obtained by the company as a result of the bribery. The 'profits' are normally calculated by deducting expenses linked to the contract from the revenue attributable to it.
[48] *Credit Lyonnais v ECGD* [1998] 1 Lloyd's Rep 19.
[49] *CBS Songs Ltd v Amstrad plc* [1988] 1 AC 1013.

foreseen that it may injure him, and it does in fact injure him'.[50] The claimant must establish that the means were unlawful, but the previous rule that unlawful means were limited to means which gave the claimant a personal right of action against the conspirators has now been struck down, therefore a wider range of unlawful means can be considered, including, for example, tax evasion.[51] There is no doubt that torts such as civil fraud constitute unlawful means and it must follow that bribery is also within this category.

13.47 An advantage of a claim for conspiracy is that it can be brought against parties other than the agent or the briber if they had a role in the combination in question. For example, other companies in a group which took steps to pay the bribe money or conceal its purpose may be liable, or corporate vehicles used by corrupt individuals may also be liable.

CLAIMS AGAINST THE BRIBER

13.48 A principal whose agent has been bribed can make claims against the briber as well as the agent, although as already noted, he will ultimately have to elect between these claims so as to ensure there is no double recovery.

13.49 Bribes are sometimes negotiated and paid via agents on both sides – ie the briber will be acting via an agent as well. In such circumstances whether the briber is liable to the principal will depend on whether the briber's agent is acting within the course of his employment rather than whether he is expressly authorised to offer bribes.[52]

13.50 Among the causes of action, which will be examined in more detail below, are:

- a claim that the transaction is ineffective, because it is void;

- rescission of the underlying transaction;

- a claim for damages for fraud and inducing a breach of contract;

- a claim for restitution of the briber's gain based on unjust enrichment;

- a claim for dishonest assistance in the agent's breach of fiduciary duty;

- a claim for damages for conspiracy.

---

[50] *Lonrho v Shell* (unreported) 6 March 1981, CA, per Lord Denning, see also *Lonhro v Fayed* [1992] 1 AC 448.
[51] *Total Network Solutions Ltd v HMRC* [2008] UKHL 19.
[52] *Armagas v Mundogas* [1986] 1 AC 717, 744–745, per Robert Goff LJ.

Transaction void

13.51 It seems clear that where an agent is bribed and then purports to enter into a contract on behalf of his principal, he has no authority to do so. An example might be where a corrupt broker signs an onerous agreement, of which his client knows nothing, 'on behalf of' the client. An agent is not generally authorised to act contrary to his principal's interests (unless otherwise agreed) and such an act would be outside the scope of his actual authority.[53] The briber will be taken to know this. Therefore the briber cannot rely on the agent's apparent authority to enter the agreement. Of course the agent is not entering into the agreement on his own behalf, so, in strict logic, no contract has been made by the briber because there is no valid counterparty.

13.52 The effect of a void contract is that no property passes under it. So, for example, any monies paid to the briber by the principal are refundable by way of restitution. More than that, it follows that since the briber never acquired any title to the money or other property transferred pursuant to the void contract, he holds it on constructive trust for the principal and it is, therefore, not available to the creditors of the briber in insolvency. However, allegations that agreements tainted by bribery are void are rarely made in practice and there is relatively little authority on the point. A more usual approach is to claim the contract is voidable, ie that the principal has the option whether or not to treat it as terminated or to affirm the contract and merely claim damages or restitution.[54]

13.53 A principal can still base a claim on equitable proprietary remedies (relying on the fact that the agent has breached his fiduciary duties) despite the fact that the transaction is void.[55] Moreover, while the contract in such cases is ineffective, the principal may be able to ratify it if he chooses.[56] As we shall see, this places him in a better position than a principal with a contract which is valid unless he chooses to set it aside, since, in that case, there are potential bars to rescission.

Rescission

13.54 If a contract induced by bribery of an agent is not already void, a principal may, on discovering bribery by his agent, rescind it, that is elect to bring it to an end.[57]

---

[53] Bowstead and Reynolds at 8-218.
[54] See the discussion in O'Sullivan, Elliott and Zakrzewski *The Law of Rescission* (Oxford, 2008), 1.78–1.80. It will be interesting to see whether the 'voidable not void' approach remains the orthodox one.
[55] *Heinl v Jyske Bank (Gibraltar Ltd)* [1999] Lloyd's Rep Bank 511 (CA), 521, 533.
[56] *Bolton Partners v Lambert* (1889) 41 Ch D 295.
[57] *Panama and South Pacific Telegraph Company v India Rubber* (1875) LR 10 Ch App 515. There are differences in the nature of the outcome of the remedy between rescission under common law and equity – see O'Sullivan, Elliott and Zakrzewski *The Law of Rescission* (Oxford, 2008), at 8.53.

13.55 In the event of rescission, the principal does not have to give any credit for the amount of the bribe, even if recovered from the agent.[58]

13.56 It is also the case that, as a matter of public policy, a briber cannot enforce performance of a contract procured by bribery, on the principle of *ex turpi causa non oritur actio* – an action does not arise from a dishonourable cause.[59]

13.57 On discovering that a bribe has been paid to his agent, a principal needs to consider whether or not to continue with the transaction – the bargain may still be worth something to the principal. Such decisions are generally commercial ones and will often depend on whether the principal believes he can affordably replace the goods or services acquired under the contract.

Bars to rescission

13.58 However, there are circumstances in which rescission is not available. For example, a principal will not be entitled to rescind the contract if the agent can show that, with full knowledge of the bribe, the principal has affirmed it. Affirmation in this context means that the principal had full knowledge of: (i) the circumstances of bribery;[60] and (ii) that it had the right to rescind, but decided not to.[61] A delay in exercising a right of rescission may also evidence an affirmation of the contract, once the principal has had notice of the bribery.[62]

13.59 Another bar to rescission may the impossibility of *restitutio ad integrum*, that is the impossibility of putting the parties back into the position they were in when the contract was made. To obtain the remedy in its common law guise it may be necessary to show that the actual benefits gained by the claimant under the contract can be returned.[63] However, a claim in equity should be available to the principal as well as a common law claim and therefore it should be possible to substitute a money value for the benefits received[64] so that rescission will rarely be prevented merely by this factor.

13.60 It has historically been accepted that another bar to rescission existed if a third party became interested in the property which was the subject of the transaction, for example by purchasing the goods sold to the briber without

---

[58] *Logicrose Ltd v Southend United Football Club Ltd* [1988] 1 WLR 1256, per Millett J.
[59] See in general *Moore Stephens v Stone Rolls Ltd* [2009] UKHL 39.
[60] That is actual knowledge, not just the means of discovering the bribery by the exercise of due diligence – *Redgrave v Hurd* (1881) 20 Ch D 1.
[61] *Clough v London and North Western Rly Co* (1871) LR7 Exch 26. The decision not to rescind does not always have to be communicated to the defendant – *Car and Universal Finance Ltd v Caldwell* [1965] 1 QB 525.
[62] *Clough v London and North Western Rly Co* (1871) LR7 Exch 26, 35.
[63] In *Smith New Court Securities Ltd v Scrimgeour Vickers (Asset Management) Ltd* [1994] 2 BCLC 212 the specific shares sold by the defendant to the claimant had been sold on, and so could not be returned. Thus, it was held, *restitutio ad integrum* was not possible at common law, however the situation could be alleviated by making a claim in equity.
[64] *O'Sullivan v Management Agency & Music Ltd* [1985] 1 QB 428 (CA).

notice of the bribery.[65] Naturally, there would be reasons to deny rescission if it were to cause validly acquired rights of innocent third parties to be defeated in a particular case. But such cases are rare. There is a strong argument that, on analysis, this 'bar' is largely fictitious given that it does not take effect in equity and common law rescission of the first sale contract will not necessarily have the effect of revoking the property rights of the innocent third party.[66]

13.61 There may also be another bar or at least limitation on the right to rescission, which is partial (but incomplete) disclosure of the commission. In *Hurstanger v Wilson*,[67] individual borrowers, who were seen as likely to be vulnerable and unsophisticated, used the services of a loan broker. They were told that the broker was to earn some commission from the lender, but the information was ambiguous. The borrowers wished to rescind the entire transaction on the basis of a secret commission and lack of their fully informed consent. The Court of Appeal held that there was a 'half-way house between the situation where there has been sufficient disclosure to negate secrecy but nevertheless the principal's informed consent has not been obtained' (per Tuckey LJ). The borrowers were not entitled to rescission as of right (although the court retained a discretion to grant it). Instead of rescission the court awarded an account of the commission from the brokers and a right to equitable compensation against the lender for instigating the broker's breach of fiduciary duty. This is quite a difficult and arguably an atypical case. It is submitted that the 'half-way house' principle introduces an unwelcome element of uncertainty to the rules applicable to fiduciaries and it remains to be seen whether it will be more widely recognised by the courts.

Damages for fraud and inducing breach of contract

13.62 The briber is as responsible for the fraud on the principal by the agent as the agent himself. It is well established that the typical bribery case makes the briber jointly liable with the agent for the tort, and the precepts previously discussed (that there is no need to show any specific representation or any reliance on such a representation) apply in the same way.[68] Again, the presumption is that the loss is the same as the amount of the bribe, although if the principal can prove some actual additional loss he may also recover for that.[69]

13.63 It is also a tort to intentionally induce a person to breach their contract, and damages are payable to the person whose interests are thus harmed. By offering a secret commission to an agent the briber can be seen as offering an

---

[65] The classic formulation is that of a 'bona fide purchaser for value without notice', although see the discussion by Berg on the subject of whether the assignee of a contractual right can take free of the principal's equitable right to rescind a contract tainted by bribery in [2001] 1 LMCLQ 27.
[66] See the discussion in O'Sullivan, Elliott and Zakrzewski *The Law of Rescission* (Oxford, 2008) at Chapter 20.
[67] [2007] 2 All ER (Comm), CA.
[68] *Mahesan v Malaysia Housing Society Ltd* [1979] AC 374.
[69] Ibid.

inducement to the agent to breach his contractual duties to the principal and thus will be liable to the principal for damages, though the damages are likely to be the same as damages for fraud.

13.64 There is also a developing tort known as interference with business by unlawful means, which involves the defendant using unlawful means with the object and effect of harming the claimant. The defendant must intend to harm the claimant, though this does not have to be his dominant purpose.[70]

Unjust enrichment claim against the briber

13.65 As explained above, a claim in unjust enrichment can be made against the agent who received the bribe. The same principles apply to claims against the briber,[71] although the facts are likely to sit rather uncomfortably within the category of 'money had and received' or even 'unjust enrichment'. After all, the briber himself does not receive the bribe; he only pays it. However, it is arguable that the briber is enriched in that he has received a valuable contract, though this does not deal with the fact that there is liability for bribery even if the briber does not manage to conclude a contract.[72]

Dishonest assistance in a breach of fiduciary duty

13.66 As discussed above, the payment of a bribe to an agent will result in a breach of the agent's fiduciary duties to his principal. The briber will be complicit with the agent in this breach of fiduciary duty and, in most circumstances, the briber will know that what is being done is wrongful and improper. If the principal can establish that the briber's state of mind at the material time was 'dishonest' then the briber will be liable to compensate the principal for dishonest assistance in the agent's breach of fiduciary duty.[73] The same will be true of any third party other than the briber itself who dishonestly assists in the agent's breach of duty, for example executives of the bribing company with knowledge of the facts or lawyers or others facilitating the transaction with knowledge of the facts.

13.67 There has been some confusion as to the proper definition of dishonesty in this context. Following the judgment of the Privy Council in *Barlow Clowes International Ltd (in liquidation) & Ors v Eurotrust International Ltd*,[74] we may take it that the nature of dishonesty is to be established by means of an objective test of what an honest person would do in the circumstances, which test takes account of the characteristics, experience

---

[70] *OBG v Allan* [2007] UKHL 21, and for discussion see *Clerk & Lindsell on Torts* (20th edn, London, 2010) 24–70, 89.
[71] Ibid.
[72] In *Grant v Gold Exploration and Development Syndicate Limited* [1900] 1 QB 233 the Court of Appeal was split on the issue of whether or not a claim for money had and received could exist against the briber.
[73] *Fyffes v Templeman* [2000] 2 Lloyd's Rep 643, per Toulson J.
[74] [2006] 1 All ER 333 (PC).

and knowledge of the individual in question.[75] Paying or offering secret commissions in the knowledge that the principal is ignorant of them, or in circumstances of 'wilful blindness' to the true facts, is likely to pass such a test, absent unusual circumstances. Note that this definition of dishonesty in civil matters is not the same as that required in criminal proceedings.[76]

Recovery of briber's profits

13.68 What of the situation where the briber has made profits from the contract over and above the value of the losses suffered by the principal? In certain cases these profits too may be recoverable. In the Canadian case of *Consul Development Pty Ltd v DPC Estates Pty Ltd*,[77] Gibbs J concluded that a person who knowingly participates in a breach of fiduciary duty is liable to account to the person to whom the duty was owed for any benefit he has received as a result of such participation.

13.69 In *Fyffes v Templeman*[78] the facts were that a shipping company, Seatrade, had bribed the agent of Fyffes. The agent procured the appointment of Seatrade by Fyffes for the shipment of bananas. Fyffes sought not only the amount of the bribe paid, and any loss it had suffered in excess of the amount of the bribe, but also the profits earned by Seatrade from the contract. All three heads of claim were accepted as claimable by the court, although, on the facts it was held that the profits were not due to Fyffes, because they would have been obtained even if no bribery had occurred. The result seems to be that on the right facts a principal may also claim against a briber for profits earned from the contract tainted by bribery on the basis that the briber is guilty of knowing assistance in a breach of the agent's fiduciary duty.[79]

Conspiracy

13.70 A briber and others (such as executives of a company which pays a bribe) are also liable for the tort of conspiracy in the same way as an agent who accepts a bribe. See above for a discussion of the principles.

---

[75] *Barlow Clowes* involved the House of Lords seeking to explain the controversial decision of the House in *Twinsectra Ltd v Yardley* [2002] UKHL 12, [2002] 2 AC 164 and to reconcile it with the decision of the Privy Council in *Royal Brunei Airlines v Philip Tan Kok Ming* [1995] 2 AC 378.
[76] Although dishonesty is not a necessary element of *mens rea* for any offence under the Bribery Act, it is necessary to establish fraud, and many other economic crimes.
[77] [1975] 132 CLR 373 at 397.
[78] [2000] 2 Lloyd's Rep 643.
[79] The principle receives support in *Ultraframe (UK) Ltd v Fielding, Northstar Systems Ltd v Fielding* [2005] EWHC 1638 (paras 1589–1594). However, the finding that Fyffes had a proprietary right in the profits was based on the principle of constructive trust in *AG for Hong Kong v Reid* discussed above. *Reid* itself is now under considerable attack. In particular the issue of whether it is binding ahead of *Lister v Stubbs* remains doubtful and may require resolution by the Supreme Court – *Sinclair Investment Holdings SA v Versailles Trade Finance Ltd* [2011] EWCA Civ 347.

ELECTION AND TRACING

Election

13.71 Where two causes of action lie against the same defendant on the same facts, the plaintiff must elect between them, but need not do so until judgment is recovered on one cause of action or the other. The House of Lords in *United Australia Ltd v Barclays Bank Ltd*[80] held that a claimant suffering a loss may pursue two defendants by means of separate causes of action but a judgment satisfied in part against one operates to reduce the quantum recoverable against the other.[81]

13.72 If the loss to the principal is greater than the amount of the bribe, then this may make a claim in fraud more attractive than a claim for restitution of the value of the bribe, although if the agent has made a profit as a result of the bribe this may also be claimable by way of account of profits. In each case the claimant will have to weigh up the pros and cons of which claim to prefer while also attempting to factor in issues of enforceability vis-à-vis each defendant. In many cases claimants may be forced to rely on an element of educated guesswork.

Tracing

13.73 Of course a principal will wish to maximise its financial recovery and trace assets lost by reason of bribery. Those engaged in bribery attempt to cover their tracks by attempting to launder the proceeds of their behaviour. An important issue will be whether the principal can identify either his original property or can establish as a matter of common law or equity that his property is identifiable in the hands of third parties.[82] The rules by which this can be done are known as the rules of tracing.

13.74 Common law tracing is possible where the asset in question has not changed its character (as when it is a physical object) or where there has been a substitution of another asset for the original asset or there are identifiable proceeds of the sale of the original or substituted asset. However, these circumstances are relatively rare.

13.75 Equitable tracing is considerably more flexible. It may be possible for bribe money paid to an agent to be traced into bank accounts containing other funds or even property subsequently purchased with the mixed funds. Once the asset or money in question has been acquired by a bona fide purchaser without notice of the principal's equitable interest, then tracing is no longer possible and the principal is left with his personal remedy against the agent or briber.

---

[80] [1941] AC 1.
[81] See also *Island Records Ltd v Tring International plc* [1996] 1 WLR 1256, *Tang Man Sit v Capacious Investment Ltd* [1996] AC 514.
[82] For a concise treatment of the rules of tracing see McGrath *Commercial Fraud In Civil Practice* (Oxford, 2008), Ch 21.

13.76 Therefore it is in the interest of the principal to try to establish, as against agent or briber, that the bribery amounted to a breach of fiduciary duty and to base claims on the right to equitable restitution insofar as possible. Of course if there are circumstances in which a constructive trust can be exercised over property acquired by the bribed agent then electing for such a remedy may prove even more worthwhile because of the availability of specific property to satisfy a judgment. However, such circumstances will be unusual, since many sophisticated fraudsters create complex international structures in which to hide ill-gotten gains.

CLAIMS AGAINST THIRD PARTIES OTHER THAN THE AGENT OR BRIBER

13.77 We have already seen that individuals connected to the briber such as third party advisers may be liable to the principal for dishonest assistance in the breach of fiduciary duty and/or conspiracy, depending on the facts.

13.78 If bribe money, or the fruits of bribery which can be treated as the property of the principal, are transferred by the agent or the briber into the hands of a third party recipient the claimant will have a proprietary claim to that property, unless the third party is a bona fide purchaser for value without notice of the breach of duty.[83]

13.79 However, if the third party no longer has the money or other property then the remedy against him is personal only, and the law relating to knowing receipt of property transferred in breach of equitable duties will apply.[84]

13.80 A person receiving money or property is not entitled to it if he knows that it is being misapplied in breach of fiduciary duties. Dishonesty is not required so long as the recipient's state of knowledge is such as to make it unconscionable for him to retain the benefit of the receipt.[85] So a bank or solicitor engaged by an agent to receive bribe money may well be liable to the principal if they know that the transaction should be notified to the principal but has not been and that therefore the agent is acting outside the scope of his authority.

CLAIMS BY PARTIES OTHER THAN THE PRINCIPAL OF THE AGENT

13.81 Consider a situation where two or more parties are bidding to win a contract or some other benefit but one bidder is shut out because of bribery by its competitor. It is possible that the honest and disappointed bidder may have

---

[83] As occurred in *Att-Gen for Hong Kong v Reid* [1994] 1 AC 324.
[84] *El Ajou v Dollar Land Holdings plc* [1994] 1 All ER 685, 700.
[85] *BCCI v Akindele* [2000] 3 WLR 1423.

a cause of action against the briber even though he had no relationship, fiduciary or otherwise, with the bribed agent (who will usually be an official of the contract-awarding body).

13.82 In the US, businesses can bring actions against their competitors when bribery has resulted in their competitors winning contracts.[86] However, the liability of parties to a contract involving bribery is less explicit in English law and there have been few reported cases in which the matter has been expressly dealt with.

Unlawful means conspiracy

13.83 However, there is a first time for everything and we can say with some confidence that there are circumstances in which a person suffering as a result of bribery may have a valid claim even if he is not the principal of the bribed agent. One theory of liability is that a corrupt bidder and a corrupt agent are engaged in an conspiracy to use unlawful means which cause harm to the disappointed bidder. In *Lonrho plc v Fayed*,[87] Lonrho's bid for House of Fraser was referred to the Monopolies Commission, but Al Fayed's was not. It was alleged by Lonrho that the Secretary of State was illegally induced not to refer the Al Fayed bid. Although that claim in itself was not decided at trial it was not struck out as untenable in principle. Intentional harm inflicted on the claimant in circumstances of bribery seems therefore to satisfy the necessary intent to injure for a claim of unlawful means conspiracy although, of course, evidence of this may not be easy to obtain.[88]

13.84 The same principles seem to apply to the tort of interference with business by unlawful means, although again this tort requires proof of intentional harm to the claimant.[89]

Breach of implied term of contract

13.85 In cases such as *Lonrho v Fayed* the allegation is that the agent of the awarding body is corrupt and it is not clear whether the awarding body itself would be liable to the claimant. This might well depend on whether the bribed agent was acting in the course of his employment.[90]

13.86 However, it is quite arguable that, at least in cases of tender, the tendering body might be under an implied obligation to conduct a fair process

---

[86] In the case of bribery of government officials see False Claims Act, 31 USC ss 3729–3733, in other cases see Racketeer Influenced and Corrupt Organisations Act, 18 USC ss 1961–1968.
[87] [1992] 1 AC 448.
[88] See, on unlawful means conspiracy in general, *Meretz Investments NV v ACP Ltd* [2007] EWCA Civ 1303; *Kuwait Oil Tanker Co SAK v AL Bader* [2000] 2 All ER (Comm) 271, 315-316; *News International plc v Clinger* (unreported) 17 November 1998, QB, para 241 of Lindsay J's judgment.
[89] *OBG v Allan* [2007] UKHL 21.
[90] *Armagas v Mundogas* [1986] 1 AC 717, 744–745 per Robert Goff LJ.

– ie at least impartially and according to the terms specified in the tender. Therefore in the case of bribery of the awarding body's agent, the awarding body might be liable to a rejected tenderer for breach of contract.[91]

Collusion in anti-competitive behaviour

13.87 It is also possible to analyse situations in which parties rig a bidding process as corrupt, certainly if the process is colluded in by an agent of the purchaser. Of course, anti-competitive behaviour is now a criminal offence in its own right[92] and it is possible for affected third parties to make claims for damages caused by breaches of competition law.[93] There seems to be no reason in principle for damages not to be available to parties suffering loss as the result of bid-rigging which involves the collusion of an agent of the purchaser.

INTERIM RELIEF

13.88 Imagine a case where a principal suspects his agent is receiving bribes. The principal fears that if he were to challenge the agent this would tip him off, causing him to hide his assets and/or destroy evidence. Issuing proceedings would also have the effect of alerting him that he has been discovered and leading to the same results.

13.89 The civil law addresses this dilemma by way of interim remedies which preserve evidence and assets prior to the commencement of proceedings. The primary interim remedies are the freezing order[94] and the search order.[95]

13.90 Freezing and search orders have been described as the 'nuclear weapons' of commercial litigation.[96] If granted, a freezing order can have the effect of freezing the respondent's[97] worldwide assets, while the search order allows the applicant's legal representatives to enter onto the respondent's premises for the purpose of preserving evidence. There are a number of other interim remedies which are most often deployed in support of a freezing injunction and/or search order and which are mentioned briefly below. Each of these orders requires the fulfilment by the applicant of specific procedures, the details of which are beyond the scope of this text.[98]

---

[91] On the issue of an implied contractual duty to conduct a fair tender process see *Blackpool & Fylde Aero Club v Blackpool Borough Council* [1990] 1 WLR 1195.
[92] Enterprise Act 2002, s 188.
[93] Competition Act 1998, s 47A, although restitutionary relief in price-fixing cases is not available to private claimants suffering loss – *Devenish Nutrition Ltd v Sanofi-Aventis SA (France) and others* [2008] EWCA Civ 1086 – the relief is damages only.
[94] Senior Courts Act 1981, s 37(1) and (3) and CPR, Part 25.1(f).
[95] Civil Procedure Act 1997, s 7 and CPR, Part 25.1(h).
[96] *Bank Mellat v Nikpour* [1985] FSR 87 per Donaldson LJ.
[97] Applications for freezing orders and search orders are generally made before a claim has been issued. At this stage, the person making the application is described as the 'applicant' while the person against whom it is made is described as the 'respondent'.
[98] See Gee *Commercial Injunctions* (5th edn, London, 2006).

Freezing order

13.91 Before turning to the process by which a freezing order (sometimes referred to as a *Mareva*[99] or freezing injunction) can be obtained, there are a number of points to note:

- the order takes effect against the respondent personally, rather than attaching to particular assets themselves. It does not give the applicant any proprietary rights against the assets covered by the order; nor does it give an applicant security for his claim;

- the order does not give the successful applicant priority over other creditors of the respondent; nor does it guarantee that the applicant will recover the value of any judgment eventually awarded;

- the order is granted as relief ancillary to the applicant's main claim. Accordingly, the freezing order will be limited in amount to the approximate value of the applicant's claim;

- the order prevents unjustifiable disposals of assets by the respondent; it does not prevent legitimate expenditure (eg ordinary living expenses, ordinary business transactions, and legal expenses).

13.92 In order to obtain a freezing order, the applicant must establish:

- *a good arguable case against the respondent* – the threshold is a relatively low one; it will suffice to show that the applicant has the better of the argument;[100]

- *a real risk that the respondent will dissipate assets if the order is not granted* – sometimes the applicant will have specific evidence of a risk of dissipation. More usually, the risk of dissipation is intrinsically linked to the (often fraudulent) nature of the claim. Evidence of dishonesty is normally sufficient to establish the risk. The risk must be 'real' and not merely speculative;

- *it must be just and convenient to make the order, in all the circumstances of the case* – if an applicant can show a good arguable case and real risk of dissipation, this ground is likely to be satisfied, absent unusual facts.

13.93 An application for a freezing order is usually made 'without notice' (ie without the respondent being present), since putting the respondent on notice of the application would serve to defeat its purpose (preservation of assets). Since the respondent does not have an opportunity to represent himself at the initial application hearing, the applicant is under an obligation to give

---

[99] After *Mareva Compania Naveria SA v International Bulk Carriers SA (The Mareva)* [1980] 1 All ER 213.
[100] *The Niedersachsen* [1983] 1 WLR 1412.

the court full and frank disclosure of all material facts relating to the case, including any facts upon which the respondent might seek to rely. If it becomes apparent that the applicant has failed in its duty to give full and frank disclosure, there is a presumption that the court will set aside the freezing order.[101]

13.94 The grant of a freezing order against the respondent may cause that respondent damage if it is found to have been granted without justification. An applicant for a freezing order must provide an undertaking that it will pay the respondent any such damages in these circumstances. The applicant is usually required to give evidence of financial standing, and may be required to provide security in support of the undertaking (particularly if it has limited assets, or is based outside the EU).

13.95 If the application for an injunction is successful, the freezing order itself must be served on the respondent within a short time. The successful applicant will also be required to undertake to issue and serve substantive proceedings on the respondent within a set period. If the application for a freezing order is unsuccessful, the applicant must nevertheless disclose its attempt to the respondent, unless it gets permission not to from the court. This emphasises the careful judgment that needs to be exercised before making the application in the first place – an unsuccessful applicant may cause the very mischief (asset dissipation) that the application was designed to avoid.

13.96 The freezing order itself will prescribe a date on which the parties must appear before the court, and at which the merits of the freezing order will be argued between them (the 'return date hearing'). At this hearing, the respondent may seek to overturn the freezing order, or obtain variations to its terms. Assuming that the freezing order is not overturned at the return date hearing, it will remain in place until trial of the substantive claim or until further order of the court.

Search order

13.97 In effect, the search order (formerly known as an *Anton Piller*[102] order) is a civil search warrant. It enables a applicant to secure evidence relating to proceedings where it is considered that there is a real possibility that the respondent would destroy such material if he were put on notice of those proceedings.

13.98 The grounds which need to be satisfied before a search order is made are as follows:

- the application must show, on its face (and subject to contrary evidence) an extremely strong case;

---

[101] *Brinks MAT v Elcombe* [1988] 1 WLR 1350, although there may well be circumstances in which this is not in the interests of justice.
[102] *Anton Piller KG v Manufacturing Processes Limited* [1976] CH 55.

- the potential or actual damage suffered or faced by the applicant must be very serious;

- there must be clear evidence that the respondent has in its possession incriminating documents or things;

- there must be a real possibility that the respondent may destroy such documents or things before an on-notice application can be made; and

- the harm likely to be caused by the execution of the search order on the respondent on his business affairs must not be out of proportion to the legitimate object of the order (namely preservation of evidence).[103]

13.99 Freezing and search orders are sometimes sought together. Most of the procedural considerations relevant to freezing orders also apply to applications for search orders, for example the without notice nature of the application, the obligation of full and frank disclosure, the need for the applicant to provide a cross-undertaking in damages, obligations as to commencement of a main claim and the need for a return date hearing.

Form and content of the search order

13.100 Typically, a search order will:

- provide for entry onto and search of identified premises;

- list the categories of document and other evidential items which an applicant is entitled to secure;

- identify which of the applicant's representatives are entitled to execute the order and enter onto the respondent's premises;

- require the respondent to co-operate with the search;

- prevent the respondent from 'tipping off' accomplices;

- prohibit the respondent from continuing with the actions complained of by the applicant until trial or further order of the court.

Supplemental orders

13.101 The applicant for freezing and/or search orders may seek additional forms of relief from the court at the without notice stage. Such relief may include some or all of the following:

---

[103] *Indicii Salus Ltd (in receivership) v Chandrasekaran* [2006] EWHC 521.

- *asset disclosure order*: this requires the respondent to provide an affidavit of his assets;

- *asset preservation order*: if there is a proprietary claim over specific assets, in particular funds, this order provides that the respondent is not entitled to pay any expenses out of such funds (including, in some cases, living and legal expenses).[104] An order of this type can be an alternative to a freezing order in circumstances where assets can be traced to a specific party and the claimant wishes to avoid some of the consequences of a freezing order such as a cross-undertaking in damages in circumstances where the likely consequences of a cross-undertaking are unknown;

- *disclosure order*: this requires the disclosure of particular documents which will assist the applicant in identifying the whereabouts of the respondent's assets, for example bank statements;

- *order for further information*: the respondent may be asked to answer questions relating to the whereabouts of particular assets;[105]

- *gagging order*: this prevents the respondent (and other parties served with the freezing order) from revealing the fact of the application and freezing order to third parties. It may afford the applicant time to pursue other freezing orders against other parties;

- *Norwich Pharmacal order*:[106] this requires third parties who have become 'mixed-up' in the wrongdoing complained of (whether innocently or otherwise) to give disclosure of information which will lead to the identification of assets or other wrongdoers;

- *Bankers Trust order*:[107] this requires disclosure by a bank of a third party's bank account; such orders can be sought to obtain evidence as a precursor to an application for a freezing order;

- *order for delivery up of passport*: while rare, this can be used to prevent a respondent from leaving the jurisdiction.

CIVIL RECOVERY BY STATES AGAINST FORMER OFFICIALS

13.102 The UK, and London in particular, are favourite places for overseas politicians to purchase property or conduct banking or investment

---

[104] *Polly Peck v Nadir* [1992] 2 Lloyd's Rep 238.
[105] In special circumstances, the respondent can be required to be cross-examined as to his assets. This usually takes place after the respondent's affidavit of assets has been received, for example where the information it contains is inaccurate.
[106] After *Norwich Pharmacal Co v Customs and Excise Commissioners* [1974] AC 133.
[107] After *Bankers Trust v Shapira* [1980] 1 WLR 1274.

transactions. As allegations of corruption among these politicians or other members of national elites emerge, especially after significant changes in government, new governments sometimes seek recovery of assets alleged to have been purchased with stolen money or to be the proceeds of corruption. There are high-profile campaign groups and media organisations which seek to expose corruption in high places and there is a growing awareness of the utility of civil recovery proceedings.

13.103 For example, in *Attorney-General of Zambia v Meer Care & Desai & Ors*,[108] the former President of Zambia and others were found liable by the High Court to the State of Zambia for figures in excess of US$45m. The main causes of action were conspiracy to defraud the Zambian state. Solicitors in London accused of dishonest assistance in the frauds were acquitted on appeal.[109]

13.104 In *Federal Republic of Nigeria v Santolina Investment Corp, Solomon & Peters, and Diepreye Alamieyeseigha*[110] the High Court found, on the basis of the criminal conviction of a Nigerian politician in the Nigerian courts, and upon the evidence in those proceedings, that properties in London were purchased by the proceeds of corruption and so were claimable by the Federal Republic of Nigeria, and that there should be summary judgment for Nigeria.

13.105 After the recent events in Tunisia, Egypt and Libya there have been allegations of corruption on a grand scale by leaders of these states. Both criminal and civil recovery proceedings may be available against any assets held in the UK. In the past, there have been extensive proceedings in London, Switzerland and elsewhere seeking to trace and repatriate assets stolen by the former president of Nigeria, General Abacha, and members of his family. Hundreds of millions were eventually recovered.

---

[108] [2007] EWHC 952 (Ch).
[109] [2008] EWCA Civ 1007.
[110] [2007] EWHC 3053 (QB).

Chapter 14

PARTICULAR PROBLEMS: HOSPITALITY, PROMOTION, FACILITATION PAYMENTS, EXTORTION AND MERGERS

INTRODUCTION

14.1 The main objective of the Bribery Act 2010 is to create effective measures against serious corruption and to cause businesses to implement adequate procedures to prevent bribery being committed on their behalf. It has been said by ministers and prosecutors that the Act is aimed at 'mavericks',[1] and that the vast majority of law-abiding businesses should not be at risk of prosecution once they take adequate anti-bribery measures.

14.2 Despite these reassurances, the scope of the conduct which might be affected by the Bribery Act is wide enough to catch hospitality offered by businesses and to catch the small 'facilitation' payments which are recognised as a common phenomenon in many places. This is a source of anxiety to many. There are also concerns about how to respond to the abuse of power by unaccountable local officials who seek bribes backed by express or implicit threats. Another issue is whether companies which acquire new businesses will acquire unknown levels of liability for past practices of the acquiree.

14.3 This chapter considers each of these topics in more depth than was possible when discussing the specific offences. It offers two detailed teaching scenarios to stimulate further thought and discussion either to individual readers or as part of an education or training programme. A deliberate decision has been made not to provide answers to all the questions asked in the scenario in the hope that they will prompt a re-examination of the Act and some of the other relevant law, guidance and good practice. At some point in the future the issues in each may be revisited.

14.4 It hardly needs repeating that any business which faces the risk that associated persons might pay bribes on its behalf should put in place adequate procedures designed to prevent this. These procedures are the subject of Chapter 9 and are not the main focus of discussion here.

---

[1] MOJ Guidance, Foreword by Secretary of State, p 2.

CORPORATE HOSPITALITY AND PROMOTIONAL EXPENSES

14.5 At the risk of stating the obvious, it may be useful to our analysis to step back and consider the purposes and context in which corporate hospitality is offered and promotional expenses incurred.

14.6 Vendors of goods or services wish to establish a good reputation for their products and for themselves. As well as advertising, many seek to establish personal rapport with their most important customers, to establish trust and to anticipate and understand their needs. This is usually beneficial to the customer as well as the vendor.

14.7 Many businesses depend on the personal reputations of their people, and whether or not customers respect, trust and get on with their people. So corporate hospitality is generally intended to allow people the opportunity to get to know each other in a more informal social setting and/or cement or commemorate cordial personal relationships. In the modern corporate world, it is rare for a particular gift to be intended to induce a business person or official away from his clear duty in relation to a purchasing or other important decision. The intention in the vast majority of cases is to develop good relations. In some contexts gifts and hospitality are not only useful but are seen as essential if one wishes to develop good business relationships.[2]

14.8 Not everyone sees corporate hospitality in this way. Some may feel it leads to cliques or nepotism, or at least to executives living the high life in defiance of their duties. The more distant one is from the process of making sales the more tempting it may be to see corporate hospitality, in general, as vaguely disreputable, perhaps even corrupt.

14.9 Promotional expenditure tends to be seen somewhat differently, although in fact the rationale for it is very similar and it is often difficult to distinguish between hospitality and promotion. Generally, when people speak of 'promotional expenses' in contrast to 'corporate hospitality' they tend to mean expenditure on specific promotional events to which potential customers are invited.[3] These are not so much directed at developing personal relationships as promoting particular products or service lines.

14.10 An example of promotional expenditure is the payment of the travel costs of potential customers who visit an industrial site, a product demonstration or a trade show, or to meet representatives of the vendor.

14.11 Like corporate hospitality, the purpose of such a visit, from the vendor's point of view, is to increase or maintain sales or to help the business in

---

[2] For example, the concept of *guanxi* which is said to underlie a great deal of business life in Chinese culture. See in general Luo, *Guanxi and Business* (Singapore, 2000).

[3] Advertising is also promotional expenditure but since it does not involve the provision of advantages to individuals it is not relevant to questions of bribery.

some other way. From the point of view of the customer it may be to educate himself about the vendor's offering, gain know-how, establish personal relationships and perhaps align the vendor more closely to the customer's needs, whether as to pricing or product specification. Despite the fact that most promotional events are, or have the potential to be, mutually beneficial, the costs are usually paid by the vendor, no doubt because vendors tend to believe they have more to gain from successful sales.

14.12 The UK government has recently been anxious to reassure businesses in particular that the Bribery Act will not be used as a stick with which to beat the normal practices of corporate hospitality or promotional expenditure.[4] The MOJ Guidance of March 2011 goes out of its way to discuss situations in which business entertainment or promotional activity should not fall foul of the Act.

14.13 However, not all corporate hospitality or promotional expenses are the same. It seems useful to at least distinguish between three types of recipient – people in the private sector, people in the domestic public sector and foreign public officials (FPOs).

Private sector hospitality

14.14 A typical corporate hospitality event in the UK involves a private-sector vendor organisation inviting employees of other private sector organisations to attend a sports or cultural event or a dinner or drinks party. At the event the staff of the vendor mix with the invitees. There is sometimes a direct sales pitch for a new product or service line, but this is often not the case. Some events are no more than a meeting over lunch or over dinner. Some can be expensive and large in scale such as private concerts, travel to major sporting events such as World Cup finals, or talks or activities with politicians or celebrities.

14.15 Of course, at these events the vendor is providing the invitees with personal advantages (food, drinks, entertainment) for a commercial rather than a social purpose.[5] The invitees are invited because the vendor hopes to improve its image and reputation and to develop relationships which ultimately lead to sales or other business advantages. So, like almost all corporate hospitality, the purpose of the provision of the advantages is to obtain business or advantages in the conduct of business.

---

[4] MOJ Guidance, p 12: 'Bona fide hospitality and promotional, or other business expenditure which seeks to improve the image of a commercial organisation, better to present products and services, or establish cordial relations, is recognised as an established and important part of doing business and it is not the intention of the Act to criminalise such behaviour.'

[5] It is best to ignore the proposition, advanced by some veterans of corporate events, that some of them can be quite dull and thus hardly qualify as 'advantages'. Not everyone will have had the opportunity to develop such world-weariness, and many officials of prosecution agencies, and jurors, will find it unattractive.

14.16 In the vast majority of cases this is not bribery. As we have seen, the general offence of provision of bribes under s 1 of the Act can be defined as the provision of advantages intending to induce or reward *improper* performance of relevant activities, or in circumstances where the provider knows or believes that the acceptance of the advantage is itself improper.[6] It will be rare for the vendors to intend any impropriety to result from the event in question or to believe that attendance by an invitee is in itself improper. Since in pure private-to-private hospitality there will be no foreign public officials involved the more expansive definition of the mental element for the s 6 offence does not apply.[7]

14.17 It is sometimes the case that corporate hospitality is offered on a conditional basis – ie in terms such as: 'If you are one of our top ten customers we will invite five of your executives to the test series'. Such an offer is not bribery, if it is addressed to the customer itself. It is merely a standard sales incentive, in the same way that supermarkets or other retailers offer discounts or other benefits to volume purchasers.

14.18 Conditional benefits may come closer to bribery if they are offered to individuals in exchange for the awarding of business by their employers or by those to whom they owe fiduciary duties. There seems nothing improper in a football club offering 50 match-day hospitality packages to a company if it will become a sponsor. The company will no doubt decide how to use these fringe benefits according to an established policy or practice (for example to reward good performance by staff, or to entertain customers).

14.19 Contrast an approach by a sports club to a company chief executive proposing that if the company agrees a sponsorship deal then the CEO, personally, will receive four free season tickets for life. The CEO is more likely to allow his personal interest in receiving the benefit to affect how he exercises his duties, and the offer makes it more likely that he will act contrary to expectations attached to his position (ie those of good faith, impartiality and arising from his position of trust).[8] In the absence of other factors there may be a reasonable inference that the club made the offer in order to get the CEO to use his influence in a manner contrary to his duties of good faith, impartiality or trust.

14.20 Inferences of impropriety get stronger as the links between significant business decisions and significant personal benefits to employees or directors become clearer. The value of a particular item of hospitality will also be a relevant factor. A free lunch is very unlikely to raise the necessary inference unless the cost is utterly spectacular. A free holiday may do so.

---

[6] That is in breach of a relevant expectation of good faith, impartiality or arising from a position of trust – Bribery Act 2010, s 4.

[7] Although of course some officials of nominally private sector organisations may be exercising public functions either for a foreign state or for a public agency or public enterprise of such a state – see the discussion in Chapter 7.

[8] Bribery Act 2010, s 3.

14.21 Even here some caution must be exercised. In some industries it is very common for senior business people to entertain according to standards which most people would think extremely lavish, and to seek out the company of others who are equally as fortunate. A meal at a three-star restaurant might be expected to turn the head of some people, but might be entirely routine for a software tycoon or a senior banker. Inferences of improper motives should only be drawn when considering all the circumstances of each case.[9]

Hospitality and the UK public sector

14.22 The situation is somewhat different when considering hospitality to officials in the UK public sector. Many such officials tend to recognise that acceptance of any more than token hospitality or gifts is potentially dangerous.[10] In the UK civil service any benefits of value received by senior civil servants must be declared and the same is true of Members of Parliament as well as officials of local authorities.

14.23 Information published by HM Government[11] indicates that some corporate hospitality directed at civil servants with apparent responsibility for commercial contracts seems to be tolerated, perhaps on the basis that it is beneficial to the public for these officials to have good personal relationships with service vendors. However, any arrangement where an official or public representative agrees to use their office to favour the interests of a particular business in exchange for money or other advantages immediately crosses the line into impropriety, because it will involve the official acting contrary to the relevant expectations. Commercial organisations dealing with public officials should exercise caution before offering them any personal benefits which are more than nominal in value. Civil servants should be equally careful about seeking or accepting such advantages.

14.24 Although not directly on the subject of hospitality, it is convenient to note here that similar caution should be exercised when considering offers of employment to former senior officials or ministers – any suspicion that the former official is being 'rewarded' for decisions taken while he was in office

---

[9] See the Joint Prosecution Guidance, p 11: 'The more lavish the hospitality or expenditure (beyond what may be reasonable standards in the particular circumstances) the greater the inference that it is intended to encourage or reward improper performance or influence an official. Lavishness is just one factor that may be taken into account in determining whether an offence has been committed. The full circumstances of each case would need to be considered. Other factors might include that the hospitality or expenditure was not clearly connected with legitimate business activity or was concealed.'

[10] Specific rules applying to acceptance of gifts or hospitality by government ministers are contained in the Ministerial Code, available at www.cabinetoffice.gov.uk/resource-library/ministerial-code. The conduct of civil servants is governed by various codes, including the Civil Service Code: www.civilservice.gov.uk/about/values/cscode/index.aspx; and specific guidance in relation to hospitality specifically is at: www.cabinetoffice.gov.uk/resource-library/guidance-civil-servants-receiving-hospitality.

[11] 'Senior Civil Servant Hospitality Details Published': www.direct.gov.uk/en/Nl1/Newsroom/DG_174932. Unhappily, at the date of writing the details of the hospitality received seems to have been removed from this website.

which favoured his new employer should be avoided. Certainly, an agreement that favours in office would mean employment when out of office would almost certainly amount to either bribery or a conspiracy to commit bribery, whether under ss 1, 2 or 6 of the Act.[12]

Hospitality and foreign public officials

14.25 As we have seen,[13] s 6 of the Act creates a special regime for FPOs, which is stricter, from the point of view of the mental element, than offences under s 1 or s 2. The relevant *mens rea*, instead of being an intention to induce or reward improper performance of relevant functions or activities, is merely an intention to influence the official in his capacity as such and to obtain or retain business or an advantage in the conduct of business.

14.26 The result, perhaps surprisingly, is that those providing corporate hospitality must be more careful when dealing with FPOs than with their counterparts in the UK. However, s 6 should not be read as outlawing all hospitality to FPOs. Transactions which are inconsequential are most unlikely to be able to support the necessary inference of intention to influence the FPO, especially if it is not possible to identify a specific decision of the FPO which the supposed bribery is intended to influence.

14.27 The MOJ Guidance[14] seems to take a relatively relaxed approach to 'normal' corporate hospitality or promotional expenditure involving FPOs. For example, it states the following at page 14:

> 'Levels of expenditure will not, therefore, be the only consideration in determining whether a section 6 offence has been committed. But in the absence of any further evidence demonstrating the required connection, it is unlikely, for example, that incidental provision of a routine business courtesy will raise the inference that it was intended to have a direct impact on decision making, particularly where such hospitality is commensurate with the reasonable and proportionate norms for the particular industry; e.g. the provision of airport to hotel transfer services to facilitate an on-site visit, or dining and tickets to an event.'

14.28 Such an approach seems sensible, and seems likely to inform the views of the Serious Fraud Office (SFO) when considering its priorities both in investigating and prosecuting.

14.29 The strictures as to employment of UK public officials mentioned above also of course apply to FPOs.

14.30 At this point it might be worthwhile to illustrate some of these issues by means of a fictional scenario.

---

[12] In the UK, the Ministerial Code of Conduct provides that former ministers must seek advice from the Independent Advisory Committee on Business Appointments on any prospective appointment undertaken within 2 years of leaving office.
[13] Chapter 7.
[14] MOJ Guidance, pp 13, 14.

Scenario A

14.31 Nigel is a founder member of Cranial Slap, a group which grew out of the South London pub rock scene to become the biggest selling heavy rock act of the mid-1970s. The band is still very successful with sell-out 'farewell' tours every 3–4 years, and healthy sales of its back catalogue.

14.32 Ten years ago Nigel bought out di Bergi Inc, an ailing film production company. Since then di Bergi has become a successful vendor of music, documentaries, guitars and amplifiers. Di Bergi carried out a partial IPO 3 years ago. Nigel still controls 51% of the shares and is chairman of the board. Nigel is said by various 'rich list' publications to have a personal fortune of over £250m. He lives in California and has other houses in Barbados, Berkshire and Tuscany, with each property benefiting from a cricket pitch due to Nigel's obsession with the game.

14.33 David is the chief executive of Mare Infirma (MI), an investment bank with a large private equity arm. He has been a fan of Cranial Slap since his early teens – indeed he went to the same school as Nigel, although 10 years later. He is keen to invest in the music business and thinks di Bergi's recorded music division would be more profitable if it was spun out of the group, taken private and put under new management. He is keen to persuade Nigel to sell the music division to MI.

14.34 Ian is another contemporary of Nigel's. He was formerly the manager of Cranial Slap but suffered a nervous breakdown. He moved to the Welsh Virgin Islands (WVI), a small self-governing archipelago, which is a British overseas territory, in 1984. He made a full recovery and eventually went into politics. He is now the WVI's Minister of Tourism and Sport.

14.35 Ian has recently been approached by Nigel, who wishes to develop a cricket venue and youth academy in the WVI. Nigel wishes to acquire land adjacent to the capital of the WVI for that purpose. Ian has not responded to Nigel's contact on this subject, fearing a recurrence of his health problems.

14.36 The following events ensue:

(i) David invites Nigel to play in a celebrity cricket match at Lord's, held to publicise MI's sponsorship of the forthcoming series of test matches. Nigel, as well as other celebrity cricket fans, are flown to and from the event in a private jet. The accommodation is five star and the event is catered by various celebrity chefs.

(ii) At the London event, Nigel and his girlfriend each receive a gift pack containing valuable watches, jewellery, electronic equipment and test match tickets (most of which they give away). Nigel receives coaching on his batting from the England cricket captain. The whole event receives significant coverage in the media.

(iii) Without explaining why, Nigel had asked David to include Ian on the guest list, and David did so. Ian dislikes cricket and anything to do with his former life in the music industry, so he does not accept the invitation.

(iv) A month later, MI (at David's suggestion) offers di Bergi Inc a speaking slot at the prestigious 'World Leaders Club' conference in Paris, which is sponsored by MI. Di Bergi nominates Nigel as the speaker.

(v) Nigel thinks the Prime Minister of the WVI should attend the Paris event and provides his own aircraft to bring him and three other officials of the WVI government to attend the event. Again, Ian does not attend. Over lunch Nigel is introduced to the UK Chancellor of the Exchequer, to whom he provides some insights on the failings of the British tax system.

(vi) A month after the Paris event David offers Nigel the chance to invest in a successful and secretive hedge fund, managed by a limited partnership spun out of MI, at a significantly reduced cost – ie waiving the management fee of 2% per annum and capping the performance fee at 15% of gains (instead of the usual 20%). David suggests at the same time that Nigel might open the books of the di Bergi music division to MI, in preparation for a buyout offer.

(vii) The sale of the music division to MI ultimately goes through on Nigel's recommendation, 6 months later, although some small shareholders allege the price paid is too low. Nigel is paid £60m for his shares, he invests £50m in MI's fund.

(viii) MI throws a party to celebrate completion of the transaction on the company yacht moored at Cannes, at a cost of £100,000. It is attended by Nigel, David, other executives of MI and di Bergi and the bankers and lawyers who worked on the deal.

(ix) A year after Nigel's investment, the hedge fund (which does not invest in the recorded music industry) has generated a 20% return on Nigel's investment. Having drunk too much at a party, David lets Nigel's involvement in the fund slip to a journalist. The minority shareholders in di Bergi are even more aggrieved and instruct lawyers to investigate their options.

14.37 Although in a classroom situation it might be interesting to investigate every possible consequence of these facts and how the Bribery Act might apply, the purpose here is merely to draw out certain points to do with corporate hospitality in particular.

14.38 It will be obvious that hospitality and other advantages have been provided at various stages, for purposes connected to business. On each occasion the hospitality and advantages were very expensive by the standards of most people. Within the terms of ss 1, 2 and 6 of the Act these benefits

Travel and events

14.39 One issue is the 'lavishness' of the hospitality provided.[15] To many people, the benefits associated with the celebrity cricket match and the post-completion party on the yacht will seem very lavish. But it is worth asking whether benefits of this kind are really significant in the circumstances. Nigel has his own private jet and, probably, his own luxury yacht, or could have the use of one if he wished. As a celebrity cricket fan he can mix with professional cricketers as often as he wants to. The gifts may not mean much to him either – some film stars, musicians, sportsmen and others frequently receive luxury goods free, either with no strings attached or as part of an endorsement arrangement.

14.40 Of course Nigel may be the type of person who covets all the free gifts, hospitality and publicity he can acquire, his wealth notwithstanding. He may be keen to economise on his Christmas list by passing on the trinkets acquired from such hospitality to friends or family.

14.41 But even then it seems relevant to ask whether the benefits mentioned above are so unusual and valuable to Nigel that receiving them would be expected to affect his judgment when considering a vitally important decision such as the price at which he and other shareholders should sell a large portion of the di Bergi business. On the present facts such a hypothesis seems strained, especially as both the events in question had clear connections to the legitimate business interests of either MI or di Bergi. The first event, in London, was not only public but occurred for the purpose of generating publicity – ie it was a promotional event for MI. The party in Cannes does not seem to have been a secret either. It is a regular enough occurrence for businesses to reward staff with large parties, though events on this scale are rarer. Although secrecy is not a prerequisite to bribery, it is usually more difficult to establish the necessary inferences of improper intent where it is absent.

14.42 However, Ian is in a different position to Nigel. He is nothing like as wealthy and has eschewed a jet-set lifestyle. Despite his acquaintance with Nigel he is also an FPO. The invitation to the cricket event at Lord's which has come, indirectly, from Nigel might be the sort of thing which could influence a person in his position in relation to Nigel's attempt to develop the academy in the WVI. Even though Ian did not take up the invitation, the timing of it in the context of Nigel's other purposes might raise an inference that Nigel (if not David) made the offer in order to influence him in his capacity as an FPO so as to obtain a business advantage.

---

[15] A factor identified as relevant by the MOJ Guidance, p 13, Joint Prosecution Guidance, p 10.

Conference

14.43 The prestige and networking opportunities presented by the invitation to the leaders' conference, though less easy to quantify in terms of money, may be more valuable to someone in Nigel's position than the trip to the cricket match. This event might be more capable of sustaining an inference of the necessary *mens rea*, on the part of MI (intention to induce or reward improper performance by Nigel). On our facts Nigel has not solicited this invitation but if he did so while indicating that there would be a commercial reward to MI as a result then there might be an inference to support the necessary *mens rea* under s 2. But an allegation of bribery of Nigel, based on the conference invitation alone, still appears weak. The value of participation in the conference seems rather low compared with the sale of the music division. Nigel may well have been a suitably qualified speaker who would have been invited anyway. Moreover, the leadership conference was a public event and the offer to participate in it was made to di Bergi as a company, not to Nigel directly.

14.44 Again, Nigel's conduct in relation to the prime minister and other officials of the WVI is more questionable. If we assume (perhaps wrongly) that these officials are not accustomed to travel by private jet, an inference of an intention to influence them might arise. Nigel might argue that this was another case of promotional expenditure, to improve di Bergi's image as a responsible and respected business in the eyes of the WVI government. The surrounding circumstances may have considerable influence on which side of the line this case will fall. If there was secrecy or an attempt to disguise the provision of the advantage then it may be difficult to avoid the impression that Nigel is attempting to buy influence.

Hedge fund fees

14.45 The offer to waive fees on the hedge fund if Nigel assists MI's bid for the music division of di Bergi is more obviously an inducement which is both personal to Nigel and likely to affect his judgment generally, including the performance of his duties as a director of di Bergi. Of course there was no guarantee that the fund would return 20% on Nigel's £50m investment in one year, and it is possible that such gains will be wiped out in subsequent years. But the saving of the 2% management fee is likely to be worth at least £1m per annum to Nigel. Although the saving of one quarter of the performance fee might be worth nothing in years when the fund does not make money, in the last year it was worth a further £2.5m. That comes to a benefit worth £3.5m in a single year. Over time, with the effect of compounding, advantages of this nature have the potential to be extremely valuable even to a person as wealthy as Nigel.

14.46 Of course we cannot assume that Nigel would be bound to do something improper to favour MI as a bidder in exchange for uncertain future benefits from a hedge-fund investment. There might be many relevant factors such as Nigel's view of the true value of his stake or his cash-flow position, or indeed his understanding of his fiduciary duty as a director of di Bergi. However, it should not be necessary to prove that Nigel would definitely have performed his activities in an improper way in exchange for the advantage to raise an inference that the offer of the advantage was intended to induce or reward such conduct[16] (or that, if Nigel requested such an advantage, it was with the intention to perform his activities improperly in consequence[17]). Absent unusual circumstances, a secretive transaction of this kind seems sufficient to raise an inference of the required mental element.

14.47 This part of the scenario is qualitatively as well as quantitatively different to the others directly relevant to MI, because there is a clear connection between a valuable advantage and an articulated quid pro quo, which results in a potentially significant conflict between Nigel's duty as a director of di Bergi and his personal interest in making more money. It perhaps serves to illustrate the type of private sector bribery which should be a priority for the UK authorities, ie activity which might have a significant effect on the proper and transparent operation of markets, the value of assets and the fiduciary duties of directors. Set against this sort of conduct, debates about the value of flights or star ratings of hotels seem less important.

14.48 Hopefully, the different considerations applicable to the public sector and foreign public officials in particular will also be clearer from this scenario. The lack of a specifically identified quid pro quo is less important because of the lower threshold for *mens rea* when dealing with FPOs. All that is required is an intention to influence, not an intention to cause improper behaviour. It is difficult to imagine that an offer to fly a senior politician of a very small and poor country to Paris in a private jet, or the package connected to the cricket match, were not intended to influence the recipients in their official capacities, especially where the provider of the advantage is, at the same time, seeking government support for a particular project.

Next steps

14.49 This scenario is capable of amendment to draw out other elements of the Act in a practical way, perhaps as part of a training programme. For example, those interested might wish to consider the following questions:

(a) Nigel spends most of his time in Beverly Hills. Di Bergi and MI are incorporated in Delaware. David is resident for tax purposes in Monaco though he spends as much time as he can in London and New York. The hedge fund is registered in the Cayman Islands and managed from Zug, Switzerland. Ian and the other BWI officials are citizens of and resident in the BWI. Could the Bribery Act apply to any of the situations or transactions discussed? How might that be the case?

---

[16] Bribery Act 2010, s 1.
[17] Ibid, s 2.

(b) If the Bribery Act does apply, what offences might have been committed, and by whom? What will be the key facts relevant to each?

(c) Would it make any difference if Nigel's ambition to develop the cricket venue in WVI were not being pursued through di Bergi but through a charitable trust set up and funded by Nigel?

(d) Would it make any difference if the person receiving the hospitality and other advantages from MI was not Nigel but the CEO of di Bergi who is not a significant shareholder of di Bergi and who, though well paid, is not in Nigel's league when it comes to personal wealth?

(e) Would it make any difference if the WVI prime minister and other officials were already planning to attend the Paris conference and the cost of their (commercial) flights would have been paid for by the WVI government had Nigel not stepped in?

(f) What investigations into the law of the WVI should be made?

(g) Assuming both di Bergi and MI have procedures in place designed to prevent bribery by persons associated with them in accordance with the Six Principles outlined by the MOJ Guidance (see the discussion in Chapter 9), what elements of these procedures might be engaged by the facts outlined at (i) to (vi) above?

(h) Would it make any difference if, a year before the events in question, Nigel had been appointed to the board of a US-based non-profit corporation aimed at discouraging drug abuse which received 80% of its funding from the US federal government?

(i) If David told Nigel that an escort agency would be sending escorts to the party in Cannes to 'entertain' him, would that affect whether the party and events surrounding it might ground a charge of bribery? Would it make a difference if the escort agency was not paid from MI's funds but by David personally?[18]

(j) What options might be open to shareholders who wish to recover what they see as losses suffered as a result of the sale of the music division, assuming the facts at (i) to (vi) above are known to them and capable of being established by credible evidence?

---

[18] Assume for these purposes that there is insufficient evidence to found any other charge related to prostitution or procuring.

FACILITATION PAYMENTS, EXTORTION AND MERGERS AND ACQUISITIONS

14.50 Like corporate hospitality, facilitation payments and extortion have been considered elsewhere in this book in the context of specific offences.[19]

14.51 To recap, a facilitation payment may be defined as a payment made with the purpose of expediting or facilitating the provision of services or routine government action which an official is normally obliged to perform.[20] Extortion is no longer a specific offence in English law, although in general parlance it continues to mean the unlawful extraction of money by a public official in the purported exercise of his office.[21] It is often difficult to distinguish extortion from mere bribe seeking by an official.

14.52 Such payments amount to bribery under s 1 or s 6 (if made for a business purpose) if they are also made either with the intention of inducing or rewarding improper performance of a relevant function or activity,[22] or in the knowledge that the acceptance of the advantage by the official itself involves improper performance of his functions,[23] or with the intention of influencing the official in his capacity as such.[24] Many such payments will be made with the requisite *mens rea*, either because it is generally known that they are illegal, or because a reasonable person would infer from the circumstances that there is something improper about them.

14.53 Facilitation payments made by a person associated with a commercial organisation make the organisation liable under s 7(1), unless a defence of adequate procedures is available under s 7(2).

---

[19] See Chapters 7, 9 and 10.
[20] The FCPA has the following definition: 'any facilitating or expediting payment to a foreign official, political party, or party official the purpose of which is to expedite or to secure the performance of a routine governmental action by a foreign official, political party, or party official' (s 78dd-1(b)). A more detailed definition of routine government action, is at s 78dd-1(f): 'A "routine governmental action," in turn, is only an action which is ordinarily and commonly performed by a foreign official in—
(i) obtaining permits, licenses, or other official documents to qualify a person to do business in a foreign country;
(ii) processing governmental papers, such as visas and work orders;
(iii) providing police protection, mail pick-up and delivery, or scheduling inspections associated with contract performance or inspections related to transit of goods across country;
(iv) providing phone service, power and water supply, loading and unloading cargo, or protecting perishable products or commodities from deterioration; or
(v) actions of a similar nature.'
Note that businesses might still fall foul of the FCPA if they do not record facilitation payments accurately in their books and records – s 78m(b).
[21] Blackstone described extortion as: 'an abuse of public justice, which consists in any officer's unlawfully taking, by colour of his office, from any man, any money or thing of value, that is not due to him, or more than is due, or before it is due.' 4 W Blackstone, *Commentaries* 141 (1769).
[22] Section 1, case 1.
[23] Section 1, case 2.
[24] Section 6.

14.54 Requests for facilitation payments are rife in certain countries. Many minor officials see such payments as a defensible way of supplementing their low salaries. These will frequently be illegal under local law, but the police are often not assiduous in investigating or prosecuting them and there are many places where the police and other legal authorities are seen as the most corrupt group of all. Some businesses may face dozens of demands for facilitation payments from government officials in a week, and believe that failure to pay these would effectively paralyse important parts of their operations.

14.55 For staff on the ground there are powerful incentives in favour of making a payment. One of the purposes of the non-exemption of facilitation payments from the law of bribery is to try to dis-incentivise this conduct insofar as those subject to UK jurisdiction are concerned. So a £10 payment to a customs official to release goods which should be released anyway, and which will perish unless released within 24 hours, is, in law, as much a bribe as a £1m payment to a government minister in exchange for a mining licence.

14.56 Whether this approach to changing practices outside the UK will be effective remains to be seen. Indeed, whether its effectiveness could even be accurately assessed given the numerous factors affecting the prevalence of petty bribery in a particular territory also remains to be seen. One difficulty is that many local employees may not feel themselves to be capable of resisting requests in circumstances where officials are nothing like as accountable for their actions as they are in the UK. Another difficulty is that in such circumstances it seems disproportionate to impose criminal liability where the paying party would much rather not have to pay and can be seen as being a victim of the requesting official.

14.57 What is clear is that commercial organisations which have operations which are vulnerable to abuse of power by officials which demand facilitation payments face an extremely difficult situation. If they sanction the practice of paying they will break the law of the UK[25] and probably the law of the country in question. If payment were to be the policy of the firm, it would be difficult to rely on the defence of adequate procedures if charged under s 7.

14.58 There are some enterprises which believe that the alternative of stopping all such payments would have a serious adverse affect on their business, at least in the short term, and would create intolerable conditions for many of their staff.

14.59 If the enterprise allows payments in certain circumstances, while discouraging them generally, it makes a rod for their own back. For example, by conscientiously recording occasions when it is felt that payments are unavoidable so that a report or complaint can be made to the authorities, and/or by making sure that facilitation payments are recorded accurately as

---

[25] For example, the Bribery Act and, potentially, the various offences under Part 7 of the Proceeds of Crime Act 2002, in particular ss 327 and 328.

such in books and records, it creates evidence which potentially incriminates it.[26] For such enterprises this is a genuine dilemma.

14.60 The MOJ Guidance[27] and Joint Prosecution Guidance[28] seem to recognise this, and recognise that UK-based enterprises are not capable of solving all the social problems of other countries single-handedly.

14.61 But there are also good reasons for not creating a special legal category for facilitation payments. Broadly these are, first, that acceptance of facilitation payments contributes to a culture where bribery is acceptable generally, and, secondly, that it is often difficult to distinguish a genuine facilitation payment from a bribe, especially in circumstances where the official in question has a degree of discretionary power.

14.62 It may be that, in the long run, improving standards of governance and economic growth will go to reducing the demand for facilitation payments in many countries. It is also to be hoped that various authorities in the UK will cooperate in assisting businesses which are particularly vulnerable to this phenomenon. In the meantime there should be no mistake: businesses subject to the jurisdiction of the UK which make facilitation payments are committing offences and taking on a material risk of prosecution.

Mergers and acquisitions

14.63 A separate issue which it is convenient to consider here is that of due diligence in corporate mergers and acquisitions (M&A). We have already explored the concept of the corporate veil,[29] which means, in essence, that each company is a separate entity even though it may be part of a group, so that its liabilities do not automatically fall on its parent or other related companies, or its owners.

14.64 This principle is not displaced by any terms of the Bribery Act. So a company which buys another company is not itself assuming the liabilities of the target company. Those liabilities stay where they were before – in the target.

14.65 The parent now has a subsidiary (the target company) which will remain liable for any offences it committed before the takeover. A protest that the crimes committed were 'under the old management' will not avail the subsidiary or the parent.[30] The legal identity of the subsidiary is the same.

---

[26] In cases where a commercial organisation becomes aware of a facilitation payment having been made then it should consider making an authorised disclosure under s 338 of POCA.
[27] MOJ Guidance, p 18 at para 46.
[28] Joint Prosecution Guidance, p 9.
[29] See Chapter 8.
[30] Although in considering remediation the authorities sometimes give weight to the fact that the offences in question are less likely to recur because of the existence of a new management team.

14.66 Corporate lawyers and accountants carry out due diligence enquiries on takeover targets as part of virtually all M&A transactions. These frequently now include specific enquiries about potential liability for criminal offences such as bribery and corruption.

14.67 Where bribery or other fraud is subsequently discovered this may give rise to civil claims against the former directors or owners. However, of course, there is no guarantee that a recovery will be made. In the meantime, the new owners face both the financial and reputational damage which comes with any investigation or conviction of a subsidiary or its officers for a criminal offence.

14.68 To draw some of these issues out, it might help to consider the following fictional scenario.

Scenario B

14.69 Peartree plc manufactures industrial fans and cooling equipment. It has approximately 1,500 employees. It is headquartered in Norwich, but now has its largest markets in developing countries. It has moved assembly of most of its products to Turkey, and equipment from that site is exported to both Europe, the Middle East and Central Asia. It has sales agents in most countries in the world. Its CEO is Alan. Alan serves on various committees and other bodies advising the government on economic policy and is on the board of his local football club. He is a prominent donor to political parties.

14.70 Ten years ago Peartree promulgated a code of ethics. The code included a commitment to abide by all relevant laws. This was also made a terms of its contracts with its sales agents.

14.71 With the advent of the Bribery Act, Peartree recognises that it needs to update and improve its ABC policies and to strengthen its team dealing with them. Lynn has recently been appointed as a compliance officer to the company. In the course of her work she discovers the following facts:

(i) Cargoes to Caravania are shipped in containers. The head of sales is Michael who, informs Lynn that officials of the Caravania customs service are 'on the take'. Each month a member of the customs staff approaches the local shipping agents of goods and asks for a fee, which varies in amount according to the volume of cargo shipped in the previous month. The fee is separate to the amount of import duty payable. The shipping agents recharge these fees to consignees, such as Peartree. On their invoices the fee is described as 'customs service charge'. Michael says that Peartree's contribution is rarely more than $200. He does not object to these payments. He says that 'everyone does it'. He believes that if any consignee refused to pay then the next cargo coming through would be delayed for an indefinite period.

(ii) Peartree is in negotiations for a sales and maintenance contract with the government of Austeristan. Obtaining a visa to enter Austeristan is an extremely time-consuming process. Peartree staff are due to visit in the next fortnight. A minister of the Austeristan government suggests that people from Peartree go to the Austeristan embassy, ask to see a 'Sonja' and pay her £50 per visa in cash, as well as the official visa application fee. If this is done the visa will be issued the next day. The minister explains that this is a way for Austeristan to provide its London-based officials with some hard currency to defray their high living costs.

(iii) Peartree is also in negotiations to take over a US-based company, Hayres International, which manufactures industrial safety systems. Hayres does a lot of business in Europe and has a division making sales in Latin America. The products sold require safety certification. The cost is generally paid by the end user of the system, ie Hayres' customers. However, in Latin America the process to obtain these is extremely slow. It can be speeded up by making what are described as 'speedy service' payments to certain officials. Hayres sales representative in Latin America, Fernando, frequently offers 'to cover initial inspection costs' when selling the equipment – he arranges certification and pays the inspectors $250 on each occasion. The charges are recorded by Fernando in annual returns as 'inspection charges'. Fernando believes that this practice is not illegal under US law, specifically the FCPA. Hayres informs Peartree of these facts as part of the M&A due diligence exercise.

(iv) The Austeristan transaction seems to be stalled, and Alan arranges a meeting with the minister of procurement. Their meeting is 2 hours after Alan is due to arrive. Alan has obtained his visa quickly by providing Sonja at the embassy with £50. On arrival Alan is wearing a diamond-encrusted Rolex watch. At the airport a uniformed man calls him into a small room and, after examining his papers, informs Alan, in broken English, that his visa lacks one of the correct stamps. He shows Alan a copy of a correctly stamped visa which is pinned to the wall, and there is a clear discrepancy. The official says that Alan can either go back to the UK and obtain the correct stamp, or he can get the stamp from airport officials, for a fee of €100 in cash. Without the stamp he cannot enter the country. Alan telephones Lynn to ask what he should do.

(v) Shortly afterwards, another official joins the first, and claims to have found a bottle of Canadian whisky and a bundle of magazines (which are several years old and include such titles as Cosmopolitan and Sports Illustrated) in Alan's bag. Alan is told that the whisky and the magazines are contraband and he has committed the very serious offence of trying to smuggle alcohol and obscene material. He is liable to be handed over to the special police force charged with guarding public morals and held in prison for several weeks without trial unless he pays an immediate cash fine of €1,000. By now, Alan's phone has been taken away by the officials, one of whom remarks: 'That is a very nice watch.'

(vi) A year later, Peartree has managed to win the Austeristan contract, although Alan sent a deputy to the signing ceremony. Someone claiming to be a former employee of Hayres has written an anonymous e-mail to Alan and various other members of the Peartree board. It states that the writer has proof of Hayres' involvement in paying hundreds of small individual kickbacks to safety and procurement officials in both Latin America and Europe, supposedly for speedy service, and that the aggregate amount of these were 'about $80,000 every year'.

14.72 Although in a classroom situation it might be interesting to investigate every possible consequence of these facts and how the Bribery Act might apply, the purpose here is merely to draw out certain points to do with facilitation payments, extortion and M&A risks in particular.

Port services fees

14.73 The port service fees may be facilitation payments or may be more serious bribes, depending on the underlying facts. Although Michael believes that the payments are evidence of the port officials being 'on the take' this should not necessarily be assumed. There seems to be at least some evidence that the fees are charged to all port users on a systematic basis and according to a reasonable basis of calculation (ie by volume of cargo). The important question will be whether the fees are lawful. Evidence of this might include whether receipts are issued, whether the payments are required to be in cash, whether there are published laws or regulations which permit them and so on. This may require local legal advice.

14.74 If the fees are not lawful then it should not be assumed that they are 'only' facilitation payments. If Michael is right that the outcome of not paying them is that the cargo will not pass through customs at all (ie it is not just a question of delay), the officials seem to be basing the exercise of their powers to decide which items can enter upon the payment of illicit fees. Arguably this is not a payment to speed up a 'routine governmental action', but to cause the carrying out of a substantive decision which constitutes an advantage in the conduct of business.

14.75 If the charges really are to avoid a bureaucratic delay then describing them as facilitation payments may be more apt. But it is fair to say that these distinctions can be very difficult to draw at a distance. As a matter of law the distinction does not matter in any event, at least as far as the UK is concerned.

14.76 So Lynn and Peartree face the familiar dilemma of whether to comply with UK law or risk losing business because of delays to shipment of their products. The current ethics code says the company will abide by all relevant laws, but says no more about facilitation payments or other subjects.

14.77 Lynn will have to take the risk of becoming unpopular with Michael and others, and the risk that in the short term the businesses' timetables in relation to this part of the world may be disrupted. She should raise this issue with the relevant authorities within Peartree and make various suggestions on how to combat the practice. These could include (but are not limited to):

- explaining the new policy of the company and UK law to the shipping agents and, if necessary, to the customs authorities;

- obtaining local legal advice as to the legality of the charges, for the purpose (in part) of relying on this as a justification for non-payment to the local authorities;

- explaining to the port authorities that as a UK company, Peartree now requires its agents to have receipts for all business costs;

- if this fails, considering approaching other port users and proposing a collective complaint to the relevant local authorities;

- if this fails, making an individual complaint;

- considering approaching the UK embassy and asking for representations to be made to the government;

- as part of her wider role, including this situation as an example of the bribery risk faced by Peartree and attempting to address it in the company's new procedures;

- as part of her wider role, considering the position of Michael, whether he has breached existing company policy or whether he should be considered a 'whistleblower' and thus protected.

14.78 While these measures are being taken Peartree should not pay the fees. It might perhaps say that they are being kept aside while legal advice is being sought, just in case the fees are valid. Although no doubt there will be oral discussions, Peartree should attempt to record all significant exchanges with local officials in writing.

14.79 If none of these measures proves to be effective, Peartree should continue to refuse to pay and should explore alternatives to mitigate the consequences, such as building in greater lead times to delivery schedules or using different routes to import the goods.

14.80 It must be a matter of individual judgment and legal advice as to whether Peartree should 'self report' the fact that, in the past, it has made these payments to the SFO. If every company encountering these practices were to take this course then the SFO would rapidly become swamped with reports of this nature. On the other hand, the SFO's own guidance mentions the fact that 'the payment(s) came to light as a result of a genuinely proactive approach involving self-reporting and remedial action' as a factor weighing against the public interest in prosecution. It will be interesting to see whether the SFO makes any public statement about the nature or value of cases which require self-reporting.

Cash for speedy visas

14.81 Usually, a cash payment to a government official such as Sonja in exchange for rapid processing of a visa application for business purposes will qualify as a facilitation payment, at least if it is known by the payer that Sonja retains the cash for herself rather than accounting for it to her employer. This assumes that the applicant was entitled to the visa – in other words it is a facilitation payment because it is only the speed of processing, rather than the outcome of the application, that is affected by the payment. Of course, facilitation or not, the payment constitutes a bribe under s 6 and possibly under s 1.

14.82 In this situation there seems to be some official authorisation for the receipt of the payments by Sonja. The minister has said that the staff are allowed (and, it may be, required) to collect small fees in exchange for rapid processing. It is possible that the minister is at the head of a bribe-taking pyramid and is merely giving cover to staff in exchange for his piece of the action. But it is probably going too far to expect a private company such as Peartree to carry out some sort of free-standing investigation of this. It is also quite a serious step to question the honesty or veracity of a minister of the government in relation to a relatively trifling matter. It would be prudent to obtain a letter from an official or some other official record of the stated policy. Beyond this, the marginal benefit of further investigation by Peartree must be questionable.

Inspection costs rebate

14.83 As the port charges case illustrates, there is a line between facilitation payments and more 'serious' bribery which is not always clear. A payment may be expressed to be for speedy service whereas in reality it is to secure the exercise of an official's discretion in favour of the payer. In the case of Hayres and the payments in Latin America, Lynn cannot assume that the payment to the safety inspectors is not to ensure that the systems pass rather than fail rather than to accelerate the inevitable certification. US$250 might well be a significant sum of money to a state official in some South American countries. Hayres has been paying this out as a flat fee in an undifferentiated way. This suggests that these payments could be more serious than mere facilitation payments, despite Hayres' view to the contrary.

14.84 If Peartree buys Hayres as a company it will no doubt seek indemnities in respect of the past liabilities of Hayres from the former owners. These should include criminal and regulatory penalties, back taxes and so on. However, the activities of Hayres in future will be liabilities of Peartree, or at least of the Hayres element of the Peartree Group (assuming Hayres remains as a separate company within the group). Any investigation, penalties or publicity will also have an effect on the reputation of Peartree as a whole even if the parent company is not itself liable and even if contractual indemnities are available to it.

14.85 On a pessimistic assessment, it may be that the practices of Hayres amount to a long-standing scheme of bribery of foreign public officials. Compared to the case of the port fees, there seem to be fewer grounds on which the practices can be excused by an 'extortion' argument. It could be said that, in effect, Hayres was gaining a competitive advantage over others in the market by paying bribes to officials so that their customers would also gain an advantage. Both the UK and the US authorities might well take an interest in such a case.

14.86 Since Hayres is a US company it may be prudent for both Peartree and Hayres to consider whether they should obtain an opinion from the US Department of Justice and perhaps even the SFO in advance of the merger.

14.87 There is some precedent for this in the US. For example, in Opinion Release 08-02 the Department of Justice agreed to a plan whereby Halliburton would not be prosecuted for any (then unknown) FCPA liability which it might acquire through its acquisition of another company. Halliburton gave an undertaking that it would carry out full due diligence investigations of the acquired company's conduct after the merger took place and make any necessary remediation if breaches of the FCPA were found, as well as putting a fully compliant ABC policy in place.[31] As yet, there is no recorded example of the UK authorities taking such a course as a matter of official policy.

Austeristan airport – visa problems

14.88 Let us assume for the moment that Alan's visa is technically invalid because Sonja was not paying attention when she issued the visa. The first official seems to be proposing a speedy service solution – in other words the expedition of a routine government action the performance of which Alan was likely to obtain in any event. As we know, this distinction does not affect potential liability but may affect the seriousness with which the offence is treated by the authorities.

14.89 Again, it is relevant to ask whether the speedy service option is legally permitted. If it is then it will not be bribery because the offer of money will not be to the official personally but to the appropriate state body.

14.90 Faced with the urgent call from Alan, Lynn may have to think very fast and follow her instinct and good sense. The stakes are clearly high, since if he fails to reach the meeting with the minister it could cause the company considerable damage. An important question may be whether there will be a

---

[31] US Department of Justice FCPA Opinion 08-02, 13 June 2008, www.justice.gov/criminal/fraud/fcpa/opinion/2008/0802.pdf.

receipt issued for the new visa stamp, or at least some record that it was obtained as part of a proper and lawful process. Faced with this dilemma many reasonable people might advise that, if there seems to be no alternative but a return to England, the money can be paid for the new stamp and the issue should be raised later with the government. If it turns out that the payment is not lawful then the company should immediately offer remediation and consider self-reporting to the UK authorities.

Austeristan airport – threat of imprisonment

14.91 The second situation at Austeristan airport is much more serious for Alan personally. Let us assume that the whisky and magazines are not his and have been planted by corrupt officials as part of an extortion scheme.[32] He is not in a position to call Lynn or any other source of advice. The threat to his liberty seems very real. He may not be at an immediate risk of violence, but it seems to him that he will not be treated very well in whichever prison he might be held in if he does not comply with the officials' demands. Requests for receipts or a vocal insistence on his rights may or may not be wise for Alan in these circumstances. Most people would accept that someone in this position can be expected to exercise their judgment in good faith about what course to take.

14.92 In these (extreme and unusual) circumstances, it seems defensible for Alan to choose the lesser of two evils and extricate himself from the situation. If it is a question of handing over his watch (as the officials seem to be suggesting) it seems a small price to pay. On his return to the UK Alan should record the incident, perhaps by way of informing the Foreign and Commonwealth Office or other authorities. It seems highly unlikely that a prosecutor would consider that it would be in the public interest to prosecute Alan. If this was ever done, Alan may be able to plead the defence of necessity.[33]

Subsequent allegations

14.93 Let us assume that the anonymous e-mail divulged sufficient information for Peartree to conclude that the author is indeed a former employee of Hayres. There is no doubt that the situation requires investigation. Lynn should probably obtain external assistance in this regard. However, she should work to identify current employees who may be able to help and, if necessary, to secure evidence. Any programme of routine document destruction should be paused in relation to the divisions or business units in question. Ultimately if the allegations are true Peartree, as the parent, and Hayres should consider what steps it should take by way of self-reporting, remediation and improvement of the ABC policy and procedures.

---

[32] Even if they were Alan's property it would, to most people, seem completely wrong to imprison him for an indefinite period merely for having them in his baggage.

[33] See the discussion in Chapter 9.

14.94 A risk which should be borne in mind is the risk that contracts won by Hayres have come about as the result of crime – ie that the proceeds represent the proceeds of crime. If so there is a risk of those proceeds being made subject to a confiscation order.[34] If either company has public reporting obligations (for example, to markets or regulators) these may well be engaged depending on the materiality of the consequences.

Next steps

14.95 Like the first scenario, this scenario is capable of amendment to draw out other elements of the Act in a practical way, perhaps as part of a training programme or seminar. For example, those interested might wish to consider the following questions:

(a) Assume UK law applies to all the UK-based actors outlined in Scenario B above. What offences may have been committed?

(b) In the visas case, imagine that the consular official, Sonja, tells applicants that in fact the minister is mistaken and the correct charge is £100, not £50. Would this matter?

(c) In the port charges case, how should Lynn respond if Michael said that the daughter of the local head of customs was about to get married, and that it would help the situation if he were to make a traditional wedding gift of £500 in cash? Michael would like to draw this from Peartree's local bank account.

(d) In the port charges case, how should Lynn respond to a suggestion that Peartree sets up a local charitable foundation for the education of port workers, to include a biannual scholarship to the University of East Anglia?

(e) In the Hayres case, imagine that the practice of paying local officials was not discovered until a week before the merger agreement was due to be executed by both parties. Alan says to Lynn: 'We can't stop the deal now, why don't we just knock some money off the price and rely on our indemnity?' Is this a sensible way forward?

(f) Would it make a difference if the main reason for Peartree purchasing Hayres was its major contracts with local authorities in European markets – the Latin American business being a very unimportant division?

(g) What investigations into the law of Austeristan should be made (if any)?

---

[34] Proceeds of Crime Act 2001, Part 6. See the discussion of the nature of the offence in Chapter 12 and the remedy of confiscation in Chapter 10.

(h) Would it make a difference to Alan's position if, instead of handing over his watch at Austeristan airport, he made a payment to a specified bank account with his company credit card and, on returning to the UK, he explained it as 'local charitable donation'?

(i) Would it make a difference if the anonymous e-mailer had asked for money in exchange for his silence, failing which he would 'go to the papers'? How should Peartree respond in such circumstances?

(j) How should all or any of these events inform Lynn's work in designing an ABC policy and procedures?

Appendix A

THE BRIBERY ACT 2010

2010 (c) 23

General bribery offences

1 Offences of bribing another person

(1) A person ("P") is guilty of an offence if either of the following cases applies.

(2) Case 1 is where –
- (a) P offers, promises or gives a financial or other advantage to another person, and
- (b) P intends the advantage –
  - (i) to induce a person to perform improperly a relevant function or activity, or
  - (ii) to reward a person for the improper performance of such a function or activity.

(3) Case 2 is where –
- (a) P offers, promises or gives a financial or other advantage to another person, and
- (b) P knows or believes that the acceptance of the advantage would itself constitute the improper performance of a relevant function or activity.

(4) In case 1 it does not matter whether the person to whom the advantage is offered, promised or given is the same person as the person who is to perform, or has performed, the function or activity concerned.

(5) In cases 1 and 2 it does not matter whether the advantage is offered, promised or given by P directly or through a third party.

2 Offences relating to being bribed

(1) A person ("R") is guilty of an offence if any of the following cases applies.

(2) Case 3 is where R requests, agrees to receive or accepts a financial or other advantage intending that, in consequence, a relevant function or activity should be performed improperly (whether by R or another person).

(3) Case 4 is where –
- (a) R requests, agrees to receive or accepts a financial or other advantage, and
- (b) the request, agreement or acceptance itself constitutes the improper performance by R of a relevant function or activity.

(4) Case 5 is where R requests, agrees to receive or accepts a financial or other advantage as a reward for the improper performance (whether by R or another person) of a relevant function or activity.

(5) Case 6 is where, in anticipation of or in consequence of R requesting, agreeing to receive or accepting a financial or other advantage, a relevant function or activity is performed improperly –

- (a) by R, or
- (b) by another person at R's request or with R's assent or acquiescence.

(6) In cases 3 to 6 it does not matter –

- (a) whether R requests, agrees to receive or accepts (or is to request, agree to receive or accept) the advantage directly or through a third party,
- (b) whether the advantage is (or is to be) for the benefit of R or another person.

(7) In cases 4 to 6 it does not matter whether R knows or believes that the performance of the function or activity is improper.

(8) In case 6, where a person other than R is performing the function or activity, it also does not matter whether that person knows or believes that the performance of the function or activity is improper.

3 Function or activity to which bribe relates

(1) For the purposes of this Act a function or activity is a relevant function or activity if –

- (a) it falls within subsection (2), and
- (b) meets one or more of conditions A to C.

(2) The following functions and activities fall within this subsection –

- (a) any function of a public nature,
- (b) any activity connected with a business,
- (c) any activity performed in the course of a person's employment,
- (d) any activity performed by or on behalf of a body of persons (whether corporate or unincorporate).

(3) Condition A is that a person performing the function or activity is expected to perform it in good faith.

(4) Condition B is that a person performing the function or activity is expected to perform it impartially.

(5) Condition C is that a person performing the function or activity is in a position of trust by virtue of performing it.

(6) A function or activity is a relevant function or activity even if it –

- (a) has no connection with the United Kingdom, and
- (b) is performed in a country or territory outside the United Kingdom.

(7) In this section "business" includes trade or profession.

4 Improper performance to which bribe relates

(1) For the purposes of this Act a relevant function or activity –

(a) is performed improperly if it is performed in breach of a relevant expectation, and
(b) is to be treated as being performed improperly if there is a failure to perform the function or activity and that failure is itself a breach of a relevant expectation.

(2) In subsection (1) "relevant expectation" –

(a) in relation to a function or activity which meets condition A or B, means the expectation mentioned in the condition concerned, and
(b) in relation to a function or activity which meets condition C, means any expectation as to the manner in which, or the reasons for which, the function or activity will be performed that arises from the position of trust mentioned in that condition.

(3) Anything that a person does (or omits to do) arising from or in connection with that person's past performance of a relevant function or activity is to be treated for the purposes of this Act as being done (or omitted) by that person in the performance of that function or activity.

5 Expectation test

(1) For the purposes of sections 3 and 4, the test of what is expected is a test of what a reasonable person in the United Kingdom would expect in relation to the performance of the type of function or activity concerned.

(2) In deciding what such a person would expect in relation to the performance of a function or activity where the performance is not subject to the law of any part of the United Kingdom, any local custom or practice is to be disregarded unless it is permitted or required by the written law applicable to the country or territory concerned.

(3) In subsection (2) "written law" means law contained in –

(a) any written constitution, or provision made by or under legislation, applicable to the country or territory concerned, or
(b) any judicial decision which is so applicable and is evidenced in published written sources.

Bribery of foreign public officials

6 Bribery of foreign public officials

(1) A person ("P") who bribes a foreign public official ("F") is guilty of an offence if P's intention is to influence F in F's capacity as a foreign public official.

(2) P must also intend to obtain or retain –

(a) business, or
(b) an advantage in the conduct of business.

(3) P bribes F if, and only if –

(a) directly or through a third party, P offers, promises or gives any financial or other advantage –
   (i) to F, or
   (ii) to another person at F's request or with F's assent or acquiescence, and
(b) F is neither permitted nor required by the written law applicable to F to be influenced in F's capacity as a foreign public official by the offer, promise or gift.

(4) References in this section to influencing F in F's capacity as a foreign public official mean influencing F in the performance of F's functions as such an official, which includes –

(a) any omission to exercise those functions, and
(b) any use of F's position as such an official, even if not within F's authority.

(5) "Foreign public official" means an individual who –

(a) holds a legislative, administrative or judicial position of any kind, whether appointed or elected, of a country or territory outside the United Kingdom (or any subdivision of such a country or territory),
(b) exercises a public function –
   (i) for or on behalf of a country or territory outside the United Kingdom (or any subdivision of such a country or territory), or
   (ii) for any public agency or public enterprise of that country or territory (or subdivision), or
(c) is an official or agent of a public international organisation.

(6) "Public international organisation" means an organisation whose members are any of the following –

(a) countries or territories,
(b) governments of countries or territories,
(c) other public international organisations,
(d) a mixture of any of the above.

(7) For the purposes of subsection (3)(b), the written law applicable to F is –

(a) where the performance of the functions of F which P intends to influence would be subject to the law of any part of the United Kingdom, the law of that part of the United Kingdom,
(b) where paragraph (a) does not apply and F is an official or agent of a public international organisation, the applicable written rules of that organisation,
(c) where paragraphs (a) and (b) do not apply, the law of the country or territory in relation to which F is a foreign public official so far as that law is contained in –
   (i) any written constitution, or provision made by or under legislation, applicable to the country or territory concerned, or

(ii) any judicial decision which is so applicable and is evidenced in published written sources.

(8) For the purposes of this section, a trade or profession is a business.

Failure of commercial organisations to prevent bribery

7 Failure of commercial organisations to prevent bribery

(1) A relevant commercial organisation ("C") is guilty of an offence under this section if a person ("A") associated with C bribes another person intending –

- (a) to obtain or retain business for C, or
- (b) to obtain or retain an advantage in the conduct of business for C.

(2) But it is a defence for C to prove that C had in place adequate procedures designed to prevent persons associated with C from undertaking such conduct.

(3) For the purposes of this section, A bribes another person if, and only if, A –

- (a) is, or would be, guilty of an offence under section 1 or 6 (whether or not A has been prosecuted for such an offence), or
- (b) would be guilty of such an offence if section 12(2)(c) and (4) were omitted.

(4) See section 8 for the meaning of a person associated with C and see section 9 for a duty on the Secretary of State to publish guidance.

(5) In this section –

"partnership" means –

- (a) a partnership within the Partnership Act 1890, or
- (b) a limited partnership registered under the Limited Partnerships Act 1907, or a firm or entity of a similar character formed under the law of a country or territory outside the United Kingdom,

"relevant commercial organisation" means –

- (a) a body which is incorporated under the law of any part of the United Kingdom and which carries on a business (whether there or elsewhere),
- (b) any other body corporate (wherever incorporated) which carries on a business, or part of a business, in any part of the United Kingdom,
- (c) a partnership which is formed under the law of any part of the United Kingdom and which carries on a business (whether there or elsewhere), or
- (d) any other partnership (wherever formed) which carries on a business, or part of a business, in any part of the United Kingdom, and, for the purposes of this section, a trade or profession is a business.

8 Meaning of associated person

(1) For the purposes of section 7, a person ("A") is associated with C if (disregarding any bribe under consideration) A is a person who performs services for or on behalf of C.

(2) The capacity in which A performs services for or on behalf of C does not matter.

(3) Accordingly A may (for example) be C's employee, agent or subsidiary.

(4) Whether or not A is a person who performs services for or on behalf of C is to be determined by reference to all the relevant circumstances and not merely by reference to the nature of the relationship between A and C.

(5) But if A is an employee of C, it is to be presumed unless the contrary is shown that A is a person who performs services for or on behalf of C.

9 Guidance about commercial organisations preventing bribery

(1) The Secretary of State must publish guidance about procedures that relevant commercial organisations can put in place to prevent persons associated with them from bribing as mentioned in section 7(1).

(2) The Secretary of State may, from time to time, publish revisions to guidance under this section or revised guidance.

(3) The Secretary of State must consult the Scottish Ministers before publishing anything under this section.

(4) Publication under this section is to be in such manner as the Secretary of State considers appropriate.

(5) Expressions used in this section have the same meaning as in section 7.
Prosecution and penalties

10 Consent to prosecution

(1) No proceedings for an offence under this Act may be instituted in England and Wales except by or with the consent of –

   (a)   the Director of Public Prosecutions,
   (b)   the Director of the Serious Fraud Office, or
   (c)   the Director of Revenue and Customs Prosecutions.

(2) No proceedings for an offence under this Act may be instituted in Northern Ireland except by or with the consent of –

   (a)   the Director of Public Prosecutions for Northern Ireland, or
   (b)   the Director of the Serious Fraud Office.

(3) No proceedings for an offence under this Act may be instituted in England and Wales or Northern Ireland by a person –

   (a)   who is acting –

(i) under the direction or instruction of the Director of Public Prosecutions, the Director of the Serious Fraud Office or the Director of Revenue and Customs Prosecutions, or
(ii) on behalf of such a Director, or Bribery Act 2010 (c. 23) 7
(b) to whom such a function has been assigned by such a Director, except with the consent of the Director concerned to the institution of the proceedings.

(4) The Director of Public Prosecutions, the Director of the Serious Fraud Office and the Director of Revenue and Customs Prosecutions must exercise personally any function under subsection (1), (2) or (3) of giving consent.

(5) The only exception is if –
(a) the Director concerned is unavailable, and
(b) there is another person who is designated in writing by the Director acting personally as the person who is authorised to exercise any such function when the Director is unavailable.

(6) In that case, the other person may exercise the function but must do so personally.

(7) Subsections (4) to (6) apply instead of any other provisions which would otherwise have enabled any function of the Director of Public Prosecutions, the Director of the Serious Fraud Office or the Director of Revenue and Customs Prosecutions under subsection (1), (2) or (3) of giving consent to be exercised by a person other than the Director concerned.

(8) No proceedings for an offence under this Act may be instituted in Northern Ireland by virtue of section 36 of the Justice (Northern Ireland) Act 2002 (delegation of the functions of the Director of Public Prosecutions for Northern Ireland to persons other than the Deputy Director) except with the consent of the Director of Public Prosecutions for Northern Ireland to the institution of the proceedings.

(9) The Director of Public Prosecutions for Northern Ireland must exercise personally any function under subsection (2) or (8) of giving consent unless the function is exercised personally by the Deputy Director of Public Prosecutions for Northern Ireland by virtue of section 30(4) or (7) of the Act of 2002 (powers of Deputy Director to exercise functions of Director).

(10) Subsection (9) applies instead of section 36 of the Act of 2002 in relation to the functions of the Director of Public Prosecutions for Northern Ireland and the Deputy Director of Public Prosecutions for Northern Ireland under, or (as the case may be) by virtue of, subsections (2) and (8) above of giving consent.

11 Penalties

(1) An individual guilty of an offence under section 1, 2 or 6 is liable –

(a) on summary conviction, to imprisonment for a term not exceeding 12 months, or to a fine not exceeding the statutory maximum, or to both,

(b) on conviction on indictment, to imprisonment for a term not exceeding 10 years, or to a fine, or to both.

(2) Any other person guilty of an offence under section 1, 2 or 6 is liable –

(a) on summary conviction, to a fine not exceeding the statutory maximum,
(b) on conviction on indictment, to a fine.

(3) A person guilty of an offence under section 7 is liable on conviction on indictment to a fine.

(4) The reference in subsection (1)(a) to 12 months is to be read –

(a) in its application to England and Wales in relation to an offence committed before the commencement of section 154(1) of the Criminal Justice Act 2003, and
(b) in its application to Northern Ireland, as a reference to 6 months.

Other provisions about offences

12 Offences under this Act: territorial application

(1) An offence is committed under section 1, 2 or 6 in England and Wales, Scotland or Northern Ireland if any act or omission which forms part of the offence takes place in that part of the United Kingdom.

(2) Subsection (3) applies if –

(a) no act or omission which forms part of an offence under section 1, 2 or 6 takes place in the United Kingdom,
(b) a person's acts or omissions done or made outside the United Kingdom would form part of such an offence if done or made in the United Kingdom, and
(c) that person has a close connection with the United Kingdom.

(3) In such a case –

(a) the acts or omissions form part of the offence referred to in subsection (2)(a), and
(b) proceedings for the offence may be taken at any place in the United Kingdom.

(4) For the purposes of subsection (2)(c) a person has a close connection with the United Kingdom if, and only if, the person was one of the following at the time the acts or omissions concerned were done or made –

(a) a British citizen,
(b) a British overseas territories citizen,
(c) a British National (Overseas),
(d) a British Overseas citizen,
(e) a person who under the British Nationality Act 1981 was a British subject,
(f) a British protected person within the meaning of that Act,
(g) an individual ordinarily resident in the United Kingdom,

(h) a body incorporated under the law of any part of the United Kingdom,
(i) a Scottish partnership.

(5) An offence is committed under section 7 irrespective of whether the acts or omissions which form part of the offence take place in the United Kingdom or elsewhere.

(6) Where no act or omission which forms part of an offence under section 7 takes place in the United Kingdom, proceedings for the offence may be taken at any place in the United Kingdom.

(7) Subsection (8) applies if, by virtue of this section, proceedings for an offence are to be taken in Scotland against a person.

(8) Such proceedings may be taken –

(a) in any sheriff court district in which the person is apprehended or in custody, or
(b) in such sheriff court district as the Lord Advocate may determine.

(9) In subsection (8) "sheriff court district" is to be read in accordance with section 307(1) of the Criminal Procedure (Scotland) Act 1995.

13 Defence for certain bribery offences etc.

(1) It is a defence for a person charged with a relevant bribery offence to prove that the person's conduct was necessary for –

(a) the proper exercise of any function of an intelligence service, or
(b) the proper exercise of any function of the armed forces when engaged on active service.

(2) The head of each intelligence service must ensure that the service has in place arrangements designed to ensure that any conduct of a member of the service which would otherwise be a relevant bribery offence is necessary for a purpose falling within subsection (1)(a).

(3) The Defence Council must ensure that the armed forces have in place arrangements designed to ensure that any conduct of –

(a) a member of the armed forces who is engaged on active service, or
(b) a civilian subject to service discipline when working in support of any person falling within paragraph (a),

which would otherwise be a relevant bribery offence is necessary for a purpose falling within subsection (1)(b).

(4) The arrangements which are in place by virtue of subsection (2) or (3) must be arrangements which the Secretary of State considers to be satisfactory.

(5) For the purposes of this section, the circumstances in which a person's conduct is necessary for a purpose falling within subsection (1)(a) or (b) are to be treated as including any circumstances in which the person's conduct –

(a) would otherwise be an offence under section 2, and

(b) involves conduct by another person which, but for subsection (1)(a) or (b), would be an offence under section 1.

(6) In this section –

"active service" means service in –
    (a) an action or operation against an enemy,
    (b) an operation outside the British Islands for the protection of life or property, or
    (c) the military occupation of a foreign country or territory,

"armed forces" means Her Majesty's forces (within the meaning of the Armed Forces Act 2006),

"civilian subject to service discipline" and "enemy" have the same meaning as in the Act of 2006,

"GCHQ" has the meaning given by section 3(3) of the Intelligence Services Act 1994,

"head" means –
    (a) in relation to the Security Service, the Director General of the Security Service, Bribery Act 2010 (c. 23) 10
    (b) in relation to the Secret Intelligence Service, the Chief of the Secret Intelligence Service, and
    (c) in relation to GCHQ, the Director of GCHQ,

"intelligence service" means the Security Service, the Secret Intelligence Service or GCHQ,

"relevant bribery offence" means –
    (a) an offence under section 1 which would not also be an offence under section 6,
    (b) an offence under section 2,
    (c) an offence committed by aiding, abetting, counselling or procuring the commission of an offence falling within paragraph (a) or (b),
    (d) an offence of attempting or conspiring to commit, or of inciting the commission of, an offence falling within paragraph (a) or (b), or
    (e) an offence under Part 2 of the Serious Crime Act 2007 (encouraging or assisting crime) in relation to an offence falling within paragraph (a) or (b).

14 Offences under sections 1, 2 and 6 by bodies corporate etc.

(1) This section applies if an offence under section 1, 2 or 6 is committed by a body corporate or a Scottish partnership.

(2) If the offence is proved to have been committed with the consent or connivance of –
    (a) a senior officer of the body corporate or Scottish partnership, or
    (b) a person purporting to act in such a capacity,

the senior officer or person (as well as the body corporate or partnership) is guilty of the offence and liable to be proceeded against and punished accordingly.

(3) But subsection (2) does not apply, in the case of an offence which is committed under section 1, 2 or 6 by virtue of section 12(2) to (4), to a senior officer or person purporting to act in such a capacity unless the senior officer or person has a close connection with the United Kingdom (within the meaning given by section 12(4)).

(4) In this section –

"director", in relation to a body corporate whose affairs are managed by its members, means a member of the body corporate,
"senior officer" means –

(a) in relation to a body corporate, a director, manager, secretary or other similar officer of the body corporate, and
(b) in relation to a Scottish partnership, a partner in the partnership.

15 Offences under section 7 by partnerships

(1) Proceedings for an offence under section 7 alleged to have been committed by a partnership must be brought in the name of the partnership (and not in that of any of the partners).

(2) For the purposes of such proceedings –

(a) rules of court relating to the service of documents have effect as if the partnership were a body corporate, and
(b) the following provisions apply as they apply in relation to a body corporate –
   (i) section 33 of the Criminal Justice Act 1925 and Schedule 3 to the Magistrates' Courts Act 1980,
   (ii) section 18 of the Criminal Justice Act (Northern Ireland) 1945 (c. 15 (N.I.)) and Schedule 4 to the Magistrates' Courts (Northern Ireland) Order 1981 (SI 1981/1675 (N.I.26)),
   (iii) section 70 of the Criminal Procedure (Scotland) Act 1995.

(3) A fine imposed on the partnership on its conviction for an offence under section 7 is to be paid out of the partnership assets.

(4) In this section "partnership" has the same meaning as in section 7.
Supplementary and final provisions

16 Application to Crown

This Act applies to individuals in the public service of the Crown as it applies to other individuals.

17 Consequential provision

(1) The following common law offences are abolished –

(a) the offences under the law of England and Wales and Northern Ireland of bribery and embracery,
(b) the offences under the law of Scotland of bribery and accepting a bribe.

(2) Schedule 1 (which contains consequential amendments) has effect.

(3) Schedule 2 (which contains repeals and revocations) has effect.

(4) The relevant national authority may by order make such supplementary, incidental or consequential provision as the relevant national authority considers appropriate for the purposes of this Act or in consequence of this Act.

(5) The power to make an order under this section –
(a) is exercisable by statutory instrument,
(b) includes power to make transitional, transitory or saving provision,
(c) may, in particular, be exercised by amending, repealing, revoking or otherwise modifying any provision made by or under an enactment (including any Act passed in the same Session as this Act).

(6) Subject to subsection (7), a statutory instrument containing an order of the Secretary of State under this section may not be made unless a draft of the instrument has been laid before, and approved by a resolution of, each House of Parliament.

(7) A statutory instrument containing an order of the Secretary of State under this section which does not amend or repeal a provision of a public general Act or of devolved legislation is subject to annulment in pursuance of a resolution of either House of Parliament.

(8) Subject to subsection (9), a statutory instrument containing an order of the Scottish Ministers under this section may not be made unless a draft of the instrument has been laid before, and approved by a resolution of, the Scottish Parliament.

(9) A statutory instrument containing an order of the Scottish Ministers under this section which does not amend or repeal a provision of an Act of the Scottish Parliament or of a public general Act is subject to annulment in pursuance of a resolution of the Scottish Parliament.

(10) In this section –

"devolved legislation" means an Act of the Scottish Parliament, a Measure of the National Assembly for Wales or an Act of the Northern Ireland Assembly,
"enactment" includes an Act of the Scottish Parliament and Northern Ireland legislation,
"relevant national authority" means –
(a) in the case of provision which would be within the legislative competence of the Scottish Parliament if it were contained in an Act of that Parliament, the Scottish Ministers, and
(b) in any other case, the Secretary of State.

18 Extent

(1) Subject as follows, this Act extends to England and Wales, Scotland and Northern Ireland.

(2) Subject to subsections (3) to (5), any amendment, repeal or revocation made by Schedule 1 or 2 has the same extent as the provision amended, repealed or revoked.

(3) The amendment of, and repeals in, the Armed Forces Act 2006 do not extend to the Channel Islands.

(4) The amendments of the International Criminal Court Act 2001 extend to England and Wales and Northern Ireland only.

(5) Subsection (2) does not apply to the repeal in the Civil Aviation Act 1982.

19 Commencement and transitional provision etc.

(1) Subject to subsection (2), this Act comes into force on such day as the Secretary of State may by order made by statutory instrument appoint.

(2) Sections 16, 17(4) to (10) and 18, this section (other than subsections (5) to (7)) and section 20 come into force on the day on which this Act is passed.

(3) An order under subsection (1) may –
   (a) appoint different days for different purposes,
   (b) make such transitional, transitory or saving provision as the Secretary of State considers appropriate in connection with the coming into force of any provision of this Act.

(4) The Secretary of State must consult the Scottish Ministers before making an order under this section in connection with any provision of this Act which would be within the legislative competence of the Scottish Parliament if it were contained in an Act of that Parliament.

(5) This Act does not affect any liability, investigation, legal proceeding or penalty for or in respect of –
   (a) a common law offence mentioned in subsection (1) of section 17 which is committed wholly or partly before the coming into force of that subsection in relation to such an offence, or
   (b) an offence under the Public Bodies Corrupt Practices Act 1889 or the Prevention of Corruption Act 1906 committed wholly or partly before the coming into force of the repeal of the Act by Schedule 2 to this Act.

(6) For the purposes of subsection (5) an offence is partly committed before a particular time if any act or omission which forms part of the offence takes place before that time.

(7) Subsections (5) and (6) are without prejudice to section 16 of the Interpretation Act 1978 (general savings on repeal).

20 Short title

This Act may be cited as the Bribery Act 2010.

Schedules

Schedule 1

Section 17(2)

Consequential Amendments

1 Ministry of Defence Police Act 1987 (c. 4)

In section 2(3)(ba) of the Ministry of Defence Police Act 1987 (jurisdiction of members of Ministry of Defence Police Force) for "Prevention of Corruption Acts 1889 to 1916" substitute "Bribery Act 2010".

2 Criminal Justice Act 1987 (c. 38)

In section 2A of the Criminal Justice Act 1987 (Director of SFO's preinvestigation powers in relation to bribery and corruption: foreign officers etc.) for subsections (5) and (6) substitute –

"(5) This section applies to any conduct –

  (a) which, as a result of section 3(6) of the Bribery Act 2010, constitutes an offence under section 1 or 2 of that Act under the law of England and Wales or Northern Ireland, or
  (b) which constitutes an offence under section 6 of that Act under the law of England and Wales or Northern Ireland."

3 International Criminal Court Act 2001 (c. 17)

The International Criminal Court Act 2001 is amended as follows.

4

In section 54(3) (offences in relation to the ICC: England and Wales) –

  (a) in paragraph (b) for "or" substitute ", an offence under the Bribery Act 2010 or (as the case may be) an offence", and
  (b) in paragraph (c) after "common law" insert "or (as the case may be) under the Bribery Act 2010".

5

In section 61(3)(b) (offences in relation to the ICC: Northern Ireland) after "common law" insert "or (as the case may be) under the Bribery Act 2010".

6 International Criminal Court (Scotland) Act 2001 (asp 13)

In section 4(2) of the International Criminal Court (Scotland) Act 2001 (offences in relation to the ICC) –

(a) in paragraph (b) after "common law" insert "or (as the case may be) under the Bribery Act 2010", and
(b) in paragraph (c) for "section 1 of the Prevention of Corruption Act 1906 (c.34) or at common law" substitute "the Bribery Act 2010".

7 Serious Organised Crime and Police Act 2005 (c. 15)

The Serious Organised Crime and Police Act 2005 is amended as follows.

8

In section 61(1) (offences in respect of which investigatory powers apply) for paragraph (h) substitute –

"(h) any offence under the Bribery Act 2010."

9

In section 76(3) (financial reporting orders: making) for paragraphs (d) to (f) substitute –

"(da) an offence under any of the following provisions of the Bribery Act 2010 –
section 1 (offences of bribing another person),
section 2 (offences relating to being bribed),
section 6 (bribery of foreign public officials),".

10

In section 77(3) (financial reporting orders: making in Scotland) after paragraph (b) insert –

"(c) an offence under section 1, 2 or 6 of the Bribery Act 2010."

11 Armed Forces Act 2006 (c. 52)

In Schedule 2 to the Armed Forces Act 2006 (which lists serious offences the possible commission of which, if suspected, must be referred to a service police force), in paragraph 12, at the end insert –

"(aw) an offence under section 1, 2 or 6 of the Bribery Act 2010."

12 Serious Crime Act 2007 (c. 27)

The Serious Crime Act 2007 is amended as follows.

13

(1) Section 53 of that Act (certain extra-territorial offences to be prosecuted only by, or with the consent of, the Attorney General or the Advocate General for Northern Ireland) is amended as follows.

(2) The existing words in that section become the first subsection of the section.

(3) After that subsection insert –

"(2) Subsection (1) does not apply to an offence under this Part to which section 10 of the Bribery Act 2010 applies by virtue of section 54(1) and (2) below (encouraging or assisting bribery)."

14

(1) Schedule 1 to that Act (list of serious offences) is amended as follows.

(2) For paragraph 9 and the heading before it (corruption and bribery: England and Wales) substitute –

"*Bribery*

9

An offence under any of the following provisions of the Bribery Act 2010 –

    (a)   section 1 (offences of bribing another person);
    (b)   section 2 (offences relating to being bribed);
    (c)   section 6 (bribery of foreign public officials)."

(3) For paragraph 25 and the heading before it (corruption and bribery: Northern Ireland) substitute –

"*Bribery*

25 An offence under any of the following provisions of the Bribery Act 2010 –

    (a)   section 1 (offences of bribing another person);
    (b)   section 2 (offences relating to being bribed);
    (c)   section 6 (bribery of foreign public officials)."

Schedule 2

Section 17(3)

Repeals and Revocations

Short title and chapter	*Extent of repeal or revocation*
Public Bodies Corrupt Practices Act 1889 (c. 69)	The whole Act
Prevention of Corruption Act 1906 (c. 34)	The whole Act
Prevention of Corruption Act 1916 (c. 64)	The whole Act
Criminal Justice Act (Northern Ireland) 1945 (c. 15 (N.I.))	Section 22.

Short title and chapter	Extent of repeal or revocation
Electoral Law Act (Northern Ireland) 1962 (c. 14 (N.I.))	Section 112(3).
Increase of Fines Act (Northern Ireland) 1967 (c. 29 (N.I.))	Section 1(8) (a) and (b).
Criminal Justice (Miscellaneous Provisions) Act (Northern Ireland) 1968 (c. 28 (N.I.))	In Schedule 2, the entry in the table relating to the Prevention of Corruption Act 1906.
Local Government Act (Northern Ireland) 1972 (c. 9 (N.I.))	In Schedule 8, paragraphs 1 and 3.
Civil Aviation Act 1982 (c. 16)	Section 19(1).
Representation of the People Act 1983 (c. 2)	In section 165(1), paragraph (b) and the word "or" immediately before it.
Housing Associations Act 1985 (c. 69)	In Schedule 6, paragraph 1 (2).
Criminal Justice Act 1988 (c. 33)	Section 47.
Criminal Justice (Evidence etc.) (Northern Ireland) Order 1988 (S.I. 1988/1847 (N.I.17))	Article 14.
Enterprise and New Towns (Scotland) Act 1990 (c. 35)	In Schedule 1, paragraph 2.
Scotland Act 1998 (c. 46)	Section 43.
Anti-terrorism, Crime and Security Act 2001 (c. 24)	Sections 108 to 110.
Criminal Justice (Scotland) Act 2003 (asp 7)	Sections 68 and 69.
Government of Wales Act 2006 (c. 32)	Section 44.
Armed Forces Act 2006 (c. 52)	In Schedule 2, paragraph 12 (1) and (m).
Local Government and Public Involvement in Health Act 2007 (c. 28	Section 217(1)(a). Section 244(4). In Schedule 14, paragraph 1.

Short title and chapter	Extent of repeal or revocation
Housing and Regeneration Act 2008 (c. 17)	In Schedule 1, paragraph 16.

Appendix B

THE BRIBERY ACT 2010: EXPLANATORY NOTES

INTRODUCTION

1 These explanatory notes relate to the Bribery Act 2010 (c. 23) which received Royal Assent on 8 April 2010. They have been prepared by the Ministry of Justice in order to assist the reader in understanding the Act. They do not form part of the Act and have not been endorsed by Parliament.

2 The notes need to be read in conjunction with the Act. They are not, and are not meant to be, a comprehensive description of the Act. So where a section or part of a section does not seem to require explanation or comment, none is given.

SUMMARY

3 The purpose of the Act is to reform the criminal law of bribery to provide for a new consolidated scheme of bribery offences to cover bribery both in the United Kingdom (UK) and abroad.

4 The Act replaces the offences at common law and under the Public Bodies Corrupt Practices Act 1889, the Prevention of Corruption Act 1906 and the Prevention of Corruption Act 1916 (known collectively as the Prevention of Corruption Acts 1889 to 1916 and which will be repealed: see Schedule 2) with two general offences. The first covers the offering, promising or giving of an advantage (broadly, offences of bribing another person). The second deals with the requesting, agreeing to receive or accepting of an advantage (broadly, offences of being bribed). The formulation of these two offences abandons the agent/principal relationship on which the previous law was based in favour of a model based on an intention to induce improper conduct. The Act also creates a discrete offence of bribery of a foreign public official and a new offence where a commercial organisation fails to prevent bribery.

5 The other main provisions of the Act include:
- replacing the requirement for the Attorney General's consent to prosecute a bribery offence with a requirement that the offences in the Act may only be instituted by, or with the consent of, the Director of the relevant prosecuting authority.
- a maximum penalty of 10 years imprisonment for all the offences, except the offence relating to commercial organisations, which will carry an unlimited fine;

- extra-territorial jurisdiction to prosecute bribery committed abroad by persons ordinarily resident in the UK as well as UK nationals and UK corporate bodies;
- a defence for conduct that would constitute a bribery offence where the conduct was necessary for the proper exercise of any function of the intelligence services or the armed forces engaged on active service.

BACKGROUND

6 The reform of the law on bribery dates back to the Nolan Committee's Report on Standards in Public Life in 1995 (Cm 2850I), which was set up in response to concerns about unethical conduct by those in public office, and its suggestion that the Law Commission might usefully take forward the consolidation of the statute law on bribery. The Law Commission first made proposals for reform of bribery in a 1998 report (Legislating the Criminal Code: Corruption, Report No. 248).

7 The Government then set up a working group of stakeholders which met over the period 1998–2000, and this was followed in June 2000 by a Government White Paper on corruption (Raising Standards and Upholding Integrity: the prevention of Corruption Cm 4759). This was positively received and led to the publication of a draft Corruption Bill in 2003 (Corruption Draft Legislation Cm 5777). That draft Bill was then subjected to pre-legislative scrutiny by a Joint Committee of Parliament which reported in July 2003 (Joint Committee on the Draft Corruption Bill Session 2002–03 Report and Evidence HL 157, HC 705). The draft Bill failed to win broad support, in particular the Joint Committee was critical of the retention of the agent/principal relationship as the basis for the offence.

8 The Government responded to the Joint Committee's report in December 2003 (The Government Reply to the Report from the Joint Committee on the Draft Corruption Bill Session 2002–03 HL 157, HC 705, Cm 6068). In its response, the Government accepted the Report's recommendations in part but expressed reservations about the suggestions made by the Committee in relation to how the offences should be structured given its rejection of the principal/agent model. A Government consultation exercise, Bribery: Reform of the Prevention of Corruption Acts and SFO powers in cases of bribery of foreign officials, followed in 2005. The Government concluded that, although there remained support for reform, there was no clear consensus on the form it should take. It was therefore decided to refer the matter back to the Law Commission for a further review.

9 The Law Commission's terms of reference were to consider the full range of options for consolidating and reforming the law on bribery. The Law Commission issued a consultation paper, Reforming Bribery (Consultation Paper No. 185), in October 2007. The Law Commission published its report Reforming Bribery (Report No. 313) on 20 November 2008.

10 The Government presented a draft Bribery Bill (Cm 7570) to Parliament on 25 March 2009 which built on the proposals in the Law Commission's report. A Joint Committee of Parliament was established to undertake pre-legislative

scrutiny of the draft Bill. It reported on 28 July 2009 (Joint Committee on the Draft Bribery Bill, First Report, Session 2008–09, HL115, HC430–I & II). The Government responded to the Joint Committee's report on 20 November 2009 (Government Response to the conclusions and recommendations of the Joint Committee Report on the Draft Bribery Bill, Cm7748).

TERRITORIAL EXTENT

11 Section 18 sets out the territorial extent of the Act. Its main substantive provisions extend throughout the UK.

Territorial application: Scotland

12 A legislative consent motion was agreed by the Scottish Parliament on 11 February 2010 under the Sewel Convention. The Convention was triggered as the Act makes provision concerning the criminal law of Scotland in relation to bribery. The Sewel Convention provides that Westminster will not normally legislate with regard to devolved matters in Scotland without the consent of the Scottish Parliament.

Territorial application: Wales

13 The Act applies to Wales as it does to the rest of the UK. It does not change the position as regards the National Assembly for Wales nor does it affect the powers of the Welsh Ministers.

Territorial application: Northern Ireland

14 The Act applies to Northern Ireland as it does to the rest of the UK. It does not change the position as regards the Northern Ireland Assembly.

COMMENTARY ON SECTIONS

Section 1: Offences of bribing another person

15 This section defines the offence of bribery as it applies to the person who offers, promises or gives a financial or other advantage to another. That person is referred to in the section as P. The meaning of "financial or other advantage" is left to be determined as a matter of common sense by the tribunal of fact. Section 1 distinguishes two cases: Case 1 *(subsection (2))* and Case 2 *(subsection (3))*.

16 Case 1 concerns cases in which the advantage is intended to bring about an improper performance by another person of a relevant function or activity, or to reward such improper performance. The nature of a "relevant function or activity" is addressed in section 3. The nature of "improper performance" is defined in section 4.

17 It is sufficient for the purposes of the offence that P intended to induce or reward impropriety in relation to a function or activity falling within section 3(2) to (5). It is not necessary that the person to whom the advantage is

offered, promised or given be the same person as the person who is to engage in the improper performance of an activity or function, or who has already done so *(subsection (4))*.

18 Case 2 concerns cases in which P knows or believes that the acceptance of the advantage offered, promised or given in itself constitutes the improper performance of a function or activity as defined in section 3.

19 Subsection (5) makes it clear that, in Cases 1 and 2, the advantage can be offered, promised or given by P directly or through someone else.

Section 2: Offences relating to being bribed

20 This section defines the offence of bribery as it applies to the recipient or potential recipient of the bribe, who is called R. It distinguishes four cases, namely Case 3 to Case 6.

21 In Cases 3, 4 and 5 there is a requirement that R "requests, agrees to receive or accepts" an advantage, whether or not R actually receives it. This requirement must then be linked with the "improper performance" of a relevant function or activity. As with section 1, the nature of this function or activity is addressed in section 3, and "improper performance" is defined in section 4.

22 The link between the request, agreement to receive or acceptance of an advantage and improper performance may take three forms:

- R may intend improper performance to follow as a consequence of the request, agreement to receive or acceptance of the advantage *(Case 3, in subsection (2))*;
- requesting, agreeing to receive or accepting the advantage may itself amount to improper performance of the relevant function or activity *(Case 4, in subsection (3))*;
- alternatively, the advantage may be a reward for performing the function or activity improperly *(Case 5, in subsection (4))*.

23 In Cases 3 and 5, it does not matter whether the improper performance is by R or by another person. In Case 4, it must be R's requesting, agreeing to receive or acceptance of the advantage which amounts to improper performance, subject to *subsection (6)*.

24 In Case 6 *(subsection (5))* what is required is improper performance by R (or another person, where R requests it, assents to or acquiesces in it). This performance must be in anticipation or in consequence of a request, agreement to receive or acceptance of an advantage.

25 *Subsection (6)* is concerned with the role of R in requesting, agreeing to receive or accepting advantages, or in benefiting from them, in Cases 3 to 6. First, this subsection makes it clear that in Cases 3 to 6 it does not matter whether it is R, or someone else through whom R acts, who requests, agrees to receive or accepts the advantage (subsection (6)(a)). Secondly, subsection (6) indicates that the advantage can be for the benefit of R, or of another person (subsection (6)(b)).

26 *Subsection (7)* makes it clear that in Cases 4 to 6, it is immaterial whether R knows or believes that the performance of the function is improper. Additionally, by subsection (8), in Case 6 where the function or activity is performed by another person, it is immaterial whether that person knew or believed that the performance of the function is improper.

Section 3: Function or activity to which bribe relates

27 This section defines the fields within which bribery can take place, in other words the types of function or activity that can be improperly performed for the purposes of sections 1 and 2. The term "relevant function or activity" is used for this purpose.

28 The purpose of the section is to ensure that the law of bribery applies equally to public and to selected private functions without discriminating between the two. Accordingly the functions or activities in question include all functions of a public nature and all activities connected with a business, trade or profession. The phrase "functions of a public nature" is the same phrase as is used in the definition of "public authority" in section 6(3)(b) of the Human Rights Act 1998 but it is not limited in the way it is in that Act. In addition, the functions or activities include all activities performed either in the course of employment or on behalf of any body of persons: these two categories straddle the public/private divide.

29 Not every defective performance of one of these functions for reward or in the hope of advantage engages the law of bribery. *Subsections (3) to (5)* make clear that there must be an expectation that the functions be carried out in good faith (condition A), or impartially (condition B), or the person performing it must be in a position of trust (condition C).

30 *Subsection (6)* provides that the functions or activities in question may be carried out either in the UK or abroad, and need have no connection with the UK. This preserves the effect of section 108(1) and (2) of the Anti-terrorism, Crime and Security Act 2001 (which is repealed by the Act).

Section 4: Improper performance to which bribe relates

31 Section 4 defines "improper performance" as performance which breaches a relevant expectation, as mentioned in condition A or B (*subsections (3) and (4)* of section 3 respectively) or any expectation as to the manner in which, or reasons for which, a function or activity satisfying condition C (subsection (5) of section 3) will be performed. Subsection (1)(b) states that an omission can in some circumstances amount to improper "performance".

32 *Subsection (3)* addresses the case where R is no longer engaged in a given function or activity but still carries out acts related to his or her former function or activity. These acts are treated as done in performance of the function or activity in question.

Section 5: Expectation test

33 Section 5 provides that when deciding what is expected of a person performing a function or activity for the purposes of sections 3 and 4, the test is what a reasonable person in the UK would expect of a person performing the relevant function or activity. *Subsection (2)* makes it clear that in deciding what a reasonable person in the UK would expect in relation to functions or activities the performance of which is not subject to UK laws, local practice and custom must not be taken into account unless such practice or custom is permitted or required by written law. *Subsection (3)* defines what is meant by "written law" for the purposes of this section.

Section 6: Bribery of foreign public officials

34 This section creates a separate offence of bribery of a foreign public official. This offence closely follows the requirements of the Organisation for Economic Cooperation and Development (OECD) *Convention on Combating Bribery of Foreign Public Officials* in *International Business Transactions*

(http://www.oecd.org/document/21/0,3343,en_2649_34859_2017813_1_1_1_1, 00.html).

35 Unlike the general bribery offences in sections 1 and 2, the offence of bribery of a foreign public official only covers the offering, promising or giving of bribes, and not the acceptance of them. The person giving the bribe must intend to influence the recipient in the performance of his or her functions as a public official, and must intend to obtain or retain business or a business advantage.

36 Foreign public officials are defined in *subsection (5)* to include both government officials and those working for international organisations. The definition draws on Article 1.4(a) of the OECD Convention. Similarly, the definition of "public international organisation" in *subsection (6)* draws on Commentary 17 to the OECD Convention.

The conduct element

37 The conduct element of the offence – what a person must do in order to commit the offence – is set out in *subsection (3)*. The offence may be committed in a number of ways.

38 If a person (P) offers, promises or gives any advantage to a foreign public official (F) with the requisite intention (see below), and the written law applicable to F neither permits nor requires F to be influenced in his or her capacity as a foreign public official by the offer, promise or gift, then P commits an offence.

39 The "written law" applicable to F is defined in *subsection (7)* as the law of the relevant part of the UK where the performance of F's functions would be subject to that law. Where the performance of F's functions would not be subject to the law of a part of the UK, the written law is either the applicable rules of a public international organisation, or the law of the country or

territory in relation to which F is a foreign public official as contained in its written constitution, provision made by or under legislation or judicial decisions that are evidenced in writing.

40 The offence will also be committed if the advantage is offered to someone other than the official, if that happens at the official's request, or with the official's assent or acquiescence.

41 It does not matter whether the offer, promise or gift is made directly to the official or through a third party *(subsection (3)(a))*.

42 The language of the OECD Convention is mirrored in the phrases "obtain or retain business" in subsection (2) and "offers, promises or gives" and "advantage" in subsection (3), and in the words "public function" in *subsection (5)(b)*.

The fault element

43 The fault element of the offence–what a person must intend in order to commit the offence–is specified in *subsections (1), (2) and (4)*.

44 *Subsections (1) and (4)* have the effect that, in order to commit the offence, a person must intend to influence a foreign public official in the performance of his or her functions as a public official, including any failure to exercise those functions and any use of his or her position, even if he or she does not have authority to use the position in that way.

45 In order to commit the offence a person must also intend to obtain or retain business or an advantage in the conduct of business *(subsection (2))*.

46 The effect of *subsection (8)* is that "business" includes what is done in the course of a trade or profession.

Section 7: Failure of commercial organisations to prevent bribery

47 Section 7 creates an offence of failing to prevent bribery which can only be committed by a relevant commercial organisation.

48 "Relevant commercial organisation" is defined *(at subsection (5))* as:
- a body incorporated under the law of any part of the UK and which carries on business whether there or elsewhere,
- a partnership that is formed under the law of any part of the UK and which carries on business there or elsewhere, or
- any other body corporate or partnership wherever incorporated or formed which carries on business in any part of the UK.

49 *Subsection (5)* also provides that "business" includes a trade or profession and includes what is done in the course of a trade or profession.

50 The offence is committed where a person (A) who is associated with the commercial organisation (C) bribes another person with the intention of obtaining or retaining business or an advantage in the conduct of business for C. *Subsection (2)* provides that it is a defence for the commercial organisation

to show it had adequate procedures in place to prevent persons associated with C from committing bribery offences. Although not explicit on the face of the Act, in accordance with established case law, the standard of proof the defendant would need to discharge in order to prove the defence is the balance of probabilities.

51 *Subsection (3)* provides that "bribery" in the context of this offence relates only to the offering, promising or giving of a bribe contrary to sections 1 and 6 (there is no corresponding offence of failure to prevent the taking of bribes). Applying ordinary principles of criminal law, the reference to offences under section 1 and 6 include being liable for such offences by way of aiding, abetting, counselling or procuring (secondary liability). *Subsection (3)* also makes clear that there is no need for the prosecution to show that the person who committed the bribery offence has already been successfully prosecuted. The prosecution must, however, show that the person would be guilty of the offence were that person prosecuted under this Act. Finally, *subsection (3)(b)* makes clear that there is no need for A to have a close connection to the UK as defined in section 12; rather, so long as C falls within the definition of "relevant commercial organisation" that should be enough to provide courts in the UK with jurisdiction.

Section 8: Meaning of associated person

52 Section 8 provides that A is associated with C for the purposes of section 7, if A performs services for, or on behalf of C. It also ensures that section 7 relates to the actual activities being undertaken by A at the time rather than A's general position. The section expressly states that A may be the commercial organisation's employee, agent or subsidiary. But where A is an employee it is to be presumed that A is performing services for or on behalf of C unless the contrary is shown.

Section 9: Guidance about commercial organisations preventing bribery

53 This section requires the Secretary of State to publish guidance on procedures that relevant commercial organisations can put in place to prevent bribery by persons associated with them *(subsection (1))*. The Secretary of State may revise such guidance or publish revised guidance from time to time *(subsection (2))*. The Scottish Ministers must be consulted before publication *(subsection (3))*. The guidance may be published in such a manner as the Secretary of State considers appropriate *(subsection (4))*. The Government has indicated its intention to publish guidance ahead of the commencement of section 7 of the Act (Hansard, House of Lords, 2 February 2010, Vol. 717, col.143).

Section 10: Consent to prosecution

54 A prosecution under the Act in England and Wales can only be brought with the consent of the Director of one of the three senior prosecuting authorities, that is to say the Director of Public Prosecutions, the Director of the Serious Fraud Office and the Director of Revenue and Customs

Prosecutions *(subsections (1) and (3))*. Under subsection (4), the relevant Director must exercise the consent function personally. However, where the Director is unavailable (for example where he or she is out of the country or is incapacitated) another person who has been designated in writing by the Director to exercise any such function may do so, but must do so personally *(subsections (5) and (6))*. Provisions of other legislation which would allow another person to exercise the functions of one of the Directors do not apply to the Directors' consent functions under section 10 *(subsection (7))*.

55 A prosecution in Northern Ireland can only be brought with the consent of the Director of Public Prosecutions for Northern Ireland or the Director of the Serious Fraud Office *(subsections (2), (3) and (8))*. Under subsection (9) the Director of Public Prosecutions for Northern Ireland must exercise the consent function personally unless the consent function is exercised by the Deputy Director (again personally) by virtue of section 30(4) and (7) of the Justice (Northern Ireland) Act 2002. *Under subsection (10)*, section 36 of the 2002 Act, which provides for the delegation of the Director's functions, does not apply in relation to the Director's functions of giving consent to prosecutions under the Act.

Section 11: Penalties

56 Any offence under the Act committed by an individual under sections 1, 2 or 6 is punishable either by a fine or imprisonment for up to 10 years (12 months on summary conviction in England and Wales or Scotland or 6 months in Northern Ireland), or both. An offence committed by a person other than an individual is punishable by a fine. In either case, the fine may be up to the statutory maximum (currently £5000 in England and Wales or Northern Ireland, £10000 in Scotland) if the conviction is summary, and unlimited if it is on indictment. The section 7 offence can only be tried upon indictment.

57 Section 154 of the Criminal Justice Act 2003, which is not yet in force, sets the maximum sentence that can be imposed by a Magistrates' Court in England and Wales at 12 months. Where an offence under this Act is committed before section 154 comes into force, the Magistrates' Court's power is limited to 6 months *(subsection (4)(a))*.

Section 12: Offences under this Act: territorial application

58 *Subsection (1)* provides that the offences in sections 1, 2 or 6 are committed in any part of the UK if any part of the conduct element takes place in that part of the UK.

59 The effect of *subsections (2) to (4)* is that, even though all the actions in question take place abroad, they still constitute the offence if the person performing them is a British national or ordinarily resident in the UK, a body incorporated in the UK or a Scottish partnership.

60 *Subsection (5)* makes it clear that for the purposes of the offence in section 7 (failure of commercial organisation to prevent bribery) it is immaterial where the conduct element of the offence occurs.

61 *Subsections (7) to (9)* provide that where proceedings are to be taken in Scotland against a person, such proceedings may be taken in any sheriff court district in which the person is apprehended or in custody, or in such sheriff district as the Lord Advocate may determine.

Section 13: Defence for certain bribery offences etc.

62 Section 13 deals with the legitimate functions of the intelligence services or the armed forces which may require the use of a financial or other advantage to accomplish the relevant function. The section provides a defence where a person charged with a relevant bribery offence can prove that it was necessary for:

- the proper exercise of any function of one of the intelligence services; or
- the proper exercise of any function of the armed forces when engaged on active service.

Although not explicit on the face of the Act, in accordance with established case law, the standard of proof the defendant would need to discharge in order to prove the defence is the balance of probabilities.

63 The head of each intelligence service is required under *subsection (2)* to ensure that each service has in place arrangements designed to ensure that the conduct of a member of the service that would otherwise amount to a relevant bribery offence is necessary for a purpose set out in *subsection (1)(a)*. A similar requirement is placed on the Defence Council under *subsection (3)* to ensure that the armed forces have arrangements in place designed to ensure that the conduct of any member of the armed forces engaged on active service or a civilian subject to service discipline working in support of military personnel so engaged is necessary for a purpose set out in *subsection (1)(b)*. Under *subsection (4)*, the arrangements must be ones that the relevant Secretary of State considers to be satisfactory.

64 *Subsection (5)* provides that a person's conduct is to be treated as necessary for the purposes of *subsection (1)(a) or (b)* in circumstances where the person's conduct would otherwise be an offence under section 2 and involves conduct on the part of another person which would amount to an offence under section 1 but for the defence in *subsection (1)*. In other words, *subsection (5)* has the effect that a recipient of a bribe paid by a member of the intelligence services or armed forces is covered by the defence in any case where the person offering or paying the bribe is able to rely on the section 13 defence.

65 As well as providing definitions for other terms used in the section, *subsection (6)* makes it clear that a "relevant bribery offence" means an offence under section 1 or 2, including one committed by aiding, abetting, counselling or procuring such an offence, and related inchoate offences. "Relevant bribery offence" does not include a section 1 offence which would also amount to an offence of bribing a foreign public official under section 6. This addresses concerns raised by the Joint Committee on the 2003 draft Corruption Bill in

relation to, in particular, compliance with the UK's obligations under the OECD Convention (see paragraph 152, HL 157 and HC 705, 31 July 2003).

Section 14: Offences under sections 1, 2 and 6 by bodies corporate etc.

66 Section 14 is aimed at individuals who consent or connive at bribery, contrary to section 1, 2 or 6, committed by a body corporate (of any kind) or Scottish partnership. It does not apply to the offence in section 7.

67 The first step is to ascertain that the body corporate or Scottish partnership has indeed been guilty of an offence under section 1, 2 or 6. That established, the section provides that a director, partner or similar senior manager of the body is guilty of the same offence if he or she has consented to or connived in the commission of the offence. In a body corporate managed by its members, the same applies to members. In relation to a Scottish partnership, the provision applies to partners.

68 It should be noted that in this situation, the body corporate or Scottish partnership and the senior manager are both guilty of the main bribery offence. This section does not create a separate offence of "consent or connivance".

69 *Subsection (3)* makes clear that for a "senior officer" or similar person to be guilty he or she must have a close connection to the UK as defined in section 12(4).

Section 15: Offences under section 7 by partnerships

70 Section 15 deals with proceedings for an offence under section 7 against partnerships. Such proceedings must be brought in the name of the partnership (and not the partners) *(subsection (1))*; certain rules of court and statutory provisions which apply to bodies corporate are deemed to apply to partnerships *(subsection (2))*; and any fine imposed on the partnership on conviction must be paid out of the partnership assets *(subsection (3))*.

Section 16: Application to Crown

71 Section 16 applies the Act to individuals in the public service of the Crown. Such individuals will therefore be liable to prosecution if their conduct in the discharge of their duties constitutes an offence under the Act.

Section 17: Consequential provision

72 This section abolishes the common law offences of bribery and embracery (bribery etc of jurors), as well as the common law offence in Scotland of accepting a bribe, and gives effect to Schedules 1 and 2, which contain consequential amendments and repeals.

73 *Subsections (4) to (10)* of this section create a power for the Secretary of State (or, as the case may be, Scottish Ministers) to make supplementary, incidental or consequential provision by order. The order making power is subject to the affirmative resolution procedure where it amends a public general Act or devolved legislation, otherwise the negative resolution procedure applies.

Section 18: Extent

74 This section provides that the Act extends to the whole of the UK and that any amendments or repeals of a provision of an enactment have the same extent as that provision. However the amendment of and repeals in the Armed Forces Act 2006 do not extend to the Channel Islands and the amendments of the International Criminal Court Act 2001 and the repeal in the Civil Aviation Act 1982 do not extend to the Channel Islands, Isle of Man or the British overseas territories

Section 19: Commencement and transitional provision etc.

75 This section provides for commencement. Details are in paragraph 107 below. A commencement order made under this section may appoint different days for different purposes and may contain transitory, transitional or saving provisions. The section also contains express saving provisions so that any offence committed or partly committed before the operative provisions of the Act come into force must be dealt with under the old law.

Section 20: Short title

76 This section deals with citation.

Schedule 1

77 This Schedule contains consequential amendments to other legislation. These are as follows.

Ministry of Defence Police Act 1987

78 Section 2 of that Act gives the Ministry of Defence Police the same powers as normal police, in relation to services property or personnel, including with regard to offences involving the bribery of such persons. That Act is amended to refer to offences under this Act rather than those under the Prevention of Corruption Acts 1889 to 1916.

Criminal Justice Act 1987

79 Section 2A of that Act gives the Director of the Serious Fraud Office power to investigate corruption offences. The amendment replaces the references to the Prevention of Corruption Acts with references to offences under this Act. The offences in question are the bribery of foreign officials (section 6), and the general bribery offence (sections 1 and 2) where the functions in question are performed outside or unconnected with the UK.

International Criminal Court Act 2001

80 Sections 54 and 61 of that Act set out the relevant domestic offences in relation to the International Criminal Court in the law of England and Wales, and Northern Ireland respectively. The amendments make clear that offences under this Act are also relevant domestic offences.

International Criminal Court (Scotland) Act 2001

81 Section 4 of that Act sets out the relevant domestic offences under Scots law in relation to the International Criminal Court. The amendment updates the references to the Prevention of Corruption Act 1906 and to the common law by substituting a reference to the offences under the Act.

Serious Organised Crime and Police Act 2005

82 Chapter 1 of Part 2 of that Act gives investigatory powers to the Director of Public Prosecutions and other prosecuting authorities in relation to offences listed in section 61. This list was amended by SI 2006/1629 to include common law bribery and offences under the Prevention of Corruption Acts. These offences are now replaced by the offences under this Act.

83 A similar amendment applies to section 76 (and section 77 in respect of Scotland), which gives the court power to make a financial reporting order in dealing with a person convicted of (among other offences) corruption offences.

Armed Forces Act 2006

84 Schedule 2 of that Act lists serious civilian offences the possible commission of which, if suspected, must be referred to a service police force. The list of civilian offences is amended to include the offences under this Act.

Serious Crime Act 2007

85 Section 53 of that Act requires the Attorney General's consent prior to commencing proceedings where there is an international element to an offence of encouraging or assisting crime under the 2007 Act. This amendment ensures that the requirement for the Attorney General's consent will not apply in the case of encouraging or assisting bribery by excluding from section 53 any offence to which section 10 (consent to prosecution) of this Act applies.

86 The Serious Crime Act also creates a power to make a "serious crime prevention order" in relation to offences listed in Schedule 1 of the Act. Part 1 of that Schedule, relating to offences in England and Wales, includes offences under the Prevention of Corruption Acts. Those offences are replaced with offences under sections 1, 2 and 6 of this Act. A corresponding amendment is made in Part 2 of the same Schedule in relation to Northern Ireland.

Schedule 2

87 This Schedule contains repeals and revocations.

88 The three Prevention of Corruption Acts are repealed in their entirety. These offences are wholly replaced by the offences under this Act.

89 Criminal Justice Act (Northern Ireland) 1945 (c. 15 (N.I)) – section 22 amended section 4 of the Public Bodies Corrupt Practices Act 1889 and section 2(1) of the Prevention of Corruption Act 1906 to provide for proceedings to be taken in Northern Ireland only with the consent of the

Attorney General for Northern Ireland. Given the 1889 and 1906 Acts will be repealed the section will become redundant.

90 Electoral Law Act (Northern Ireland) 1962 (c.14 (N.I.)) – section 112(3) amended paragraphs (c) and (d) of section 2 of the 1889 Act and will be redundant following the repeal of the 1889 Act.

91 Increase of Fines Act (Northern Ireland) 1967 (c. 29 (N.I.)) – section 1(8)(a) and (b) provide that a court may impose a fine whether greater or less than the amount limited by section 2 of the Public Bodies Corrupt Practices Act 1889 or section 1(1) of the Prevention of Corruption Act 1906 respectively. These references will become redundant once those two Acts are repealed.

92 Criminal Justice (Miscellaneous Provisions) Act (Northern Ireland) 1968 (c. 28 (N.I)) – the entry in the table in Schedule 2 relating to the Prevention of Corruption Act 1906 increased the penalty in Northern Ireland for the offence under section 1(1) of the 1906 Act from 4 months imprisonment to 6 months imprisonment. That entry will become redundant upon repeal of the 1906 Act.

93 Local Government Act (Northern Ireland) 1972 (c.9 (N.I.)) – paragraph 1 of Schedule 8 amended the 1889 Act and will be redundant following the repeal of the 1889 Act.

94 Civil Aviation Act 1982 (c. 16) – section 19(1) designates the Civil Aviation Authority as a public authority for the purposes of the Prevention of Corruption Acts 1889-1916 and will be redundant once they are repealed.

95 Representation of the People Act 1983 (c. 2) – section 165(1) makes certain provision where a candidate at a Parliamentary or local election engages as agent or canvasser an individual who has been convicted and disenfranchised, including under the Public Bodies Corrupt Practices Act 1889. That entry becomes redundant upon repeal of the 1889 Act.

96 Housing Associations Act 1985 (c. 69) – paragraph 1(2) of Schedule 6 provides that the Housing Corporation is a public body for the purposes of the Prevention of Corruption Acts 1889 to 1916. That paragraph becomes redundant upon repeal of those Acts.

97 Criminal Justice Act 1988 (c. 33) – section 47 inserts provisions about penalties into the three Prevention of Corruption Acts, and becomes redundant upon repeal of those Acts.

98 Criminal Justice (Evidence etc.) (Northern Ireland) Order 1988 (SI 1988/1847 (N.I.17)) article 14(1) amended paragraph (a) of section 2 of the 1889 Act and will be redundant following the repeal of the 1889 Act.

99 Enterprise and New Towns (Scotland) Act 1990 (c. 35) – paragraph 2 of Schedule 1 provides that Scottish Enterprise and Highlands and Islands Enterprise are public bodies for the purposes of the Prevention of Corruption Acts 1889 to 1916. That paragraph becomes redundant upon repeal of those Acts.

100 Scotland Act 1998 (c. 46) – section 43 provides that the Scottish Parliament shall be a public body for the purposes of the Prevention of Corruption Acts 1889 to 1916. This section will be redundant once those Acts are repealed.

101 Anti-terrorism, Crime and Security Act 2001 (c. 24) – sections 108 to 110, which extend the geographical scope of the offences under the Prevention of Corruption Acts 1889 to 1916, will be redundant once those Acts are repealed.

102 Criminal Justice (Scotland) Act 2003 (asp7) – sections 68 and 69, which extend the geographical scope of the offences under the Prevention of Corruption Acts 1889 to 1916, will be redundant once those Acts are repealed.

103 Government of Wales Act 2006 (c.32) – section 44 provides that the Welsh Assembly and the Assembly Commission shall be public bodies for the purposes of the Prevention of Corruption Acts 1889 to 1916. This section will be redundant once those Acts are repealed.

104 Armed Forces Act 2006 (c. 52) – those paragraphs in the list in Schedule 2 which refer to offences under the Prevention of Corruption Acts are repealed. This repeal is a corollary of the amendment to that list in Schedule 1 to this Act.

105 Local Government and Public Involvement in Health Act 2007 (c. 28) – section 217(1)(a) gives the Secretary of State power to define an "entity under the control of a local authority" and an "entity jointly controlled by bodies that include a local authority" for the purposes of section 4(2) of the Prevention of Corruption Act 1916. Section 217(1)(a) becomes redundant upon the repeal of the 1916 Act. Paragraph 1 of Schedule 14 to the 2007 Act, which contains amendments to the 1916 Act and section 244(4) which makes provision as to the extent of a repeal contained in that paragraph, are also repealed.

106 Housing and Regeneration Act 2008 (c.17) – paragraph 16 of Schedule 1 provides that the Home and Communities Agency is a public body for the purposes of the Prevention of Corruption Acts 1889 to 1916. This section will be redundant once those Acts are repealed.

Commencement

107 Sections 16, 17(4) to (10), 18, 19(1) to (4) and 20 of the Act came into force on Royal Assent. The remainder of the Act will be brought into force by one or more commencement orders

Hansard References

108 The following table sets out the dates and Hansard references for each stage of the Bribery Bill's passage through Parliament.

Stage	Date	Hansard Reference
House of Lords		
Introduction	19 November 2009	Vol 715 Col 27
Second Reading	9 December 2009	Vol 715 Col 1085–1126
Comittee	7 January 2010 13 January 2010	Vol 716 GC21–GC72 Vol 716 GC83–GC118
Report	2 February 2010	Vol 717 Col 117–187
Third Reading	8 January 2010	Vol 717 Col 481–502
House of Commons		
First Reading		No debate
Second Reading		Vol 506 Col 945–983
Committee	16 March 2010 18 March 2010 23 March 2010	Hansard Public Bill Comittee
Report	7 April 2010	Vol 508 Col 1005–1009
Third Reading	7 April 2010	Vol 508 Col 1009–1015
Consideration of Amendments		
Lords consideration of Commons amendments	8 April 2010	Vol 718 Col 1704–1713
Royal Assent	8 April 2010	Lords: Vol 718 Col 1738
		Commons: Vol 508 Col 1256

Appendix C

MINISTRY OF JUSTICE GUIDANCE, SECTION 9 OF THE BRIBERY ACT 2010

INTRODUCTION

1   The Bribery Act 2010 received Royal Assent on 8 April 2010. A full copy of the Act and its Explanatory Notes can be accessed at: www.opsi.gov.uk/acts/acts2010/ukpga_20100023_en_1. The Act creates a new offence under section 7 which can be committed by commercial organisations[1] which fail to prevent persons associated with them from committing bribery on their behalf. It is a full defence for an organisation to prove that despite a particular case of bribery it nevertheless had adequate procedures in place to prevent persons associated with it from bribing. Section 9 of the Act requires the Secretary of State to publish guidance about procedures which commercial organisations can put in place to prevent persons associated with them from bribing. This document sets out that guidance.

2   The Act extends to England & Wales, Scotland and Northern Ireland. This guidance is for use in all parts of the United Kingdom. In accordance with section 9(3) of the Act, the Scottish Ministers have been consulted regarding the content of this guidance. The Northern Ireland Assembly has also been consulted.

3   This guidance explains the policy behind section 7 and is intended to help commercial organisations of all sizes and sectors understand what sorts of procedures they can put in place to prevent bribery as mentioned in section 7(1).

4   The guidance is designed to be of general application and is formulated around six guiding principles, each followed by commentary and examples. The guidance is not prescriptive and is not a one-size-fits-all document. The question of whether an organisation had adequate procedures in place to prevent bribery in the context of a particular prosecution is a matter that can only be resolved by the courts taking into account the particular facts and circumstances of the case. The onus will remain on the organisation, in any case where it seeks to rely on the defence, to prove that it had adequate procedures in place to prevent bribery. However, departures from the suggested procedures contained within the guidance will not of itself give rise to a presumption that an organisation does not have adequate procedures.

---

[1]   See paragraph 35 below on the definition of the phrase 'commercial organisation'.

5   If your organisation is small or medium sized the application of the principles is likely to suggest procedures that are different from those that may be right for a large multinational organisation. The guidance suggests certain procedures, but they may not all be applicable to your circumstances. Sometimes, you may have alternatives in place that are also adequate.

6   As the principles make clear commercial organisations should adopt a risk-based approach to managing bribery risks. Procedures should be proportionate to the risks faced by an organisation. No policies or procedures are capable of detecting and preventing all bribery. A risk-based approach will, however, serve to focus the effort where it is needed and will have most impact. A risk-based approach recognises that the bribery threat to organisations varies across jurisdictions, business sectors, business partners and transactions.

7   The language used in this guidance reflects its non-prescriptive nature. The six principles are intended to be of general application and are therefore expressed in neutral but affirmative language. The commentary following each of the principles is expressed more broadly.

8   All terms used in this guidance have the same meaning as in the Bribery Act 2010. Any examples of particular types of conduct are provided for illustrative purposes only and do not constitute exhaustive lists of relevant conduct.

GOVERNMENT POLICY AND SECTION 7 OF THE BRIBERY ACT

9   Bribery undermines democracy and the rule of law and poses very serious threats to sustained economic progress in developing and emerging economies and to the proper operation of free markets more generally. The Bribery Act 2010 is intended to respond to these threats and to the extremely broad range of ways that bribery can be committed. It does this by providing robust offences, enhanced sentencing powers for the courts (raising the maximum sentence for bribery committed by an individual from 7 to 10 years imprisonment) and wide jurisdictional powers (see paragraphs 15 and 16 on page 9).

10   The Act contains two general offences covering the offering, promising or giving of a bribe (active bribery) and the requesting, agreeing to receive or accepting of a bribe (passive bribery) at sections 1 and 2 respectively. It also sets out two further offences which specifically address commercial bribery. Section 6 of the Act creates an offence relating to bribery of a foreign public official in order to obtain or retain business or an advantage in the conduct of business[2], and section 7 creates a new form of corporate liability for failing to

---

[2]   Conduct amounting to bribery of a foreign public official could also be charged under section 1 of the Act. It will be for prosecutors to select the most appropriate charge.

prevent bribery on behalf of a commercial organisation. More detail about the sections 1, 6 and 7 offences is provided under the separate headings below.

11   The objective of the Act is not to bring the full force of the criminal law to bear upon well run commercial organisations that experience an isolated incident of bribery on their behalf. So in order to achieve an appropriate balance, section 7 provides a full defence. This is in recognition of the fact that no bribery prevention regime will be capable of preventing bribery at all times. However, the defence is also included in order to encourage commercial organisations to put procedures in place to prevent bribery by persons associated with them.

12   The application of bribery prevention procedures by commercial organisations is of significant interest to those investigating bribery and is relevant if an organisation wishes to report an incident of bribery to the prosecution authorities – for example to the Serious Fraud Office (SFO) which operates a policy in England and Wales and Northern Ireland of co-operation with commercial organisations that self-refer incidents of bribery (see 'Approach of the SFO to dealing with overseas corruption' on the SFO website). The commercial organisation's willingness to co-operate with an investigation under the Bribery Act and to make a full disclosure will also be taken into account in any decision as to whether it is appropriate to commence criminal proceedings.

13   In order to be liable under section 7 a commercial organisation must have failed to prevent conduct that would amount to the commission of an offence under sections 1 or 6, but it is irrelevant whether a person has been convicted of such an offence. Where the prosecution cannot prove beyond reasonable doubt that a sections 1 or 6 offence has been committed the section 7 offence will not be triggered.

14   The section 7 offence is in addition to, and does not displace, liability which might arise under sections 1 or 6 of the Act where the commercial organisation itself commits an offence by virtue of the common law 'identification' principle.[3]

Jurisdiction

15   Section 12 of the Act provides that the courts will have jurisdiction over the sections 1, 2[4] or 6 offences committed in the UK, but they will also have jurisdiction over offences committed outside the UK where the person

---

[3]   See section 5 and Schedule 1 to the Interpretation Act 1978 which provides that the word 'person' where used in an Act includes bodies corporate and unincorporate. Note also the common law 'identification principle' as defined by cases such as *Tesco Supermarkets v Nattrass* [1972] AC 153 which provides that corporate liability arises only where the offence is committed by a natural person who is the directing mind or will of the organisation.
[4]   Although this particular offence is not relevant for the purposes of section 7.

committing them has a close connection with the UK by virtue of being a British national or ordinarily resident in the UK, a body incorporated in the UK or a Scottish partnership.

16 However, as regards section 7, the requirement of a close connection with the UK does not apply. Section 7(3) makes clear that a commercial organisation can be liable for conduct amounting to a section 1 or 6 offence on the part of a person who is neither a UK national or resident in the UK, nor a body incorporated or formed in the UK. In addition, section 12(5) provides that it does not matter whether the acts or omissions which form part of the section 7 offence take part in the UK or elsewhere. So, provided the organisation is incorporated or formed in the UK, or that the organisation carries on a business or part of a business in the UK (wherever in the world it may be incorporated or formed) then UK courts will have jurisdiction (see more on this at paragraphs 34 to 36).

Section 1: Offences of bribing another person

17 Section 1 makes it an offence for a person ('P') to offer, promise or give a financial or other advantage to another person in one of two cases:

- Case 1 applies where P intends the advantage to bring about the improper performance by another person of a relevant function or activity or to reward such improper performance.

- Case 2 applies where P knows or believes that the acceptance of the advantage offered, promised or given in itself constitutes the improper performance of a relevant function or activity.

18 'Improper performance' is defined at sections 3, 4 and 5. In summary, this means performance which amounts to a breach of an expectation that a person will act in good faith, impartially, or in accordance with a position of trust. The offence applies to bribery relating to any function of a public nature, connected with a business, performed in the course of a person's employment or performed on behalf of a company or another body of persons. Therefore, bribery in both the public and private sectors is covered.

19 For the purposes of deciding whether a function or activity has been performed improperly the test of what is expected is a test of what a reasonable person in the UK would expect in relation to the performance of that function or activity. Where the performance of the function or activity is not subject to UK law (for example, it takes place in a country outside UK jurisdiction) then any local custom or practice must be disregarded – unless permitted or required by the written law applicable to that particular country. Written law means any written constitution, provision made by or under legislation applicable to the country concerned or any judicial decision evidenced in published written sources.

20 By way of illustration, in order to proceed with a case under section 1 based on an allegation that hospitality was intended as a bribe, the prosecution would need to show that the hospitality was intended to induce conduct that amounts to a breach of an expectation that a person will act in good faith, impartially, or in accordance with a position of trust. This would be judged by what a reasonable person in the UK thought. So, for example, an invitation to foreign clients to attend a Six Nations match at Twickenham as part of a public relations exercise designed to cement good relations or enhance knowledge in the organisation's field is extremely unlikely to engage section 1 as there is unlikely to be evidence of an intention to induce improper performance of a relevant function.

Section 6: Bribery of a foreign public official

21 Section 6 creates a standalone offence of bribery of a foreign public official. The offence is committed where a person offers, promises or gives a financial or other advantage to a foreign public official with the intention of influencing the official in the performance of his or her official functions. The person offering, promising or giving the advantage must also intend to obtain or retain business or an advantage in the conduct of business by doing so. However, the offence is not committed where the official is permitted or required by the applicable written law to be influenced by the advantage.

22 A 'foreign public official' includes officials, whether elected or appointed, who hold a legislative, administrative or judicial position of any kind of a country or territory outside the UK. It also includes any person who performs public functions in any branch of the national, local or municipal government of such a country or territory or who exercises a public function for any public agency or public enterprise of such a country or territory, such as professionals working for public health agencies and officers exercising public functions in state-owned enterprises. Foreign public officials can also be an official or agent of a public international organisation, such as the UN or the World Bank.

23 Sections 1 and 6 may capture the same conduct but will do so in different ways. The policy that founds the offence at section 6 is the need to prohibit the influencing of decision making in the context of publicly funded business opportunities by the inducement of personal enrichment of foreign public officials or to others at the official's request, assent or acquiescence. Such activity is very likely to involve conduct which amounts to 'improper performance' of a relevant function or activity to which section 1 applies, but, unlike section 1, section 6 does not require proof of it or an intention to induce it. This is because the exact nature of the functions of persons regarded as foreign public officials is often very difficult to ascertain with any accuracy, and the securing of evidence will often be reliant on the co-operation of the state any such officials serve. To require the prosecution to rely entirely on section 1 would amount to a very significant deficiency in the ability of the legislation to address this particular mischief. That said, it is not the Government's intention to criminalise behaviour where no such mischief occurs, but merely to

formulate the offence to take account of the evidential difficulties referred to above. In view of its wide scope, and its role in the new form of corporate liability at section 7, the Government offers the following further explanation of issues arising from the formulation of section 6.

Local law

24   For the purposes of section 6 prosecutors will be required to show not only that an 'advantage' was offered, promised or given to the official or to another person at the official's request, assent or acquiescence, but that the advantage was one that the official was not permitted or required to be influenced by as determined by the written law applicable to the foreign official.

25   In seeking tenders for publicly funded contracts Governments often permit or require those tendering for the contract to offer, in addition to the principal tender, some kind of additional investment in the local economy or benefit to the local community. Such arrangements could in certain circumstances amount to a financial or other 'advantage' to a public official or to another person at the official's request, assent or acquiescence. Where, however, relevant 'written law' permits or requires the official to be influenced by such arrangements they will fall outside the scope of the offence. So, for example, where local planning law permits community investment or requires a foreign public official to minimise the cost of public procurement administration through cost sharing with contractors, a prospective contractor's offer of free training is very unlikely to engage section 6. In circumstances where the additional investment would amount to an advantage to a foreign public official and the local law is silent as to whether the official is permitted or required to be influenced by it, prosecutors will consider the public interest in prosecuting. This will provide an appropriate backstop in circumstances where the evidence suggests that the offer of additional investment is a legitimate part of a tender exercise.

Hospitality, promotional, and other business expenditure

26   Bona fide hospitality and promotional, or other business expenditure which seeks to improve the image of a commercial organisation, better to present products and services, or establish cordial relations, is recognised as an established and important part of doing business and it is not the intention of the Act to criminalise such behaviour. The Government does not intend for the Act to prohibit reasonable and proportionate hospitality and promotional or other similar business expenditure intended for these purposes. It is, however, clear that hospitality and promotional or other similar business expenditure can be employed as bribes.

27   In order to amount to a bribe under section 6 there must be an intention for a financial or other advantage to influence the official in his or her official role and thereby secure business or a business advantage. In this regard, it may be in some circumstances that hospitality or promotional expenditure in the

form of travel and accommodation costs does not even amount to 'a financial or other advantage' to the relevant official because it is a cost that would otherwise be borne by the relevant foreign Government rather than the official him or herself.

28 Where the prosecution is able to establish a financial or other advantage has been offered, promised or given, it must then show that there is a sufficient connection between the advantage and the intention to influence and secure business or a business advantage. Where the prosecution cannot prove this to the requisite standard then no offence under section 6 will be committed. There may be direct evidence to support the existence of this connection and such evidence may indeed relate to relatively modest expenditure. In many cases, however, the question as to whether such a connection can be established will depend on the totality of the evidence which takes into account all of the surrounding circumstances. It would include matters such as the type and level of advantage offered, the manner and form in which the advantage is provided, and the level of influence the particular foreign public official has over awarding the business. In this circumstantial context, the more lavish the hospitality or the higher the expenditure in relation to travel, accommodation or other similar business expenditure provided to a foreign public official, then, generally, the greater the inference that it is intended to influence the official to grant business or a business advantage in return.

29 The standards or norms applying in a particular sector may also be relevant here. However, simply providing hospitality or promotional, or other similar business expenditure which is commensurate with such norms is not, of itself, evidence that no bribe was paid if there is other evidence to the contrary; particularly if the norms in question are extravagant.

30 Levels of expenditure will not, therefore, be the only consideration in determining whether a section 6 offence has been committed. But in the absence of any further evidence demonstrating the required connection, it is unlikely, for example, that incidental provision of a routine business courtesy will raise the inference that it was intended to have a direct impact on decision making, particularly where such hospitality is commensurate with the reasonable and proportionate norms for the particular industry; eg the provision of airport to hotel transfer services to facilitate an on-site visit, or dining and tickets to an event.

31 Some further examples might be helpful. The provision by a UK mining company of reasonable travel and accommodation to allow foreign public officials to visit their distant mining operations so that those officials may be satisfied of the high standard and safety of the company's installations and operating systems are circumstances that fall outside the intended scope of the offence. Flights and accommodation to allow foreign public officials to meet with senior executives of a UK commercial organisation in New York as a matter of genuine mutual convenience, and some reasonable hospitality for the individual and his or her partner, such as fine dining and attendance at a

baseball match are facts that are, in themselves, unlikely to raise the necessary inferences. However, if the choice of New York as the most convenient venue was in doubt because the organisation's senior executives could easily have seen the official with all the relevant documentation when they had visited the relevant country the previous week then the necessary inference might be raised. Similarly, supplementing information provided to a foreign public official on a commercial organisation's background, track record and expertise in providing private health care with an offer of ordinary travel and lodgings to enable a visit to a hospital run by the commercial organisation is unlikely to engage section 6. On the other hand, the provision by that same commercial organisation of a five-star holiday for the foreign public official which is unrelated to a demonstration of the organisation's services is, all things being equal, far more likely to raise the necessary inference.

32 It may be that, as a result of the introduction of the section 7 offence, commercial organisations will review their policies on hospitality and promotional or other similar business expenditure as part of the selection and implementation of bribery prevention procedures, so as to ensure that they are seen to be acting both competitively and fairly. It is, however, for individual organisations, or business representative bodies, to establish and disseminate appropriate standards for hospitality and promotional or other similar expenditure.

Section 7: Failure of commercial organisations to prevent bribery

33 A commercial organisation will be liable to prosecution if a person associated with it bribes another person intending to obtain or retain business or an advantage in the conduct of business for that organisation. As set out above, the commercial organisation will have a full defence if it can show that despite a particular case of bribery it nevertheless had adequate procedures in place to prevent persons associated with it from bribing. In accordance with established case law, the standard of proof which the commercial organisation would need to discharge in order to prove the defence, in the event it was prosecuted, is the balance of probabilities.

Commercial organisation

34 Only a 'relevant commercial organisation' can commit an offence under section 7 of the Bribery Act. A 'relevant commercial organisation' is defined at section 7(5) as a body or partnership incorporated or formed in the UK irrespective of where it carries on a business, or an incorporated body or partnership which carries on a business or part of a business in the UK irrespective of the place of incorporation or formation. The key concept here is that of an organisation which 'carries on a business'. The courts will be the final arbiter as to whether an organisation 'carries on a business' in the UK taking into account the particular facts in individual cases. However, the following paragraphs set out the Government's intention as regards the application of the phrase.

35 As regards bodies incorporated, or partnerships formed, in the UK, despite the fact that there are many ways in which a body corporate or a partnership can pursue business objectives, the Government expects that whether such a body or partnership can be said to be carrying on a business will be answered by applying a common sense approach. So long as the organisation in question is incorporated (by whatever means), or is a partnership, it does not matter if it pursues primarily charitable or educational aims or purely public functions. It will be caught if it engages in commercial activities, irrespective of the purpose for which profits are made.

36 As regards bodies incorporated, or partnerships formed, outside the United Kingdom, whether such bodies can properly be regarded as carrying on a business or part of a business 'in any part of the United Kingdom' will again be answered by applying a common sense approach. Where there is a particular dispute as to whether a business presence in the United Kingdom satisfies the test in the Act, the final arbiter, in any particular case, will be the courts as set out above. However, the Government anticipates that applying a common sense approach would mean that organisations that do not have a demonstrable business presence in the United Kingdom would not be caught. The Government would not expect, for example, the mere fact that a company's securities have been admitted to the UK Listing Authority's Official List and therefore admitted to trading on the London Stock Exchange, in itself, to qualify that company as carrying on a business or part of a business in the UK and therefore falling within the definition of a 'relevant commercial organisation' for the purposes of section 7. Likewise, having a UK subsidiary will not, in itself, mean that a parent company is carrying on a business in the UK, since a subsidiary may act independently of its parent or other group companies.

Associated person

37 A commercial organisation is liable under section 7 if a person 'associated' with it bribes another person intending to obtain or retain business or a business advantage for the organisation. A person associated with a commercial organisation is defined at section 8 as a person who 'performs services' for or on behalf of the organisation. This person can be an individual or an incorporated or unincorporated body. Section 8 provides that the capacity in which a person performs services for or on behalf of the organisation does not matter, so employees (who are presumed to be performing services for their employer), agents and subsidiaries are included. Section 8(4), however, makes it clear that the question as to whether a person is performing services for an organisation is to be determined by reference to all the relevant circumstances and not merely by reference to the nature of the relationship between that person and the organisation. The concept of a person who 'performs services for or on behalf of' the organisation is intended to give section 7 broad scope so as to embrace the whole range of persons connected to an organisation who might be capable of committing bribery on the organisation's behalf.

38 This broad scope means that contractors could be 'associated' persons to the extent that they are performing services for or on behalf of a commercial organisation. Also, where a supplier can properly be said to be performing services for a commercial organisation rather than simply acting as the seller of goods, it may also be an 'associated' person.

39 Where a supply chain involves several entities or a project is to be performed by a prime contractor with a series of sub-contractors, an organisation is likely only to exercise control over its relationship with its contractual counterparty. Indeed, the organisation may only know the identity of its contractual counterparty. It is likely that persons who contract with that counterparty will be performing services for the counterparty and not for other persons in the contractual chain. The principal way in which commercial organisations may decide to approach bribery risks which arise as a result of a supply chain is by employing the types of anti-bribery procedures referred to elsewhere in this guidance (eg risk-based due diligence and the use of anti-bribery terms and conditions) in the relationship with their contractual counterparty, and by requesting that counterparty to adopt a similar approach with the next party in the chain.

40 As for joint ventures, these come in many different forms, sometimes operating through a separate legal entity, but at other times through contractual arrangements. In the case of a joint venture operating through a separate legal entity, a bribe paid by the joint venture entity may lead to liability for a member of the joint venture if the joint venture is performing services for the member and the bribe is paid with the intention of benefiting that member. However, the existence of a joint venture entity will not of itself mean that it is 'associated' with any of its members. A bribe paid on behalf of the joint venture entity by one of its employees or agents will therefore not trigger liability for members of the joint venture simply by virtue of them benefiting indirectly from the bribe through their investment in or ownership of the joint venture.

41 The situation will be different where the joint venture is conducted through a contractual arrangement. The degree of control that a participant has over that arrangement is likely to be one of the 'relevant circumstances' that would be taken into account in deciding whether a person who paid a bribe in the conduct of the joint venture business was 'performing services for or on behalf of' a participant in that arrangement. It may be, for example, that an employee of such a participant who has paid a bribe in order to benefit his employer is not to be regarded as a person 'associated' with all the other participants in the joint venture. Ordinarily, the employee of a participant will be presumed to be a person performing services for and on behalf of his employer. Likewise, an agent engaged by a participant in a contractual joint venture is likely to be regarded as a person associated with that participant in the absence of evidence that the agent is acting on behalf of the contractual joint venture as a whole.

42 Even if it can properly be said that an agent, a subsidiary, or another person acting for a member of a joint venture, was performing services for the organisation, an offence will be committed only if that agent, subsidiary or person intended to obtain or retain business or an advantage in the conduct of business for the organisation. The fact that an organisation benefits indirectly from a bribe is very unlikely, in itself, to amount to proof of the specific intention required by the offence. Without proof of the required intention, liability will not accrue through simple corporate ownership or investment, or through the payment of dividends or provision of loans by a subsidiary to its parent. So, for example, a bribe on behalf of a subsidiary by one of its employees or agents will not automatically involve liability on the part of its parent company, or any other subsidiaries of the parent company, if it cannot be shown the employee or agent intended to obtain or retain business or a business advantage for the parent company or other subsidiaries. This is so even though the parent company or subsidiaries may benefit indirectly from the bribe. By the same token, liability for a parent company could arise where a subsidiary is the 'person' which pays a bribe which it intends will result in the parent company obtaining or retaining business or vice versa.

43 The question of adequacy of bribery prevention procedures will depend in the final analysis on the facts of each case, including matters such as the level of control over the activities of the associated person and the degree of risk that requires mitigation. The scope of the definition at section 8 needs to be appreciated within this context. This point is developed in more detail under the six principles set out on pages 20 to 31.

Facilitation payments

44 Small bribes paid to facilitate routine Government action – otherwise called 'facilitation payments' – could trigger either the section 6 offence or, where there is an intention to induce improper conduct, including where the acceptance of such payments is itself improper, the section 1 offence and therefore potential liability under section 7.

45 As was the case under the old law, the Bribery Act does not (unlike US foreign bribery law) provide any exemption for such payments. The 2009 Recommendation of the Organisation for Economic Co-operation and Development[5] recognises the corrosive effect of facilitation payments and asks adhering countries to discourage companies from making such payments. Exemptions in this context create artificial distinctions that are difficult to enforce, undermine corporate anti-bribery procedures, confuse anti-bribery communication with employees and other associated persons, perpetuate an existing 'culture' of bribery and have the potential to be abused.

---

5 Recommendation of the Council for Further Combating Bribery of Foreign Public Officials in International Business Transactions.

46   The Government does, however, recognise the problems that commercial organisations face in some parts of the world and in certain sectors. The eradication of facilitation payments is recognised at the national and international level as a long term objective that will require economic and social progress and sustained commitment to the rule of law in those parts of the world where the problem is most prevalent. It will also require collaboration between international bodies, governments, the anti-bribery lobby, business representative bodies and sectoral organisations. Businesses themselves also have a role to play and the guidance below offers an indication of how the problem may be addressed through the selection of bribery prevention procedures by commercial organisations.

47   Issues relating to the prosecution of facilitation payments in England and Wales are referred to in the guidance of the Director of the Serious Fraud Office and the Director of Public Prosecutions.[6]

Duress

48   It is recognised that there are circumstances in which individuals are left with no alternative but to make payments in order to protect against loss of life, limb or liberty. The common law defence of duress is very likely to be available in such circumstances.

Prosecutorial discretion

49   Whether to prosecute an offence under the Act is a matter for the prosecuting authorities. In deciding whether to proceed, prosecutors must first decide if there is a sufficiency of evidence, and, if so, whether a prosecution is in the public interest. If the evidential test has been met, prosecutors will consider the general public interest in ensuring that bribery is effectively dealt with. The more serious the offence, the more likely it is that a prosecution will be required in the public interest.

50   In cases where hospitality, promotional expenditure or facilitation payments do, on their face, trigger the provisions of the Act prosecutors will consider very carefully what is in the public interest before deciding whether to prosecute. The operation of prosecutorial discretion provides a degree of flexibility which is helpful to ensure the just and fair operation of the Act.

51   Factors that weigh for and against the public interest in prosecuting in England and Wales are referred to in the joint guidance of the Director of the Serious Fraud Office and the Director of Public Prosecutions referred to at paragraph 47.

---

[6]   Bribery Act 2010: Joint Prosecution Guidance of the Director of the Serious Fraud Office and the Director of Public Prosecutions.

THE SIX PRINCIPLES

The Government considers that procedures put in place by commercial organisations wishing to prevent bribery being committed on their behalf should be informed by six principles. These are set out below. Commentary and guidance on what procedures the application of the principles may produce accompanies each principle.

These principles are not prescriptive. They are intended to be flexible and outcome focussed, allowing for the huge variety of circumstances that commercial organisations find themselves in. Small organisations will, for example, face different challenges to those faced by large multi-national enterprises. Accordingly, the detail of how organisations might apply these principles, taken as a whole, will vary, but the outcome should always be robust and effective anti-bribery procedures.

As set out in more detail below, bribery prevention procedures should be proportionate to risk. Although commercial organisations with entirely domestic operations may require bribery prevention procedures, we believe that as a general proposition they will face lower risks of bribery on their behalf by associated persons than the risks that operate in foreign markets. In any event procedures put in place to mitigate domestic bribery risks are likely to be similar if not the same as those designed to mitigate those associated with foreign markets.

A series of case studies based on hypothetical scenarios is provided at Appendix A. These are designed to illustrate the application of the principles for small, medium and large organisations.

Principle 1: Proportionate procedures

A commercial organisation's procedures to prevent bribery by persons associated with it are proportionate to the bribery risks it faces and to the nature, scale and complexity of the commercial organisation's activities. They are also clear, practical, accessible, effectively implemented and enforced.

Commentary

1.1 The term 'procedures' is used in this guidance to embrace both bribery prevention policies and the procedures which implement them. Policies articulate a commercial organisation's anti-bribery stance, show how it will be maintained and help to create an anti-bribery culture. They are therefore a necessary measure in the prevention of bribery, but they will not achieve that objective unless they are properly implemented. Further guidance on implementation is provided through principles 2 to 6.

1.2 Adequate bribery prevention procedures ought to be proportionate to the bribery risks that the organisation faces. An initial assessment of risk across the organisation is therefore a necessary first step. To a certain extent the level of risk will be linked to the size of the organisation and the nature and complexity of its business, but size will not be the only determining factor. Some small organisations can face quite significant risks, and will need more extensive procedures than their counterparts facing limited risks. However, small organisations are unlikely to need procedures that are as extensive as those of a large multi-national organisation. For example, a very small business may be able to rely heavily on periodic oral briefings to communicate its policies while a large one may need to rely on extensive written communication.

1.3 The level of risk that organisations face will also vary with the type and nature of the persons associated with it. For example, a commercial organisation that properly assesses that there is no risk of bribery on the part of one of its associated persons will accordingly require nothing in the way of procedures to prevent bribery in the context of that relationship. By the same token the bribery risks associated with reliance on a third party agent representing a commercial organisation in negotiations with foreign public officials may be assessed as significant and accordingly require much more in the way of procedures to mitigate those risks. Organisations are likely to need to select procedures to cover a broad range of risks but any consideration by a court in an individual case of the adequacy of procedures is likely necessarily to focus on those procedures designed to prevent bribery on the part of the associated person committing the offence in question.

1.4 Bribery prevention procedures may be stand alone or form part of wider guidance, for example on recruitment or on managing a tender process in public procurement. Whatever the chosen model, the procedures should seek to ensure there is a practical and realistic means of achieving the organisation's stated anti-bribery policy objectives across all of the organisation's functions.

1.5 The Government recognises that applying these procedures retrospectively to existing associated persons is more difficult, but this should be done over time, adopting a risk-based approach and with due allowance for what is practicable and the level of control over existing arrangements.

Procedures

1.6 Commercial organisations' bribery prevention policies are likely to include certain common elements. As an indicative and not exhaustive list, an organisation may wish to cover in its policies:

- its commitment to bribery prevention (see Principle 2)

- its general approach to mitigation of specific bribery risks, such as those arising from the conduct of intermediaries and agents, or those associated with hospitality and promotional expenditure, facilitation payments or political and charitable donations or contributions; (see Principle 3 on risk assessment)

- an overview of its strategy to implement its bribery prevention policies.

1.7 The procedures put in place to implement an organisation's bribery prevention policies should be designed to mitigate identified risks as well as to prevent deliberate unethical conduct on the part of associated persons. The following is an indicative and not exhaustive list of the topics that bribery prevention procedures might embrace depending on the particular risks faced:

- The involvement of the organisation's top-level management (see Principle 2).

- Risk assessment procedures (see Principle 3).

- Due diligence of existing or prospective associated persons (see Principle 4).

- The provision of gifts, hospitality and promotional expenditure; charitable and political donations; or demands for facilitation payments.

- Direct and indirect employment, including recruitment, terms and conditions, disciplinary action and remuneration.

- Governance of business relationships with all other associated persons including pre and post contractual agreements.

- Financial and commercial controls such as adequate bookkeeping, auditing and approval of expenditure.

- Transparency of transactions and disclosure of information.

- Decision making, such as delegation of authority procedures, separation of functions and the avoidance of conflicts of interest.

- Enforcement, detailing discipline processes and sanctions for breaches of the organisation's anti-bribery rules.

- The reporting of bribery including 'speak up' or 'whistle blowing' procedures.

- The detail of the process by which the organisation plans to implement its bribery prevention procedures, for example, how its policy will be applied to individual projects and to different parts of the organisation.

- The communication of the organisation's policies and procedures, and training in their application (see Principle 5).

- The monitoring, review and evaluation of bribery prevention procedures (see Principle 6).

Principle 2: Top-level commitment

The top-level management of a commercial organisation (be it a board of directors, the owners or any other equivalent body or person) are committed to preventing bribery by persons associated with it. They foster a culture within the organisation in which bribery is never acceptable.

Commentary

2.1 Those at the top of an organisation are in the best position to foster a culture of integrity where bribery is unacceptable. The purpose of this principle is to encourage the involvement of top-level management in the determination of bribery prevention procedures. It is also to encourage top-level involvement in any key decision making relating to bribery risk where that is appropriate for the organisation's management structure.

Procedures

2.2 Whatever the size, structure or market of a commercial organisation, top-level management commitment to bribery prevention is likely to include (1) communication of the organisation's anti-bribery stance, and (2) an appropriate degree of involvement in developing bribery prevention procedures.

Internal and external communication of the commitment to zero tolerance to bribery

2.3 This could take a variety of forms. A formal statement appropriately communicated can be very effective in establishing an anti-bribery culture within an organisation. Communication might be tailored to different audiences. The statement would probably need to be drawn to people's attention on a periodic basis and could be generally available, for example on an organisation's intranet and/or internet site. Effective formal statements that demonstrate top level commitment are likely to include:

- a commitment to carry out business fairly, honestly and openly• a commitment to zero tolerance towards bribery• the consequences of breaching the policy for employees and managers• for other associated persons the consequences of breaching contractual provisions relating to bribery prevention (this could include a reference to avoiding doing business with others who do not commit to doing business without bribery as a 'best practice' objective)

- articulation of the business benefits of rejecting bribery (reputational, customer and business partner confidence)

- reference to the range of bribery prevention procedures the commercial organisation has or is putting in place, including any protection and procedures for confidential reporting of bribery (whistle-blowing)

- key individuals and departments involved in the development and implementation of the organisation's bribery prevention procedures• reference to the organisation's involvement in any collective action against bribery in, for example, the same business sector.

Top-level involvement in bribery prevention

2.4 Effective leadership in bribery prevention will take a variety of forms appropriate for and proportionate to the organisation's size, management structure and circumstances. In smaller organisations a proportionate response may require top-level managers to be personally involved in initiating, developing and implementing bribery prevention procedures and bribery critical decision making. In a large multi-national organisation the board should be responsible for setting bribery prevention policies, tasking management to design, operate and monitor bribery prevention procedures, and keeping these policies and procedures under regular review. But whatever the appropriate model, top-level engagement is likely to reflect the following elements:

- Selection and training of senior managers to lead anti-bribery work where appropriate.

- Leadership on key measures such as a code of conduct.

- Endorsement of all bribery prevention related publications.

- Leadership in awareness raising and encouraging transparent dialogue throughout the organisation so as to seek to ensure effective dissemination of anti-bribery policies and procedures to employees, subsidiaries, and associated persons, etc.

- Engagement with relevant associated persons and external bodies, such as sectoral organisations and the media, to help articulate the organisation's policies.

- Specific involvement in high profile and critical decision making where appropriate.

- Assurance of risk assessment.

- General oversight of breaches of procedures and the provision of feedback to the board or equivalent, where appropriate, on levels of compliance.

Principle 3: Risk Assessment

The commercial organisation assesses the nature and extent of its exposure to potential external and internal risks of bribery on its behalf by persons associated with it. The assessment is periodic, informed and documented.

Commentary

3.1 For many commercial organisations this principle will manifest itself as part of a more general risk assessment carried out in relation to business objectives. For others, its application may produce a more specific stand alone bribery risk assessment. The purpose of this principle is to promote the adoption of risk assessment procedures that are proportionate to the organisation's size and structure and to the nature, scale and location of its activities. But whatever approach is adopted the fuller the understanding of the bribery risks an organisation faces the more effective its efforts to prevent bribery are likely to be.

3.2 Some aspects of risk assessment involve procedures that fall within the generally accepted meaning of the term 'due diligence'. The role of due diligence as a risk mitigation tool is separately dealt with under Principle 4.

Procedures

3.3 Risk assessment procedures that enable the commercial organisation accurately to identify and prioritise the risks it faces will, whatever its size, activities, customers or markets, usually reflect a few basic characteristics. These are:

- Oversight of the risk assessment by top level management.

- Appropriate resourcing – this should reflect the scale of the organisation's business and the need to identify and prioritise all relevant risks.

- Identification of the internal and external information sources that will enable risk to be assessed and reviewed.

- Due diligence enquiries (see Principle 4).

- Accurate and appropriate documentation of the risk assessment and its conclusions.

3.4 As a commercial organisation's business evolves, so will the bribery risks it faces and hence so should its risk assessment. For example, the risk assessment that applies to a commercial organisation's domestic operations might not apply when it enters a new market in a part of the world in which it has not done business before (see Principle 6 for more on this).

Commonly encountered risks

3.5 Commonly encountered external risks can be categorised into five broad groups – country, sectoral, transaction, business opportunity and business partnership:

- *Country risk:* this is evidenced by perceived high levels of corruption, an absence of effectively implemented anti-bribery legislation and a failure of the foreign government, media, local business community and civil society effectively to promote transparent procurement and investment policies.

- *Sectoral risk:* some sectors are higher risk than others. Higher risk sectors include the extractive industries and the large scale infrastructure sector.

- *Transaction risk:* certain types of transaction give rise to higher risks, for example, charitable or political contributions, licences and permits, and transactions relating to public procurement.

- *Business opportunity risk:* such risks might arise in high value projects or with projects involving many contractors or intermediaries; or with projects which are not apparently undertaken at market prices, or which do not have a clear legitimate objective.

- *Business partnership risk:* certain relationships may involve higher risk, for example, the use of intermediaries in transactions with foreign public officials; consortia or joint venture partners; and relationships with politically exposed persons where the proposed business relationship involves, or is linked to, a prominent public official.

3.6 An assessment of external bribery risks is intended to help decide how those risks can be mitigated by procedures governing the relevant operations or business relationships; but a bribery risk assessment should also examine the extent to which internal structures or procedures may themselves add to the level of risk. Commonly encountered internal factors may include:

- deficiencies in employee training, skills and knowledge,

- bonus culture that rewards excessive risk taking,

- lack of clarity in the organisation's policies on, and procedures for, hospitality and promotional expenditure, and political or charitable contributions,

- lack of clear financial controls,

- lack of a clear anti-bribery message from the top-level management.

Principle 4: Due diligence

The commercial organisation applies due diligence procedures, taking a proportionate and risk based approach, in respect of persons who perform or will perform services for or on behalf of the organisation, in order to mitigate identified bribery risks.

Commentary

4.1 Due diligence is firmly established as an element of corporate good governance and it is envisaged that due diligence related to bribery prevention will often form part of a wider due diligence framework. Due diligence procedures are both a form of bribery risk assessment (see Principle 3) and a means of mitigating a risk. By way of illustration, a commercial organisation may identify risks that as a general proposition attach to doing business in reliance upon local third party intermediaries. Due diligence of specific prospective third party intermediaries could significantly mitigate these risks. The significance of the role of due diligence in bribery risk mitigation justifies its inclusion here as a Principle in its own right.

4.2 The purpose of this Principle is to encourage commercial organisations to put in place due diligence procedures that adequately inform the application of proportionate measures designed to prevent persons associated with them from bribing on their behalf.

Procedures

4.3 As this guidance emphasises throughout, due diligence procedures should be proportionate to the identified risk. They can also be undertaken internally or by external consultants. A person 'associated' with a commercial organisation as set out at section 8 of the Bribery Act includes any person performing services for a commercial organisation. As explained at paragraphs 37 to 43 in the section 'Government Policy and section 7', the scope of this definition is broad and can embrace a wide range of business relationships. But the appropriate level of due diligence to prevent bribery will vary enormously depending on the risks arising from the particular relationship. So, for example, the appropriate level of due diligence required by a commercial organisation when contracting for the performance of information technology services may be low, to reflect low risks of bribery on its behalf. In contrast, an organisation that is selecting an intermediary to assist in establishing a business in foreign markets will typically require a much higher level of due diligence to mitigate the risks of bribery on its behalf.

4.4 Organisations will need to take considerable care in entering into certain business relationships, due to the particular circumstances in which the relationships come into existence. An example is where local law or convention dictates the use of local agents in circumstances where it may be difficult for a commercial organisation to extricate itself from a business relationship once established. The importance of thorough due diligence and risk mitigation prior to any commitment are paramount in such circumstances. Another relationship that carries particularly important due diligence implications is a merger of commercial organisations or an acquisition of one by another.

4.5 'Due diligence' for the purposes of Principle 4 should be conducted using a risk-based approach (as referred to on page 27). For example, in lower risk situations, commercial organisations may decide that there is no need to conduct much in the way of due diligence. In higher risk situations, due diligence may include conducting direct interrogative enquiries, indirect investigations, or general research on proposed associated persons. Appraisal and continued monitoring of recruited or engaged 'associated' persons may also be required, proportionate to the identified risks. Generally, more information is likely to be required from prospective and existing associated persons that are incorporated (eg companies) than from individuals. This is because on a basic level more individuals are likely to be involved in the performance of services by a company and the exact nature of the roles of such individuals or other connected bodies may not be immediately obvious. Accordingly, due diligence may involve direct requests for details on the background, expertise and business experience, of relevant individuals. This information can then be verified through research and the following up of references, etc.

4.6 A commercial organisation's employees are presumed to be persons 'associated' with the organisation for the purposes of the Bribery Act. The organisation may wish, therefore, to incorporate in its recruitment and human resources procedures an appropriate level of due diligence to mitigate the risks of bribery being undertaken by employees which is proportionate to the risk associated with the post in question. Due diligence is unlikely to be needed in relation to lower risk posts.

Principle 5: Communication (including training)

The commercial organisation seeks to ensure that its bribery prevention policies and procedures are embedded and understood throughout the organisation through internal and external communication, including training, that is proportionate to the risks it faces.

Commentary

5.1 Communication and training deters bribery by associated persons by enhancing awareness and understanding of a commercial organisation's procedures and to the organisation's commitment to their proper application.

Making information available assists in more effective monitoring, evaluation and review of bribery prevention procedures. Training provides the knowledge and skills needed to employ the organisation's procedures and deal with any bribery related problems or issues that may arise.

Procedures

Communication

5.2 The content, language and tone of communications for internal consumption may vary from that for external use in response to the different relationship the audience has with the commercial organisation. The nature of communication will vary enormously between commercial organisations in accordance with the different bribery risks faced, the size of the organisation and the scale and nature of its activities.

5.3 Internal communications should convey the 'tone from the top' but are also likely to focus on the implementation of the organisation's policies and procedures and the implications for employees. Such communication includes policies on particular areas such as decision making, financial control, hospitality and promotional expenditure, facilitation payments, training, charitable and political donations and penalties for breach of rules and the articulation of management roles at different levels. Another important aspect of internal communications is the establishment of a secure, confidential and accessible means for internal or external parties to raise concerns about bribery on the part of associated persons, to provide suggestions for improvement of bribery prevention procedures and controls and for requesting advice. These so called 'speak up' procedures can amount to a very helpful management tool for commercial organisations with diverse operations that may be in many countries. If these procedures are to be effective there must be adequate protection for those reporting concerns.

5.4 External communication of bribery prevention policies through a statement or codes of conduct, for example, can reassure existing and prospective associated persons and can act as a deterrent to those intending to bribe on a commercial organisation's behalf. Such communications can include information on bribery prevention procedures and controls, sanctions, results of internal surveys, rules governing recruitment, procurement and tendering. A commercial organisation may consider it proportionate and appropriate to communicate its anti-bribery policies and commitment to them to a wider audience, such as other organisations in its sector and to sectoral organisations that would fall outside the scope of the range of its associated persons, or to the general public.

Training

5.5 Like all procedures training should be proportionate to risk but some training is likely to be effective in firmly establishing an anti-bribery culture whatever the level of risk. Training may take the form of education and awareness raising about the threats posed by bribery in general and in the sector or areas in which the organisation operates in particular, and the various ways it is being addressed.

5.6 General training could be mandatory for new employees or for agents (on a weighted risk basis) as part of an induction process, but it should also be tailored to the specific risks associated with specific posts. Consideration should also be given to tailoring training to the special needs of those involved in any 'speak up' procedures, and higher risk functions such as purchasing, contracting, distribution and marketing, and working in high risk countries. Effective training is continuous, and regularly monitored and evaluated.

5.7 It may be appropriate to require associated persons to undergo training. This will be particularly relevant for high risk associated persons. In any event, organisations may wish to encourage associated persons to adopt bribery prevention training.

5.8 Nowadays there are many different training formats available in addition to the traditional classroom or seminar formats, such as e-learning and other web-based tools. But whatever the format, the training ought to achieve its objective of ensuring that those participating in it develop a firm understanding of what the relevant policies and procedures mean in practice for them.

Principle 6: Monitoring and review

The commercial organisation monitors and reviews procedures designed to prevent bribery by persons associated with it and makes improvements where necessary.

Commentary

6.1 The bribery risks that a commercial organisation faces may change over time, as may the nature and scale of its activities, so the procedures required to mitigate those risks are also likely to change. Commercial organisations will therefore wish to consider how to monitor and evaluate the effectiveness of their bribery prevention procedures and adapt them where necessary. In addition to regular monitoring, an organisation might want to review its processes in response to other stimuli, for example governmental changes in countries in which they operate, an incident of bribery or negative press reports.

Procedures

6.2 There is a wide range of internal and external review mechanisms which commercial organisations could consider using. Systems set up to deter, detect and investigate bribery, and monitor the ethical quality of transactions, such as internal financial control mechanisms, will help provide insight into the effectiveness of procedures designed to prevent bribery. Staff surveys, questionnaires and feedback from training can also provide an important source of information on effectiveness and a means by which employees and other associated persons can inform continuing improvement of anti-bribery policies.

6.3 Organisations could also consider formal periodic reviews and reports for top-level management. Organisations could also draw on information on other organisations' practices, for example relevant trade bodies or regulators might highlight examples of good or bad practice in their publications.

6.4 In addition, organisations might wish to consider seeking some form of external verification or assurance of the effectiveness of anti-bribery procedures. Some organisations may be able to apply for certified compliance with one of the independently-verified anti-bribery standards maintained by industrial sector associations or multilateral bodies. However, such certification may not necessarily mean that a commercial organisation's bribery prevention procedures are 'adequate' for all purposes where an offence under section 7 of the Bribery Act could be charged.

APPENDIX A: BRIBERY ACT 2010 CASE STUDIES

Introduction

These case studies (which do not form part of the guidance issued under section 9 of the Act) look at how the application of the six principles might relate to a number of hypothetical scenarios commercial organisations may encounter. The Government believes that this illustrative context can assist commercial organisations in deciding what procedures to prevent persons associated with them from bribing on their behalf might be most suitable to their needs.

These case studies are illustrative. They are intended to complement the guidance. They do not replace or supersede any of the principles. The considerations set out below merely show in some circumstances how the principles can be applied, and should not be seen as standard setting, establishing any presumption, reflecting a minimum baseline of action or being appropriate for all organisations whatever their size. Accordingly, the considerations set out below are not:

- comprehensive of all considerations in all circumstances;

- conclusive of adequate procedures;

- conclusive of inadequate procedures if not all of the considerations are considered and/or applied.

All but one of these case studies focus on bribery risks associated with foreign markets. This is because bribery risks associated with foreign markets are generally higher than those associated with domestic markets. Accordingly case studies focussing on foreign markets are better suited as vehicles for the illustration of bribery prevention procedures.

Case study 1 – Principle 1 – Facilitation payments

A medium sized company ('A') has acquired a new customer in a foreign country ('B') where it operates through its agent company ('C'). Its bribery risk assessment has identified facilitation payments as a significant problem in securing reliable importation into B and transport to its new customer's manufacturing locations. These sometimes take the form of 'inspection fees' required before B's import inspectors will issue a certificate of inspection and thereby facilitate the clearance of goods.

A could consider any or a combination of the following:

- Communication of its policy of non-payment of facilitation payments to C and its staff.

- Seeking advice on the law of B relating to certificates of inspection and fees for these to differentiate between properly payable fees and disguised requests for facilitation payments.

- Building realistic timescales into the planning of the project so that shipping, importation and delivery schedules allow where feasible for resisting and testing demands for facilitation payments.

- Requesting that C train its staff about resisting demands for facilitation payments and the relevant local law and provisions of the Bribery Act 2010.

- Proposing or including as part of any contractual arrangement certain procedures for C and its staff, which may include one or more of the following, if appropriate:

    - questioning of legitimacy of demands
    - requesting receipts and identification details of the official making the demand
    - requests to consult with superior officials
    - trying to avoid paying 'inspection fees' (if not properly due) in cash and directly to an official
    - informing those demanding payments that compliance with the demand may mean that A (and possibly C) will commit an offence under UK law
    - informing those demanding payments that it will be necessary for C to inform the UK embassy of the demand.

- Maintaining close liaison with C so as to keep abreast of any local developments that may provide solutions and encouraging C to develop its own strategies based on local knowledge.

- Use of any UK diplomatic channels or participation in locally active non-governmental organisations, so as to apply pressure on the authorities of B to take action to stop demands for facilitation payments.

Case study 2 – Principle 1 – Proportionate Procedures

A small to medium sized installation company is operating entirely within the United Kingdom domestic market. It relies to varying degrees on independent consultants to facilitate business opportunities and to assist in the preparation of both pre-qualification submissions and formal tenders in seeking new business. Such consultants work on an arms-length-fee-plus-expenses basis. They are engaged by sales staff and selected because of their extensive network of business contacts and the specialist information they have. The reason for engaging them is to enhance the company's prospects of being included in tender and pre-qualification lists and of being selected as main or sub-contractors. The reliance on consultants and, in particular, difficulties in monitoring expenditure which sometimes involves cash transactions has been identified by the company as a source of medium to high risk of bribery being undertaken on the company's behalf.

In seeking to mitigate these risks the company could consider any or a combination of the following:

- Communication of a policy statement committing it to transparency and zero tolerance of bribery in pursuit of its business objectives. The statement could be communicated to the company's employees, known consultants and external contacts, such as sectoral bodies and local chambers of commerce.

- Firming up its due diligence before engaging consultants. This could include making enquiries through business contacts, local chambers of commerce, business associations, or internet searches and following up any business references and financial statements.

- Considering firming up the terms of the consultants' contracts so that they reflect a commitment to zero tolerance of bribery, set clear criteria for provision of bona fide hospitality on the company's behalf and define in detail the basis of remuneration, including expenses.

- Consider making consultants' contracts subject to periodic review and renewal.

- Drawing up key points guidance on preventing bribery for its sales staff and all other staff involved in bidding for business and when engaging consultants

- Periodically emphasising these policies and procedures at meetings – for example, this might form a standing item on meeting agendas every few months.

- Providing a confidential means for staff and external business contacts to air any suspicions of the use of bribery on the company's behalf.

Case study 3 – Principles 1 and 6 – Joint venture

A medium sized company ('D') is interested in significant foreign mineral deposits. D proposes to enter into a joint venture with a local mining company ('E'). It is proposed that D and E would have an equal holding in the joint venture company ('DE'). D identifies the necessary interaction between DE and local public officials as a source of significant risks of bribery.

D could consider negotiating for the inclusion of any or a combination of the following bribery prevention procedures into the agreement setting up DE:

- Parity of representation on the board of DE.

- That DE put in place measures designed to ensure compliance with all applicable bribery and corruption laws. These measures might cover such issues as:

    – gifts and hospitality
    – agreed decision making rules
    – procurement
    – engagement of third parties, including due diligence requirements
    – conduct of relations with public officials
    – training for staff in high risk positions
    – record keeping and accounting.

- The establishment of an audit committee with at least one representative of each of D and E that has the power to view accounts and certain expenditure and prepare regular reports.

- Binding commitments by D and E to comply with all applicable bribery laws in relation to the operation of DE, with a breach by either D or E being a breach of the agreement between them. Where such a breach is a material breach this could lead to termination or other similarly significant consequences.

Case study 4 – Principles 1 and 5 – Hospitality and Promotional expenditure

A firm of engineers ('F') maintains a programme of annual events providing entertainment, quality dining and attendance at various sporting occasions, as an expression of appreciation of its long association with its business partners. Private bodies and individuals are happy to meet their own travel and accommodation costs associated with attending these events. The costs of the travel and accommodation of any foreign public officials attending are, however, met by F.

F could consider any or a combination of the following:

- Conducting a bribery risk assessment relating to its dealings with business partners and foreign public officials and in particular the provision of hospitality and promotional expenditure.

- Publication of a policy statement committing it to transparent, proportionate, reasonable and bona fide hospitality and promotional expenditure.

- The issue of internal guidance on procedures that apply to the provision of hospitality and/or promotional expenditure providing:
    - that any procedures are designed to seek to ensure transparency and conformity with any relevant laws and codes applying to F
    - that any procedures are designed to seek to ensure transparency and conformity with the relevant laws and codes applying to foreign public officials
    - that any hospitality should reflect a desire to cement good relations and show appreciation, and that promotional expenditure should seek to improve the image of F as a commercial organisation, to better present its products or services, or establish cordial relations
    - that the recipient should not be given the impression that they are under an obligation to confer any business advantage or that the recipient's independence will be affected
    - criteria to be applied when deciding the appropriate levels of hospitality for both private and public business partners, clients, suppliers and foreign public officials and the type of hospitality that is appropriate in different sets of circumstances
    - that provision of hospitality for public officials be cleared with the relevant public body so that it is clear who and what the hospitality is for
    - for expenditure over certain limits, approval by an appropriately senior level of management may be a relevant consideration
    - accounting (book-keeping, orders, invoices, delivery notes, etc).

- Regular monitoring, review and evaluation of internal procedures and compliance with them.

- Appropriate training and supervision provided to staff.

Case study 5 – Principle 3 – Assessing risks

A small specialist manufacturer is seeking to expand its business in one of several emerging markets, all of which offer comparable opportunities. It has no specialist risk assessment expertise and is unsure how to go about assessing the risks of entering a new market.

The small manufacturer could consider any or a combination of the following:

- Incorporating an assessment of bribery risk into research to identify the optimum market for expansion.

- Seeking advice from UK diplomatic services and government organisations such as UK Trade and Investment.

- Consulting general country assessments undertaken by local chambers of commerce, relevant non-governmental organisations and sectoral organisations.

- Seeking advice from industry representatives.

- Following up any general or specialist advice with further independent research.

Case study 6 – Principle 4 – Due diligence of agents

A medium to large sized manufacturer of specialist equipment ('G') has an opportunity to enter an emerging market in a foreign country ('H') by way of a government contract to supply equipment to the state. Local convention requires any foreign commercial organisations to operate through a local agent. G is concerned to appoint a reputable agent and ensure that the risk of bribery being used to develop its business in the market is minimised.

G could consider any or a combination of the following:

- Compiling a suitable questionnaire for potential agents requiring for example, details of ownership if not an individual; CVs and references for those involved in performing the proposed service; details of any directorships held, existing partnerships and third party relationships and any relevant judicial or regulatory findings.

- Having a clear statement of the precise nature of the services offered, costs, commissions, fees and the preferred means of remuneration.

- Undertaking research, including internet searches, of the prospective agents and, if a corporate body, of every person identified as having a degree of control over its affairs.

- Making enquiries with the relevant authorities in H to verify the information received in response to the questionnaire.

- Following up references and clarifying any matters arising from the questionnaire or any other information received with the agents, arranging face to face meetings where appropriate.

- Requesting sight or evidence of any potential agent's own anti-bribery policies and, where a corporate body, reporting procedures and records.

- Being alert to key commercial questions such as:

    – Is the agent really required?
    – Does the agent have the required expertise?
    – Are they interacting with or closely connected to public officials?
    – Is what you are proposing to pay reasonable and commercial?

- Renewing due diligence enquiries on a periodic basis if an agent is appointed.

Case study 7 – Principle 5 – Communicating and training

A small UK manufacturer of specialist equipment ('J') has engaged an individual as a local agent and adviser ('K') to assist with winning a contract and developing its business in a foreign country where the risk of bribery is assessed as high.

J could consider any or a combination of the following:

- Making employees of J engaged in bidding for business fully aware of J's anti-bribery statement, code of conduct and, where appropriate, that details of its anti-bribery policies are included in its tender.

- Including suitable contractual terms on bribery prevention measures in the agreement between J and K, for example: requiring K not to offer or pay bribes; giving J the ability to audit K's activities and expenditure; requiring K to report any requests for bribes by officials to J; and, in the event of suspicion arising as to K's activities, giving J the right to terminate the arrangement.

- Making employees of J fully aware of policies and procedures applying to relevant issues such as hospitality and facilitation payments, including all financial control mechanisms, sanctions for any breaches of the rules and instructions on how to report any suspicious conduct.

- Supplementing the information, where appropriate, with specially prepared training to J's staff involved with the foreign country.

Case study 8 – Principle 1, 4 and 6 – Community benefits and charitable donations

A company ('L') exports a range of seed products to growers around the globe. Its representative travels to a foreign country ('M') to discuss with a local farming co-operative the possible supply of a new strain of wheat that is resistant to a disease which recently swept the region. In the meeting, the head of the co-operative tells L's representative about the problems which the relative unavailability of antiretroviral drugs cause locally in the face of a high HIV infection rate.

In a subsequent meeting with an official of M to discuss the approval of L's new wheat strain for import, the official suggests that L could pay for the necessary antiretroviral drugs and that this will be a very positive factor in the Government's consideration of the licence to import the new seed strain. In a further meeting, the same official states that L should donate money to a certain charity suggested by the official which, the official assures, will then take the necessary steps to purchase and distribute the drugs. L identifies this as raising potential bribery risks.

L could consider any or a combination of the following:

- Making reasonable efforts to conduct due diligence, including consultation with staff members and any business partners it has in country M in order to satisfy itself that the suggested arrangement is legitimate and in conformity with any relevant laws and codes applying to the foreign public official responsible for approving the product. It could do this by obtaining information on:

    - M's local law on community benefits as part of Government procurement and, if no particular local law, the official status and legitimacy of the suggested arrangement,
    - the particular charity in question including its legal status, its reputation in M, and whether it has conducted similar projects, and
    - any connections the charity might have with the foreign official in question, if possible.

- Adopting an internal communication plan designed to ensure that any relationships with charitable organisations are conducted in a transparent and open manner and do not raise any expectation of the award of a contract or licence.

- Adopting company-wide policies and procedures about the selection of charitable projects or initiatives which are informed by appropriate risk assessments.

- Training and support for staff in implementing the relevant policies and procedures of communication which allow issues to be reported and compliance to be monitored.

- If charitable donations made in country M are routinely channelled through government officials or to others at the official's request, a red flag should be raised and L may seek to monitor the way its contributions are ultimately applied, or investigate alternative methods of donation such as official 'off-set' or 'community gain' arrangements with the government of M.

- Evaluation of its policies relating to charitable donations as part of its next periodic review of its anti-bribery procedures.

Case study 9 – Principle 4 – Due diligence of agents

A small UK company ('N') relies on agents in country ('P') from which it imports local high quality perishable produce and to which it exports finished goods. The bribery risks it faces arise entirely as a result of its reliance on agents and their relationship with local businessmen and officials. N is offered a new business opportunity in P through a new agent ('Q'). An agreement with Q needs to be concluded quickly.

N could consider any or a combination of the following:

- Conducting due diligence and background checks on Q that are proportionate to the risk before engaging Q; which could include:
    - making enquiries through N's business contacts, local chambers of commerce or business associations, or internet searches
    - seeking business references and a financial statement from Q and reviewing Q's CV to ensure Q has suitable experience.

- Considering how best to structure the relationship with Q, including how Q should be remunerated for its services and how to seek to ensure Q's compliance with relevant laws and codes applying to foreign public officials.

- Making the contract with Q renewable annually or periodically.

- Travelling to P periodically to review the agency situation.

Case study 10 – Principle 2 – Top level commitment

A small to medium sized component manufacturer is seeking contracts in markets abroad where there is a risk of bribery. As part of its preparation, a senior manager has devoted some time to participation in the development of a sector wide anti-bribery initiative.

The top level management of the manufacturer could consider any or a combination of the following:

- The making of a clear statement disseminated to its staff and key business partners of its commitment to carry out business fairly, honestly and openly, referencing its key bribery prevention procedures and its involvement in the sectoral initiative.

- Establishing a code of conduct that includes suitable anti-bribery provisions and making it accessible to staff and third parties on its website.

- Considering an internal launch of a code of conduct, with a message of commitment to it from senior management.

- Senior management emphasising among the workforce and other associated persons the importance of understanding and applying the code of conduct and the consequences of breaching the policy or contractual provisions relating to bribery prevention for employees and managers and external associated persons.

- Identifying someone of a suitable level of seniority to be a point-person for queries and issues relating to bribery risks.

Case study 11 – Proportionate procedures

A small export company operates through agents in a number of different foreign countries. Having identified bribery risks associated with its reliance on agents it is considering developing proportionate and risk based bribery prevention procedures.

The company could consider any or a combination of the following:

- Using trade fairs and trade publications to communicate periodically its anti-bribery message and, where appropriate, some detail of its policies and procedures.

- Oral or written communication of its bribery prevention intentions to all of its agents.

- Adopting measures designed to address bribery on its behalf by associated persons, such as:

    - requesting relevant information and conducting background searches on the internet against information received
    - making sure references are in order and followed up
    - including anti-bribery commitments in any contract renewal
    - using existing internal arrangements such as periodic staff meetings to raise awareness of 'red flags' as regards agents' conduct, for example evasive answers to straightforward requests for information, overly elaborate payment arrangements involving further third parties, ad hoc or unusual requests for expense reimbursement not properly covered by accounting procedures.

- Making use of any external sources of information (UKTI, sectoral organisations) on bribery risks in particular markets and using the data to inform relationships with particular agents.

- Making sure staff have a confidential means to raise any concerns about bribery.

www.justice.gov.uk/guidance/bribery.htm

Appendix D

MINISTRY OF JUSTICE GUIDANCE, THE BRIBERY ACT 2010, QUICK START GUIDE

The Bribery Act 2010 modernises the law on bribery. It comes into force on 1 July 2011. This document offers a quick guide to the things you need to know to prepare your business for implementation.

The Government has also produced detailed guidance about the Act and the procedures that organisations can put in place to prevent bribery, as well as a set of illustrative case studies which you may find of further assistance (available here: www.justice.gov.uk/guidance/bribery.htm).

KEY POINTS

- This Act deals only with bribery – not other forms of white collar crime

- Your organisation may be liable for failing to prevent a person from bribing on your behalf but only if that person performs services for you in business. It is very unlikely therefore that you will be liable for the actions of someone who simply supplies goods to you

- There is a full defence if you can show you had adequate procedures in place to prevent bribery. But you do not need to put bribery prevention procedures in place if there is no risk of bribery on your behalf

- Hospitality is not prohibited by the Act

- Facilitation payments are bribes under the Act just as they are under the old law

WHAT IS COVERED BY THE ACT?

The Act is concerned with bribery. Very generally, this is defined as giving someone a financial or other advantage to encourage that person to perform their functions or activities improperly or to reward that person for having already done so. So this could cover seeking to influence a decision-maker by giving some kind of extra benefit to that decision maker rather than by what can legitimately be offered as part of a tender process.

The Act is not concerned with fraud, theft, books and record offences, Companies Act offences, money laundering offences or competition law. Further detail about what is covered by the Act can be found in 'The Bribery Act 2010 – Guidance about procedures which relevant commercial organisations can put into place to prevent persons associated with them from bribing (section 9 of the Bribery Act 2010)' – www.justice.gov.uk/guidance/bribery.htm.

WHEN COULD MY ORGANISATION BE LIABLE?

Your organisation could be liable if a very senior person in the organisation (for example, a managing director) commits a bribery offence. This person's activities would then be attributed to the organisation.

Your organisation could also be liable where someone who performs services for it – like an employee or agent – pays a bribe specifically to get business, keep business, or gain a business advantage for your organisation. But you will have a full defence for this particular offence, and can avoid prosecution, if you can show you had adequate procedures in place to prevent bribery (see page 4, 'What do I need to do to rely on the defence?' for further information about this defence).

It is important to note that no one can be prosecuted in England and Wales unless one of the two most senior prosecutors (the Director of Public Prosecutions or the Director of the Serious Fraud Office) is personally satisfied that a conviction is more likely than not, and that prosecution is in the public interest.

WHAT DO I NEED TO DO TO RELY ON THE DEFENCE?

You will not commit the offence of failing to prevent bribery if you can show that your organisation had 'adequate procedures' in place to prevent bribery. What counts as adequate will depend on the bribery risks you face ('How do I assess risk?', see page 5) and the nature, size and complexity of your business. So, a small or medium sized business which faces minimal bribery risks will require relatively minimal procedures to mitigate those risks. The following six principles will help you decide what, if anything, you need to do differently:

1 Proportionality: The action you take should be proportionate to the risks you face and to the size of your business. So you might need to do more to prevent bribery if your organisation is large, or if you are operating in an overseas market where bribery is known to be commonplace, compared to what you might do if your organisation is small, or is operating in markets where bribery is not prevalent.

2 Top Level Commitment: Those at the top of an organisation are in the best position to ensure their organisation conducts business without bribery. If you are running a business, you will want to show that you have been active in making sure that your staff (including any middle management) and the key people who do business with you and for you understand that you do not tolerate bribery. You may also want to get personally involved in taking the necessary proportionate action to address any bribery risks.

3 Risk Assessment: Think about the bribery risks you might face. For example, you might want to do some research into the markets you operate in and the people you deal with, especially if you are entering into new business arrangements and new markets overseas ('How do I assess risk', see page 5).

4 Due Diligence: Knowing exactly who you are dealing with can help to protect your organisation from taking on people who might be less than trustworthy. You may therefore want to ask a few questions and do a few checks before engaging others to represent you in business dealings.

5 Communication: Communicating your policies and procedures to staff and to others who will perform services for you enhances awareness and helps to deter bribery by making clear the basis on which your organisation does business. You may, therefore, want to think about whether additional training or awareness raising would be appropriate or proportionate to the size and type of your business.

6 Monitoring and Review: The risks you face and the effectiveness of your procedures may change over time. You may want, therefore, to keep an eye on the anti- bribery steps you have taken so that they keep pace with any changes in the bribery risks you face when, for example, you enter new markets.

HOW DO I ASSESS RISK?

Many organisations will face little or no risk of bribery, especially if their business is undertaken primarily in the UK. If you operate overseas, the risks may be higher. Factors such as the particular country you want to do business in, the sector which you are dealing in, the value and duration of your project, the kind of business you want to do and the people you engage to do your business will all be relevant.

There are simple practical steps you can take to assess and mitigate risks. These are mostly obvious, and are similar to (or even the same as) those you probably take anyway (for example, to make sure you can trust the people you work with). For example, you might use simple internet searches to find out about the levels of corruption or bribery in the particular country you propose to do business in. You could consult UK diplomatic posts or UK Trade and Investment for advice. You could also consult business representative bodies here and in the relevant country for up to date local knowledge. We sct out some contacts below including a Government-sponsored Business Anti-Corruption Portal aimed at small and medium sized businesses involved in overseas trade.

DO I NEED COMPLEX PROCEDURES IN PLACE EVEN IF THERE IS NO RISK?

No. If there is very little risk of bribery being committed on behalf of your organisation then you may not feel the need for any procedures to prevent bribery. If, having assessed the position, there is a risk of bribery then, if you want to rely on the defence, the procedures you adopt should be proportionate to that risk.

There is no need for extensive written documentation or policies. You may already have proportionate procedures through existing controls over company expenditure, accounting and commercial or agent contracts for example. In larger organisations it will be important to ensure that management in charge of the day to day business is fully aware and committed to the objective of preventing bribery. In micro-businesses it may be enough for simple oral reminders to key staff about the organisation's anti-bribery policies.

In addition, although parties to a contract are of course free to agree whatever terms are appropriate, the Act does not require you to comply with the anti-bribery procedures of your business partners in order to be able to rely on the defence.

DO I NEED TO DO DUE DILIGENCE ON ALL MY SUPPLIERS?

You only have to think about doing due diligence on persons who will actually perform services for you, or on your behalf. Someone who simply supplies goods to you is unlikely to do that. It is very unlikely, therefore, that you will need to consider doing due diligence on persons further down a supply chain.

Where you decide to undertake due diligence, how much you need to do will depend on your risk assessment. If you assess the risk as low then all you may need to do is satisfy yourself that people performing services for you (for example, an agent) are genuine and someone you can trust to do your business without bribing. You could do this by making enquiries with business contacts, local chambers of commerce or business associations or via the internet for example.

Where you think the risks are higher, then you may need to do more. You might ask your agent for a CV, financial statements or accounts, and other references. You might then follow those up to ensure they are genuine. The aim is to satisfy yourself that the person that is to represent your organisation can be trusted not to use bribery on your behalf, but this does not necessarily require sophisticated and costly techniques. Personal contact, allowing you to assess the person for yourself, can be very helpful.

DO I NEED TO EMPLOY CONSULTANTS OR LAWYERS TO PROVIDE ADVICE ON THE RISKS I FACE, THE PROCEDURES I ADOPT, OR THE LEVEL OF DUE DILIGENCE I SHOULD UNDERTAKE?

No. There is no duty to engage lawyers or consultants in helping you assess what risks you face, what procedures you might adopt or what sort of due diligence you undertake – especially where you consider the risks to be low or non-existent. The Act does not require external verification of any bribery prevention measures you have put in place.

CAN I PROVIDE HOSPITALITY, PROMOTIONAL OR OTHER BUSINESS EXPENDITURE UNDER THE ACT?

Yes. The Government does not intend that genuine hospitality or similar business expenditure that is reasonable and proportionate be caught by the Act, so you can continue to provide bona fide hospitality, promotional or other business expenditure.

In any case where it was thought the hospitality was really a cover for bribing someone, the authorities would look at such things as the level of hospitality offered, the way in which it was provided and the level of influence the person receiving it had on the business decision in question. But, as a general proposition, hospitality or promotional expenditure which is proportionate and reasonable given the sort of business you do is very unlikely to engage the Act. So you can continue to provide tickets to sporting events, take clients to dinner, offer gifts to clients as a reflection of your good relations, or pay for reasonable travel expenses in order to demonstrate your goods or services to clients if that is reasonable and proportionate for your business.

WHAT ABOUT FACILITATION PAYMENTS?

Facilitation payments, which are payments to induce officials to perform routine functions they are otherwise obligated to perform, are bribes. There was no exemption for such payments under the previous law nor is there under the Bribery Act.

As was the case under the old law, prosecutors will carefully consider all the facts and surrounding circumstances of cases which come to their attention to assess whether a payment amounts to a bribe and, if so, whether a prosecution is in the public interest.

You can continue to pay for legally required administrative fees or fast-track services. These are not facilitation payments.

FURTHER INFORMATION

www.justice.gov.uk

www.bis.gov.uk

www.businesslink.gov.uk

www.justice.gov.uk/guidance/bribery.htm

Appendix E

JOINT PROSECUTION GUIDANCE ON THE BRIBERY ACT 2010

INTRODUCTION

The Bribery Act 2010 ("the Act") will come into force on a day to be notified by the Secretary of State for Justice. The Act applies to the whole of the UK and provides for wide extra-territorial jurisdiction to deal with bribery committed outside the UK.

In England and Wales, proceedings for offences under the Act require the personal consent of the Director of Public Prosecutions or the Director of the Serious Fraud Office. They will make their decisions in accordance with the Code for Crown Prosecutors ("The Code") applying the two stage test of whether there is sufficient evidence to provide a realistic prospect of conviction and, if so, whether a prosecution is in the public interest.

The purpose of this guidance is to set out the Directors' approach to prosecutorial decision-making in respect of offences under the Act. The guidance is not intended to be exhaustive and prosecutors should be mindful of the wide range of circumstances and culpability which may arise in any particular case.

This guidance is subject to the Code for Crown Prosecutors and when considering corporate prosecutions, it should be read in conjunction with the Guidance on Corporate Prosecutions, which sets out the approach to the prosecution in England and Wales of corporate offenders.

Scotland and Northern Ireland are separate legal jurisdictions and this guidance therefore does not apply to decisions about prosecutions in those jurisdictions. However, there has been liaison with the Lord Advocate and the Director of Public Prosecutions for Northern Ireland during the development of this guidance.

THE ACT IN ITS WIDER CONTEXT

In his foreword to the 2004 United Nations Convention against Corruption (UNCAC) the then UN Secretary General (Kofi Annan) described the serious effects of corruption:

"Corruption is an insidious plague that has a wide range of corrosive effects on societies. It undermines democracy and the rule of law, leads to violations of human rights, distorts markets, erodes the quality of life and allows organised crime, terrorism and other threats to human security to flourish ... Corruption is a key element in economic under-performance and a major obstacle to poverty alleviation and development."

The UK is a signatory to a number of international anti-corruption instruments including the UN Convention against Corruption, the OECD Convention on Combating Bribery of Foreign Public Officials (1997) and the Council of Europe Criminal Law Convention on Corruption (1998) and additional Protocol (2005).

The Act reflects the UK's continued commitment to combat bribery and provides a modern, comprehensive scheme of bribery offences. The Act covers all forms of bribery but there is a clear focus on commercial bribery, evidenced by the fact that two of its four offences are business related. The Government intends that over time the Act will contribute to international and national efforts towards ensuring a shift away from a culture of bribery that may persist in certain sectors or markets and help ensure high ethical standards in international business transactions.

The Serious Fraud Office is the lead agency in England and Wales for investigating (jointly with the police in some cases) and prosecuting cases of overseas corruption. The SFO promotes active engagement with businesses and "self-reporting" by companies (see Approach of the SFO to dealing with overseas corruption). The Crown Prosecution Service also prosecutes bribery offences investigated by the police, committed either overseas or in England and Wales.

The statutory "adequate procedures" defence to a failure of commercial organisations to prevent bribery (section 7) encourages such bodies to put procedures in place to prevent bribery by persons associated with them. The Act is not intended to penalise ethically run companies that encounter an isolated incident of bribery. Section 7 and, to a degree, section 6 (bribery of foreign public officials) are designed to balance corporate responsibility for ensuring ethical conduct in the modern international business environment with the public interest in prosecuting where appropriate.

THE LEGAL FRAMEWORK

The Bribery Act 2010 received Royal Assent on 8 April 2010. A full copy of the Act and its Explanatory Notes can be accessed at: www.legislation.gov.uk.

In summary, the Act:

- provides a revised framework to combat bribery in the public or private sectors, removing the need to prove acts were done corruptly or dishonestly;

- abolishes the offences of bribery at common law and the statutory offences in the Public Bodies Corrupt Practices Act 1889 and the Prevention of Corruption Act 1906 (s17 and Schedule 2);

- creates two general offences of bribing another person ("active bribery") (s1) and being bribed ("passive bribery") (s2);

- creates a discrete offence of bribery of a foreign public official (s6);

- creates a new offence of failure of commercial organisations to prevent bribery by persons associated with them (s7);

- requires the Secretary of State to publish guidance about procedures that relevant commercial organisations can put in place to prevent bribery by persons associated with them (s9);

- replaces the need for Attorney General's consent (for the statutory offences abolished) with the requirement for the consent of the Director of the relevant prosecuting authority (for the new offences under the Act) (s10);

- provides a maximum penalty of 10 years' imprisonment or an unlimited fine for all the offences for individuals, and an unlimited fine only for commercial organisations (s11);

- provides jurisdiction to prosecute bribery committed abroad by any person (individual or corporate) who has a 'close connection' with the UK (s12);

- provides a limited defence for certain action taken by an intelligence service or by the armed forces (s13);

- provides that senior officers of a body corporate may be prosecuted if an offence is proved to have been committed by a corporate body with their consent or connivance (s14);

- applies equally to individuals in the public service of the Crown as it applies to other individuals (s16) but not to Crown bodies.

Transitional provisions

Prosecutors should note that the Act does not affect any liability, investigation, legal proceeding or penalty in respect of the common law offence of bribery or the statutory offences under the Public Bodies Corrupt Practices Act 1889 and the Prevention of Corruption Act 1906 committed wholly or partly before the commencement of the Act (s19).

THE OFFENCES AND APPLICATION OF THE CODE FOR CROWN PROSECUTORS

Scope of the Act

The Act takes a robust approach to tackling commercial bribery, which is one of its principal objectives. The offences are not, however, limited to commercial bribery. There may be many examples outside the commercial sphere where individuals attempt to influence the application of rules, regulations and normal procedures. Examples would include attempts to influence decisions by local authorities, regulatory bodies or elected representatives on matters such as planning consent, school admission procedures or driving tests.

General approach to bribery prosecutions

Bribery is a serious offence. There is an inherent public interest in bribery being prosecuted in order to give practical effect to Parliament's criminalisation of such behaviour. As with other criminal offences, however, prosecutors will make their decisions in accordance with the Full Code Test as set out in the Code for Crown Prosecutors. It has two stages: (i) the evidential stage; and (ii) the public interest stage. The evidential stage must be considered before the public interest stage.

A case which does not pass the evidential stage must not proceed, no matter how serious or sensitive it may be. Where there is sufficient evidence to justify a prosecution, prosecutors must always go on to consider whether a prosecution is required in the public interest. Assessing the public interest is not simply a matter of adding up the number of factors on each side and seeing which side has the greater number. The absence of a factor does not necessarily mean that it should be taken as a factor tending in the opposite direction. Each case will have to be rigorously considered on its own facts and merits in accordance with the Code.

Prosecutors dealing with bribery cases are reminded of the UK's commitment to abide by Article 5 of the OECD Convention on Combating Bribery of Foreign Public Officials in International Business Transactions:

> "Investigation and prosecution of the bribery of a foreign public official ... shall not be influenced by considerations of national economic interest, the potential effect upon relations with another State or the identity of the natural or legal persons involved".

Key terms used in the Act

Offers and requests

The Act uses everyday language of offering, promising or giving ("active bribery"), requesting, agreeing to receive or accepting an advantage ("passive bribery").

This language is wide enough to include cases in which an offer, promise or request can only be inferred from the circumstances. The Law Commission used the example of an interview held over an open briefcase full of money that could be seen as an implied offer. It will be a matter for the tribunal of fact to decide whether such an inference can be drawn from the evidence in each case.

It is also clear that, except where the allegation is that an advantage was given or received, there is no need for a transaction to have been completed. The Act focuses on conduct not results.

Financial or other advantage

All the offences under the Act refer either directly or indirectly to a "financial or other advantage". The Act does not define the term. It is left to be determined as a matter of common sense by the tribunal of fact. Prosecutors should therefore approach prosecutions under the Act on the basis that "advantage" should be understood in its normal, everyday meaning.

Improper performance

The concept of improper performance (section 4) is central to the general bribery offences and also indirectly to the offence of failure of commercial organisations to prevent bribery, since an offence under section 7 requires a general bribery offence to have been committed.

Improper performance involves a breach of an expectation of "good faith", "impartiality" or "trust" (section 3(3) to (5)) in respect of the function or activity carried out. The test of what is expected is a test of what a reasonable person in the United Kingdom would expect in relation to the performance of the type of function or activity concerned (section 5(1)).

The Law Commission (*Reforming Bribery, Law Comm No 313*) was confident of the jury's ability to apply this test on the basis of the ordinary meaning of the words rather than as something that needed to be defined in the Act:

> "… the expectation in question is that which would be had, in the circumstances by people of moral integrity … it will be for the tribunal of fact to decide what that expectation amounted to, in the circumstances" (paragraph 3.176).

Associated person

A commercial organisation ('C') can be liable only for bribes by an "associated person" ('A') as defined in section 8.

Whether A is associated with C is determined by the nature of what is done (disregarding any bribe under consideration) rather than the capacity in which it is done. It is necessary to take into account all the relevant circumstances, not just the nature of the relationship. Services can be performed by one legal person on behalf of another legal person.

A may therefore, for example, be the commercial organisation's employee, agent or subsidiary of the organisation. Where A is an employee it is presumed that A is performing services for or on behalf of C unless the contrary is shown.

Section 1: Offences of bribing another person

The legal elements

The ways in which the offence of bribing another person can be committed are contained in two 'Cases' set out in section 1(2) and 1(3) of the Act. The necessary conduct element is when a person "offers, promises or gives" a "financial or other advantage", either directly or through a third party. The offence also requires a "wrongfulness element".

In Case 1, the wrongfulness element is committed where the advantage is intended to induce (or be a reward for) improper performance of a relevant function or activity.

In Case 2, the wrongfulness element is committed where the person knows or believes that the acceptance of the advantage offered, promised or given in itself constitutes the improper performance of a relevant function or activity.

Prosecutors will need to consider any direct evidence (documentary or otherwise) there may be of actual intention (Case 1) or knowledge or belief (Case 2) as well as whether they can be inferred from the circumstances including the value of the advantage.

Prosecutors should draft separate charges or counts based on Cases 1 and 2 to avoid duplicity, as their wrongfulness elements are different; and should also make it clear if charges or counts are alternatives.

Public Interest Considerations

A prosecution will usually take place unless the prosecutor is sure that there are public interest factors tending against prosecution which outweigh those tending in favour.

Factors tending in favour of prosecution:

The Code sets out a number of general factors tending in favour of prosecution. When applied in the context of bribery offences, the following may be particularly relevant:

- A conviction for bribery is likely to attract a significant sentence (Code 4.16a);

- Offences will often be premeditated and may include an element of corruption of the person bribed (Code 4.16e and k);

- Offences may be committed in order to facilitate more serious offending (4.16i);

- Those involved in bribery may be in positions of authority or trust and take advantage of that position (Code 4.16n).

Factors tending against prosecution:

The factors tending against prosecution may include cases where:

- The court is likely to impose only a nominal penalty (Code 4.17a);

- The harm can be described as minor and was the result of a single incident (Code 4.17e);

- There has been a genuinely proactive approach involving self-reporting and remedial action (additional factor (a) in the Guidance on Corporate Prosecutions).

Section 2: Offences relating to being bribed

The legal elements

Section 2 provides a number of ways in which the offence of being bribed can be committed and distinguishes four 'Cases', namely Case 3 to Case 6 as set out in section 2 (2) to (5). The Explanatory Notes to the Act explain in more detail how the offence may be committed. Section 2 uses the same concepts as in section 1 of "financial or other advantage"; "relevant function or activity"; and "improper performance".

Prosecutors should draft separate charges or counts based on Cases 3 to 6 to avoid duplicity, as their wrongfulness elements are different; and should also make it clear if charges or counts are alternatives.

Public Interest Considerations

The factors tending in favour of and against prosecution for section 1 (see above) are equally applicable to the offence under section 2.

Section 6: Bribery of foreign public officials

The legal elements

Section 6 creates a discrete offence of bribery of a foreign public official (as defined in section 6(5)).

The offence is committed where a person offers, promises or gives a financial or other advantage to a foreign public official with the intention of influencing the official in the performance of his or her official functions.

That person must also intend to obtain or retain business or an advantage in the conduct of business. The official must be neither permitted nor required by the applicable written law (section 6(7)) to be influenced by the advantage).

Bribery of foreign public officials may also be prosecuted, in appropriate cases, under section 1, making use of the extended extra-territorial jurisdiction. This may be the case, for example, if it is difficult to prove that the person bribed is a foreign public official. It should be noted, however, that under section 1 it will be necessary to prove the improper performance element.

Specific issues under section 6 (note they may also apply to section 1 offences)

Facilitation payments

Facilitation payments are unofficial payments made to public officials in order to secure or expedite the performance of a routine or necessary action. They are sometimes referred to as 'speed' or 'grease' payments. The payer of the facilitation payment usually already has a legal or other entitlement to the relevant action.

There is no exemption in respect of facilitation payments. They were illegal under the previous legislation and the common law and remain so under the Act.

Public Interest Considerations

Prevention of bribery of foreign public officials is a significant policy aspect of the Act. In the context of facilitation payments, the following public interest factors tending in favour of and against prosecution may be relevant. A prosecution will usually take place unless the prosecutor is sure that there are public interest factors tending against prosecution which outweigh those tending in favour.

Factors tending in favour of prosecution:

- Large or repeated payments are more likely to attract a significant sentence (Code 4.16a);

- Facilitation payments that are planned for or accepted as part of a standard way of conducting business may indicate the offence was premeditated (Code 4.16e);

- Payments may indicate an element of active corruption of the official in the way the offence was committed (Code 4.16k);

- Where a commercial organisation has a clear and appropriate policy setting out procedures an individual should follow if facilitation payments are requested and these have not been correctly followed.

Factors tending against prosecution:

- A single small payment likely to result in only a nominal penalty (Code 4.17a);

- The payment(s) came to light as a result of a genuinely proactive approach involving self-reporting and remedial action (additional factor (a) in the Guidance on Corporate Prosecutions);

- Where a commercial organisation has a clear and appropriate policy setting out procedures an individual should follow if facilitation payments are requested and these have been correctly followed;

- The payer was in a vulnerable position arising from the circumstances in which the payment was demanded.

Hospitality and promotional expenditure

Hospitality or promotional expenditure which is reasonable, proportionate and made in good faith is an established and important part of doing business. The Act does not seek to penalise such activity.

Hospitality and promotional expenditure could, however, form the basis of offences under s1 (bribing another person) or s6 (bribing a foreign public official) and constitute a bribe for the purpose of s7 (failure to prevent bribery). Under section 1 there must be an element of "improper performance". Under section 6, it will be necessary to show that the provision of hospitality or promotional expenditure was intended to influence the foreign public official so as to obtain or retain business, or an advantage in the conduct of business.

The more lavish the hospitality or expenditure (beyond what may be reasonable standards in the particular circumstances) the greater the inference that it is intended to encourage or reward improper performance or influence an official. Lavishness is just one factor that may be taken into account in determining whether an offence has been committed. The full circumstances of each case would need to be considered. Other factors might include that the hospitality or expenditure was not clearly connected with legitimate business activity or was concealed.

Public Interest Considerations

Prevention of bribery of foreign public officials is a significant policy aspect of the Act. When considering the public interest stage, the factors tending in favour of and against prosecution referred to in respect of "active bribery" (section 1) are likely to be relevant. A prosecution will usually take place unless the prosecutor is sure that there are public interest factors tending against prosecution which outweigh those tending in favour.

Section 7: Failure of commercial organisations to prevent bribery

The legal elements

A "relevant commercial organisation" will be liable to prosecution if a person associated with it bribes another person intending to obtain or retain business or an advantage in the conduct of business for that organisation, but only if the associated person is or would be guilty of an offence under section 1 or 6 (section 2 "passive bribery" is not relevant to a section 7 offence).

Section 7 does not require a prosecution for the predicate offences under section 1 or 6, but there needs to be sufficient evidence to prove the commission of such an offence to the normal criminal standard. For this purpose it is not necessary for the associated person to have a close connection with the United Kingdom (section 7(3)(b)).

The jurisdiction for this offence is wide (see section 12 of the Act). Provided that the commercial organisation is incorporated or formed in the UK, or that the organisation carries out its business or part of its business in the UK, courts in the UK will have jurisdiction, irrespective of where in the world the acts or omissions which form part of the offence may be committed.

The offence is not a substantive bribery offence. It does not involve vicarious liability and it does not replace or remove direct corporate liability for bribery. If it can be proved that someone representing the corporate 'directing mind' bribes or receives a bribe or encourages or assists someone else to do so then it may be appropriate to charge the organisation with a section 1 or 6 offence in the alternative or in addition to any offence under section 7 (or a section 2 offence if the offence relates to being bribed).

The defence of adequate procedures

It is a defence if a relevant commercial organisation can show it had adequate procedures in place to prevent persons associated with it from bribing. The standard of proof the defendant would need to discharge in order to prove the defence is on the balance of probabilities. Whether the procedures are adequate will ultimately be a matter for the courts to decide on a case by case basis.

As stated in the Code (4.5) prosecutors must consider what the defence case may be, and how it is likely to affect the prospects of conviction, under the evidential stage. Clearly, the defence under s7(2) of adequate procedures is likely to be highly relevant when considering whether there is sufficient evidence to provide a realistic prospect of conviction.

Prosecutors must look carefully at all the circumstances in which the alleged bribe occurred including the adequacy of any anti-bribery procedures. A single instance of bribery does not necessarily mean that an organisation's procedures are inadequate. For example, the actions of an agent or an employee may be wilfully contrary to very robust corporate contractual requirements, instructions or guidance.

Section 9 Guidance

Section 9 of the Act requires the Secretary of State to publish guidance on procedures that relevant commercial organisations can put in place to prevent bribery by persons associated with them. *"Guidance about commercial organisations preventing bribery (section 9 of the Bribery Act 2010)"* has been published by the Ministry of Justice. Prosecutors must take it into account when considering whether the procedures put in place by commercial organisations are adequate to prevent persons performing services for or on their behalf from bribing.

The Ministry of Justice's guidance also provides some explanation of the Government policy behind the formulation of the offences and gives assistance on the particular concepts relevant to the application of sections 1, 6 and 7 in the context of commercial bribery. Prosecutors may find this helpful when reviewing cases involving commercial bribery.

Public Interest Considerations

The factors tending in favour of and against prosecution referred to above in respect of section 1 may be equally applicable to the section 7 offence. The additional factors in the Guidance on Corporate Prosecutions will also be particularly relevant in determining whether or not it is in the public interest to prosecute.

OBTAINING THE CONSENT OF THE DPP OR DIRECTOR SFO

The DPP or the Director of the Serious Fraud Office must give personal consent to a prosecution under the Act as set out in section 10 of the Act. Prosecutors should follow any relevant internal procedures when submitting cases for consideration.

USEFUL LINKS

Bribery Act 2010 and Explanatory Notes

Code for Crown Prosecutors

Guidance on Corporate Prosecutions

Approach of the SFO to dealing with overseas corruption (currently being revised)

OECD Convention on Combating Bribery of Foreign Public Officials (1997)

UN Convention against Corruption

Appendix F

OECD CONVENTION ON COMBATING BRIBERY OF FOREIGN PUBLIC OFFICIALS IN INTERNATIONAL BUSINESS TRANSACTIONS

ADOPTED BY THE NEGOTIATING CONFERENCE ON 21 NOVEMBER 1997

Preamble

The Parties,

Considering that bribery is a widespread phenomenon in international business transactions, including trade and investment, which raises serious moral and political concerns, undermines good governance and economic development, and distorts international competitive conditions;

Considering that all countries share a responsibility to combat bribery in international business transactions;

Having regard to the Revised Recommendation on Combating Bribery in International Business Transactions, adopted by the Council of the Organisation for Economic Co-operation and Development (OECD) on 23 May 1997, C(97)123/FINAL, which, *inter alia*, called for effective measures to deter, prevent and combat the bribery of foreign public officials in connection with international business transactions, in particular the prompt criminalisation of such bribery in an effective and co-ordinated manner and in conformity with the agreed common elements set out in that Recommendation and with the jurisdictional and other basic legal principles of each country;

Welcoming other recent developments which further advance international understanding and co-operation in combating bribery of public officials, including actions of the United Nations, the World Bank, the International Monetary Fund, the World Trade Organisation, the Organisation of American States, the Council of Europe and the European Union;

Welcoming the efforts of companies, business organisations and trade unions as well as other non-governmental organisations to combat bribery;

Recognising the role of governments in the prevention of solicitation of bribes from individuals and enterprises in international business transactions;

Recognising that achieving progress in this field requires not only efforts on a national level but also multilateral co-operation, monitoring and follow-up;

Recognising that achieving equivalence among the measures to be taken by the Parties is an essential object and purpose of the Convention, which requires that the Convention be ratified without derogations affecting this equivalence;

HAVE AGREED AS FOLLOWS:

ARTICLE 1

THE OFFENCE OF BRIBERY OF FOREIGN PUBLIC OFFICIALS

1. Each Party shall take such measures as may be necessary to establish that it is a criminal offence under its law for any person intentionally to offer, promise or give any undue pecuniary or other advantage, whether directly or through intermediaries, to a foreign public official, for that official or for a third party, in order that the official act or refrain from acting in relation to the performance of official duties, in order to obtain or retain business or other improper advantage in the conduct of international business.

2. Each Party shall take any measures necessary to establish that complicity in, including incitement, aiding and abetting, or authorisation of an act of bribery of a foreign public official shall be a criminal offence. Attempt and conspiracy to bribe a foreign public official shall be criminal offences to the same extent as attempt and conspiracy to bribe a public official of that Party.

3. The offences set out in paragraphs 1 and 2 above are hereinafter referred to as "bribery of a foreign public official".

4. For the purpose of this Convention:

    a) "foreign public official" means any person holding a legislative, administrative or judicial office of a foreign country, whether appointed or elected; any person exercising a public function for a foreign country, including for a public agency or public enterprise; and any official or agent of a public international organisation;

    b) "foreign country" includes all levels and subdivisions of government, from national to local;

c) "act or refrain from acting in relation to the performance of official duties" includes any use of the public official's position, whether or not within the official's authorised competence.

ARTICLE 2

RESPONSIBILITY OF LEGAL PERSONS

Each Party shall take such measures as may be necessary, in accordance with its legal principles, to establish the liability of legal persons for the bribery of a foreign public official.

ARTICLE 3

SANCTIONS

1. The bribery of a foreign public official shall be punishable by effective, proportionate and dissuasive criminal penalties. The range of penalties shall be comparable to that applicable to the bribery of the Party's own public officials and shall, in the case of natural persons, include deprivation of liberty sufficient to enable effective mutual legal assistance and extradition.

2. In the event that, under the legal system of a Party, criminal responsibility is not applicable to legal persons, that Party shall ensure that legal persons shall be subject to effective, proportionate and dissuasive non-criminal sanctions, including monetary sanctions, for bribery of foreign public officials.

3. Each Party shall take such measures as may be necessary to provide that the bribe and the proceeds of the bribery of a foreign public official, or property the value of which corresponds to that of such proceeds, are subject to seizure and confiscation or that monetary sanctions of comparable effect are applicable.

4. Each Party shall consider the imposition of additional civil or administrative sanctions upon a person subject to sanctions for the bribery of a foreign public official.

ARTICLE 4

JURISDICTION

1. Each Party shall take such measures as may be necessary to establish its jurisdiction over the bribery of a foreign public official when the offence is committed in whole or in part in its territory.

2. Each Party which has jurisdiction to prosecute its nationals for offences committed abroad shall take such measures as may be necessary to establish its jurisdiction to do so in respect of the bribery of a foreign public official, according to the same principles.

3. When more than one Party has jurisdiction over an alleged offence described in this Convention, the Parties involved shall, at the request of one of them, consult with a view to determining the most appropriate jurisdiction for prosecution.

4. Each Party shall review whether its current basis for jurisdiction is effective in the fight against the bribery of foreign public officials and, if it is not, shall take remedial steps.

ARTICLE 5

ENFORCEMENT

Investigation and prosecution of the bribery of a foreign public official shall be subject to the applicable rules and principles of each Party. They shall not be influenced by considerations of national economic interest, the potential effect upon relations with another State or the identity of the natural or legal persons involved.

ARTICLE 6

STATUTE OF LIMITATIONS

Any statute of limitations applicable to the offence of bribery of a foreign public official shall allow an adequate period of time for the investigation and prosecution of this offence.

ARTICLE 7

MONEY LAUNDERING

Each Party which has made bribery of its own public official a predicate offence for the purpose of the application of its money laundering legislation shall do so on the same terms for the bribery of a foreign public official, without regard to the place where the bribery occurred.

ARTICLE 8

ACCOUNTING

1. In order to combat bribery of foreign public officials effectively, each Party shall take such measures as may be necessary, within the framework of its laws and regulations regarding the maintenance of books and records, financial statement disclosures, and accounting and auditing standards, to prohibit the establishment of off-the-books accounts, the making of off-the-books or inadequately identified transactions, the recording of non-existent expenditures, the entry of liabilities with incorrect identification of their object, as well as the use of false documents, by companies subject to those laws and regulations, for the purpose of bribing foreign public officials or of hiding such bribery.

2. Each Party shall provide effective, proportionate and dissuasive civil, administrative or criminal penalties for such omissions and falsifications in respect of the books, records, accounts and financial statements of such companies.

ARTICLE 9

MUTUAL LEGAL ASSISTANCE

1. Each Party shall, to the fullest extent possible under its laws and relevant treaties and arrangements, provide prompt and effective legal assistance to another Party for the purpose of criminal investigations and proceedings brought by a Party concerning offences within the scope of this Convention and for non-criminal proceedings within the scope of this Convention brought by a Party against a legal person. The requested Party shall inform the requesting Party, without delay, of any additional

information or documents needed to support the request for assistance and, where requested, of the status and outcome of the request for assistance.

2. Where a Party makes mutual legal assistance conditional upon the existence of dual criminality, dual criminality shall be deemed to exist if the offence for which the assistance is sought is within the scope of this Convention.

3. A Party shall not decline to render mutual legal assistance for criminal matters within the scope of this Convention on the ground of bank secrecy.

ARTICLE 10

EXTRADITION

1. Bribery of a foreign public official shall be deemed to be included as an extraditable offence under the laws of the Parties and the extradition treaties between them.

2. If a Party which makes extradition conditional on the existence of an extradition treaty receives a request for extradition from another Party with which it has no extradition treaty, it may consider this Convention to be the legal basis for extradition in respect of the offence of bribery of a foreign public official.

3. Each Party shall take any measures necessary to assure either that it can extradite its nationals or that it can prosecute its nationals for the offence of bribery of a foreign public official. A Party which declines a request to extradite a person for bribery of a foreign public official solely on the ground that the person is its national shall submit the case to its competent authorities for the purpose of prosecution.

4. Extradition for bribery of a foreign public official is subject to the conditions set out in the domestic law and applicable treaties and arrangements of each Party. Where a Party makes extradition conditional upon the existence of dual criminality, that condition shall be deemed to be fulfilled if the offence for which extradition is sought is within the scope of Article 1 of this Convention.

ARTICLE 11

RESPONSIBLE AUTHORITIES

For the purposes of Article 4, paragraph 3, on consultation, Article 9, on mutual legal assistance and Article 10, on extradition, each Party shall notify to the Secretary-General of the OECD an authority or authorities responsible for making and receiving requests, which shall serve as channel of communication for these matters for that Party, without prejudice to other arrangements between Parties.

ARTICLE 12

MONITORING AND FOLLOW-UP

The Parties shall co-operate in carrying out a programme of systematic follow-up to monitor and promote the full implementation of this Convention. Unless otherwise decided by consensus of the Parties, this shall be done in the framework of the OECD Working Group on Bribery in International Business Transactions and according to its terms of reference, or within the framework and terms of reference of any successor to its functions, and Parties shall bear the costs of the programme in accordance with the rules applicable to that body.

ARTICLE 13

SIGNATURE AND ACCESSION

1. Until its entry into force, this Convention shall be open for signature by OECD Members and by Non-Members which have been invited to become full participants in its Working Group on Bribery in International Business Transactions.

2. Subsequent to its entry into force, this Convention shall be open to accession by any non-signatory which is a member of the OECD or has become a full participant in the Working Group on Bribery in International Business Transactions or any successor to its functions. For each such non-signatory, the Convention shall enter into force on the sixtieth day following the date of deposit of its instrument of accession.

ARTICLE 14

RATIFICATION AND DEPOSITARY

1. This Convention is subject to acceptance, approval or ratification by the Signatories, in accordance with their respective laws.

2. Instruments of acceptance, approval, ratification or accession shall be deposited with the Secretary-General of the OECD, who shall serve as Depositary of this Convention.

ARTICLE 15

ENTRY INTO FORCE

1. This Convention shall enter into force on the sixtieth day following the date upon which five of the ten countries which have the ten largest export shares set out in DAFFE/IME/BR(97)18/FINAL (annexed), and which represent by themselves at least sixty per cent of the combined total exports of those ten countries, have deposited their instruments of acceptance, approval, or ratification. For each signatory depositing its instrument after such entry into force, the Convention shall enter into force on the sixtieth day after deposit of its instrument.

2. If, after 31 December 1998, the Convention has not entered into force under paragraph 1 above, any signatory which has deposited its instrument of acceptance, approval or ratification may declare in writing to the Depositary its readiness to accept entry into force of this Convention under this paragraph 2. The Convention shall enter into force for such a signatory on the sixtieth day following the date upon which such declarations have been deposited by at least two signatories. For each signatory depositing its declaration after such entry into force, the Convention shall enter into force on the sixtieth day following the date of deposit.

ARTICLE 16

AMENDMENT

Any Party may propose the amendment of this Convention. A proposed amendment shall be submitted to the Depositary which shall communicate it to the other Parties at least sixty days before convening a meeting of the Parties to consider the proposed amendment. An amendment adopted by consensus of the Parties, or by such other means as the Parties may determine by consensus, shall enter into force sixty days after the deposit of an instrument of ratification, acceptance or approval by all of the Parties, or in such other circumstances as may be specified by the Parties at the time of adoption of the amendment.

ARTICLE 17

WITHDRAWAL

A Party may withdraw from this Convention by submitting written notification to the Depositary. Such withdrawal shall be effective one year after the date of the receipt of the notification. After withdrawal, co-operation shall continue between the Parties and the Party which has withdrawn on all requests for assistance or extradition made before the effective date of withdrawal which remain pending.

Annex: Statistics on OECD Exports

1990–1996 US$	million	1990–1996	1990–1996
		% of Total OCDE	% of 10 largest
United States	287 118	15.9%	19.7%
Germany	254 746	14.1%	17.5%
Japan	212 665	11.8%	14.6%
France	138 471	7.7%	9.5%
United Kingdom	121 258	6.7%	8.3%
Italy	112 449	6.2%	7.7%
Canada	91 215	5.1%	6.3%
Korea[1]	81 364	4.5%	5.6%
Netherlands	81 264	4.5%	5.6%
Belgium-Luxembourg	78 598	4.4%	5.4%
Total 10 largest	**1 459 148**	**81.0%**	**100%**

Spain	42 469	2.4%	
Switzerland	40 395	2.2%	
Sweden	36 710	2.0%	
Mexico[(1)]	34 233	1.9%	
Australia	27 194	1.5%	
Denmark	24 145	1.3%	
Austria*	22 432	1.2%	
Norway	21 666	1.2%	
Ireland	19 217	1.1%	
Finland	17 296	1.0%	
Poland[(1)]**	12 652	0.7%	
Portugal	10 801	0.6%	
Turkey*	8 027	0.4%	
Hungary**	6 795	0.4%	
New Zealand	6 663	0.4%	
Czech Republic***	6 263	0.3%	
Greece*	4 606	0.3%	
Iceland	949	0.1%	
Total OCDE	**1 801 661**	**100%**	

Notes: * 1990–1995; ** 1991–1996; *** 1993–1996

Source: OECD, (1) IMF

Concerning Belgium-Luxembourg: Trade statistics for Belgium and Luxembourg are available only on a combined basis for the two countries. For purposes of Article 15, paragraph 1 of the Convention, if either Belgium or Luxembourg deposits its instrument of acceptance, approval or ratification, or if both Belgium and Luxembourg deposit their instruments of acceptance, approval or ratification, it shall be considered that one of the countries which have the ten largest exports shares has deposited its instrument and the joint exports of both countries will be counted towards the 60 per cent of combined total exports of those ten countries, which is required for entry into force under this provision.

Appendix G

COMMENTARIES ON THE OECD CONVENTION

COMMENTARIES ON THE CONVENTION ON COMBATING BRIBERY OF FOREIGN PUBLIC OFFICIALS IN INTERNATIONAL BUSINESS TRANSACTIONS

ADOPTED BY THE NEGOTIATING CONFERENCE ON 21 NOVEMBER 1997

General:

1. This Convention deals with what, in the law of some countries, is called "active corruption" or "active bribery", meaning the offence committed by the person who promises or gives the bribe, as contrasted with "passive bribery", the offence committed by the official who receives the bribe. The Convention does not utilise the term "active bribery" simply to avoid it being misread by the non-technical reader as implying that the briber has taken the initiative and the recipient is a passive victim. In fact, in a number of situations, the recipient will have induced or pressured the briber and will have been, in that sense, the more active.

2. This Convention seeks to assure a functional equivalence among the measures taken by the Parties to sanction bribery of foreign public officials, without requiring uniformity or changes in fundamental principles of a Party's legal system.

ARTICLE 1. THE OFFENCE OF BRIBERY OF FOREIGN PUBLIC OFFICIALS:

Re paragraph 1:

3. Article 1 establishes a standard to be met by Parties, but does not require them to utilise its precise terms in defining the offence under their domestic laws. A Party may use various approaches to fulfil its obligations, provided that conviction of a person for the offence does not require proof of elements beyond those which would be required to be proved if the offence were defined as in this paragraph. For example, a statute prohibiting the bribery of agents

generally which does not specifically address bribery of a foreign public official, and a statute specifically limited to this case, could both comply with this Article. Similarly, a statute which defined the offence in terms of payments "to induce a breach of the official's duty" could meet the standard provided that it was understood that every public official had a duty to exercise judgement or discretion impartially and this was an "autonomous" definition not requiring proof of the law of the particular official's country.

4. It is an offence within the meaning of paragraph 1 to bribe to obtain or retain business or other improper advantage whether or not the company concerned was the best qualified bidder or was otherwise a company which could properly have been awarded the business.

5. "Other improper advantage" refers to something to which the company concerned was not clearly entitled, for example, an operating permit for a factory which fails to meet the statutory requirements.

6. The conduct described in paragraph 1 is an offence whether the offer or promise is made or the pecuniary or other advantage is given on that person's own behalf or on behalf of any other natural person or legal entity.

7. It is also an offence irrespective of, *inter alia*, the value of the advantage, its results, perceptions of local custom, the tolerance of such payments by local authorities, or the alleged necessity of the payment in order to obtain or retain business or other improper advantage.

8. It is not an offence, however, if the advantage was permitted or required by the written law or regulation of the foreign public official's country, including case law.

9. Small "facilitation" payments do not constitute payments made "to obtain or retain business or other improper advantage" within the meaning of paragraph 1 and, accordingly, are also not an offence. Such payments, which, in some countries, are made to induce public officials to perform their functions, such as issuing licenses or permits, are generally illegal in the foreign country concerned. Other countries can and should address this corrosive phenomenon by such means as support for programmes of good governance. However, criminalisation by other countries does not seem a practical or effective complementary action.

10. Under the legal system of some countries, an advantage promised or given to any person, in anticipation of his or her becoming a foreign public official, falls within the scope of the offences described in Article 1, paragraph 1 or 2. Under the legal system of many countries, it is considered technically distinct from the offences covered by the present Convention. However, there is a commonly shared concern and intent to address this phenomenon through further work.

Re paragraph 2:

11. The offences set out in paragraph 2 are understood in terms of their normal content in national legal systems. Accordingly, if authorisation, incitement, or one of the other listed acts, which does not lead to further action, is not itself punishable under a Party's legal system, then the Party would not be required to make it punishable with respect to bribery of a foreign public official.

Re paragraph 4:

12. "Public function" includes any activity in the public interest, delegated by a foreign country, such as the performance of a task delegated by it in connection with public procurement.

13. A "public agency" is an entity constituted under public law to carry out specific tasks in the public interest.

14. A "public enterprise" is any enterprise, regardless of its legal form, over which a government, or governments, may, directly or indirectly, exercise a dominant influence. This is deemed to be the case, *inter alia*, when the government or governments hold the majority of the enterprise's subscribed capital, control the majority of votes attaching to shares issued by the enterprise or can appoint a majority of the members of the enterprise's administrative or managerial body or supervisory board.

15. An official of a public enterprise shall be deemed to perform a public function unless the enterprise operates on a normal commercial basis in the relevant market, *i.e.,* on a basis which is substantially equivalent to that of a private enterprise, without preferential subsidies or other privileges.

16. In special circumstances, public authority may in fact be held by persons (e.g., political party officials in single party states) not formally designated as public officials. Such persons, through their *de facto* performance of a public function, may, under the legal principles of some countries, be considered to be foreign public officials.

17. "Public international organisation" includes any international organisation formed by states, governments, or other public international organisations, whatever the form of organisation and scope of competence, including, for example, a regional economic integration organisation such as the European Communities.

18. "Foreign country" is not limited to states, but includes any organised foreign area or entity, such as an autonomous territory or a separate customs territory.

19. One case of bribery which has been contemplated under the definition in paragraph 4.c is where an executive of a company gives a bribe to a senior

official of a government, in order that this official use his office – though acting outside his competence – to make another official award a contract to that company.

ARTICLE 2. RESPONSIBILITY OF LEGAL PERSONS:

20. In the event that, under the legal system of a Party, criminal responsibility is not applicable to legal persons, that Party shall not be required to establish such criminal responsibility.

ARTICLE 3. SANCTIONS:

Re paragraph 3:

21. The "proceeds" of bribery are the profits or other benefits derived by the briber from the transaction or other improper advantage obtained or retained through bribery.

22. The term "confiscation" includes forfeiture where applicable and means the permanent deprivation of property by order of a court or other competent authority. This paragraph is without prejudice to rights of victims.

23. Paragraph 3 does not preclude setting appropriate limits to monetary sanctions.

Re paragraph 4:

24. Among the civil or administrative sanctions, other than non-criminal fines, which might be imposed upon legal persons for an act of bribery of a foreign public official are: exclusion from entitlement to public benefits or aid; temporary or permanent disqualification from participation in public procurement or from the practice of other commercial activities; placing under judicial supervision; and a judicial winding-up order.

ARTICLE 4. JURISDICTION:

Re paragraph 1:

25. The territorial basis for jurisdiction should be interpreted broadly so that an extensive physical connection to the bribery act is not required.

Re paragraph 2:

26. Nationality jurisdiction is to be established according to the general principles and conditions in the legal system of each Party. These principles deal with such matters as dual criminality. However, the requirement of dual criminality should be deemed to be met if the act is unlawful where it occurred, even if under a different criminal statute. For countries which apply nationality jurisdiction only to certain types of offences, the reference to "principles" includes the principles upon which such selection is based.

ARTICLE 5. ENFORCEMENT:

27. Article 5 recognises the fundamental nature of national regimes of prosecutorial discretion. It recognises as well that, in order to protect the independence of prosecution, such discretion is to be exercised on the basis of professional motives and is not to be subject to improper influence by concerns of a political nature. Article 5 is complemented by paragraph 6 of the Annex to the 1997 OECD Revised Recommendation on Combating Bribery in International Business Transactions, C(97)123/FINAL (hereinafter, "1997 OECD Recommendation"), which recommends, *inter alia*, that complaints of bribery of foreign public officials should be seriously investigated by competent authorities and that adequate resources should be provided by national governments to permit effective prosecution of such bribery. Parties will have accepted this Recommendation, including its monitoring and follow-up arrangements.

ARTICLE 7. MONEY LAUNDERING:

28. In Article 7, "bribery of its own public official" is intended broadly, so that bribery of a foreign public official is to be made a predicate offence for money laundering legislation on the same terms, when a Party has made either active or passive bribery of its own public official such an offence. When a Party has made only passive bribery of its own public officials a predicate offence for money laundering purposes, this article requires that the laundering of the bribe payment be subject to money laundering legislation.

ARTICLE 8. ACCOUNTING:

29. Article 8 is related to section V of the 1997 OECD Recommendation, which all Parties will have accepted and which is subject to follow-up in the OECD Working Group on Bribery in International Business Transactions. This paragraph contains a series of recommendations concerning accounting requirements, independent external audit and internal company controls the implementation of which will be important to the overall effectiveness of the fight against bribery in international business. However, one immediate consequence of the implementation of this Convention by the Parties will be

that companies which are required to issue financial statements disclosing their material contingent liabilities will need to take into account the full potential liabilities under this Convention, in particular its Articles 3 and 8, as well as other losses which might flow from conviction of the company or its agents for bribery. This also has implications for the execution of professional responsibilities of auditors regarding indications of bribery of foreign public officials. In addition, the accounting offences referred to in Article 8 will generally occur in the company's home country, when the bribery offence itself may have been committed in another country, and this can fill gaps in the effective reach of the Convention.

ARTICLE 9. MUTUAL LEGAL ASSISTANCE:

30. Parties will have also accepted, through paragraph 8 of the Agreed Common Elements annexed to the 1997 OECD Recommendation, to explore and undertake means to improve the efficiency of mutual legal assistance.

Re paragraph 1:

31. Within the framework of paragraph 1 of Article 9, Parties should, upon request, facilitate or encourage the presence or availability of persons, including persons in custody, who consent to assist in investigations or participate in proceedings. Parties should take measures to be able, in appropriate cases, to transfer temporarily such a person in custody to a Party requesting it and to credit time in custody in the requesting Party to the transferred person's sentence in the requested Party. The Parties wishing to use this mechanism should also take measures to be able, as a requesting Party, to keep a transferred person in custody and return this person without necessity of extradition proceedings.

Re paragraph 2:

32. Paragraph 2 addresses the issue of identity of norms in the concept of dual criminality. Parties with statutes as diverse as a statute prohibiting the bribery of agents generally and a statute directed specifically at bribery of foreign public officials should be able to co-operate fully regarding cases whose facts fall within the scope of the offences described in this Convention.

ARTICLE 10. EXTRADITION

Re paragraph 2:

33. A Party may consider this Convention to be a legal basis for extradition if, for one or more categories of cases falling within this Convention, it requires an extradition treaty. For example, a country may consider it a basis for

extradition of its nationals if it requires an extradition treaty for that category but does not require one for extradition of non-nationals.

ARTICLE 12. MONITORING AND FOLLOW-UP:

34. The current terms of reference of the OECD Working Group on Bribery which are relevant to monitoring and follow-up are set out in Section VIII of the 1997 OECD Recommendation. They provide for:

i) receipt of notifications and other information submitted to it by the [participating] countries;

ii) regular reviews of steps taken by [participating] countries to implement the Recommendation and to make proposals, as appropriate, to assist [participating] countries in its implementation; these reviews will be based on the following complementary systems:

- a system of self evaluation, where [participating] countries' responses on the basis of a questionnaire will provide a basis for assessing the implementation of the Recommendation;
- a system of mutual evaluation, where each [participating] country will be examined in turn by the Working Group on Bribery, on the basis of a report which will provide an objective assessment of the progress of the [participating] country in implementing the Recommendation.

iii) examination of specific issues relating to bribery in international business transactions;
...

v) provision of regular information to the public on its work and activities and on implementation of the Recommendation.

35. The costs of monitoring and follow-up will, for OECD Members, be handled through the normal OECD budget process. For Non-Members of the OECD, the current rules create an equivalent system of cost sharing, which is described in the Resolution of the Council Concerning Fees for Regular Observer Countries and Non-Member Full Participants in OECD Subsidiary Bodies, C(96)223/FINAL.

36. The follow-up of any aspect of the Convention which is not also follow-up of the 1997 OECD Recommendation or any other instrument accepted by all the participants in the OECD Working Group on Bribery will be carried out by the Parties to the Convention and, as appropriate, the participants party to another, corresponding instrument.

ARTICLE 13. SIGNATURE AND ACCESSION:

37. The Convention will be open to Non-Members which become full participants in the OECD Working Group on Bribery in International Business Transactions. Full participation by Non-Members in this Working Group is encouraged and arranged under simple procedures. Accordingly, the requirement of full participation in the Working Group, which follows from the relationship of the Convention to other aspects of the fight against bribery in international business, should not be seen as an obstacle by countries wishing to participate in that fight. The Council of the OECD has appealed to Non-Members to adhere to the 1997 OECD Recommendation and to participate in any institutional follow-up or implementation mechanism, i.e., in the Working Group. The current procedures regarding full participation by Non-Members in the Working Group may be found in the Resolution of the Council concerning the Participation of Non-Member Economies in the Work of Subsidiary Bodies of the Organisation, C(96)64/REV1/FINAL. In addition to accepting the Revised Recommendation of the Council on Combating Bribery, a full participant also accepts the Recommendation on the Tax Deductibility of Bribes of Foreign Public Officials, adopted on 11 April 1996, C(96)27/FINAL.

RECOMMENDATION OF THE COUNCIL FOR FURTHER COMBATING BRIBERY OF FOREIGN PUBLIC OFFICIALS IN INTERNATIONAL BUSINESS TRANSACTIONS

ADOPTED BY THE COUNCIL ON 26 NOVEMBER 2009

THE COUNCIL,

Having regard to Articles 3, 5a) and 5 b) of the Convention on the Organisation for Economic Cooperation and Development of 14 December 1960;

Having regard to the Convention on Combating Bribery of Foreign Public Officials in International Business Transactions of 21 November 1997 (hereinafter "the OECD Anti-Bribery Convention");

Having regard to the Revised Recommendation of the Council on Bribery in International Business Transactions of 23 May 1997 [C(97)123/FINAL] (hereinafter "the 1997 Revised Recommendation") to which the present Recommendation succeeds;

Having regard to the Recommendation of the Council on Tax Measures for Further Combating Bribery of Foreign Public Officials in International Business Transactions of 25 May 2009 [C(2009)64], the Recommendation of the Council on Bribery and Officially Supported Export Credits of 14

December 2006 [C(2006)163], the Recommendation of the Development Assistance Committee on Anti-corruption Proposals for Bilateral Aid Procurement of 7 May 1996 [DCD/DAC(96)11/FINAL], and the OECD Guidelines for Multinational Enterprises of 27 June 2000 [C(2000)96/REV1];

Considering the progress which has been made in the implementation of the OECD Anti-Bribery Convention and the 1997 Revised Recommendation and reaffirming the continuing importance of the OECD Anti-Bribery Convention and the Commentaries to the Convention;

Considering that bribery of foreign public officials is a widespread phenomenon in international business transactions, including trade and investment, raising serious moral and political concerns, undermining good governance and sustainable economic development, and distorting international competitive conditions;

Considering that all countries share a responsibility to combat bribery of foreign public officials in international business transactions;

Reiterating the importance of the vigorous and comprehensive implementation of the OECD Anti-Bribery Convention, particularly in relation to enforcement, as reaffirmed in the Statement on a Shared Commitment to Fight Against Foreign Bribery, adopted by Ministers of the Parties to the OECD Anti-Bribery Convention on 21 November 2007, the Policy Statement on Bribery in International Business Transactions, adopted by the Working Group on Bribery on 19 June 2009, and the Conclusions adopted by the OECD Council Meeting at Ministerial Level on 25 June 2009 [C/MIN(2009)5/FINAL];

Recognising that the OECD Anti-Bribery Convention and the United Nations Convention against Corruption (UNCAC) are mutually supporting and complementary, and that ratification and implementation of the UNCAC supports a comprehensive approach to combating the bribery of foreign public officials in international business transactions;

Welcoming other developments which further advance international understanding and co-operation regarding bribery in international business transactions, including actions of the Council of Europe, the European Union and the Organisation of American States;

Welcoming the efforts of companies, business organisations and trade unions as well as other non-governmental organisations to combat bribery;

Recognising that achieving progress in this field requires not only efforts on a national level but also multilateral co-operation, as well as rigorous and systematic monitoring and follow-up;

GENERAL

I. **NOTES** that the present Recommendation for Further Combating Bribery of Foreign Public Officials in International Business Transactions shall apply to OECD Member countries and other countries party to the OECD Anti-Bribery Convention (hereinafter "Member countries").

II. **RECOMMENDS** that Member countries continue taking effective measures to deter, prevent and combat the bribery of foreign public officials in connection with international business transactions.

III. **RECOMMENDS** that each Member country take concrete and meaningful steps in conformity with its jurisdictional and other basic legal principles to examine or further examine the following areas:

   i) awareness-raising initiatives in the public and private sector for the purpose of preventing and detecting foreign bribery;
   ii) criminal laws and their application, in accordance with the OECD Anti-Bribery Convention, as well as sections IV, V, VI and VII, and the Good Practice Guidance on Implementing Specific Articles of the Convention on Combating Bribery of Foreign Public Officials in International Business Transactions, as set out in Annex I to this Recommendation;
   iii) tax legislation, regulations and practice, to eliminate any indirect support of foreign bribery, in accordance with the 2009 Council Recommendation on Tax Measures for Further Combating Bribery of Foreign Public Officials in International Business Transactions, and section VIII of this Recommendation;
   iv) provisions and measures to ensure the reporting of foreign bribery, in accordance with section IX of this Recommendation;
   v) company and business accounting, external audit, as well as internal control, ethics, and compliance requirements and practices, in accordance with section X of this Recommendation;
   vi) laws and regulations on banks and other financial institutions to ensure that adequate records would be kept and made available for inspection and investigation;
   vii) public subsidies, licences, public procurement contracts, contracts funded by official development assistance, officially supported export credits, or other public advantages, so that advantages could be denied as a sanction for bribery in appropriate cases, and in accordance with sections XI and XII of this Recommendation;
   viii) civil, commercial, and administrative laws and regulations, to combat foreign bribery;
   ix) international co-operation in investigations and other legal proceedings, in accordance with section XIII of this Recommendation.

CRIMINALISATION OF BRIBERY OF FOREIGN PUBLIC OFFICIALS

IV. **RECOMMENDS,** in order to ensure the vigorous and comprehensive implementation of the OECD Anti-Bribery Convention, that Member countries should take fully into account the Good Practice Guidance on Implementing Specific Articles of the Convention on Combating Bribery of Foreign Public Officials in International Business Transactions, set forth in Annex I hereto, which is an integral part of this Recommendation.

V. **RECOMMENDS** that Member countries undertake to periodically review their laws implementing the OECD Anti-Bribery Convention and their approach to enforcement in order to effectively combat international bribery of foreign public officials.

VI. **RECOMMENDS,** in view of the corrosive effect of small facilitation payments, particularly on sustainable economic development and the rule of law that Member countries should:

   i) undertake to periodically review their policies and approach on small facilitation payments in order to effectively combat the phenomenon;
   ii) encourage companies to prohibit or discourage the use of small facilitation payments in internal company controls, ethics and compliance programmes or measures, recognising that such payments are generally illegal in the countries where they are made, and must in all cases be accurately accounted for in such companies' books and financial records.

VII. **URGES** all countries to raise awareness of their public officials on their domestic bribery and solicitation laws with a view to stopping the solicitation and acceptance of small facilitation payments.

TAX DEDUCTIBILITY

VIII. **URGES** Member countries to:

   i) fully and promptly implement the 2009 Council Recommendation on Tax Measures for Further Combating Bribery of Foreign Public Officials in International Business Transactions, which recommends in particular "that Member countries and other Parties to the OECD Anti-Bribery Convention explicitly disallow the tax deductibility of bribes to foreign public officials, for all tax purposes in an effective manner", and that "in accordance with their legal systems" they "establish an effective legal and administrative framework and provide guidance to facilitate reporting by tax authorities of suspicions of foreign bribery arising out of the performance of their duties, to the appropriate domestic law enforcement authorities";

viii) support the monitoring carried out by the Committee on Fiscal Affairs as provided under the 2009 Council Recommendation on Tax Measures for Further Combating Bribery of Foreign Public Officials in International Business Transactions.

REPORTING FOREIGN BRIBERY

IX. **RECOMMENDS** that Member countries should ensure that:

i) easily accessible channels are in place for the reporting of suspected acts of bribery of foreign public officials in international business transactions to law enforcement authorities, in accordance with their legal principles;

ii) appropriate measures are in place to facilitate reporting by public officials, in particular those posted abroad, directly or indirectly through an internal mechanism, to law enforcement authorities of suspected acts of bribery of foreign public officials in international business transactions detected in the course of their work, in accordance with their legal principles;

iii) appropriate measures are in place to protect from discriminatory or disciplinary action public and private sector employees who report in good faith and on reasonable grounds to the competent authorities suspected acts of bribery of foreign public officials in international business transactions.

ACCOUNTING REQUIREMENTS, EXTERNAL AUDIT, AND INTERNAL CONTROLS, ETHICS AND COMPLIANCE

X. **RECOMMENDS** that Member countries take the steps necessary, taking into account where appropriate the individual circumstances of a company, including its size, type, legal structure and geographical and industrial sector of operation, so that laws, rules or practices with respect to accounting requirements, external audits, and internal controls, ethics and compliance are in line with the following principles and are fully used in order to prevent and detect bribery of foreign public officials in international business, according to their jurisdictional and other basic legal principles.

A. Adequate accounting requirements

i) Member countries shall, in accordance with Article 8 of the OECD Anti-Bribery Convention, take such measures as may be necessary, within the framework of their laws and regulations regarding the maintenance of books and records, financial statement disclosures, and accounting and auditing standards, to prohibit the establishment of off-thebooks accounts, the making of off-the-books or inadequately identified transactions, the recording of non-existent expenditures, the entry of liabilities with incorrect identification of their object, as well as the use of false documents, by companies subject to those laws and regulations, for the purpose of bribing foreign public officials or of hiding such bribery;

ii) Member countries should require companies to disclose in their financial statements the full range of material contingent liabilities;

iii) Member countries shall, in accordance with Article 8 of the OECD Anti-Bribery Convention, provide effective, proportionate and dissuasive civil, administrative or criminal penalties for such omissions and falsifications in respect of the books, records, accounts and financial statements of such companies.

B. Independent External Audit

i) Member countries should consider whether requirements on companies to submit to external audit are adequate;

ii) Member countries and professional associations should maintain adequate standards to ensure the independence of external auditors which permits them to provide an objective assessment of company accounts, financial statements and internal controls;

iii) Member countries should require the external auditor who discovers indications of a suspected act of bribery of a foreign public official to report this discovery to management and, as appropriate, to corporate monitoring bodies;

iv) Member countries should encourage companies that receive reports of suspected acts of bribery of foreign public officials from an external auditor to actively and effectively respond to such reports;

v) Member countries should consider requiring the external auditor to report suspected acts of bribery of foreign public officials to competent authorities independent of the company, such as law enforcement or regulatory authorities, and for those countries that permit such reporting, ensure that auditors making such reports reasonably and in good faith are protected from legal action.

C. Internal controls, ethics, and compliance
   Member countries should encourage:

i) companies to develop and adopt adequate internal controls, ethics and compliance programmes or measures for the purpose of preventing and detecting foreign bribery, taking into account the Good Practice Guidance on Internal Controls, Ethics, and Compliance, set forth in Annex II hereto, which is an integral part of this Recommendation;

ii) business organisations and professional associations, where appropriate, in their efforts to encourage and assist companies, in particular small and medium size enterprises, in developing internal controls, ethics, and compliance programmes or measures for the purpose of preventing and detecting foreign bribery, taking into account the Good Practice Guidance on Internal Controls, Ethics, and Compliance, set forth in Annex II hereto;

iii) company management to make statements in their annual reports or otherwise publicly disclose their internal controls, ethics and compliance programmes or measures, including those which contribute to preventing and detecting bribery;

iv) the creation of monitoring bodies, independent of management, such as audit committees of boards of directors or of supervisory boards;

v) companies to provide channels for communication by, and protection of, persons not willing to violate professional standards or ethics under instructions or pressure from hierarchical superiors, as well as for persons willing to report breaches of the law or professional standards or ethics occurring within the company in good faith and on reasonable grounds, and should encourage companies to take appropriate action based on such reporting;

vi) their government agencies to consider, where international business transactions are concerned, and as appropriate, internal controls, ethics, and compliance programmes or measures in their decisions to grant public advantages, including public subsidies, licences, public procurement contracts, contracts funded by official development assistance, and officially supported export credits.

PUBLIC ADVANTAGES, INCLUDING PUBLIC PROCUREMENT

XI. **RECOMMENDS**:

i) Member countries' laws and regulations should permit authorities to suspend, to an appropriate degree, from competition for public contracts or other public advantages, including public procurement contracts and contracts funded by official development assistance, enterprises determined to have bribed foreign public officials in contravention of that Member's national laws and, to the extent a Member applies procurement sanctions to enterprises that are determined to have bribed domestic public officials, such sanctions should be applied equally in case of bribery of foreign public officials;[1]

ii) In accordance with the 1996 Development Assistance Committee Recommendation on Anti-corruption Proposals for Bilateral Aid Procurement, Member countries should require anti-corruption provisions in bilateral aid-funded procurement, promote the proper implementation of anti-corruption provisions in international development institutions, and work closely with development partners to combat corruption in all development cooperation efforts;[2]

iii) Member countries should support the efforts of the OECD Public Governance Committee to implement the principles contained in the 2008 Council Recommendation on Enhancing Integrity in Public Procurement [C(2008)105], as well as work on transparency in public procurement in other international governmental organisations such as the United Nations, the World Trade Organisation (WTO), and the European Union, and are encouraged to adhere to relevant international standards such as the WTO Agreement on Government Procurement.

OFFICIALLY SUPPORTED EXPORT CREDITS

XII. **RECOMMENDS**:

i) Countries Party to the OECD Anti-Bribery Convention that are not OECD Members should adhere to the 2006 OECD Council Recommendation on Bribery and Officially Supported Export Credits;

ii) Member countries should support the efforts of the OECD Working Party on Export Credits and Credit Guarantees to implement and monitor implementation of the principles contained in the 2006 OECD Council Recommendation on Bribery and Officially Supported Export Credits.

INTERNATIONAL CO-OPERATION

XIII. **RECOMMENDS** that Member countries, in order to effectively combat bribery of foreign public officials in international business

---

[1] Member countries' systems for applying sanctions for bribery of domestic officials differ as to whether the determination of bribery is based on a criminal conviction, indictment or administrative procedure, but in all cases it is based on substantial evidence.

[2] This paragraph summarises the DAC recommendation, which is addressed to DAC members only, and addresses it to all OECD Members and eventually non-member countries which adhere to the Recommendation.

transactions, in conformity with their jurisdictional and other basic legal principles, take the following actions:

i) consult and otherwise co-operate with competent authorities in other countries, and, as appropriate, international and regional law enforcement networks involving Member and non-Member countries, in investigations and other legal proceedings concerning specific cases of such bribery, through such means as the sharing of information spontaneously or upon request, provision of evidence, extradition, and the identification, freezing, seizure, confiscation and recovery of the proceeds of bribery of foreign public officials;
ii) seriously investigate credible allegations of bribery of foreign public officials referred to them by international governmental organisations, such as the international and regional development banks;
iii) make full use of existing agreements and arrangements for mutual international legal assistance and where necessary, enter into new agreements or arrangements for this purpose;
iv) ensure that their national laws afford an adequate basis for this co-operation, in particular in accordance with Articles 9 and 10 of the OECD Anti-Bribery Convention;
v) consider ways for facilitating mutual legal assistance between Member countries and with non-Member countries in cases of such bribery, including regarding evidentiary thresholds for some Member countries.

FOLLOW-UP AND INSTITUTIONAL ARRANGEMENTS

XIV. **INSTRUCTS** the Working Group on Bribery in International Business Transactions, to carry out an ongoing programme of systematic follow-up to monitor and promote the full implementation of the OECD Anti-Bribery Convention and this Recommendation, in co-operation with the Committee for Fiscal Affairs, the Development Assistance Committee, the Investment Committee, the Public Governance Committee, the Working Party on Export Credits and Credit Guarantees, and other OECD bodies, as appropriate. This follow-up will include, in particular:

i) continuation of the programme of rigorous and systematic monitoring of Member countries' implementation of the OECD Anti-Bribery Convention and this Recommendation to promote the full implementation of these instruments, including through an ongoing system of mutual evaluation, where each Member country is examined in turn by the Working Group on Bribery, on the basis of a report which will provide an objective assessment of the progress of the Member country in implementing the OECD Anti-Bribery Convention and this Recommendation, and which will be made publicly available;

ii) receipt of notifications and other information submitted to it by the Member countries concerning the authorities which serve as channels of communication for the purpose of facilitating international cooperation on implementation of the OECD Anti-Bribery Convention and this Recommendation;
iii) regular reporting on steps taken by Member countries to implement the OECD Anti-Bribery Convention and this Recommendation, including non-confidential information on investigations and prosecutions;
iv) voluntary meetings of law enforcement officials directly involved in the enforcement of the foreign bribery offence to discuss best practices and horizontal issues relating to the investigation and prosecution of the bribery of foreign public officials;
v) examination of prevailing trends, issues and counter-measures in foreign bribery, including through work on typologies and cross-country studies;
vi) development of tools and mechanisms to increase the impact of monitoring and follow-up, and awareness raising, including through the voluntary submission and public reporting of non-confidential enforcement data, research, and bribery threat assessments;
vii) provision of regular information to the public on its work and activities and on implementation of the OECD Anti-Bribery Convention and this Recommendation.

XV. **NOTES** the obligation of Member countries to co-operate closely in this follow-up programme, pursuant to Article 3 of the Convention on the Organisation for Economic Co-operation and Development of 14 December 1960, and Article 12 of the OECD Anti-Bribery Convention.

CO-OPERATION WITH NON MEMBERS

XVI. **APPEALS** to non-Member countries that are major exporters and foreign investors to adhere to and implement the OECD Anti-Bribery Convention and this Recommendation and participate in any institutional follow-up or implementation mechanism.

XVII. **INSTRUCTS** the Working Group on Bribery in International Business Transactions to provide a forum for consultations with countries which have not yet adhered, in order to promote wider participation in the OECD Anti-Bribery Convention and this Recommendation, and their follow-up.

RELATIONS WITH INTERNATIONAL GOVERNMENTAL AND NON-GOVERNMENTAL ORGANISATIONS

XVIII. INVITES the Working Group on Bribery in International Business Transactions, to consult and co-operate with the international organisations and international financial institutions active in the fight against bribery of foreign public officials in international business transactions, and consult regularly with the non-governmental organisations and representatives of the business community active in this field.

ANNEX I:

GOOD PRACTICE GUIDANCE ON IMPLEMENTING SPECIFIC ARTICLES OF THE CONVENTION ON COMBATING BRIBERY OF FOREIGN PUBLIC OFFICIALS IN INTERNATIONAL BUSINESS TRANSACTIONS

Having regard to the findings and recommendations of the Working Group on Bribery in International Business Transactions in its programme of systematic follow-up to monitor and promote the full implementation of the OECD Convention on Combating Bribery in International Business Transactions (the OECD Anti Bribery Convention), as required by Article 12 of the Convention, good practice on fully implementing specific articles of the Convention has evolved as follows:

A) ARTICLE 1 OF THE OECD ANTI BRIBERY CONVENTION: THE OFFENCE OF BRIBERY OF FOREIGN PUBLIC OFFICIALS

Article 1 of the OECD Anti-Bribery Convention should be implemented in such a way that it does not provide a defence or exception where the foreign public official solicits a bribe.

Member countries should undertake public awareness-raising actions and provide specific written guidance to the public on their laws implementing the OECD Anti-Bribery Convention and the Commentaries to the Convention.

Member countries should provide information and training as appropriate to their public officials posted abroad on their laws implementing the OECD Anti-Bribery Convention, so that such personnel can provide basic information to their companies in foreign countries and appropriate assistance when such companies are confronted with bribe solicitations.

B) ARTICLE 2 OF THE OECD ANTI BRIBERY CONVENTION: RESPONSIBILITY OF LEGAL PERSONS

Member countries' systems for the liability of legal persons for the bribery of foreign public officials in international business transactions should not restrict the liability to cases where the natural person or persons who perpetrated the offence are prosecuted or convicted.

Member countries' systems for the liability of legal persons for the bribery of foreign public officials in international business transactions should take one of the following approaches:

a. the level of authority of the person whose conduct triggers the liability of the legal person is flexible and reflects the wide variety of decision-making systems in legal persons; or

b. the approach is functionally equivalent to the foregoing even though it is only triggered by acts of persons with the highest level managerial authority, because the following cases are covered:

    –   A person with the highest level managerial authority offers, promises or gives a bribe to a foreign public official;
    –   A person with the highest level managerial authority directs or authorises a lower level person to offer, promise or give a bribe to a foreign public official; and
    –   A person with the highest level managerial authority fails to prevent a lower level person from bribing a foreign public official, including through a failure to supervise him or her or through a failure to implement adequate internal controls, ethics and compliance programmes or measures.

C) RESPONSIBILITY FOR BRIBERY THROUGH INTERMEDIARIES

Member countries should ensure that, in accordance with Article 1 of the OECD Anti Bribery Convention, and the principle of functional equivalence in Commentary 2 to the OECD Anti-Bribery Convention, a legal person cannot avoid responsibility by using intermediaries, including related legal persons, to offer, promise or give a bribe to a foreign public official on its behalf.

D) ARTICLE 5: ENFORCEMENT

Member countries should be vigilant in ensuring that investigations and prosecutions of the bribery of foreign public officials in international business transactions are not influenced by considerations of national economic interest, the potential effect upon relations with another State or the identity of the natural or legal persons involved, in compliance with Article 5 of the OECD Anti Bribery Convention.

Complaints of bribery of foreign public officials should be seriously investigated and credible allegations assessed by competent authorities.

Member countries should provide adequate resources to law enforcement authorities so as to permit effective investigation and prosecution of bribery of foreign public officials in international business transactions, taking into consideration Commentary 27 to the OECD Anti Bribery Convention.

ANNEX II

GOOD PRACTICE GUIDANCE ON INTERNAL CONTROLS, ETHICS, AND COMPLIANCE

This Good Practice Guidance acknowledges the relevant findings and recommendations of the Working Group on Bribery in International Business Transactions in its programme of systematic follow-up to monitor and promote the full implementation of the OECD Convention on Combating Bribery of Foreign Public Officials in International Business Transactions (hereinafter "OECD Anti-Bribery Convention"); contributions from the private sector and civil society through the Working Group on Bribery's consultations on its review of the OECD anti-bribery instruments; and previous work on preventing and detecting bribery in business by the OECD as well as international private sector and civil society bodies.

INTRODUCTION

This Good Practice Guidance (hereinafter "Guidance") is addressed to companies for establishing and ensuring the effectiveness of internal controls, ethics, and compliance programmes or measures for preventing and detecting the bribery of foreign public officials in their international business transactions (hereinafter "foreign bribery"), and to business organisations and professional associations, which play an essential role in assisting companies in these efforts. It recognises that to be effective, such programmes or measures should be interconnected with a company's overall compliance framework. It is intended to serve as non-legally binding guidance to companies in establishing effective internal controls, ethics, and compliance programmes or measures for preventing and detecting foreign bribery.

This Guidance is flexible, and intended to be adapted by companies, in particular small and medium sized enterprises (hereinafter "SMEs"), according to their individual circumstances, including their size, type, legal structure and geographical and industrial sector of operation, as well as the jurisdictional and other basic legal principles under which they operate.

A) GOOD PRACTICE GUIDANCE FOR COMPANIES

Effective internal controls, ethics, and compliance programmes or measures for preventing and detecting foreign bribery should be developed on the basis of a risk assessment addressing the individual circumstances of a company, in particular the foreign bribery risks facing the company (such as its geographical and industrial sector of operation). Such circumstances and risks should be regularly monitored, re-assessed, and adapted as necessary to ensure the continued effectiveness of the company's internal controls, ethics, and compliance programme or measures. Companies should consider, *inter alia*, the following good practices for ensuring effective internal controls, ethics, and compliance programmes or measures for the purpose of preventing and detecting foreign bribery:

1. strong, explicit and visible support and commitment from senior management to the company's internal controls, ethics and compliance programmes or measures for preventing and detecting foreign bribery;

2. a clearly articulated and visible corporate policy prohibiting foreign bribery;

3. compliance with this prohibition and the related internal controls, ethics, and compliance programmes or measures is the duty of individuals at all levels of the company;

4. oversight of ethics and compliance programmes or measures regarding foreign bribery, including the authority to report matters directly to independent monitoring bodies such as internal audit committees of boards of directors or of supervisory boards, is the duty of one or more senior corporate officers, with an adequate level of autonomy from management, resources, and authority;

5. ethics and compliance programmes or measures designed to prevent and detect foreign bribery, applicable to all directors, officers, and employees, and applicable to all entities over which a company has effective control, including subsidiaries, on, *inter alia*, the following areas:

    i) gifts;
    ii) hospitality, entertainment and expenses;
    iii) customer travel;
    iv) political contributions;
    v) charitable donations and sponsorships;
    vi) facilitation payments; and

vii) solicitation and extortion;

6. ethics and compliance programmes or measures designed to prevent and detect foreign bribery applicable, where appropriate and subject to contractual arrangements, to third parties such as agents and other intermediaries, consultants, representatives, distributors, contractors and suppliers, consortia, and joint venture partners (hereinafter "business partners"), including, *inter alia*, the following essential elements:

    i) properly documented risk-based due diligence pertaining to the hiring, as well as the appropriate and regular oversight of business partners;
    ii) informing business partners of the company's commitment to abiding by laws on the prohibitions against foreign bribery, and of the company's ethics and compliance programme or measures for preventing and detecting such bribery; and
    iii) seeking a reciprocal commitment from business partners.

7. a system of financial and accounting procedures, including a system of internal controls, reasonably designed to ensure the maintenance of fair and accurate books, records, and accounts, to ensure that they cannot be used for the purpose of foreign bribery or hiding such bribery;

8. measures designed to ensure periodic communication, and documented training for all levels of the company, on the company's ethics and compliance programme or measures regarding foreign bribery, as well as, where appropriate, for subsidiaries;

9. appropriate measures to encourage and provide positive support for the observance of ethics and compliance programmes or measures against foreign bribery, at all levels of the company;

10. appropriate disciplinary procedures to address, among other things, violations, at all levels of the company, of laws against foreign bribery, and the company's ethics and compliance programme or measures regarding foreign bribery;

11. effective measures for:

    i) providing guidance and advice to directors, officers, employees, and, where appropriate, business partners, on complying with the company's ethics and compliance programme or measures, including when they need urgent advice on difficult situations in foreign jurisdictions;
    ii) internal and where possible confidential reporting by, and protection of, directors, officers, employees, and, where appropriate, business partners, not willing to violate professional standards or ethics under instructions or pressure from hierarchical superiors, as well as for

directors, officers, employees, and, where appropriate, business partners, willing to report breaches of the law or professional standards or ethics occurring within the company, in good faith and on reasonable grounds; and

iii) undertaking appropriate action in response to such reports;

12. periodic reviews of the ethics and compliance programmes or measures, designed to evaluate and improve their effectiveness in preventing and detecting foreign bribery, taking into account relevant developments in the field, and evolving international and industry standards.

B) ACTIONS BY BUSINESS ORGANISATIONS AND PROFESSIONAL ASSOCIATIONS

Business organisations and professional associations may play an essential role in assisting companies, in particular SMEs, in the development of effective internal control, ethics, and compliance programmes or measures for the purpose of preventing and detecting foreign bribery. Such support may include, *inter alia*:

1. dissemination of information on foreign bribery issues, including regarding relevant developments in international and regional forums, and access to relevant databases;

2. making training, prevention, due diligence, and other compliance tools available;

3. general advice on carrying out due diligence; and

4. general advice and support on resisting extortion and solicitation.

RECOMMENDATION OF THE COUNCIL ON TAX MEASURES FOR FURTHER COMBATING BRIBERY OF FOREIGN PUBLIC OFFICIALS IN INTERNATIONAL BUSINESS TRANSACTIONS

ADOPTED BY THE COUNCIL ON 25 MAY 2009

THE COUNCIL,

Having regard to Article 5, b) of the Convention on the Organisation for Economic Cooperation and Development of 14 December 1960;

Having regard to the Recommendation of the Council on the Tax Deductibility of Bribes to Foreign Public Officials [C(96)27/FINAL] (hereafter the "1996 Recommendation"), to which the present Recommendation succeeds;

Having regard to the Revised Recommendation of the Council on Bribery in International Business Transactions [C(97)123/FINAL];

Having regard to the Convention on Combating Bribery of Foreign Public Officials in International Business Transactions to which all OECD Members and eight non-Members are Parties, as at the time of the adoption of this Recommendation (hereafter the "OECD Anti-Bribery Convention");

Having regard to the Commentaries on the OECD Anti-Bribery Convention;

Having regard to the Recommendation of the Council concerning the Model Tax Convention on Income and on Capital (hereafter the "OECD Model Tax Convention") [C(97)195/FINAL];

Welcoming the United Nations Convention Against Corruption to which most parties to the OECD Anti-Bribery Convention are State parties, and in particular Article 12.4, which provides that "Each State Party shall disallow the tax deductibility of expenses that constitute bribes";

Considering that the 1996 Recommendation has had an important impact both within and outside the OECD, and that significant steps have already been taken by governments, the private sector and non-governmental agencies to combat the bribery of foreign public officials, but that the problem still continues to be widespread and necessitates strengthened measures;

Considering that explicit legislation disallowing the deductibility of bribes increases the overall awareness within the business community of the illegality of bribery of foreign public officials and within the tax administration of the need to detect and disallow deductions for payments of bribes to foreign public officials; and

Considering that sharing information by tax authorities with other law enforcement authorities can be an important tool for the detection and investigation of transnational bribery offences;

On the proposal of the Committee on Fiscal Affairs and the Investment Committee;

I. RECOMMENDS that:

(i) Member countries and other Parties to the OECD Anti-Bribery Convention explicitly disallow the tax deductibility of bribes to foreign public officials, for all tax purposes in an effective manner. Such disallowance should be established by law or by any other binding means which carry the same effect, such as:

- prohibiting tax deductibility of bribes to foreign public officials;
- prohibiting tax deductibility of all bribes or expenditures incurred in furtherance of corrupt conduct in contravention of the criminal law or any other laws of the Party to the Anti-Bribery Convention.

Denial of tax deductibility is not contingent on the opening of an investigation by the law enforcement authorities or of court proceedings.

(ii) Each Member country and other Party to the OECD Anti-Bribery Convention review, on an ongoing basis, the effectiveness of its legal, administrative and policy frameworks as well as practices for disallowing tax deductibility of bribes to foreign public officials. These reviews should assess whether adequate guidance is provided to taxpayers and tax authorities as to the types of expenses that are deemed to constitute bribes to foreign public officials, and whether such bribes are effectively detected by tax authorities.

(iii) Member countries and other Parties to the OECD Anti-Bribery Convention consider to include in their bilateral tax treaties, the optional language of paragraph 12.3 of the Commentary to Article 26 of the OECD Model Tax Convention, which allows *"the sharing of tax information by tax authorities with other law enforcement agencies and judicial authorities on certain high priority matters (e.g. to combat money laundering, corruption, terrorism financing)"* and reads as follows:

> *"Notwithstanding the foregoing, information received by a Contracting State may be used for other purposes when such information may be used for such other purposes under the laws of both States and the competent authority of the supplying State authorises such use."*

II. further RECOMMENDS Member countries and other Parties to the OECD Anti-Bribery Convention, in accordance with their legal systems, to establish an effective legal and administrative framework and provide guidance to facilitate reporting by tax authorities of suspicions of foreign bribery arising out of the performance of their duties, to the appropriate domestic law enforcement authorities.

III. INVITES non-Members that are not yet Parties to the OECD Anti-Bribery Convention to apply this Recommendation to the fullest extent possible.

IV. INSTRUCTS the Committee on Fiscal Affairs together with the Investment Committee to monitor the implementation of the Recommendation and to promote it in the context of contacts with non-Members and to report to Council as appropriate.

RECOMMENDATION OF THE COUNCIL ON BRIBERY AND OFFICIALLY SUPPORTED EXPORT CREDITS

ADOPTED BY THE COUNCIL ON 14 DECEMBER 2006

THE COUNCIL

Having regard to the Convention on the Organisation for Economic Co-operation and Development of 14th December 1960 and, in particular, to Article 5 b) thereof;

Having regard to the Convention on Combating Bribery of Foreign Public Officials in International Business Transactions (hereafter the Anti-Bribery Convention) and to the 1997 Revised Recommendation of the Council on Combating Bribery in International Business Transactions [C(97)123] (hereafter the 1997 Recommendation);

Having regard to the 2006 Action Statement on Bribery and Officially Supported Export Credits;

Considering that combating bribery in international business transactions is a priority issue and that the Working Party on Export Credits and Credit Guarantees is the appropriate forum to ensure the implementation of the Anti-Bribery Convention and the 1997 Recommendation in respect of international business transactions benefiting from official export credit support;

Noting that the application by Members of the measures set out in Paragraph 2 in no way mitigates the responsibility of the exporter and other parties in transactions benefiting from official support to: (i) comply with all applicable laws and regulations, including national provisions for combating bribery of foreign public officials in international business transactions, or (ii) provide the proper description of the transaction for which support is sought, including all relevant payments;

On the proposal of the Working Party on Export Credits and Credit Guarantees (hereafter the ECG):

1. RECOMMENDS that Members take appropriate measures to deter bribery[3] in international business transactions benefiting from official export credit support, in accordance with the legal system of each member country and the

---

[3] As defined in the Anti-Bribery Convention.

character of the export credit[4] and not prejudicial to the rights of any parties not responsible for the illegal payments, including:

a) Informing exporters and, where appropriate, applicants, requesting support about the legal consequences of bribery in international business transactions under its national legal system including its national laws prohibiting such bribery and encouraging them to develop, apply and document appropriate management control systems that combat bribery.

b) Requiring exporters and, where appropriate, applicants, to provide an undertaking/ declaration that neither they, nor anyone acting on their behalf, such as agents, have been engaged or will engage in bribery in the transaction.

c) Verifying and noting whether exporters and, where appropriate, applicants, are listed on the publicly available debarment lists of the following international financial institutions: World Bank Group, African Development Bank, Asian Development Bank, European Bank for Reconstruction and Development and the Inter-American Development Bank[5].

d) Requiring exporters and, where appropriate, applicants, to disclose whether they or anyone acting on their behalf in connection with the transaction are currently under charge in a national court or, within a five-year period preceding the application, have been convicted in a national court or been subject to equivalent national administrative measures for violation of laws against bribery of foreign public officials of any country.

e) Requiring that exporters and, where appropriate, applicants, disclose, upon demand: (i) the identity of persons acting on their behalf in connection with the transaction, and (ii) the amount and purpose of commissions and fees paid, or agreed to be paid, to such persons.

f) Undertaking enhanced due diligence if: (i) the exporters and, where appropriate, applicants, appear on the publicly available debarment lists of one of the international financial institutions referred to in c) above; or (ii) the Member becomes aware that exporters and, where appropriate, applicants or anyone acting on their behalf in connection with the transaction, are currently under charge in a national court, or, within a fiveyear period preceding the application, has been convicted in a national

---

[4] It is recognised that not all export credit products are conducive to a uniform implementation of the Recommendation. For example, on short-term whole-turnover and multi-buyer export credit insurance policies, Members may, where appropriate, implement the Recommendation on an export credit policy basis rather than on a transaction basis.

[5] The implementation of paragraph 1 c) may take the form of a self-declaration from exporters and, where appropriate, applicants, as to whether they are listed on the publicly available IFI debarment lists.

court or been subject to equivalent national administrative measures for violation of laws against bribery of foreign public officials of any country; or (iii) the Member has reason to believe that bribery may be involved in the transaction.

g) In case of a conviction in a national court or equivalent national administrative measures for violation of laws against bribery of foreign public officials of any country within a five-year period, verifying whether appropriate internal corrective and preventive measures[6] have been taken, maintained and documented.

h) Developing and implementing procedures to disclose to their law enforcement authorities instances of credible evidence[7] of bribery in the case that such procedures do not already exist.

i) If there is credible evidence at any time that bribery was involved in the award or execution of the export contract, informing their law enforcement authorities promptly.

j) If, before credit, cover or other support has been approved, there is credible evidence that bribery was involved in the award or execution of the export contract, suspending approval of the application during the enhanced due diligence process. If the enhanced due diligence concludes that bribery was involved in the transaction, the Member shall refuse to approve credit, cover or other support.

k) If, after credit, cover or other support has been approved bribery has been proven, taking appropriate action, such as denial of payment, indemnification, or refund of sums provided.

2. INSTRUCTS the ECG to continue to:

a) Exchange information on how the Anti-Bribery Convention and 1997 Recommendation are being taken into account in national official export credit systems.

b) Collate and map the information exchanged with a view to considering further steps to combat bribery in respect of officially supported export credits.

c) Exchange views with appropriate stakeholders.

---

[6] Such measures could include: replacing individuals that have been involved in bribery, adopting an appropriate anti-bribery management control systems, submitting to an audit and making the results of such periodic audits available.

[7] For the purpose of this Recommendation, credible evidence is evidence of a quality which, after critical analysis, a court would find to be reasonable and sufficient grounds upon which to base a decision on the issue if no contrary evidence were submitted.

3. INVITES the Parties to the Anti-Bribery Convention which are not OECD Members to adhere to this Recommendation.

RECOMMENDATION OF THE DEVELOPMENT ASSISTANCE COMMITTEE ON ANTI-CORRUPTION PROPOSALS FOR BILATERAL AID PROCUREMENT

Recommendation endorsed by the Development Assistance Committee at its High Level Meeting, 6–7 May 1996

1. DAC Members share a concern with corruption:

– It undermines good governance.

– It wastes scarce resources for development, whether from aid or from other public or private sources, with far-reaching effects throughout the economy.

– It undermines the credibility of, and public support for, development co-operation and devalues the reputation and efforts of all who work to support sustainable development.

– It compromises open and transparent competition on the basis of price and quality.

2. The DAC, therefore, firmly endorses the need to combat corruption through effective prohibition, co-ordinated in a multilateral framework to ensure harmonised implementation. Other meaningful and concrete measures are also required to ensure transparency, accountability and probity in the use of public resources in DAC Members' own systems and those of partner countries, who themselves are increasingly concerned with this problem.

3. In its efforts to curb corruption, the DAC recognises that opportunities may exist for corrupt practices in aid-funded procurement. Together with other efforts to deal with corruption, the DAC hereby expresses its firm intention to work to eliminate corruption in aid procurement.

4. The DAC therefore recommends that Members introduce or require anti-corruption provisions governing bilateral aid-funded procurement. This work should be carried out in coordination with other work being undertaken in the OECD and elsewhere to eliminate corruption, and in collaboration with recipient countries. The DAC also recommends that its Members work to ensure the proper implementation of their anti-corruption provisions and that they draw to the attention of the international development institutions to which they belong, the importance of proper implementation of the anti-corruption provisions envisaged in their rules of operation.

5. The DAC will follow up on the effect given to this Recommendation within one year.

6. DAC Members will work closely with development partners to combat corruption in all **development co-operation efforts.**

OECD GUIDELINES FOR MULTINATIONAL ENTERPRISES – SECTION VI

VI. COMBATING BRIBERY

Enterprises should not, directly or indirectly, offer, promise, give, or demand a bribe or other undue advantage to obtain or retain business or other improper advantage. Nor should enterprises be solicited or expected to render a bribe or other undue advantage. In particular, enterprises should:

1. Not offer, nor give in to demands, to pay public officials or the employees of business partners any portion of a contract payment. They should not use subcontracts, purchase orders or consulting agreements as means of channelling payments to public officials, to employees of business partners or to their relatives or business associates.

2. Ensure that remuneration of agents is appropriate and for legitimate services only. Where relevant, a list of agents employed in connection with transactions with public bodies and stateowned enterprises should be kept and made available to competent authorities.

3. Enhance the transparency of their activities in the fight against bribery and extortion. Measures could include making public commitments against bribery and extortion and disclosing the management systems the company has adopted in order to honour these commitments. The enterprise should also foster openness and dialogue with the public so as to promote its awareness of and co-operation with the fight against bribery and extortion.

4. Promote employee awareness of and compliance with company policies against bribery and extortion through appropriate dissemination of these policies and through training programmes and disciplinary procedures.

5. Adopt management control systems that discourage bribery and corrupt practices, and adopt financial and tax accounting and auditing practices that prevent the establishment of "off the books" or secret accounts or the creation of documents which do not properly and fairly record the transactions to which they relate.

6. Not make illegal contributions to candidates for public office or to political parties or to other political organisations. Contributions should fully comply with public disclosure requirements and should be reported to senior management.

Appendix H

UNITED NATIONS CONVENTION AGAINST CORRUPTION

UNITED NATIONS *Office on Drugs and Crime*

UNITED NATIONS CONVENTION AGAINST CORRUPTION

UNITED NATIONS OFFICE ON DRUGS AND CRIME

Vienna

UNITED NATIONS CONVENTION AGAINST CORRUPTION

UNITED NATIONS

New York, 2004

FOREWORD

Corruption is an insidious plague that has a wide range of corrosive effects on societies. It undermines democracy and the rule of law, leads to violations of human rights, distorts markets, erodes the quality of life and allows organized crime, terrorism and other threats to human security to flourish.

This evil phenomenon is found in all countries—big and small, rich and poor—but it is in the developing world that its effects are most destructive. Corruption hurts the poor disproportionately by diverting funds intended for development, undermining a Government's ability to provide basic services, feeding inequality and injustice and discouraging foreign aid and investment. Corruption is a key element in economic underperformance and a major obstacle to poverty alleviation and development.

I am therefore very happy that we now have a new instrument to address this scourge at the global level. The adoption of the United Nations Convention against Corruption will send a clear message that the international community is determined to prevent and control corruption. It will warn the corrupt that betrayal of the public trust will no longer be tolerated. And it will reaffirm the importance of core values such as honesty, respect for the rule of law, accountability and transparency in promoting development and making the world a better place for all.

The new Convention is a remarkable achievement, and it complements another landmark instrument, the United Nations Convention against Transnational Organized Crime, which entered into force just a month ago. It is balanced, strong and pragmatic, and it offers a new framework for effective action and international cooperation.

The Convention introduces a comprehensive set of standards, measures and rules that all countries can apply in order to strengthen their legal and regulatory regimes to fight corruption. It calls for preventive measures and the criminalization of the most prevalent forms of corruption in both public and private sectors. And it makes a major breakthrough by requiring Member States to return assets obtained through corruption to the country from which they were stolen.

These provisions—the first of their kind—introduce a new fundamental principle, as well as a framework for stronger cooperation between States to prevent and detect corruption and to return the proceeds. Corrupt officials will in future find fewer ways to hide their illicit gains. This is a particularly important issue for many developing countries where corrupt high officials have plundered the national wealth and where new Governments badly need resources to reconstruct and rehabilitate their societies.

For the United Nations, the Convention is the culmination of work that started many years ago, when the word corruption was hardly ever uttered in official circles. It took systematic efforts, first at the technical, and then gradually at the political, level to put the fight against corruption on the global agenda. Both the Monterrey International Conference on Financing for Development and the Johannesburg World Summit on Sustainable Development offered opportunities for Governments to express their determination to attack corruption and to make many more people aware of the devastating effect that corruption has on development.

The Convention is also the result of long and difficult negotiations. Many complex issues and many concerns from different quarters had to be addressed. It was a formidable challenge to produce, in less than two years, an instrument that reflects all those concerns. All countries had to show flexibility and make concessions. But we can be proud of the result.

Allow me to congratulate the members of the bureau of the Ad Hoc Committee for the Negotiation of a Convention against Corruption on their hard work and leadership, and to pay a special tribute to the Committee's late Chairman, Ambassador Héctor Charry Samper of Colombia, for his wise guidance and his dedication. I am sure all here share my sorrow that he is not with us to celebrate this great success.

The adoption of the new Convention will be a remarkable achievement. But let us be clear: it is only a beginning. We must build on the momentum achieved to ensure that the Convention enters into force as soon as possible. I urge all

Member States to attend the Signing Conference in Merida, Mexico, in December, and to ratify the Convention at the earliest possible date.

If fully enforced, this new instrument can make a real difference to the quality of life of millions of people around the world. And by removing one of the biggest obstacles to development it can help us achieve the Millennium Development Goals. Be assured that the United Nations Secretariat, and in particular the United Nations Office on Drugs and Crime, will do whatever it can to support the efforts of States to eliminate the scourge of corruption from the face of the Earth. It is a big challenge, but I think that, together, we can make a difference.

Kofi A. Annan

Secretary-General

GENERAL ASSEMBLY RESOLUTION 58/4 OF 31 OCTOBER 2003

UNITED NATIONS CONVENTION AGAINST CORRUPTION

The General Assembly,

Recalling its resolution 55/61 of 4 December 2000, in which it established an ad hoc committee for the negotiation of an effective international legal instrument against corruption and requested the Secretary-General to convene an intergovernmental open-ended expert group to examine and prepare draft terms of reference for the negotiation of such an instrument, and its resolution 55/188 of 20 December 2000, in which it invited the intergovernmental open-ended expert group to be convened pursuant to resolution 55/61 to examine the question of illegally transferred funds and the return of such funds to the countries of origin,

Recalling also its resolutions 56/186 of 21 December 2001 and 57/244 of 20 December 2002 on preventing and combating corrupt practices and transfer of funds of illicit origin and returning such funds to the countries of origin,

Recalling further its resolution 56/260 of 31 January 2002, in which it requested the Ad Hoc Committee for the Negotiation of a Convention against Corruption to complete its work by the end of 2003,

Recalling its resolution 57/169 of 18 December 2002, in which it accepted with appreciation the offer made by the Government of Mexico to host a high-level political conference for the purpose of signing the convention and requested the Secretary-General to schedule the conference for a period of three days before the end of 2003,

Recalling also Economic and Social Council resolution 2001/13 of 24 July 2001, entitled "Strengthening international cooperation in preventing and combating the transfer of funds of illicit origin, derived from acts of corruption, including the laundering of funds, and in returning such funds",

Expressing its appreciation to the Government of Argentina for hosting the informal preparatory meeting of the Ad Hoc Committee for the Negotiation of a Convention against Corruption in Buenos Aires from 4 to 7 December 2001,

Recalling the Monterrey Consensus, adopted by the International Conference on Financing for Development, held in Monterrey, Mexico, from 18 to 22 March 2002,[1] in which it was underlined that fighting corruption at all levels was a priority,

Recalling also the Johannesburg Declaration on Sustainable Development, adopted by the World Summit on Sustainable Development, held in Johannesburg, South Africa, from 26 August to 4 September 2002,[2] in particular paragraph 19 thereof, in which corruption was declared a threat to the sustainable development of people,

Concerned about the seriousness of problems and threats posed by corruption to the stability and security of societies, undermining the institutions and values of democracy, ethical values and justice and jeopardizing sustainable development and the rule of law,

1. *Takes note* of the report of the Ad Hoc Committee for the Negotiation of a Convention against Corruption,[3] which carried out its work at the headquarters of the United Nations Office on Drugs and Crime in Vienna, in which the Ad Hoc Committee submitted the final text of the draft United Nations Convention against Corruption to the General Assembly for its consideration and action, and commends the Ad Hoc Committee for its work;

2. *Adopts* the United Nations Convention against Corruption annexed to the present resolution, and opens it for signature at the High-level Political Signing Conference to be held in Merida, Mexico, from 9 to 11 December 2003, in accordance with resolution 57/169;

---

[1] Report of the International Conference on Financing for Development, Monterrey, Mexico, 18–22 March 2002 (United Nations publication, Sales No. E.02.II.A.7), chap. I, resolution 1, annex.

[2] Report of the World Summit on Sustainable Development, Johannesburg, South Africa, 26 August – 4 September 2002 (United Nations publication, Sales No. E.03.II.A.1 and corrigendum), chap. I, resolution 1, annex.

[3] A/58/422 and Add.1.

3. *Urges* all States and competent regional economic integration organizations to sign and ratify the United Nations Convention against Corruption as soon as possible in order to ensure its rapid entry into force;

4. *Decides* that, until the Conference of the States Parties to the Convention established pursuant to the United Nations Convention against Corruption decides otherwise, the account referred to in article 62 of the Convention will be operated within the United Nations Crime Prevention and Criminal Justice Fund, and encourages Member States to begin making adequate voluntary contributions to the above-mentioned account for the provision to developing countries and countries with economies in transition of the technical assistance that they might require to prepare for ratification and implementation of the Convention;

5. *Also decides* that the Ad Hoc Committee for the Negotiation of a Convention against Corruption will complete its tasks arising from the negotiation of the United Nations Convention against Corruption by holding a meeting well before the convening of the first session of the Conference of the States Parties to the Convention in order to prepare the draft text of the rules of procedure of the Conference of the States Parties and of other rules described in article 63 of the Convention, which will be submitted to the Conference of the States Parties at its first session for consideration;

6. *Requests* the Conference of the States Parties to the Convention to address the criminalization of bribery of officials of public international organizations, including the United Nations, and related issues, taking into account questions of privileges and immunities, as well as of jurisdiction and the role of international organizations, by, inter alia, making recommendations regarding appropriate action in that regard;

7. *Decides* that, in order to raise awareness of corruption and of the role of the Convention in combating and preventing it, 9 December should be designated International Anti-Corruption Day;

8. *Requests* the Secretary-General to designate the United Nations Office on Drugs and Crime to serve as the secretariat for and under the direction of the Conference of the States Parties to the Convention;

9. *Also requests* the Secretary-General to provide the United Nations Office on Drugs and Crime with the resources necessary to enable it to promote in an effective manner the rapid entry into force of the United Nations Convention against Corruption and to discharge the functions of secretariat of the Conference of the States Parties to the Convention, and to support the Ad Hoc Committee in its work pursuant to paragraph 5 above;

10. *Further requests* the Secretary-General to prepare a comprehensive report on the High-level Political Signing Conference to be held in Merida, Mexico, in accordance with resolution 57/169, for submission to the General Assembly at its fifty-ninth session.

ANNEX

UNITED NATIONS CONVENTION AGAINST CORRUPTION

PREAMBLE

The States Parties to this Convention,

Concerned about the seriousness of problems and threats posed by corruption to the stability and security of societies, undermining the institutions and values of democracy, ethical values and justice and jeopardizing sustainable development and the rule of law,

Concerned also about the links between corruption and other forms of crime, in particular organized crime and economic crime, including money-laundering,

Concerned further about cases of corruption that involve vast quantities of assets, which may constitute a substantial proportion of the resources of States, and that threaten the political stability and sustainable development of those States,

Convinced that corruption is no longer a local matter but a transnational phenomenon that affects all societies and economies, making international cooperation to prevent and control it essential,

Convinced also that a comprehensive and multidisciplinary approach is required to prevent and combat corruption effectively,

Convinced further that the availability of technical assistance can play an important role in enhancing the ability of States, including by strengthening capacity and by institution-building, to prevent and combat corruption effectively,

Convinced that the illicit acquisition of personal wealth can be particularly damaging to democratic institutions, national economies and the rule of law,

Determined to prevent, detect and deter in a more effective manner international transfers of illicitly acquired assets and to strengthen international cooperation in asset recovery,

Acknowledging the fundamental principles of due process of law in criminal proceedings and in civil or administrative proceedings to adjudicate property rights,

Bearing in mind that the prevention and eradication of corruption is a responsibility of all States and that they must cooperate with one another, with the support and involvement of individuals and groups outside the public sector, such as civil society, non-governmental organizations and community-based organizations, if their efforts in this area are to be effective,

Bearing also in mind the principles of proper management of public affairs and public property, fairness, responsibility and equality before the law and the need to safeguard integrity and to foster a culture of rejection of corruption,

Commending the work of the Commission on Crime Prevention and Criminal Justice and the United Nations Office on Drugs and Crime in preventing and combating corruption,

Recalling the work carried out by other international and regional organizations in this field, including the activities of the African Union, the Council of Europe, the Customs Cooperation Council (also known as the World Customs Organization), the European Union, the League of Arab States, the Organisation for Economic Cooperation and Development and the Organization of American States,

Taking note with appreciation of multilateral instruments to prevent and combat corruption, including, inter alia, the Inter-American Convention against Corruption, adopted by the Organization of American States on 29 March 1996,[4] the Convention on the Fight against Corruption involving Officials of the European Communities or Officials of Member States of the European Union, adopted by the Council of the European Union on 26 May 1997,[5] the Convention on Combating Bribery of Foreign Public Officials in International Business Transactions, adopted by the Organisation for Economic Cooperation and Development on 21 November 1997,[6] the Criminal Law Convention on Corruption, adopted by the Committee of Ministers of the Council of Europe on 27 January 1999,[7] the Civil Law Convention on Corruption, adopted by the Committee of Ministers of the Council of Europe

---

[4] See E/1996/99.
[5] Official Journal of the European Communities, C 195, 25 June 1997.
[6] See Corruption and Integrity Improvement Initiatives in Developing Countries (United Nations publicaion, Sales No. E.98.III.B.18).
[7] Council of Europe, European Treaty Series, No. 173. [5] Ibid, No. 174.

on 4 November 1999,[8] and the African Union Convention on Preventing and Combating Corruption, adopted by the Heads of State and Government of the African Union on 12 July 2003,

Welcoming the entry into force on 29 September 2003 of the United Nations Convention against Transnational Organized Crime,[9]

Have agreed as follows:

CHAPTER I

GENERAL PROVISIONS

Article 1. Statement of purpose

The purposes of this Convention are:

(a) To promote and strengthen measures to prevent and combat corruption more efficiently and effectively;

(b) To promote, facilitate and support international cooperation and technical assistance in the prevention of and fight against corruption, including in asset recovery;

(c) To promote integrity, accountability and proper management of public affairs and public property.

Article 2. Use of terms

For the purposes of this Convention:

(a) "Public official" shall mean: (i) any person holding a legislative, executive, administrative or judicial office of a State Party, whether appointed or elected, whether permanent or temporary, whether paid or unpaid, irrespective of that person's seniority; (ii) any other person who performs a public function, including for a public agency or public enterprise, or provides a public service, as defined in the domestic law of the State Party and as applied in the pertinent area of law of that State Party; (iii) any other person defined as a "public official" in the domestic law of a State Party. However, for the purpose of some specific measures contained in chapter II of this Convention, "public official" may mean any person who

---

[8] Ibid., No. 174.
[9] General Assembly resolution 55/25, annex I.

performs a public function or provides a public service as defined in the domestic law of the State Party and as applied in the pertinent area of law of that State Party;

(b) "Foreign public official" shall mean any person holding a legislative, executive, administrative or judicial office of a foreign country, whether appointed or elected; and any person exercising a public function for a foreign country, including for a public agency or public enterprise;

(c) "Official of a public international organization" shall mean an international civil servant or any person who is authorized by such an organization to act on behalf of that organization;

(d) "Property" shall mean assets of every kind, whether corporeal or incorporeal, movable or immovable, tangible or intangible, and legal documents or instruments evidencing title to or interest in such assets;

(e) "Proceeds of crime" shall mean any property derived from or obtained, directly or indirectly, through the commission of an offence;

(f) "Freezing" or "seizure" shall mean temporarily prohibiting the transfer, conversion, disposition or movement of property or temporarily assuming custody or control of property on the basis of an order issued by a court or other competent authority;

(g) "Confiscation", which includes forfeiture where applicable, shall mean the permanent deprivation of property by order of a court or other competent authority;

(h) "Predicate offence" shall mean any offence as a result of which proceeds have been generated that may become the subject of an offence as defined in article 23 of this Convention;

(i) "Controlled delivery" shall mean the technique of allowing illicit or suspect consignments to pass out of, through or into the territory of one or more States, with the knowledge and under the supervision of their competent authorities, with a view to the investigation of an offence and the identification of persons involved in the commission of the offence.

Article 3. Scope of application

1. This Convention shall apply, in accordance with its terms, to the prevention, investigation and prosecution of corruption and to the freezing, seizure, confiscation and return of the proceeds of offences established in accordance with this Convention.

2. For the purposes of implementing this Convention, it shall not be necessary, except as otherwise stated herein, for the offences set forth in it to result in damage or harm to state property.

Article 4. Protection of sovereignty

1. States Parties shall carry out their obligations under this Convention in a manner consistent with the principles of sovereign equality and territorial integrity of States and that of non-intervention in the domestic affairs of other States.

2. Nothing in this Convention shall entitle a State Party to undertake in the territory of another State the exercise of jurisdiction and performance of functions that are reserved exclusively for the authorities of that other State by its domestic law.

CHAPTER II

PREVENTIVE MEASURES

Article 5. Preventive anti-corruption policies and practices

1. Each State Party shall, in accordance with the fundamental principles of its legal system, develop and implement or maintain effective, coordinated anti-corruption policies that promote the participation of society and reflect the principles of the rule of law, proper management of public affairs and public property, integrity, transparency and accountability.

2. Each State Party shall endeavour to establish and promote effective practices aimed at the prevention of corruption.

3. Each State Party shall endeavour to periodically evaluate relevant legal instruments and administrative measures with a view to determining their adequacy to prevent and fight corruption.

4. States Parties shall, as appropriate and in accordance with the fundamental principles of their legal system, collaborate with each other and with relevant international and regional organizations in promoting and developing the measures referred to in this article. That collaboration may include participation in international programmes and projects aimed at the prevention of corruption.

Article 6. Preventive anti-corruption body or bodies

1. Each State Party shall, in accordance with the fundamental principles of its legal system, ensure the existence of a body or bodies, as appropriate, that prevent corruption by such means as:

(a) Implementing the policies referred to in article 5 of this Convention and, where appropriate, overseeing and coordinating the implementation of those policies;

(b) Increasing and disseminating knowledge about the prevention of corruption.

2. Each State Party shall grant the body or bodies referred to in paragraph 1 of this article the necessary independence, in accordance with the fundamental principles of its legal system, to enable the body or bodies to carry out its or their functions effectively and free from any undue influence. The necessary material resources and specialized staff, as well as the training that such staff may require to carry out their functions, should be provided.

3. Each State Party shall inform the Secretary-General of the United Nations of the name and address of the authority or authorities that may assist other States Parties in developing and implementing specific measures for the prevention of corruption.

Article 7. Public sector

1. Each State Party shall, where appropriate and in accordance with the fundamental principles of its legal system, endeavour to adopt, maintain and strengthen systems for the recruitment, hiring, retention, promotion and retirement of civil servants and, where appropriate, other non-elected public officials:

(a) That are based on principles of efficiency, transparency and objective criteria such as merit, equity and aptitude;

(b) That include adequate procedures for the selection and training of individuals for public positions considered especially vulnerable to corruption and the rotation, where appropriate, of such individuals to other positions;

(c) That promote adequate remuneration and equitable pay scales, taking into account the level of economic development of the State Party;

(d) That promote education and training programmes to enable them to meet the requirements for the correct, honourable and proper performance of public functions and that provide them with specialized and appropriate

training to enhance their awareness of the risks of corruption inherent in the performance of their functions. Such programmes may make reference to codes or standards of conduct in applicable areas.

2. Each State Party shall also consider adopting appropriate legislative and administrative measures, consistent with the objectives of this Convention and in accordance with the fundamental principles of its domestic law, to prescribe criteria concerning candidature for and election to public office.

3. Each State Party shall also consider taking appropriate legislative and administrative measures, consistent with the objectives of this Convention and in accordance with the fundamental principles of its domestic law, to enhance transparency in the funding of candidatures for elected public office and, where applicable, the funding of political parties.

4. Each State Party shall, in accordance with the fundamental principles of its domestic law, endeavour to adopt, maintain and strengthen systems that promote transparency and prevent conflicts of interest.

Article 8. Codes of conduct for public officials

1. In order to fight corruption, each State Party shall promote, inter alia, integrity, honesty and responsibility among its public officials, in accordance with the fundamental principles of its legal system.

2. In particular, each State Party shall endeavour to apply, within its own institutional and legal systems, codes or standards of conduct for the correct, honourable and proper performance of public functions.

3. For the purposes of implementing the provisions of this article, each State Party shall, where appropriate and in accordance with the fundamental principles of its legal system, take note of the relevant initiatives of regional, interregional and multilateral organizations, such as the International Code of Conduct for Public Officials contained in the annex to General Assembly resolution 51/59 of 12 December 1996.

4. Each State Party shall also consider, in accordance with the fundamental principles of its domestic law, establishing measures and systems to facilitate the reporting by public officials of acts of corruption to appropriate authorities, when such acts come to their notice in the performance of their functions.

5. Each State Party shall endeavour, where appropriate and in accordance with the fundamental principles of its domestic law, to establish measures and systems requiring public officials to make declarations to appropriate authorities regarding, inter alia, their outside activities, employment, investments, assets and substantial gifts or benefits from which a conflict of interest may result with respect to their functions as public officials.

6. Each State Party shall consider taking, in accordance with the fundamental principles of its domestic law, disciplinary or other measures against public officials who violate the codes or standards established in accordance with this article.

Article 9. Public procurement and management of public finances

1. Each State Party shall, in accordance with the fundamental principles of its legal system, take the necessary steps to establish appropriate systems of procurement, based on transparency, competition and objective criteria in decision-making, that are effective, inter alia, in preventing corruption. Such systems, which may take into account appropriate threshold values in their application, shall address, inter alia:

(a) The public distribution of information relating to procurement procedures and contracts, including information on invitations to tender and relevant or pertinent information on the award of contracts, allowing potential tenderers sufficient time to prepare and submit their tenders;

(b) The establishment, in advance, of conditions for participation, including selection and award criteria and tendering rules, and their publication;

(c) The use of objective and predetermined criteria for public procurement decisions, in order to facilitate the subsequent verification of the correct application of the rules or procedures;

(d) An effective system of domestic review, including an effective system of appeal, to ensure legal recourse and remedies in the event that the rules or procedures established pursuant to this paragraph are not followed;

(e) Where appropriate, measures to regulate matters regarding personnel responsible for procurement, such as declaration of interest in particular public procurements, screening procedures and training requirements.

2. Each State Party shall, in accordance with the fundamental principles of its legal system, take appropriate measures to promote transparency and accountability in the management of public finances. Such measures shall encompass, inter alia:

(a) Procedures for the adoption of the national budget;

(b) Timely reporting on revenue and expenditure;

(c) A system of accounting and auditing standards and related oversight;

(d) Effective and efficient systems of risk management and internal control; and

(e) Where appropriate, corrective action in the case of failure to comply with the requirements established in this paragraph.

3. Each State Party shall take such civil and administrative measures as may be necessary, in accordance with the fundamental principles of its domestic law, to preserve the integrity of accounting books, records, financial statements or other documents related to public expenditure and revenue and to prevent the falsification of such documents.

Article 10. Public reporting

Taking into account the need to combat corruption, each State Party shall, in accordance with the fundamental principles of its domestic law, take such measures as may be necessary to enhance transparency in its public administration, including with regard to its organization, functioning and decision-making processes, where appropriate. Such measures may include, inter alia:

(a) Adopting procedures or regulations allowing members of the general public to obtain, where appropriate, information on the organization, functioning and decision-making processes of its public administration and, with due regard for the protection of privacy and personal data, on decisions and legal acts that concern members of the public;

(b) Simplifying administrative procedures, where appropriate, in order to facilitate public access to the competent decision-making authorities; and

(c) Publishing information, which may include periodic reports on the risks of corruption in its public administration.

Article 11. Measures relating to the judiciary and prosecution services

1. Bearing in mind the independence of the judiciary and its crucial role in combating corruption, each State Party shall, in accordance with the fundamental principles of its legal system and without prejudice to judicial independence, take measures to strengthen integrity and to prevent opportunities for corruption among members of the judiciary. Such measures may include rules with respect to the conduct of members of the judiciary.

2. Measures to the same effect as those taken pursuant to paragraph 1 of this article may be introduced and applied within the prosecution service in those States Parties where it does not form part of the judiciary but enjoys independence similar to that of the judicial service.

Article 12. Private sector

1. Each State Party shall take measures, in accordance with the fundamental principles of its domestic law, to prevent corruption involving the private sector, enhance accounting and auditing standards in the private sector and, where appropriate, provide effective, proportionate and dissuasive civil, administrative or criminal penalties for failure to comply with such measures.

2. Measures to achieve these ends may include, inter alia:

(a) Promoting cooperation between law enforcement agencies and relevant private entities;

(b) Promoting the development of standards and procedures designed to safeguard the integrity of relevant private entities, including codes of conduct for the correct, honourable and proper performance of the activities of business and all relevant professions and the prevention of conflicts of interest, and for the promotion of the use of good commercial practices among businesses and in the contractual relations of businesses with the State;

(c) Promoting transparency among private entities, including, where appropriate, measures regarding the identity of legal and natural persons involved in the establishment and management of corporate entities;

(d) Preventing the misuse of procedures regulating private entities, including procedures regarding subsidies and licences granted by public authorities for commercial activities;

(e) Preventing conflicts of interest by imposing restrictions, as appropriate and for a reasonable period of time, on the professional activities of former public officials or on the employment of public officials by the private sector after their resignation or retirement, where such activities or employment relate directly to the functions held or supervised by those public officials during their tenure;

(f) Ensuring that private enterprises, taking into account their structure and size, have sufficient internal auditing controls to assist in preventing and detecting acts of corruption and that the accounts and required financial statements of such private enterprises are subject to appropriate auditing and certification procedures.

3. In order to prevent corruption, each State Party shall take such measures as may be necessary, in accordance with its domestic laws and regulations regarding the maintenance of books and records, financial statement disclosures and accounting and auditing standards, to prohibit the following acts carried out for the purpose of committing any of the offences established in accordance with this Convention:

(a) The establishment of off-the-books accounts;

(b) The making of off-the-books or inadequately identified transactions;

(c) The recording of non-existent expenditure;

(d) The entry of liabilities with incorrect identification of their objects;

(e) The use of false documents; and

(f) The intentional destruction of bookkeeping documents earlier than foreseen by the law.

4. Each State Party shall disallow the tax deductibility of expenses that constitute bribes, the latter being one of the constituent elements of the offences established in accordance with articles 15 and 16 of this Convention and, where appropriate, other expenses incurred in furtherance of corrupt conduct.

Article 13. Participation of society

1. Each State Party shall take appropriate measures, within its means and in accordance with fundamental principles of its domestic law, to promote the active participation of individuals and groups outside the public sector, such as civil society, non-governmental organizations and community-based organizations, in the prevention of and the fight against corruption and to raise public awareness regarding the existence, causes and gravity of and the threat posed by corruption. This participation should be strengthened by such measures as:

(a) Enhancing the transparency of and promoting the contribution of the public to decision-making processes;

(b) Ensuring that the public has effective access to information;

(c) Undertaking public information activities that contribute to non-tolerance of corruption, as well as public education programmes, including school and university curricula;

(d) Respecting, promoting and protecting the freedom to seek, receive, publish and disseminate information concerning corruption. That freedom may be subject to certain restrictions, but these shall only be such as are provided for by law and are necessary:

  (i) For respect of the rights or reputations of others;
  (ii) For the protection of national security or *ordre public* or of public health or morals.

2. Each State Party shall take appropriate measures to ensure that the relevant anti-corruption bodies referred to in this Convention are known to the public and shall provide access to such bodies, where appropriate, for the reporting, including anonymously, of any incidents that may be considered to constitute an offence established in accordance with this Convention.

Article 14. Measures to prevent money-laundering

1. Each State Party shall:

(a) Institute a comprehensive domestic regulatory and supervisory regime for banks and non-bank financial institutions, including natural or legal persons that provide formal or informal services for the transmission of money or value and, where appropriate, other bodies particularly susceptible to money-laundering, within its competence, in order to deter and detect all forms of money-laundering, which regime shall emphasize requirements for customer and, where appropriate, beneficial owner identification, record-keeping and the reporting of suspicious transactions;

(b) Without prejudice to article 46 of this Convention, ensure that administrative, regulatory, law enforcement and other authorities dedicated to combating money-laundering (including, where appropriate under domestic law, judicial authorities) have the ability to cooperate and exchange information at the national and international levels within the conditions prescribed by its domestic law and, to that end, shall consider the establishment of a financial intelligence unit to serve as a national centre for the collection, analysis and dissemination of information regarding potential money-laundering.

2. States Parties shall consider implementing feasible measures to detect and monitor the movement of cash and appropriate negotiable instruments across their borders, subject to safeguards to ensure proper use of information and without impeding in any way the movement of legitimate capital. Such measures may include a requirement that individuals and businesses report the cross-border transfer of substantial quantities of cash and appropriate negotiable instruments.

3. States Parties shall consider implementing appropriate and feasible measures to require financial institutions, including money remitters:

(a) To include on forms for the electronic transfer of funds and related messages accurate and meaningful information on the originator;

(b) To maintain such information throughout the payment chain; and

(c) To apply enhanced scrutiny to transfers of funds that do not contain complete information on the originator.

4. In establishing a domestic regulatory and supervisory regime under the terms of this article, and without prejudice to any other article of this Convention, States Parties are called upon to use as a guideline the relevant initiatives of regional, interregional and multilateral organizations against money-laundering.

5. States Parties shall endeavour to develop and promote global, regional, subregional and bilateral cooperation among judicial, law enforcement and financial regulatory authorities in order to combat money-laundering.

CHAPTER III

CRIMINALIZATION AND LAW ENFORCEMENT

Article 15. Bribery of national public officials

Each State Party shall adopt such legislative and other measures as may be necessary to establish as criminal offences, when committed intentionally:

(a) The promise, offering or giving, to a public official, directly or indirectly, of an undue advantage, for the official himself or herself or another person or entity, in order that the official act or refrain from acting in the exercise of his or her official duties;

(b) The solicitation or acceptance by a public official, directly or indirectly, of an undue advantage, for the official himself or herself or another person or entity, in order that the official act or refrain from acting in the exercise of his or her official duties.

Article 16. Bribery of foreign public officials and officials of public international organizations

1. Each State Party shall adopt such legislative and other measures as may be necessary to establish as a criminal offence, when committed intentionally, the promise, offering or giving to a foreign public official or an official of a public international organization, directly or indirectly, of an undue advantage, for the official himself or herself or another person or entity, in order that the official act or refrain from acting in the exercise of his or her official duties, in order to obtain or retain business or other undue advantage in relation to the conduct of international business.

2. Each State Party shall consider adopting such legislative and other measures as may be necessary to establish as a criminal offence, when committed intentionally, the solicitation or acceptance by a foreign public official or an official of a public international organization, directly or indirectly, of an

undue advantage, for the official himself or herself or another person or entity, in order that the official act or refrain from acting in the exercise of his or her official duties.

Article 17. Embezzlement, misappropriation or other diversion of property by a public official

Each State Party shall adopt such legislative and other measures as may be necessary to establish as criminal offences, when committed intentionally, the embezzlement, misappropriation or other diversion by a public official for his or her benefit or for the benefit of another person or entity, of any property, public or private funds or securities or any other thing of value entrusted to the public official by virtue of his or her position.

Article 18. Trading in influence

Each State Party shall consider adopting such legislative and other measures as may be necessary to establish as criminal offences, when committed intentionally:

(a) The promise, offering or giving to a public official or any other person, directly or indirectly, of an undue advantage in order that the public official or the person abuse his or her real or supposed influence with a view to obtaining from an administration or public authority of the State Party an undue advantage for the original instigator of the act or for any other person;

(b) The solicitation or acceptance by a public official or any other person, directly or indirectly, of an undue advantage for himself or herself or for another person in order that the public official or the person abuse his or her real or supposed influence with a view to obtaining from an administration or public authority of the State Party an undue advantage.

Article 19. Abuse of functions

Each State Party shall consider adopting such legislative and other measures as may be necessary to establish as a criminal offence, when committed intentionally, the abuse of functions or position, that is, the performance of or failure to perform an act, in violation of laws, by a public official in the discharge of his or her functions, for the purpose of obtaining an undue advantage for himself or herself or for another person or entity.

Article 20. Illicit enrichment

Subject to its constitution and the fundamental principles of its legal system, each State Party shall consider adopting such legislative and other measures as may be necessary to establish as a criminal offence, when committed intentionally, illicit enrichment, that is, a significant increase in the assets of a public official that he or she cannot reasonably explain in relation to his or her lawful income.

Article 21. Bribery in the private sector

Each State Party shall consider adopting such legislative and other measures as may be necessary to establish as criminal offences, when committed intentionally in the course of economic, financial or commercial activities:

(a) The promise, offering or giving, directly or indirectly, of an undue advantage to any person who directs or works, in any capacity, for a private sector entity, for the person himself or herself or for another person, in order that he or she, in breach of his or her duties, act or refrain from acting;

(b) The solicitation or acceptance, directly or indirectly, of an undue advantage by any person who directs or works, in any capacity, for a private sector entity, for the person himself or herself or for another person, in order that he or she, in breach of his or her duties, act or refrain from acting.

Article 22. Embezzlement of property in the private sector

Each State Party shall consider adopting such legislative and other measures as may be necessary to establish as a criminal offence, when committed intentionally in the course of economic, financial or commercial activities, embezzlement by a person who directs or works, in any capacity, in a private sector entity of any property, private funds or securities or any other thing of value entrusted to him or her by virtue of his or her position.

Article 23. Laundering of proceeds of crime

1. Each State Party shall adopt, in accordance with fundamental principles of its domestic law, such legislative and other measures as may be necessary to establish as criminal offences, when committed intentionally:

   (a)

   (i) The conversion or transfer of property, knowing that such property is the proceeds of crime, for the purpose of concealing or disguising the illicit origin of the property or of helping any person who is involved in the commission of the predicate offence to evade the legal consequences of his or her action;

(ii) The concealment or disguise of the true nature, source, location, disposition, movement or ownership of or rights with respect to property, knowing that such property is the proceeds of crime;

(b) Subject to the basic concepts of its legal system:

(i) The acquisition, possession or use of property, knowing, at the time of receipt, that such property is the proceeds of crime;
(ii) Participation in, association with or conspiracy to commit, attempts to commit and aiding, abetting, facilitating and counselling the commission of any of the offences established in accordance with this article.

2. For purposes of implementing or applying paragraph 1 of this article:

(a) Each State Party shall seek to apply paragraph 1 of this article to the widest range of predicate offences;

(b) Each State Party shall include as predicate offences at a minimum a comprehensive range of criminal offences established in accordance with this Convention;

(c) For the purposes of subparagraph *(b)* above, predicate offences shall include offences committed both within and outside the jurisdiction of the State Party in question. However, offences committed outside the jurisdiction of a State Party shall constitute predicate offences only when the relevant conduct is a criminal offence under the domestic law of the State where it is committed and would be a criminal offence under the domestic law of the State Party implementing or applying this article had it been committed there;

(d) Each State Party shall furnish copies of its laws that give effect to this article and of any subsequent changes to such laws or a description thereof to the Secretary-General of the United Nations;

(e) If required by fundamental principles of the domestic law of a State Party, it may be provided that the offences set forth in paragraph 1 of this article do not apply to the persons who committed the predicate offence.

Article 24. Concealment

Without prejudice to the provisions of article 23 of this Convention, each State Party shall consider adopting such legislative and other measures as may be necessary to establish as a criminal offence, when committed intentionally after the commission of any of the offences established in accordance with this Convention without having participated in such offences, the concealment or continued retention of property when the person involved knows that such property is the result of any of the offences established in accordance with this Convention.

Article 25. Obstruction of justice

Each State Party shall adopt such legislative and other measures as may be necessary to establish as criminal offences, when committed intentionally:

(a) The use of physical force, threats or intimidation or the promise, offering or giving of an undue advantage to induce false testimony or to interfere in the giving of testimony or the production of evidence in a proceeding in relation to the commission of offences established in accordance with this Convention;

(b) The use of physical force, threats or intimidation to interfere with the exercise of official duties by a justice or law enforcement official in relation to the commission of offences established in accordance with this Convention. Nothing in this subparagraph shall prejudice the right of States Parties to have legislation that protects other categories of public official.

Article 26. Liability of legal persons

1. Each State Party shall adopt such measures as may be necessary, consistent with its legal principles, to establish the liability of legal persons for participation in the offences established in accordance with this Convention.

2. Subject to the legal principles of the State Party, the liability of legal persons may be criminal, civil or administrative.

3. Such liability shall be without prejudice to the criminal liability of the natural persons who have committed the offences.

4. Each State Party shall, in particular, ensure that legal persons held liable in accordance with this article are subject to effective, proportionate and dissuasive criminal or non-criminal sanctions, including monetary sanctions.

Article 27. Participation and attempt

1. Each State Party shall adopt such legislative and other measures as may be necessary to establish as a criminal offence, in accordance with its domestic law, participation in any capacity such as an accomplice, assistant or instigator in an offence established in accordance with this Convention.

2. Each State Party may adopt such legislative and other measures as may be necessary to establish as a criminal offence, in accordance with its domestic law, any attempt to commit an offence established in accordance with this Convention.

3. Each State Party may adopt such legislative and other measures as may be necessary to establish as a criminal offence, in accordance with its domestic law, the preparation for an offence established in accordance with this Convention.

Article 28. Knowledge, intent and purpose as elements of an offence

Knowledge, intent or purpose required as an element of an offence established in accordance with this Convention may be inferred from objective factual circumstances.

Article 29. Statute of limitations

Each State Party shall, where appropriate, establish under its domestic law a long statute of limitations period in which to commence proceedings for any offence established in accordance with this Convention and establish a longer statute of limitations period or provide for the suspension of the statute of limitations where the alleged offender has evaded the administration of justice.

Article 30. Prosecution, adjudication and sanctions

1. Each State Party shall make the commission of an offence established in accordance with this Convention liable to sanctions that take into account the gravity of that offence.

2. Each State Party shall take such measures as may be necessary to establish or maintain, in accordance with its legal system and constitutional principles, an appropriate balance between any immunities or jurisdictional privileges accorded to its public officials for the performance of their functions and the possibility, when necessary, of effectively investigating, prosecuting and adjudicating offences established in accordance with this Convention.

3. Each State Party shall endeavour to ensure that any discretionary legal powers under its domestic law relating to the prosecution of persons for offences established in accordance with this Convention are exercised to maximize the effectiveness of law enforcement measures in respect of those offences and with due regard to the need to deter the commission of such offences.

4. In the case of offences established in accordance with this Convention, each State Party shall take appropriate measures, in accordance with its domestic

law and with due regard to the rights of the defence, to seek to ensure that conditions imposed in connection with decisions on release pending trial or appeal take into consideration the need to ensure the presence of the defendant at subsequent criminal proceedings.

5. Each State Party shall take into account the gravity of the offences concerned when considering the eventuality of early release or parole of persons convicted of such offences.

6. Each State Party, to the extent consistent with the fundamental principles of its legal system, shall consider establishing procedures through which a public official accused of an offence established in accordance with this Convention may, where appropriate, be removed, suspended or reassigned by the appropriate authority, bearing in mind respect for the principle of the presumption of innocence.

7. Where warranted by the gravity of the offence, each State Party, to the extent consistent with the fundamental principles of its legal system, shall consider establishing procedures for the disqualification, by court order or any other appropriate means, for a period of time determined by its domestic law, of persons convicted of offences established in accordance with this Convention from:

(a) Holding public office; and

(b) Holding office in an enterprise owned in whole or in part by the State.

8. Paragraph 1 of this article shall be without prejudice to the exercise of disciplinary powers by the competent authorities against civil servants.

9. Nothing contained in this Convention shall affect the principle that the description of the offences established in accordance with this Convention and of the applicable legal defences or other legal principles controlling the lawfulness of conduct is reserved to the domestic law of a State Party and that such offences shall be prosecuted and punished in accordance with that law.

10. States Parties shall endeavour to promote the reintegration into society of persons convicted of offences established in accordance with this Convention.

Article 31. Freezing, seizure and confiscation

1. Each State Party shall take, to the greatest extent possible within its domestic legal system, such measures as may be necessary to enable confiscation of:

(a) Proceeds of crime derived from offences established in accordance with this Convention or property the value of which corresponds to that of such proceeds;

(b) Property, equipment or other instrumentalities used in or destined for use in offences established in accordance with this Convention.

2. Each State Party shall take such measures as may be necessary to enable the identification, tracing, freezing or seizure of any item referred to in paragraph 1 of this article for the purpose of eventual confiscation.

3. Each State Party shall adopt, in accordance with its domestic law, such legislative and other measures as may be necessary to regulate the administration by the competent authorities of frozen, seized or confiscated property covered in paragraphs 1 and 2 of this article.

4. If such proceeds of crime have been transformed or converted, in part or in full, into other property, such property shall be liable to the measures referred to in this article instead of the proceeds.

5. If such proceeds of crime have been intermingled with property acquired from legitimate sources, such property shall, without prejudice to any powers relating to freezing or seizure, be liable to confiscation up to the assessed value of the intermingled proceeds.

6. Income or other benefits derived from such proceeds of crime, from property into which such proceeds of crime have been transformed or converted or from property with which such proceeds of crime have been intermingled shall also be liable to the measures referred to in this article, in the same manner and to the same extent as proceeds of crime.

7. For the purpose of this article and article 55 of this Convention, each State Party shall empower its courts or other competent authorities to order that bank, financial or commercial records be made available or seized. A State Party shall not decline to act under the provisions of this paragraph on the ground of bank secrecy.

8. States Parties may consider the possibility of requiring that an offender demonstrate the lawful origin of such alleged proceeds of crime or other property liable to confiscation, to the extent that such a requirement is consistent with the fundamental principles of their domestic law and with the nature of judicial and other proceedings.

9. The provisions of this article shall not be so construed as to prejudice the rights of bona fide third parties.

10. Nothing contained in this article shall affect the principle that the measures to which it refers shall be defined and implemented in accordance with and subject to the provisions of the domestic law of a State Party.

Article 32. Protection of witnesses, experts and victims

1. Each State Party shall take appropriate measures in accordance with its domestic legal system and within its means to provide effective protection from potential retaliation or intimidation for witnesses and experts who give testimony concerning offences established in accordance with this Convention and, as appropriate, for their relatives and other persons close to them.

2. The measures envisaged in paragraph 1 of this article may include, inter alia, without prejudice to the rights of the defendant, including the right to due process:

(a) Establishing procedures for the physical protection of such persons, such as, to the extent necessary and feasible, relocating them and permitting, where appropriate, non-disclosure or limitations on the disclosure of information concerning the identity and whereabouts of such persons;

(b) Providing evidentiary rules to permit witnesses and experts to give testimony in a manner that ensures the safety of such persons, such as permitting testimony to be given through the use of communications technology such as video or other adequate means.

3. States Parties shall consider entering into agreements or arrangements with other States for the relocation of persons referred to in paragraph 1 of this article.

4. The provisions of this article shall also apply to victims insofar as they are witnesses.

5. Each State Party shall, subject to its domestic law, enable the views and concerns of victims to be presented and considered at appropriate stages of criminal proceedings against offenders in a manner not prejudicial to the rights of the defence.

Article 33. Protection of reporting persons

Each State Party shall consider incorporating into its domestic legal system appropriate measures to provide protection against any unjustified treatment for any person who reports in good faith and on reasonable grounds to the competent authorities any facts concerning offences established in accordance with this Convention.

Article 34. Consequences of acts of corruption

With due regard to the rights of third parties acquired in good faith, each State Party shall take measures, in accordance with the fundamental principles of its domestic law, to address consequences of corruption. In this context, States

Parties may consider corruption a relevant factor in legal proceedings to annul or rescind a contract, withdraw a concession or other similar instrument or take any other remedial action.

Article 35. Compensation for damage

Each State Party shall take such measures as may be necessary, in accordance with principles of its domestic law, to ensure that entities or persons who have suffered damage as a result of an act of corruption have the right to initiate legal proceedings against those responsible for that damage in order to obtain compensation.

Article 36. Specialized authorities

Each State Party shall, in accordance with the fundamental principles of its legal system, ensure the existence of a body or bodies or persons specialized in combating corruption through law enforcement. Such body or bodies or persons shall be granted the necessary independence, in accordance with the fundamental principles of the legal system of the State Party, to be able to carry out their functions effectively and without any undue influence. Such persons or staff of such body or bodies should have the appropriate training and resources to carry out their tasks.

Article 37. Cooperation with law enforcement authorities

1. Each State Party shall take appropriate measures to encourage persons who participate or who have participated in the commission of an offence established in accordance with this Convention to supply information useful to competent authorities for investigative and evidentiary purposes and to provide factual, specific help to competent authorities that may contribute to depriving offenders of the proceeds of crime and to recovering such proceeds.

2. Each State Party shall consider providing for the possibility, in appropriate cases, of mitigating punishment of an accused person who provides substantial cooperation in the investigation or prosecution of an offence established in accordance with this Convention.

3. Each State Party shall consider providing for the possibility, in accordance with fundamental principles of its domestic law, of granting immunity from prosecution to a person who provides substantial cooperation in the investigation or prosecution of an offence established in accordance with this Convention.

4. Protection of such persons shall be, mutatis mutandis, as provided for in article 32 of this Convention.

5. Where a person referred to in paragraph 1 of this article located in one State Party can provide substantial cooperation to the competent authorities of another State Party, the States Parties concerned may consider entering into agreements or arrangements, in accordance with their domestic law, concerning the potential provision by the other State Party of the treatment set forth in paragraphs 2 and 3 of this article.

Article 38. Cooperation between national authorities

Each State Party shall take such measures as may be necessary to encourage, in accordance with its domestic law, cooperation between, on the one hand, its public authorities, as well as its public officials, and, on the other hand, its authorities responsible for investigating and prosecuting criminal offences. Such cooperation may include:

(a) Informing the latter authorities, on their own initiative, where there are reasonable grounds to believe that any of the offences established in accordance with articles 15, 21 and 23 of this Convention has been committed; or

(b) Providing, upon request, to the latter authorities all necessary information.

Article 39. Cooperation between national authorities and the private sector

1. Each State Party shall take such measures as may be necessary to encourage, in accordance with its domestic law, cooperation between national investigating and prosecuting authorities and entities of the private sector, in particular financial institutions, relating to matters involving the commission of offences established in accordance with this Convention.

2. Each State Party shall consider encouraging its nationals and other persons with a habitual residence in its territory to report to the national investigating and prosecuting authorities the commission of an offence established in accordance with this Convention.

Article 40. Bank secrecy

Each State Party shall ensure that, in the case of domestic criminal investigations of offences established in accordance with this Convention, there are appropriate mechanisms available within its domestic legal system to overcome obstacles that may arise out of the application of bank secrecy laws.

Article 41. Criminal record

Each State Party may adopt such legislative or other measures as may be necessary to take into consideration, under such terms as and for the purpose that it deems appropriate, any previous conviction in another State of an alleged offender for the purpose of using such information in criminal proceedings relating to an offence established in accordance with this Convention.

Article 42. Jurisdiction

1. Each State Party shall adopt such measures as may be necessary to establish its jurisdiction over the offences established in accordance with this Convention when:

(a) The offence is committed in the territory of that State Party; or

(b) The offence is committed on board a vessel that is flying the flag of that State Party or an aircraft that is registered under the laws of that State Party at the time that the offence is committed.

2. Subject to article 4 of this Convention, a State Party may also establish its jurisdiction over any such offence when:

(a) The offence is committed against a national of that State Party; or

(b) The offence is committed by a national of that State Party or a stateless person who has his or her habitual residence in its territory; or

(c) The offence is one of those established in accordance with article 23, paragraph 1 *(b)* (ii), of this Convention and is committed outside its territory with a view to the commission of an offence established in accordance with article 23, paragraph 1 *(a)* (i) or (ii) or *(b)* (i), of this Convention within its territory; or

(d) The offence is committed against the State Party.

3. For the purposes of article 44 of this Convention, each State Party shall take such measures as may be necessary to establish its jurisdiction over the offences established in accordance with this Convention when the alleged offender is present in its territory and it does not extradite such person solely on the ground that he or she is one of its nationals.

4. Each State Party may also take such measures as may be necessary to establish its jurisdiction over the offences established in accordance with this Convention when the alleged offender is present in its territory and it does not extradite him or her.

5. If a State Party exercising its jurisdiction under paragraph 1 or 2 of this article has been notified, or has otherwise learned, that any other States Parties are conducting an investigation, prosecution or judicial proceeding in respect of the same conduct, the competent authorities of those States Parties shall, as appropriate, consult one another with a view to coordinating their actions.

6. Without prejudice to norms of general international law, this Convention shall not exclude the exercise of any criminal jurisdiction established by a State Party in accordance with its domestic law.

CHAPTER IV

INTERNATIONAL COOPERATION

Article 43. International cooperation

1. States Parties shall cooperate in criminal matters in accordance with articles 44 to 50 of this Convention. Where appropriate and consistent with their domestic legal system, States Parties shall consider assisting each other in investigations of and proceedings in civil and administrative matters relating to corruption.

2. In matters of international cooperation, whenever dual criminality is considered a requirement, it shall be deemed fulfilled irrespective of whether the laws of the requested State Party place the offence within the same category of offence or denominate the offence by the same terminology as the requesting State Party, if the conduct underlying the offence for which assistance is sought is a criminal offence under the laws of both States Parties.

Article 44. Extradition

1. This article shall apply to the offences established in accordance with this Convention where the person who is the subject of the request for extradition is present in the territory of the requested State Party, provided that the offence for which extradition is sought is punishable under the domestic law of both the requesting State Party and the requested State Party.

2. Notwithstanding the provisions of paragraph 1 of this article, a State Party whose law so permits may grant the extradition of a person for any of the offences covered by this Convention that are not punishable under its own domestic law.

3. If the request for extradition includes several separate offences, at least one of which is extraditable under this article and some of which are not extraditable by reason of their period of imprisonment but are related to

offences established in accordance with this Convention, the requested State Party may apply this article also in respect of those offences.

4. Each of the offences to which this article applies shall be deemed to be included as an extraditable offence in any extradition treaty existing between States Parties. States Parties undertake to include such offences as extraditable offences in every extradition treaty to be concluded between them. A State Party whose law so permits, in case it uses this Convention as the basis for extradition, shall not consider any of the offences established in accordance with this Convention to be a political offence.

5. If a State Party that makes extradition conditional on the existence of a treaty receives a request for extradition from another State Party with which it has no extradition treaty, it may consider this Convention the legal basis for extradition in respect of any offence to which this article applies.

6. A State Party that makes extradition conditional on the existence of a treaty shall:

(a) At the time of deposit of its instrument of ratification, acceptance or approval of or accession to this Convention, inform the Secretary-General of the United Nations whether it will take this Convention as the legal basis for cooperation on extradition with other States Parties to this Convention; and

(b) If it does not take this Convention as the legal basis for cooperation on extradition, seek, where appropriate, to conclude treaties on extradition with other States Parties to this Convention in order to implement this article.

7. States Parties that do not make extradition conditional on the existence of a treaty shall recognize offences to which this article applies as extraditable offences between themselves.

8. Extradition shall be subject to the conditions provided for by the domestic law of the requested State Party or by applicable extradition treaties, including, inter alia, conditions in relation to the minimum penalty requirement for extradition and the grounds upon which the requested State Party may refuse extradition.

9. States Parties shall, subject to their domestic law, endeavour to expedite extradition procedures and to simplify evidentiary requirements relating thereto in respect of any offence to which this article applies.

10. Subject to the provisions of its domestic law and its extradition treaties, the requested State Party may, upon being satisfied that the circumstances so warrant and are urgent and at the request of the requesting State Party, take a

person whose extradition is sought and who is present in its territory into custody or take other appropriate measures to ensure his or her presence at extradition proceedings.

11. A State Party in whose territory an alleged offender is found, if it does not extradite such person in respect of an offence to which this article applies solely on the ground that he or she is one of its nationals, shall, at the request of the State Party seeking extradition, be obliged to submit the case without undue delay to its competent authorities for the purpose of prosecution. Those authorities shall take their decision and conduct their proceedings in the same manner as in the case of any other offence of a grave nature under the domestic law of that State Party. The States Parties concerned shall cooperate with each other, in particular on procedural and evidentiary aspects, to ensure the efficiency of such prosecution.

12. Whenever a State Party is permitted under its domestic law to extradite or otherwise surrender one of its nationals only upon the condition that the person will be returned to that State Party to serve the sentence imposed as a result of the trial or proceedings for which the extradition or surrender of the person was sought and that State Party and the State Party seeking the extradition of the person agree with this option and other terms that they may deem appropriate, such conditional extradition or surrender shall be sufficient to discharge the obligation set forth in paragraph 11 of this article.

13. If extradition, sought for purposes of enforcing a sentence, is refused because the person sought is a national of the requested State Party, the requested State Party shall, if its domestic law so permits and in conformity with the requirements of such law, upon application of the requesting State Party, consider the enforcement of the sentence imposed under the domestic law of the requesting State Party or the remainder thereof.

14. Any person regarding whom proceedings are being carried out in connection with any of the offences to which this article applies shall be guaranteed fair treatment at all stages of the proceedings, including enjoyment of all the rights and guarantees provided by the domestic law of the State Party in the territory of which that person is present.

15. Nothing in this Convention shall be interpreted as imposing an obligation to extradite if the requested State Party has substantial grounds for believing that the request has been made for the purpose of prosecuting or punishing a person on account of that person's sex, race, religion, nationality, ethnic origin or political opinions or that compliance with the request would cause prejudice to that person's position for any one of these reasons.

16. States Parties may not refuse a request for extradition on the sole ground that the offence is also considered to involve fiscal matters.

17. Before refusing extradition, the requested State Party shall, where appropriate, consult with the requesting State Party to provide it with ample opportunity to present its opinions and to provide information relevant to its allegation.

18. States Parties shall seek to conclude bilateral and multilateral agreements or arrangements to carry out or to enhance the effectiveness of extradition.

Article 45. Transfer of sentenced persons

States Parties may consider entering into bilateral or multilateral agreements or arrangements on the transfer to their territory of persons sentenced to imprisonment or other forms of deprivation of liberty for offences established in accordance with this Convention in order that they may complete their sentences there.

Article 46. Mutual legal assistance

1. States Parties shall afford one another the widest measure of mutual legal assistance in investigations, prosecutions and judicial proceedings in relation to the offences covered by this Convention.

2. Mutual legal assistance shall be afforded to the fullest extent possible under relevant laws, treaties, agreements and arrangements of the requested State Party with respect to investigations, prosecutions and judicial proceedings in relation to the offences for which a legal person may be held liable in accordance with article 26 of this Convention in the requesting State Party.

3. Mutual legal assistance to be afforded in accordance with this article may be requested for any of the following purposes:

(a) Taking evidence or statements from persons;

(b) Effecting service of judicial documents;

(c) Executing searches and seizures, and freezing;

(d) Examining objects and sites;

(e) Providing information, evidentiary items and expert evaluations;

(f) Providing originals or certified copies of relevant documents and records, including government, bank, financial, corporate or business records;

(g) Identifying or tracing proceeds of crime, property, instrumentalities or other things for evidentiary purposes;

(h) Facilitating the voluntary appearance of persons in the requesting State Party;

(i) Any other type of assistance that is not contrary to the domestic law of the requested State Party;

(j) Identifying, freezing and tracing proceeds of crime in accordance with the provisions of chapter V of this Convention;

(k) The recovery of assets, in accordance with the provisions of chapter V of this Convention.

4. Without prejudice to domestic law, the competent authorities of a State Party may, without prior request, transmit information relating to criminal matters to a competent authority in another State Party where they believe that such information could assist the authority in undertaking or successfully concluding inquiries and criminal proceedings or could result in a request formulated by the latter State Party pursuant to this Convention.

5. The transmission of information pursuant to paragraph 4 of this article shall be without prejudice to inquiries and criminal proceedings in the State of the competent authorities providing the information. The competent authorities receiving the information shall comply with a request that said information remain confidential, even temporarily, or with restrictions on its use. However, this shall not prevent the receiving State Party from disclosing in its proceedings information that is exculpatory to an accused person. In such a case, the receiving State Party shall notify the transmitting State Party prior to the disclosure and, if so requested, consult with the transmitting State Party. If, in an exceptional case, advance notice is not possible, the receiving State Party shall inform the transmitting State Party of the disclosure without delay.

6. The provisions of this article shall not affect the obligations under any other treaty, bilateral or multilateral, that governs or will govern, in whole or in part, mutual legal assistance.

7. Paragraphs 9 to 29 of this article shall apply to requests made pursuant to this article if the States Parties in question are not bound by a treaty of mutual legal assistance. If those States Parties are bound by such a treaty, the corresponding provisions of that treaty shall apply unless the States Parties agree to apply paragraphs 9 to 29 of this article in lieu thereof. States Parties are strongly encouraged to apply those paragraphs if they facilitate cooperation.

8. States Parties shall not decline to render mutual legal assistance pursuant to this article on the ground of bank secrecy.

9.

(a) A requested State Party, in responding to a request for assistance pursuant to this article in the absence of dual criminality, shall take into account the purposes of this Convention, as set forth in article 1;

(b) States Parties may decline to render assistance pursuant to this article on the ground of absence of dual criminality. However, a requested State Party shall, where consistent with the basic concepts of its legal system, render assistance that does not involve coercive action. Such assistance may be refused when requests involve matters of a *de minimis* nature or matters for which the cooperation or assistance sought is available under other provisions of this Convention;

(c) Each State Party may consider adopting such measures as may be necessary to enable it to provide a wider scope of assistance pursuant to this article in the absence of dual criminality.

10. A person who is being detained or is serving a sentence in the territory of one State Party whose presence in another State Party is requested for purposes of identification, testimony or otherwise providing assistance in obtaining evidence for investigations, prosecutions or judicial proceedings in relation to offences covered by this Convention may be transferred if the following conditions are met:

(a) The person freely gives his or her informed consent;

(b) The competent authorities of both States Parties agree, subject to such conditions as those States Parties may deem appropriate.

11. For the purposes of paragraph 10 of this article:

(a) The State Party to which the person is transferred shall have the authority and obligation to keep the person transferred in custody, unless otherwise requested or authorized by the State Party from which the person was transferred;

(b) The State Party to which the person is transferred shall without delay implement its obligation to return the person to the custody of the State Party from which the person was transferred as agreed beforehand, or as otherwise agreed, by the competent authorities of both States Parties;

(c) The State Party to which the person is transferred shall not require the State Party from which the person was transferred to initiate extradition proceedings for the return of the person;

(d) The person transferred shall receive credit for service of the sentence being served in the State from which he or she was transferred for time spent in the custody of the State Party to which he or she was transferred.

12. Unless the State Party from which a person is to be transferred in accordance with paragraphs 10 and 11 of this article so agrees, that person, whatever his or her nationality, shall not be prosecuted, detained, punished or subjected to any other restriction of his or her personal liberty in the territory of the State to which that person is transferred in respect of acts, omissions or convictions prior to his or her departure from the territory of the State from which he or she was transferred.

13. Each State Party shall designate a central authority that shall have the responsibility and power to receive requests for mutual legal assistance and either to execute them or to transmit them to the competent authorities for execution. Where a State Party has a special region or territory with a separate system of mutual legal assistance, it may designate a distinct central authority that shall have the same function for that region or territory. Central authorities shall ensure the speedy and proper execution or transmission of the requests received. Where the central authority transmits the request to a competent authority for execution, it shall encourage the speedy and proper execution of the request by the competent authority. The Secretary-General of the United Nations shall be notified of the central authority designated for this purpose at the time each State Party deposits its instrument of ratification, acceptance or approval of or accession to this Convention. Requests for mutual legal assistance and any communication related thereto shall be transmitted to the central authorities designated by the States Parties. This requirement shall be without prejudice to the right of a State Party to require that such requests and communications be addressed to it through diplomatic channels and, in urgent circumstances, where the States Parties agree, through the International Criminal Police Organization, if possible.

14. Requests shall be made in writing or, where possible, by any means capable of producing a written record, in a language acceptable to the requested State Party, under conditions allowing that State Party to establish authenticity. The Secretary-General of the United Nations shall be notified of the language or languages acceptable to each State Party at the time it deposits its instrument of ratification, acceptance or approval of or accession to this Convention. In urgent circumstances and where agreed by the States Parties, requests may be made orally but shall be confirmed in writing forthwith.

15. A request for mutual legal assistance shall contain:

(a) The identity of the authority making the request;

(b) The subject matter and nature of the investigation, prosecution or judicial proceeding to which the request relates and the name and functions of the authority conducting the investigation, prosecution or judicial proceeding;

(c) A summary of the relevant facts, except in relation to requests for the purpose of service of judicial documents;

(d) A description of the assistance sought and details of any particular procedure that the requesting State Party wishes to be followed;

(e) Where possible, the identity, location and nationality of any person concerned; and

(f) The purpose for which the evidence, information or action is sought.

16. The requested State Party may request additional information when it appears necessary for the execution of the request in accordance with its domestic law or when it can facilitate such execution.

17. A request shall be executed in accordance with the domestic law of the requested State Party and, to the extent not contrary to the domestic law of the requested State Party and where possible, in accordance with the procedures specified in the request.

18. Wherever possible and consistent with fundamental principles of domestic law, when an individual is in the territory of a State Party and has to be heard as a witness or expert by the judicial authorities of another State Party, the first State Party may, at the request of the other, permit the hearing to take place by video conference if it is not possible or desirable for the individual in question to appear in person in the territory of the requesting State Party. States Parties may agree that the hearing shall be conducted by a judicial authority of the requesting State Party and attended by a judicial authority of the requested State Party.

19. The requesting State Party shall not transmit or use information or evidence furnished by the requested State Party for investigations, prosecutions or judicial proceedings other than those stated in the request without the prior consent of the requested State Party. Nothing in this paragraph shall prevent the requesting State Party from disclosing in its proceedings information or evidence that is exculpatory to an accused person. In the latter case, the requesting State Party shall notify the requested State Party prior to the disclosure and, if so requested, consult with the requested State Party. If, in an exceptional case, advance notice is not possible, the requesting State Party shall inform the requested State Party of the disclosure without delay.

20. The requesting State Party may require that the requested State Party keep confidential the fact and substance of the request, except to the extent necessary to execute the request. If the requested State Party cannot comply with the requirement of confidentiality, it shall promptly inform the requesting State Party.

21. Mutual legal assistance may be refused:

(a) If the request is not made in conformity with the provisions of this article;

(b) If the requested State Party considers that execution of the request is likely to prejudice its sovereignty, security, *ordre public* or other essential interests;

(c) If the authorities of the requested State Party would be prohibited by its domestic law from carrying out the action requested with regard to any similar offence, had it been subject to investigation, prosecution or judicial proceedings under their own jurisdiction;

(d) If it would be contrary to the legal system of the requested State Party relating to mutual legal assistance for the request to be granted.

22. States Parties may not refuse a request for mutual legal assistance on the sole ground that the offence is also considered to involve fiscal matters.

23. Reasons shall be given for any refusal of mutual legal assistance.

24. The requested State Party shall execute the request for mutual legal assistance as soon as possible and shall take as full account as possible of any deadlines suggested by the requesting State Party and for which reasons are given, preferably in the request. The requesting State Party may make reasonable requests for information on the status and progress of measures taken by the requested State Party to satisfy its request. The requested State Party shall respond to reasonable requests by the requesting State Party on the status, and progress in its handling, of the request. The requesting State Party shall promptly inform the requested State Party when the assistance sought is no longer required.

25. Mutual legal assistance may be postponed by the requested State Party on the ground that it interferes with an ongoing investigation, prosecution or judicial proceeding.

26. Before refusing a request pursuant to paragraph 21 of this article or postponing its execution pursuant to paragraph 25 of this article, the requested State Party shall consult with the requesting State Party to consider whether assistance may be granted subject to such terms and conditions as it deems necessary. If the requesting State Party accepts assistance subject to those conditions, it shall comply with the conditions.

27. Without prejudice to the application of paragraph 12 of this article, a witness, expert or other person who, at the request of the requesting State Party, consents to give evidence in a proceeding or to assist in an investigation, prosecution or judicial proceeding in the territory of the requesting State Party shall not be prosecuted, detained, punished or subjected to any other restriction of his or her personal liberty in that territory in respect of acts, omissions or convictions prior to his or her departure from the territory of the requested State Party. Such safe conduct shall cease when the witness, expert or other person having had, for a period of fifteen consecutive days or for any period

agreed upon by the States Parties from the date on which he or she has been officially informed that his or her presence is no longer required by the judicial authorities, an opportunity of leaving, has nevertheless remained voluntarily in the territory of the requesting State Party or, having left it, has returned of his or her own free will.

28. The ordinary costs of executing a request shall be borne by the requested State Party, unless otherwise agreed by the States Parties concerned. If expenses of a substantial or extraordinary nature are or will be required to fulfil the request, the States Parties shall consult to determine the terms and conditions under which the request will be executed, as well as the manner in which the costs shall be borne.

29. The requested State Party:

(a) Shall provide to the requesting State Party copies of government records, documents or information in its possession that under its domestic law are available to the general public;

(b) May, at its discretion, provide to the requesting State Party in whole, in part or subject to such conditions as it deems appropriate, copies of any government records, documents or information in its possession that under its domestic law are not available to the general public.

30. States Parties shall consider, as may be necessary, the possibility of concluding bilateral or multilateral agreements or arrangements that would serve the purposes of, give practical effect to or enhance the provisions of this article.

Article 47. Transfer of criminal proceedings

States Parties shall consider the possibility of transferring to one another proceedings for the prosecution of an offence established in accordance with this Convention in cases where such transfer is considered to be in the interests of the proper administration of justice, in particular in cases where several jurisdictions are involved, with a view to concentrating the prosecution.

Article 48. Law enforcement cooperation

1. States Parties shall cooperate closely with one another, consistent with their respective domestic legal and administrative systems, to enhance the effectiveness of law enforcement action to combat the offences covered by this Convention. States Parties shall, in particular, take effective measures:

(a) To enhance and, where necessary, to establish channels of communication between their competent authorities, agencies and services in order to facilitate the secure and rapid exchange of information concerning all

aspects of the offences covered by this Convention, including, if the States Parties concerned deem it appropriate, links with other criminal activities;

(b) To cooperate with other States Parties in conducting inquiries with respect to offences covered by this Convention concerning:

(i) The identity, whereabouts and activities of persons suspected of involvement in such offences or the location of other persons concerned;
(ii) The movement of proceeds of crime or property derived from the commission of such offences;
(iii) The movement of property, equipment or other instrumentalities used or intended for use in the commission of such offences;

(c) To provide, where appropriate, necessary items or quantities of substances for analytical or investigative purposes;

(d) To exchange, where appropriate, information with other States Parties concerning specific means and methods used to commit offences covered by this Convention, including the use of false identities, forged, altered or false documents and other means of concealing activities;

(e) To facilitate effective coordination between their competent authorities, agencies and services and to promote the exchange of personnel and other experts, including, subject to bilateral agreements or arrangements between the States Parties concerned, the posting of liaison officers;

(f) To exchange information and coordinate administrative and other measures taken as appropriate for the purpose of early identification of the offences covered by this Convention.

2. With a view to giving effect to this Convention, States Parties shall consider entering into bilateral or multilateral agreements or arrangements on direct cooperation between their law enforcement agencies and, where such agreements or arrangements already exist, amending them. In the absence of such agreements or arrangements between the States Parties concerned, the States Parties may consider this Convention to be the basis for mutual law enforcement cooperation in respect of the offences covered by this Convention. Whenever appropriate, States Parties shall make full use of agreements or arrangements, including international or regional organizations, to enhance the cooperation between their law enforcement agencies.

3. States Parties shall endeavour to cooperate within their means to respond to offences covered by this Convention committed through the use of modern technology.

Article 49. Joint investigations

States Parties shall consider concluding bilateral or multilateral agreements or arrangements whereby, in relation to matters that are the subject of investigations, prosecutions or judicial proceedings in one or more States, the competent authorities concerned may establish joint investigative bodies. In the absence of such agreements or arrangements, joint investigations may be undertaken by agreement on a case-by-case basis. The States Parties involved shall ensure that the sovereignty of the State Party in whose territory such investigation is to take place is fully respected.

Article 50. Special investigative techniques

1. In order to combat corruption effectively, each State Party shall, to the extent permitted by the basic principles of its domestic legal system and in accordance with the conditions prescribed by its domestic law, take such measures as may be necessary, within its means, to allow for the appropriate use by its competent authorities of controlled delivery and, where it deems appropriate, other special investigative techniques, such as electronic or other forms of surveillance and undercover operations, within its territory, and to allow for the admissibility in court of evidence derived therefrom.

2. For the purpose of investigating the offences covered by this Convention, States Parties are encouraged to conclude, when necessary, appropriate bilateral or multilateral agreements or arrangements for using such special investigative techniques in the context of cooperation at the international level. Such agreements or arrangements shall be concluded and implemented in full compliance with the principle of sovereign equality of States and shall be carried out strictly in accordance with the terms of those agreements or arrangements.

3. In the absence of an agreement or arrangement as set forth in paragraph 2 of this article, decisions to use such special investigative techniques at the international level shall be made on a case-by-case basis and may, when necessary, take into consideration financial arrangements and understandings with respect to the exercise of jurisdiction by the States Parties concerned.

4. Decisions to use controlled delivery at the international level may, with the consent of the States Parties concerned, include methods such as intercepting and allowing the goods or funds to continue intact or be removed or replaced in whole or in part.

CHAPTER V

ASSET RECOVERY

Article 51. General provision

The return of assets pursuant to this chapter is a fundamental principle of this Convention, and States Parties shall afford one another the widest measure of cooperation and assistance in this regard.

Article 52. Prevention and detection of transfers of proceeds of crime

1. Without prejudice to article 14 of this Convention, each State Party shall take such measures as may be necessary, in accordance with its domestic law, to require financial institutions within its jurisdiction to verify the identity of customers, to take reasonable steps to determine the identity of beneficial owners of funds deposited into high-value accounts and to conduct enhanced scrutiny of accounts sought or maintained by or on behalf of individuals who are, or have been, entrusted with prominent public functions and their family members and close associates. Such enhanced scrutiny shall be reasonably designed to detect suspicious transactions for the purpose of reporting to competent authorities and should not be so construed as to discourage or prohibit financial institutions from doing business with any legitimate customer.

2. In order to facilitate implementation of the measures provided for in paragraph 1 of this article, each State Party, in accordance with its domestic law and inspired by relevant initiatives of regional, interregional and multilateral organizations against money-laundering, shall:

(a) Issue advisories regarding the types of natural or legal person to whose accounts financial institutions within its jurisdiction will be expected to apply enhanced scrutiny, the types of accounts and transactions to which to pay particular attention and appropriate account-opening, maintenance and record-keeping measures to take concerning such accounts; and

(b) Where appropriate, notify financial institutions within its jurisdiction, at the request of another State Party or on its own initiative, of the identity of particular natural or legal persons to whose accounts such institutions will be expected to apply enhanced scrutiny, in addition to those whom the financial institutions may otherwise identify.

3. In the context of paragraph 2 *(a)* of this article, each State Party shall implement measures to ensure that its financial institutions maintain adequate

records, over an appropriate period of time, of accounts and transactions involving the persons mentioned in paragraph 1 of this article, which should, as a minimum, contain information relating to the identity of the customer as well as, as far as possible, of the beneficial owner.

4. With the aim of preventing and detecting transfers of proceeds of offences established in accordance with this Convention, each State Party shall implement appropriate and effective measures to prevent, with the help of its regulatory and oversight bodies, the establishment of banks that have no physical presence and that are not affiliated with a regulated financial group. Moreover, States Parties may consider requiring their financial institutions to refuse to enter into or continue a correspondent banking relationship with such institutions and to guard against establishing relations with foreign financial institutions that permit their accounts to be used by banks that have no physical presence and that are not affiliated with a regulated financial group.

5. Each State Party shall consider establishing, in accordance with its domestic law, effective financial disclosure systems for appropriate public officials and shall provide for appropriate sanctions for non-compliance. Each State Party shall also consider taking such measures as may be necessary to permit its competent authorities to share that information with the competent authorities in other States Parties when necessary to investigate, claim and recover proceeds of offences established in accordance with this Convention.

6. Each State Party shall consider taking such measures as may be necessary, in accordance with its domestic law, to require appropriate public officials having an interest in or signature or other authority over a financial account in a foreign country to report that relationship to appropriate authorities and to maintain appropriate records related to such accounts. Such measures shall also provide for appropriate sanctions for non-compliance.

Article 53. Measures for direct recovery of property

Each State Party shall, in accordance with its domestic law:

(a) Take such measures as may be necessary to permit another State Party to initiate civil action in its courts to establish title to or ownership of property acquired through the commission of an offence established in accordance with this Convention;

(b) Take such measures as may be necessary to permit its courts to order those who have committed offences established in accordance with this Convention to pay compensation or damages to another State Party that has been harmed by such offences; and

(c) Take such measures as may be necessary to permit its courts or competent authorities, when having to decide on confiscation, to recognize another

State Party's claim as a legitimate owner of property acquired through the commission of an offence established in accordance with this Convention.

Article 54. Mechanisms for recovery of property through international cooperation in confiscation

1. Each State Party, in order to provide mutual legal assistance pursuant to article 55 of this Convention with respect to property acquired through or involved in the commission of an offence established in accordance with this Convention, shall, in accordance with its domestic law:

(a) Take such measures as may be necessary to permit its competent authorities to give effect to an order of confiscation issued by a court of another State Party;

(b) Take such measures as may be necessary to permit its competent authorities, where they have jurisdiction, to order the confiscation of such property of foreign origin by adjudication of an offence of money-laundering or such other offence as may be within its jurisdiction or by other procedures authorized under its domestic law; and

(c) Consider taking such measures as may be necessary to allow confiscation of such property without a criminal conviction in cases in which the offender cannot be prosecuted by reason of death, flight or absence or in other appropriate cases.

2. Each State Party, in order to provide mutual legal assistance upon a request made pursuant to paragraph 2 of article 55 of this Convention, shall, in accordance with its domestic law:

(a) Take such measures as may be necessary to permit its competent authorities to freeze or seize property upon a freezing or seizure order issued by a court or competent authority of a requesting State Party that provides a reasonable basis for the requested State Party to believe that there are sufficient grounds for taking such actions and that the property would eventually be subject to an order of confiscation for purposes of paragraph 1 *(a)* of this article;

(b) Take such measures as may be necessary to permit its competent authorities to freeze or seize property upon a request that provides a reasonable basis for the requested State Party to believe that there are sufficient grounds for taking such actions and that the property would eventually be subject to an order of confiscation for purposes of paragraph 1 *(a)* of this article; and

(c) Consider taking additional measures to permit its competent authorities to preserve property for confiscation, such as on the basis of a foreign arrest or criminal charge related to the acquisition of such property.

Article 55. International cooperation for purposes of confiscation

1. A State Party that has received a request from another State Party having jurisdiction over an offence established in accordance with this Convention for confiscation of proceeds of crime, property, equipment or other instrumentalities referred to in article 31, paragraph 1, of this Convention situated in its territory shall, to the greatest extent possible within its domestic legal system:

(a) Submit the request to its competent authorities for the purpose of obtaining an order of confiscation and, if such an order is granted, give effect to it; or

(b) Submit to its competent authorities, with a view to giving effect to it to the extent requested, an order of confiscation issued by a court in the territory of the requesting State Party in accordance with articles 31, paragraph 1, and 54, paragraph 1 *(a)*, of this Convention insofar as it relates to proceeds of crime, property, equipment or other instrumentalities referred to in article 31, paragraph 1, situated in the territory of the requested State Party.

2. Following a request made by another State Party having jurisdiction over an offence established in accordance with this Convention, the requested State Party shall take measures to identify, trace and freeze or seize proceeds of crime, property, equipment or other instrumentalities referred to in article 31, paragraph 1, of this Convention for the purpose of eventual confiscation to be ordered either by the requesting State Party or, pursuant to a request under paragraph 1 of this article, by the requested State Party.

3. The provisions of article 46 of this Convention are applicable, mutatis mutandis, to this article. In addition to the information specified in article 46, paragraph 15, requests made pursuant to this article shall contain:

(a) In the case of a request pertaining to paragraph 1 *(a)* of this article, a description of the property to be confiscated, including, to the extent possible, the location and, where relevant, the estimated value of the property and a statement of the facts relied upon by the requesting State Party sufficient to enable the requested State Party to seek the order under its domestic law;

(b) In the case of a request pertaining to paragraph 1 *(b)* of this article, a legally admissible copy of an order of confiscation upon which the request is based issued by the requesting State Party, a statement of the facts and information as to the extent to which execution of the order is requested, a statement specifying the measures taken by the requesting

State Party to provide adequate notification to bona fide third parties and to ensure due process and a statement that the confiscation order is final;

(c) In the case of a request pertaining to paragraph 2 of this article, a statement of the facts relied upon by the requesting State Party and a description of the actions requested and, where available, a legally admissible copy of an order on which the request is based.

4. The decisions or actions provided for in paragraphs 1 and 2 of this article shall be taken by the requested State Party in accordance with and subject to the provisions of its domestic law and its procedural rules or any bilateral or multilateral agreement or arrangement to which it may be bound in relation to the requesting State Party.

5. Each State Party shall furnish copies of its laws and regulations that give effect to this article and of any subsequent changes to such laws and regulations or a description thereof to the Secretary-General of the United Nations.

6. If a State Party elects to make the taking of the measures referred to in paragraphs 1 and 2 of this article conditional on the existence of a relevant treaty, that State Party shall consider this Convention the necessary and sufficient treaty basis.

7. Cooperation under this article may also be refused or provisional measures lifted if the requested State Party does not receive sufficient and timely evidence or if the property is of a *de minimis* value.

8. Before lifting any provisional measure taken pursuant to this article, the requested State Party shall, wherever possible, give the requesting State Party an opportunity to present its reasons in favour of continuing the measure.

9. The provisions of this article shall not be construed as prejudicing the rights of bona fide third parties.

Article 56. Special cooperation

Without prejudice to its domestic law, each State Party shall endeavour to take measures to permit it to forward, without prejudice to its own investigations, prosecutions or judicial proceedings, information on proceeds of offences established in accordance with this Convention to another State Party without prior request, when it considers that the disclosure of such information might assist the receiving State Party in initiating or carrying out investigations, prosecutions or judicial proceedings or might lead to a request by that State Party under this chapter of the Convention.

Article 57. Return and disposal of assets

1. Property confiscated by a State Party pursuant to article 31 or 55 of this Convention shall be disposed of, including by return to its prior legitimate owners, pursuant to paragraph 3 of this article, by that State Party in accordance with the provisions of this Convention and its domestic law.

2. Each State Party shall adopt such legislative and other measures, in accordance with the fundamental principles of its domestic law, as may be necessary to enable its competent authorities to return confiscated property, when acting on the request made by another State Party, in accordance with this Convention, taking into account the rights of bona fide third parties.

3. In accordance with articles 46 and 55 of this Convention and paragraphs 1 and 2 of this article, the requested State Party shall:

(a) In the case of embezzlement of public funds or of laundering of embezzled public funds as referred to in articles 17 and 23 of this Convention, when confiscation was executed in accordance with article 55 and on the basis of a final judgement in the requesting State Party, a requirement that can be waived by the requested State Party, return the confiscated property to the requesting State Party;

(b) In the case of proceeds of any other offence covered by this Convention, when the confiscation was executed in accordance with article 55 of this Convention and on the basis of a final judgement in the requesting State Party, a requirement that can be waived by the requested State Party, return the confiscated property to the requesting State Party, when the requesting State Party reasonably establishes its prior ownership of such confiscated property to the requested State Party or when the requested State Party recognizes damage to the requesting State Party as a basis for returning the confiscated property;

(c) In all other cases, give priority consideration to returning confiscated property to the requesting State Party, returning such property to its prior legitimate owners or compensating the victims of the crime.

4. Where appropriate, unless States Parties decide otherwise, the requested State Party may deduct reasonable expenses incurred in investigations, prosecutions or judicial proceedings leading to the return or disposition of confiscated property pursuant to this article.

5. Where appropriate, States Parties may also give special consideration to concluding agreements or mutually acceptable arrangements, on a case-bycase basis, for the final disposal of confiscated property.

Article 58. Financial intelligence unit

States Parties shall cooperate with one another for the purpose of preventing and combating the transfer of proceeds of offences established in accordance with this Convention and of promoting ways and means of recovering such proceeds and, to that end, shall consider establishing a financial intelligence unit to be responsible for receiving, analysing and disseminating to the competent authorities reports of suspicious financial transactions.

Article 59. Bilateral and multilateral agreements and arrangements

States Parties shall consider concluding bilateral or multilateral agreements or arrangements to enhance the effectiveness of international cooperation undertaken pursuant to this chapter of the Convention.

CHAPTER VI

TECHNICAL ASSISTANCE AND INFORMATION EXCHANGE

Article 60. Training and technical assistance

1. Each State Party shall, to the extent necessary, initiate, develop or improve specific training programmes for its personnel responsible for preventing and combating corruption. Such training programmes could deal, inter alia, with the following areas:

(a) Effective measures to prevent, detect, investigate, punish and control corruption, including the use of evidence-gathering and investigative methods;

(b) Building capacity in the development and planning of strategic anticorruption policy;

(c) Training competent authorities in the preparation of requests for mutual legal assistance that meet the requirements of this Convention;

(d) Evaluation and strengthening of institutions, public service management and the management of public finances, including public procurement, and the private sector;

(e) Preventing and combating the transfer of proceeds of offences established in accordance with this Convention and recovering such proceeds;

(f) Detecting and freezing of the transfer of proceeds of offences established in accordance with this Convention;

(g) Surveillance of the movement of proceeds of offences established in accordance with this Convention and of the methods used to transfer, conceal or disguise such proceeds;

(h) Appropriate and efficient legal and administrative mechanisms and methods for facilitating the return of proceeds of offences established in accordance with this Convention;

(i) Methods used in protecting victims and witnesses who cooperate with judicial authorities; and

(j) Training in national and international regulations and in languages.

2. States Parties shall, according to their capacity, consider affording one another the widest measure of technical assistance, especially for the benefit of developing countries, in their respective plans and programmes to combat corruption, including material support and training in the areas referred to in paragraph 1 of this article, and training and assistance and the mutual exchange of relevant experience and specialized knowledge, which will facilitate international cooperation between States Parties in the areas of extradition and mutual legal assistance.

3. States Parties shall strengthen, to the extent necessary, efforts to maximize operational and training activities in international and regional organizations and in the framework of relevant bilateral and multilateral agreements or arrangements.

4. States Parties shall consider assisting one another, upon request, in conducting evaluations, studies and research relating to the types, causes, effects and costs of corruption in their respective countries, with a view to developing, with the participation of competent authorities and society, strategies and action plans to combat corruption.

5. In order to facilitate the recovery of proceeds of offences established in accordance with this Convention, States Parties may cooperate in providing each other with the names of experts who could assist in achieving that objective.

6. States Parties shall consider using subregional, regional and international conferences and seminars to promote cooperation and technical assistance and to stimulate discussion on problems of mutual concern, including the special problems and needs of developing countries and countries with economies in transition.

7. States Parties shall consider establishing voluntary mechanisms with a view to contributing financially to the efforts of developing countries and countries with economies in transition to apply this Convention through technical assistance programmes and projects.

8. Each State Party shall consider making voluntary contributions to the United Nations Office on Drugs and Crime for the purpose of fostering, through the Office, programmes and projects in developing countries with a view to implementing this Convention.

Article 61. Collection, exchange and analysis of information on corruption

1. Each State Party shall consider analysing, in consultation with experts, trends in corruption in its territory, as well as the circumstances in which corruption offences are committed.

2. States Parties shall consider developing and sharing with each other and through international and regional organizations statistics, analytical expertise concerning corruption and information with a view to developing, insofar as possible, common definitions, standards and methodologies, as well as information on best practices to prevent and combat corruption.

3. Each State Party shall consider monitoring its policies and actual measures to combat corruption and making assessments of their effectiveness and efficiency.

Article 62. Other measures: implementation of the Convention through economic development and technical assistance

1. States Parties shall take measures conducive to the optimal implementation of this Convention to the extent possible, through international cooperation, taking into account the negative effects of corruption on society in general, in particular on sustainable development.

2. States Parties shall make concrete efforts to the extent possible and in coordination with each other, as well as with international and regional organizations:

(a) To enhance their cooperation at various levels with developing countries, with a view to strengthening the capacity of the latter to prevent and combat corruption;

(b) To enhance financial and material assistance to support the efforts of developing countries to prevent and fight corruption effectively and to help them implement this Convention successfully;

(c) To provide technical assistance to developing countries and countries with economies in transition to assist them in meeting their needs for the implementation of this Convention. To that end, States Parties shall endeavour to make adequate and regular voluntary contributions to an account specifically designated for that purpose in a United Nations funding mechanism. States Parties may also give special consideration, in accordance with their domestic law and the provisions of this Convention, to contributing to that account a percentage of the money or of the corresponding value of proceeds of crime or property confiscated in accordance with the provisions of this Convention;

(d) To encourage and persuade other States and financial institutions as appropriate to join them in efforts in accordance with this article, in particular by providing more training programmes and modern equipment to developing countries in order to assist them in achieving the objectives of this Convention.

3. To the extent possible, these measures shall be without prejudice to existing foreign assistance commitments or to other financial cooperation arrangements at the bilateral, regional or international level.

4. States Parties may conclude bilateral or multilateral agreements or arrangements on material and logistical assistance, taking into consideration the financial arrangements necessary for the means of international cooperation provided for by this Convention to be effective and for the prevention, detection and control of corruption.

CHAPTER VII

MECHANISMS FOR IMPLEMENTATION

Article 63. Conference of the States Parties to the Convention

1. A Conference of the States Parties to the Convention is hereby established to improve the capacity of and cooperation between States Parties to achieve the objectives set forth in this Convention and to promote and review its implementation.

2. The Secretary-General of the United Nations shall convene the Conference of the States Parties not later than one year following the entry into force of this Convention. Thereafter, regular meetings of the Conference of the States Parties shall be held in accordance with the rules of procedure adopted by the Conference.

3. The Conference of the States Parties shall adopt rules of procedure and rules governing the functioning of the activities set forth in this article, including

rules concerning the admission and participation of observers, and the payment of expenses incurred in carrying out those activities.

4. The Conference of the States Parties shall agree upon activities, procedures and methods of work to achieve the objectives set forth in paragraph 1 of this article, including:

(a) Facilitating activities by States Parties under articles 60 and 62 and chapters II to V of this Convention, including by encouraging the mobilization of voluntary contributions;

(b) Facilitating the exchange of information among States Parties on patterns and trends in corruption and on successful practices for preventing and combating it and for the return of proceeds of crime, through, inter alia, the publication of relevant information as mentioned in this article;

(c) Cooperating with relevant international and regional organizations and mechanisms and non-governmental organizations;

(d) Making appropriate use of relevant information produced by other international and regional mechanisms for combating and preventing corruption in order to avoid unnecessary duplication of work;

(e) Reviewing periodically the implementation of this Convention by its States Parties;

(f) Making recommendations to improve this Convention and its implementation;

(g) Taking note of the technical assistance requirements of States Parties with regard to the implementation of this Convention and recommending any action it may deem necessary in that respect.

5. For the purpose of paragraph 4 of this article, the Conference of the States Parties shall acquire the necessary knowledge of the measures taken by States Parties in implementing this Convention and the difficulties encountered by them in doing so through information provided by them and through such supplemental review mechanisms as may be established by the Conference of the States Parties.

6. Each State Party shall provide the Conference of the States Parties with information on its programmes, plans and practices, as well as on legislative and administrative measures to implement this Convention, as required by the Conference of the States Parties. The Conference of the States Parties shall examine the most effective way of receiving and acting upon information, including, inter alia, information received from States Parties and from

competent international organizations. Inputs received from relevant non-governmental organizations duly accredited in accordance with procedures to be decided upon by the Conference of the States Parties may also be considered.

7. Pursuant to paragraphs 4 to 6 of this article, the Conference of the States Parties shall establish, if it deems it necessary, any appropriate mechanism or body to assist in the effective implementation of the Convention.

Article 64. Secretariat

1. The Secretary-General of the United Nations shall provide the necessary secretariat services to the Conference of the States Parties to the Convention.

2. The secretariat shall:

(a) Assist the Conference of the States Parties in carrying out the activities set forth in article 63 of this Convention and make arrangements and provide the necessary services for the sessions of the Conference of the States Parties;

(b) Upon request, assist States Parties in providing information to the Conference of the States Parties as envisaged in article 63, paragraphs 5 and 6, of this Convention; and

(c) Ensure the necessary coordination with the secretariats of relevant international and regional organizations.

CHAPTER VIII

FINAL PROVISIONS

Article 65. Implementation of the Convention

1. Each State Party shall take the necessary measures, including legislative and administrative measures, in accordance with fundamental principles of its domestic law, to ensure the implementation of its obligations under this Convention.

2. Each State Party may adopt more strict or severe measures than those provided for by this Convention for preventing and combating corruption.

Article 66. Settlement of disputes

1. States Parties shall endeavour to settle disputes concerning the interpretation or application of this Convention through negotiation.

2. Any dispute between two or more States Parties concerning the interpretation or application of this Convention that cannot be settled through negotiation within a reasonable time shall, at the request of one of those States Parties, be submitted to arbitration. If, six months after the date of the request for arbitration, those States Parties are unable to agree on the organization of the arbitration, any one of those States Parties may refer the dispute to the International Court of Justice by request in accordance with the Statute of the Court.

3. Each State Party may, at the time of signature, ratification, acceptance or approval of or accession to this Convention, declare that it does not consider itself bound by paragraph 2 of this article. The other States Parties shall not be bound by paragraph 2 of this article with respect to any State Party that has made such a reservation.

4. Any State Party that has made a reservation in accordance with paragraph 3 of this article may at any time withdraw that reservation by notification to the Secretary-General of the United Nations.

Article 67. Signature, ratification, acceptance, approval and accession

1. This Convention shall be open to all States for signature from 9 to 11 December 2003 in Merida, Mexico, and thereafter at United Nations Headquarters in New York until 9 December 2005.

2. This Convention shall also be open for signature by regional economic integration organizations provided that at least one member State of such organization has signed this Convention in accordance with paragraph 1 of this article.

3. This Convention is subject to ratification, acceptance or approval. Instruments of ratification, acceptance or approval shall be deposited with the Secretary-General of the United Nations. A regional economic integration organization may deposit its instrument of ratification, acceptance or approval if at least one of its member States has done likewise. In that instrument of ratification, acceptance or approval, such organization shall declare the extent of its competence with respect to the matters governed by this Convention. Such organization shall also inform the depositary of any relevant modification in the extent of its competence.

4. This Convention is open for accession by any State or any regional economic integration organization of which at least one member State is a Party to this Convention. Instruments of accession shall be deposited with the Secretary-General of the United Nations. At the time of its accession, a regional economic integration organization shall declare the extent of its competence with respect to matters governed by this Convention. Such organization shall also inform the depositary of any relevant modification in the extent of its competence.

Article 68. Entry into force

1. This Convention shall enter into force on the ninetieth day after the date of deposit of the thirtieth instrument of ratification, acceptance, approval or accession. For the purpose of this paragraph, any instrument deposited by a regional economic integration organization shall not be counted as additional to those deposited by member States of such organization.

2. For each State or regional economic integration organization ratifying, accepting, approving or acceding to this Convention after the deposit of the thirtieth instrument of such action, this Convention shall enter into force on the thirtieth day after the date of deposit by such State or organization of the relevant instrument or on the date this Convention enters into force pursuant to paragraph 1 of this article, whichever is later.

Article 69. Amendment

1. After the expiry of five years from the entry into force of this Convention, a State Party may propose an amendment and transmit it to the Secretary-General of the United Nations, who shall thereupon communicate the proposed amendment to the States Parties and to the Conference of the States Parties to the Convention for the purpose of considering and deciding on the proposal. The Conference of the States Parties shall make every effort to achieve consensus on each amendment. If all efforts at consensus have been exhausted and no agreement has been reached, the amendment shall, as a last resort, require for its adoption a two-thirds majority vote of the States Parties present and voting at the meeting of the Conference of the States Parties.

2. Regional economic integration organizations, in matters within their competence, shall exercise their right to vote under this article with a number of votes equal to the number of their member States that are Parties to this Convention. Such organizations shall not exercise their right to vote if their member States exercise theirs and vice versa.

3. An amendment adopted in accordance with paragraph 1 of this article is subject to ratification, acceptance or approval by States Parties.

4. An amendment adopted in accordance with paragraph 1 of this article shall enter into force in respect of a State Party ninety days after the date of the deposit with the Secretary-General of the United Nations of an instrument of ratification, acceptance or approval of such amendment.

5. When an amendment enters into force, it shall be binding on those States Parties which have expressed their consent to be bound by it. Other States Parties shall still be bound by the provisions of this Convention and any earlier amendments that they have ratified, accepted or approved.

Article 70. Denunciation

1. A State Party may denounce this Convention by written notification to the Secretary-General of the United Nations. Such denunciation shall become effective one year after the date of receipt of the notification by the Secretary-General.

2. A regional economic integration organization shall cease to be a Party to this Convention when all of its member States have denounced it.

Article 71. Depositary and languages

1. The Secretary-General of the United Nations is designated depositary of this Convention.

2. The original of this Convention, of which the Arabic, Chinese, English, French, Russian and Spanish texts are equally authentic, shall be deposited with the Secretary-General of the United Nations.

IN WITNESS WHEREOF, the undersigned plenipotentiaries, being duly authorized thereto by their respective Governments, have signed this Convention.

Published with the financial support of the Government of Japan

UNITED NATIONS *Office on Drugs and Crime*

Vienna International Centre, PO Box 500, A 1400 Vienna, Austria

Tel: +(43) (1) 26060-0, Fax: +(43) (1) 26060-5866, www.unodc.org

Printed in Austria

V.04-56160—September 2004—2,000

Appendix I

LIST OF USEFUL WEBSITES

There are many sources of information and good practice available in this area. Among these are the following.

GOOD PRACTICE GUIDES/RESEARCH MATERIALS

www.bis.gov.uk/policies/trade-policy-unit/anti-corruption

Department of Business, Innovation and Skills, *Combating International Corruption*

www.business-anti-corruption.com/

Global Advice Network, *Business Anti-Corruption Portal*

www.iccwbo.org/policy/anticorruption/id870/index.html

International Chamber of Commerce Rules of Conduct and Recommendations for Combating Extortion and Bribery

www.oecd.org/document/42/0,3746,en_2649_34855_41799402_1_1_1_1,00.html

OECD Good Practice Guidance on Internal Controls, Ethics and Compliance

www.traceinternational.org/news/TRACEDueDiligenceGuidebook.asp

TRACE International Due Diligence Guidebook

www.transparency.org.uk/working-with-companies/adequate-procedures

Transparency International, *Adequate Procedures: Guidance to the UK Bribery Act 2010*

www.transparency.org/global_priorities/private_sector/business_principles

Transparency International, *Business Principles for Countering Bribery*

www.unodc.org/unodc/en/corruption/anti-corruption-policies-and-measures-of-the-fortune-global-500.html

United Nations Office on Drugs and Crime, *Anti-Corruption Policies and Measures of the Fortune Global 500*

www.transparency.org/policy_research/surveys_indices/cpi

Transparency International Corruption Perceptions Index

http://info.worldbank.org/governance/wgi/sc_country.asp

World Bank Worldwide Governance Indicators

LEGISLATION/GUIDANCE

www.legislation.gov.uk/ukpga/2010/23/contents

The Bribery Act 2010

http://conventions.coe.int/treaty/Commun/QueVoulezVous.asp?NT=173&CL=ENG

Council of Europe Criminal Law Convention On Corruption

http://conventions.coe.int/Treaty/Commun/QueVoulezVous.asp?NT=174&CM=8&DF=02/06/2011&CL=ENG

Council of Europe Civil Law Convention On Corruption

www.oecd.org/topic/0,3699,en_2649_37447_1_1_1_1_37447,00.html

OECD Convention and associated material

www.justice.gov.uk/guidance/making-and-reviewing-the-law/bribery.htm

UK Ministry of Justice (guidance)

www.unodc.org/unodc/en/treaties/CAC/index.html

UN Convention Against Corruption, and associated material

PROSECUTORS/REGULATORS
UK

www.sfo.gov.uk

Serious Fraud Office

www.cityoflondon.police.uk/CityPolice/Departments/ECD/anticorruptionunit

City of London Police – Anti-Corruption Unit

www.fsa.gov.uk

Financial Services Authority

www.soca.gov.uk

Serious Organised Crime Agency (SOCA)

Overseas

http://ec.europa.eu/anti_fraud/index_en.html

European Anti-Fraud Office (OLAF)

www.justice.gouv.fr/le-ministere-de-la-justice-10017/organismes-rattaches-10028/service-central-de-la-prevention-de-la-corruption-12081.html

French Ministry of Justice Anti-Corruption Service

www.bmz.de/en/what_we_do/issues/goodgovernance/korruption/index.html

German Federal Ministry for Economic Cooperation – Anti-Corruption Materials

www.icac.org.hk/en/home/index.html#

Hong Kong Independent Commission Against Corruption

www.justice.gov/criminal/fraud/fcpa/

US Dept of Justice – FCPA

www.sec.gov/index.htm

US Securities and Exchange Commission

BLOGS/COMMENTARY

www.thebriberyact.com

Thoughtful commentary from two UK practitioners

www.fcpablog.com

Comprehensive resource on FCPA enforcement trends and case-law

http://openairblog.wordpress.com

Opinionated, passionate commentary on the FCPA, Bribery Act and ABC matters generally from a US-based lawyer

http://blogs.wsj.com/corruption-currents

Blog by two journalists of the Wall Street Journal, specialising in corruption and economic crime from an international perspective

www.ipaidabribe.com

Indian website which encourages citizens to make reports of demands for bribes, provides resources to resist them and makes use of 'crowdsourcing' to campaign for change

INDEX

References are to paragraph numbers.

ABC policy
   outline   9.151
Accept
   meaning   3.12, 8.63
Acceptance of advantage   2.48, 2.49
   examples   2.56
   expectations of impartiality   2.54
   improper   2.54, 2.55
   indirectness   2.59
   third parties   2.59
Accessory liability   12.3
Acquiescence
   meaning   3.48
Activities connected with business   4.27
Activities performed by or on behalf of
   body of persons   4.34
Activities performed in course of
   person's employment   4.30–4.33
Adequate procedures   9.1
   adequate   9.7, 9.8
   anti-bribery policy   9.124
   burden of proof   9.2
   clear, practical and accessible   9.46–9.48
   communication   9.112
   conflicts of interest   9.62
   due diligence   9.101
   employee negligence   9.11
   employment   9.56
   facilitation payments   9.54, 9.55
   fault, and   9.10
   financial controls   9.57, 9.58
   gifts/hospitality   9.52, 9.53
   government policy on
      interpretation of Act   9.21–9.24
   investigations   9.62
   list of topics   9.49–9.51
   monitoring   9.117
      recording procedures at work   9.122, 9.123
   outline   9.151
   proportionate procedures   9.29
      proportionality   9.31
      sub-principles   9.30
   recruitment   9.56
   review   9.117
      recording procedures at work   9.122, 9.123
   risk assessment   9.80
   section 9   9.1–9.4

Adequate procedures—*continued*
   six principles   9.25
      Appendix A   9.27
      structure   9.26
   speak up procedures   9.59–9.61
   statutory guidance   9.4–9.6
      parts   9.17
      Quick Start Guide   9.18
      six principles   9.25–9.28
      status of   9.13–9.16
   top level commitment   9.69
      CEO   9.72, 9.73
      compliance officer   9.73, 9.74
      very large organisations   9.77
   training   9.112
Agent
   meaning   8.63
Agent/principal relationship   13.10
Aiding and abetting   12.7
   abetting   12.10
Ancillary orders   10.83
Anti-terrorism, Crime and Security Act
   2001   1.53
   bribery and corruption
      foreign officers   1.54
   bribery and corruption committed
      outside UK   1.54
   presumption of corruption not to
      apply   1.54
Assent
   meaning   3.48
Attempt   12.38
   more than merely
      preparatory   12.39–12.41
   specific intent   12.42–12.44
Attorney-General
   role of   10.2

Belief
   meaning   2.46
Breach of expectation of good faith   5.10
   mistake, and   5.16
Breach of expectation of
   impartiality   5.18–5.20
Breach of expectations   6.8
   impartiality   6.14
   position of trust cases   6.11
Breach of relevant expectations   5.5
   reasonable person test   5.6, 5.7

Breach of relevant expectations—*continued*
types of expectation ... 5.9
Bribery
common law ... 1.27
corruption, and ... 1.67–1.71
existing law ... 1.26
previous attempts at reform ... 1.58
'public office' ... 1.28
slow pace of reform ... 1.66
statutory offences ... 1.32
undue reward ... 1.29, 1.31
Bribery Act
historical background ... 1.1
interpreting ... 1.72–1.74
need for ... 1.5, 1.6
radicalism of ... 1.1–1.4
Bribes for boarding ... 2.69, 2.70
Bribing another person ... 2.1
actus reus ... 2.6, 2.7
mens rea ... 2.6, 2.7
provider ... 2.2
threshold conditions ... 2.5
Business
meaning ... 4.27

Carrying on business
meaning ... 8.24–8.27
Civil liability ... 13.1
account of profits ... 13.40
agent/principal relationship ... 13.10
agents, claims against ... 13.27
arbitration ... 13.7, 13.8
breach of contract ... 13.28
breach of fiduciary duty ... 13.40
bribery as civil wrong ... 13.9
civil bribery, definition ... 13.18
civil fraud ... 13.32
civil recovery by states against former officials ... 13.102
claims against briber ... 13.48
claims against third parties other than agent or briber ... 13.77
claims by parties other than principal of agent ... 13.81
collusion in anti-competitive behaviour ... 13.87
conspiracy ... 13.43, 13.70
constructive trust ... 13.40
dishonest assistance in breach of fiduciary duty ... 13.66
election ... 13.71
fiduciary duties ... 12.15–12.17, 13.15
fraud, damages for ... 13.62
freezing order ... 13.91
inducing breach of contract, damages for ... 13.62
interim relief ... 13.88
jurisdiction ... 13.6
overview of claims ... 13.24
principal, knowledge of ... 13.23
proof of bribery ... 13.19
recovery of briber's profits ... 13.68
rescission ... 13.54

Civil liability—*continued*
restitution ... 13.34
search order ... 13.97
supplemental orders ... 13.101
tracing ... 13.73
transaction void ... 13.51
unjust enrichment ... 13.34
unjust enrichment claim against briber ... 13.65
unlawful means conspiracy ... 13.83
Civil procedure ... 13.5
Civil recovery orders
Proceeds of Crime Act 2002 ... 10.95
agreements with SFO to accept ... 10.101
Commercial organisations
A, a person associated with C ... 8.61
performing services for or on behalf of C ... 8.62
adequate procedures, defence of ... 8.134
burden of proof ... 8.138
object is prevention ... 8.141
procedures must be 'adequate' ... 8.143
agents ... 8.63
Bribery Act offences ... 8.13, 8.14
bribery by A to obtain/retain business for C
additional mens rea required by section 7(1) ... 8.127
no need for A to be prosecuted ... 8.130
no need for A to have UK connection ... 8.132
section 1 offence by A ... 8.123
section 6 offence by A ... 8.124
carrying on business ... 8.24
carrying on part of business ... 8.28
corporate liability under section 7 ... 8.10
corporate veil ... 8.54
directors ... 8.78, 8.79
employees ... 8.78, 8.79
expanded jurisdiction ... 8.15
failure to prevent bribery by ... 8.1
corporate bodies, liability of ... 8.1
corporate criminal liability ... 8.2
joint ventures ... 8.102
key issues ... 8.18
non-UK corporation ... 8.28, 8.29
non-UK partnerships ... 8.28, 8.29
partners ... 8.78, 8.79
recipient, and ... 3.25–3.29
relevant ... 8.20
section 1 and section 6 offences ... 8.16
shareholders ... 8.77
subsidiaries ... 8.96
functions ... 8.98
meaning ... 8.96
parent company liability ... 8.97
suppliers ... 8.84
UK corporations ... 8.23–8.25
UK partnerships ... 8.23–8.25
UK subsidiary of foreign company ... 8.49
vicarious liability ... 8.12
Compensation order ... 10.84, 10.85

Index

Compromise of position	2.49, 3.24
knows or believes	2.50
Confiscation order	10.86
Consent to prosecution	10.1
Conspiracy	12.23, 13.43, 13.70
agreement	12.26–12.28
forms	12.24
impossibility	12.29
intention to agree and fulfil agreement	12.30
meaning	12.23
sentences	12.37
uses of	12.34
Conspiracy to defraud	12.57
Corporate bodies	2.69
connivance	2.69
consent	2.69
offences by	2.69
senior officers	2.69
Corporate criminal liability	
Bribery Act offences	8.13, 8.14
directing mind	8.3, 8.4
identification doctrine	8.5
mens rea, and	8.2
Corporate hospitality	14.5
promotional expenses	14.5
Corporate prosecutions	10.35
Attorney-General's Guidance	10.36
Joint Prosecution Guidance	10.50
SFO policy	10.37
Innospec	10.39
Corporate veil	8.54
joint venture, and	8.110
Corruption	
bribery, and	1.67–1.71
existing criminal law	1.26
Counselling	12.7
meaning	12.11
Debarment from public procurement	10.110
proposed amendment of UK regulations	10.117
Defences	9.1
military and security service personnel	9.126
Directors of prosecuting agencies	
role of	10.2
Disqualification of directors	10.106–10.108
Due diligence	9.99
level of	9.103
policy	9.105
red flags	9.109–9.111
varying according to incorporation	9.107, 9.108
Duress	9.139–9.142
Election	13.71, 13.72
civil bribery, and	12.69, 12.70
Encouraging or assisting crime	12.16
'acting reasonably'	12.19
jurisdiction	12.22
meaning	12.17
Serious Crime Act 2007	12.16

Expectation test	6.1
breach of expectations	6.8
key issues	6.1
objective test, as	6.2
performance of functions outside UK	6.18
burden of proof	6.22
customary activities	6.23
legal conduct	6.20, 6.21
tolerated practices	6.23
reasonable person, meaning	6.5–6.7
two questions for reasonable person	6.3, 6.4
Extortion	14.50
Extradition	12.88–12.90
Facilitation payments	14.50
False accounting	12.71
failure to keep accurate records	12.77
mens rea	12.75
'person'	12.73
Fiduciary duties	13.15
Financial or other advantage	2.17
another person	2.21
de minimis	2.20
examples	2.19
Financial reporting order	10.90, 10.91
Financial Services Authority	
role of	10.120
Foreign public officials	7.1
administrative position	7.23
advantage need not be for 'improper performance'	7.71
advantage to	7.98
advantage to another at request	7.98
bodies corporate, offences by	7.120
compliance with OECD Convention	7.3
directly or through third party	7.94
exercising public function for foreign country	7.41
facilitation payments	7.115
financial or other advantage	7.96, 7.97
functional definition	7.38
gives	7.95
hospitality	7.77
institutional definition	7.22
intention to influence	
actions exceeding authority	7.87
omissions exceeding authority	7.87
intention to influence in official capacity	7.68
intention to obtain or retain advantage in conduct of business	7.88
intention to obtain or retain business	7.88
judicial position	7.23
legislative position	7.23
local law, role of	7.101
applicable law	7.108
meaning	7.19
offers	7.95

Foreign public officials—*continued*

officials of political parties	7.32
omissions and actions exceeding authority	7.87
political candidates	7.32
private relationships with FPOs	7.84
promises	7.95
promotional expenses	7.77
providing advantage	7.94
applicable law	7.108
public agency	7.44
public enterprise	7.49
example	7.58
public international organisations	7.65
role of OECD Convention in interpreting section 6	7.13
Article 1	7.14
same mens rea as section 1, whether	7.74
scheme of section 6	7.8
senior officers of bodies corporate, offences by	7.120
sovereign wealth funds	7.63
support staff	7.28
territory outside UK	7.35

Fraud — 12.45

abuse of position	12.54–12.56
dishonesty	12.51
gain	12.52
loss	12.52

Functions and activities

civil law	4.70
connections to UK	4.75
expectations applicable to	4.41
good faith	4.45–4.48
impartiality	4.49
position of trust	4.56
fuzziness at margins	4.64
private sector	4.9
public sector	4.9
threshold condition	4.1–4.4
two-stage definition	4.6–4.8
United Kingdom, connections to	4.75, 4.76

Functions of public nature — 4.14

core public authorities	4.16
existing English law	4.14
'foreign public official'	4.18
hybrid public authorities	4.17
meaning	4.18
Members of Parliament	4.23–4.26

Give

meaning	2.14, 2.15

Hospitality

corporate	14.5
foreign public officials, and	14.25
conference	14.43
events	14.39
hedge fund fees	14.45
scenario A	14.31
travel	14.39

Hospitality—*continued*

private sector	14.14
UK public sector, and	14.22–14.24

Improper performance — 5.1

breach of expectation arising from position of trust	5.21
breach of expectation of good faith	5.10
breach of expectation of impartiality	5.18–5.20
breach of relevant expectation	5.5
connections to past protected functions	5.33–5.35
meaning	2.27–2.31
reasonable person	5.36
relevant function or activity	5.2–5.4

In anticipation of

meaning	3.53

In consequence of

meaning	3.54

Induce

meaning	2.36–2.38

Inducing breach of contract

damages for	12.61

Inducing or rewarding improper performance — 2.8

officer, promise or give	2.9

Innocent abroad — 2.75

Intending to induce improper performance — 2.22

intention	2.23

Intending to reward improper performance — 2.41

Intention

improper performance	2.27
inference	2.25
proof of	2.23, 2.24

International organisations

officials of	7.58

Joint Prosecution Guidance 2011 — 10.24

Joint ventures — 8.102

corporate veil, and	8.110
example	8.106
form of	8.103
not incorporated	8.116

Knowledge

meaning	2.51

Law Commission

Legislating the Criminal Code – Corruption	1.58
Report of 2008	1.60, 1.61

Members of Parliament — 4.23–4.26

Mergers and acquisitions — 14.63

cash for speedy visas	14.81
inspection costs rebate	14.83
port service fees	14.73
scenario B	14.69

Index

Mergers and acquisitions—*continued*
  threat of imprisonment   14.91
  visa problems   14.88
Military and security service personnel   9.126
  armed forces   9.131–9.133
  defence for   9.126
  intelligence services   9.131–9.133
  police and informants   9.136, 9.137
  proper exercise of any function   9.134, 9.136
    relevant bribery offence   9.128–9.130
Misconduct in public office   12.79
  meaning   12.80
Money laundering   12.58
  criminal conduct   12.61
  criminal property   12.60
  main offences   12.66
  regulated sector   12.70

Necessity   9.143
  'acting reasonably'   9.148
  loss of liberty, and   9.147

OECD Convention
  comparison of Article 1 OECD Convention with section 6, Bribery Act 2010   7.125
  compliance with   7.3
  role of interpreting section 6   7.13
Offer
  meaning   2.11, 2.13
Offer, promise or give   2.9
Omission to act   12.13

Part of a business
  meaning   8.37
Penalties   10.55
  mode of trial   10.55
Position of trust   4.56
  breach of expectation arising from   5.21
    examples   5.30–5.32
    reasonable person test   5.25
    reasons for which function or activity carried out   5.28
    relevant activities   5.22
  by virtue of performing function or activity   5.24
  civil law, and   4.70
  example   4.60, 4.65
  fuzziness at the margins   4.64
  meaning   5.21
  performances of function or activity   4.61
Prevention of Corruption Act 1906   1.41, 1.48
  presumption of corruption   1.49–1.52
  punishment of corrupt transactions with agents   1.41
Private sector hospitality   14.14
Procuring   12.7
  meaning   12.12
Promise
  meaning   2.12, 2.13

Promotional expenses   14.5
Proportionality   9.31
  meaning   9.32
  reasonable person standard   9.44
  risk assessment   9.37–9.40
  risk-based approach   9.35–9.40
  size-based approach   9.35, 9.36
  types   9.33, 9.34
  'very small business'   9.41
Prosecution of individuals   10.16
  Code for Crown Prosecution   10.17
  giving assistance to prosecutors   10.31–10.34
  Joint Prosecution Guidance 2011   10.24
Prosecutors' priorities   10.12
Public Bodies Corrupt Practices Act 1889   1.33
  corruption in office a misdemeanour   1.33
  'corruptly'   1.37–1.40
  public body   1.34–1.36
Public enterprise
  meaning   7.50–7.52
Public procurement
  debarment from   10.110

Reasonable person   5.36
  meaning   6.5–6.7
Receipt of bribes   3.1
  assent or acquiescence   3.48
  compromise of position cases   3.24
  conduct   3.43, 3.44
  financial or other advantage   3.15
  improper performance   3.36–3.42
  in anticipation of   3.51
  in consequence   3.19, 3.20, 3.51
    example   3.21
  intending that relevant function or activity is performed improperly in consequence   3.16–3.18
  lack of intention as to improper performance   3.23
  offence complete without actual improper performance   3.22
  offences   3.2
  position of person performing function or activity   3.55–3.58
  'requests, agrees to receive or accepts'   3.6
    communication   3.10, 3.11
    example   3.13, 3.14
  reward, as   3.35
  threshold conditions   3.3
Relevant commercial organisation
  meaning   8.20
Relevant function or activity   2.35
  meaning   5.2–5.4
Request
  meaning   3.8, 3.9
Rescission   13.54
  bars to   13.58

Reward
  meaning   3.35
Reward offence   2.41
Risk assessment   9.80
  commission-based
    remuneration   9.90–9.92
  documenting   9.83
  external risks   9.85
  how much information is enough   9.96
  incentives   9.93, 9.94
  internal risks   9.85
  methodology   9.84
  outside consultancies   9.98
  regulatory environment   9.95

Sentencing   10.59
  Innospec, and   10.78
  maximum sentences   10.63
  range of sentences
    companies   10.76
    individual   10.66
  recent cases   10.109
  suspended sentences   10.72
Serious crime prevention order   10.92–10.94
Sovereign wealth funds   7.63

Territorial application of Act   11.1
  commercial organisations failure to
    prevent bribery   11.42
  nationality jurisdiction   11.20
    British citizen   11.26
    British national (overseas)   11.29
    British overseas citizen   11.30
    British overseas territories
      citizen   11.28

Territorial application of Act—*continued*
  nationality jurisdiction—*continued*
    British overseas territories
      incorporated bodies   11.40
    British protected person   11.32
    British subject under British
      Nationality Act 1981   11.31
    Crown dependency
      incorporated bodies   11.40
    Individual ordinarily resident in
      UK   11.34
    UK incorporated body   11.37–11.39
  providing bribes to foreign public
    official   11.8
  provision of bribes   11.8
  receipt of bribes   11.15
  Scots criminal procedure   11.46
  territorial jurisdiction   11.4
Transnational bribery
  case for fighting   1.8
  counterarguments   1.16
  failed states, and   1.15
  human nature, and   1.16
  instability, and   1.14
  local culture, and   1.18, 1.19, 1.21–1.23
  poverty, and   1.14
  social trust, and   1.9
  unfair social conditions, and   1.17

UK subsidiary of foreign company   8.49
  hand in bribery   8.59–8.62
Unincorporated associations   4.35

Vicarious liability
  commercial organisation, and   8.12